HISTOR

GIACOMO CASANOVA

Chevalier de Seingalt

HISTORY OF MY LIFE

FIRST TRANSLATED INTO ENGLISH IN ACCORDANCE
WITH THE ORIGINAL FRENCH MANUSCRIPT

by Willard R. Trask

VOLUMES 11 AND 12

———

THE JOHNS HOPKINS UNIVERSITY PRESS
Baltimore and London

English translation copyright © 1971 by Harcourt Brace
Jovanovich, Inc.
Printed in the United States of America on acid-free paper

Originally published as *Histoire de Ma Vie,* Edition intégrale, by
Jacques Casanova de Seingalt, Vénitien, by F. A. Brockhaus,
Wiesbaden, Librairie Plon, Paris, 1960. © F. A. Brockhaus,
Wiesbaden, 1960.

This edition originally published in the United States as a Helen and
Kurt Wolff book by Harcourt Brace Jovanovich, Inc.
Johns Hopkins Paperbacks edition, 1997
9 8 7 6 5 4 3 2

The Johns Hopkins University Press
2715 North Charles Street
Baltimore, Maryland 21218-4363
The Johns Hopkins Press Ltd., London

Library of Congress Catalog Card Number 97-70304

A catalog record for this book is available from the British Library.

ISBN 0-8018-5667-1 (pbk.: Vols. 11 and 12)

HISTORY OF MY LIFE
Volume 11

CONTENTS

Volume 11

vii

LIST OF PLATES

Volume 11

VOLUME 11

CHAPTER I

1768. My amour with Doña Ignacia, the gentleman-cobbler's daughter. My imprisonment in Buen Retiro and my triumph. I am recommended to the Venetian Ambassador by a State Inquisitor of the Republic.

I ENTER the ballroom with the beautiful Doña Ignacia, we take several turns around it, everywhere meeting the guard of soldiers with fixed bayonets who were walking slowly about, ready to apprehend any who should break the peace by quarreling. We dance minuets and contradances until ten o'clock, then we go to supper, both remaining silent, she, perhaps, in order not to encourage me to take liberties, I because, speaking very little Spanish, I did not know what to say. After supper I go to the box where I was to see La Pichona,[1] and I see only maskers whom I did not know. We go back to dancing, until permission to dance the fandango[2] is at last given, and I fall to with my *pareja*,[3] who danced it very well and who is surprised to find herself so well accompanied in it by a foreigner. At the end of the seductive dance, which had set us both on fire, I escort her to the place where refreshments were served, I ask her if she has been pleased with me, and I tell her that she has made me so

3

much in love with her that I should die if she did not find
a way to make me happy and confide it to me, assuring
her that I was a man to run all risks. She replies that she
could not think of making me happy except by becoming
happy herself, and that she would write me how I could
accomplish that in a letter which she would sew between
the cloth and the lining of the hood of her domino, and
so I must put off sending for it until the next day. Telling
her that she will find me ready for anything, I escort her
outside, I go to find the carriage with her beyond the
plazuela,[4] where I had left it. We get into it, her mother
wakes, the coachman drives off, I take both her hands,
intending nothing but to kiss them; but, supposing that
I was going to subject her to something which she considered too much, she holds them in so strong a grip that I
should have sought in vain to free them if I had attempted it. Still grasping my hands, she gives her mother
an account of all the pleasures she had enjoyed at the
ball; she did not release them until, as we entered the
Calle del Desengaño,[5] her mother told the coachman to
stop, for she did not want to give the neighbors occasion
to gossip by getting out at her own door. She asked me
not to get out, and, after thanking me, they walked to
their house. I at once went home and to bed.

The next day I sent for the domino, in which I found
Doña Ignacia's letter where she had said it would be. In
her letter, which was very short, she told me that Don
Francisco de Ramos[6] would call on me at my lodging,
that he was her lover, and that it would be from him that
I should learn the way to make her happy, for my happiness could be only the consequence of hers.

Don Francisco lost no time. My page announced him to
me the next morning at eight o'clock. He told me that
Doña Ignacia, with whom he talked every night from the
street, she being at her window, had confided to him that
she had gone to the ball with me and her mother, and
that, being certain that I could have conceived only a

fatherly fondness for her, she had persuaded him to present himself to me, assuring him that I would treat him as if he were my son. So it was she who gave him the courage to unbosom himself to me and to ask me to lend him a hundred doblones,[7] which could put him in a position to marry her before the end of the Carnival. He told me that he was employed in the office of the Mint,[8] and that his salary, which was then very small, would be increased later, that his father and mother were in Toledo, that he would be alone in Madrid with his dear wife, and that he would have no other friend than I, never even imagining that I could have any inclination toward Doña Ignacia except that which a father could have toward a daughter.

I replied that he had divined my feelings, but that for the moment I did not have the hundred doblones, and that I did not even know how long it might be before I could have that amount. I assured him of my discretion, and, telling him that I should be pleased whenever he honored me with a call, I saw him leave extremely disappointed. He was a young man perhaps twenty-two years of age, ugly and ill built. Making light of what had happened, for I felt only a passing fancy for Doña Ignacia, I went to pay my homage to La Pichona, who had so cordially invited me to call on her the first time I had attended the ball. I had made inquiries about her. I had learned that she had been an actress, and that she owed her wealth to the Duke of Medina Celi,[9] who, having gone to see her one day when it was very cold, found that she had no brazier because she had no money to buy charcoal. The Duke, who was extremely rich, feeling ashamed to have called on a woman so poor, the next day sent her a silver brazier containing a hundred thousand pesos duros[10] in gold, which came to fifty thousand zecchini. So since that time she had lived very comfortably and received good company.

I go to call on her, she receives me cordially, but I see

that she is very sad. I tell her that I had not failed to go
to her box, and that I had not found her. She replies that
the Duke of Medina Celi had died [11] on that day after
three days' illness, and, since he was her only friend, she
had not had the strength to go out.

"Was he very old?"

"No, sixty. You saw him yourself. He didn't look his
age."

"Where did I see him?"

"Wasn't it he who brought you to my box?"

"That man? He didn't tell me his name. That was the
first time I saw him."

His death shocked me. All his possessions went to a
son,[12] who, as might be expected, was a great miser. But
his miserly son in his turn had a son who was a spendthrift.

This is what I have observed always and everywhere.
The miser's son is a spendthrift, and the spendthrift's
son is a miser. It seems to me natural that the characters
of the father and the son are in perpetual contradiction.
An intelligent author[13] tries to ascertain the reason why
a father usually loves his grandson far more than his son:
he thinks he has found it in nature. It is natural, he says,
that a man should love the enemy of his enemy. It seems
to me that, advanced as a generalization, this is a barbarous reason, for, beginning with myself, I have found that
the son loves his father. I grant, however, that the father's love of his son is infinitely greater than the son's
of his father. I was told that the House of Medina Celi
had thirty hats,[14] which means thirty grandeeships of
Spain.

A young man who frequented the coffeehouse, to which
I never went, came upstairs to my room without much
ceremony to offer me his services in a country which was
new to me and with which he was very well acquainted.

"I am," he said, "Count Marazzani,[15] of Piacenza, I
am not rich, I have come to Madrid to seek my fortune; I

begged her to accept a doblón de a ocho,[23] which she refused without haughtiness, only asking me confidently to
give it to her lover when he came to call on me.

"How shall I make sure not to offend him?"

"Tell him that it is the first of the hundred he asked
you for. He is poor, and I am certain that at this moment
he must be in despair because he has not seen me at my
window; he may spend the whole night in the street. I
will tell him tomorrow night that I came to the ball with
you only to please my father."

Convinced that she had resolved to give herself to me,
I found the girl dancing the fandango with me so voluptuously that she could not have promised me everything
more eloquently in words. What a dance! It burns, it
inflames, it carries away. Nevertheless, people tried to
assure me that the majority of Spanish men and women
who dance it mean no harm by it. I pretended to believe
them. Before getting out of the carriage at her house,
she asked me to go to mass at La Soledad [24] on the next
day but one at eight o'clock. I did not tell her that it was
there that I had seen her the first time, receiving the
sacrament. She also asked me to come that evening to her
house, where she would give me a letter if she could not
manage to be alone with me.

Having slept until noon, when I woke I saw Marazzani,
come to dine with me. He had watched me all evening at
the ball, and, always in disguise, he had seen me sup with
Doña Ignacia. He said that, trying to find out who she
was, he had questioned all the connoisseurs in Madrid,
and I patiently put up with his extremely indiscreet
curiosity; but when he told me that if he had had money
he would have had me followed, I talked to him in a way
which made him turn pale. He at once begged my pardon,
promising that he would permit himself no more curiosity
about her. He proposed a party with a well-favored and
celebrated courtesan named Spiletta, who did not sell her
favors cheaply, and I refused. Doña Ignacia occupied me

entirely. I thought her very worthy to succeed to Charlotte.[25]

I arrived at La Soledad before her; she saw me in the
corner of a confessional as soon as she entered with the
girl who had been her companion the first time. She came
and knelt down two paces from me; she never looked at
me; the one who constantly examined me was her friend,
who was extremely ugly but of the same age. I saw Don
Francisco in the church, so I left it before Doña Ignacia
did. He joined me, and he congratulated me somewhat
bitterly on the good fortune I had had to go to the ball a
second time with the sovereign of his soul. He confessed
that he had followed us all night, and that he could have
left the ball well enough pleased if he had not seen us
dance the fandango, for he had thought we looked too
much like a pair of happy lovers. I told him with a laugh
that love was subject to delusions, and that as an intelligent man he should not allow his soul to harbor any suspicions. At the same moment, begging his pardon, I gave
him a doblón de a ocho as a payment on account. He
accepts it, utterly astonished, he calls me his father, his
good angel, and he promises me eternal gratitude. He
leaves, assuring me he was certain that, as soon as I
could, I would give him the entire sum he needed in order
to marry Doña Ignacia after Easter, for the Carnival was
about to end, and weddings were forbidden in Lent.

Toward nightfall I called on the shoemaker, who at
once treated me to some of the excellent ratafia which I
had given to Doña Antonia, his wife, who, together with
her daughter, did nothing but talk of the obligation
under which the Count of Aranda had laid the nation by
what he had done.[26]

"Nothing," said Doña Antonia, "is more innocent
than a ball, nothing is better for the health, and it was
forbidden before that great man occupied the exalted
post in which he can do whatever he pleases, and yet he is
hated because he banished *los padres de la Compañía*,[27]

and he forbade heel-length cloaks and *sombreros gachos*.[28] But the poor bless him, for all the money which the ball at los Caños del Peral [29] brings in goes to the poor.''

''And so,'' said Don Diego the cobbler, ''those who go to the ball do a work of charity.''

''I have two cousins,'' Doña Ignacia said to me, ''girls who, so far as their conduct goes, are angels. I told them I had been to the ball with you, and, since they are poor, they had no hope of going; you could easily make them happy by inviting them to go with me on the last day of the Carnival. Their mother would let them come, and the more willingly because the ball ends at midnight in order not to infringe on Ash Wednesday.''

''I am ready, my good Doña Ignacia, to give you so innocent a pleasure. In that case the Señora would not have to spend the night in the carriage waiting for you.''

''You are very kind; but you must be introduced to my aunt, who is a woman who carries religion to the point of scrupulosity. When she has made your acquaintance I am sure that she will not object when I propose the party to her, for one sees in you a man of good conduct who cannot have the slightest evil designs on her daughters. Go there today; they live in the first house in the next street, where you will see a small sign on the door saying that laces are mended there. Take some laces with you in your pocket, and say that it was my mother who gave you their address. Tomorrow morning on my way home from mass I will do the rest, and you shall come here at noon to learn how we can all meet on the last day of the Carnival.''

I did all this in accordance with Doña Ignacia's instructions. I took some laces to her cousins, and the next day my beauty told me that everything was arranged. I told her that I should have all the dominoes at my inn, that the three of them had only to come there together, going in by the back door, that we would dine in my room, that we would mask afterward to go to the ball,

and that after the ball I would see them all home. I said
that I would dress the elder of her cousins as a man, for
she would look just like one, and that she should tell her
so beforehand; she said with a laugh that she would not
tell her, but that she was sure she would do whatever I
told her to do.

The younger of the two cousins was ugly, but she had
the look of her sex. The ugliness of the elder was surprising. Extraordinarily tall, she looked like an ill-favored
man dressed as a woman. The contrast amused me, for
Doña Ignacia was a perfect beauty and seduction itself
when she sent her pious airs to the devil.

I saw to having dominoes and everything necessary in
a closet adjoining my room, without my page knowing
anything about it; and on Tuesday morning I gave him
a peso duro with which to go and spend the last day of
the Carnival wherever he pleased, telling him that he
need not be back to serve me until the next day at noon. I
bought myself a pair of shoes, I ordered a good dinner
for four at an inn nearby, and I arranged for the waiter
in the coffeehouse to wait on me. I also got rid of Marazzani by giving him enough to go to dine wherever he
pleased, and I prepared to laugh myself and to inspire
laughter in Doña Ignacia, whom love was certain to make
my mistress that day. The party was a complete novelty,
consisting of three pious girls, two of them revoltingly
ugly, and the third, as pretty as possible, whom I had
already initiated and who had become softened and
tamed.

They came at noon, and until one o'clock, when we sat
down at table, I treated them to nothing but sage and
moral discourses with much unction. I had wine from
La Mancha,[30] which was exquisite but which is as strong
as Hungarian wine. The poor girls were not used to
spending two hours at table and not rising until their appetites were satisfied. Unaccustomed to unmixed wine,
they did not get drunk, but they became heated and suc-

for he was hungry and had not a copper; I told him to
tell him that I would give him nothing, for in prison he
was no longer in my service. So I saw all my fellow pris-
oners eat the wretched soup and bread and drink water,
except two priests and a man who was addressed as *cor-
regidor* ("magistrate"), the three of whom ate well.

It was at three o'clock that one of the Cavaliere
Mengs's servants brought me a dinner which would have
fed four amply. He wanted to leave the dinner and come
back in the evening to take away the dishes and bring me
supper; but in the evil humor in which I was I did not
want to have to bestow my leavings either on the rabble
whose companion I had become or on the soldiers. I made
the servant wait, and I ate and drank, setting everything
out on a bench; then I told him to take everything that
was left back to the house and not to return until the next
day, for I did not want supper. The servant obeyed, and
the rabble treated him to catcalls. Marazzani said to me
harshly that I might at least have kept the bottle of wine.
I did not answer him.

At five o'clock Manuzzi[43] entered gloomily with the
officer of the guard. After he had condoled with me and
I had thanked him, I asked the officer if I was permitted
to write to those who could not leave me in this plight
except because they knew nothing of it, and, he having
answered me that it would be tyranny not to let me do so,
I asked him if it was within the rights of a soldier, to
whom I had given an écu to buy me some paper at
eight o'clock that morning, to steal my money and disap-
pear.

"What soldier?"

I ask his name of everyone, and so does he, but in vain;
no one has the least idea, the guard had been changed.
The officer promises me that he will have my écu returned
to me and the soldier punished. The officer at once has
writing materials, a table, and a candle brought me, and
Manuzzi promises me that at eight o'clock he will send a

servant in the Ambassador's livery to take my letters and
deliver them to their addresses, assuring me that the Ambassador will act for me privately, for he did not think
he could do so openly. Before they leave I take from my
pocket three écus, and I tell the rabble that I will give
them to those who will tell the name of the soldier who
had stolen the écu from me. At that, Marazzani was the
first to name him, two others bore him out, and the officer,
who knew him, wrote down his name, laughing a little,
and learning to know me. I was spending three écus to
recover one. They left, and I fell to writing. The patience
I had to show is unbelievable. Some came to read what I
was writing and, when they did not understand it, demanded that I explain it. One came to snuff my candle,
and put it out. I imagined I was in the galleys, and I
bore it without complaining. A soldier had the impertinence to tell me that if I would give him an écu he
would make everyone keep quiet, and I did not answer
him. But despite all these damned souls I finished my
letters and sealed them. There was no art in my letters.
They breathed the venom which was circulating in my
soul.

I wrote the Ambassador Mocenigo that he was obliged
by his position to defend a subject of his prince whom
the ministers of a foreign power were murdering in order
to seize everything he possessed. I told him to reflect that
he could not refuse me his protection unless he knew how
I could have broken the laws of the Republic, for my difference with the State Inquisitors arose from nothing
but the fact that Signora Zorzi preferred me to Signor
Condulmer,[44] who, jealous of my good fortune, had had
me imprisoned under the Leads.

I wrote to Señor Manuel de Roda,[45] a learned man, the
Minister of Grace and Justice, that I did not want his
grace but only his justice.

"Serve God, Monseigneur, and your master the King,
by preventing the Alcalde Messa from murdering a Vene-

tian who has done nothing contrary to the laws and who came to Spain only in the belief that he was coming to a country inhabited by honest men and not by murderers whom the posts they are given authorize to murder with impunity. The man who writes to you has in his pocket a purse filled with doblones, and is imprisoned in a room in which he has already been robbed. He fears that he will be murdered tonight for the sake of his purse and everything he possesses.''

I wrote the Duke of Losada to inform the King his master that certain servants of his, without his knowledge but in his name, were murdering a Venetian who had broken no law; whose only crime was to be rich enough not to need anyone so long as he remained in Spain. I put it to him that he ought to ask the King to send an order at once which would prevent such a murder.

The strongest of my four letters was the one I wrote to the Count of Aranda. I told him that if the murderers ended by killing me I should believe before I died that it was by his order, because I had vainly told the officer who arrested me that I had come to Madrid with a letter from a Princess recommending me to him.

"I have done nothing," I told him. "What compensation am I to receive, when you have me released from this inferno, for the ill treatment I have already undergone? Either have me released at once, or order your executioners to dispatch me quickly, for if they take it into their heads to send me to a *presidio,* I will kill myself first with my own hand."

Keeping copies of my letters, I dispatched them by the Ambassador's lackey, whom the all-powerful Manuzzi did not fail to send me. But I spent the cruelest of nights. The beds were full, but even had they not been, I should not have wanted to get into one. I asked in vain for straw, but even if it had been brought me I should not have known where to put it. The floor was soaked with urine, for, with two or three exceptions, no one had a chamber pot. Burning with anger, I would not spend a copper for some small comfort, and my giving three écus to have the officer told the name of the thieving soldier had only irritated the rabble all the more. I spent the whole night sitting on a bench without a back.

At seven o'clock in the morning Manuzzi came in. I at once asked him to arrange for me to go to the guardroom with himself and the officer to eat something, for I felt that I was dying; and it was done at once. I drank some chocolate, and I made their hair stand on end with my account of my sufferings. Manuzzi told me that my letters could not be taken to their addresses except in the course of the day; and he said with a laugh that I had written the Ambassador a harsh letter. I then showed him copies of the others, and the inexperienced young man said that the proper tone for obtaining what one asked for was mildness. He did not know that there are situations in which it is absolutely impossible for a man to use a mild tone. Manuzzi whispered to me that the Ambassador would dine that day at the Count of Aranda's, and that he had promised him he would speak to him privately in my favor; but that he was afraid that my ferocious letter would have irritated the Spaniard. I warned him not to say anything to the Ambassador about my letter.

An hour after he left, just when, sitting among the rabble, I was pretending not to notice the impertinences addressed to me on the score of my haughtiness, which offended them all, I see Doña Ignacia, accompanied by her father the noble cobbler, come in with the kind captain who had done me so many favors. Their visit wounded me to the soul, but I had to make the best of it, and gratefully, for it proceeded from merit, magnanimity, virtue, and humanity in the worthy man and in the pious and amorous Doña Ignacia who were paying it to me.

Though sadly, and in very bad Spanish, I managed to make them understand how deeply I felt the honor they were doing me. Doña Ignacia never said a word; it was the only way she had to keep the tears from welling from her beautiful eyes; but Don Diego summoned all his eloquence to tell me that he would never have come to see me if he was not absolutely certain that a mistake had been made, or that it was some horrible calumny, of the kind which deceives judges for a few days. From this he drew the conclusion that in a few days I would be released from this foul place and that I would receive a satisfaction proportionate to the insult which had been put upon me. I replied that I hoped so; but what surprised me, and touched me to the soul, was what this very poor man did when he left, embracing me. He put into my hands a roll, whispering to me that there were twelve doblones de a ocho in it, which I should return to him when I could. My hair stood on end. I whispered to him that I had fifty in my pocket which I did not dare show him because I feared the thieves by whom I was surrounded. At that, he put his roll back in his pocket, and he wept. I promised to visit him as soon as I should be set free. He went; he had not sent in his name. He was well dressed, he was taken to be a man of substance. Such characters are not uncommon in Spain. The noble, heroic act is the craze of the Castilian.

Mengs's servant came at noon with a dinner which was more choice and less abundant; which was what I wanted. I ate in his presence in half an hour, and he went away, carrying my compliments to his master. At one o'clock a man entered and told me to come with him. He took me to a small room, in which I saw my carbine and pistols. The Alcalde Messa, seated at a table covered with notebooks, with two clerks, told me to sit down; then he ordered me to reply truthfully to all his questions, for my answers would be written down. I told him that I understood very little Spanish, and that I would never answer anything except in writing to a person who would question me in Italian, French, or Latin. This reply, ut-

tered in a firm voice, astonished him. He talked to me for
a whole hour, I understood everything he said, but all
that he ever got by way of reply was:

"I do not understand what you are saying. Find a
judge who knows one of my languages, and then I will
answer; but I will not dictate; I will write my answer
myself."

He grew angry, I paid no attention to his outbursts.
Finally he gave me a pen, and he told me to write in
Italian my name, my rank, and what I had come to Spain
to do. I could not refuse him that satisfaction, but I wrote
only a score of lines:

"*I am So-and-so, a subject of the Republic of Venice,
a man of letters, moderately rich; I am traveling for my
pleasure; I am known to the Ambassador of my country,
to the Count of Aranda, to Prince della Cattolica, to the
Marqués de Mora, to the Duke of Losada; I have not
broken the least of His Catholic Majesty's[46] laws, and
nevertheless I find myself being murdered, and confined
with criminals and thieves by ministers who would deserve to be treated far more harshly than I. If I have
done nothing against the laws, His Catholic Majesty must
know that he has no right over me except to order me to
leave his domains, and I will obey the instant I receive
that order. My weapons which I see here have traveled
with me for eleven years, I carry them only to defend
myself against highway robbers, and at the Puerta de
Alcalá they were seen in my carriage and they were not
confiscated; which shows that their confiscation now is
only a pretext to murder me.*"

After writing this document I give it to the Alcalde,
who sends for a man who faithfully translates the whole
of it into Spanish for him. The Alcalde rises, looks at me
with eyes venomous with anger, and says:

"*Valgame Dios* ['*So help me God*'], *you will repent of
having written this document.*"

So saying, he has me escorted back to the room in which I had been, and he leaves.

At eight o'clock Manuzzi came to tell me that the Count of Aranda had been the first to ask the Ambassador if he knew me, and that the Ambassador had told him nothing but good about me, ending by assuring him that he was sorry he could not be of use to me in the matter of an affront to which I had been subjected, because I was in disfavor with the State Inquisitors. The Count of Aranda replied that a great affront had indeed been put on me, but it was not such as to make an intelligent man lose his head.

"*'I should have known nothing about it,'* he said to him, *'if he had not written me a furious letter, and he wrote others in the same style to Don Manuel de Roda and to the Duke of Losada. He is in the right, but one does not write such letters.'* That is all he said to him."

"Then my troubles are over, if it is true that he said I am in the right."

"You may be sure that he said it."

"If he said it he will do what is right, and, as for my letters, everyone has his style. I became angry and maddened because I have been treated like a dog; look at this room, I have no bed, and, running with urine as it is, I cannot lie on the floor; I shall spend a second night sitting on this bench without a back. Do you think it possible that I do not want to eat the hearts of all my executioners? If I do not leave this inferno tomorrow I will kill myself or go mad."

Manuzzi understood that I could not but be in a state of desperation; he promised he would come to see me early the next morning, and he advised me to pay for a bed. I would not take his advice. The lice horrified me, and I feared for my purse, my watch, my snuffbox, and everything I had. I spent a terrible night dozing on the same bench, constantly starting awake when, losing my balance, I was on the verge of falling into the stinking filth on the floor.

Manuzzi came at eight o'clock and I saw that he was really terrified at the sight of my face. He had come in a carriage, bringing with him some excellent chocolate, which he ordered heated, which I drank with pleasure, and which gave me a little courage. But the door opens, and in comes an officer, followed by two others. The first officer asks for me; I approach him, saying that it is I.

"His Excellency the Count of Aranda," he says, "is outside, and greatly regrets the misfortune which has befallen you. He learned of it yesterday from the letter you wrote him. If you had written to him at once, nothing would have happened to you."

I told him the story of the soldier who had robbed me of an écu. He asked who he was, and as soon as he was informed of everything he summoned the captain, reprimanded him, ordered him to give me an écu, which I accepted with a laugh, and to send someone to find the soldier so that he could be flogged in my presence. The officer was Count Rojas,[47] Colonel of the regiment which was at Buen Retiro. I then told him in detail the whole story of my arrest and all the sufferings I had endured in the accursed place in which I had been put. I told him that if I were not given back my freedom, my weapons, and my honor in the course of that day, I would kill myself or go mad, for a man had to lie down once a day, and I had not been able to lie either on a bed or on the floor because of the filth he would have seen if he had arrived an hour earlier.

I saw the worthy man surprised by the fury with which I spoke to him. Noticing it, I asked him to excuse me, assuring him that when I was not overcome by rage I was entirely different. Manuzzi told him what my natural temperament was, and the Colonel condoled with me. He sighed, and he gave me his word of honor that I should leave the place in the course of the day, that my weapons would be returned to me, and that I would sleep in my own bed.

"After that," he said, "you shall go to thank the Count of Aranda, who has come here purposely and who has ordered me to tell you that you shall not return to your lodging until afternoon, for His Excellency wants you to have a satisfaction sufficient to restore your peace of mind and make you forget this insult, if it is one, for what is done in the name of the law insults no one, and in your case the Alcalde Messa was deceived by the scoundrel who was in your service."

"There he is," I said. "I ask you as a favor to have him removed from here, since he is known to be a monster."

He went out, and two minutes later two soldiers came to take him, and I did not see him again. I never troubled to learn what had become of the wretch. It was then that he had me go to the guardroom to see the flogging which was given the thieving soldier. I saw the Count of Aranda forty paces from me, walking up and down followed by a number of officers and one of the King's Bodyguard. All this kept us occupied for two hours and a half. Before leaving, the Colonel invited me to dine at his house with Mengs when he next invited him. I had to return to the room, where I found a folding bed set up on planks, which looked clean. A noncommissioned officer told me it was for me, and I instantly lay down on it, but Manuzzi, before leaving me, embraced me again and again. I was convinced that he was my true friend, and it still saddens me when I think that I did him a wrong[48] for which I am not surprised that he never forgave me, for I have never been able to forgive myself for it. The reader will see, however, that the young man carried his vengeance too far.

After this scene the rabble in the room no longer dared to look at me. Marazzani came to my bedside to beg for my good offices, but I did not let him suppose that I had any influence. I said that in Spain a foreigner was doing a great deal if he was able to look after himself. I was brought dinner as usual, and at three o'clock the Alcalde Messa came to tell me to go with him because, having made a mistake, he had received an order to escort me back to my apartment, where he hoped that I should find everything I had left there. At the same time he showed me my carbine and my pistols which he handed to one of his men to carry to my room. The officer of the guard gave me back my sword; the Alcalde, in a black cloak, took his place at my left and, followed by thirty constables, escorted me to the coffeehouse in the Calle de la Cruz, where he removed the seal on the door of my room, which the landlord came to open, and where I was easily able to tell the Alcalde that everything was as I had left it. He said to me as he left that, if I had not had a traitor in my service, I should never have been led to believe that His Catholic Majesty's ministers were murderers.

"Anger, Señor Alcalde, made me write the same thing to four ministers. I believed it, and I no longer believe it. Let us forget everything; but admit that, if I had not known how to write, you would have sent me to the galleys."

"Alas, it is possible."

I washed, and I changed all my clothes; more from duty than from affection, I paid a visit to the truly noble cobbler, who, on seeing me, called himself the most fortunate of men and the most foresighted, for he was certain that a mistake must have been made; but Doña Ignacia was beside herself with joy, for she had felt none of her father's certainty. When he learned what kind of satisfaction I had received, he said that a Grandee of Spain could ask no more. I invited them to come to dine with me somewhere as soon as I sent them word, and they promised to do so. Gratitude having entered in, I found myself much more in love with Doña Ignacia than I had been before.

On leaving the Calle del Desengaño I went to see Mengs, who, knowing Spain, expected anything rather than to see me. But when he heard the story of the whole day, in which I had had so many triumphs, he congratulated me as he should. He was in gala dress, a very unusual thing; and he told me that he had gone to see Don Manuel de Roda, hoping to be useful to me with him, but that he had not been able to speak to him. He gave me a letter from Venice which he had received that day, and which I quickly unsealed, recognizing Signor Dandolo's[49] hand; in it I find a sealed letter, addressed to Signor Mocenigo, Ambassador. Signor Dandolo wrote me that, after reading the enclosed letter, the Ambassador would no longer fear to displease the State Inquisitors by giving me introductions, for the person who had written him the letter recommended me to him in the name of one of the three Inquisitors.[50] At that, Mengs says that it is in my power to make my fortune in Spain, provided that I behave myself, and especially now that the ministers were under an obligation to treat me in a way to make me forget the outrage to which I had been subjected. He advises me to take the letter to the Ambassador that very moment, and to use his carriage, for after sixty hours of continual torture I could not stand. Needing to go to bed, I excuse myself from returning to his house for supper, but I promise to dine there the next day. The Ambassador was not in. I leave the letter with Manuzzi, and I go home, where I go to bed to enjoy ten hours of the deepest sleep.

Manuzzi comes very early in the morning, with his face the picture of joy, to bring me the news that Signor Girolamo Zulian[51] wrote the Ambassador on behalf of Signor da Mula that he could introduce me everywhere, for my quarrel with the tribunal was in no way prejudicial to my honor.

''The Ambassador expects to present you at Court at

Aranjuez[52] next week, and he wants you to dine with him today with a large company.''

"I am engaged to dine with Mengs."

"I shall go to invite Mengs at once, and, if he declines, you must disappoint him, for you must be aware of the fine effect your entrance at the Ambassador's is bound to produce on the day after your triumph."

"You are right. Go to Mengs; and I will dine at the Ambassador's."

CHAPTER II

*Campomanes. Olavides. Sierra Morena. Aran-
juez. Mengs. The Marchese Grimaldi. Toledo.
Signora Pelliccia. Return to Madrid and to the
house of Doña Ignacia's father.*

IN THE principal vicissitudes of my life particular
circumstances combined to make my poor mind a trifle
superstitious. I feel humiliated when, reflecting upon myself, I recognize this truth. But how can I help it? It is in
the nature of things that Fortune should do to a man
who surrenders himself to her whims what a child does to
an ivory sphere on a billiard table when he pushes it one
way and another, only to burst out laughing when he
sees it fall into a pocket; but it is not in the nature of
things, it seems to me, that Fortune should do to such a
man what a skillful player, who calculates the force, the
speed, the distance, and the regularity of the reaction,
does to the billiard ball; it is not in the nature of things,
as I conceive it to be, that I should do Fortune the honor
to believe that she is skilled in geometry, or that I should
posit in that metaphysical being the physical laws to
which I find that all nature is subject. Despite this reasoning, what I observe astonishes me. The very same Fortune

I ought to regard with contempt, as synonymous with chance, becomes an object to be respected, as if she wanted to reveal herself to me as a goddess, in the most decisive events in my life. She has amused herself by constantly showing me that she is not blind, as people say; she has never cast me into the depths except to raise me proportionately high, and she seems never to have made me rise very high except to give herself the pleasure of seeing me fall. It seems that she has exercised absolute dominion over me only in order to convince me that she reasons and that she is the ruler of all things; to convince me of it, she employed striking means to compel me to act, and to make me understand that my will, far from declaring me free, was only an instrument which she used to make what she would of me.

I could not hope to attain to anything in Spain without the help of my country's Ambassador, and he, in his pusillanimity, would never have dared to do anything without the letter which I presented to him; and the letter would have led to nothing if it had not arrived precisely at the moment when my arrest, and the reparation which the Count of Aranda ordered to be given me, had made my adventure the talk of the day.

The letter made the Ambassador blush for not having acted in my favor before it arrived; but he did not despair of making people believe that the Count of Aranda had given me such ample reparation only because he had demanded it. His favorite, Count Manuzzi, had brought me an invitation to dinner from him, and luck would have it that I was engaged to dine with Mengs. Manuzzi had the good sense to go to Mengs with an invitation from the Ambassador, which greatly flattered the vain man with whom I had taken refuge, though in vain. The invitation became in his eyes a token of gratitude, which made up to him for the mortification he had suffered from having to let me be taken from his house. After accepting the invitation, and learning from Manuzzi that I had already been invited, he wrote me a note to tell me that he would come for me in his carriage at one o'clock.

I went to call on the Count of Aranda, who, after making me wait a quarter of an hour, came out with some papers.

"The thing is over," he said to me serenely, "and I believe that you can be satisfied. Here are four letters, which I return to you to read."

I see my three letters to him, to the Duke of Losada, and to the Minister of Grace and Justice.

"Why, my Lord, must I read these letters? This is the statement submitted to the Señor Alcalde."

"I know that. Read them all, and you will see that, despite your having been entirely in the right, it is not allowable to write in such a way."

"I beg your pardon. A man who has resolved to kill himself, as I had done, cannot write otherwise. I thought that everything done to me was by Your Excellency's order."

"You did not know me. However, you will go to thank Don Manuel de Roda, who wants to make your acquaintance without fail, and I will take it as a favor if you will go sometime at your convenience to the Alcalde, not to apologize to him but to say something pleasant which will make him forget the insulting things you say to him in your statement. If you inform Princess Lubomirska[1] of this affair, tell her that as soon as I heard of it I set it to rights."

After having thus done my duty to the Count of Aranda, I called on Colonel Rojas, who told me in so many words that I had made a great mistake to tell the Count of Aranda that I was satisfied.

"What could I demand?"

"Everything. The Alcalde's resignation. A sum of money in compensation for what you were made to suffer in that horrible place. You are in a country where you do not need to hold your tongue unless you have to deal with the Inquisition.''

Colonel Rojas, who is now a general, is one of the most amiable men I met in Spain.

I returned to my apartment, and Mengs came to fetch me. The Ambassador paid me countless attentions, and heaped praise on the painter Mengs for having tried, by giving me asylum in his house, to save me from a misfortune which would overwhelm any man. It was at table that I gave a detailed account of all that I had suffered at Buen Retiro, and of the conversation I had just had with the Count of Aranda, who had returned my letters to me. Everyone wanted to read them, and everyone expressed his opinion. The guests were the French Consul, the Abbé Béliardi,[2] Don Rodrigo de Campomanes,[3] who was very celebrated, and the equally celebrated Don Pablo de Olavides.[4] Each of them gave his opinion on my letters, which the Ambassador condemned, calling them ferocious; but Campomanes maintained that my letters, which contained no insults, were just what was needed to make the reader see that I was in the right, even if he were the King. Olavides and Béliardi were of the same opinion. Mengs was of the Ambassador's, and invited me to go to stay in his house and so have done with the calumnies of spies, of which Madrid was full. I did not accept Mengs's invitation until after I had been urged for some time and after having heard the Ambassador himself say that I really must give the Cavaliere Mengs that satisfaction for, in addition to its being a great honor to me, it would be a satisfaction which was due to him.

What really pleased me at the dinner was making the acquaintance of Campomanes and Olavides. They were both men of an intelligence very uncommon in Spain, for, though not learned, they were well aware of all the prejudices and abuses which accompany religion there, and they not only publicly mocked them, they acted openly to destroy them. It was Campomanes who had furnished

the Count of Aranda with all the matter of complaint
against the Jesuits, whom the Count had driven out of
Spain in one day. Campomanes squinted, the Count of
Aranda squinted, and the General of the Jesuits
squinted; at table I laughed at the dissension among the
three strabismics,[5] one of whom, as was only to be expected, had been crushed by the two others. I asked
Campomanes why he hated the Jesuits, and he replied
that he hated them no more than he did the other religious orders, which, if he could have had his way, he
would have destroyed one and all. He was the author of
everything that had been published against the mortmains,[6] enjoying, as he did, the friendship of the Venetian Ambassador, who had communicated to him all that
the Senate had done against the monks—information
which Campomanes would not have needed if he had read
and put into practice all that our Fra Paolo Sarpi[7] wrote
on the subject in perfect honesty. Far-seeing, courageous,
active, Treasurer of the Supreme Council of Castile, of
which Aranda was President, Campomanes was recognized to be a man who did not act as he did from private
interest, but for the good of the State. So the statesmen
respected and valued him; but the monks, the priests, the
bigots, and all the rabble infected with the fear of offending God and the saints by acting against the temporal
interests of the ecclesiastics and the beneficiaries of mortmain hated Campomanes with a mortal hatred. The Inquisition must have sworn to destroy him, and everyone
said that in two or three years Campomanes would either
have to become a bishop or be shut up in the prisons of
the Inquisition for life. This prediction was fulfilled only
in part. Campomanes was imprisoned by the Inquisition
four years later,[8] remained in prison for three years, and
did not leave it until he made a formal retraction. His
friend Olavides was treated more harshly;[9] and even the
Count of Aranda would not have escaped the horrible
monster's fury if, profoundly intelligent and foresighted,

he had not asked to be appointed Ambassador to France,[10] which the King at once granted him, glad thus to find himself rid of the obligation to hand him over to the accursed fury of the monks.

Carlos III, who died mad,[11] as almost all kings must die, had done things which even those who knew him could not believe, for he was weak, gross, stubborn, excessively devoted to religion, and inalterably determined to die a hundred deaths before he would stain his soul with the smallest of mortal sins. Everyone sees that such a man must have been completely the slave of his confessor. The excesses committed by the Jesuits[12] in Portugal, the Indies, and France had already made them hated and openly condemned in all the four quarters of the globe; and the crime of the Jesuit confessor of Don Fernando VI,[13] which had brought about the ruin of Ensenada,[14] had taught his successor Carlos III that he must not have a Jesuit as his confessor, since the interest of the State demanded the destruction of *los Teatinos*.[15]

So they were called in Spain, and the Theatines were called *Cayetanos*.[16]

The same confessor, then, who quieted all the King's scruples against the great operation of destroying a whole religious order, was also obliged to yield to the King and give him the reins when, at the same time, the Count of Aranda showed him that he must set limits to the excessive power of the Inquisition, whose great work was to keep Christians in ignorance and to maintain in force abuses, superstitions, and the *pia mendacia* ("pious falsehoods") ;[17] the confessor's policy could not but give him the reins. He was certain that he could plunge the King back into the abyss of superstition whenever he pleased; and he succeeded. However, I was never able to learn if, two years after my departure, the King was given a new confessor,[18] for, unhappily for poor mankind, it is decreed that a pious king will never do anything but what his confessor will let him do, and it is

obvious that the confessor's chief interest can never be
the good of the State, since religion, as it exists, is directly opposed to it. If I am told that a wise king can
always keep matters of State out of his confession, I will
admit it; but I am not talking of a wise king, for if he is
such, as a Christian he need go to confession only once a
year and hear the voice of his confessor only in the words
he utters to absolve him; if the king needs to talk with
him to clear up doubts he is a fool; doubts and scruples
are the same thing; he who goes to confession should
know his religion before he goes to it. No doubts, no discussions with his confessor. Louis XIV would have been
the greatest king on earth, greater than Frederick II,
King of Prussia, if he had not had the weakness to chatter
with his confessors.

At that time the Spanish Cabinet was engaged in a
promising undertaking. A thousand families had been
brought from various Swiss cantons and been sent to live
in the fine deserted countryside called *las sierras de
Morena*,[19] a name famous in Europe, being well known
to all who have read Cervantes' masterpiece, the magnificent romance which tells the story of Don Quixote. Nature had endowed the place with all the gifts which
should have made it populous, an excellent climate, fertile
soil, pure water, advantageous situation, for the *sierras*
(which means "mountains") are between the Kingdoms
of Andalusia and Granada; nevertheless this beautiful
countryside, this vast and delicious abode, was deserted.
The King of Spain resolves that for a limited time he
will make a present of the products of the soil to colonists,
he invites them to come, paying for their journey, they
come, they go there, and the Government makes every
effort to lodge them and to set up an excellent administration for them, both spiritual and temporal. This enterprise had the support of Señor Olavides, a man of
intelligence and education. It was he who conferred with
the ministers in Madrid to establish order in the settle-

ment, to provide it with judges who would render prompt justice, with priests of course, for these Swiss were all Catholics, with a governor, with artisans in all the necessary trades to build houses, churches, and above all a theater or circus in which to give bullfights, a favorite spectacle in Spain, and so beautiful, so humane, so natural, and so reasonable that the thinkers of that country cannot understand how there can possibly be nations in the world who can do without it. So in the Sierra Morena the worthy emigrants from Switzerland found a huge circular amphitheater, so that on certain days they could enjoy that delicious spectacle.

Don Pablo de Olavides in the memorials which he had presented for the greater prosperity of the promising colony had said that all establishments of monks should be excluded, and he gave very good reasons for it; but even if he had demonstrated it infallibly, compass in hand, it took no more to make every monk in Spain his enemy, and even the Bishop[20] of whose diocese Morena was a part. The priests of Spain said that he was right, but the monks cried out against such impiety, and persecutions were already beginning; and the subject was raised at the Ambassador's table.

After letting them talk as long as they pleased, I said as modestly as I could that the colony would vanish like a dream within a few years, for several reasons both material and moral. The principal reason which I alleged was that the Swiss was a mortal of a different species from other men.

"He is," I said, "a plant which, transplanted from the soil in which it was born, dies. The Swiss are subject to a disease called *Heimweh*,[21] which means 'return,' what the Greeks called *nostalgia*;[22] when they are away from their country, after a certain period of time the disease overtakes them, the only remedy is returning to their country; if they do not employ it they die."

I said that it might be worth trying to combine them

with another colony of Spanish men and women, in order
to bind them by marriages; I said that at least in the beginning they must be given Swiss priests and judges, and
above all they must be declared free from all inquisition
into matters of conscience, for the true Swiss had customs
and laws in regard to making love[23] which were inseparable from their nature, and ceremonies of which the
Spanish church would never approve, which would make
the disease of *Heimweh* attack them in a very short time.

My discourse, which Don Olavides at first took to be
only banter, in the end persuaded him that all I had
said might be true. He asked me to set down my reflections in writing, and to communicate any thoughts I
might have on the subject only to him. I promised to give
him all my ideas to read, and Mengs set a day when he
could dine at his house. It was on the next day that I had
my few belongings carried to Mengs's, and that I began
working on the subject of the colonies, treating them
from the point of view both of the natural sciences and of
philosophy.

The next day I went to call on Don Manuel de Roda,
who—a very rare thing in Spain—was a man of letters.
He was fond of Latin poetry, he had some appreciation
of Italian poetry, but he gave the preference to the Spanish. He received me with great courtesy, he asked me to
come to see him, and he expressed his regret for the vexa-
tion my imprisonment in Buen Retiro had caused me.
The Duke of Losada congratulated me on the Venetian
Ambassador's speaking well of me to everyone, and encouraged me to think that I might draw profit from my
talents by proposing myself for some employment in
which I could be useful to the Government, and he promised me his full support. Prince della Cattolica had me
to dinner with the Venetian Ambassador. In three weeks,
lodging at Mengs's and often dining at the Ambassador's,
I made a quantity of valuable acquaintances. I thought
of finding employment in Spain, for, receiving no letters

from Lisbon, I did not dare to go there simply on the chance that something would turn up. The Portuguese lady[24] no longer wrote to me, I had no way of knowing what had become of her.

To pass the evenings I had fallen into the habit of calling on Signora Sabatini,[25] on a Spanish lady who had a *tertulia,* that is, whose evening receptions were frequented by men of letters, all of them paltry, and on the Duke of Medina Sidonia,[26] Master of the Horse to the King, man of letters, sound and reliable, to whom I had been presented by Don Domingo Varnier,[27] valet to the King, whose acquaintance Mengs had procured me. I often went to see Doña Ignacia, but since I could never be alone with her I was bored. When I found an opportunity to tell her that she should think of some excursion with her ugly cousins, for in the country I could give her proofs of my constancy, she replied that she wanted it as much as I did, but at that season she must banish all such ideas, for Holy Week was drawing near, God had died for us, we must think not of criminal pleasures but of doing penance. After Easter we could think of our love. Such is the character of almost all the pious beauties in Spain.

Two weeks before Easter the King of Spain left Madrid for Aranjuez with the whole Court. The Venetian Ambassador invited me to go there to stay in his house, so that he could have a good opportunity to present me. On the day before we were to leave, I succumbed to a fever as I sat beside Mengs in his carriage on the way to visit the widow of the painter Amigoni.[28] The fever, which came on with chills such as it is impossible to conceive, made me shake so much that my head struck the roof of the carriage. My teeth were chattering, I could not utter a word. Mengs, in terror, ordered the coachman to return home at speed, I was quickly put to bed, where four or five hours later a violent sweat which continued

for ten or twelve hours without intermission expelled
from my body at least twenty pints of water, for it ran
over the floor after passing through two mattresses and a
straw pallet. Forty-eight hours later the fever ended, but
weakness kept me in bed for a week. On the Saturday
before Easter I took a carriage and went to Aranjuez,
where I was very well received and very well lodged by
the Ambassador; but a small pustule which, on leaving
Madrid, I had near the place where I had had the fistula
was so much irritated on the road by the jolting of the
carriage that when I arrived in Aranjuez in the evening
it made me extremely uncomfortable. During the night
the pustule swelled to the size of a big pear, so that, the
day being Easter, I could not get up to go to mass. In
five days the tumor became an abscess as big as a melon;
it terrified not only the Ambassador and Manuzzi but an
old French surgeon of the King's, who swore that he had
never seen the like. As for me, being the only one who
was not terrified, for the abscess caused me no pain and
was not hard, I told the surgeon to open it. I described to
him, in the presence of a physician, the kind of fever I
had just had in Madrid, and I convinced him that the
abscess could come only from a quantity of lymph which
had accumulated in that place and which, as soon as it
was discharged, would leave me in perfect health. The
physician having declared my reasoning sound, the surgeon exercised his art; he made a six-inch opening, after
putting under me a large sheet folded thirty-two times.
Though my abscess could have contained only a pint of
liquid, it is none the less true that the lymph which left
my body through it in the course of four days was as
abundant as that which had come out of me as sweat during the fever I had had at Mengs's house. At the end of
the four days almost no trace remained of the opening
which the surgeon had made. I had to stay in bed because
of my weakness; but I was very much surprised when I

received in my bed a letter from Mengs which an express messenger brought me. I open it, and here is what I find in bad Italian, which I have before me now:

"Yesterday the priest of my parish posted on the door of his church the names of all those who are lodged in his district and who, not believing in God, did not take the sacrament at Easter. Among the names I saw yours, and I had to swallow a reproof from the priest, who said bitterly that he was surprised to see that I granted hospitality to heretics[29] in my house. I did not know what to answer him, for it is true that you could have stayed in Madrid one day longer and done the duty of a Christian, if only because of the consideration you owed me. What I owe to the King my master, the care I must take to preserve my reputation and my peace in the future oblige me meanwhile to inform you that my house is no longer yours. On your return to Madrid you will go to lodge where you please, and my servants will deliver your belongings to whomever you authorize to come for them. I am, etc. . . . Antonio Rafael Mengs."

This letter had such an effect on me that Mengs would certainly not have written it with impunity if he had not been seven long Spanish leagues[30] distant from me. I told the messenger to go. He replied that he was ordered to wait for my answer, whereupon I tore the letter in two, and I told him it was all the answer such a letter deserved. At that he left in great surprise. Without losing time, and in the heat of my anger, I dressed and I went in a sedan chair to the church in Aranjuez, where I confessed to a Franciscan monk, who gave me the sacrament at six o'clock the next morning. The monk had the goodness to write me a certificate that I had been confined to bed from the moment of my arrival *al sitio*,[31] and that despite my weakness I had done my Easter duty at his church, having confessed to him the day before. He then told me the name of the parish priest who had posted me on the door of his church.

Back at the Ambassador's house, I wrote the priest that the certificate I was sending him would make him understand the reason which had obliged me to put off receiving the sacrament at Easter, in consequence of which I asked him to remove my name from the list in which he had unjustly had the kindness to dishonor me. I asked him to take the enclosure to the Cavaliere Mengs.

I wrote Mengs that I deserved the insult he had put on me by turning me out of his house, since I had been stupid enough to do him the honor of going there; but as a Christian who had just done his Easter duty I must not only forgive him but teach him a verse known to all men of honor, but not to him, which said: *Turpius ejicitur quam non admittitur hospes* ("It is more shameful to turn out a guest than not to admit him").[32]

After sending off my letter I told the whole story to the Ambassador, who answered me only that Mengs was esteemed for nothing but his talent, for in other respects all Madrid knew that he was full of absurdities. The man had lodged me in his house only from vanity, at a moment when all Madrid, the Count of Aranda, and the ministers were sure to hear of it and when many would believe that it was partly out of respect for him that I had been escorted back to my lodging. He even told me, in an access of pride, that I should have made the Alcalde Messa escort me not to the coffeehouse where I was staying,[33] but back to his house, since it was from his house that I had been taken away. He was a man ambitious for fame, a great worker, jealous, and the enemy of all the painters of his time who could pretend to a talent equal to his, and he was wrong, for, though a great painter in coloring and drawing, he did not have the very first qualification to make a great painter, namely, invention.

"Just as," I said to him one day, "every great poet must be a painter, so every painter must be a poet."

He took my dictum in bad part, for he wrongly thought that I had uttered it only to reproach him with his deficiency. He was extremely ignorant, and he wanted to pass for learned; he was a drunkard, lascivious, bad-tempered, jealous, and avaricious, and he wanted to pass for virtuous. A great worker, he found it necessary not to dine, for he liked to drink until his reason was totally extinguished. This was why, when he was invited to dine anywhere, he drank only water.

He spoke four languages, all of them badly; but he refused to admit it. He had begun to hate me a few days before I left Madrid because chance had shown me too much of all his failings, and because he had been too often obliged to admit the justice of my criticisms. His ill breeding made him resent being under vital obligations to me. I one day prevented him from sending a memorial to the Court, which was to have been seen by the King and in which he signed himself *el más ínclito* when he wanted to call himself "the most humble"; I told him that he would be laughed at, for *ínclito* did not mean "humble" but "illustrious"; he flew into a rage, he said I must not imagine I knew Spanish better than he did, and he was in despair when someone who arrived told him that he ought to thank me, for so gross an error would have made him eternally ridiculous. Another time I prevented him from sending a critical comment on a diatribe by someone who said that we had not on earth a single antediluvian monument. Mengs had thought he would confound the author by writing in the margin that the ruins of the Tower of Babylon[34] were still to be seen: a twofold blunder, because the pretended ruins are not visible, and, even if they were, the building of that unique tower took place after the Flood. When he found himself convinced, he erased his note, but hating me with all his heart, for he was certain that I must know the full extent of his ignorance. He had a mania for discussing metaphysical problems; his passion was reasoning on beauty in general and defining it, and the things he said on the subject were enormously stupid.

Excessively splenetic, in his fits of rage he beat his children even at the risk of crippling them. I more than once snatched his eldest son[35] from his hands at moments when I thought I should see him tear him to pieces with his teeth. He boasted that his Bohemian father, a bad painter, had brought him up stick in hand, and, having himself become a good painter by this treatment, he was convinced that he must deliberately use the same means to make his children become something. He took offense when someone wrote to him and he saw in the address neither his title of Cavaliere[36] nor his Christian names. I told him one day that I had not felt offended when he failed to add the title of Cavaliere to my name, in the addresses of the letters he had written me at Florence and Madrid, and that I nevertheless had the honor to have been decorated with the same order as he. He made no answer. As for his Christian names, his reason for valuing them was very strange. He said that, since he was named Anton Raphael, and was a painter, people who failed to give him those names refused him, according to his mad idea, the qualities in painting of Antonio da Correggio[37] and Raffaello d'Urbino,[38] which he united in himself.

I one day ventured to tell him that I thought the hand of one of the principal figures which I saw in a painting of his was faulty because the fourth finger was shorter than the index finger. He told me it ought to be so, and he showed me his hand; I laughed and showed him mine, saying that I was sure my hand was formed like that of all the children descended from Adam.

"Then from whom do you suppose I am descended?"

"I have no idea; but it is certain that you are not of my species."

"It is you who are not of mine, nor of that of the rest of mankind, for the hands of men and women are generally constructed like mine."

"I wager a hundred pistoles you are wrong."

With that he rises, throwing his palette and brushes on

the floor, he rings, his servants come up, he looks at their hands, and he is furious to see that they all have the fourth finger longer than the index. That time—a most unusual thing—I saw him laugh and end the argument with a jest:

"I am delighted that I can boast I am unique in something."

A sensible thing which Mengs said to me one day, and which I have never forgotten, was the following: he had painted a Magdalen whose beauty was really surprising. For ten or twelve days he had said to me every morning:

"This evening the picture will be finished."

He worked on it until evening, and the next day I found him still working on the same picture. So one day I asked him if he had been wrong the day before when he had told me that the painting was already finished.

"No," he replied, "it might seem to be finished in the eyes of ninety-nine out of a hundred connoisseurs who examined it; but the one who most interests me is the hundredth, and I look at it with his eyes. Understand that there is not a picture in the world which is finished more than relatively. This Magdalen will never be finished until I stop working on it, but it will not really be so, for it is certain that if I worked on it another day it would be more finished. Understand that even in your Petrarch there is not one sonnet which can be called really finished. Nothing of what comes from the hands or the minds of men is perfect in this world except a mathematical calculation."

I embraced my dear Mengs after hearing him talk to me in this fashion; but I did not embrace him on another day when he told me he wished he had been Raffaello d'Urbino. He was his great painter.

"How," I asked him, "can you want to have been? Such a desire is contrary to nature, for having existed, you would exist no longer. You cannot entertain that desire unless you imagine yourself enjoying its fulfill-

The Abscess

Bullfight

ment in the bliss of Paradise, and in that case I congratulate you.''

''Not at all: I should like to have been Raffaello, and I should care nothing about existing today, either in body or in soul.''

''That is absurd. Think about it. You cannot have that desire and at the same time have the faculty of thought.''

He flew into a rage and treated me to insults which made me laugh. Another time he compared the work of a poet composing a tragedy with that of a painter composing a picture in which the whole tragedy was depicted in a single scene. After analyzing a great number of differences, I ended by telling him that the tragic poet had to employ all the attention of his soul even in the smallest details, whereas the painter could employ colors on the surfaces of the objects and at the same time discuss various subjects with friends around him.

''This proves,'' I said, ''that your painting is more the work of your hands than a product of your soul. That fact proves its inferiority. Find me a poet who can tell his cook what he wants for supper while composing epic verse.''

Mengs worsted in an argument became brutal; he declared himself insulted. Yet the man, who died before the age of fifty years,[39] will go down to posterity as a philosopher, a great stoic, learned, and endowed with all the virtues—and all because of his biography,[40] which one of his inordinate admirers wrote and had printed in beautiful type in a large quarto volume dedicated to the King of Spain. It is a tissue of falsehoods. Let us leave him for the present, and speak of my own concerns. I shall speak of Mengs when I meet him again in Rome two or three years hence.

I still had to stay in bed because of my weakness. Manuzzi managed to induce me to go with him to Toledo to see all the antiquities which still exist in that ancient city. We were to be back in Aranjuez on the fifth day. He was eager to be away because the Ambassador was to give a great dinner for all the ministers, which, not having been presented, he could not attend.

"My exclusion," he said, "will not be remarked on when it is known that I am not in Aranjuez."

Thoroughly persuaded, and delighted to see Toledo, I set out with him early the next day, and we were there by evening. At the gate of that capital of New Castile, which is on top of a mountain, I saw a naumachia.[41] The Tagus, which carries gold, surrounds it on two sides. We lodged well enough for that country at an inn on a great square, and we went out in the morning with a guide, who took us to the Alcázar:[42] it is the Louvre of Toledo, the great royal palace in which the King of the Moors lived. Its majestic name could have no other vowel than the queen of the alphabet. After that we went to the cathedral,[43] worthy to be seen for the riches it contains. I saw the tabernacle in which the holy sacrament is carried in procession on Corpus Christi, so heavy that thirty men are used to carry it. The Archbishop of the city has an income of three hundred thousand écus, and its clergy has four hundred thousand. A canon, showing me vessels in which there were relics, said that in one of them were the thirty coins which Judas had received for selling Our Lord; I asked him to show them to me, and, looking at me balefully, he replied that the King himself would not dare to admit to such curiosity. The priests in Spain are a rabble which it is necessary to treat with more respect than anywhere else. The next morning we were shown some collections[44] of curiosities of natural history and medicine, where we were at least permitted to laugh. We were shown a dissected dragon, "which proves," the owner of it said to me, "that the dragon is not a fabulous animal"; and after the dragon we were shown a basilisk, whose eyes, instead of terrifying us, made us laugh. This grave nobleman showed us a Freemason's apron, assuring us that the person who had presented it to his father had been a member of a lodge.

"Which proves," he told us, "that those who say that the sect has never existed and does not exist are wrong."

On my return to Aranjuez, finding myself in very good health, I began paying my court to all the ministers, and the Ambassador presented me to the Marchese Grimaldi,[45] with whom I had several conferences on the subject of the Sierra Morena, where the colony was doing badly. The Swiss families could not thrive there. I gave him a plan intended to show him that the colony should be composed of Spanish families.

"Spain," he said, "is scantily populated everywhere; so it would be necessary to impoverish one place in order to enrich another."

"Not at all, for ten male emigrants who die in Asturias without marrying because of their poverty would die in the Sierra Morena after producing fifty children, and those fifty children in the next generation would produce two hundred, who would produce a thousand, and all would be well."

My project was being studied, and the Marchese Grimaldi assured me that if the thing was done I should be appointed governor.

An Italian *opera buffa* was delighting the Court, except the King,* who had no liking for music. He cared for nothing but hunting. An Italian musician, who enjoyed the Venetian Ambassador's patronage, wanted to compose the music for a new drama, flattering himself that he would deserve universal applause and receive substantial presents in recompense for his work. The time was too

---

* The King of Spain had the face of a sheep, and the sheep is the animal which has no idea of oral harmony. If one listens to the voices of a hundred sheep in a flock, one will hear a hundred different semitones. (C.'s marginal note.)

short to write to Italy; I offered to write one for him then and there, I was taken at my word, and the next day I gave him the first act. The chapelmaster composed the music for it in four days, and the Venetian Ambassador invited all the ministers to the rehearsal of the first act in the great hall of his palace. The music was declared in exquisite taste; the two other acts were already written, he hurried, and in two weeks my opera[46] was performed, and the musician had reason to be well content. As for me, I was considered to be above a poet who worked to be paid; I was paid in applause. And to tell the truth, I should have thought myself insulted if payment had been offered me. It was enough for me to see the Ambassador delighted to have me in his entourage, and to see myself valued by the ministers as a man capable of contributing to the pleasures of the Court.

The composition of the opera had necessitated my making the acquaintance of the actresses. The leading one was a Roman named Pelliccia.[47] Her talent was mediocre, she was neither pretty nor ugly, she squinted a little. Her sister, who was younger than she, was pretty; yet the pretty one attracted and interested nobody; the elder made herself liked by all who spoke to her. She had magic in her face; her squint eyes were touching, her subtle, modest laughter charmed; her easy manner gained her the good will of all.

She had a husband who was a painter, but a bad one, a well-meaning, rather ugly man, whose manner was more that of her servant than of her husband. He was extremely submissive to his wife, and she treated him with consideration. The woman did not inspire love in me, but true friendship. I went to see her every day, I wrote words for her for Roman airs which she sang with much grace, she received me unreservedly and with no artifice, as if I had been her friend from childhood.

One day when there was to be a rehearsal of a short act for which I had written the words, I talked to her on the stage about the great names of the personages who were present, and who had come only to hear the new music which was to be performed. The impresario of the opera, who was named Marescalchi,[48] had contracted with the Governor of Valencia[49] to spend the month of September in that city with his troupe to play comic operas in a small theater which the Governor of that Kingdom had had built expressly for the purpose. The city of Valencia had never seen an Italian *opera buffa,* the impresario Marescalchi hoped to make a great fortune there. La Pelliccia wanted to obtain from some great nobleman of the Court a letter of recommendation for Valencia, and, knowing none of them, she asked me if she could address herself to the Venetian Ambassador in the hope that he would favor her by asking someone for a letter for her. I advised her to go and ask for one from the Duke of Arcos,[5] who was twenty paces from us and who kept his eyes fixed on her.

"There stands a great nobleman, my dear, who is dying to oblige you in some way; go yourself now and ask him to do you the favor; I am sure he will not refuse you; it is no more than asking him for a pinch of snuff."

"I haven't the courage. Present me."

"No, no—that would spoil everything. He mustn't even imagine that it is I who gave you the advice. Do as I say; seize the moment; he is there in the wings, all alone, and he looks at no one but you. After I have left you— one minute after—approach him, and ask him for the favor; you will be granted it."

I go toward the orchestra, and a minute later I see the Duke advance toward the actress and speak to her politely and decently, and, in the course of the conversation, I notice that La Pelliccia blushes as she says something to him; I see the Duke with the air of a man who consents, and I see him draw back his hand, which La Pelliccia wanted to kiss. The thing is done. After the opera she told me that he had promised she should have the

letter for which she had asked him on the day the opera
was first performed. He kept his word. He gave her a
sealed letter addressed to a merchant in the city, whose
name was Don Diego Valencia.[51] She was not to go there
until September; so there was time enough. We were in
the middle of May. We will speak of this strange letter in
its proper place.

I amused myself in Aranjuez by frequently seeing Don
Domingo Varnier, the King's valet, a valet of the Prince
of Asturias, who now reigns,[52] and a chamberwoman to
the Princess, who was adored and who had had the
strength of mind to get a great deal of cumbersome eti-
quette done away with and to change the solemn and serious tone at Court for a pleasant affability. I was charmed
to see His Catholic Majesty dine every day at eleven
o'clock, always eat the same thing, go hunting[53] at the
same hour, and return with his brother,[54] too exhausted
to do anything. The King was very ugly, but he was
handsome in comparison with his brother, whose face was
positively frightening. The King's brother never traveled
without an image of the Blessed Virgin which Mengs had
made for him. It was a painting two feet high by three
and a half feet wide. The Blessed Virgin was seated on
the grass and had her bare feet crossed in the Moorish
fashion; her most holy legs were visible halfway up the
calves. It was a painting which excited the soul by way
of the senses. The Infante was in love with it, and he took
to be devotion what was nothing but the most criminal of
voluptuous instincts, for it was impossible that, when he
contemplated the image, he did not burn with longing to
have in his arms, warm and alive, the goddess whom he
saw painted on the canvas. But the Infante never suspected it. He was delighted to be in love with the mother
of his God. For him this love was the assurance of his
eternal salvation. Such are the Spaniards. Objects intended to interest them must be striking, and they never

interpret anything except in a way favorable to their dominant passion.

In Madrid, before going to Aranjuez, I saw a picture of the Blessed Virgin suckling the Infant Jesus. Her bare breast, excellently painted, fired the imagination. The picture was the retable of the high altar of a chapel in the Carrera de San Gerónimo.[55] The chapel was filled all day with pious men who went there to worship the mother of God, whose representation was perhaps interesting only because of her beautiful bosom; the offerings given at the sanctuary were so abundant that, in the century and a half during which the painting had been there, a great number of gold and silver lamps and candelabra had been made and a considerable income set aside for the maintenance of these objects, which fed on oil and wax. At the door of the chapel there were always a quantity of carriages and a soldier with fixed bayonet to keep order and prevent quarrels among the coachmen, who were constantly arriving and leaving, for there was not a nobleman who, passing the sacred place in his carriage, did not order his coachman to stop so that he could get out and go, if only for a moment, to do homage to the goddess and contemplate *beata ubera quae lactaverunt aeterni patris filium* ("the blessed paps which suckled the son of the eternal father").[56] Since I knew men, this devotion did not surprise me; but here is what surprised me on my return to Madrid at the end of May in the same year 1768.

Having to pay a visit to the Abate Pico,[57] I order the coachman to avoid the Carrera because of the carriages which might be in front of the chapel and delay my journey. The coachman replies that for some time there have been few carriages there, so he continues on his way, and, sure enough, I see only two or three. Getting out at the Abate's, I ask the coachman the reason for this suspension of devotion, and he replies that men are getting more wicked every day. I make light of his reason, and, after drinking some of his excellent chocolate with the illustrious and intelligent Abate, I ask him the reason why the chapel was losing its reputation. He bursts out laughing, and he asks me to excuse him if he does not dare tell me the reason; but he asks me to go myself and receive the indulgence, and he assures me that my curiosity will be allayed. I went there the same day, and in an instant I saw it all. The Blessed Virgin's bosom was no longer visible. A handkerchief painted by the most criminal of all painters had spoiled the superb picture. There was nothing to be seen—not even the nipple, not the suckling mouth of the Child God, not the bulge of the breast, so that the Virgin, who, before the alteration, had a reason for gazing at her son's divine lips as they sucked the ambrosia, now seemed to look at nothing but the wretched handkerchief with which, contrary to the laws of costume, a profane brush had made her as ugly as the picture. This disaster had happened at the end of the Carnival. The old chaplain having died, the new one saw fit to call the most beautiful and most holy of all the bosoms God has created scandalous. As a fool, the chaplain may have been right, but as a Spanish Christian, he was wrong, and the falling off in the offerings must already have made him repent. My reflections on this incident, and my insatiable curiosity to know men by making them talk, impelled me to call on the chaplain, who, as I saw it, must be old and stupid.

I go there one morning, and I find a priest thirty years of age, extremely lively and prepossessing, who, though he does not know me, at once offers me a cup of chocolate, which I refuse, as a foreigner must do in Spain, for not only is it usually bad, but it is pressed upon one everywhere and at all hours of the day with such urgency that if one accepted I believe one would die of it.

Without making a long exordium, I go to the point, I tell him that I am passionately devoted to painting and that I am distressed at his having had a superb picture ruined.

"That may be so, but its beauty was precisely what made it unfit to represent a woman whose appearance should excite the soul to adore and contemplate her immaculateness, and never to sensual passion. Let all beautiful pictures perish if all of them together can cause the smallest mortal sin."

"Who gave you permission to commit this murder? The State Inquisitors in Venice, even Signor Barbarigo,[58] though very devout and a theologian, would have had you imprisoned under the Leads. Love of the bliss of Paradise must not injure the fine arts, and I am sure that St. Luke the Evangelist, as a painter,[59] is speaking against you to the Blessed Virgin, whose portrait, as you must know, he painted with only three colors."

"Sir, I needed to ask no one's permission. It is I who have to say mass every day at this altar,[60] and I am not ashamed to tell you that I could not consecrate; you will forgive me my weakness. That beautiful breast troubled my imagination."

"Who obliged you to look at it?"

"I did not look at it, and the enemy of God presented it to my mind nevertheless."

"Why did you not rather mutilate yourself, like the wise Origen,[61] *qui se castravit propter regnum coelorum* ['who castrated himself for the sake of the Kingdom of Heaven']?[62] Believe me, your genitals, too weak because it seems they are too strong, are not worth the painting you have destroyed."

"Signore, you insult me."

"Not at all, for I have no such intention. Either ask the Cavaliere Mengs to make you a new picture of the Blessed Virgin such as will inspire the devotion of her devotees, whom you have very much offended, or renounce a benefice which you were not born to enjoy."

"I will do neither."

The young priest showed me to the door so uncere-
moniously that I left certain that he was plotting some
Spanish revenge on me through the terrible Inquisition.
It occurred to me that he could easily find out my name
and make difficulties for me. So I at once resolved to forestall the blow. About this time I had made the acquaintance of a Frenchman named De Ségur,[63] who had just
come out of the prisons of the Inquisition, where he had
been confined for three years. His crime was that he had
on a table in the drawing room of his house a stone basin,
to which he went every morning to wash his hands and
face. On the edge of the basin there was a statue of a
naked child a foot and a half high. The statue was filled
with water, which he caused to come out of the child's
little virile member as from a faucet, when he wanted to
wash. To someone who deifies everything the child might
well appear to be the image of our Redeemer, for the
sculptor had surrounded its head with the kind of crown
which is called a halo and which sculptors and painters
affix to the heads of saints. Poor Ségur was accused of
impiety before the Inquisition, it was judged a crime that
he should dare to wash with water which might seem to be
the Saviour's urine. The jest cost him three years of
penitence. *Aliena spectans doctus evasi mala* ("Taught
by those which befell others, I avoided misfortunes").[64]

I presented myself to the Grand Inquisitor,[65] who was
a bishop. I told him all that I had said to the chaplain,
repeating every word but suppressing my bantering tone,
and I ended by asking his pardon if by any chance the
chaplain could have been offended. I assured him of my
orthodoxy. I should never have believed that the Grand
Inquisitor in Madrid would be an agreeable man, though
his face was as ugly as possible. The prelate did nothing
but laugh from the beginning to the end of my narrative,
for he would not hear me as if in confession. He said that
the chaplain was himself guilty and absolutely incapable
of fulfilling his function, for, by supposing others to be as

weak as himself, he had done grave harm to religion; he said that I had nevertheless done wrong to go there and irritate him. Since I had had to tell him my name, he ended by reading me, still with a smiling countenance, an accusation against me drawn up by someone who had witnessed the occurrence. He gently chided me for having called the Duke of Medina Sidonia's Franciscan confessor an ignoramus because he had refused to grant that a priest should say mass a second time on a feast day even after dining, if his sovereign, who had not heard it, ordered him to say it.

"You were right," the Bishop said, "but even so you should not have called the Duke's confessor an ignoramus in his presence. For the future, avoid all arguments on the subject of religion, in respect to both doctrine and discipline. I can tell you, so that when you leave Spain you will take with you a true idea of the Inquisition, that the parish priest who posted your name among those of the excommunicated was reprimanded, for it was his duty to inform you beforehand and above all to find out if you were ill, and we know that you really were so."

At these words I kissed his hand, going down on one knee, and I left well enough satisfied.

Let us return to Aranjuez, for what I have just written happened on my return to Madrid. As soon as I learned that the Ambassador could not lodge me in Madrid, where I thought of staying, for I was hoping for the governorship of Sierra Morena, I wrote to my good friend the cobbler Don Diego that I needed a well-furnished room with a good bed, closet, also a servant, an honest man who would be willing to ride behind my carriage, and a carriage engaged at so much a month, which, if he would vouch for me, I would pay in advance. I informed him what I wanted to pay for my apartment, and I asked him to write to me as soon as he had found it for me, for I should not leave Aranjuez until I knew where I was to go when I arrived in Madrid. The cobbler answered me at once that he was sure he could do what I wanted, and that he would inform me of the place as soon as he had found it.

The *población* ("colonization") of Sierra Morena occupied me a good deal, for I was writing on the maintenance of order, which was the chief requisite for making the colony prosper. My writings, which were only demonstrative arguments, were valued by the Minister Grimaldi and flattered the Ambassador Mocenigo, for he thought that if I succeeded in going to govern the colony it could only increase the reputation of his embassy. My labors, however, did not keep me from amusing myself, and above all from frequenting the courtiers who could acquaint me with the characters of the individuals who made up the royal family. Don Varnier, a frank, reliable, intelligent man, gave me all the information I wanted.

I asked him one day if it was true that the King's attachment to Gregorio Squillace[66] was due to his loving, or having loved, his wife, and he assured me that it was a slander imagined by those who stated as true whatever had some semblance of truth.

"If the epithet 'the Chaste,' " he said, "is to be added to the name of a king by the mouth of Truth, and not by adulation, it has never become any king better than it does Carlos III. He has never in his life had to do with another woman than the late Queen, and that not so much because it was the duty of a husband but because it was the duty of a Christian. He does not want to commit a sin because he does not want to sully his soul and because he does not want to suffer the shame of admitting his weakness to his confessor. In the best of health, strong, vigorous, having never in his life had the slightest illness, not even a fever, he has a temperament which makes him very much inclined to the act of Venus, for as long as she lived he never for one day failed to pay his marital duty to the Queen. On the days when it was forbidden him for cleanliness' sake, he tired himself more than usual at hunting, to calm the impulses of concupiscence. Imagine his despair when he found himself a widower, and resolved to die rather than to suffer the humiliation of taking a mistress. His resource was to hunt, and to keep himself so occupied every hour of the day, that he has no time left to think of a woman. It was difficult, for he likes neither to write nor to read nor to listen to music or to light conversation. Here is what he did, what he does, and what he will do until he dies. At seven o'clock he dresses, he goes to the wardrobe, his hair is dressed, and he prays until eight. He goes to mass, he drinks his chocolate, then he takes a pinch of Spanish snuff, which he pushes into his big nose; it is the one pinch of snuff he takes each day. At nine o'clock he works with his ministers until eleven, he dines alone until a quarter to twelve, and until twelve he goes to see the Princess of Asturias. At twelve he gets into his carriage, and he goes hunting. At seven he eats a bite wherever he happens to be, and at eight he returns to the castle so tired that he often falls asleep before he gets into bed. In this way he never needs a woman. He thought of remarrying, and he asked for Madame Adélaïde of France,[67] who, having seen his portrait, absolutely refused him. That annoyed him, and he has not thought of marrying since. Woe betide anyone who should propose a mistress to him.''

Speaking of whether his character was humane or severe, kindly or harsh, Don Domingo said that his ministers were right to keep him inaccessible, for if someone managed to take him by surprise and beg for some favor, he made it a point of honor never to refuse anything, for it was only then that he felt he was the King.

''Believe me, the most intractable, the most difficult of sovereigns are those who give public audience to all comers. They are the ones who are the most often deceived; nothing can be got from them; their one thought is always to refuse what a petitioner asks for. The inac-

cessible sovereign, on the other hand, when someone
manages to speak to him, listens attentively and considers
how best to let him have what he asks for. The place
where Carlos III is often found alone is out hunting.
There he is in a good humor, and he takes pleasure in
satisfying the person who speaks to him. His great fault
is his firmness, for in him it is obstinacy; when he wants
something done, and has supposed it possible, done it
must be; failures do not discourage him. His consideration for his brother the Infante is very great; he can
refuse him nothing; but he insists on being always the
master. It is thought that he will grant him permission
to contract a marriage of conscience,[68] for he fears that
he will damn himself and he has no love for bastards. The
Infante has already fathered three.''

At Aranjuez I observed the immense number of people
who were there waiting on the ministers to obtain posts.

''They all return home after the King's journey,'' said
Don Domingo, ''without having obtained anything.''

''Then they are asking for impossibilities?''

''Not at all. They ask for nothing. 'What do you
want?' a minister asks them. 'What Your Excellency
thinks will be suitable for me.' 'But what can you do?' 'I
don't know. Your Excellency can look into my talents,
my capacity, and give me the employment for which
Your Excellency may consider me fit.' 'Away with you,
I haven't the time.' ''

But so it goes everywhere. Carlos III died mad; now
the Queen of Portugal has gone mad.[69] The King of England was mad, and has, they say, recovered.[70]

I took leave of the Venetian Ambassador three days
before his departure, and I hastily embraced Manuzzi,
who never failed to give me proofs of most sincere friendship. I have to admit it, to my confusion. Don Diego, the
cobbler, had written me that for the money I wanted to
spend I should also have a Biscayan maidservant,[71] who,
when I wished, would cook for me well enough. The ad-

dress he sent me was that of a house in the Calle de Alcalá.[72] I left Aranjuez in the morning, and I arrived at my lodging early in the afternoon. Aranjuez is the same distance from Madrid as Fontainebleau is from Paris.[73]

I arrive, I get out, I go to the second floor, I find the Biscayan maid, who spoke French, I look at my apartment, and I find, besides the closet, a second room with a bed in which to put up a friend if I wished; I praise the cobbler. I have my belongings brought up; my lackey arrives, and he seems to be honest; I praise Don Diego. Curious to see the skill of the cook from Bilbao,[74] I order her to prepare supper for me, without company, and I offer her money, whereupon she tells me that she has some, and that she will give me the bill the next day. I go out with my manservant to fetch my belongings from Mengs's. His valet delivers everything to mine, who goes for two porters, and sets off. I do not ask if Mengs is at home, I try to give his valet a doblón, and he refuses it.

I go at once to the Calle del Desengaño to see both Doña Ignacia and her father, whom I had to thank and to reimburse, and I find no one. A woman next door tells me that he has moved. I am astonished that he did not write to tell me so, and I go back to my lodging in the Calle de Alcalá, which was three hundred paces distant. I arrange everything as I want it in my room, I ask Felipe (such was my valet's name) where Don Diego had gone to lodge, and he answers that it is far away and that he will take me there the next day. I ask him where my landlord lives, and he says it is on the floor above me, but that I can be sure he will not make the slightest noise. He had gone out, and would not come home until ten o'clock.

I have everything I need to write with set out on a small table, telling Felipe to go away and not come back until nine o'clock to serve my supper. I order him to fetch me some wine from where I knew it was good, and I fall to writing. At nine o'clock he comes to tell me that

my supper is served in the other room, I go there with a
ravenous appetite, for I had eaten nothing, and I am
astonished to see a small table ready laid, with a cloth of
a cleanliness which I had not yet seen in Spain in the
houses of the citizenry. But the supper finally proves to
me that Don Diego is a hero. The cook from Bilbao
cooked like a Frenchwoman. Five dishes, *criadillas*,[75]
which I loved to distraction, everything excellent—it
seemed to me impossible that I should have such a good
cook into the bargain, though I was paying a good deal
for the apartment.

Toward the end of supper Felipe told me that my landlord had come home, and that, if I would permit it, he
wanted to see me.

"Let him come in."

I see the cobbler and his daughter. He had rented the
house expressly to lodge me.

CHAPTER III

*My amour with Doña Ignacia. Signor
Mocenigo returns to Madrid.*

YOU ILL-FATED Counts and Marquises who are
pleased to crush the self-esteem of a man who by his
lofty acts tries to convince you that he is as noble as you,
beware of him if you succeed in denying his claims, in
humbling him; fired by a just disdain, he will tear you
limb from limb, and he will be in the right. Respect the
man who, calling himself a gentleman though he is not
one in your terms, imagines that to play the part he must
do lofty deeds. Respect the man who gives nobility a definition which makes you laugh. He does not say that it
consists in a series of generations from father to son, of
which he himself is the latest heir; he makes light of
genealogies. He defines the gentleman by saying that he
is a man who demands respect and who believes that
there is no way to be respected but to respect others, to
live decently, to deceive no one, never to lie when the person who is listening to him believes that he is speaking
sincerely, and to put his honor above his life. This last

part of his definition of the gentleman should make you fear that he will kill you like an assassin if you succeed in dishonoring him by treachery or by surprise. In the physical world anything which strikes is subjected to the same force in reaction; but in the moral world the reaction is stronger than the action. The reaction from being imposed upon is scorn; the reaction from scorn is hatred; the reaction from hatred is murder, as it is from a stain which covers with dishonor a man who wants to be honored and who does everything to deserve it.

The cobbler Don Diego saw that he might have made himself ridiculous in my eyes when he had told me that he was noble; but, feeling that he was truly so in the meaning which he gave to the word, he wanted to convince me more and more that he had not imposed on me. The noble deed he had done[1] for me at Buen Retiro had already shown me the nature of his soul; but that was not enough for him, he wanted to go on in the same way. He finds one of my letters laying a servile task on him, such as anyone can perform more or less competently, and he is not content to serve me as a banker, for example, would have done. He forms the plan of himself becoming the tenant-in-chief of a house, in order to rent the best part of it to me. He sees that he can do this without exceeding his resources, and even at a profit eventually, assuming that his apartment would not remain unoccupied long; and he does it; and he enjoys my surprise, sure that the esteem I should conceive for him would show that I rated his magnanimous act at its due value.

He was not mistaken; I gave him every proof of it in avowals of friendship. I saw Doña Ignacia proud of what her father had done. We sat for an hour, talking, emptying a bottle, and we made all our business arrangements. The only thing I would not grant him, and on which I made him yield, was that I would not have the Biscayan woman at his expense. I rented his apartment for six months, paying the whole sum in advance; and I asked

him to let the cook continue to think that it was not I
who paid her but he; I asked him also to pay her what she
would spend to provide me with meals every day, at least
until the Ambassador arrived. In addition, having assured
him that it was a real penance for me to eat alone, I invited him to dine and sup with me every day, and hence to
order my Biscayan always to prepare meals for two persons. He tried in vain to think of excuses, he had to accept my conditions, reserving the right to be represented
by his daughter when, having much work to do, he had
not time to dress to dine with me. It is easy to understand
that this last condition was not displeasing to me; and
indeed I expected it.

I went upstairs to his lodging the next morning. This
third floor was the attic, which was, however, divided into
four sections by partitions. In the large room in which he
worked at repairing shoes and boots with an apprentice,
he had his bed, in which he slept with his wife. In the
adjoining room, which was smaller, I saw Doña Ignacia's
bed, a stool to kneel on before a great crucifix, a picture
four feet high representing St. Ignatius of Loyola,[2]
whose young and handsome face inspired fleshly love,
and rosaries and prayer books, with a pail full of holy
water. Another smaller room was occupied by her very
ugly younger sister, whom I believe I have not yet mentioned, and the fourth was the kitchen, in which there
was an alcove containing the cook's bed. He told me that
he was more comfortably lodged than in the other house,
and that the apartment he rented me paid him four
times the rent of the whole house.

"But the furniture——"

"In four years it will all be paid for. This house will
be my daughter's dowry, and it is to you that I owe this
excellent investment."

"I am very glad of it; but it seems to me that you are
making brand-new shoes there."

"That is true; but observe that I am working on the

last which was given me, so that I am obliged neither to put them on the feet of the person who is to wear them nor to be concerned as to whether they fit him or not.''

''How much are you paid for them?''

''A peso duro[3] and a half.''

''More than the usual price, I think.''

''Certainly; but the difference between the shoes I make and those which are made by ordinary shoemakers *de nuevo* is very great, both in the quality of the leather and the good workmanship.''

''I will have a last made, and you shall make me shoes, if you please; but I warn you that they must be of the finest leather you have and with soles of grain morocco.''

''It costs more and does not last as long.''

''That makes no difference. In summer I have to wear very light shoes.''

I at once had a last made, and it was he who worked for me until I left. He said he would sup with me, but that at dinner I should have his daughter, and I replied that I should value his daughter's company as highly as his own.

I called on the Count of Aranda, who, though coldly, received me well enough. I gave him an account of everything I had done at Aranjuez, and of the trouble which the parish priest and Mengs had made for me together.

''I heard of it. This second scrape was worse than the first, and I should not have known how to get you out of it if you had not quickly done what you did, which obliged the priest to cross out your name at once. Just now people are putting up placards which they think will upset me; but they are wrong. I am perfectly calm.''

''What do they want of Your Excellency?''

''They want me to permit long cloaks and slouch hats. Didn't you know that?''

''I arrived yesterday.''

''That accounts for it. Don't come here at noon on Sun-

day, for according to yesterday's placard this house will
be blown up."

"I am curious to see how high it will go. I shall have
the honor to be in your reception room at noon."

"I think you will not find yourself alone."

I went there, and I never saw it so full. The Count
talked to everyone. On the last placard, which threatened
the Count with death if he did not withdraw his decrees,
there were two very forceful verses, which in Spanish
have a particular wit and grace. The man who had written the placard, and who was sure to be hanged if he
were to be found out, said:

> *Si me cogen me horqueran*
> *Pero no me cogeran*
>
> ("If they catch me they
> will hang me, but they will
> not catch me")

Dining with me, Doña Ignacia constantly let me know
how glad she was to have me in her house; but she remained completely unresponsive to the amorous pleas
which I made to her when Felipe, after serving a dish,
went upstairs to fetch another. She blushed, she sighed,
and, forced to speak, she begged me to forget all that
had happened between us during the Carnival. I smiled,
saying that I was sure she knew it was not in my power
to forget that I had loved her while I still loved her. I
added, half seriously, half tenderly, that, even if it were
in my power, I should not want to forget it all. Since I
knew that she was neither inconstant nor a hypocrite, I
saw very well that her reserve was due to nothing but the
resolves she had made to live in future in the grace of her
God, whom she had too greatly offended by loving me;
but I knew what to expect, and that her resistance could
not last long. However, I had to proceed step by step. I
had had to do with other pious women, whose tempera-

ments were not as strong as hers, who did not love me as much, and whom I had nevertheless conquered. I felt sure of Doña Ignacia.

After dinner she remained with me for a quarter of an hour, never seeing me amorous. I dressed after taking a siesta, and I went out without seeing her, and when, after supper, she came downstairs to join her father, who had supped with me, I treated her with the utmost gentleness, showing no sign that I had taken offense at her resolve to love me no more. The next day I acted in the same way. She told me at dinner that she had dismissed Don Francisco during the first days of Lent, and she asked me not to receive him if he came to call on me.

The next day, which was Pentecost, after calling on the Count of Aranda, whose palace was to be blown up, I went home, where Don Diego, very neatly dressed, dined with me; I did not see his daughter. I asked him if she was dining out, and he replied with a laugh which was not Spanish that she had shut herself up in her room, where she was apparently keeping the feast of the Holy Ghost by praying; but that she would certainly come down to sup with me, since he was invited to sup at his brother's house, where he would remain until at least midnight.

"My dear Don Diego, do not stand on ceremony, I beg you, for I am speaking to you sincerely. Before you go out, tell Doña Ignacia that I willingly relinquish my rights in favor of those which God may have over her conscience. Tell her that if she finds it a burden to interrupt her devotions to sup with me, she shall sup with me another day. I shall not mind supping alone. Will you tell her that?"

"Since you wish it, I will tell her so."

After the siesta I saw him in my room, telling me contentedly that Doña Ignacia would be glad to take advantage of the freedom I granted her that day, in which she would see no one.

"That's the way to behave! I'm delighted. Tomorrow I shall thank her."

I had to exercise a great deal of self-control to answer him thus, for such excessive devotion displeased me and even made me fear that I should lose the love which attached me to the charming girl and the esteem I felt for her. However, the worthy Don Diego very nearly made me laugh when, as he left, he told me that an intelligent father must forgive excessive devotion in his young daughter, as he must a strong amorous passion. Could I expect so odd a dictum from the lips of a Spanish cobbler?

It was raining and windy, I decided not to go out. I told Felipe to dismiss my carriage and to go away after telling the cook that I would not sup until ten o'clock. I sat down to write. It was Doña Ignacia's mother who brought me a light. But suddenly I had a promising idea. When the Biscayan came at ten o'clock to say that my supper was on the table, I told her to take it away, for I did not feel like eating.

At eleven o'clock I went to bed, and I slept better. The next morning at nine Doña Ignacia entered my room to tell me how sorry she had been when she learned that morning that I had not supped.

"All alone, sad, and disconsolate, I did well to abstain from eating supper."

"You look downcast."

"I shall look better when you wish it."

The hairdresser came in, she left me. I went to the splendid mass at the Buen Suceso,[4] where I saw the most beautiful courtesans in Madrid. I dined well with Don Diego, who at dessert told his daughter that she had been the cause of my not supping. She replied that it would not happen again. I asked her if she wanted to go to Nuestra Señora de Atocha[5] with me, and she expressed her readiness, looking at her father, who told her that true devotion was inseparable from cheerfulness and from the confidence one should have in God, in oneself, and in the probity of the decent people with whom one had to do, and, that being so, she should believe that I could be an honest man despite my not having had the good fortune to be born a Spaniard.

This conclusion made me burst out laughing, which was not taken in bad part. Doña Ignacia kissed her father's hand and asked me frankly if I would take her cousin with me too.

"What need," her father asked her, "have you of your cousin? I answer for Don Jaime." [6]

"I am obliged to you," I said, "but if her cousin would like to come, and if Doña Ignacia wants her, I shall enjoy it all the more, provided it is her elder cousin, whose character pleases me better than that of the younger."

This arrangement made, her father left, and I sent Felipe to the stable to have four mules harnessed; Doña Ignacia, looking at once content and contrite, asked me to forgive her her weaknesses.

"Everything, my beautiful angel, provided that you too will forgive me for loving you."

"Oh, my dear friend! I am afraid I shall go mad if I continue to fight a battle which rends my soul."

"No battle, dear heart. Either love me as I love you, or ask me to leave your house and never again to appear in your sight. I shall have the strength to obey you; but I warn you that you will not be happy."

"That I know. No, no. Remain where you are, this house is yours; but now allow me to tell you that you are mistaken when you suppose that my elder cousin has a better character than the younger one. I know what made you think so on the last night of the Carnival; but you do not know all. The younger is a goodhearted creature, and, ugly though she is, she succumbed to a man who was able to touch her heart; but the elder is ten times uglier, and her spite because she has never been able to win anyone's love makes her malicious. Let me tell you that she believes you love her, and that she nevertheless speaks ill of you; she says you are a seducer, that I was unable to resist you, but that you will not succeed with her.''

''Tell me no more, I beg you; we must punish her. Send for the younger one.''

''Very well. Thank you.''

''Does she know that we love each other?''

''Alas, yes.''

''Why did you tell her so?''

''She guessed it, but she has a kind heart, and she only pities me. She wants us to perform a devotion together to the Blessed Virgin at La Soledad,[7] which will cure us both of a love which damns us.''

''Then she is in love too?''

''Yes, but unhappily, poor child, for she alone loves. Imagine what torture!''

''Indeed it is. I pity her, for, such as she is, I do not know a man who would want her. If ever there was one, there's a girl who shouldn't love. But you——''

''But I. Say no more. My soul is exposed to a greater danger than hers, for I do not know if I am pretty, but I am courted; I must either resist or be damned; and there are men whom it is impossible to resist. God is my witness that during Holy Week I went to see a girl who had smallpox, hoping that I should catch it and become ugly. God did not will it, and then my confessor at La Soledad reprimanded me severely, and gave me a penance I should never have expected.''

''Tell me what it was, please.''

''Yes, I can tell you. After telling me that a beautiful face is the sign of a beautiful soul, and that it is a gift from God, for which the person who is granted it must thank him every day, for beauty is a charm which recommends the possessor of it to everyone; it followed, he went on, that by having tried to become ugly I had made myself unworthy of the gift which God had given me, and had become guilty of ingratitude to the Creator. So he told me that as a penance for my crime I must put a touch of rouge on my cheeks whenever I think I am too pale. I had to promise him I would, and I bought a pot of rouge; but until now I have not felt any need to use it. Add that my father might notice it, and then I should feel extremely embarrassed if I had to tell him that it is at my confessor's bidding."

"Is your confessor young?"

"He is seventy."

"Do you tell him all the particulars of your sins of weakness?"

"Of course! I tell him everything, for every particular, however small, is a mortal sin."

"Does he question you?"

"No, for he knows that I tell him everything. It is a great torment, a great shame; but it must be borne. I have had this confessor for two years; before him I had one who was unbearable. He asked me things which made me indignant, which insulted me. I left him."

"What did he ask you?"

"Oh, please excuse me from telling you."

"What need have you to go to confession so often?"

"What need? Would to God that I did not need it! Yet I go only once a week."

"That is too often."

"It is not too often, for when I am in mortal sin I cannot sleep. I am afraid I shall die while I am sleeping."

"I am sorry for you, my dear, for the fear must make you unhappy. I have a privilege which you have not. I count much more than you do on the mercy of God."

Her cousin arrived and we left. Nothing is more certain than that a devout girl who does the work of the flesh with her lover feels a hundred times more pleasure than a girl who is without prejudices. This truth is too much in the nature of things for me to think it necessary to prove it to my reader.

We found many carriages at the entrance to the small church, which consequently was filled with the devout of both sexes and every rank. I saw the Duchess of Villa-darias,[8] famous for her andromania. When the uterine fury seized her nothing could restrain her. She laid hands on the man who aroused her instinct, and he had to satisfy her. It had happened to her several times in public places, and the people who were present had had to flee. I had met her at a ball, she was still pretty and fairly young; she was on her knees when I entered with my two devout companions, and she at once fixed her eyes on me, as if trying to recognize me, for she had seen me only in a domino. My pious charges, delighted to be there, prayed for half an hour, then got up to leave, and the Duchess got up too. Outside of the church, she asked me if I knew her; and when I named her she asked me why I did not go to see her and if I called on the Duchess of Benavente.[9] I said that I did not, but I assured her that I would go to make my bow to her.

On our way to take a walk in Los Balbazes,[10] I explained to the two cousins the nature of the Duchess's malady. Doña Ignacia, in horror, asked me if I would keep my word to her, and I saw her breathe again when I answered no.

I laugh when I think of certain facts which a paltry philosophy insists on putting among problems, whereas they have been solved ever since reason has existed. The question is put which of the two sexes has more reason to be interested in the work of the flesh in respect to the pleasure obtained from performing it. The answer has always been the female sex. Homer made Jupiter and Juno dispute on the subject;[11] Tiresias,[12] who had been a woman, handed down a correct decision, but one which is laughable because it seems that the two pleasures are weighed in a pair of scales. A summary judgment has led practical minds to declare that the woman's pleasure must be greater because the feast is celebrated in her own

house, and this reason is very plausible, for she has only
to let the thing be done, without exerting herself; but
what makes the truth palpable to the mind of a physiolo-
gist is that if the woman did not have more pleasure than
the man, nature would not have her play a greater part
in the thing than he; she would not have more to do than
he, and more organs, for, taking into consideration only
the sack which women have between the rectal intestine
and the bladder, which is called the womb and which is
an organ absolutely foreign to her brain and hence inde-
pendent of her reason, it is certain that one can perfectly
well conceive the birth of a human being without a man's
having sown the seed of it, but never unless a receptacle
has contained it and brought it to the condition of being
able to resist the air before it sees the light.

Now it is well to reflect that this creature the womb,[13]
which has only one issue, which connects it with the
vagina, becomes furious when it finds that it is not occupied by the matter for which nature has made it and
placed it in the most crucial of all the regions of the
female body. It has an instinct which does not listen to
reason; and if the individual in which it is situated op-
poses its will it raises the devil and inflicts most violent
disorders on the tyrant who will not satisfy it; the hunger to which it is subject is far worse than canine;[14] if
the woman does not give it the food it demands through
the channel which she alone controls, it often becomes
furious and so gains an ascendancy over her which no
strength can resist. It threatens her with death, it makes
her an andromaniac like the Duchess I have named, another Duchess whom I knew in Rome twenty-five years
ago, two great Venetian ladies, and twenty more, who
all together led me to conclude that the womb is an
animal so self-willed, so irrational, so untamable that a
wise woman, far from opposing its whims, should defer
to them, humbling herself and submitting by an act of

virtue to the law to which God had subjected her at her birth. Yet this ferocious organ is susceptible to a degree of management; it is not malicious except when a fanatical woman irritates it: to one such it gives convulsions; another it drives mad; another it turns into a mirror or a monster of piety, St. Theresa,[15] St. Agreda;[16] and it makes a quantity of Messalinas,[17] who, however, are not more unfortunate than the innumerable women who spend their nights half sleeping, half awake, holding in their arms St. Anthony of Padua,[18] St. Aloysius Gonzaga,[19] St. Ignatius,[20] and the Infant Jesus. It is to be noted that these poor unfortunates tell everything in confession to the priest or the monk who governs their consciences; and that very rarely does the sacred tyrant disabuse them. He fears to uproot the plant by cultivating it.

After examining all these evils to which we men are not subject, I ask if it is to be presumed that Nature *semper sibi consona* ("always in conformity with herself"),[21] never in error in her reactions and her compensations, has not given the female sex a pleasure equal in intensity to the vexatious evils which are attached to it. What I can affirm is this: the pleasure which I have felt when the woman I loved made me happy was certainly great, but I know that I should not have wanted it if, to procure it, I had had to run the risk of becoming pregnant. The woman takes that risk even after she has experienced pregnancy several times; so she finds that the pleasure is worth the pain. After all this examination I ask myself if I would consent to be born again as a woman, and, curiosity aside, I answer no. I have enough other pleasures as a man which I could not have as a woman, and which make me prefer my sex to the other. However, I admit that, to have the great privilege of being reborn, I would be satisfied, and I would bind myself in writing, especially today, to be born again not

only as a woman but as an animal of any species; provided, of course, that I should be reborn with my memory,
for without that it would no longer be I.

At Los Balbazes we ate ices. My two young ladies returned to my lodging very well satisfied with the pleasure
I had procured them that day without offending the Lord
God, whom they loved with all their hearts, despite his
forbidding them to love a man who was not their husband. Doña Ignacia, whom I loved very much, and who
was such as to be loved by the most fastidious of men,
delighted that she had spent the whole day in my company without my making any attempt on her, but apparently fearing that I would not observe the same
restraint at supper, asked me to have her cousin sup with
us; I consented, and even with pleasure. The cousin was
as stupid as she was ugly, her one quality was that she
was kind and sympathetic; she was the same age as Doña
Ignacia; after she had confided to me that she had told
her all that had happened between us, I did not mind her
being present at our meetings; she could be no obstacle
to me. Doña Ignacia thought that I would not dare to
attempt anything in her presence.

A third place had already been laid at the table, when
I heard someone on the stairs. She said it was her father;
I went to the door myself to ask him to come down and
sup with us; he accepted with pleasure. The man was
likable. The moral maxims which he uttered from time to
time amused me; he made it a point of honor to parade
his confidence; he believed that I loved his daughter, but
in all honor, relying on my probity or on her piety; I
always thought that he would have considered himself
insulted and would never have left her alone with me if
he had discovered that during the Carnival we had already done all that love had commanded us to do.

So it was he who kept up the conversation at table,
seated beside his niece and opposite his daughter, who
was next to me. It was very hot, I asked him to take off

his coat so that I should be free to do likewise, and to persuade his daughter to sup as if she were in her own room, and, so far as his daughter was concerned, he managed it without too much difficulty, for she had a very beautiful bosom, but he had his hands full getting his niece to do the same thing; she finally gave in, very much ashamed to display nothing but bones under a dark skin; but I did her the kindness never to look at her. Doña Ignacia told her father how much she had enjoyed the adoration at Nuestra Señora de Atocha, and our visit to Los Balbazes, then she told him that she had seen the Duchess of Villadarias, who had invited me to call on her. At that the worthy man began discoursing on the lady's malady in a jesting vein, and mentioned a number of cases, which he and I discussed at length, and which the two cousins pretended not to understand. The good wine from La Mancha kept us at table for two hours; he told his niece that she could sleep with his daughter in the room next to mine, in which there was a wide bed, his daughter's bed in her room upstairs being very narrow and the night being torrid. I told them it would be an honor. Doña Ignacia blushed and said to her father that it would not be proper, for the room was separated from mine only by a door of which the upper half was glazed. I looked at Don Diego and smiled.

The worthy man then treated his daughter to a harangue which almost made me laugh. He reproached her with her pride, her maliciousness, her piety, her suspicious nature. He said that I must be at least twenty years older than she, and that her suspicion was a greater sin than any that she could have committed by some small amorous favor which she might have brought herself to grant.

"I am sure," he said, "that on Sunday you will forget to accuse yourself of the sin of having suspected that Don Jaime was capable of doing anything improper."

She looked at me, asked me to excuse her, and said that

she would go to bed where we were. The cousin said nothing against it, and the father went upstairs very well pleased to have given me another proof of his nobility.

I decided to punish myself in order to exacerbate the love of Doña Ignacia, who loved me and who had perhaps determined on a resistance which would have grieved me. I bade them good night in the sweetest of terms, assuring them that they could be at their ease, and I went to my room, where I at once got into bed after putting out my candle. But I at once got up again to see if they might not take advantage of the opportunity to display their secret beauties, which they had no need to suspect that I was observing. The ugly cousin talked in a low voice to Doña Ignacia, who was already about to take off her petticoat, and a moment later she blew out the candle. I went to bed. The next morning at six o'clock I get up, and through the glass panes I see the bed made and the room tidied; not a sign of the two cousins. It was the third day of Whitsun week, they had certainly gone to mass at La Soledad.

Doña Ignacia came home alone at ten o'clock, I was writing, being dressed and ready to go out to mass at eleven. She told me that she had spent three hours in church with her cousin, whom she had left at her door.

"I imagine you went to confession."

"No. I went to it on Sunday, and I will go next Sunday too."

"I am delighted that your confession will not be longer on my account."

"You are mistaken."

"Mistaken! I understand you. Let me tell you that I will not be a party to our damning ourselves for mere desires. I did not come to your house either to torment you or to become a martyr. What you did with me on the last day of the Carnival made me fall completely in love with you, and you horrify me when I think that my affection and yours have become something of which you re-

Gold Snuffbox

*The Torre de San Juan Prison in the
Citadel of Barcelona*

pent. I spent a very bad night, and I must take care of my health. I must think of forgetting you, and I must begin by avoiding your presence. I will keep your house, but tomorrow I will begin to lodge elsewhere. Believe me, if you know your religion as you should, you must approve of my decision. Inform your confessor of it on Sunday, and you will see that he will approve of it.''

''What you say is true, but I cannot consent to it. It is for you to say if you will leave me, I will bear it in silence; I will let my father say what he will, but I tell you that I shall be the unhappiest girl in all Madrid.''

After these words she lowered her beautiful eyes, she shed tears, and she touched my heart.

''Doña Ignacia, I love you, and I hope that the passion you have inspired in me will not be the cause of my damnation; I can neither see you without loving you nor love you without giving you the proofs of it which love imperiously orders me to give you in the way which my happiness demands. If I go away, you say that you will be unhappy, and I cannot bring myself to do it; if I remain and you do not change your behavior, it is I who will be unhappy and who will even lose my health. Now tell me what I must do. Am I to go or to stay? Choose.''

''Stay.''

''Then you will be kind and loving to me, as you were before, perhaps for my misfortune.''

''Alas! I have had to repent of it and to promise *God* that I would not succumb to it again. I tell you to stay because I am sure that in a week or ten days we will become so used to each other that I will love you only as a father or a brother, and you will be able to clasp me in your arms as if I were your sister or your daughter.''

''And you say you are sure of that?''

''Yes, my dear friend, sure of it.''

''You are deceiving yourself.''

''Let me deceive myself. Will you believe that I am happy in deceiving myself?''

"Good God! What do I hear? I see that it is true. Oh, ill-omened piety!"

"Why 'ill-omened'?"

"Nothing, my dear friend; it would take me too long, and I might endanger—— Let us say no more about it. I will remain in your house."

I went out unfeignedly distressed, more on the girl's account than on mine, though I saw myself cheated of what she would have granted me if she had not been under the domination of a misunderstood religion. I saw that I must get her out of my head, for even if I had the luck to enjoy her again one day, taking her by surprise at some moment when my words or my caresses had troubled her soul, Sunday would come, and a new promise to her confessor would send her back to me sullen and intractable. She admitted that she loved me, and she hoped she could come to love me in a different way. A monstrous desire, which can exist in a sincere soul only if it is the slave of a religion which makes it see crime where nature cannot allow crime to be.

I return home at noon, and Don Diego thinks he is pleasing me by dining with me. His daughter does not come down until the dessert. I ask her to sit down, politely, but gloomily and coldly. Don Diego asks her if I had got up during the night to go to her bed, he laughs at her, she replies that she had not insulted me by the slightest suspicion and that her hesitation had been only from force of habit. I put an end to her explanations by praising her modesty and assuring her that she would have reason to guard herself against me if the laws of duty did not have more power over me than the desires inspired in me by her charms. Don Diego pronounced this declaration of love sublime and worthy of a knight of the ancient Round Table. I had to laugh. His daughter told him that I was mocking her, and he replied that he was sure I was not and that he even believed I had known her for some time before I came to his house to

ask to take her to the ball. At that she swore he was
wrong.

"You have sworn it in vain," I said. "Your father
knows more about it than you do."

"What! You had seen me? But where?"

"At La Soledad, when you had received the Blessed
Sacrament and were coming out of the church after the
mass with your young cousin, whom you met at the door.
I followed you at a distance, and you can guess the rest."

Doña Ignacia was as dumfounded as her father was
triumphant and proud of his perspicacity. He said that
he was going *a los toros* ("to the bullfights"), that it
was a delightful day, and that one must go early, for all
Madrid would be there. I had never been to a bullfight,
he advises me to go, and he tells his daughter to go with
me. She asks me fondly if her company will give me
pleasure. I reply that it will, but on condition that she
will take her cousin with her, for I was in love with her.
Her father bursts out laughing; his daughter says she
believes it; she sends for her, and we go to the great
amphitheater[22] outside the Puerta de Alcalá, which was
to be the scene of the magnificent and cruel festival which
is the delight of the nation. There was no time to lose.
Nearly all the boxes were either occupied or engaged. We
took places in one in which there were only two ladies,
one of whom, to my amusement, was the same Duchess of
Villadarias whom we had seen the day before at the
Atocha. My young ladies sit in front, as was only right,
and I on a higher bench directly behind the Duchess, who
thus had her head between my knees.

She compliments me in French on the fortunate chance
which made us meet at churches and spectacles. Doña Ignacia was beside her, she praises her, she asks me if she
is my mistress or my wife, and I reply that she is a beauty
for whom I sighed in vain. She laughs, she refuses to believe it, and she begins talking to Doña Ignacia and
treating her to the most charming sallies on love, suppos-

ing that she is as well versed in the subject as herself.
She whispers to her, the other blushes, the Duchess becomes ardent, she laughs heartily, she tells me that she is
the most beautiful young lady in Madrid, she says that
she will not ask me who she is, but that she will be happy
if I will go to dine in her house in the country with the
delightful girl. I promise to go, for I cannot do otherwise,
but I decline to set a day. However, she makes me promise that I will visit her the next afternoon at four o'clock.
What terrified me was that she said she would be alone.
It indicated a formal assignation—with all its consequences; she was pretty, but she was too notorious; my
visit would have occasioned too much talk. The bullfight
began, and with it silence fell, for the spectacle absorbs
all the attention of the true Spaniard.

A bull comes out of a small door in a fury, and swiftly
enters the arena, then stops and looks to right and left,
as if to discover who can be challenging it. It sees a man
on horseback who gallops toward it with a long lance in
his hand; the bull runs to meet him, and the *picadero*[23]
gives it a thrust of his lance, avoiding it; the angered
bull pursues him, and if it has not plunged one of its
horns into the horse's belly at the first encounter it does
so at the second or the third or the fourth, and often at
each of them, so that the horse runs about the arena spill-
ing out and dragging its entrails, covering the ground
with the blood which spurts from its wounds, until it falls
dead. It is seldom that the bull receives a lance thrust so
well placed that it drops dead on the spot. When that
happens those who preside over the festival grant the bull
to the brave and skillful *picadero* who has killed him.

It very often happens that a bull in its rage kills the
horse and its rider. This atrocity is watched without com-
punction; it makes the foreigner shudder. After one bull,
another is sent in, as well as another horse. What distressed me at this barbarous spectacle, which I attended
several times, is that the horse, with which I sympathized

far more than with the bull, was always sacrificed,
slaughtered by the cowardice of its wretched rider. What
I admired in the cruel spectacle was the nimbleness and
daring of the Spaniards who run about the arena on
foot against the raging bull, which, though held back by
men who control it with ropes, nevertheless does not fail
to attack now one, now another of those who wound it
and who then escape its fury without ever turning their
backs to it. These bold men have no defense but an unfolded black cloak fastened to the end of a pike. When
they see that the bull is ready to charge at them, they
hold out the pike, showing the bull the spread cloak;
the outwitted animal then turns from the man to charge
at the cloak, and the challenger escapes with astonishing
agility. He runs, turning somersaults and making dangerous leaps, sometimes jumping over the barriers. This
occupies the spectator and may give him some pleasure,
but, taking everything into consideration, the spectacle
struck me as gloomy and terrifying. It is expensive. The
receipts often come to four or five thousand pistoles. In
every city in Spain there is an amphitheater built for
these combats. When the King is in Madrid the whole
Court attends except himself, who prefers hunting. Carlos III went hunting every day of the year except Good
Friday.

On the way back to my apartment the two cousins
thanked me endlessly. I kept the ugly girl to supper and
she remained to spend the night, as on the day before;
but Don Diego dined out and our supper was a sad occasion, for, being in a bad humor, I could find nothing
amusing to say. Doña Ignacia too became gloomy and
thoughtful when, on her asking if I would really go to
see the Duchess, I replied that it would be bad manners
on my part not to go.

"We will go to dine with her in the country one day
too," I said.

"Certainly not!"

"Why?"

"Because she is mad. She whispered things to me at which I should have taken offense if I had not reflected that she thought she was doing me honor by treating me as her equal."

We rose from table and, having dismissed Felipe, we sat on the balcony to wait for Don Diego and also to enjoy a little breeze which, in the hot weather we were having, was delicious. Seated beside each other on the tiles, enlivened by the good food we had eaten, excited by love, invited by the mysterious darkness which, without preventing lovers from seeing, makes them hope that they will be seen by no one, we looked at each other amorously. I let my arm fall on Doña Ignacia, and I pressed my lips to her beautiful mouth. Letting me clasp her more closely, she asked me if I should go to see the Duchess the next day.

"No," I said, "if you promise me you will not go to confession Sunday."

"What will my father confessor say if I do not go?"

"Nothing, if he knows his business. But let us discuss it a little, I beg you."

We were both in the most decisive posture, and the cousin, who had seen us ready to surrender ourselves to love, had retired to the corner of the balcony, where she stood with her back to us. Without stirring, without changing my position, without drawing back my hand, which was enjoying the palpitation of her amorous heart, I ask her if at this moment she is thinking of repenting on Sunday of the tender sin she is already prepared to commit.

"No, I am not thinking now of the confusion I shall feel when I confess it; but if you make me think of it, I reply that I shall certainly confess it."

"And after you have confessed it will you continue to love me, as you do at this moment?"

"I must hope that God will grant me the strength not to offend him again."

"I must warn you, my dear friend, that if you continue to love me God will not grant you the strength. But since I foresee that, on your side, you will endeavor to deserve that grace, I am in despair, for I foresee too that at least on Sunday evening you will refuse to commit the sweet sin with me which we are about to commit at this moment."

"Alas, my dear friend! That is true! But why think of it now?"

"My dear heart, your quietism is a far more heinous sin than the work of the flesh which love makes so precious to us. I cannot be your accomplice in a sin which my religion forbids, despite the fact that I adore you and that I am at this moment the happiest of men. One thing or the other, then. Either promise me that you will stop going to confession for as long as I remain in Madrid, or allow me now to make myself the unhappiest of mortals by retiring, for I cannot truly surrender myself to love when I am thinking of the pain which your resistance will cause me on Sunday."

While preaching her this terrible sermon, I tenderly clasped her in my arms, giving her every kind of caress in all the effervescence of love; but before coming to the act I again asked her if she promised me she would abstain from going to confession on Sunday.

"Oh, my dear friend, now you are cruel, you make me unhappy. I cannot in conscience promise you that."

At this reply I become motionless, I proceed no further, I deliberately make her unhappy in order to put her in a condition to be perfectly happy in the future; it costs me an effort, but I bear everything, being certain that my pain will not last long. Doña Ignacia, whom I had nevertheless not pushed away, is in despair to see me inactive; modesty forbids her to urge me openly; but she allows

herself to redouble her caresses, to reproach me with seduction and cruelty. Just then her cousin turns and tells
us that Don Diego is entering the house.

We having returned to a decent position, and the
cousin having sat down beside me, Don Diego paid his respects to me, then he left, wishing us a good night's sleep.
I did the same in the saddest tone to the charming Doña
Ignacia, whom I adored, whom I pitied, and whom I had
to treat in this way in order to make her as happy as I
was.

After putting out my candles I spent half an hour spy-
ing on her through the glass panes. Sitting in an armchair with a look of the utmost dejection, she never
answered a word to all that her cousin said to her, which
I could not hear. The cousin having gone to bed, I
thought she would make up her mind to come to mine,
and I got into it; but I was mistaken. The next morning
very early they left my room, and Don Diego came down
at noon to dine with me and to tell me that his daughter
was suffering from a very bad headache so that she had
not even gone to mass. She was in bed in a state of col-
lapse.

"She must be persuaded to eat something."

"On the contrary. She will be well this evening if she
eats nothing, and she will sup with you."

After taking a siesta, I went to keep her company, sitting down beside her and, for three whole hours, saying
to her everything that such a lover as I could say to a
girl whom he must force to change her behavior in order
to make her happy; and she kept her eyes closed through
it all, never answering me, only sighing when I said something very touching to her. I left her to go for a walk in
the Prado San Jerónimo,[24] telling her that if she did not
come down to sup with me I should take it that she no
longer wanted to see me. Frightened by my threat, she
came to table when I no longer expected her, but pale and
weak. She ate very little, and she never said a word, be-

cause she was convinced, and she did not know what to
say to me. The tears which now and again welled from
her beautiful eyes, though her pretty face never under-
went the least contraction, pierced my soul. The pain she
caused me was incredible; I thought I could not bear it,
for I loved her, and I had no diversion in Madrid which
could make up to me for this abstinence. Before going up
to her room, she asked me if I had paid the Duchess the
visit I had promised her, and she seemed less sad when I
told her I had not gone there, of which Felipe could
assure her, for it was he who had delivered the letter in
which I asked the lady to excuse me for not being able to
have the honor of paying my court to her that day.

"But you will go some other day."

"No, my dear friend, for I see that it would grieve
you."

I tenderly kissed Doña Ignacia, sighing, and she left
me as unhappy as she was herself.

I saw very well that what I demanded of her was far
too much; but I had reason to hope that I should bring
her to terms, for I had had proof of her great inclination
to love. I did not think it was with God that I was vying
for her, but with her confessor. It was she herself who
had told me that she would feel in a false position toward
her confessor if she stopped going to confession; and, full
of probity and feelings of Spanish honor, she could
neither bring herself to deceive her confessor nor resolve
to combine her love with what she believed she owed to
her religion. She thought rightly.

On Friday and Saturday she did no more and no less.
Her father, who had seen that we were in love with each
other, made her dine and sup with me, counting on her
sense of duty and on mine. He did not come down except
when I sent him an invitation to do so. On Saturday evening his daughter left me more sadly than ever, turning
her head away when I wanted to give her the kiss which
I thought would assure her of my constancy. I saw what

was in the wind. She had to go to receive the Blessed Sacrament the next day. I admired the candor of her soul, I pitied her, seeing the battle which the two passions must be fighting within her. I began to feel afraid, and to repent that I had acted in a way which would make me lose the whole because I had not been content with a part.

Wanting to convince myself of the thing with my own eyes, the next morning I get up early, I dress unaided, and I wait for her to go out. I knew that she would go to fetch her cousin; I leave the house after her, I go straight to La Soledad, and I take my stand behind the sacristy door, from where I saw everyone who was in the church and where no one could see me. A quarter of an hour later I see the two cousins come in, pray together, rise, and separate. One goes to wait near one confessional, the other near another. I watched only Doña Ignacia. When her turn came she entered the box, and I saw the confessor, after giving an absolution to his right, bend his head to the left to listen to Doña Ignacia. The confession bored me, revolted me, for it never ended; what could she be saying to him? I saw the confessor speaking to his penitent from time to time. I was on the verge of leaving. It had been going on for an hour. I had heard three masses. At last I see her rise. I had already seen her ugly cousin at the high altar, receiving the Eucharist.

Doña Ignacia, with her eyes lowered and the look of a saint, goes and kneels on my side of the church, where I cannot see her; I suppose she is hearing the mass which is being said at the altar four paces from her. I expected to see her, at the end of the mass, at the high altar to receive the Sacrament, but not a bit of it. I see her rejoin her cousin at the church door and leave. "It is love. She made a sincere confession," I said to myself, "she confessed her passion, her confessor demanded sacrifices of her which she could not promise him, and the monster, true to his calling, refused her absolution. I am lost.

What will happen? My peace, and the peace of this worthy girl, truly devout and ardently in love, demand that I leave her father's home. Wretch! I should have contented myself with having her from time to time by surprise. Today I shall see her dining with me in tears. I must deliver her from this hell.''

I go home extremely sad, extremely displeased with myself, and I dismiss the hairdresser because I want to go to bed, I tell the Biscayan cook not to serve me dinner until I call her; I hear Doña Ignacia come in, I do not want to see her, I lock my door, I get into bed, and I sleep until one o'clock. I get up, I order dinner served and send word that the father or the daughter is to come down and dine with me, and I see the daughter, wearing a black bodice with silk ribbons at every seam. In all Europe there is not a more seductive garment when the woman has a beautiful bosom and a narrow waist. Seeing her so pretty, noticing her serene manner, I cannot keep from complimenting her. Not expecting to see her in this mood, I forget the kiss which she had refused me the night before, I embrace her, and I find her as gentle as a lamb. But Felipe was coming down, I say nothing to her, and we sit down at table. I reflect on the change, I weigh it, I conclude that the Spanish girl has jumped the ditch; she has made up her mind. Now I am happy; but I must say nothing, pretend to know nothing, and watch her come to me.

Without concealing anything of the content which was flooding my soul, I talk to her of love whenever Felipe leaves me free, and I see her not only untrammeled but ardent. Before we get up from table she asks me if I still love her, and, in ecstasy at my reply, she asks me to take her to *los toros*. Quick, the hairdresser! I put on a taffeta coat with Lyons embroidery[25] which I had never worn, and we go to the bullfight on foot, not having the patience to wait for my carriage and being afraid that we shall not find places; but we find two in a big box, and she is glad not to see me, as she had done the time before, next to her rival. After the bullfight, the day being delightful, she wants me to take her to the Prado, where we find all the most fashionable people of both sexes in Madrid. Holding my arm, she seemed proud to display herself as mine, and she filled me with joy.

But along comes the Venetian Ambassador, on foot as we were, with his favorite Manuzzi, and meets us. They had arrived from Aranjuez that day, and I knew nothing about it. They accost me with all the Spanish ceremoniousness, and the Ambassador pays me a compliment which is infinitely flattering to Doña Ignacia, who pretends not to have heard it. After accompanying us for a time, he leaves, saying that he will be glad if I will come to dine with him the next day.

Toward nightfall we go to eat ices, and we return to the house, where we find Don Diego, who congratulates his daughter on being in a good humor and on having spent an enjoyable day with me. I ask him to sup with us, he accepts, and he amuses us with countless little tales of gallantry, each of which reveals more of his noble character. But before he goes up to his room these are the exact words, literally translated, with which he surprised me:

"Amigo Don Jaime, I leave you to enjoy the coolness of the night with my daughter on the balcony, I am delighted that you love her, and I assure you that, to become my son-in-law, you have only to do what is necessary to enable me to declare myself certain *de vuestra nobleza* ['of your nobility']." [26]

"I should be only too happy, my charming friend," I said to his daughter as soon as he left us alone, "if that were possible, but I must tell you that in my country only those are styled noble whose birth gives them the right to govern the State. I should be noble if I had been born in Spain; but such as I am, I adore you, and I have reason to believe that you will make me entirely happy here and now.''

"Yes, my dear friend, entirely; but I want to be so too. No infidelity.''

"None. On my word of honor.''

"Come, then,'' she said. "Let us shut the door to the balcony.''

"Let us wait a quarter of an hour. Put out the candles, and do not shut the door. Tell me, my angel, whence comes[27] my happiness? I should never have expected it.''

"If it is a happiness, you owe it to a tyranny which was driving me to despair. God is good, and he does not want me to become my own executioner, I am sure. When I told my confessor that it was absolutely impossible for me to stop loving you, and at the same time possible for me not to do anything wrong with you, he told me that I could not have such confidence in myself, and the more so since I had already been weak. That being the case, he wanted me to promise him that I would not be alone with you again. I told him that I could not promise him that, and he refused to absolve me. I suffered that indignity for the first time in my life with a firmness of mind of which I did not believe myself capable, and, putting myself in the hands of God, I said: 'Lord, thy will be done.' While hearing mass, I made my decision. As long as you love me, I will be yours alone, and when you leave Spain I will find another confessor. What comforts me is that my soul is perfectly at peace. My cousin, to whom I told everything, is astonished; but she is very unintelligent. She does not understand that I am led astray only for the moment.''

After this declaration, which made me see all the beauty of her soul, I took her in my arms and I led her to my bed, where she remained with me, free from any scruples, until the first rays of dawn. She left me more in love than ever.

CHAPTER IV

I commit an indiscretion which makes Ma-
nuzzi my bitterest enemy. His revenge. My
departure from Madrid. Saragossa. Valencia.
La Nina. My arrival in Barcelona.

IT IS now that the truth makes me contrite, for I am
obliged to tell it and to confess myself guilty of an indiscretion which, however, may lead the reader to judge
wrongly of me if he takes it to be characteristic.

I dined the next day at the Venetian Ambassador's,
where I had the pleasure of learning that at Court the
ministers and all those who had made my acquaintance
had formed so good an opinion of me that I could not
wish it better. Three or four days later the King returned
to Madrid with the entire royal family and with the ministers, on whom I constantly called in pursuit of the
Sierra Morena project. I was preparing to make a journey there. Manuzzi, who continued to give me proofs of
the sincerest friendship, was to accompany me for his
own pleasure, with an adventuress who went by the name
of Portocarrero and who said she was the niece or the
daughter of the late Cardinal,[1] which allowed her to
assert great pretensions, but who in secret was nothing

but the concubine of the Abbé Béliardi,[2] the French Consul in Madrid.

My affairs being in this posture, the Genius who opposed my Guardian Genius brought to Madrid the Baron de Fraiture,[3] of Liège, Grand Huntsman to the Principality,[4] a profligate, a gamester, and as great a scoundrel as those who today say that he was honest. He had known me at Spa, where I had told him that I was going to Portugal, and he was on his way to meet me there, counting heavily on my friendship to make such acquaintances as would fill his purse with the money of dupes.

Nothing in all my life has ever shown cheating gamesters that I was of their tribe; nevertheless, they always insisted on believing me a sharper. I could not but be one. They thought they were doing me honor. How could they believe I was stupid when I had all the outward signs, all the appearance and manner, of a man of intelligence? They talked to me openly, and, what is amusing, I did not deny the allegation, I equivocated; I had to do so, or declare myself insulted. Baron de Fraiture, then, who stopped at Madrid as soon as he learned that I was there, came to see me, appeared most happy to have found me, flattered me, and by his politeness obliged me to give him a good reception. It seemed to me that a few small favors and some acquaintances which I might procure for him could never compromise me. He introduced his traveling companion. He was a fat Frenchman, idle, lazy, ignorant, but a Frenchman. All the rest passes unobserved except by those who look closely, and they are very few who look closely into the character of a Frenchman who has a good appearance, who dresses well, who is gay at table, who loves women, and who can stand up to a debauch. This companion of Fraiture's was a cavalry captain in the French service, one of those who has had the good fortune to obtain an endless leave of absence.

On the fourth or fifth day Fraiture told me frankly that he had no money, and he asked me for thirty or forty pistoles, saying that he would consider himself indebted to me for them; I thanked him for being open with me, and I frankly told him that I could do nothing for him in the way of money, for I should soon be in need of it myself.

"But we will do some good piece of business, and you will be sure to have money."

"I do not know about that, and in the meanwhile I cannot go without the necessities of life."

"We do not know what to do to quiet our landlord. Come and talk to him."

"If I talk to him I shall do you more harm than good, for he will ask me if I vouch for you, and I will tell him that you are one of those noblemen who need no one to vouch for them; but the evasion will not prevent your landlord from thinking that if I do not vouch for you it shows that I am doubtful."

Since I had introduced Count Manuzzi to him on the promenade, Fraiture persuaded me to take him to call on the Count, and it was in him that, a week or ten days later, he confided. Manuzzi, obliging and himself a professional sharper, did not give him money; but he introduced him to a man who lent him some against pledges and without interest. They played a few times, they won something, without my ever taking part in it. Occupied by the colony and by Doña Ignacia, I wanted to be left in peace; my spending a single night away from the house would have alarmed her beautiful soul, which she was sacrificing to love.

During this time Signor Querini,[5] the new Venetian Ambassador, arrived in Madrid to replace Signor Mocenigo, whom the Republic had appointed Ambassador to the Court of Versailles. Querini was a man of letters, a talent not shared by Mocenigo, who loved only music and Greek friendship.

The new Ambassador became favorable to me, and I

was convinced that in a few days I should be able to count on him even more than on Signor Mocenigo.

Meanwhile Baron de Fraiture and his friend had to think of leaving Spain; they found no gaming at the Ambassador's or elsewhere, no hope of any at the Escorial,[6] they must go back to France; but they owe at their inn, they need money for the journey, and they have none. I can give them nothing. Manuzzi imagines that he cannot do so either, we are sorry for their misfortune, but the obligation to think of ourselves first of all obliges us to be cruel to everyone else on earth.

But now for a surprise. Manuzzi comes to me one morning with a look of uneasiness and dismay which he tries in vain to hide.

"What is the matter?"

"I am beset despite myself. Baron Fraiture, to whom I have not been at home for a week, for, since I could not give him money, he distressed me, wrote me a note last evening in which he said that he will blow out his brains today if I do not lend him a hundred pistoles, and I am sure he will take that desperate step if I refuse him."

"He said the same to me three days ago, and I told him that I wager a hundred pistoles he will not kill himself. Angered by my flippant reply, he proposed to fight a duel with me; I replied that, in his state of desperation, he would have too great an advantage over me, or I over him, and I left him. Answer him as I did, or do not answer him at all!"

"I cannot. Here are a hundred pistoles. Take them to him from me, and have him give you a properly drawn note, so that he can be made to return the amount at Liège, where, after all, he has property."

Admiring his noble act, I undertake the commission, I go to him, I find him flurried, at his wits' end, and I am not surprised, for I attribute his dismay to his situation. I think I shall restore him to life and good humor by telling him that I have brought the hundred pistoles he needs to leave Madrid, and that it was Count Manuzzi who was doing him the favor; but not a bit of it, he accepts the money, he writes me out a note in the terms which I prescribe, and he remains sad and gloomy. However, he assures me that he will leave with his friend for Barcelona the next day, and that from there he will go to Avignon, where his friend has a relative. I wish him a good journey, I take the note to Manuzzi, who I see is still uneasy, and I remain to dine with the Ambassador. It was for the last time.

Three days later I go to dine with the two Ambassadors,[7] for they were living together in the Calle ancha de San Bernardo, and I am amazed when the porter tells me that no one is at home to me there and that I should do well not to present myself at the door in future, for he had orders to refuse me entrance whenever I should do so.

At this thunderbolt, of which I could not guess the cause, I go home, and I sit down and proceed to write a note to Manuzzi, a very short one for I had only to tell him what had happened and to ask him the reason for it. I seal it, I send it to him by Felipe, who brings it back to me unopened. An order had come from Count Manuzzi himself not to receive it. A fresh surprise. What has happened? I can divine nothing; but I am determined to die or to have an explanation. I dine very thoughtfully with Doña Ignacia, who is uneasy, but to whom there is no reason to tell the cause of my own uneasiness; and after dinner, just as I was about to take a siesta, in comes Manuzzi's lackey, who hands me a letter and leaves without waiting for me to read it.

In the letter I find another, which I read before reading Manuzzi's. I see that it is signed: "The Baron de Fraiture." The desperate wretch demanded a hundred pistoles of Manuzzi as an unsecured loan, promising that, if he gives them to him, he will unmask an enemy of his

in the man who he thought was most attached to his
interests and his person.

Manuzzi, calling me a traitor and ingrate, told me that,
curious to know this enemy, he had at once arranged to
meet Fraiture in the Prado San Gerónimo, where, after
obtaining his word of honor that he would lend him the
money, he had proved to him that the enemy was I, since
it was from me that he had learned that the name he bore
was genuine, but that all the titles he assumed were
false. And here he entered into the appalling detail of all
that I had told him, and so circumstantially that, since
Fraiture could only have heard it from me, Manuzzi
could be left in no doubt of my perfidy. He ended his
letter by saying (and it was too much) that he advised
me to leave Madrid within a week at the latest.

My reader cannot imagine the prostration of soul in
which I was left after reading this letter. It was the first
time in my life that I found myself guilty[8] of a monstrous
indiscretion and one committed for no reason, of a gra-
tuitous and infernal ingratitude which I did not find in
my character, of a crime, in short, of which I did not
believe myself capable.[9] Grieving, confused, ashamed of
myself, recognizing the full extent of my wrongdoing,
and knowing that, not deserving forgiveness, I must not
even ask for it, I sank into the blackest gloom. Yet it
seemed to me that Manuzzi, though justifiably angry, had
made a great mistake by ending his letter with the absurd
advice that I should leave Madrid in a week, for, knowing
what kind of man I was, he ought to be certain that I
would scorn his advice. He was not powerful enough to
demand any such submission of me, and on my side I
must not, after committing one base action, commit another which would declare me not only the vilest of men
but also incapable of giving him any other kind of satisfaction. Plunged in the blackest melancholy, I spent the
whole day unable to decide on a course, and at nine

o'clock I kissed my dear mistress, asking her to eat her supper with her family and to leave, for I had to come to terms with the greatest trial I had had to bear in my life.

After sleeping well enough to restore my soul to a condition in which it could adopt the course most becoming to my guilt, I got up, and I wrote the friend whom I had offended the most sincere of confessions in a letter than which he could ask for nothing more submissive. In conclusion I told him that if he had a generous soul he should accept my letter as the fullest satisfaction; but that if by chance it did not suffice him he had only to inform me of whatever he demanded, assuring him that I would accede to everything except to a course which could make me suspected of fearing any treachery.

"I am willing," I said, "to leave it in your power to have me murdered; but I will not leave Madrid except when I choose and when I have nothing more to do there."

After sealing my letter with a commonplace seal, I had Felipe, whose handwriting he did not know, write the address, and, to make sure that Manuzzi would receive it, I sent him to put it in the royal box at El Pardo,[10] where the King had gone. I remained in my room all day with Doña Ignacia, who, seeing me recovered from my depression of the evening before, no longer insisted on knowing the cause of it. I also spent the next day at home, hoping for an answer, but in vain. On the next day but one, which was a Sunday, I go out to call on Prince della Cattolica, I stop at the door, and the porter comes politely to my carriage to whisper to me that His Excellency has reasons for asking me not to call at his house again. I did not expect it; but after this blow I expect all the others. I go to the house of the Abbé Béliardi, and it is his lackey in his anteroom who, after announcing me, comes out to tell me that he is not at home.

As I get back into my carriage, I see Don Domingo Varnier, who tells me he has something to say to me; I ask him if he would like to go on to mass with me, he gets in, and he tells me that the Venetian Ambassador, the former one, had told the Duke of Medina Sidonia that it was his duty to inform him that I was a scoundrel. The Duke had replied that as soon as he became aware of it himself he would no longer permit me access to him. These three dagger thrusts, entering my heart in the course of less than half an hour, leave me completely at a loss; I make no answer, I go to mass with my friend; but afterward I believe I should have died if I had not relieved myself by giving him a full account of the cause of the Ambassador's anger. He advised me to tell no one about it, for it could only enrage Manuzzi, who had become, with some show of reason, my bitter enemy.

Back at the house I wrote Manuzzi to renounce a too cowardly revenge, for he put me under the necessity of becoming indiscreet to all those who thought it their part to insult me in order to flatter the Ambassador's hatred. I send my letter, unsealed, to Signor Gasparo Soderini,[11] Secretary of Embassy, sure that he would transmit it to him. After that I dined with my mistress, and after dinner I took her to the bullfight, where by chance I found a place in a box next to one in which were Manuzzi and the two Ambassadors. I bowed to them, then did not look at them again.

It was on the next day that the Marchese Grimaldi refused to grant me an audience. I had nothing more to hope for. The Duke of Losada received me, for he despised the Ambassador because of his masculine loves, but he told me that he had already been instructed not to receive me again. He said that, in view of this persecution, I had nothing more to hope for at Court.

Such a fury was unbelievable. It was thus that Manuzzi displayed the power he had over his ambassadorial wife. To avenge himself, he had overleaped the boundaries of shame. I wanted to see if he had forgotten Don Manuel de Roda and the Marquis of Mora, but, calling on them, I found that they had been informed. I had no one left but the Count of Aranda, and I was thinking of going there, when an Adjutant came to tell me that His Excellency wanted to speak to me. At that I leaped to the most terrible conclusions.

The Count had signified at what hour I was to appear. I find that deep-minded man all alone, and I see that he looks serene; I gain courage. He makes me sit down near him, a favor which he had never granted me before; I feel reassured.

"What have you done to your Ambassador?"

"Nothing to him directly; but I have offended his lover where it hurts him most, and that out of sheer stupidity. I made an indiscreet confidence, with no intention of harming him, to a wretch who has gone and sold it to him for a hundred pistoles. Manuzzi, in his anger, has loosed on me the man of position, the man who idolizes him, the man whom he can make do whatever he wishes."

"You did wrong; but what is done is done. You must understand that you can no longer hope to succeed in your project, for as soon as it came to giving you a post the King, informed that you are a Venetian, would ask the Ambassador about you."

"Must I leave, My Lord?"

"No, but the Ambassador has urged it on me. I replied that I have not the power to expel you so long as you do nothing contrary to the laws. He told me that your lies and slanders insult the honor of a Venetian subject whom it is his duty to protect and whom he knows intimately. I replied that if you are a slanderer, you must be attacked in the usual way and delivered to the rigor of the law if you cannot justify yourself. He ended by asking me to order you not to speak of him or of his protégé to the Venetian subjects who are now in Madrid, and it seems to me that you might grant him so much. Aside from that, you can, living as you live, stay in Madrid as long as you please, with nothing to fear, and the more so since he will leave in the course of this week.'' [12]

That was the entire conversation I had with the Count, and it was on that day I made up my mind to amuse myself and give up paying court to anyone. Friendship alone made me go to call on Varnier from time to time because I was fond of him, on the Duke of Medina Sidonia because I respected him, and on the architect Sabatini,[13] who always received me cordially, as did his wife. Doña Ignacia possessed me entirely, and she often congratulated me on having got rid of all the business which occupied me before Fraiture left. After the departure of the Ambassador, who, not having received permission[14] to visit Venice, went to Paris by way of Navarre, I wanted to see if Signor Querini would treat me as his uncle had done, and I laughed when his porter paid me the unwelcome compliment of informing me that his house was closed to me.

Six or seven weeks after the Ambassador's departure I left Madrid. I had to bring myself to it, despite the affection which kept me still in love with Doña Ignacia, for, aside from my having nothing more to hope for in Spain, I could not think of Lisbon, for I received no more letters and I had no more money. Carriage, table, theaters, and all the other little expenditures necessary to maintain life had brought me, though Doña Ignacia did not know it, to the end of my resources. I thought of selling a watch and a snuffbox in order to go to Marseilles, where I was sure to get money enough to sail for Constantinople. It seemed to me that I could not but make my fortune there without turning Turk;[15] but I should have been wrong. I was entering on the age which Fortune scorns.

In my distress I made the acquaintance of a learned Abate, the Auditor to the Papal Nuncio.[16] He was the Abate Pinzi,[17] who introduced me to a Genoese bookseller named Corrado, a rich man and so honest that, in a just

estimation, his virtues and his candor outweighed the
dishonesty of ten thousand Genoese.[18] It was to this man
that I went to sell a repeating watch and a snuffbox the
gold in which was worth twenty-five louis. Don Corrado
would not hear of my selling my possessions; he lent me
twenty doblones de a ocho, contenting himself with my
word that I would send them back to him when I should
be in a position to return them. Unfortunately for me, I
could never have the pleasure of doing so. He had no
children except a ravishingly pretty daughter, the only
heir to his entire fortune, whom he married to the son
of the Venetian painter Tiepoletto,[19] who, though his
talent was of the slightest, was a young man of excellent
qualities.

Nothing is sweeter than the life which a man in love
leads with a woman who loves him equally and who re-
sponds to his every desire; but nothing is more bitter
than separation when love has lost none of its strength.
The pain seems infinitely greater than the pleasure they
have had. The pleasure no longer exists, they feel only
the pain. They are so unhappy that, to escape it, they
wish they had never been happy. We spent the last days
with Doña Ignacia in pleasures which were always followed by sorrow and in the tears which seemed to lessen
it. Don Diego did not cry, he congratulated us on the tenderness of our hearts. Through Felipe, whom I left in
Madrid, I had news of Doña Ignacia until the middle of
the next year. She became the wife of a rich shoemaker,
her interest dictating that she resign herself to the mortification which a misalliance caused her father.

Having promised the Marquis of Mora and Colonel
Rojas that I would go to see them in Saragossa, I wanted
to keep my word. I arrived there all alone at the beginning of September, and I spent two weeks there. I saw
the manners and customs of the Aragonese.[20] The Count
of Aranda's laws had no currency in that city; in the
streets both by day and by night I encountered men who,

wearing hats with wide, turned-down brims, and black
cloaks which came down to their heels, were nothing short
of maskers, for the same cloaks covered their faces to the
eyes. One saw nothing. Under his cloak the masker carried *el spadino*;[21] it was a sword half again as long as
honest men commonly carry in France, in Italy, and in
Germany. These maskers were treated with great respect.
They were most often scoundrels, but they might be great
noblemen. At Saragossa I saw the great devotion paid to
Nuestra Señora del Pilar.[22] I saw processions in which
gigantic wooden statues were carried. I was taken to receptions where I found monks. I was introduced to a very
fat lady who, I was told, was a cousin of the Blessed
Palafox,[23] at which I was expected to fall into a trans-
port of reverence; and I made the acquaintance of a
Canon Pignatelli,[24] who was the presiding judge of the
Inquisition and who every morning sent to prison the
bawd who on the previous evening had arranged for him
to sup with a whore,[25] who had then spent the night with
him. He woke up, and, after thus exercising his judicial
authority, he went to confession, he said mass, then he
dined, the devil in the flesh overcame him, another girl
was procured for him, he enjoyed her, and the next morning he did over again what he had done the day before;
and it was the same thing every day. Always struggling
between God and the devil, the Canon was the happiest
of men after dinner and the unhappiest in the morning.

The bullfights at Saragossa were finer than at Madrid;
the bulls were not restrained by ropes, they moved about
the arena freely, and there was greater slaughter. The
Marquis of Mora and Count Rojas gave me very fine
dinners. The Marquis was by far the most amiable of
Spaniards; he died very young two years later.[26] I was
shown courtesans; but, with the image of Doña Ignacia
pursuing me everywhere, it was impossible for me to find
any woman worthy of love. The great Church of Nuestra
Señora del Pilar is on the ramparts of the city. The

Saragossans consider this fortification impregnable; they
are more than certain that, in case of a siege, the enemy
might enter everywhere else, but never there.

Traveling from Saragossa to Valencia, where I had
promised Signora Pelliccia I would be at this time, I saw
on a hill the ancient city of Sagunto. *Eminet excelso con-
surgens colle Sagunthos* ("Saguntum towers, rising from
a high hill").[27]

"I want to go up there," I said to a priest who was
with me and to the driver, who wanted to arrive in Valencia that evening, and who put the well-being of his
mules above all the antiquities on earth.

What objections, what remonstrances on the part of
the priest and the driver!

"You will see nothing but ruins."

"I like them better when they are ancient than all the
most beautiful modern buildings. Here is an écu; we will
go to Valencia tomorrow."

The driver said that I was an *hombre de bien* ("true
gentleman").

I saw the crenellations on top of the walls, which were
in large part intact; yet it was a monument dating from
the Second Punic War. I saw inscriptions on two gates,
incomprehensible to me and to many more, but which La
Condamine[28] or Séguier,[29] the Marchese Maffei's old
friend, would certainly have copied. My admiration for
this monument to an entire people, who had the courage
to burn themselves rather than break faith with the Romans by surrendering to Hannibal, ravished my soul and
drew a laugh from the priest, who would not have said
a mass to become the owner of the place, whose very name
has been destroyed, despite its title to respect and its
being easier to pronounce than Murviedro,[30] which,
though it comes from the Latin *muri veteres* ("old
walls"), does not please me; but time is an untamable
and ferocious monster bent on devouring everything:

mors etiam saxis nominibusque venit ("death comes also to stones and names").[31]

"This place," the priest said to me, "was always named Murviedro."

"That is impossible, for common sense does not permit a thing to be called old which must indubitably have been new at its birth. It is as if you were to tell me that your New Castile is not old because it is called New."

"However, it is certain that Old Castile must be older than New Castile." [32]

"Sir, that is not so. The new one will never be 'old,' and the old one is less ancient than the new."

After that the priest said no more to me and thought me a madman.

I tried my best, but in vain, to find the bust of Hannibal and the inscription in honor of Caesar Claudius, successor to Gallienus,[33] but I saw the remains of the amphitheater.[34]

The next day I saw the road paved in mosaic which had been discovered only twenty years earlier. I arrived at Valencia at nine o'clock in the morning, and I found myself very poorly lodged, for the impresario of the opera, the Bolognese Marescalchi, had taken all the good rooms for the actresses and actors who were to arrive from Madrid. He had with him his brother the Abate, whom I found erudite for his age. We went for a walk, and he laughed when I asked him to go to a coffeehouse. In the whole city there was not a place where a man who wants to rest can sit down and order something to drink to have a reason for giving the proprietor of the establishment four or five sous. Must we go to a pothouse and order wine? The idea is revolting: the place is ill-kept, the company one finds there is vicious or unsociable, and the wine is detestable, positively a poison not only for foreigners but for Spaniards as well, who can have excellent wine at home but who have good reason to drink only water in taverns. I found it inconceivable. In Spain, where the wines are excellent, especially on the coast where I was, close to Málaga and Alicante,[35] a foreigner cannot get a passable glass of wine except with the greatest difficulty. But what is the reason? It is the ignorance of the vintners, who are rogues everywhere on earth, but merciless scoundrels in Spain and at the same time fools, for their doctoring makes the wine undrinkable. During the first three days which I spent in that famous city, the birthplace of Alexander VI,[36] whom Father Pétau[37] calls *non adeo sanctus* ("not so saintly"), I saw everything, always in the company of the learned Abate Marescalchi. I saw that everything famous and beautiful in the world, if we judge by the descriptions and drawings of writers and artists, always loses when we go to see it and examine it closely. Valencia, situated in an excellent climate, very near to the Mediterranean, watered by the Guadalaviar,[38] in a smiling and fertile countryside rich in all the most delectable gifts which nature can offer mankind, animated by the healthiest and mildest air, distant only an hour from the famous *amenum stagnum*[39] ("lovely lake") which abounds in the most exquisite fish, inhabited by a numerous, very distinguished, and very rich nobility, where the women are, if not the cleverest, at least the most beautiful in all Spain, where there is an Archbishop and a clergy with an income of at least a million—this Valencia is a most unpleasant city for a foreigner because in it he can enjoy none of the comforts of life which he finds for his money everywhere else. In Valencia one is badly lodged, one eats badly, one cannot drink, one cannot converse because there is no society, nor argue with anyone, for, despite its university,[40] one does not find a single being there who deserves the name of man of letters. As for its material aspect, its five great bridges[41] over the Guadalaviar, its churches, its public buildings, the Arsenal, the Exchange, the Town Hall, its twelve gates, its ten thousand wells aroused no admira-

tion in me in a city where the streets are not paved and
where, to take a walk, one has to leave it. It is true that
one is then very well satisfied, it seems one is in the
Earthly Paradise, especially in the direction of the sea.

What did please me was the great number of one-horse
cabriolets which are waiting everywhere to serve those
who want to take a drive or even travel to some city at
two or three days' distance. One is conveyed very rapidly, and very cheaply, to Málaga, to Alicante, to Carta-
gena, to Tarragona,[42] and even, if one wishes, to Barcelona, which is fifty leagues away. If I had been in a
good humor I should have taken a trip through the Kingdoms of Murcia and Granada,[43] whose physical beauty
surpasses that of all the provinces we have in Italy. Poor
Spaniards! The beauty of their country, its fertility and
richness, are the cause of their indolence, and the mines
of Peru and Potosí are those of their poverty, their pride,
and all their prejudices.[44] It is paradoxical, but my
reader knows that what I say is true. To become the most
flourishing of all the kingdoms on earth, Spain would
need to be conquered, shaken to its foundations, and
nearly destroyed, it would be reborn fit to be the land of
the blessed.

I went to pay my respects to the sweet, modest, and
noble Pelliccia. The first performance was to be given on
the next day but one. It was not difficult, for the same
operas were given which had been performed for the
Court at the Sitios. This means at Aranjuez, at the Escorial, at La Granja,[45] for the Count of Aranda never
dared to give the theater in Madrid permission to show
the public an Italian *opera buffa*. The novelty would have
been too great, the Inquisition would have opened its
haggard eyes too wide. The balls at Los Caños del Peral
had astonished it; but they had to be done away with
two years later. So long as there is an Inquisition in
Spain[46] she will never be happy.

Signora Pelliccia had scarcely arrived before she sent

Don Diego Valencia the letter of recommendation which
the Duke of Arcos had given her three months before.
She had not seen that great nobleman since Aranjuez.
We dined—she, her husband, her sister, and an accomplished violinist who married her sister soon afterward.
She has scarcely risen, when Don Diego Valencia is announced: he was the banker to whom the Duke had recommended her.

"Señora," Don Diego says to her, "delighted by My
Lord the Duke of Arcos's doing me the favor of sending
you to me, I come to offer you my services and also to
inform you of the orders which he gives me and of which
you may not know."

"Señor, I hope that nothing will happen to me which
will oblige me to inconvenience you; I am very grateful
for the favor My Lord the Duke has shown me, and for
the trouble you have been at to come here to my lodging;
I shall have the honor of going to thank you."

"That is not necessary, Señora. You should know that,
as for any money you might need, I am ordered to furnish you with a total sum of no more than twenty-five
thousand doblones."

"Twenty-five thousand doblones?"

"No more, Señora. Have the goodness to read his
letter, for I think you should assure yourself of it."

He hands her the letter. It was four lines long:

"Don Diego, you[47] will furnish Doña Pelliccia when
she orders you up to the amount of twenty-five thousand
doblones, on my account. The Duke of Arcos."

She shows me the letter, we all read it and sit there
mute and amazed. She returns the letter to the banker,
who rises, bows to her, and goes. It is almost unbelievable.

It is only in Spain that such gestures are to be seen,
and they are not uncommon. I have already spoken of the
one in the same style to which Medina Celi had treated
La Pichona.[48] Some thinkers make bold to disapprove of
these divine actions, whereas it is at most permissible to

criticize them; they put them among vicious actions; they attribute them to prodigality or to pride. As for pride, I admit that it may often be the cause of them, but at that moment it becomes beautiful, for it can only act in concert with a great, heroic, rare soul, entirely above the vulgar; and I do not deny that it may come from the vice which we call prodigality, for the prodigal, as long as he can continue it, never ceases to be one; he throws away, he scatters, he is equally the prodigal with everyone; he sometimes stops, but only when he sees himself on the verge of ruin, whereupon he becomes a miser. The Spaniard is ambitious by nature, and does nothing except in the hope of being admired and declared superior to his equals. He wants those who examine and judge him to consider him worthy of the throne, and to attribute virtues to him which no man can practice except disinterestedly. He is so afraid of being thought a prodigal that even Medina Celi, even Arcos, who spent immense sums, never made expenditures which could be called foolish and always refused a hundred pistoles to a man who asked for them if it seemed there was not a good reason for giving them.

After Don Diego left, the Duke's recommendation became the subject of our conversation. La Pelliccia said that the Duke had wanted to teach her what sort of man he was of whom she had asked a recommendation, at the same time doing her the honor to believe her incapable of abusing the confidence he had in her.

"For it is certain," she said, "that I would die of hunger before I would take a single pistole from Don Diego."

The violinist said that the Duke would consider himself slighted, and that she must take something; her husband pleased me by saying that she must either take it all or take nothing. As for me, I thought as La Pelliccia did: nothing, for if the Duke wanted to make her rich by a present so extraordinary he could find means to do so without her being obliged to reproach herself with having abused his generosity and perhaps giving him occasion to believe that she had duped him.

"I am sure," I said to her, "that the Duke will consider himself obliged to make your fortune precisely because you will have made yourself estimable by your delicacy."

It was what she did, to the great displeasure of the banker. But the city, the public, which at once learned the whole story, did not believe what it considered beyond likelihood. The charming woman let people believe what they pleased, and returned to Madrid two weeks later without having asked Don Diego for a copper. But it was not believed in Madrid, or at the Court. The King believed what everyone said, which was repeated to him by Don Almerico Pini,[49] who kept His Catholic Majesty amused with news of Madrid. He thought he ought to save the Duke of Arcos from ruin by ordering Signora Pelliccia to leave. At the same time the same order was given to La Marcucci,[50] a dancer from Lucca, with whom another extremely rich Spanish Grandee[51] was in love.

The two had to obey the order, and the Spanish Grandee who loved the dancer immediately paid her his last visit, leaving her a bill of exchange on Lyons for a hundred thousand francs. The Duke of Arcos, on the contrary, considered himself aggrieved, ill-treated, and entitled to consider the King's order most unjust, for he had known the Roman Pelliccia only from having spoken with her once or twice in public and he had never spent anything on her. Seeing himself become the cause of the good woman's misfortune, he felt it his duty not to put up with it. Since he could not oppose the King's order, and wanted neither to humiliate himself nor to sink to asking the monarch to spare her, he took the one course worthy of his great soul. He went to her house for the first time, to ask her to forgive him if he had been the innocent cause of her misfortune, and to do what he be-

The Marquis d'Argens

The Harbor of Marseilles

lieved had become his duty. So saying, he left her a hundred doblones de a ocho for her journey, giving her a
sealed letter addressed to the Spirito Santo Bank[52] in
Rome, and Signora Pelliccia thought herself entitled to
accept from so great a nobleman a present in money
which he in some sort owed her and a letter whose contents she could not know. But she knew it when she was
in Rome. Signor Belloni[53] paid her eighty thousand Roman scudi. She invested them, and she settled in her
native city, where for twenty-nine years she has maintained an establishment which shows that she is worthy
of the good fortune which befell her.

At El Pardo on the day after La Pelliccia left, the
King said to the Duke of Arcos that he ought not to be
sad but should forget the woman whom he had banished
from Spain for his good.

"Your Majesty, by sending her the order to leave,
obliged me to make a truth of what was only a tale, for
I knew the woman only from having spoken to her in
public, and I had never given her the slightest present."

"Then you did not give her twenty-five thousand doblones?"

"Yes, Sire; but not until day before yesterday. Your
Majesty is the *amo* ['master'], but it is certain that if you
had not made her leave, I should never have gone to her
house, and she would never have cost me a copper."

The King, very much surprised, did not answer a word
and learned how much to believe the gossip of Madrid. I
was informed of this incident, just as I have now written
it, by Señor Moñino,[54] who was later known by the Castilian title of Floridablanca and who[55] now lives in exile
in Murcia, his native province.

After Marescalchi's departure, when I was preparing
to leave for Barcelona, I saw *a los toros,* outside the city,
a woman whose appearance was impressive. I asked a
Chevalier of Alcántara,[56] who was standing beside me,
who she was.

"She is," he replied, "the famous Nina." [57]

"Why 'famous'?"

"If you haven't heard of her before, her story is too long to tell you here."

A minute or two later a well-dressed but unprepossessing-looking man leaves the side of the impressive beauty who was engaging my eyes, approaches the Chevalier who had spoken to me, and whispers something to him. The Chevalier modestly tells me that the lady whose name I had asked him wanted to know who I was. Foolishly flattered by her curiosity, I myself answer the messenger that, if the lady would permit it, I would myself tell her who I was after the performance.

"I judge from your accent that you are Italian, as she is."

"Yes, Sir, I am a Venetian."

"So is she."

After this exchange with her emissary, the Chevalier told me in a few words that she was a dancer with whom the Count of Ricla,[58] Captain-General (for there was no longer a Viceroy) of the Principality of Barcelona, was in love and whom he was keeping in Valencia for a few weeks until he could arrange her return to Barcelona, where the Bishop would not tolerate her presence because of the scandal. He told me that he had allowed her fifty doblones a day.

"But she does not spend them, I hope."

"She cannot, but she indulges in some folly every day which costs him a great deal of money."

Extremely curious to make the acquaintance of such a woman, and far from fearing that the acquaintance would be sure to cause me unhappiness, I could not wait for the performance to be over so that I could speak with her.

It was on the stairs that I approached her, paying her the usual sort of compliment, which she unabashedly returned, resting her hand, which despite her rings and her

bracelets proved to be very beautiful, on mine. Arrived at
her carriage, to which six mules were harnessed, she says
that she will be glad if I will come to breakfast with her
the next day; I promise to do myself the honor.

I do not fail to keep the appointment. I find her in a
very large house, a hundred paces outside the city, the
whole of which she rented and which was well furnished
though without taste, and open to the air of the countryside, with gardens in front and behind. I see menservants
in livery, maids coming and going, and I hear an imperi-
ous voice scolding in the apartment into which I was
shown. The scolding voice was La Nina's, who was dressing down a man who was standing in amazement in front
of an array of merchandise on a big table. She asks me
to forgive her for being angry with the fool of a Spaniard
who insisted on maintaining that his laces, which I saw
there, were excellent. She wants me to look at them and
give my opinion, and I say that I am no judge of lace.
The man, losing patience, says to her that if the laces
do not please her she has only to leave them to him, and
he asks her if she wants the fabrics.

"I will keep the fabrics, and as for your laces I want
to convince you that it is not to save money that I refuse
them. Look!"

And she picks up a great pair of scissors and cuts them
to bits. The man who had been with her at the bullring
the day before told me that it was a pity, and that everyone in Valencia would call her mad.

"Be still, pimp."

Treating him to which fine epithet, she gives him a slap
with the back of her hand. He leaves, calling her a
whore.[59] She bursts out laughing. She tells the trembling
Spaniard to write out a bill at once for all that she had
bought, and he instantly obeys, avenging himself well for
all the insults to which she had treated him. She signs,
objecting to none of the prices, and she tells him to go to
Don Diego Valencia, who will pay him at once. The man

leaves, chocolate is brought, she makes me sit down beside her, and she sends to tell the man who had called her a whore to come at once to drink chocolate with us.

"Do not be surprised," she says, "at the way I treat him, for he is nothing but a clown whom Ricla keeps with me to spy on what I do. I treat him badly on purpose, so that he will write him everything."

To tell the truth I thought I was dreaming, or that the woman must be mad. In all my life I had never seen or imagined that a woman of such a character could exist. The unfortunate Bolognese, who was a musician and whose name was Molinari,[60] came and drank his chocolate without saying a word. He left afterward, and she spent a whole hour with me talking of Spain, of Italy, of Portugal, where she had married a dancer named Bergonzi. She told me that she was the daughter of Pelandi, the famous charlatan who sold the "Oil of Strazzon" in Venice, and whom I might have known. And in fact I had known him, just as everyone in Venice must have known him on the platform where he sold his balsam.[61]

After this confidence, which she imparted with so little reserve as to make it not one, she asked me to do her the favor of coming to sup with her, for supper was her favorite meal; I promised I would do so, and I went for a walk, reflecting on this strange phenomenon and on the great good fortune which the woman treated in such a fashion. After what I had seen I had to believe that she really had fifty doblones a day. She was of the most surprising beauty, but since I was of the opinion that beauty alone is not enough to make a man love, I did not understand how the Viceroy of Catalonia could be in love with her to such a degree. As for Molinari, after what I had seen and heard I had no doubt that he must be an infamous scoundrel, the most despicable of men. I would go to supper there to enjoy the performance, for, beautiful though she was,[62] she had not aroused the least sensation in me.

Toward nightfall I make my way to her house. It was the beginning of October; but in Valencia the weather was as hot as it is with us in August. She was walking in the garden with her jackanapes,[63] both of them nearly undressed, for she had on only a shift and petticoat and he only drawers. She invites me to make myself comfortable in the same way; but I offer excuses which she accepts as good, and I am glad, for the presence of the base scoundrel utterly shocked and revolted me. It was she who amused me until suppertime with talk than which nothing could be more lewd. She told me any number of stories of fuc. . . . ,[64] in which she was the principal figure, which had happened to her in the twenty-two years of her life.

All these stories would have had the effect they should have had on me, though without arousing love, were it not for the presence of the fellow with his revolting countenance and his abysmal stupidity. At table we were all very hungry; the supper was choice, with both meat and fish, the wine was excellent, I was well satisfied, and I should have been glad to go home; but she had no such intention. The wine had affected her, the clown was drunk, she wanted to be gay. She sent everyone away, she insisted on his undressing, and performed experiments on him which are too filthy and disgusting to commit to paper. The buffoon was young, and his drunkenness did not prevent him from attaining a state which did him honor under Nina's ministrations. It was obvious that the lascivious Nina wanted me to serve her in an orgy in the wretched scoundrel's presence; but his presence deprived me of the ability to satisfy Nina, who, without looking at me, had stripped naked. When she saw that I persisted in being inactive, she made use of the man, inviting me, if I wanted to amuse myself, to come and see how he went about it. I went reluctantly, suffering the torments of the damned, not from any desire to do what he was doing, for I was in a state of impotence, but from anger at seeing such a beautiful woman surrender herself to a man whose only merit was that of a donkey.

After she made him work until his powers were exhausted, she washed her parts, then she forced him to drink, and the swine vomited up his whole supper; she ran off into the other room, shrieking with laughter, and I followed her, for the stench was making me nauseous. After laughing her fill, seated beside me stark naked, she asked me how I had liked the entertainment. At that, my honor and my self-esteem demanded that I justify myself. I told her that my antipathy to the base fellow was so great that it had raised an insuperable obstacle to the effect which her charms should have on any man with eyes.

"I think it possible, for he is very ugly; but he is not here now, and yet you are still nothing. One would not think it to look at you."

"And rightly, my dear Nina, for I am as good as any other man; but at the moment it would be impossible. He has left me too disgusted. No, I beg you, it is no use, nothing will come of it; but it can happen tomorrow, if you do not offend my sight with a monster who is unworthy to enjoy you."

"You are mistaken, he does not enjoy it. I make him work. If I could suppose that he loved me, I would die rather than satisfy him, for I loathe him."

"What! You do not love him, and you use him to give yourself the pleasure of love?"

"As I would use a dildo." [65]

I found nothing in all that Nina said but the pure truth of a depraved nature. She urged me to come to supper the next day, saying that she wanted to see if what I said was true or false, and assuring me that Molinari would be ill.

"He will have got over the effect of the wine, and he will be well."

"No, he will be ill. Come, and come every evening."

"I leave day after tomorrow. I have already reserved my place."

"My friend, you shall not leave. You will leave in a week, after I do."

"That is impossible."

"You shall not leave, I tell you; it would be an insult which I would not stomach."

I did not contradict her, and I went home firmly intending to leave in spite of her. Though at my age I was no longer a novice in anything, I went to bed astonished at the woman's licentiousness, at her freedom of speech and action, and, even more, at her frankness, for she had confessed to me what no woman had ever confessed to anyone.

"I use him to do that because I am sure he does not love me. If I knew he loved me I would die rather than satisfy him, for I loathe him."

I knew about that sort of thing, but no woman had ever put it into words to me.

The next day at seven o'clock in the evening I went to her house. She told me with affected regret that we should sup alone, for Molinari had a very bad colic.

"You told me before that he would be ill. Have you poisoned him?"

"I wouldn't put it beyond me, but God preserve me from doing it."

"But you assured me he would be ill, and he is ill. So you must have given him something."

"No. Let us not speak of it. Let us play cards; afterward we will sup, and we will amuse ourselves until tomorrow, and tomorrow evening we will do it again."

"No, for I shall leave at seven o'clock."

"You shall not leave, and the coachman will not complain to you, for he has been paid. Here is his receipt."

All this being said in the playful tone of a love determined to have its way, I did not think it offensive. Being in no hurry to leave, I took it in good part, calling her a madcap and saying that I was not worth the present she had made me.

"It is astonishing," I said, "that, being what you are, and with such a fine house, you do not receive company."

"Everyone is afraid. They fear Ricla, who is in love and jealous and to whom the knave with the colic writes everything I do. He says he doesn't, but I am sure of it; I am even delighted that he writes to him, and sorry that until now he has had nothing of consequence to report."

"He will write him that I sup with you alone."

"So much the better. Are you afraid?"

"No. But I think you ought to tell me if I have reason to be afraid."

"None at all, for he can blame only me."

"But I should not want to be the cause of a falling out which would harm you."

"On the contrary, the more I irritate him, the more he will love me, and making it up will cost him dear."

"Then you do not love him?"

"I love him to ruin him; but he is so rich that it is impossible."

I saw before me a woman beautiful as an angel, black as a devil, an atrocious whore[66] born to punish every man who to his misfortune fell in love with her. I had known others of the same sort, but never one to equal her. I thought of turning her wickedness to profit by laying her under contribution. She sent for cards and invited me to play what is called primero.[67] It is a game of chance, but so complicated that the most careful player always wins. In less than a quarter of an hour I saw that I played it better than she did; but her luck was so great that when we stopped to go to supper I counted up the points and I found that I was the loser by eighteen or twenty pistoles, which I immediately paid her and which she took, at the same time promising me my revenge. We supped well, and after supper I joined her in all the amorous follies for which she asked and of which I was capable, for my great days were over. However, she declared herself satisfied, and she let me go home when I told her I needed to sleep.

The next day I went to her house earlier, we played, and she lost, and she lost on all of the five or six days she remained in Valencia, so the hussy yielded me a profit of nearly two hundred doblones, which at the time I could not regard with indifference. The spy had already recovered from his colic the next day, and he always supped with us, but his presence was no hindrance to me after she stopped prostituting herself with him in my presence. She had taken the opposite course. She gave herself to me, telling him to go and write to Count Ricla, whereupon he withdrew.

She finally received a letter from the Count, which she gave me to read. He told her in good Italian that she could return to Barcelona without fear, for the Bishop had received an order from the Court to consider her simply an actress who was traveling by way of Barcelona, so she could spend all the rest of the winter there and be sure that she would be left in peace, provided that she lived quietly and caused no scandal. She told me that during the whole of my stay in Barcelona I could visit her only at night after the Count had gone; which he always did at ten o'clock. She assured me that I ran no risk. I should perhaps not have stopped there at all had she not told me that, if I should be short of money, she would lend me as much as I needed. She insisted that I leave a day before her and stop to wait for her at the inn in Tarragona, which I did. I spent the day very pleasantly in that city full of ancient monuments.

I had a very choice supper prepared for Nina, as she had ordered me to do, as well as a room for her next to mine, so that I could sleep with her without causing a scandal. She left in the morning, after telling me not to leave until toward nightfall so that I should be in Barcelona the following morning, where I was to lodge at the

"Santa Maria." [68] She also ordered me not to go to see her until after she had written me a note. I did everything she prescribed, and I arrived in Barcelona at daybreak. It is only twenty leagues from Tarragona. The proprietor of the "Santa Maria" inn lodged me very comfortably. He was an old Swiss. He told me privately that he had received orders from La Nina to treat me well and show me every consideration.

CHAPTER V

My imprudent conduct. Passano. My deten-
tion in the Tower. My departure from Bar-
celona. La Castel-Bajac at Montpellier. Nîmes.
My arrival at Aix-en-Provence.

I THOUGHT this action of La Nina's very imprudent, even though the innkeeper seemed to be a sensible,
discreet man; for after all she was the mistress of the
Captain-General, who might be a man of intelligence
but who, as a Spaniard, could not be of an easygoing nature in the matter of a love affair. Indeed, she had described him to me as ardent, suspicious, and jealous by
temperament; but the thing was done.

I went to bed, I slept until two o'clock, and on waking
I found an excellent dinner, a local manservant, and the
innkeeper, come to tell me that he vouched for him. I
withdraw to my room with him, and I ask him if it is by
Nina's order that he has found me the manservant, and
he replies that it is, and that he has also seen to arranging
for the weekly hire of the carriage I see at the door.

"I am surprised that La Nina goes to so much trouble,
for it is only I who have the right to regulate my expenditures."

"Señor, everything is paid for."

"Everything is paid for? I beg you to believe no such thing, for I will never allow it."

"You shall settle matters with her, but meanwhile you may be sure that I will not accept a copper."

At that moment I foresaw many difficulties, but the unpleasant thought did not possess me long enough. I had a letter of recommendation from the Marquis of Mora to Don Miguel de Cevaillos[1] and another from Colonel Rojas to Don Diego de la Secada.[2] I went at once to deliver the letters. The next morning Don Diego came to see me and took me to call on the Count of Peralada;[3] and on the day after that Don Miguel presented me to the Count of Ricla, Captain-General in command of the Principality of Catalonia, Cavaliere of San Gennaro,[4] and the lover of the vicious beauty who made it appear that she was keeping me.

The Count of Peralada was a young, rich nobleman, handsome of countenance, short and ill-built, a great debauchee who loved bad company, an enemy of religion, morals, and public order, violent and proud of his birth, directly descended from the Count of Peralada who had served Philip II so well that he had earned a patent in which that famous King declared him Count "by the grace of God." It was the first parchment I read in his anteroom, on a table covered with glass. He kept it there so that all those who went to see him could read it during the quarter of an hour he kept them waiting, perhaps for no other reason. He received me with the free, easy manner of a great nobleman who renounces everything due to him because of his high birth. He thanked Don Diego for having brought me to call on him, and he talked to me at length about Colonel Rojas. He asked me if I had made the acquaintance of the Englishwoman he was keeping in Saragossa, and when I said that I had, he whispered to me that he had slept with her. After taking me to see his stables, where he had splendid horses, he invited me to dinner the next day.

My reception from the Captain-General was very different; he received me standing, so that he would not have to offer me a chair, and, having heard me address him in Italian, he replied in Spanish, giving me the title "Usía"[5] in return for the "Excellency" which, as in duty bound, I had given him. He talked to me at length about Madrid, and he complained of the Venetian Ambassador Mocenigo, who, instead of going to Paris by way of Barcelona, as he had promised him he would do, had gone by way of Bordeaux. I thought I might excuse the Ambassador by telling the Count that the other route saved him fifty leagues; but he replied that keeping *la palabra* ("his word") would have been better. He asked me if I expected to make a long stay in Barcelona, and I surprised him by replying that, with his permission, I should stay there as long as I found that I was enjoying it.

"I hope," he said, "that you will enjoy it, but I warn you that the pleasures which my nephew Peralada can procure you will not give you a good reputation in Barcelona."

Since the Count had made this remark to me in public, I thought I might repeat it to Señor de Peralada the same day at table. It delighted him. He told me, as if boasting of it, that he had made three journeys to Madrid, and that each time the Court had ordered him to return to Catalonia. However, I followed the Count of Ricla's advice; I refused all the parties which Peralada offered me with girls, both in the country and at supper at his house. On the fifth day an officer came to invite me to dine at the Captain-General's, an invitation which very much pleased me, for I feared that, having heard of the life I lived in Valencia with his Nina, he would hold it against me. At table he addressed me several times, but always with a seriousness which forbade me to venture on a jest.

After a week during which, to my surprise, Nina never wrote me to visit her, I received a note in which she told me to come to her house at ten o'clock in the evening, on foot and without a servant. It is certain that, not being in love with her, I ought not to have gone; by not going, I should have been both prudent and wise, and I should have shown the Count of Ricla a respect which I owed him; but I was neither wise nor prudent. I had not yet had misfortunes enough in my life to have learned to be so. During the week I had constantly seen La Nina at the theater,[6] but I had never bowed to her.

At the appointed hour I went there alone, wearing a greatcoat and with only my sword. She was with her sister, who was fifteen or sixteen years older than she and who was married to a comic dancer called Squizza (Schizza[7] in Italian), because he had scarcely any nose. She had just supped with the Captain-General, who had left at a quarter before ten o'clock; it was his unchanging hour. She said she was delighted that I had dined with him, and the more so because it was she who had mentioned me to him, praising me and congratulating herself on my having kept her good company for a week or ten days in Valencia.

"Excellent, my dear friend; but I think you ought not to have me call on you at unwonted hours."

"It is to avoid giving the neighbors any occasion for malicious gossip."

"On the contrary, it is to give them one, and to put suspicions into the Count's mind."

"He cannot learn of it."

I left at midnight, after a conversation than which nothing more decorous could be imagined. Her sister, though she was far from scrupulous, had never left us alone together, and in her presence Nina neither did nor said anything which could make her suppose we had been much more intimately acquainted in Valencia. During the following days I went there every evening; she begged me to come, it gave her pleasure; nothing happened between us which would displease the Count if he chose to inquire into it. I went, and I feared nothing. But now for what ought to have made me stop going there.

An officer of the Walloon Guards[8] comes up to me one day at noon outside the city, where I was walking alone. He politely asks me to excuse him if, without the warrant of any friendship between us, he was going to speak to me about something which should be of concern to me, though he had no connection with it and no right to interfere in it.

"Speak, Señor, I cannot but take in good part whatever you may be kind enough to say to me."

"Very well. You are a foreigner, perhaps you do not know this city or Spanish customs, and so you do not know that you run a great risk by going every night to call on La Nina as soon as the Count leaves."

"What risk can I run? I would wager that the Count knows it, and that he has no objection to it."

"It is certain that he knows it, and that he perhaps pretends to her that he does not know it, for he fears her as much as he loves her. If she does not tell you that he objects to it, either she is deceiving you or he is deceiving her, for it is impossible that he loves her without being jealous of her. Take my advice, and pardon me. Go there no more!"

"I thank you, but I shall not take your advice. It would be discourteous to her, who receives me very well, and who enjoys my company as much as I enjoy hers. I shall not stop going there until she orders me to stop, or until the Count lets me know that my visits to his mistress offend him."

"He will never do that, for he would consider it humiliating."

The worthy officer then recounted to me all the in-

justices and arbitrary acts of violence which he had committed since he had fallen in love with the woman, who
made him do whatever she wanted. Men whom he suspected of loving her dismissed from his service, others
banished, others sent to prison, on specious pretexts.

"This man," he added, "who holds so high a post and
who before he knew that Messalina was a model of justice
and virtue, has become, since he made her acquaintance,
unjust, violent, blind, scandalous."

Such a discourse should have affected me, but not at all.
On leaving the officer I told him for politeness' sake that
I would gradually stop going there, but I had no intention of doing so. When I asked him how he had learned
that I went to Nina's, he answered with a smile that it
was the talk of every coffeehouse. That same evening I
went to her house, and I told her nothing about it. I still
cannot understand it, for I was neither in love with her
nor curious about her.

On November 14 I arrive at her house at the usual
hour, and I see a man who is showing her miniatures; I
look at him, and I see the infamous scoundrel Passano,
or Pogomas.[9] The blood rushes to my head, but I control
myself. I take Nina by the hand, I lead her into the next
room, I tell her to send the vile creature away at once or I
will leave at once and never return there in all my life.

"He is a painter."

"I know that, I am acquainted with him, I will tell
you everything afterward, send him away now, or I will
leave."

She calls her sister and tells her to dismiss the painter
at once and tell him not to set foot in her house again. It
was done instantly; her sister told us that when he left
he had said that I would repent of it. I spent an hour
telling her most of the grounds for complaint which I had
against the monster.

The next day, November 15, I go to her house at the
usual time, and I spend the two hours in the gayest con-

versation, Schizza's wife being always present. Midnight strikes, I leave. The door of her house was under the arcade which continued to the end of the street. I have scarcely gone twenty paces under the arcade, the night being very dark, when I am attacked by two men. I give a great leap back, I unsheathe my sword, shouting "Murder!" and thrusting it into the nearest body, after which I jump out of the arcade into the middle of the street across the low wall which bounded it. At the same time I hear the report of a gun or a pistol, I run, I fall, I rise without troubling to pick up my hat, and, still running and holding my naked sword in my hand, not knowing if I was wounded, I arrive at my inn breathless, I lay my sword, stained with blood up to the middle, on the counter, ordering the innkeeper to take charge of it. I tell the good old man all that has just happened to me, and at the same time I am relieved to find that the gun shot or pistol shot had missed me; but I find two unmistakable holes in my greatcoat, below the armpit.

"I am going to bed," I said to him, "and I leave you my greatcoat too. Tomorrow morning you shall come to the magistrate with me as my witness, to lay a charge of murder, for if a man has been killed it will be seen that I did it only to defend my life."

"I think you would do better to leave at once."

"Then you do not believe the thing happened as I have told you it did?"

"I believe every word of it; but leave, for I see from where the blow has come, and God knows what will happen to you."

"Nothing will happen to me. If I left, I should be pronounced guilty. Take care of my sword and my cloak. There has been an attempt to murder me. It is for the murderers to be afraid."

I go up to bed, and at seven o'clock in the morning I hear a knock on my door. I open it, and a police officer enters with the innkeeper.

"Give me all your papers," he says, "dress, and come with me. If you resist I will send downstairs for my men."

"By whose order have you come to demand my papers?"

"By order of the Government. They will be returned to you if there is nothing to prevent their being returned to you."

"And where am I to go with you?"

"To the Citadel, where you will be under arrest."

I open my trunk, and the man is astonished to see that it was at least two-thirds filled with notebooks. I take out my coats and my shirts, which I entrust to the innkeeper, and I leave him my trunk, giving him the keys to it. The officer tells me to pack a portmanteau with what I may need for the night, and he orders the innkeeper to send me a bed. He asks me if I have any papers in my pockets, and I say I have not, showing him that I have only my passports. He says with a bitter smile that it is above all my passports that he wants.

"My passports are sacred; I will give them to no one but the Governor-General, or you shall take my life. Respect your King: here is his passport, here is the Count of Aranda's, and here is the Venetian Ambassador's. They order you to respect me. You shall not have them until you have tied me hand and foot."

"Calm yourself. When you give them to me it is as if you gave them to His Excellency, and if you resist I will not have you tied hand and foot, but I will have you taken to the Palace,[10] where you will be obliged to hand them over in public. Give them to me, and I will write you a receipt."

The innkeeper told me that I would do better to yield, that I risked nothing, and that my passports could only speak in my favor, and I was persuaded. He wrote me a receipt, which I put in my portfolio, which he was kind enough to let me keep, and I left the inn with him, being followed by six constables, but at a distance. Remembering Madrid, I thought I was being treated humanely. The officer having told me that I could order the innkeeper to send me food, I told him to send me dinner and supper. He lent me an overcoat, for I did not want mine with two bullet holes in it, and on the way I told the police officer all that had happened to me at midnight. He listened attentively, never answering a word.

At the Citadel he turned me over to a military officer, who put me in a second-floor room without furniture, whose ungrated windows looked out on the square. A soldier locked me into it. A moment later a soldier brought me my night bag, and a quarter of an hour later I was brought an excellent bed with a coverlet of crimson damask and two others, for on the 16th of November the cold was beginning to be felt. Left alone, I gave myself to reflection.

"What sort of prison is this? What can it have to do with what happened to me at midnight? Nothing. My papers are to be examined, for reasons which, being completely innocent, I cannot guess, and I am put in a decent prison until they have been examined. So far so good. The attack on me is another matter. Even if the man I wounded has died, I have nothing to fear. The innkeeper's advice shows me that I have everything to fear if the cutthroats were ordered to kill me by someone who has unlimited power. He is right, but I must not suppose that. Should I have done well to take his advice and leave at once? No, because after such an incident I might have been followed, caught, and put in a far worse prison. This one is extremely mild. It will take only three or four days to examine my papers; I shall be freed, and they will be returned to me. My passports will be seen, and they will show that I am to be treated with respect. The attempt on my life cannot have come from a tyrannical order on the part of the only man who can give such an order in Barcelona, for he would not now be treating me so mildly. If the order came from him, he must have been informed at once that the attempt failed, and having me arrested was not the expedient to which he would best have resorted this morning. Should I write to Nina? Is one allowed to write here?''

Thus rehearsing a hundred arguments, lying on my bed, for I had not a single chair, and being able to reach no conclusion, I hear a noise outside and I open the window to see what it is. To my great surprise I see the scoundrel Passano conducted by a corporal and two soldiers into a room on the ground floor twenty paces from where I was. As he entered it the knave raised his eyes, and, seeing me, he laughed. This sudden apparition left me completely at a loss. Now I understood nothing. ''He told Nina's sister that I would repent. He must have made some slanderous accusation against me, and he is apparently being put in prison to testify to it.'' It was all that I could suppose.

I was brought a choice dinner, and the soldier, persuaded by a peso duro, which is worth exactly a hundred French sous, had a table and chair brought me. The same soldier brought me as much paper and as many pencils as I wanted; it was forbidden to bring pen and ink without the officer's permission. He also brought me candles and a candlestick; I passed my time making geometrical calculations. I had him sup with me, and he promised to speak well of me the next day to a soldier who was a friend of his and who would serve me faithfully. The guard was changed at eleven o'clock. My prison was mild; it cost me a great deal; but I had nearly three hundred doblones in my purse. I consoled myself by thinking that it would all be over at any moment. On the morning of the fourth day an officer enters my room and tells me sadly that he brings bad news.

''I did not expect it in this place. What now, Señor?''

''I am ordered to put you in the Tower.'' [11]

''Me?''

"None other."

"Then I have been found to be a great criminal. Let us go, Señor."

He orders two soldiers to carry everything I had there to the Tower, and two others and a corporal conduct me to the Tower, which was a hundred paces from where I was. It was raining in torrents. I see a round cell, a sort of cellar paved with stone, with four or five slits high up and two inches wide, through which came a sufficiency of light. The officer said that I had only to order what I wanted to eat once a day, for at night no one was allowed to have his cell opened. I think he called it a *calabozo*.[12]

"Who will bring me lights?"

"Keep an oil lamp always burning, and that will suffice you, for books are not allowed here. When you are brought your dinner, the officer on duty will come to open the pasty or the fowl, for there might be letters in them; and here it is permitted neither to write nor to receive letters."

"Were you given these orders expressly for me?"

"No, these are the customary regulations here. You will have a sentinel always in sight at your door, to whom you may talk."

"Then the door will be open?"

"Certainly not."

"And cleanliness?"

"The officer who will have dinner brought to you will come up with a soldier who for a trifle will make your bed and take away anything that may inconvenience you."

"May I make architectural plans with a pencil?"

"As many as you please."

"Then order paper brought me. Here is some money."

"I can do you the favor. I will tell the officer who will go on guard duty."

When he saw that I had everything there which had been in the room in the barracks, he went away sadly,

trying to encourage me and advising me to be patient, as
if I could have been anything else. He shut the heavy
door himself, and through a square, grated window ten
inches wide I saw a soldier standing guard.

The officer who came at noon brought me paper and
cut up a fowl for me. He put the fork into the dishes in
which there were ragouts to see if there were letters at
the bottom of them. There was food enough for six. I told
him that he would do me honor if he would dine with
me; he replied that it was absolutely forbidden, and he
made the same reply when I asked him for the news-
paper. The lucky soldiers were my guards, for I gave
them food and excellent wine. I was very curious to know
if I was living at my own expense, or if it was Nina who
was paying; but that was impossible, for the waiter from
the inn had to leave my dinner at the guardhouse.

It was there that in forty-two days I wrote in pencil
and without books my entire confutation[13] of the *History
of the Government of Venice* written by Amelot de la
Houssaye,[14] putting off quoting from it until, restored to
freedom, I could work with the author I was refuting
under my eyes. What surprised me one day, and almost
made me laugh, was the soldier whom I saw on guard
duty at my door. The thing seemed to me impossible.
Here is the story.

An Italian named Tadini[15] came to Warsaw while I
was there, with letters of recommendation to Tomatis
and to me. He said that he was an oculist. The person
who recommended him to me was an actress in Dresden,
who recommended him as such. Tomatis sometimes gave
him dinner; not being rich, I could only give him kind
words and a cup of coffee when he came at my breakfast
time. He talked to everyone about his operations; he deni-
grated the oculist who had been established in Warsaw
for twenty years, saying that he did not know how to remove a cataract, and the other countered by calling him
a charlatan who did not know how the eye was con-

structed. Tadini asked me to speak in his favor to a lady
whose cataract, which the other had removed, had re-
curred; she was blind in the eye which had been operated
on and which was again covered over; but she saw all
that she needed to see with the other. I told Tadini that I
would have no part in the matter. He told me that he had
spoken to her, and that he had mentioned me as someone
who could vouch for him.

"You did very wrong, for in that respect I would not
vouch for the most learned of men, and I know nothing
about you. In your profession you should need no one's
recommendation; you should cry aloud *operibus credite*
['let my works bear witness'].[16] That should be your
motto."

Tadini, put out by my argument, shows me a quantity
of testimonials which I might have read if the first one
he handed me had not been from a person who bore witness *urbi et orbi* ("to the city and the world")[17] that
Signor Tadini had cured him of *gutta serena*.[18] I laugh,
and I ask him to leave. Some days later I find him dining
with me at the house of the lady whose left eye was covered by a large cataract. I am cordial to him, and I let
him talk his fill, but intending to find an opportunity to
warn the lady not to trust him. I saw that she had almost
resolved to have the cataract removed; but since he had
mentioned me she wanted me to be present beforehand at
a discussion between him and the other oculist, who arrived at dessert. It was then that I prepared to listen
with great pleasure to the argument between the two
professors. The old oculist, who was German but who
spoke French well, attacked Tadini in Latin. Tadini
stopped him by saying that the lady should be able to
understand what they were saying, and I said that Tadini
was right. Tadini did not understand a word of Latin.

The German oculist began reasonably enough by saying it was true that removing the cataract assured the
doctor and the patient that it would not return, but that

the operation was less certain and, in addition, might
leave the patient blind even so, because of the irreparable
loss of the crystalline humor. Tadini, instead of denying
this, for the German was wrong, was stupid enough to
take from his pocket a small box in which were small
round objects which looked like lenses; they were highly
polished and made of very pure crystal.

"What are they?" the old oculist asked.

"They are what I possess the skill to put under the
cornea to replace the crystalline lens."

At that the German burst into laughter so loud, so long,
and so often repeated that the lady could not but do
likewise. For my part, ashamed to be thought the sponsor
of so stupid a beast, I looked at him sadly, saying nothing.
Tadini, taking my silence as proof that I was persuaded
that the German had no reason to laugh at him, thought
he could retrieve the situation by calling on me to give
my opinion.

"My opinion is that, the difference between a tooth
and the crystalline lens being very great, you are wrong
to believe that one can replace the crystalline lens in the
eye between the retina and the vitreous humor as you
have perhaps placed a false tooth in a jaw."

"Sir, I have never replaced anyone's teeth."

So saying, the unmannerly brute rises and leaves. We
continued to laugh, and the lady was thoroughly determined to see no more of the dangerous man; but the oculist was not satisfied with despising the impostor in silence, he thought him a danger; he had him summoned
before the medical faculty to take an examination in his
knowledge of the structure of the eye, and he printed in
the gazette a humorous article on inserting the crystalline lens into the eye between the cornea and the retina,
naming the wonderful artist who was then in Warsaw
and who performed the operation as easily as a dentist
replaced a tooth. The desperate Tadini waited for the
oculist I forget where, and, sword in hand, forced him to

take refuge in a house. He must have left on foot the same day, for he did not return to the room in which he was lodging.

So what a surprise it was, and how I wanted to laugh, when, going to the little window of the *calabozo,* where I was dying of boredom, I saw the oculist Tadini, dressed in white, with a bayonet fixed to the muzzle of his gun! I have never decided which of us should have been the more surprised—whether I seeing the oculist as the sentry at the door of my cell, or he seeing me in the depths of a tower and in a way under his guard. The fact is that he was thunderstruck when, despite the darkness, he recognized me, and that he felt no desire to laugh, whereas I did nothing but laugh during the whole of the two hours he stayed there. I gave him a good dinner and good wine and an écu, promising that I would do as much for him each time he came to guard me, but I had him only four times, for there were intrigues to be posted at my door in the daytime. Tadini amused me by telling me of all the misfortunes which had befallen him during the three years since we had seen each other in Warsaw. He had been to Cracow, Vienna, Munich, Strassburg, Paris, Toulouse, and finally to Barcelona, where the Catalan laws[19] had shown no mercy on his qualifications as an oculist. Having no recommendations, nor a diploma from any university to testify to his knowledge of the eye, and having refused to take an examination which was to be given in Latin, for the Latin language had nothing to do with diseases of the eye, he was not allowed simply to go elsewhere a free man, he was made a soldier. He confided to me that he would desert at the first opportunity. He consoled me by saying that since Warsaw he had said no more about his crystalline lenses, though he felt certain that they would succeed; he was convinced of it; and he had not performed the experiment, which, despite the lack of arguments for it, was absolutely necessary. I never learned what became of the poor fellow.

On December 28, the Feast of the Holy Innocents,[20] exactly six weeks after the day I was imprisoned, the officer on duty entered my cell and told me to dress and go with him.

"Am I to be released?"

"I know nothing about it. I shall deliver you to an official of the Government, who is in the guardhouse."

I dress quickly, I put what I had in my portmanteau, I leave everything there, I follow him, he turns me over to the same officer who had brought me there, who takes me to the Palace, where a chancellery clerk shows me my trunk, gives me the keys to it, and tells me that all the papers which had been in it were there. After that he gives me my three passports, saying that they are authentic.

"I know that, and I knew it."

"There were strong reasons for believing the contrary. Look at this."

He shows me a document from Madrid, dated December 23 and signed by a name which I do not remember, certifying the authenticity of my three passports. I read it,[21] I hand it back to him, and I thank him. He goes on as follows:

"*Vuestra Señoría*[22] is justified so far as the passports are concerned. I am ordered to tell you that you must leave Barcelona in three days, and the Principality of Catalonia in eight. However, you are at liberty to go to Madrid to complain at the Court, if you think you have grounds for complaint."

"Señor, I shall go to France. Will you be so good as to give me in writing the order you have just conveyed to me?"

"That is not necessary. My name is Manuel Badillo,[23] Secretary to the Government. Señor ...... here will escort you to the 'Santa Maria' and to the same room from which he took you. You will find everything there that you left there, and everything you have left in the Tower. You are free. Good-by, Señor. Tomorrow I will send you a passport signed by His Excellency and my-self.''

I return to the officer dressed in blue the receipt for my passports, and, followed by a manservant carrying my trunk, we go to the ''Santa Maria.'' On the way I see a placard announcing the opera for that evening, and I look forward with pleasure to attending it.

The host of the ''Santa Maria'' is glad to see me, he has a fire lighted for me at once, for an unusually strong north wind was chilling the air, he assures me that no one has entered my room except himself, and in the offi-cer's presence he gives me back my naked sword, but from which the blood had been cleaned, and my great-coat. What surprises me is the hat I had lost when I fell during my escape. The other officer, after seeing that everything I had had in the Tower had been brought, asks me if I acknowledge that all my belongings have been returned to me. I reply that I am sure of it.

''Señor, I wish you good day, and a good journey, whether to France or to Madrid.''

That, my dear reader, is the whole of the strange story of what befell me in Barcelona; you have never read anything more true, or more faithfully narrated, and it is known in all its circumstances to a number of people who still live in that city, all of them worthy of credit. Here is what followed.

I tell the innkeeper that I will dine at noon, and I go out with the same manservant with whom Nina had fur-nished me. I go to the post office to see if I shall find the letters which must have been sent to me marked *poste restante*, and I find five or six. Yet another surprise: the same Government which summarily seizes a man's person and all his papers does not permit itself to remove the letters addressed to him from the post office. The letters were all dated long before, from Paris, Venice, Warsaw, and Madrid. I had no reason to suppose that a single letter to me had been intercepted.

I go back to the inn to read my letters at my ease and to have a talk with the innkeeper which I expected would be of great interest to me. The first thing for which I ask him is my reckoning, and he replies that I owe him nothing. He shows me the whole account from before my imprisonment duly paid, and he tells me that he had been instructed by the same emissary to take nothing from me for anything he would supply me with in prison and, after that, until I left Barcelona.

"Then you knew how long I was to remain in the Tower?"

"I never knew anything. I was paid at the end of every week."

"At whose behest?"

"You know."

"Have you received any notes for me?"

"None."

"And the manservant?"

"I paid him and dismissed him; at present I have no orders in that respect."

"I want him to accompany me as far as Perpignan."

"I believe you are doing well to leave Spain, for in Madrid you will not obtain justice."

"What was said about the attempt on my life?"

"They said that the shot which was heard was fired by you; and that it must have been you who bloodied your sword, for no one was found either killed or wounded."

"That's as amusing as it is extraordinary. And my hat?"

"It was sent to me three days later; I sent everything to the Government, together with your sword and your greatcoat, on the morning of your arrest, as you ordered me to do."

"What an imbroglio! But was it known that I was in the Tower?"

"The whole town knew it. But two good reasons were given for it; one publicly, and the other was whispered about. The public one was that your passports were forged. The secret one, which, if you ask me, was the true one, was that you spent your nights at Nina's. I swore to everyone that you had never spent a night away; but that makes no difference. You went there. However, as it turns out, you did well not to leave when I tried to persuade you to go, for now you are justified in every respect."

"I shall go to the opera this evening, but not in the parterre. See to engaging me a box."

"I will do so. I hope you will not go to La Nina's."

"I shall not, that is certain."

Toward noon a young man, a banker's clerk, brought me a letter which gave me a fresh surprise. I open it, and I find the bills of exchange which I had drawn in Genoa in favor of Signor Agostino Grimaldi della Pietra.[24] His letter was short. Here is a translation of it, which I make from the original today:

"Passano is vainly trying to persuade me to send these bills to Barcelona to get you arrested. I send them to you as a present, and to convince you that I am not a man to increase the troubles of those whom Fortune persecutes. Genoa, this 30th November 1768."

Here was the fourth Genoese[25] whose conduct toward me had been truly heroic. Must I, I asked myself, for the sake of four such men of honor, forgive the Genoese Passano? Certainly not. I must deliver them from such an unworthy fellow countryman. But my wish to do so came to nothing. I learned some years later that the monster died in poverty in Genoa. But Signor Grimaldi's letter gave me urgent reason to find out where Passano was then. He had remained a prisoner in the barracks when I was taken to the Tower; I had to know where he was, either to attempt to crush him if he was in a position to harm me, or, having such a cutthroat as my enemy, to be on my guard. I confided my concern to the innkeeper, who ordered my manservant to make inquiries. Here is what I learned before I left Barcelona, though I could never learn more.

Ascanio Pogomas, for so he called himself, had been set free toward the end of November and had left by sea on a ship which sailed for Toulon three or four days after his release from the Citadel. On the same day I wrote Signor Grimaldi a four-page letter in which he must have found the quintessence of gratitude. It was a matter of so couching my thanks that they would pay him for a thousand zecchini[26] which I acknowledged that I owed him by my two bills, with which, if he had done what the monster told him to do, he would have caused me great distress.

But now for another piece of news which set Barcelona talking.

Two hours after noon all the placards advertising the opera for that evening were changed. The new placards announced that the theater would be closed until the day after New Year's because two of the leading actors were ill. Such an order could only come directly from the Viceroy, for everyone still called him so, saying that Catalonia was a Kingdom, not a Principality.[27] I said nothing, but I laid the suspension to my door. My character being what it is, I made a resolve of which I thought myself incapable: I resolved not to go out. It was a way to make the Count of Ricla blush for his tyranny, to reproach him for his blindness and the iniquities into which he had been driven by the unfortunate love which had reduced him to becoming the most unjust of men whereas before he was considered the justest. Petrarch says:

> *Amor che fa gentile un cor vilano*
>
> ("Love which makes a base heart gentle").[28]

Love had done the opposite to Ricla, whom it had found a decent man.

Nor did I write to the infamous Nina, whose black soul I had recognized on the first day I had made her acquaintance in Valencia. I left her free to boast that she had kept me. It was none the less true that she had worked my ruin and deliberately brought me to the verge of an abyss which was to have cost me my life. My reader will learn more about this dark business four months hence.

I should have left the same day, but for a superstitious fancy on my part. I wanted my departure from Spain to take place on the last day of the unlucky year that I had spent there. I devoted the whole of the three days to writing some thirty letters to all my most valued friends and acquaintances. Don Miguel de Cevaillos, Don Diego de la Secada, and the Count of Peralada all came to see me, but without meeting one another. Señor de la Secada was the uncle of the Countess A B [29] whom I had known in Milan. The three noblemen all related to me a most remarkable and singular circumstance, as are all the others which enter into the story I am telling. On the 26th of the same month, that is, two days before I was released from prison, the Abate Marchisio,[30] Envoy from the Duke of Modena, asked the Count of Ricla, in the presence of several people, if he could visit me to give me a letter which he could deliver into no hands but mine, which he regretted, for he had to leave for Madrid the next morning. Everyone was astonished that the Count made no reply to the Abate, who did in fact leave the next morning, the day before my release. I wrote to the Abate, whom I did not know, in Madrid, and I received no answer. I was never able to learn what the letter was which he had to deliver to me personally.

Everything in this affair being mysterious and inconceivable, it follows that I was involved in it only because of the despotism of the jealous Count Ricla, whom the infamous Nina had amused herself by convincing that I was in love with her and that she granted me her favors. Sending my passports to Madrid was nothing but a pretext, for in a week or ten days they could have been sent there and returned, supposing that someone had accused me of having forged them. It might have been a calumny on the part of Pogomas, supposing that he had learned that I had a passport from the King of Spain, which I could never have had without first having one from the Venetian Ambassador. The wretch might have said that I could not possibly have such a passport since I was in disfavor with the State Inquisitors. Despite his notion and his conclusion from it, I had nevertheless obtained one, and in the following fashion:

Having resolved at the end of August to leave my charming Doña Ignacia and Madrid for ever, I applied for a passport to the Count of Aranda, who answered me that, since he was bound by the regulations, he could not give it to me until I had first received a passport from the Venetian Ambassador; he said that the Ambassador could not refuse it to me. Satisfied with this decision, I go to the residence of the Ambassador, Signor Querini, who was then at San Ildefonso.[31] I tell the porter that I need to speak to Signor Olivieri,[32] the Secretary of Embassy; he announces me, and the idiot takes it on himself not to receive me. I write him the next day that I had not gone to Signor Querini's residence to pay court to him, the Secretary, but to demand a passport which he could not refuse me. I write him my name, and the very insignificant title of Doctor of Law, which he could not refuse me, and I ask him to leave it with the porter, to whom I would go for it the next day. The next day the porter tells me by word of mouth that the Ambassador had left an order that I was not to be given a passport.

It was then that I wrote to the Marchese Grimaldi[33] at San Ildefonso, and at the same time to the Duke of Losada, asking them both to tell the Venetian Ambassador to send me a passport, for, failing that, I should make

public the shameful means which his uncle the Ambassador[34] had adopted to disgrace me. I do not know if the
Duke and the Marchese showed my letter to the Ambassador, Querini, but I know that Secretary Olivieri sent me
the passport, which Doña Ignacia put into my hands. I
read the passport, and I see my name without any title at
all, a thing which is noticed in Spain, for only a servant
is refused the *Don*, as we refuse him the *Signor* and the
French the *Monsieur*, while I was accorded only the
Sieur. Burning with anger at this mark of contempt, I
wrote a letter to Don Domingo Varnier, who, being on
duty, was then at Court, and I send him my diploma as a
Prothonotary[35] in which I am styled Cavaliere of the
Golden Spur and Doctor of Law. In addition I send him
the offending passport, and I ask him to convey my letter
and my complaint to the Marchese Grimaldi if the Ambassador continued to insult me. Three days later he sent
me back my diploma, saying that he had not needed to
speak to the Minister, for the Ambassador had been convinced as soon as he saw my titles, of which he had not
known before. He ended his letter by saying that the
Secretary of Embassy would send me such a passport as
I had a right to demand, whereupon it would rest with
me to obtain one from the King through the Minister of
Foreign Affairs. The next day I received the passport in
the form in which I wanted it; I sent it to Don Varnier
in San Ildefonso, who sent it back to me with the King's,
signed by the Marchese Grimaldo de' Grimaldi,[36] which
enabled me to obtain a passport from the Count of
Aranda, who, when I told him the story, deigned to smile.
Correspondence between Madrid and the Court when it
is at one of the three Sitios[37] costs nothing. It is all at the
King's expense. The organization, or the regulation, of
the letter post is also different from what I have found
all over Europe. Everyone can write letters to any country in the world and drop them in the public box without
paying a copper; the letters are sent with the greatest

punctuality; but one pays very high to obtain the answers from the post office. An answer from Petersburg costs a ducat. If the person to whom it is sent leaves it there, lacking the ducat or from parsimony, he cannot obtain one from Cadiz which would cost him only ten sous. If he goes to ask for it, he is refused it unless he also takes all the other letters addressed to him. The same thing is done in Naples.

On the last day of the year I left Barcelona, with my manservant sitting behind my barouche. I had contracted to reach Perpignan by short stages on the third day of the year 1769. My coachman was a Piedmontese. Perpignan is forty short leagues from Barcelona.[38] The next day at the inn where I dined the coachman came in with my servant and asked me if I had any reason to suspect that I was being followed.

"It is possible. Why do you ask?"

"There are three villainous-looking men, on foot and armed, whom I noticed yesterday when we left Barcelona, who spent last night in the stable of the inn where we lodged, who ate here today, and who left three quarters of an hour ago. They talk to no one, they strike me as being shady characters."

"What can we do to protect ourselves from being murdered, or to free ourselves from a suspicion which troubles me?"

"Set out late and stop at an inn I know a league this side of the usual stopping place, to which the fellows will have gone to wait for us. If I see them coming back to lodge in the poor inn at which we shall be, I shall have no more doubt; they are cutthroats bent on harming us."

I find his reasoning sound. I leave later, I travel most of the way on foot, and at five o'clock we stop where we find very poor accommodations but where we do not see[39] their three faces. At eight o'clock, when I was supping, my servant comes in and tells me that the three cutthroats are in the stable, where they are drinking with our coachman. My hair stands on end at the news, for there was no more doubt. We had nothing to fear at the inn, but very much to fear at the border, which we were to reach that evening. I urge my servant to show no sign, and to arrange for the coachman to come to speak to me when the fellows fall asleep. It was at ten o'clock that the coachman came; he told me point-blank that the men would murder us as soon as we got to the French border.

"After drinking a bottle at my expense," he said, "one of them asked me why I had not gone to the other post station, where we should have been better lodged, and I replied that you were cold and that it was late. I could have asked them why they did not stop there themselves, and where they are going, but I took good care not to. I only asked them if the road to Perpignan was good, and they answered that it is excellent and that one is not even aware that one is crossing the Pyrenees. They are asleep on bales of straw, wrapped in their cloaks, near my mules. We will leave before daybreak; but after them, of course, and we will dine at the usual stopping place; but after dinner, if you will trust me, we will leave after them, and I will drive at a trot by another road, and we shall be in France at midnight. I am sure of what I say."

If I could have engaged an escort of four armed men I should not have taken the coachman's advice; but in the situation I was in I had to do as he said. We found the three bravoes where the driver had told me they would be, and as we went downstairs I had glanced at them. They looked what they were. They left a quarter of an hour later, and a half hour after them my worthy coachman drove back for a quarter of a league, then hired a peasant to guide him, who got up behind to tell him if he went wrong. We made eleven leagues in seven hours; it was ten o'clock when we arrived at a good inn in a considerable village in France, where we had nothing more to fear. I slept well and dined there the next day, and

that evening I was at the post house inn in Perpignan,
sure that I had saved my life and that I owed it to my
coachman. I could not guess from where the order to
murder me might have come; but the reader will see how
I learned everything three weeks later. At Perpignan I
dismissed my manservant, whom I recompensed liberally,
and I wrote my brother in Paris my good luck in escaping from the plots of three cutthroats. I told him to answer me at Aix-en-Provence, *poste restante,* where I
should spend two weeks in order to see the Marquis
d'Argens,⁴⁰ who ought to be there.

The next day I slept at Narbonne, and on the day
after that at Béziers. From Narbonne to Béziers is only
five leagues; but the excellent dishes which the most
amiable of all hostesses had had prepared for me at dinner persuaded me to sup there with her and her whole
family. Béziers was a city whose delightful situation was
apparent despite the season. Fortunate site, a fit retreat
for a philosopher who had renounced all the vanities of
the world, and no less so for a voluptuary who wanted
to enjoy all the pleasures of the senses without having to
be very rich. The inhabitants of the place are all intelligent, the women are extremely beautiful, and the cuisine
is as exquisite for flesh food as it is for fish. One drinks
excellent wines, which the accursed vintners have not
tampered with. I spent the next day in Pézenas, and on
the day after that I arrived in Montpellier, going to
lodge at the "White Horse," ⁴¹ where I intended to spend
a week.

It was there that I left my coachman, giving him a
gratuity of a doblón de a ocho, which encouraged him to
remain an honest man. I supped at the public table,
where there were as many made dishes as guests. Nowhere in France does one eat better than in Montpellier.
The next morning I went to breakfast at a coffeehouse,
where I struck up an acquaintance with a stranger who,
when he heard me say that I wanted to meet some pro-

fessors,[42] himself took me to the house of one who enjoyed a considerable reputation and who had the urban-
ity which the man of letters in France rightly believes to
be the finest jewel in Apollo's[43] crown. The true man of
letters must be the friend of all who love letters, and he
is so in France even more than in Italy; in Germany he
is mysterious and reserved; he is too much inclined to
think he must assert no pretensions, and because of this
mistaken idea he does not gain the friendship of those
who go to admire him at close range and to imbibe his
doctrine.

I am told that the troupe of actors is very good; I go,
and I find it so. I breathed again, finding myself in
France after so many misfortunes had assailed me in
Spain; I seemed to be reborn, and in fact I felt rejuve-
nated. I congratulated myself that at the play I had seen
several very pretty girls and not one of them had roused
desires in me. I wanted to find La Castel-Bajac,[44] more in
the hope of rejoicing in her prosperous state than to
renew a liaison which, if she had become reconciled with
her husband, I thought criminal. I did not know how to
go about finding her. I had written to her under the
name of Mademoiselle Blasin; but that was not her name;
she had always refused to tell me it. By making particular inquiries I feared I should be indiscreet and do her
harm. Knowing that her husband must be an apothecary,
I decided to become acquainted with them all; in this way
I found her on the third day. I talked with all of them
about the different practice of pharmacy in foreign countries, and as soon as I had reason to suppose that the one
with whom I was speaking might be her husband I left,
hoping that he would tell his wife about the traveler
whom she might have known; I was sure that she could
not but be curious about him. When the apothecary was
not in his shop, I at once learned all his family affairs
from the shopboy, and if the circumstances did not fit my
case I went to another shop.

In this way I found her. On the third day I received a note from her, saying that she had seen me talking with her husband in a shop which she named. She told me to return there at such-and-such an hour and to be guided in my replies by her husband's questions, never telling him anything more than that I had known her under the name of Mademoiselle Blasin, and always as a seller of laces, in England, at Spa, at Leipzig, at Vienna, and that I had taken an interest in her in the last of those cities only to procure her the protection of the Ambassador.[45] She ended her note by saying that her husband himself would have the pleasure of surprising me by presenting his wife to me.

I followed her instructions. I went to his shop immediately after dinner, and the good man asked me if I had anywhere known a young seller of laces from Montpellier by the name of Blasin.

"Yes, but I do not know if she was from Montpellier. Pretty, well-behaved, and doing a good business. I saw her several times here and there in Europe, and in Vienna I was able to be of use to her. Her conduct gained her the affection and esteem of all the ladies with whom she had dealings. It was even at the house of a Duchess that I met her in England."

"Would you know her if you saw her?"

"Of course! Such a pretty woman! Is she in Montpellier? If she is, mention me to her. My name is So-and-so."

"You shall speak to her yourself."

He tells me to follow him upstairs, and he introduces me.

"What, Mademoiselle! You are here? I am delighted to see you again."

"Monsieur, she is not 'Mademoiselle'; she is my wife, by your leave, and I beg you not to let that keep you from kissing her."

"With great pleasure. So you found a husband in Montpellier! I congratulate you both, and I am grateful to Chance. Tell me if you had a good journey from Vienna to Lyons.''

She then began telling me everything she wanted to, and she found me as good an actor as herself. Our pleasure at seeing each other again was very great; but the pleasure the apothecary felt when he saw the respect with which I treated her was even greater. We conversed for an hour, in so natural a way that her husband never for a moment suspected that there had been a bond of love between us. She asked me if I thought of spending the Carnival in Montpellier, and she expressed regret when I told her that I should leave the next day. Her husband said that it could not be, to which she added that it should not be and that I absolutely must do her husband the ''honor'' of giving him two days so that I could come to their family dinner on the next day but one. After standing on ceremony for some time, I let myself be persuaded.

Instead of two days I gave them four. I dined and supped there. I thought her husband's mother as worthy of respect for her intelligence as for her age; like her son, she appeared to have forgotten everything which could prevent her from feeling all the affection for her daughter-in-law which the latter could ask. She told me herself, at times when we were alone, that she was happy, and if she said so she must have been so, for it is not possible in this world to be happy without feeling it. She never went out except to take the air with her mother, and she dearly loved her husband. During those four days I tasted the pure joy of true friendship, and the memory of the sweet life we had led together never once had the power to rekindle in us the desire to renew it. We did not need to communicate our thoughts to each other in order to know them. On the day on which I dined with her she told me that if I needed fifty louis she knew where to find them, and I answered that she should keep them for some other time when I should have the pleasure of seeing her again. I left Montpellier certain that my

156 History of My Life

visit had increased the esteem which her husband and her mother-in-law felt for her. I congratulated myself that I could be happy without doing wrong.

On the day after I said good-by to one who owed me her happiness, I slept at Nîmes, where I spent three days with a most learned naturalist. He was Monsieur Séguier,[46] the intimate friend of the Marchese Maffei, of Verona, until his death. In the wonders of his collection he showed me the immensity of nature. Nîmes is a French city in which a stranger can profitably stay. There is excellent food for the mind in considerable monuments,[47] and for the heart in the fair sex. I was invited to a ball, where I enjoyed the privilege of a foreigner, a privilege unknown in Spain and Germany, where being a foreigner is counted against one.

On leaving Nîmes I decided to go to spend the whole of the Carnival at Aix, the seat of a Parlement,[48] where the nobility enjoys a distinguished reputation. I wanted to make the acquaintance of it. I lodged at the "Three Dolphins," [49] if I am not mistaken; there I found a Spanish Cardinal who was on his way to Rome for the conclave to elect a Pope in place of Rezzonico.[50]

CHAPTER VI

My stay in Aix-en-Provence; serious illness;
the unknown woman who takes care of me.
The Marquis d'Argens. Cagliostro. My depar-
ture. Letter from Henriette. Marseilles. His-
tory of La Nina. Nice. Turin. Lugano. Madame
de . . . .

MY ROOM being separated from His Eminence's
only by a very thin partition, I heard him at supper
severely reprimanding someone who must be his principal
servant and in charge of their journey. The reason which
provoked the Cardinal's just anger was that the man
economized at dinner and supper as if his master were
the poorest beggar in Spain.

"My Lord, I do not economize at all, but it is impossible to spend more, unless I make the innkeepers
charge me twice the proper prices of the meals they give
you, which you yourself declare to abound in everything
you can want in the way of game, fish, and wines."

"That may be so, but with a little ingenuity you could
send messengers ahead to order meals in places where I
then would not stop, and which would be paid for nevertheless, you could have dishes prepared for twelve when
we would only be six, and above all you could see to it
that three tables are always served, one for us, one for

my officers, and the third for my servants. I see here that
you tip the postilions only twenty sous; I blush for it; in
addition to what is prescribed for the guides, you must
give at least an écu each time, and when you are given
change from a louis you must leave it on the table. I have
seen you put it in your pocket. That sort of thing is beggarly. It will be said at Versailles, at Madrid, at Rome—
for everything becomes known—that Cardinal de la
Cerda is a beggar or a miser. Understand that I am
neither. Either stop dishonoring me, or leave.''

Such is the character of the great Spanish nobleman;
but, all in all, the Cardinal was right. I saw him set off
the next day. What a man! Not only was he short, ill-
built, tanned, but his face was so ugly and so common-
looking that I understood his need to make himself
respected by lavishness and to distinguish himself by his
decorations, for otherwise he would have been taken for a
groom. Any man who has a revolting exterior must do
everything to keep the eyes which see him from examining his person. External ornaments are an excellent remedy for this sorry gift of nature. Display is the only
weapon which the ugly command to fight beauty.

The next day I inquired for the Marquis d'Argens.[1] I
was told that he was in the country, visiting his brother
the Marquis d'Éguilles,[2] President of the Parlement; and
I went there. The Marquis, famous rather for the unvarying friendship with which the late Frederick II[3] honored
him than for his writings,[4] which no one reads any longer,
was already old. Very voluptuous, a perfect gentleman,
amusing, amiable, a determined Epicurean, he lived with
the actress Cochois,[5] whom he had married and who had
proved worthy of it. As a wife, she considered it her duty
to be her husband's first servant. In any case, the Marquis
d'Argens was deeply learned, thoroughly versed in Greek
and Hebrew, endowed by nature with a most excellent
memory, and hence full of erudition. He received me very
well in consequence of what his friend Lord Marischal[6]

had written to him, he at once presented me to his wife and to President d'Éguilles, his brother, an illustrious member of the Parlement of Aix, moderately rich, a lover of literature, whose virtuous life followed rather from his character than from his religion—which is saying a great deal, for he was sincerely devout, though a man of intelligence. A friend to the Jesuits to the point of himself being a Jesuit "of the short robe," [7] as it is called, he dearly loved his brother, pitying him and hoping that efficacious grace would bring him back to the bosom of the Church. His brother smilingly encouraged him to hope, and they both took care not to offend each other by talking of religion. I was presented to the numerous company, which consisted of relatives, both men and women, all of them amiable and polished, as are all the Provençal nobility, which possesses these attributes in the highest degree. There was a small stage on which plays were performed, the fare was excellent, there were strolls in the garden despite the season. In Provence winter is unpleasant only when it is windy; unfortunately a north wind blows very often.

A lady from Berlin, the widow of a nephew of the Marquis d'Argens, was there with her brother, whose name was Gotzkowski.[8] Very young and very gay, he had thrown himself into all the pleasure afforded by the President's house, without paying any attention to all the religious devotions which were performed every day. A professed heretic when he happened to think of the Church, and playing the flute in his room when everyone in the house was attending the mass which the Jesuit confessor of the whole family celebrated every day, he laughed at everything; but the same was not true of the young widow his sister. Not only had she turned Catholic, she had become so devout that the whole household considered her a saint. It had been the Jesuit's doing. She was not more than twenty-two years of age. I learned from her brother that her husband, whom she adored, dying in

her arms and lucid until his last moment, like all who die
of consumption, had said to her, as his last words, that
he could not hope to see her again in eternity unless she
made up her mind to become a Catholic.

His words having thus been engraved in her memory,
she had determined she would leave Berlin to visit her
relatives on her late husband's side. No one had dared to
oppose her wish. She persuaded her nineteen-year-old
brother to accompany her, and, as soon as she was in Aix
and her own mistress, she confided her vocation to her
relatives, all of them devout believers. The disclosure had
brought joy to the house; she was made much of, she was
caressed, she was assured that there was no other way for
her to see her husband again *in body* and in soul, the
Jesuit had been able to "proselytize" her, as the Marquis
d'Argens said to me, without needing to "catechumen-
ize" her, for she had already been baptized and she had
abjured. This budding saint was ugly. Her brother at
once became my friend. It was he who, coming to Aix
every day, introduced me at every house.

We were at least thirty at table. Excellent fare without
profusion, the tone of good society, restrained and polished conversation which excluded not only equivocal
allusions to the game of love but anything which could
bring it to mind. I noticed that when such a remark escaped the Marquis d'Argens all the women made wry
faces, and the father confessor quickly changed the subject. I should never have supposed that the man was
either a Jesuit or a confessor, for, dressing as an abbé
does in the country, he looked and acted neither part.
The Marquis d'Argens had told me what he was. However, his presence in no way damped my natural gaiety.
I told in decent terms the story of the image of the
Blessed Virgin giving suck to the Infant Jesus, to which
the Spaniards lost all their devotion when the scrupulous
parish priest had her bosom covered by too opaque a veil.

I cannot explain what it was about the tone I gave my narrative which made all the ladies laugh. Their laughter so displeased the Jesuit that he took it upon himself to inform me that it was not permissible to tell stories in public which could bear an indecent interpretation. I thanked him by bowing, and the Marquis d'Argens, to change the subject, asked me what was the Italian name for a large force-meat pie which Madame d'Argens was serving and which the whole company declared excellent. I replied that we should call it *una crostata,* but that I did not know the name for the *béatilles* ("titbits") with which it was filled. They were little sausages, sweetbreads, mushrooms, artichoke hearts, fatted goose livers, and I know not what else. The Jesuit declared that by calling them *béatilles* I was making a mock of eternal bliss.[9] I could not keep from laughing loudly, and Monsieur d'Éguilles saw fit to come to my defense by saying that in good French *béatilles* was the generic term for all titbits of the sort.

Having thus differed from the director of his conscience, the Marquis wisely thought it best to talk of something else, and unfortunately he put the fat in the fire by asking me what Cardinal I thought would be made Pope.

"I would wager," I replied, "that it will be Father Ganganelli,[10] for he is the only Cardinal in the conclave who is a monk."

"By what necessity must it be a monk who is elected Pope?"

"Because only a monk is capable of committing the excess which Spain demands of the new Pontiff."

"You mean the suppression of the Jesuit order?"

"Exactly."

"Her demand will not be met."

"I hope so, for in the Jesuits I love my teachers; but I greatly fear it. I have seen a terrible letter. But aside from that, Cardinal Ganganelli will be Pope for a reason which will make you laugh but which is nevertheless very strong."

"What reason is that? Tell us, and we will laugh."

"He is the only Cardinal who doesn't wear a wig, and observe that since that Holy See has existed no Pope has ever worn a wig."

Since I said all this playfully, there was much laughter; but afterwards I was called on to speak seriously concerning the suppression of the order, and, when I repeated all that I had learned from the Abate Pinzi,[11] I saw the Jesuit turn pale.

"The Pope," he said, "cannot suppress the Jesuit order."

"Apparently, Abate, you did not study under the Jesuits, for their dictum is that the Pope can do everything, *et aliquid pluris* ['and somewhat more']."

Everyone thereupon thought that I did not know I was talking to a Jesuit; he did not answer me, and we spoke of other things. I was urged to stay for the performance of *Polyeucte*;[12] but I excused myself. I returned to Aix with Gotzkowski, who told me his sister's whole story and acquainted me with the characters of several members of Monsieur d'Éguilles's circle, with the result that I saw I could never adapt myself to it. But for this young man, who introduced me to some very agreeable people, I should have gone to Marseilles. Assemblies, suppers, balls, and very pretty girls made me spend the whole of the Carnival and part of Lent in Aix, always with Gotzkowski, who went back and forth from the country nearly every day to join me in parties of pleasure.

I had presented a copy of Homer's *Iliad* to Monsieur d'Argens, who knew Greek as well as he knew French, and an *Argenis*[13] in Latin to his adopted daughter,[14] who knew Latin. My *Iliad* had Porphyry's[15] scholia; it was a rare edition and very well bound. He had come to Aix to thank me, and I had to go again to dine in the

country. Returning to Aix in an open chaise against a
very strong north wind and without an overcoat, I
arrived there chilled to the bone; and instead of going to
bed I went with Gotzkowski to call on a woman who had
a daughter fourteen years of age and beautiful as a star,
who defied all the connoisseurs to make her see the light.
Gotzkowski had tried the thing several times and had
never succeeded; I laughed at him because I knew it was
buffoonery[16] on the minx's part, and I went there with
him that evening, determined to succeed, as I had done
in England and at Metz. I believe I have written those
two stories in their proper places.[17]

So we both set about the enterprise like seasoned
warriors, the girl being at our disposal and, far from
resisting, saying that she asked nothing better than that
some man should rid her of her tiresome burden. Having
at once seen that the difficulty we encountered came from
her holding herself in a wrong posture, I should either
have beaten her, as I had done to one of her sort in
Venice twenty-five years earlier, or else have left; but not
a bit of it, like a fool I determined to triumph over her by
force, imagining that I was raping her. The age for exploits of that sort was long behind me. After vainly ex-
hausting myself for two hours on end, I returned to my
inn, leaving my friend there. I went to bed with a very
severe pain in my right side, and after sleeping for six
hours I woke feeling as ill as possible. Pleurisy had set
in. An old physician who took care of me refused to bleed
me. A violent cough began to torment me; the next morning I began spitting blood, and the disease made such
strides in six or seven days that I confessed and received
the last sacraments. It was on the tenth day, after I had
been in a torpor for three, that the skillful old physician
vouched for my life and assured all those who were concerned for me that I would recover; but I did not stop
spitting blood until the eighteenth day. I then began a
convalescence which lasted three weeks, and which I

found more trying than the illness, for a sick person suffers but is not bored. To be bored without doing anything takes intelligence, and an invalid has almost none. During the whole of this acute illness I was cared for and waited on day and night by a woman whom I neither knew nor had any idea who had sent her to me. In the state of apathy in which I was, I never tried to find out where she had come from; I saw that I was served to perfection, I waited to be cured in order to reward her and dismiss her. She was not old; but she was not of a figure to make me think of amusing myself; she had continued to sleep in my room until she saw that I was cured, and it was after Easter that, beginning to go out, I thought of paying her and sending her away.

When I dismissed her, well recompensed, I asked her who had sent her to nurse me, and she replied that it had been my physician. She left. Some days later I thanked the physician for having found me the woman, to whom I perhaps owed my life, and he replied that she had deceived me, for he did not know her. I asked the innkeeper's wife if she knew her, and she said she did not. No one could tell me either who the woman was or at whose instigation she had come to me. I did not learn it until I left Aix, and the reader will learn it in a quarter of an hour.

After my convalescence I did not fail to go to the post for my letters; and here is a strange piece of news which I learned by reading a letter from my brother, who wrote me from Paris in reply to the letter I had written him from Perpignan. He thanked me heartily for the letter I had written him because he had learned from it that I had not been murdered on the frontier of Catalonia.

"The person," he wrote me, "who gave me the fatal news as beyond doubt is one of your best friends, Count Manuzzi, an attaché at the Venetian Embassy."

Reading this revealed everything to me. My "best friend" had carried revenge so far as to hire three cut-

throats to take my life. It was at that point that he made
his first mistake. He was so sure of my death that he announced it as having already happened; if he had waited,
he would have seen that, by announcing it before he was
certain of it, he unmasked himself. When I came upon
him in Rome two years later, and tried to convince him of
his baseness, he denied everything, saying that he had
received the news of it in Barcelona. But we will speak of
that when we come to it.

The company at the public table being excellent, I
dined and supped there every day. One day at dinner
there was talk of a pair of pilgrims, a man and a woman,
who had just arrived, who were Italians, who had come
from Santiago de Compostela[18] on foot, and who must
be persons of high rank, for, when they entered the city,
they had distributed a great deal of money among the
poor. The lady, we were told, was charming, only eighteen years of age; very tired, she had gone to bed at once.
They were staying at our inn; we all became curious
about them. As an Italian, it was for me to lead the band
of us to visit the pair, who must be either fanatical zeal-
ots or rogues.

We find the female pilgrim sitting in an armchair, with
the look of a person tired to exhaustion, and claiming our
attention by her extreme youth, her beauty, which her
melancholy increased, and a crucifix of some yellow
metal, six inches long, which she held in her hands. She
puts it down when we appear, and she rises to greet us
graciously. The male pilgrim, who was fastening cockle
shells[19] to his short cloak of black oiled cloth, does not
stir; he seemed, glancing at his wife, to be telling us that
we should be concerned only for her. He appeared to
be five or six years older than she, he was short, well
enough built, and his not unhandsome face expressed
boldness, effrontery, cynicism, and deceit, in all which
he differed entirely from his wife, whose countenance
breathed nobility. The two strange creatures, who spoke

French only well enough to make themselves understood with difficulty, showed their relief when I spoke to them in Italian. She told me that she was a native of Rome, and she did not need to tell me so, for her pretty speech assured me of it; as for him, I put him down as a Sicilian, despite his telling me that he was from Naples. His passport, dated at Rome, gave his name as Balsamo;[20] hers was Serafina Feliciani, a name which she never changed. The reader will find Balsamo become Cagliostro ten years hence.

She told us that she was going back to Rome with her husband, glad to have made her devotions to St. James of Compostela and to Our Lady of the Pillar,[21] having gone there on foot and returned the same way, always living on alms, having vainly sought poverty in order to have and to gain more merit in the eyes of God, whom she had so greatly offended in her lifetime.

"It was in vain," she said to me, "that I never asked for more than a copper, I was always given silver and gold, so that, to fulfill our vow, whenever we entered a city we always had to give the poor all the money we had left, which, if we had kept it, would have made us guilty of failing to trust in Eternal Providence."

She told us that her husband, who was very strong, had not suffered, but that she had endured the greatest torments, having always to travel on foot and sleep in bad beds, almost always fully dressed for fear of contracting some skin disease of which it would prove very difficult to be cured.

It seemed to me likely that she mentioned this detail only to make us curious to see the cleanliness of her skin elsewhere than on her arms and hands, whose whiteness and perfect cleanliness she let us see gratis in the meanwhile. Her face had only one defect: her slightly rheumy eyelids marred the tenderness of her beautiful blue eyes. She told us that she intended to rest for three days and then leave for Rome, traveling by way of Turin to make her devotions at the adoration of the Most Holy Sudary.[22] She knew that there were several of them in Europe, but she had been assured that the true one was the one to be seen in Turin; it was the very cloth which St. Veronica had used to wipe the sweating[23] face of our Saviour, who had left the imprint of his divine countenance on it.

We left very well pleased with the pretty pilgrim, but doubting her devotion. As for me, still weak from my illness, I formed no designs on her; but all those who were with me would gladly have supped with her, if they had thought that her favors would await them afterward. The next morning the male pilgrim came to ask me if I would rather come up to breakfast with his wife and himself, or if they should come down; it would have been impolite to answer "Neither"; so I said I should be glad if they would come down. It was at this breakfast that, when I asked him what his profession was, the pilgrim replied that it was making drawings in ink in what is called "chiaroscuro." His ability consisted only in copying an engraving, and not at all in invention; but he assured me that he excelled in his art, for he could copy any engraving so accurately that he defied anyone to find the slightest difference between the copy and the original.

"I congratulate you. It is an admirable talent, with which, since you are not rich, you can earn a good living wherever you may be pleased to settle."

"Everyone tells me that, and everyone is mistaken. With my talent a man starves. Practicing my profession, I work a whole day in Naples and Rome, and I earn only a half a testone;[24] that is not a living."

After this explanation, he showed me some fans he had decorated, than which nothing could be more beautiful. It was done with ink, and they looked as if they were engraved. To convince me, he showed me the copy he had made from a Rembrandt,[25] which, if anything, was more beautiful than the original. Yet, excellent at his craft though he was, he swears to me that it does not bring him in enough to live; but I do not believe him. He was one of these lazy geniuses who prefer a vagabond life to hard work. I offer him a louis for one of his fans, and he refuses it, begging me to accept it gratis and to take up a collection for him at the public table, for he wanted to leave on the next day but one. I accepted his present, and I promised to make the collection for him.

I got together fifty or sixty écus for him, which his wife came to receive in person at the table, where we were still sitting. Far from acting immodestly, the young woman had an air of virtue. Invited to write down her name for a chance in a lottery, she excused herself, saying that in Rome girls who were brought up to be decent and virtuous were not taught to write. Everyone laughed, except myself, for, feeling sorry for her, I did not want to see her put to shame; but the thing made me certain that she must be a peasant.

It was she who, the next morning, came to my room to ask me for a letter of recommendation for Avignon, and I immediately wrote two for her, one to Monsieur Audifret, banker, the other to the proprietor of the "Saint-Omer" inn.[26] After supper that evening she gave me back the letter to Monsieur Audifret, saying that her husband had told her that he did not need it. At the same time she urges me to examine the letter she has returned and make sure that it is the one I had given her, and after looking at it I say there is no doubt that it is the same. At that she laughs and tells me I am mistaken, for it is only a copy. I refuse to admit it. She sends upstairs for her husband, who, with my letter in his hand, convinces me of the amazing imitation, which was much more difficult than copying an engraving. I expressed my admiration, saying that he could draw great profit from his talent; but that if he was not careful it could cost him his life.

The couple left the next day. The reader will learn at the proper time—which will be ten years hence—where and how I saw the man again, under the name of Count Pellegrini, with the good Serafina, his wife and his familiar spirit. As I write this, he is in prison, which he will never leave, and his wife is perhaps happy in a convent. I have heard that he is dead.[27]

As soon as my health was perfectly restored I went to take leave of the Marquis d'Argens at the house of President d'Éguilles. After dinner I spent three hours with the learned old man, who kept me well amused with countless anecdotes of the King of Prussia's private life, all of which would be new if I had the time and the wish to publish them. He was a monarch who had great qualities and great weaknesses, like nearly all great men; but the weaknesses were less in weight and in bulk. The King of Sweden who was assassinated [28] provoked hatred and then defied it to do its worst. He had the soul of a despot, and he had had to be one in order to satisfy his ruling passion, which was to get himself talked about and to be accounted a great man. His enemies all willingly risked death in order to deprive him of life. It would seem that he should have foreseen his fate, for his acts of oppression always drove his victims to desperation.

The Marquis d'Argens presented me with all his works.[29] When I asked him if I could really boast that I had them all, he said that I had, except the account of a period of his life which he had written in his youth[30] and allowed to be printed, and which he now regretted having written.

"Why?"

"Because with the mania of wanting to write the truth, I made myself eternally ridiculous. If the urge ever comes to you, resist it as you would a temptation; for I can assure you that you will repent, because as a gentleman you cannot write anything but the truth, and as an honest writer you are obliged not only not to leave anything that may have happened to you unrecorded, but also not to spare yourself in all the sins you have

committed, while, as a sound philosopher, you must bring
out all your good actions. You must blame and praise
yourself by turns. All your confessions will be taken at
face value, and you will not be believed when you tell
truths which are to your credit. Besides all that, you will
make enemies when you have to reveal secrets which will
do no honor to the people who will have had dealings with
you. If you do not give their names, they will be guessed,
which comes to the same thing. Believe me, my friend, if
a man may not talk about himself, still less may he write
about himself. It is permitted only to a man whom
slander forces to justify himself. Believe me: never think
of writing your biography.''

Convinced by his solid arguments, I promised him that
I would never be guilty of that folly; nevertheless, I
began my biography seven years ago, and by now I have
promised myself that I will finish it, although I am already repentant. I write in the hope that my history will
never be published; I flatter myself that in my last illness, grown wise at last, I will have all my notebooks
burned in my presence. If that does not happen, the
reader will forgive me when he learns that writing my
memoirs was the only remedy I thought I could employ
to keep from going mad or dying of chagrin over the
vexations to which I was subjected by the scoundrels who
inhabited Count Waldstein's castle[31] at Dux. By keeping
myself busy writing ten or twelve hours a day, I have
prevented black melancholy from killing me or driving
me mad. We will speak of this when the time comes.[32]

On the day after Corpus Christi[33] I left Aix for Marseilles; but before leaving I must say something about
the procession with which the feast is celebrated in every
Catholic Christian city, but which at Aix-en-Provence
has features so peculiar that any stranger whom they do
not amaze must be a dolt. As everyone knows, at this procession the Being of Beings, displayed in body and spirit
in the Eucharist and carried by the Bishop, is escorted

by all the religious and secular confraternities. This is
the case everywhere, and I will say no more about it. But
what deserves to be observed and recorded, and what
cannot but surprise, are the masquerades, the antics, and
the buffoonery which are indulged in and performed. The
Devil, Death, the Deadly Sins, most comically dressed,
fighting one another in their rage at having to pay homage to the Creator on that day; the shouts, the catcalls,
the booing of the populace deriding these personages, and
the din of the songs with which the crowd mockingly hail
them, playing all kinds of tricks on them, make up a
spectacle far more unbridled than the Saturnalia[34] and
than anything which we read was anywhere indulged in
by the most frantic paganism. All the peasants from five
or six leagues around are in Aix on that day to honor
God. It is his feast day. God goes in procession only once
a year; he has to be entertained, made to laugh on that
day. This is implicitly believed, and anyone who should
question it would be impious, for the Bishop, who cannot
but be aware of what goes on, is himself the ringleader
in it. Monsieur de Saint-Marc,[35] an important member
of the Parlement, solemnly told me that it was excellent,
for the day brought at least a hundred thousand francs
into the city. Recognizing the cogency of his argument, I
said not a word to the contrary.

During all the time I stayed in Aix, I constantly
thought of Henriette.[36] Already knowing her real name,
I had not forgotten the message she had sent me by Marcolina, and I was always expecting to find her at some
gathering in Aix, at which I should have played toward
her whatever role she wished. I several times heard her
name spoken in different connections, but I took care not
to question the person who had mentioned it, for fear of
suggesting that I knew the lady. I always thought that
she must be in the country; and, determined to pay her a
visit, I had stayed on in Aix after my severe illness only
in order to arrive at her house in perfect health. So I

left Aix with a letter in my pocket in which I announced
my arrival, intending to stop at the door of her country
house, send it in to her, and not to get out of my carriage
until she invited me to do so.

I had instructed the postilion accordingly. It was a
league and a half before the Croix d'Or.[37] We arrive
there. It was eleven o'clock. I give my letter to a man
who had come to see what we wanted, and he tells me
that he will send it to her.

"Madame is not here?"

"No, Monsieur. She is in Aix."

"Since when?"

"For the last six months."

"Where does she live in Aix?"

"In her town house. She will be here in three weeks to
spend the summer, as she always does."

"Will you be so good as to let me write a letter?"

"You have only to get out, and I will open Madame's
apartment for you. You will find everything you need
there."

I get out, and no sooner have I entered the house
than I am surprised to see the woman who had taken
care of me during my illness.

"Do you live here?"

"Yes, Monsieur."　,

"Since when?"

"For the past ten years."

"And how is it that you came to nurse me?"

"If you will go upstairs, I will go up too, and I will tell
you the truth."

She told me that her mistress had sent for her and had
ordered her to go to the inn in which I was lying ill, to
enter my room boldly, and to take care of me as if it were
of her own self, and that if I should ask who had sent her
she should answer that it was the physician.

"What! The physician told me he had no idea who you
are."

"He may have told you the truth, and he may have been ordered by Madame to answer you as I did. I know nothing more; but I am amazed that you did not see Madame in Aix."

"It is certain that she receives no one."

"You are right, but she goes everywhere."

"It is astonishing. I must have seen her, and I cannot understand how I can have failed to recognize her. You have been with her for ten years. Has she changed? Has she had some illness which has changed her features? Has she aged?"

"On the contrary. She has put on flesh. To see her, you would think she was a woman of thirty."

"I will write to her."

She leaves; and, astonished to the point of confusion by this extraordinary situation, I consider if I can, if I should, go to Aix at once, that very day. "She is at home; she receives no one; who can prevent her from receiving me? If she does not receive me, I will go away; but Henriette still loves me; she sent me a nurse; she is hurt by my not having recognized her; she knows that I have left Aix, she is sure that I am here at this moment, and she is waiting for the last act of the play to bring me to her house. Shall I go, or shall I write to her?"

I decide to write and to tell her that I will wait in Marseilles for her answer, to be addressed to me at the post office. I give my letter to my nurse, and money to send it at once by express messenger, and I go to dine in Marseilles. Not wanting to be known, I go to lodge at a poor inn, where I am very glad to see Signora Schizza, Nina's sister. She had arrived there from Barcelona with her husband three or four days before, and she was about to leave for Leghorn. She had dined, her husband was not there, I was extremely curious to learn a great many things, I asked her to come to talk with me in my room until my dinner was brought.

"What is your sister doing? Is she still in Barcelona?"

"My sister is still in Barcelona, but she will not stay there long, for the Bishop will not have her either in his city or in his diocese, and the Bishop is more powerful than Count Ricla. She returned from Valencia only as a woman who cannot be refused passage through Catalonia on her way back to Italy; but one does not stay nine or ten months in a city through which one is only passing. She will certainly leave within a month; but she is not sorry; for she is certain that the Count will keep her lavishly wherever she goes, and she may succeed in ruining him. Meanwhile she is well pleased to have ruined his reputation."

"I have some idea of the way her mind works, but after all she cannot be the enemy of a man who by now must already have made her rich."

"Not a bit of it. She has nothing but some diamonds. But do you suppose the monster can feel gratitude? Do you suppose she has human feelings? She is a perfect monster, and no one knows better than I that she is a monster because she cannot be anything else. She forced the Count to commit innumerable injustices for no other reason than that all Spain should talk about her and know that she has made herself the mistress of his body, his wealth, his soul, and his will. The more flagrant the injustices she makes him commit, the more certain she is that she will be talked about, and that is all she wants. Her obligations to me are beyond reckoning, for she owes me everything, even her life, yet she is so wicked that, instead of having my husband confirmed in his appointment with an increase in salary, which would have cost her only a word, she had him dismissed."

"I am amazed that, with such a character, she treated me so generously."

"Yes, I know the whole story; but if you knew it too you would not feel in the least grateful to her for what she did for you. She paid your expenses at the inn and in the Tower only to convince people in general that, to the

Count's shame, you were her lover, and everyone in Barcelona knows that there was an attempt to murder you at her door and that the cutthroat whom you wounded died.''

"But she cannot have ordered my murder, or been an accomplice in it, for that would be against nature.''

"That I know; but is there anything in Nina which is not against nature? What I can tell you for certain is what I saw with my own eyes. During the hour the Count spent with her she did nothing but talk about you, your intelligence, your good manners, comparing the Spaniards with you to their disadvantage. The Count, annoyed, kept telling her to have done and talk of something else; but it was no use; in the end he left cursing you, and two days before what happened to you he told her that he would do her a favor she did not expect; and I can assure you that when we heard the shot a moment after you left she said with the utmost calm that it was certainly the favor the unfortunate nobleman had promised her. I told her that you might have been killed; and she replied that it was so much the worse for the Count, for his turn would come to find the man who would kill him. She began laughing at the thought of the sensation the news would produce in Barcelona the next day. However, at eight o'clock the next morning I saw her very well pleased when your servant came to tell her that you had been arrested and taken to the Citadel.''

"My servant! I never knew that he had any communication with her.''

"You were not meant to know it; but I assure you that the man loved you.''

"I was convinced of it. But go on.''

"She then wrote the proprietor of your inn a note which she did not show me but in which she must have ordered him to supply you with everything you needed. Your servant told us that he had seen your bloodstained sword and the hole in your cloak, and she was very glad to hear it; but never believe that it was because she loved you, for she said that, having escaped being murdered, you might take your revenge. What puzzled us was to guess on what pretext the Count had had you arrested.

"That evening we did not see him. He came the next day at eight o'clock, and the infamous creature received him with smiles and an air of the greatest contentment. She said she had heard that he had had you imprisoned, and that he had done well, for he could only have done it to safeguard you from what might be attempted against you by the same enemies who had tried to take your life. He replied drily that your being arrested had nothing to do with what had happened to you that night. He said that you were in custody for only a few days, for your papers would be examined, and you would be set free as soon as nothing was found in them to make you deserve a more rigorous imprisonment. She asked him who the man you had wounded was; and he replied that the police were making inquiries, for neither a wounded man nor any traces of blood had been found. He told her that your hat had been found and had been sent to you. I left her alone with him until midnight. Three days later everyone knew that you had been imprisoned in the Tower. That evening she asked the Count the reason for it, and he replied that all three of your passports might be forged, since the one you had from the Venetian Ambassador, dated at San Ildefonso, could not but be so. Everyone knew that, since you were in disfavor with your country, it was impossible that your Ambassador had given you a passport; and it was certain that, if the Venetian one was forged, the ones from the King and the Count of Aranda must be forged too, for foreigners are not given passports unless they first present one from their country's Ambassador. He[38] said that, on this supposition, you had to be strictly confined, and that you would not be released until your passports came back

from the Court confirmed by those who were responsible
for them. That was all.

"It was the arrest of the painter Pogomas which made
us certain that it could only be he who had denounced
you to the Government as a forger, to avenge himself for
your having had him turned out of our house. The
painter remained under arrest in the Citadel, and we
thought that he must be being held to substantiate his
accusation. This reasoning made us suppose that you
would be released as soon as we learned that Pogomas
had been removed from the Citadel only to be sent to
Genoa. This meant that your passports had returned
from the Court recognized as authentic; however, seeing
that you were still kept there, Nina no longer knew what
to think, and the Count made no reply to her further
questions concerning your imprisonment. False as she is,
she approved of his secrecy, respecting the reasons he
might have for keeping silent on the subject.

"We finally learned that you had been unconditionally
released. Nina was sure she would see you in the parterre
and would triumph in her box before an audience which
would consider her the person who had obliged the Captain-General to restore you to freedom. She was preparing to show herself in her box in her most splendid attire,
when she was astonished to learn that there would be no
more performances for three days. It was not until that
evening that she learned from the Count himself that
your passports and your papers had been returned to
you and that you had been ordered to leave; she praised
her mad lover's prudence. She saw that you would not
dare go to her house, and she believed that you must have
received secret orders, even to being forbidden to write to
her, when she saw that you had gone without writing her
a note. She said that if you had had the courage to ask
her she would have left with you. But she was greatly
surprised when she learned from your manservant a

week later that you had only escaped the cutthroats by a
sort of miracle. She laughingly told the Count the story,
to which he replied that he knew nothing about it. Give
thanks to God that you were able to leave Spain alive.
Your becoming acquainted with the monster in Valencia
should have cost you your life; the state of misfortune in
which you find me is her doing, and God is justly punish-
ing me for having brought her into the world."

"What do you mean?"

"I mean what I say. Nina is my daughter."

"Is it possible? Everyone thinks she is your sister."

"She is my sister too, for she is the daughter of my
father."

"What! Your father loved you?"

"Yes, I was sixteen years old when he made me big
with her. She is the child of sin; and a just God decrees
that it shall be she who punishes me. My father died to
escape her vengeance; but perhaps I shall cut her throat
before she cuts mine. I should have strangled her in the
cradle."

Overcome with horror, I did not know what to say to
this dreadful narrative, the truth of which was not to be
doubted. I asked her if Nina knew that she was her
daughter, and she replied that her father himself had
told her so when she was eleven years old, and that it
was the same worthy father who had had her virginity
and who would certainly have given her a child too if he
had not died in the same year.

On hearing this second outrage committed by the charlatan Pelandi, I could not help laughing. The man had
the misfortune to fall in love with his daughters and his
granddaughters. I thought to myself that, in a state of
nature, the thing would not arouse horror, and that all
the horror that was felt for it came only from education
and force of habit. I asked the woman how Count Ricla
had come to fall in love with Nina.

"Listen. It is not a long story, and it is a strange one.

She had no sooner arrived in Barcelona two years ago, coming from Lisbon, where she had left her husband Bergonzi, than she was engaged as a figurante in the ballets because of her beautiful face, for, so far as talent goes, she can't dance a step. All she can do is make the turning leap called *rebaltade*; when she makes it she has the pleasure of hearing the parterre applaud her because they see her underdrawers up to the waist. You must know that there is a theatrical regulation here which makes any dancer who shows her drawers to the audience in a caper liable to a fine of an écu. Nina, who knew nothing about it, did her *rebaltade,* the audience applauded, she did another, even higher, and at the end of the ballet the censor told her that at the end of the month she would be docked two écus because of her shameless capers. She cursed and swore, but she could not get the better of the law. Do you know what she did the next day to avenge herself? She appeared without drawers, and she did her *rebaltade* the same as ever, which raised a storm of laughter in the parterre such as had never been heard in Barcelona. Count Ricla, who, in his stage box, had seen her better than anyone, being equally overcome by horror and admiration, told the censor, for whom he sent at once, that the audacious flouter of the law must be exemplarily punished otherwise than by fines.

" 'Meanwhile,' he said, 'have her brought to me.'

"Whereupon Nina marches into the Viceroy's box with her impudent air and asks him what he wants with her.

" 'You are a shameless creature who has failed in respect to the public and the laws and who deserves to be severely punished.'

" 'What have I done?'

" 'You made the same jump as you did day before yesterday.'

" 'That is true, but I did not break your Catalan law, for no one can say that he saw my drawers. To make sure

that no one would see them, I didn't put any on. Could I
do any more in obedience to your accursed law, which has
already cost me two écus? Answer me.'

"The Viceroy and all the grave personages of his
entourage had to make an effort to keep from laughing,
for, as you know, gravity does not countenance laughter.
The diabolical Nina was in the right after all, and to discuss whether the law had been broken or not would have
entailed bringing up the most laughable details in order
to prove Nina twice guilty. So the Viceroy merely told
her that if she ever took it into her head to dance without
underdrawers again she would be sent to prison on bread
and water for a month. She obeyed.

"A week later a new ballet of my husband's was given
which pleased the audience so much that an encore was
demanded. The Count sent word that the audience was to
be satisfied, and the dancers, male and female, were told
in their dressing rooms to return to the stage and take
their positions. Nina, who had nearly undressed, tells my
husband that he will have to do without her. It was not
possible; she had a role which was necessary to the ballet.
She laughs at his arguments, she refuses. My husband
tells the censor for what reason he cannot satisfy the
audience; the censor goes into Nina's box, he tries to persuade her, he does not succeed, he scolds her, he threatens
her, it is no use; he speaks roughly to her; at that Nina
gets up and pushes him out the door so forcefully that
the little fellow almost falls down. He repairs to His
Excellency's box, tells him what has happened, and two
soldiers instantly go to bring Nina before the Governor
as she is, not in her shift, but in a state of undress to
offend decency and to prove the undoing of a man who,
if he was to punish her, did not need to see her so nearly
naked. You know how beautiful the vixen is. In an un-
steady voice the Governor says what he has to say to her,
but Nina boldly tells him in so many words that he can
have her killed but that he cannot make her dance.

Daily Life on the Piazza San Carlo, Turin

Literary Reading

." 'To the devil with Spain, the audience, and the whole earth, I do not want to dance, and you are in the wrong to try to force me to, since it is not in my contract that I must appear in the same ballet twice on the same evening; and I am so outraged by your tyrannical proceedings and the insult you have put upon me by an act of abominable despotism that I now tell you that I will not dance on this stage either tonight or tomorrow or ever. I do not ask a copper of you, let me go home, and know that I am a Venetian and free. I admit that, despite that, you can subject me to all kinds of ill-treatment. I will bear it firmly, and if you do not have me killed I will avenge myself by going to proclaim to all Italy how you treat decent women in your country.'

"The astonished Governor declared that Nina was mad. He sent for my husband again and told him to give the ballet without her, and not to count on her in future, for she was no longer engaged. He then told Nina to go, and gave orders that she was not to be interfered with. She went back to her box, where she dressed and returned to our house, where she was living. My husband gave the ballet as well as he could, but the Governor, Count Ricla, found that he had fallen violently in love with the shameless creature. She had a valuable ring, which she was thinking of selling in order to return to Italy at once.

"It was Molinari,[39] a very bad singer, who came the next morning to tell her that His Excellency wanted to see her on the next day at a small country house, to assure himself that she was not mad, or that, having spoken to him as he had never in his life been spoken to before, she was so. It was just what Nina wanted; she felt sure that she would complete her conquest of him. She told Molinari to tell His Excellency that he would find her well-behaved and amenable. That first interview, under Molinari's proc . . . . ship,[40] was followed by all the rest. To keep the nobleman and assure herself that he will never escape from her chains, she ill-treats him from

time to time, and thus she makes him happy when she is
gracious to him. He cannot leave her.''

This is all that I learned from the incestuous Schizza,
who was then perhaps forty years of age. Two years
hence my reader will find himself in Bologna, where he
will see Nina again. We will speak of her at that time.

The next day I found Henriette's answer at the post
office. Here is a copy of it:

''Nothing, my old friend, is more like a romance than
our meeting at my country house six years ago and our
present encounter twenty-two years[41] after our parting
in Geneva. We have both aged. Will you believe that,
though I still love you, I am very glad that you did not
recognize me? It is not that I have become ugly, but
putting on flesh has given me a different countenance. I
am a widow, happy, and well enough off to tell you that
if you should be short of money with the bankers you will
find it in Henriette's purse. Do not come back to Aix to
recognize me, for your return might give rise to specula-
tion; but if you come back some time hence, we can see
each other, though not as old acquaintances. I feel happy
when I think that I may have helped to prolong your life
by putting with you a woman whose kind heart and
whose fidelity I knew. I am very glad that she told you all.
If you would like to maintain a correspondence with me,
I shall do all that I can to make it a regular one. I am
very curious to know what you did after your escape
from the Leads. I promise, now that you have given me
such strong proof of your discretion, that I will tell you
the whole story of what brought about our meeting at
Cesena,[42] and of my return to my country. The first is a
secret from everyone. Only Monsieur d'Antoine[43] knows
a part of it. I am grateful to you for not having made
any inquiries about me here, though Marcolina[44] must
have told you all that I asked her to. Tell me what became
of that charming girl. Farewell.''

Her letter made up my mind for me. Henriette had

grown wise; the force of temperament had diminished in her as it had in me. She was happy, I was not. If I went back to Aix for her, people would have guessed things which no one should know; and what would I have done? I could only become a burden to her. I wrote her a long letter in reply, and I accepted the correspondence which she proposed. I gave her a general account of all my vicissitudes, and she told me all the details of her life in thirty or forty letters which I shall add [45] to these memoirs if Henriette dies before me. She is still alive today, old and happy.

The next day I called on Madame Audibert[46] and I went with her to pay a visit to Madame N. N.,[47] who by then had three children whom her husband adored; I gave her the good news of Marcolina which I had received from Venice and of which I shall speak in the year 1774, when I return to my country. I also told her the story of what had happened to me with Croce, and of the death of Charlotte,[48] which greatly touched her. She gave me very recent news of Rosalie,[49] who, with her husband's fortune, had become very rich. Alas! I could not hope to see her again, for in Genoa the sight of Signor Agostino Grimaldi would not have amused me.[50] My dear ex-niece mortified me without being aware of it. She told me that she found me aged. A man can easily rise above the unwelcome feeling this compliment may arouse in him; nevertheless it is still displeasing to one who has not renounced gallantry. She gave me a fine dinner, and her husband made me offers which I was ashamed to accept. I still had fifty louis, and, having decided to go to Turin, I had resources there. At Marseilles I found the Duke of Villars[51] whom Tronchin was keeping alive by his art. That nobleman, the Governor of Provence, invited me to supper, where I was surprised to find the Marquis d'Aragon,[52] who held the bank. I punted for small stakes, I lost, and the Marquis invited me to dine with his wife, an old Englishwoman, who had brought him, as I think I said before, a dowry of forty thousand guineas and twenty thousand which would revert to a son she had in London. It was from this fortunate Neapolitan that I was not ashamed to borrow another fifty louis.

I left Marseilles alone, having taken a place in a carriage which was going to Antibes, and from there I went to Nice, where I joined company with an Abate to go to Turin by way of the Colle di Tenda,[53] which is the highest of all the Alps. Going by this route, I had the satisfaction of seeing the beauty of the country which is called Piedmont. I arrived in Turin, where the Cavaliere Raiberti[54] and the Comte de la Pérouse[55] received me with the greatest satisfaction. They both found me aged, but after all I could only be relatively so at my then age of forty-four years. I struck up a close friendship with Sir XXX,[56] the English Envoy, a charming man, well read, rich, with excellent taste, who kept a choice table, whom everyone loved, among others a Parmesan dancer named Campioni,[57] than whom it was difficult to see a prettier woman.

As soon as I told my friends my idea of going to Switzerland to print at my expense a confutation in Italian of the *History of the Venetian Government* by Amelot de la Houssaye, they all eagerly undertook to find me subscribers who would pay me in advance for a certain number of copies. The most generous of all was the Comte de la Pérouse, who gave me twenty-five Piedmontese gold pistoles for fifty copies. I left a week later with two thousand Piedmontese lire in my purse for copies thus paid for in advance, which enabled me to print the entire work, which I had sketched out in the Tower in the Citadel of Barcelona, but which I had to write in full with the author whom I wanted to refute at hand, together with the *History of Venice* by the Procurator Nani.[58] Provided with these books, I set out, resolved to go to have my work printed in Lugano, where there was a good press and no censorship. In addition I knew that the proprietor of the press was a man of letters, and that there was excellent fare there and good society. Not far from Milan, very near to Varese, where the Duke of Modena went to spend the season, close to Coire, to Como, to Chiavenna, and to Lake Maggiore, in which were the famous Borromean Islands, I should be in a place where I could very easily amuse myself; I went there, and I at once went to lodge at the inn which was considered the best. Its proprietor was Taglioretti,[59] who immediately gave me the best of all his rooms.

The next morning I went to see Doctor Agnelli,[60] the printer, who was a priest, a theologian, and a man of good reputation. I made a formal agreement with him, in which he promised to give me four sheets a week, each in twelve hundred copies, I undertook to pay him each week, and he reserved the right of censorship, hoping, however, that he would always be of the same opinion as I. I began at once by giving him a preface and a fore-word which would keep him busy for a week, after choosing my paper and prescribing the size I wanted, large octavo.

When I got back to the inn for dinner the innkeeper announces the Bargello,[61] who wanted to speak to me. The Bargello was the chief constable. Though Lugano belonged to the thirteen cantons, its police had the same organization as those of Italian cities. Curious to know what this ill-omened personage could want with me, and in any case having no choice but to listen to him, I have him shown in. Hat in hand, he tells me that he has come to offer me his services, to assure me that, though a for-eigner, I should enjoy every privilege in his city with no fear for my safety in the streets if I had enemies or for my personal liberty if I had difficulties with the Venetian Government.

"I thank you, and I am sure that what you tell me is true, for I know that I am in Switzerland."

"I make bold to tell you that the custom is that all for-

eigners who come here, and who want to be sure that the
asylum they are granted is inviolable, pay a trifling sum
in advance, either by the week or the month or the year.''

"And if they should not want to pay?"

"They could not count themselves safe."

"Very good. I will tell you that I fear nothing, and
that consequently I count myself safe, and more than
safe, without going to the trouble of paying."

"Excuse me, but I know that you are on bad terms
with the State of Venice."

"You are mistaken, my friend."

"Oh, no I'm not."

"See if you can find someone who will wager two hundred zecchini that I have nothing to fear from Venice,
and I will put them up in an hour."

The Bargello is taken aback, the innkeeper, who was
present, tells him that he may well be mistaken, and he
leaves in great astonishment. The innkeeper, very glad to
have overheard the dialogue, told me that, since I intended to stay in Lugano three or four months, I might
well show the Captain, or High Bailiff, who was equivalent to the Governor and who had all authority, the courtesy of going to call on him. He was, he said, a very
honest and amiable Swiss gentleman, with a young wife
who was very intelligent and as beautiful as possible.

"Oh, in that case I assure you I will go there tomorrow."

Toward noon the next day I go there, I am announced,
I enter, and I see Monsieur de ===[62] with his charming
wife and a little boy five or six years old. We stand there
motionless, staring at one another.

Marazzani punished. My departure from Lugano. Turin. Monsieur Dubois in Parma. Leghorn. Departure of Orlov with the fleet. Pisa. Stratico. Siena. The Marchesa Chigi. My departure from Siena with an Englishwoman.

THEY ARE my life's finest moments—these happy, unforeseen, unexpected, purely fortuitous meetings, due to chance alone, and hence all the more precious. Monsieur de R. was the first to break the silence and embrace me fondly. We quickly exchanged the excuses we thought we owed each other as old friends, for in other respects we had both done our duty, I not having known his name, and he thinking that other Italians might bear the same name as I. It went without saying that I had to take pot luck at dinner with them that very day, and in the course of it our old acquaintance was entirely renewed and everything we had to say to each other was said. His Republic had given him this extremely lucrative governorship; he was only sorry that it would last but two years. He was delighted, as I was, that Fortune had placed him there at a time when he could be of use to me, and he assured me that I could count upon him in anything that lay in his power. I could ask nothing more. He learned with the greatest delight that, being there to print a work of which I was the author, I should have to make a stay of four or five months, and he was greatly disappointed when I told him that I could accept his offer of his table at most once a week, for, the work being only sketched out, I had to write at night what I would give to be printed during the day, when I should be equally busy correcting proofs.

Madame could not get over her surprise. It was nine years since I had left her at Soleure, so beautiful that I should never have believed that a few more years could make her more beautiful, yet I found her so. I congratulated her on it, and she seemed to know that I was not flattering her; she kept calling my attention to their only offspring, a boy whose mother she had become four years[1] after my departure. She loved him more than the light of her eyes, so she seemed to be on the way to making a spoiled child of him. However, I am told that he is now most likable. In a quarter of an hour Madame de R. informed me of all that had happened at Soleure after my departure which could be of interest to me. The principal piece of news was that Lebel [2] and his wife had gone to settle in Besançon, where she believed that they were very prosperous. As for the story of all that had happened to me in nine years, Madame de R. saw from the summary I gave her that it would be enough to keep her entertained for several days during the long stay I was to make in Lugano.

A truth which the charming woman told me, namely, that she did not find the look of youth in me which I had had in Soleure, was enough to make me renounce any idea I might have had of resuming an amorous relationship with her. "So much the better," I said to myself on the way back to my inn, "I will be her friend, and I will make myself worthy to be Monsieur de R.'s." The work which I intended to publish could not permit me the least distraction, and a love affair would have absorbed the

better part of my time. I set to work the next morning,
being interrupted for only an hour by a visit from Monsieur de R. On the following day I received the first sheet,
which I corrected, and I was well enough pleased. I spent
the whole of the first month in my room, going out only
on feast days to hear mass, to dine at Madame de R.'s,
and to take the air with her and her baby. Since I worked
fourteen hours a day, at the end of a month the printer
delivered the first volume to me; meanwhile I had got the
whole of the second ready. A month later I finished the
entire work, divided into three volumes, which the
printer delivered to me at the end of October. In less than
a year I sold my whole edition.

My purpose in printing this work was to earn a pardon
from the Venetian State Inquisitors. After traveling
from one end of Europe to the other, I was so overcome
by a longing to return to my native country that it
seemed to me I could no longer live anywhere else. Amelot de la Houssaye had written his *History of the Government of Venice* as an inveterate enemy of the Venetians;
his history was a satire, which contained learned dis-
quisitions interlarded with slanders. In all the seventy
years during which Amelot's work had been in everyone's
hands, no one had taken the trouble to refute it. A Venetian living in Venice who wanted to challenge the author's lies by pointing them out in print would not have
obtained permission from the Government, whose rule is
not to let anyone discuss it, either in praise or in blame.
Hence until then no writer had dared to refute the satirical historian, for instead of the reward he had deserved
he could expect nothing but punishment. I thought it
was my part to undertake such a work. The reasons I
might have for complaining of a government from which
a body which despotically persecuted me drew its powers
freed me from any suspicion of partiality; and the irref-
utability with which I was sure I could expose Amelot's
lies and blunders to all Europe made me sure of a reward

which, since it consisted only in an act of justice, seemed
to me certain. Permission to return to my country was
due me, after fourteen years in which a despotic power
forced me to remain absent from it. I thought the State
Inquisitors could not but seize the opportunity to repair
their injustice on the pretext of giving me a reward
which my patriotism had deserved. The reader will see
that I guessed rightly; but they made me wait for it five
more years. Signor Bragadin having died, I had only two
friends left in Venice, Signor Dandolo and Signor Barbaro. It was they who secretly procured me fifty subscribers even in Venice.

During all the time I spent in Lugano the only house I
frequented was Monsieur de R.'s. I had several conversations with the Abate Riva,[3] a man both learned and wise,
to whom I had been recommended by the celebrated Signor Angelo Querini,[4] a relative of his. The Abate enjoyed so great a reputation for prudence among his com-
patriots that he was chosen to be the arbiter in almost all
the differences which arose among them and which they
would otherwise have had to take to court. The brood of
chicaning lawyers loathed him and considered him their
greatest enemy. Their hatred was his aureole. His nephew,
Count Giovanni Battista,[5] devoted in equal measure to
the Muses, to Bacchus, and to Venus, was my only friend,
though I could not drink glass for glass with him. He lent
me all the girls whom he had initiated, and they only
loved him the more, for I gave them money. It was with
him and two very pretty sisters that I made a voyage
to the Borromean Islands in Lake Maggiore.

I knew that Count Federico Borromeo,[6] who had honored me with his friendship in Turin, was there, and,
sure that I should be well received, I went there with my
friend and the two pretty girls, one of whom was to pass
as his wife. In this way her sister would be properly
accounted for. At Count Borromeo's they slept together.
That nobleman, though ruined, lived there like a prince.

It is impossible so to describe these islands as to give the reader any adequate idea of how delicious they are. One enjoys a perpetual spring there; it is never either hot or cold. The Count treated us to delicate fare; and he amused our young ladies by a fishing party. Very ugly, old, disgraced, ruined, he was still able to please. On the way back to Lugano on the fourth day, when I tried to give room to a carriage on a viaduct, my horse slipped over the edge and fell ten feet. Having hit my head against a large stone, I thought I had cracked my skull. A copious bleeding, performed as soon as I got back to Lugano, freed me from all apprehension. It was the last time I rode horseback.

During this time the inspectors sent by all the thirteen cantons[7] arrived in Lugano. The Luganese call them Ambassadors, Monsieur de R. called them *avoyés*. They all lodged at Taglioretti's. I ate with them during the whole of the week they spent there. The one from Bern[8] gave me news of my poor friend M. F.[9] and his family which pleased me. His charming daughter Sara[10] had become the wife of Monsieur de V., and she was happy.

It was after the inspectors left that one fine morning I saw in my room the unfortunate Marazzani,[11] whom I no sooner saw than I took him by the collar. He shouts, he vainly uses all his strength to defend himself, I drag him outside, he falls, and I fall on him before he has time to use either his walking stick or his sword; I slap him, I pummel him, the innkeeper comes running at the noise, and the servants force me to contain my fury. I tell the innkeeper not to let him get away, and to send for the Bargello to put him in prison. I go back to my room, leaving him shouting protests, and I try to dress quickly to go and tell the whole story to Monsieur de R. The Bargello arrives, he comes to ask me why he is to put the man in prison, and I reply that he will learn the reason from Monsieur de R., to whom I am going at once. Here is the reason for my anger.

The reader may remember that I had left the wretch in Buen Retiro when the Alcalde Messa had released me from that inferno and escorted me to my inn. I learned afterward that he had been sent to a Presidio[12] in Africa, where he served the King of Spain as a rower on a galley with the pay of a soldier; but, not knowing what to do about it, I blotted him from my memory. Yet the man was guilty of no crime. His only offense had been that he was without a sponsor, without money, and without employment in the city of Madrid, where at that time the police regulations were very strict and especially in respect to vagabonds.

Eight months later at Barcelona I saw among the dancers at the opera La Bellucci,[13] a Venetian girl whom I had loved before her marriage. I had left her husband in Riga, where he still is today; I felt that I should like to go and give her news of him, and also, if she liked, to renew our old relationship. I go there the next day; she cries out for joy when she sees me, she returns my embrace, and she says she is happy that I have had the good luck to escape from the terrible misfortune into which tyranny had plunged me.

"I do not know what misfortune you mean."

"The Presidio, where you were sentenced to hard labor, which usually costs those who are not used to it their lives."

"I was never sentenced to labor in any Presidio. Who told you this tale, which is an insult to me?"

"A Count Marazzani, who spent three weeks here, who had the same misfortune, and who, luckier than you, managed to escape."

"The shameless scoundrel lied to you, but the slander will cost him dear."

From that moment on the fact that the man existed never arose in my memory without my burning with the desire to find him somewhere and make him pay for such a black calumny. It was at Lugano that his destiny

brought him into my presence. What I had done had
sprung from a first impulse, and it seemed to me that I
had done nothing, for after all I had only engaged in a
fist fight with him, in which I had perhaps received as
much as I gave. He was in prison, and I went to see what
punishment Monsieur de R. could inflict on the scoundrel
to give me some slight satisfaction.

As soon as Monsieur de R. was informed of the facts,
he said that he could neither keep him in prison nor
banish him from the city unless I would lodge a complaint
with him in which I would ask him for protection from
the man, who I had good reason to believe had come to
Lugano expressly to murder me. He told me that I could
substantiate my accusation by citing the genuine complaints I had against him and by putting the most sinister
interpretation on his appearing in my room without having had himself announced.

"Do that," he said, "and we shall see what he answers;
I will ask him for his passport; I will drag the thing out;
I will order him treated harshly; but in the end I shall
only be able to banish him from the city, unless he gives
good security for himself and his behavior."

It was all I could ask of the worthy man; I drew up the
complaint, and the next morning I insisted on having the
pleasure of seeing him brought before him in chains in
my presence. He said that it was certainly not true that
he had entered my room to murder me, and that he had
said in Barcelona that I was in a Presidio, sentenced to
hard labor, only because he had been told as much, and
that if it was not true he was very glad that he had been
misinformed. The Captain told him that hearsay cannot
excuse anyone who publicly repeats a calumny which
casts doubt on a man's honor, and that he could not in
justice refuse me the reparation which I demanded. He
also told him that my suspicion that he had entered my
room to murder me might be well founded, since I alleged
that he had given a false name at the inn, which I under-

took to prove, offering security, which would compensate
him if it turned out that he was, as he claimed to be,
Count Marazzani. In consequence, he told him, he would
remain in prison only until an answer came from Piacenza to say whether he was or was not what he said he
was.

"If you are Count Marazzani," he said, "Monsieur
Casanova will give you whatever satisfaction you wish,
and if you are not I promise you that your only punishment will be banishment from Lugano and the entire district."

He had to go to prison, where the Bargello did not have
to be asked twice to make it unpleasant for him, since
the scoundrel had not a copper. Monsieur de R. wrote to
the agent of the thirteen cantons in Parma to obtain the
requisite information; but the shameless scoundrel, knowing that the answer could not be what he wanted, wrote
me a letter intended to touch me in which he confessed
that he was a poor commoner from Bobbio,[14] and that
though his name was Marazzani he had no connection
with the Marazzani family of Piacenza. He begged me to
let him go somewhere else.

After showing this letter to Monsieur de R., I had him
set free, but under orders to leave Lugano within twenty-
four hours. He remained in prison only four days, and,
considering myself amply satisfied, I gave him some
money and a letter of recommendation to Baron Sellentin,[15] who was in Augsburg recruiting soldiers for the
King of Prussia. We will return to this fellow at the
proper time and place.

The Chevalier de Brézé[16] came to the fair at Lugano[17]
to buy horses; he spent two weeks there, constantly in my
company at Madame de R.'s, whose charms had conquered him. Three or four days after his departure I left
Lugano too, having resolved to spend the winter in Turin,
where the friends I had and the English Envoy[18] led me
to hope for every enjoyment. About this time I received

a bill of exchange for a hundred ducats from Prince Lubomirski, who, after the death of the Grand Marshal to the Crown, Bielinski,[19] had been raised to that exalted post. The hundred ducats were the price of fifty copies of my work which I had sent him.

Arrived in Turin, I found at the post office a letter from the same noble Venetian, Signor Girolamo Zulian,[20] who, with the permission of the State Inquisitors, had recommended me to the Ambassador, Mocenigo, in Madrid. In the letter I found another, addressed to Signor Berlendis,[21] Resident of the Republic in Turin, who, when I delivered it to him, thanked me for having thus spared him the difficulty he would otherwise have had in receiving me. Berlendis, rich and with an excessive inclination for the fair sex, maintained a splendid establishment. That was enough to have it said in Venice that he did honor to his position as Resident of the Republic. To represent Venice at foreign courts intelligence was no requirement. On the contrary, it was the man who had it and tried to use it who would fall into disfavor with the Senate, which does nothing but what the College[22] commands. In Venice "the College" means the council of the Ministers of the State Cabinet. Berlendis could not but be well regarded, for he had no pretensions to intelligence.

Sure that it could only do me good, I persuaded him, after giving him two copies of my work, to send it officially to the State Inquisitors. I thought the answer he received,[23] and which he gave me to read, very strange. The Secretary of the redoubtable Tribunal told him that he had done very well to send the Tribunal a work the mere title page of which was enough to prove the author's audacious temerity. He told him that it would be examined, and that in the meanwhile he was to keep a close watch on me and above all not to favor me in any way which could lead the Court to suppose that he was protecting me as a Venetian. The Secretary expressed the

mind of the Tribunal. Its members at that time were not
those who had opened the way to the Ambassador in
Madrid for me. I thought it my part to be as circumspect
as Berlendis, never going to see him except sometimes
early in the morning to drink coffee. A Corsican Abate,
his son's tutor, interested me much more than he did. He
was a man of letters, a good writer in prose and a good
poet. He is the Abate Andrais,[24] who now lives in England a free man.

I spent my time in Turin very tranquilly in the company of Epicureans. The old Cavaliere Raiberti, the
Comte de la Pérouse, a charming Abate di Rubione,[25] a
pleasure-loving Count Rica,[26] the English Envoy, and
some literary work kept me very pleasantly occupied; no
love affairs. Frequent suppers with very pretty girls
quenched our desires before they had become strong
enough to make us unhappy. A milliner who was La
Pérouse's mistress died about that time after swallowing
her lover's portrait instead of the Eucharist. The incident inspired me to write two sonnets, which pleased me
and still please me. I had a literary controversy with
Baretti,[27] who died while he was still in London and
whose motto should have been: *Ille Bioneis sermonibus
et sale nigro* ("Another [enjoys] Bion's satiric discourses
with their caustic raillery").[28] He wrote in pure Italian,
and his only claim to fame was the biting wit which filled
everything he wrote, for he was completely without learning and without sound literary judgment. He had a
thorough command of English, yet he made it unpleasing
by trying to combine it with the beauties of Italian.

During this time[29] I thought I could make my fortune
by going to Leghorn and offering my services to Count
Alexis Orlov,[30] who was in command of the fleet which
was to go to Constantinople and which might have gone
there if it had been commanded by an Englishman.

The English Envoy, Sir XXX,[31] gave me a strong letter of recommendation for Leghorn addressed to his

country's Consul there. I left Turin with very little money in my pocket and without a letter of credit on any banker. The Englishman Aston[32] recommended me to an English man of business who had settled in Leghorn, but his recommendation did not go so far as to authorize me to ask him for money. Another letter, from the Abate Andrais, recommended me to the Corsican Rivarola,[33] also settled in Leghorn, a man of intelligence and a great friend of Paoli's.[34] The Englishman Aston was then engaged in a strange affair in Turin. He had fallen in love in Venice with a very beautiful woman, I forget whether Greek or Neapolitan. The woman's husband was a Turinese named Sclopis,[35] who put nothing in the way of the rich and generous Englishman's amour, but who was becoming an inconvenience to the lover and his wife precisely at the moments when common decency demanded that he should not be. Such a husband is more trying than a jealous one, and unfortunately the lover cannot talk sense to him, for he is the husband. Aston, in a situation the embarrassment of which an English gentleman, generous and in love, cannot tolerate, determined, with his beauty's approval, to speak plainly to her husband. He asked him if he needed a thousand guineas, and he offered them to him on condition that he would let him travel for three years with the lady without going to the trouble of escorting her. Signor Sclopis accepted the proposal, and signed an agreement in writing. The three years having expired, Sclopis, who was in Turin, wrote his wife, who was in Venice, to return to him, and wrote Aston not to prevent her from doing so. His wife answered that she would no longer live with him, and Aston gave him to understand that he neither could nor would send her away; and, thinking that the cuckold would no doubt apply to the English Envoy, he informed Sir XXX of the matter and asked him for his good offices; Sir XXX at once spoke to the Cavaliere Raiberti, who was then Minister of Foreign Affairs. Sclopis spoke to him at the same time, demanding that he write to the Resident in Turin, the Commendatore Camerana,[36] to demand her officially from the Venetian Government, and persuaded Berlendis to add to his letter that, his (Sclopis's) claim being perfectly justified, his demand should be honored and his wife made to leave Venice, even against her will. There is no doubt that the thing would have been done if the Commendatore Camerana had demanded her at the same time, but the Cavaliere Raiberti, more a man of honor than a scrupulous Christian in respect to the laws which consider marriage a sacrament, not only did not write to the Resident Camerana, but, informed of the matter by XXX, and having a view of it directly contrary to that of the Venetian Resident Berlendis, cordially received Aston, who had come to Turin to pursue it, having left Signora Sclopis in Venice under the protection of the English Resident.[37] Sclopis was ashamed to complain publicly, for the agreement he had signed covered him with opprobrium; but Berlendis made everyone laugh by saying publicly that the husband Sclopis was in the right, and that it was shameful that he was not given his due without delay, for after all he was the husband; and, there being no legal divorce between his wife and himself, he could not be prevented from living with her again, and the more so because the three years for which he had been weak enough to cede his rights in her had passed.

"What would you say," I asked Berlendis on the day before I left, "if Sclopis, whom you are protecting, had sent word to Aston that he would stop plaguing him in return for a thousand guineas which he would give him for another three years' lease?"

"It is too infamous; I do not believe it."

"You are wrong. The thing is well known, and you are making yourself ridiculous, or, if that were possible, suspect of something which would dishonor you; but take comfort, no one believes that, for you are known to be

rich and a gentleman. I advise you to abandon what you
call the just cause of Signor Sclopis, who is unworthy to
enjoy the privileges of a sacrament which he is willing to
sell.''

Berlendis blushed fiery red. *Erubuit: salva res est*
("He has blushed: all is well").[38] I left, and two years
later in Bologna I found Aston and La Sclopis, whose
beauty I admired. She had a charming little Aston in her
lap. I gave her news of her sister; but I will speak of
that in the proper place.

I traveled from Turin to Parma with a Venetian, who,
like myself, was wandering about outside his country,
unable to live there for reasons known to the State Inquisitors. He had turned actor to earn his living, and he
was going to Parma with two actresses, one of whom
was worthy to be loved. When he learned who I was, he
became my intimate friend; and he would have allowed
me to share in all the pleasures which our traveling companions could have offered us; but I was not in the mood
for amusement. I was going to Leghorn with chimerical
ideas. I thought I could make myself indispensable to
Count Alexis Orlov in his intended conquest of Constantinople; I imagined that, without me, he would never
pass the Dardanelles,[39] that such was the decree of Fate,
like the one she had pronounced in regard to the taking
of Troy, which could never have been accomplished without the presence of Achilles.[40] Meanwhile, I took a great
liking to the young Venetian, whose name was Angelo
Bentivoglio,[41] and whom the State Inquisitors never
forgave for a crime than which philosophy knows none
more trifling. I will speak of him when my reader finds
me back in Venice, four years hence.

Arriving in Parma about noon, I said good-by to Bentivoglio and his two companions. I was at once told that the
Court was at Colorno;[42] but I had no business at the
Court. Determined to leave the next day for Bologna, I
invited myself to dinner with the hunchbacked Dubois-

Chatellerault,[43] Director of the Infante's[44] Mint, a man
of intelligence, vain, and with a great deal of talent. My
reader may remember that I had known him twenty-two
years earlier, during the happy days when I was in love
with Henriette; I had seen him only twice since then,
each time only for a moment. He received me with the
cries of joy with which one greets an old acquaintance,
and showed himself greatly obliged to me for my courtesy in spending my few hours in Parma with him. I told
him that I was on my way to Leghorn, where Count
Orlov was expecting me, and that I should travel day and
night, for at the time we were speaking he must be setting sail. He assured me that he was ready to leave, and
he showed me letters which he had just received from
Leghorn; but with a little smile I assured him that he
would not leave without me, whereupon Monsieur Dubois
gave me a bow of politic admiration. He wanted to talk
about the expedition, which was then setting all Europe
to calculating; but my reserve made him change the subject. He showed me his fine engravings, which were indeed masterpieces, and he did me the honor to have me
dine with his housekeeper. We spoke a great deal about
Henriette, whose identity he boasted that he had managed to discover, and, though he spoke of her with great
respect, I never gave him time to get anything out of me.
So he spent the whole afternoon talking to me about himself, complaining of all the sovereigns in Europe, except
the King of Prussia, who had created him a Baron though
he did not know him and though he had never had anything to do with him either directly or indirectly.

He complained most of all of the Infante Duke of
Parma, in whose service he was and who, never making
up his mind to establish a mint, gave him nothing to do;
he would not have entered his service if he could have
foreseen that he would be like a canon in a chapter who
was there only to enjoy his emoluments. He complained
bitterly of the Court of Louis XV, at which he had asked

for nothing but a glass of water, and had not obtained it.
The "glass of water" was the order of St. Michael,[45]
which was given to men of talent who certainly were no
more worthy than he. Finally he complained of the Republic of Venice, which had not properly rewarded him
for what he had done for it. He had spent a year in
Venice setting up a coining press in the Republic's
mint,[46] and he had done it well. After the operation Venice was able to strike edge-rolled coins, like all the other
powers in Europe, and the present he had been given
was a mere trifle. He had spent eight times what he had
received. After telling him that he had every reason in
the world to complain, I asked him to arrange for some
banker to give me fifty zecchini, which I would return
at whatever bank in Leghorn I was directed to; he answered very generously that there was no need of my
going to a banker for such a trifle, for he could give me
the amount himself. I accepted his offer, promising to
return the money to him soon, but I was never in a position to repay this small debt. I do not know if he is still
alive; but even if he should live to Nestor's age,[47] I have
no hope that I shall ever be in a position again to return
that small sum to him. I grow poorer every day, and I
know that I am at the end of my career.

The next day I arrived in Bologna, and the day after
that in Florence, where I found the Cavaliere Morosini,[48]
nephew of the Procurator, a young man of nineteen, who
was traveling with Count Stratico,[49] Professor of Mathematics at the University of Padua. He was with the
young nobleman as his tutor. He gave me a letter for his
brother,[50] a Dominican monk, Professor of Belles-Lettres
at the University of Pisa. I stopped in Pisa for two hours
only to make the acquaintance of this monk, who was as
celebrated for his wit as for his learning. I found him
even greater than he was famed to be, and I promised
him I would spend some time in that city on another occasion expressly to enjoy his company. I stopped for an

hour at the baths,[51] and I made the acquaintance of the
"Pretender-in-vain" to the throne of Great Britain.[52] I
arrived in Leghorn, where I found Count Orlov only because the weather was stormy.

The English Consul [53] immediately presented me; he
was staying in his house. When he saw me, he seemed
delighted to have the pleasure of seeing me again, for he
had been well acquainted with me in Petersburg; and he
seemed even better pleased when the Consul showed him
the letter he had received from the English Envoy in
Turin. He hastily told me that he would be delighted to
have me with him on his own ship, so I should have my
things taken on board, for he would leave as soon as the
wind allowed; and, having a great deal to do, he left me
with the Consul, who asked me in what capacity I was
going to Constantinople with the Admiral.

"That is what I want to know before I have my few
things taken on board his ship. You can understand that
I must talk to him and that he must talk to me. Would
one ever have believed that a Russian would have become
such a Frenchman?"

"You cannot talk to him until tomorrow morning."

I go very early the next morning and I send him in a
note in which he reads that before having my trunk sent
on board his ship it was indispensable that I talk with
him privately for at least a quarter of an hour. He was
writing in bed, his Adjutant told me, so he asked me to
wait.

"Gladly."

In comes Dall'Oglio,[54] Agent to the King of Poland in
Venice and his old friend; he knew me from Berlin, and
indeed had known me from my birth through old connections.

"What are you doing here?" he asked me.

"I must speak to the Admiral."

"He is extremely busy."

After giving me which news, he goes in. It is a piece of

impertinence. Can he tell me more clearly that he is not busy for him? A moment later I see the Marchese Marucci,[55] with his order of St. Anne[56] and his stiff manner, who, congratulating me on my being in Leghorn, tells me that he is reading my confutation of Amelot, in which he had not expected to find himself.

He was right not to expect it, for there was nothing in common between him and my work; but he was not the sort of man to see nothing in the world except things he expected. If he had not gone in to the Admiral, I would have told him so. He told me he did not expect it only to make me understand that he had not found himself in it as he would have wished to be, and I knew it. I did not care: *nescit vox missa reverti* ("words once uttered cannot be recalled").[57] But I was annoyed to see that these gentlemen were inside, while I was outside. I began to dislike my project. Five hours later the Admiral comes out, followed by a great many people, to go to call on someone, saying pleasantly that we should speak at table or after dinner.

"After dinner," I replied.

He came back at two o'clock and sat down to dinner, at which the guests were those who sat down first. Fortunately I was one of them. Orlov, constantly repeating "Eat, gentlemen, eat," did nothing but read letters, handing them to a secretary after making notes on them in pencil. After dinner, during which I never spoke, when everyone was taking coffee standing, he looked at me as if startled, and, with a "by the way," took me by the hand and led me to a window niche, where he told me to have my trunk sent on board his ship at once, for if the wind held as it was he would leave before dawn.

"Permit me to ask you in what capacity you will take me with you; what post shall I have?"

"I have no post to give you, but that may come. Come on board as my friend."

"A most honorable condition, which would certainly

always make me run the most obvious risk to my life in
order to defend yours, but which will avail me nothing
after the expedition, and even during the expedition, for
you alone in your goodness would show me marks of confidence and esteem; all the others would have no regard
for me at all. I should be considered no more than a man
to make you laugh, and I should perhaps kill the first
man who dared to show me the slightest sign of contempt.
I need a post which makes it my duty to serve you in
your uniform. I can be useful to you in every way. I
know the country to which you are going, I speak the
language, I am in good health, and I am not lacking in
courage. I do not want your valuable friendship for
nothing, I want the honor of earning it.''

"My dear friend, I have no definite employment to
give you."

"Then I wish you a good voyage, and I shall go to
Rome. I hope you will never repent of not having taken
me with you. Without me you will never pass the Dardanelles."

"Is that a prophecy?"

"It is an oracle."

"We shall see, my dear Calchas." [58]

This was literally the dialogue which I had with the
worthy Count, who did not pass the Dardanelles. No one
can know if he would have passed them if I had been
with him.

The next morning I delivered the letters I had to Signor
Rivarola and to the English man of business; the fleet
sailed. On the following day I went to Pisa, where I spent
a week very agreeably with Father Stratico, who two or
three years later[59] became a Bishop by a very bold stroke
which might have ruined him. He took it upon himself to
deliver the funeral oration for Father Ricci,[60] who was
the last General of the Jesuits. His oration, which praised
the deceased, not ironically but in the most serious style,
put Pope Ganganelli under the necessity of either pun-

ishing the orator, which would have been taken very ill, or of giving the world an example of heroic virtue by rewarding him; His Holiness found the latter course preferable to the former. Father Stratico himself told me, four or five years after he obtained the bishopric, that, knowing the human heart, he was sure that the Holy Father would punish his daring by a splendid reward.

In Pisa the monk initiated me into the charming society in which he delighted. He had chosen two or three well-born girls who combined beauty with talent, so that he could teach them to sing improvisations in which he accompanied them on the guitar. He had taught them the art of Corilla,[61] who was then famous and who six years later was crowned *Poetessa* by night on the Capitol[62] in Rome, the same place where our greatest poets had been crowned, which caused a great scandal, for after all Corilla's talent, though unique of its kind, consisted in nothing but a splendid show. The crowned Corilla was attacked in scathing satires, and the authors of them were even more in the wrong than those who profaned the Capitol by crowning her, for all the poisoned darts with which black envy made every effort to lacerate the celebrated woman found nothing to say but that chastity was not her favorite virtue, which proved the ignorance of the poets who assailed her. All the women poets who have existed from the time of Homer, from the time of the Sibyls, until ours were all votaries of Venus. But for that, their names would not have come down to posterity, for they could not become famous except by being immortalized by the pens of those who enjoyed their favors.[63] No one would have heard of Corilla if she had not been able to make men her lovers, and she would never have been crowned in Rome if she had not enslaved Prince Gonzaga Solferino,[64] who later married the pretty Rangoni, the daughter of the Roman Consul whom I knew in Marseilles.

To the door of the temple[65] in which the woman was

crowned the following verses were affixed the day before
the august ceremony took place:

> *Arce in Tarpeia, Caio regnante, sedentem*
> *Nunquam vidit equum, Roma videbit equam.*
> *Corillam patres obscura nocte coronant.*
> *Quid mirum? Tenebris nox tegit omne nefas.*

> ("In the reign of Caius a horse was never
> seen on the Tarpeian rock; Rome will now
> see a mare there. The Senators crown Corilla
> in the darkness of night. No wonder! Night
> hides all evil in its shadows.")

She should have been crowned by the light of day, or
never; night was chosen, and it was a mistake. The day
after her coronation these verses were posted up all over
the city:

> *Corillam patres turba plaudente coronant*
> *Altricem memores germinis esse lupam.*
> *Proh scelus! impuri redierunt saecla Neronis*
> *Indulget scortis laurea serta Pius.*

> ("The Senators crown Corilla before an ap-
> plauding crowd, remembering that the she-
> wolf [66] nurses her cubs. What infamy! The
> time of filthy Nero has returned. Pius [Pope
> Pius VI] bestows the laurel wreath on prosti-
> tutes.")

The thing is an ineffaceable stain on the pontificate of
that Pope,[67] who still reigns, for it is certain that in
future no poet will aspire to an honor which until that
day Rome, far from scattering broadcast, had conferred
only very rarely on geniuses who seemed to rise above
human nature; hence this distich was posted on the
Vatican:

> *Sacra fronde vilis frontem meretricula cingit;*
> *Quis vatum tua nunc praemia Phoebe velit?*

("The base harlot binds her brow with the
sacred branch; what poet will now want your
prizes, Apollo?")

A young Abate put a large sheet of paper containing
the following four verses into Corilla's hands just as,
trembling with fright, she entered the theater of Apollo,
where she was awaited by a considerable number of
Cardinals, by the Senator, and by the Conservatori of
Rome. She took the paper, thinking it was a eulogy, and
since the quatrain was in Latin it was read to her by
Prince Gonzaga, who did not expect the next to the last
word:

> *Quis pallor tenet ora? Tuos tremor occupat artus?*
> *Ad Tarpeia times tecta movere pedes?*
> *Femina pone metum: sint pronae Heliconis alumnae*
> *Si nec Apollo tibi praesto, Priapus erit.*

("Why is your face so pale? Are your limbs trembling? Do you fear to move on to the Capitol?
Woman, be not afraid! May the Heliconian Muses
favor you. If Apollo is not your guardian, Priapus
will be." [68]

The impertinent Abate was looked for, but he had dis-
appeared. On the next day but one after her coronation
Corilla and her lovers all left Rome, ashamed to have
succeeded in solemnizing such a scandal. The Abate
Pizzi,[69] guardian of the sacred forests of the Arcadians,[70]
who had been the chief promoter of the *Poetessa*'s apoth-
eosis, inundated with pamphlets and caustic satires from
every direction, did not dare to leave his house for several
months. But after this long digression let us return to
Father Stratico, to whom I owed eight happy days in
Pisa.

The monk, who, though not handsome, perfectly possessed the art of making himself loved, persuaded me to
go to spend a week in Siena, promising me every pleasure
of the heart and the mind from two letters of recommen-

dation which he would give me, one to the Marchesa Chigi,[71] the other to the Abate Ciaccheri.[72] Having nothing better to do than to find pleasures where I could, I accepted his offer, and I went to Siena by the shortest road, not troubling to visit Florence.

The next morning I took Father Stratico's letter to the Abate Ciaccheri. He promised me all the amusements in his power, and he kept his word; but above all, as soon as I told him that I had a letter to the Marchesa Chigi, he himself took me to call on the lady, who made an unresisting conquest of me as soon as, still standing, she quickly read to herself the letter from her "dear Stratico." This was the epithet she accorded him as soon as she recognized his handwriting.

The lady was still beautiful. Though past her prime, she must have been sure that she could still please, for she knew how to make up for her want of youth by obliging ways, by graces, by an easy and affable manner, by her intelligence, by the pretty turn she gave to her remarks, and by the charms which she added to the beautiful language of her country by her own eloquence, which shone the more because she treated it as nothing, without the slightest pretension. I have told my reader beforehand what I found in her the next day, for I spent the first day entirely in studying her.

"Let us sit down," she said; "you will spend a week here, according to what my dear Stratico tells me; it is little for us, and hence too much for you. I hope he has not given you too favorable a report of us."

"He told me nothing, Signora, except that I must stay here a week, promising me that I should find here the charms of the heart and the mind; but I did not believe him. I have come to see if he told me the truth, at the same time resolved to keep my word to him. You see that I have not let him make up my mind for me."

"So much the better; but Stratico should have sentenced you to at least a month, without mercy."

"Why without mercy? What risk could I have run?"

"Of being bored to death, or leaving a piece of your heart in Siena."

"All that can happen in a week; but I defy either of those dangers, for Stratico protected me from the first of them by counting on you, and from the second by counting on me. You will receive my homage, and so that I may offer it to you pure, it will be only of the mind. My heart will leave this place as free as it is now; for since it cannot hope for a return, its defeat would make me unhappy."

"Is it possible that you are among the despairing?"

"Yes, fortunately; for I owe all my peace to my despair."

"But how unfortunate for you if you are mistaken!"

"Not as great a misfortune, Signora, as you suppose. Apollo assures me of an admirable subterfuge, he gives me an infallible way of escape. He leaves me only the freedom to enjoy the moment; but since it is a favor the god does me, I use it to the top of my bent. *Carpe diem* ['Seize the day'] [73] is my motto."

"It is the voluptuous Horace's; but I approve of it only in so far as it is convenient. The pleasure which follows on desires, and sometimes even on desires unsatisfied, is preferable, for it is infinitely more acute."

"True, but one cannot count on it. That distresses the philosopher who calculates. God preserve you, Signora, from learning that cruel truth from experience. The good to be preferred to all other goods is the good one enjoys; the good which one desires is often limited merely to the pleasure of desiring. It is a figment of the soul, the vanity of which I have too often experienced in my life. Yet I congratulate you if you have not yet learned that Horace is right."

At that the Marchesa, with a gracious smile, excused herself from either admitting or denying it. Ciaccheri, who had not said a word, told us that the most fortunate thing that could happen to us was never to agree; the Marchesa admitted it, laughing at Ciaccheri's subtle thought; and I denied it.

"If I admit it," I said, "I renounce the happiness which you make dependent upon never being in agreement. I would rather contradict you, Signora, than renounce the hope of pleasing you. The Abate Ciaccheri is a spoilsport who has thrown the apple of discord between us; but if we go on as we have begun, I will settle in Siena."

The Marchesa, very well pleased to have given me a good taste of her wit, then talked of everything and nothing, of Pisa, of Stratico, of Leghorn, of Rome, of the pleasure of traveling, and asked me if I wanted to make my way with the prettiest women in Siena by attending all the great assemblies, offering to take me everywhere; and, in all seriousness, I asked her not to think of going to that trouble.

"I want to be able to say, Signora, that during the week I spent in Siena I paid court to no one but you, and that no one but the Abate Ciaccheri showed me the monuments of the city and introduced me to its men of letters."

Flattered by this ultimatum, she invited me to dine next day, with the Abate, at a charming house which she owned a hundred paces from the city and which she called Vico.[74]

The older I grew, the more what attached me to women was intelligence. It became the medium which my blunted senses needed in order to enter into play. In men of a temperament different from mine, what happens is exactly the opposite. A sensual man who grows old wants only the material, women skilled in the arts of Venus, and not philosophical discourses. As we left the Marchesa's house I told Ciaccheri that if I stayed in Siena she would be the only woman I would see, and that the outcome should be as God willed. The Abate Ciaccheri

could not but agree that I was right. In the course of the
week he showed me everything worth seeing in the city,
and made me acquainted with all the men of letters, who
did not fail to call on me. Toward evening he took me to a
house, where, he said, everything was free and easy—no
formality, no introductions; people talked to be amusing,
there was singing, there was instrumental music, beautiful verses were read aloud, one girl composed them to
make up for her ugliness, her very pretty younger sister
enjoyed their beauties and was content to afford a subject for them to those whom all of her charming person
fired with love. The two sisters had two brothers, one of
whom played the harpsichord, the other was a painter.
Such was the house to which Ciaccheri took me to spend
the evening, with another Abate, a young professor,
whose name was Pistoi.[75] I saw neither father nor mother
nor servants. But if the younger of the two sisters was a
perfect beauty, the other was ugly without being either
hunchbacked or lame or squint-eyed or dirty; but she
was ugly, and all ugliness repels. Nevertheless the ugly
girl did not lose heart, but talked to me sweetly and modestly about poetry, and asked me to recite her something
of mine, promising me something of hers in exchange. I
recited whatever came into my head, and she replied with
a poem in the same style and of a beauty which I praised
as it deserved, pretending to believe that she was the
author of it. Ciaccheri, who had been her teacher, seeing
that I could not believe the girl was so clever, suggested
bouts-rimés.[76] It was the pretty sister who proposed the
rhymes, and, all four working at the same time, it was the
ugly one who, having finished, was the first to put down
her pen. The rhymes were for a sonnet. The girl's sonnet,
in verses of eight syllables, was the prettiest; I am astonished, and, still doubting, I compose an improvisation in
her honor, and I present it to her written down; she returns the eulogy immediately on the same rhymes, and at
that I become serious. I ask her her name, and she replies

that, both as a shepherdess in the Arcadian Academy and as her family name, she is Maria Fortuna.[77]

"What! You are she?"

I had read some stanzas of hers in praise of Metastasio, which she had had printed. I tell her so, she rises and fetches the reply which the immortal poet had sent her in his own hand. Overcome with admiration, I no longer talk to anyone else, and all her ugliness vanishes. If I had had a delicious conversation with the Marchesa that morning, my conversation with Maria Fortuna turned my head. Going back to my inn with Ciaccheri, I thanked him again and again for the pleasure he had given me to enjoy. She was a girl in whom he had happened to discover poetic genius, and in three years he had taught her all that she knew. I asked him if she improvised as Corilla did, and he said that she wanted to but that he would not let her do it, for, he said, it would be a shame to spoil the girl by indulging her in it.

Supping with me, Ciaccheri had no difficulty in persuading me that he would spoil his pupil if he let her improvise, for I was of the same opinion. The intelligence of a poet, called upon to discourse in verse on some subject without first meditating on it and deciding upon the heads of his argument, cannot produce good things except by chance, for though his mind pursues the subject he has been given to discuss, he usually finds himself led astray by the rhyme, to which he is enslaved despite his great knowledge of the language in which he is speaking. He finds himself obliged to use the first rhyme which chance offers him, and not having time to look for one which will more properly express his thought, he cannot say what he wanted to say, and he says what he did not want to say and what he would not have said if he had been composing pen in hand. Improvisation enjoyed some reputation among the Greeks only because Greek poetry, like the Latin, rejected rhyme. It was just tolerated in prose. But that did not lead to our great Latin

The Arrival

The Seducer

poets' being willing to *speak* in verse; they could only produce lifeless ones, of which they were ashamed afterward. Horace often spent a sleepless night in order to say in a vigorous verse the thing he wanted to say, and when he had found it wrote it on the wall and went to sleep content and at peace. The verses that cost him nothing were the prosaic ones which he uses in masterly fashion in several of his *Epistles*. We can learn from this that the Latin poets like the Greeks heard the quantity of the first syllable in all their words, even in dissyllables —a truth which we cannot conceive, for we know perfectly well that *sine* is a word of two short syllables; but we do not know the reason for it when we consider that we could not pronounce it otherwise if its two syllables were long.

I have written this discourse because it belongs entirely to the Abate Ciaccheri, the learned and charming poet. He confessed to me that he was in love with his ugly pupil, and that he would never have expected to fall in love with her when he began teaching her to compose verses. I told him that I could easily believe it, for *sublata lucerna* ("when the lamp has been taken away");[78] but he laughed.

"No *sublata lucerna*," he said; "it is with her face that I fell in love, for it is inseparable from her."

I believe that a Tuscan can more easily write in beautiful poetic language than an Italian from another province, since he has the beautiful language from his birth, and the language spoken in Siena is dainty, more copious, more graceful, and more energetic than the Florentine, though the latter claims the first place and indeed holds it because of its purity, which it owes to its Academy,[79] as it does its richness, which is the cause of our treating subjects much more eloquently than the French do, for we have a choice among many synonyms; whereas it would be hard to find a dozen in the language of Voltaire, who laughed at those of his countrymen who said that it

was not true that the French language was poor, for it
had all the words it needed. He who has only what he
needs is poor; and the obstinacy of the French Academy
in refusing to adopt foreign words proves nothing except
that pride goes with poverty. We continue to take all the
words which please us from foreign languages; we like to
grow constantly richer; we even take pleasure in stealing
from the poor : such is the character of the rich.

The Marchesa Chigi gave us a choice dinner in her
pretty house, the architect of which had been Palladio.[80]
On our way there Ciaccheri had warned me not to mention the pleasure I had enjoyed the evening before at La
Fortuna's; but at dinner the Marchesa said to him that
she was sure he had taken me there, and he did not have
the face to deny it. After that I did not conceal from her
all the pleasure I had had there; and I pronounced a
splendid eulogy on his pupil's great talent.

"Stratico," she said to me, "admires it as you do, and,
having read something of hers, I certainly give her all
the praise she deserves; it is a pity that one cannot go to
their house except secretly."

"Why is that?" I asked, a little taken aback.

"What!" she said to Ciaccheri, "didn't you tell him
whose house it is?"

"I did not consider it necessary, for her father never
shows himself, or even her mother."

"I can well believe it, but it makes no difference."

"Who, pray," I asked, "are her father and mother?
He's not the executioner, I imagine."

"He's worse. He's the Bargello.[81] You can see that it
is not possible for a foreigner to come here and at the
same time to frequent that house, where he will never find
decent company. It is certainly not a prejudice, for honest as the Bargello may be, he must always be the man of
his trade, and no communication between his house and
decent houses is permissible."

I saw Ciaccheri a little mortified by this discourse,

which was not without justification, and I thought it my part to say that I would not go there again until the eve of my departure, to take leave of the charming family, which one would never believe to be that of a man of such an occupation.

The Marchesa then said that his daughter, the pretty one, had been pointed out to her in the street, and that she had really thought her ravishingly beautiful; she added that it was a pity that a girl of such great beauty, and of irreproachable morals, could only hope to be married in another city to a man of her father's trade. I said that I had known a certain Coltellini,[82] the son or brother of the Bargello of Florence, and that I would write to him to propose the marriage; and the Marchesa declared that it would be suitable. This Coltellini, whose acquaintance I had made at Calzabigi's in Vienna, was endowed with the rarest qualities. I have been told that he is dead. Nothing is more odious in all Italy than a Bargello, except in Modena, where the spineless nobility frequent his house and take pot luck with him; which is surprising, for a Bargello must by his profession be a spy, a liar, untrustworthy, a scoundrel, and everyone's enemy, for the scorned hate the scorners.

As the result of these conversations I spent the whole of my week in Siena with the Marchesa Chigi and Ciaccheri, who introduced me to all the Professors. The anatomist Tabarrani[83] made me a present of his book, and I gave him mine. In Siena a Count Piccolomini,[84] if I remember rightly, was pointed out to me; he was a wit, well read, and most likable, but an oddity because he spent six months of the year at home without ever going out or receiving visitors or speaking to anyone, even his servants, always reading and writing; but he made up for it during the other six months, which he spent in company of all sorts, talking from morning to night. He was a Chevalier of St. Stephen,[85] and he may still be alive.

The Marchesa promised me she would come to Rome during the summer, where she had a more than intimate friend in Bianconi,[86] who had given up the practice of medicine to become Chargé d'Affaires for the Court of Saxony. She did come to Rome, but I did not see her. On the day before I left, the coachman who was to take me to Rome alone, and who, having made that agreement with me, could not dispose of the other seat in his calèche without my permission, came to ask me if I wanted a traveling companion, who would save me three zecchini.

"I want no one."

"You are keeping me from earning a zecchino, and you are making a mistake, for it is a pretty girl, who has just arrived."

"All alone?"

"No indeed. She is with a gentleman who has a horse and who wants to ride it to Rome."

"Then the girl arrived here with someone?"

"No indeed, she arrived on horseback too, and she does not want to ride any farther. She was exhausted and went straight to bed. Her gentleman will give me four zecchini to take the lady to Rome. Do it. I am a poor man."

"Then her gentleman will ride along with us at a slow pace."

"Let him ride as he chooses, it makes no difference to me, or to you."

"You say she is young and pretty?"

"So I hear, I have not seen her."

"What sort of man is her companion?"

"A good-looking man who scarcely speaks Italian."

"Has he sold the horse on which the young lady arrived?"

"No, for it was hired, and the peasant who owned it has already left."

"What luggage have they?"

"He has only a small trunk; he will spare his horse by putting it behind the carriage."

"I will decide nothing before I talk with him, for the whole thing seems strange to me."

"I will tell him to come and talk with you."

In comes a young Frenchman in uniform, spruce, cocky, not unprepossessing, who tells me just what the coachman had told me, and ends by saying he is sure I will not refuse to take his wife with me.

"Your wife, Monsieur?"

"Oh, thank God you speak my language! Yes, my wife, who is English and not at all demanding. She will be no trouble to you."

"Very well. I should not want to delay my departure. Can she be ready at five o'clock?"

"You can be sure of it."

The next morning at the appointed hour I see her in the carriage. I pay her a brief compliment; I sit down beside her, and we set off.

CHAPTER VIII

*Miss Betty. Count de l'Étoile. Sir B. M. made
to see reason.*

IT WAS the fourth adventure which I had had of
this kind, and which was not unusual if one was traveling alone and in a hired carriage; but this one seemed
more like something out of a romance than the three
others. I had about two hundred zecchini, and I was
forty-five years old; I still loved the fair sex, though with
much less ardor, much more experience, and less courage
for daring enterprises, for, looking more like a father
than a lover, I believed I no longer had rights or justifi-
able claims. The young woman beside me was perfectly
charming, very nicely dressed in the English style,
blonde, rather thin, with small breasts which a gauze
gorget allowed me to glimpse, a childish timidity which
expressed itself in fear of discommoding me, a noble, delicate countenance, and a modesty of manner which was
almost virginal.

"I hope, Madame, that you speak French."

"And a little Italian too, Monsieur."

"I am very fortunate that Fate has appointed me to escort you to Rome."

"Perhaps I am more fortunate than you."

"I was told that you arrived on horseback."

"Yes. It was foolish, and I shall never do it again."

"I should think your husband should have sold his horse and accompanied you in a two-seated soufflet[1] like this one."

"He cannot sell the horse. He hired it at Leghorn, and he has to deliver it in Rome to an address which he was given. From Rome we shall go to Naples together by carriage."

"You enjoy traveling."

"Very much, but much more comfortably."

So saying, the beautiful little blonde, whose white face showed not the slightest sign that there was blood in her veins, went red to the ears. Sure that I had troubled her beautiful soul, I begged her pardon and I fell silent. I spent an hour and more thinking of the young creature, in whom I was beginning to take a violent interest, but, knowing myself, I held myself in check. I knew that my impulse did not spring from virtue, and, despite the very questionable circumstances under which we had met, I waited to see things more clearly at Buonconvento,[2] where the coachman had told me we should dine, and where the lady's horseback-riding husband was to wait for us.

We arrived there at exactly ten o'clock. Coachmen in Italy never drive at more than a walk; one can travel faster on foot. They make only three miles an hour;[3] one is bored to death, and when the weather is hot one falls ill if one does not stop for five or six hours at the height of the day. The coachman told me that, not wanting to go farther than San Quirico,[4] where the inn was very good, he would not leave until four o'clock. So we had six full hours before us to rest and to shelter ourselves from the heat in a room which faced north.

The lady, astonished not to see her husband, kept looking about for him. I ask where he is, and the innkeeper tells us that he had had his horse fed a measure of oats, meanwhile eating a pigeon and drinking a glass of wine, and had ordered him to tell us that he would go on to wait for us at San Quirico, where he would have a good supper prepared for us. This seems to me a trifle odd, but I let it pass as the sort of thing Frenchmen do. But the lady thinks it rude, she tells me so, she begs me to excuse the thoughtlessness of a man who, having met me only the evening before, treated me as if I were an old friend.

"It is a mark of your husband's confidence in me," I replied; "I cannot take offense at it; it is very French."

"You are right; for it is certainly not English."

The innkeeper asks me if it is the coachman who pays for my food or I, and I reply that it is I. The young woman uneasily asks the innkeeper to go and ask the coachman if he is obliged to feed her. The innkeeper comes back with the coachman, who, to convince the lady that he is under no such obligation, takes from his pocket the agreement her husband had made with him. I read it, and I see that it is signed "Count de l'Étoile," [5] who undertakes to pay him four zecchini, two on leaving Siena and two more on arriving in Rome, in return for conveying his wife the Countess there in five days. There is no stipulation that the coachman shall pay for her meals. Enough said, the innkeeper knows what his situation is, they both leave. No sooner have we entered the room than the charming lady begs me to ask the innkeeper to prepare dinner only for me, for, having supped too heavily, she should go without dinner.

I see it all instantly, and, divining how ashamed the girl must feel to be treated in this way by the man who called himself her husband, I undertake to put her at ease by marshaling all the powers of sympathy in words which only friendship can find and utter.

"Madame, I divine that you have no money with you, and I beg you not to deprive yourself of dinner for that reason. Your husband the Count will repay me, if he insists on it. You must understand that if I told the innkeeper to prepare dinner only for me, I should dishonor your husband, and you, and myself most of all.''

''Monsieur, I understand that; you are right. You must let the innkeeper prepare dinner for two, but I will not dine. I already feel ill, and I beg you to permit me to lie down on the bed.''

''I am more than sorry to hear it, but pray make yourself comfortable. This room is excellent, I will have the table set in the other; lie down if you wish and sleep if you can. I will order dinner served three hours from now, I hope that you will be feeling better. Forgive your husband this little oversight too.''

Not leaving her time to answer me, I went out, I shut her door, and I went to tell the innkeeper what I wanted to eat at three o'clock. He was intelligent; I taught him how to make a pudding,[6] and to broil slices of fillet of beef on a grill. After that I went and lay down too. The Englishwoman, whose figure I had not seen before I got into the carriage, was a beauty. Her self-possession was perfect; her distress, her shame had won me over completely. I felt that I should certainly fight a duel with her self-styled husband, whom I no longer believed to be her husband. It must, I thought, be an elopement, a seduction; and, superstitious as always, I was sure that it had been her guardian angel who had sent me to protect her from I knew not what, to rescue her, to take care of her, to save her from the insults to which brutality, avarice, and her situation could subject her. Thus did I foster my budding passion. I laughed at the name ''Count de l'Étoile,'' and when I considered that the adventurer might well have abandoned the girl to my care for ever, I thought it a little too serious; but I felt sure that I would never abandon her. With these romantic ideas, I fell asleep.

It was the innkeeper's wife who woke me by saying

softly that three o'clock had struck. I told her to wait a
little longer before serving dinner, and I go quietly to see
if the Englishwoman is asleep. And asleep she was; but a
slight noise which the door made when I tried to close it
woke her. She asked me if I had dined, I replied that if
she did not come to the table I did not care to dine, and
that I hoped that, after sleeping five hours, she felt better. She said very sweetly that she would come, and I
went out to order dinner served.

She ate little, but with a good appetite, astonished to
find two English dishes, and the pudding made with
good butter. She asked the innkeeper's wife if the cook
was English, and, when she answered that the cook was I,
she showed, though saying nothing, that she was overcome with gratitude. She became gay, she congratulated
me on my appetite, she drank when I did, but sparingly
and always doing justice to the excellent Montepulciano[7]
which the innkeeper gave us, as well as to the Montefiascone.[8] I was tipsy, and she was not, for she only sipped
while I emptied glasses. She spoke to me in the Italian
she had learned during the six months she had spent in
Florence; she told me that she had been born in London,
that she had learned French in school, and I thought I
should die for joy when, on my asking her if she knew
La Cornelys, she answered that she had known her
daughter Sophie at the school to which they had both
gone, but not her mother.

"Tell me if Sophie has grown tall."

"No. She's short, but very pretty, and full of talent."

"She must be seventeen years old [9] now."

"Yes, just my age."

With these words she stops, she lowers her eyes, and
she blushes.

"Do you feel ill?"

"Not at all; I'm afraid to tell you that Sophie is the
very image of you."

"Why should you be afraid? I've been told so more

than once. It's a coincidence. But it's been a long time since you saw Sophie, hasn't it?''

''A year and a half. She was going back to her mother's on Soho Square to be married, I heard; I don't remember to whom.''

''You have told me a very interesting piece of news, Madame.''

The innkeeper comes in with the bill, on which I see three paoli[10] which the rider had expended for himself and his horse.

''He told me,'' says the innkeeper, ''that you would pay.''

The English beauty blushes, I pay, and we leave. Her blushing gave me the greatest pleasure; it convinced me that she was not an accomplice in her husband's practices. I was dying to learn by what chance she had left London, how she could have become the wife of a Frenchman, how she had left Leghorn without luggage, what she was going to do in Rome; but I feared to embarrass her by asking her questions; for, if she had wanted to, she could have told me her story, at least in brief, when she told me that she had last seen Miss Cornelys a year and a half before. Having three hours to spend before we reached San Quirico, I got her to talk about my daughter Sophie. When she said that she had lived with Sophie for a whole year in the same school, I asked her if Miss Nancy Stein was still there. The reader may remember that she had dined with me, a charming child ten or eleven years old whom I had devoured with kisses and whose father had given my daughter a ring.[11]

On hearing Nancy's name she sighed, saying that she was there when she had entered the school, but that she had left seven or eight months later.

''Was she still pretty?''

''A perfect beauty; but beauty is often but a fatal gift of nature which only spurs men on to make the innocent possessor of it unhappy. In eight months Nancy became my intimate friend; we loved each other dearly; our sympathy perhaps arose from the fact that the same destiny was setting the same snares for us. Nancy, the tender, sincere Nancy, is perhaps unhappier than I am.''

''Why do you say unhappy? Can you complain of your destiny? Can you be unhappy with the beautiful letter of recommendation which nature has given you?''

''Alas, Monsieur! Let us talk of something else, I beg you.''

I see her emotion in her eyes. I silently pity her, and, becoming more and more interested in her, I lead her back to the subject of Miss Nancy.

''Should you consider yourself at liberty to tell me why you think Nancy may have become unhappy?''

''She went away with a young man with whom she had fallen in love, unable to hope that she could ever be his with her father's consent; and after that nothing was heard of her; you see that my love for her cannot but make me fear.''

''You are right. I feel that I would sacrifice myself for her if I found her in need of help.''

''Where did you meet her?''

''In my own house. She was only twelve years old. She dined there, and her father came there to eat oysters with her.''

''I know about that. He gave Miss Cornelys a pretty ring. Ah, Monsieur, it is you! If you knew how often I have heard Sophie talk about you! Nancy loved you as much as she loved her father. She congratulated Sophie on your fondness for her. I heard her say that you had gone to Russia, and that afterward you had fought a duel with a general in Poland. Is that true? Would that I could send my dear friend Sophie news of you! Alas, I cannot hope to do so now!''

''It is all true, Madame; but why can you not hope for so trifling a pleasure as sending news of yourself to anyone you please in England? I am most keenly interested in you; trust me, and you can send your news to anyone you choose."

"I am infinitely obliged to you."

After this expression of gratitude, she fell silent, and I left her to her thoughts. At seven o'clock we arrived in San Quirico, where the Count de l'Étoile came to the carriage and embraced his wife most joyfully and lovingly, giving her countless kisses in public; which made all the bystanders believe that she was his wife and that I must be her father; the alternative would have been that she was a trollop and I could only be her pi . . .[12] At this greeting from the Count I see the young Englishwoman looking very happy and satisfied and meeting all his ardor halfway; she does not reproach him, she goes upstairs with him, giving not the least sign that she remembers all the politeness I had shown her. I attribute it to love, to youth, and to a certain thoughtlessness; it was annoying, but, dismissing the thought, I go upstairs with my night bag. The innkeeper serves us immediately, for the coachman wanted to leave at three o'clock in the morning, in order to reach Radicofani[13] before the heat of the day began. It was a journey of six hours.

We sat down at table, and the supper was excellent; I had no doubt that it would be, for the Count, having arrived six hours before us, had given the innkeeper time enough to prepare it; but what astonished me and made me a little angry was that the young Englishwoman, who appeared to be more in love with him than he was with her, did not even mention me. It was not until the roast that she said that it was not as good as the sliced fillet of beef which she had eaten at dinner. The gaiety, the jests, the horseplay in which the young man saw fit to indulge at table cannot be described. The Englishwoman laughed at the top of her lungs, and I had to laugh too. For a moment I thought he might be a well-born, rich, undisciplined young officer, of the type who treats everything with that kind of levity and for whom nothing is important; I had known any number of such odd characters in Paris—intolerable and at the same time amusing, frivolous triflers yet sometimes dangerous, keeping their honor in their pockets, only to display it at a moment's notice and risk it as the whim took them. On this supposition, I was very ill pleased with myself, for I thought that the Frenchman, treating me too cavalierly, took me for an outright dupe and insulted me while perhaps thinking that he did me honor. Assuming that the Englishwoman was his wife, I saw myself being treated as a man of no consequence, and I did not want to play the role. Inferior though it was, it was obviously the role which everyone who saw me must attribute to me.

Clean sheets were brought, there were two beds, I told the innkeeper's wife to give me another room. The Count would not hear of it, and his insistence was polite, the lady saying nothing; but no less politely I obliged him to let me leave him and his wife together in perfect freedom. I had my bag taken into the next room, and I even bolted my door. I thought it odd that neither of my traveling companions had a night bag. I concluded that all their luggage must have been sent on to Rome. The little trunk must contain the few things they needed, and since they did not order it brought up they were hardy enough to do without it. I go quietly to bed, much less interested in the lady than I had been all day. The change pleased me.

I am waked before dawn by a servant bringing me a light; I dress quickly and, hearing that they are dressing in the other room, I open the door and, without going in, wish them good morning. A quarter of an hour later I hear quarreling in the courtyard. It was the Frenchman talking in broken Italian to the coachman; I open the window, and I see that it is serious. Though it was not yet light, I make out the coachman holding the Frenchman's horse by the bridle, which the Frenchman was trying to wrest from his hands. I guess what is the matter, for I had read the agreement; the driver wanted money,

and he was right. I surmise that the Frenchman has not a
copper; I expect to see them come up to my room; and I
prepare to do my duty without mercy. The Frenchman
enters first and says to me:

"This b . . . . .[14] doesn't understand me; however, he
may be right. Be so good as to give him two zecchini,
which I will return to you in Rome; as chance would
have it, I have run out of money; he has nothing to fear,
for he has my trunk; but he says he needs the money. Do
me the favor, Monsieur; in Rome you shall know better
who I am."

So saying, he goes downstairs; he does not trouble to
wait for my answer, the coachman does not follow him;
hardly believing my eyes, I see him mount his horse in
silk stockings and ride away. The lady was there before
me, looking nonplused, and the coachman neither moved
nor spoke. I sit down on the bed, drying my hands, and,
after considering the adventure, I surrender to the hy-
sterical laughter which overwhelms my entire imagination. I see the thing as so amusing, so new, so comical that
I cannot take it in all at once.

"Laugh, Madame, I beg you, for, despite my sympathy, your sadness is out of place; laugh, I say, or I
will not get up from this bed."

"It is laughable, but I have not the wit to laugh at it."

"At least sit down."

I give the coachman two zecchini, I tell him that no
harm will be done if we arrive a quarter of an hour later,
and that I want coffee. The Englishwoman's desolate
look wrung my heart.

"I understand," I said, "that you have good reason
to be sad, and I am even willing to put your sadness to
your credit; but I beg you to overcome it during our
journey, in which I promise you that I will deal with
every contingency. I ask you for only one favor, which I
very much need. If you refuse it, you will see me become
as sad as you are, and that will not be amusing."

"What favor can I do you?"

"Tell me on your honor as an Englishwoman if that strange individual is your husband or your lover."

"Very well. I will tell you the truth, and gladly. He will not be my husband until we reach Rome, but there he will be."

"I breathe again. He will not be your husband, and so much the better for you. I am sure that he has seduced you; I see that you are in love with him, but I hope you will get over it."

"That is impossible, unless he deceives me."

"He has already deceived you. I am sure he has told you he is rich, that he is well-born, that he will make you happy, and every word of it is false."

"How can you know it is false?"

"As I know a great many other things, which only experience of the world teaches. He is a lunatic, unprincipled, brazen, willful, who may perhaps even marry you; but it will only be to become your master and to use you to support himself."

"He loves me, and I cannot but be convinced of it."

"What convinces you is not love, my dear child, but caprice and libertinism. You see that he does not know me, and he leaves you in my care. Do you think that a true lover can thus abandon the woman he loves?"

"He is not jealous; Frenchmen are not, you know."

"A Frenchman who is a man of honor is no different from an Englishman, an Italian, and a man of any other nationality. Do you think that if he loved you he would have left you without a copper at the mercy of a man who might have threatened to abandon you in the street or have demanded favors from you which would horrify you? What would you do at this moment if I were such a brute? You understand my meaning. Answer me, you are not in danger."

"I would defend myself."

"Very well. I would leave you here at the inn. What

would you do here? Learn that, though you are very
pretty, and though you have refined feelings, there are
men who, pretty as you are, would have nothing to do
with you unless you sacrificed your feelings to them, and
who, if you continued to act like a woman whose feelings
entitle her to respect, would not give you a scudo. The man
whom it is your misfortune to love did not know me, and
he exposed you to wretchedness and shame. That will not
happen, for I am the man you needed; but permit me to
tell you that it is something of a miracle. Do you now
think the fellow loves you? He is a monster. I am most
sorry to see you crying, or rather, to have made you cry;
but it was necessary, and I do not repent of having been
cruel, for the way I shall treat you will justify me. Know
that I find you exceedingly attractive, and that I am concerned for you only because you inspire me with the most
ardent desires; but know too that I will not ask you for
one kiss, and that even in Rome I will not abandon you;
but before we get to Rome I will convince you that the
Count not only does not love you but is a scoundrel."

"You will convince me of that?"

"Yes, I give you my word of honor for it. But dry
your tears, and let us try to spend the day as we did
yesterday. You cannot imagine how glad I am that you
have fallen to my charge. It is of my friendship that I
want to convince you; if love does not follow, I shall bear
it patiently."

The innkeeper brought me the bill for the whole supper, as I expected he would do; but I paid without once
looking at the lovelorn girl, I even feared I had said too
much to her. Too strong a dose of medicine, instead of
curing her, might do her harm. I was dying to learn her
story, and I flattered myself that I should manage to do
so before we reached Rome. We set off, and we did not
speak a word until we came to the inn at La Scala,[15]
where we got out.

I thought I should do well to hire two post horses, be-

cause going from La Scala to Radicofani with the coachman's horses would take four hours, whereas with post
horses it could be done in two. So I told the coachman
to go on and wait for us there, and I ordered the post
horses for ten o'clock. It was only six o'clock, and I much
preferred spending four hours where I was to leaving at
once, for I should have overtaken the libertine who had
deceived the poor girl. The arrangement greatly pleased
the coachman, who saw himself relieved of the effort of
dragging his carriage over the mountain and his purse
spared the cost of a third horse.[16] The young Englishwoman broke the silence to say that, since I had decided
to travel post, it would be better to do so at once, for
from ten o'clock to noon the heat would be intense.

"That is true," I said, "but Count de l'Étoile, whom
we should certainly find at Radicofani, would not be glad
to see me."

"Why so? On the contrary."

A feeling of pity kept me from answering her, for the
reason I should have given her would have made her shed
more tears. I considered the girl's love literally a sickness
which blinded her intelligence; it did not let her see her
seducer in his true role of her destroyer, and she hastened
to her ruin because she had not strength enough to deny
her instinct. To cure her, I could not use the gentle eloquence which persuades; I needed the harsh reasoning
which convinces; it was a tooth which I could not extract
except with the tongs, feeling no pity for her pain and
disregarding the tears it would make her shed. But was
what impelled me to act in this way virtue? Was it love
for the innocent beauty whom I had before my eyes and
whose grief pierced my soul? All that entered in; but
since it was more than clear that if I had found her ugly
and sullen I might well have left her to die of starvation,
it followed that my efforts were only for myself. So farewell virtue! She was a delicate morsel which I wanted
to snatch from another in order to gobble it down myself;

but I did not tell myself so; when I suspected it, I turned my thoughts elsewhere; in all sincerity I was playing a false role, which I could not play well except by imagining that I was not playing it.

After the coachman left, I invited the Englishwoman to take a walk in a countryside than which poetry can invent none more beautiful. Betty (such was her name) tried to persuade me that the English countryside would be still more beautiful if the grape grew there, and to distract her I pretended to yield to her arguments, the charm of which ravished my soul. She spoke the Florentine language with the oddities and the faults which come from too much stress, which, combined with her English accent, treated my ear to a music which filled me with delight. I languished, seeing her parted lips which I dared not kiss; for that was the goal of it all. Love which wants to praise knows no other language.

We had walked for two hours when, hearing all the bells of the church pealing and seeing the people going there, Betty told me that she had never seen a Catholic service, and I was delighted to give her the pleasure. It was a feast day. She attended the high mass with perfect modesty, doing whatever she saw the others do; no one would have supposed that she was English. Leaving the church, she said that our rite was much more fit to prosper, and to make religion loved, than the English one, and she thought that the English peasant girls were nothing in comparison with those she had just seen, their elaborate attire having surprised her. She asked me what time it was, and, when I thoughtlessly said that I was surprised she did not have a watch, she replied with a blush that the Count had asked her for it to leave as a pledge with the innkeeper who had given him the horse. I at once repented of having asked her such a tactless question, for her blush could only come from a painful feeling of shame. Betty knew that she was guilty, and she was incapable of lying.

We left with three horses at exactly ten o'clock, and a breeze which tempered the heat allowed us to arrive at Radicofani at noon very well satisfied with our journey. The innkeeper, who was at the same time the post master, at once asked me if I would pay the three paoli which he was owed by the Frenchman who had passed through, who had eaten and drunk, and who had paid nothing. As soon as I told him that I would pay I saw that he was less uneasy; but that was not all.

"The gentleman," he said, "beat three postilions with his naked sword, and one of them, who was wounded in the face, has already followed him, and it will cost him dear. He beat them because they tried to keep him from leaving without paying me and without paying at the stable for the oats his horse ate."

"You were wrong to try to use force with him, for he does not look like a thief, and you should have believed that I would pay you when I arrived."

"You are mistaken. There was no need for me to believe it. I have been cheated that way countless times in my life. If you want to dine, your table is laid for you. If your coachman had arrived a quarter of an hour earlier, all would have been well."

I saw that Betty was in despair. Her whole soul appeared in her face, and her silence made me respect her. Far from taking her to task for her lover's vagaries, I tried to amuse her by light talk, and I urged her to dine well and to cheer her soul with the excellent muscat of which the innkeeper brought us a large flagon. But my efforts to cure her despondency would have been vain if I had not summoned the coachman and told him that I wanted to leave as soon as we had finished dinner.

"We shall only go as far as Centino," [17] he answered, "and we'll be there in two hours. Let us wait till it is cooler."

"Certainly not. The Signora's husband may need help.

The wounded postilion has followed him, and God knows
what may happen to him."

"Very well, we will leave."

Betty looked at me, with her face the picture of gratitude, and to give me a token of it she pretended to be
very hungry. She had already learned that it was a way
to thank me. While we dined, I have one of the postilions
he had beaten come up and tell me the story. The scoundrel was a braggart; he admitted that the Count had
beaten him with the flat of his sword, but he boasted that
he had thrown a stone at him which must have hurt him;
I gave him a paolo, and I promised him a scudo if he
would go to Centino to testify against his fellow postilion, and he undertook to do so. He instantly began argu-
ing on the Count's side, which made Betty laugh. He said
that the wound on his face was only a scratch, and that
in any case he had asked for it, for he should not have
resisted him. By way of consolation, he assured us that
the Frenchman had been hit three or four times by
stones, which did not console Betty. I saw that the thing
was turning into a comedy, and that nothing would come
of it. The postilion, now a partisan of the Count, left at
once, and we followed him a half hour later.

But Betty was very much disappointed when, arriving
in Centino, we found that the Count had gone on to
Acquapendente,[18] that the wounded postilion had followed him, and the postilion who was on our side had
gone there too. It was no use my telling Betty that there
was nothing to fear, that the Count was no fool and
would know how to defend himself, and the more so
because his having been stoned proved that he had acted
only in self-defense; Betty did not answer me, and I saw
that she was in despair. Perhaps she was afraid that,
since she would have to spend the night alone with me, I
would demand some recompense for the money and the
effort I was expending on her. I think, I calculate, I see
the truth. I ask Betty if she wants us to go on to Acqua-

pendente at once. At my question her brow clears, she opens her arms, and I embrace her.

Ah, nature! I do not stop to consider from what source the kiss I had received had come; I rise, I call the coachman, who had already put his horses in the stable, and I tell him that I want to go to Acquapendente at once. He rudely answers that I am free to go there by post, but that he will not leave.

"Very well. Order two horses at once."

It was at that moment that Betty, overcome with gratitude, and seeing herself so well paid for a mere kiss, would, I believe, have granted me all that I could have asked, for she fell into my arms. I laughed, enjoying her joy, and, assuring her that I could have no will but hers, I did no more than cover her lips and eyes with kisses. She seemed to esteem me the more for my moderation. The horses were already harnessed to the carriage, and, after paying the innkeeper for the supper which he said he had prepared, we set off. The coachman told us that he would be at Acquapendente too at eight o'clock, for we must leave at daybreak the next morning in order to dine at Montefiascone.[19]

It took us only three quarters of an hour to reach Acquapendente, where we found the wild Count, who gaily and happily embraced the unfortunate Betty, who I saw was in ecstasies to find him safe and sound. He at once told us triumphantly that he had given all the scoundrels in Radicofani a thrashing, while he himself had only been hit by a few stones, from which he had adroitly protected his head.

"But where," I asked him, "is the wounded postilion?"

"Drinking my health with the other one; they all asked me to forgive them."

"At the price of a scudo," Betty said to him.

"A scudo? You shouldn't have given it to them. They'll let themselves be beaten all over again."

Before supper he showed us the bruises on his thighs and the sides of his chest; the young scoundrel was a very handsome man. Betty's adoring manner vexed me; but I put up with it the more willingly after the tokens she had given me of the power which gratitude had over her. At supper he talked and acted as wildly as he had the evening before; he insisted that I should not go to bed in another room; but I did so. I clearly saw that I should have embarrassed Betty, who was not yet hardened to the libertine freedom into which the wretch wanted to initiate her.

The next morning the Count told me he would order us a good supper at Viterbo,[20] and that it would be well if I lent him a zecchino so that he could pay for his dinner at Montefiascone. He offhandedly showed me a bill of exchange for three thousand écus which he had in a portfolio. I said that I was convinced of it without reading it.

Betty, after seeing that, despite the tears I had made her shed, she could count on my doing as she wished, had begun to treat me on a footing of friendship. She talked more openly, and she had almost granted me the right to question her freely, reserving to herself that of correcting my mistaken conjectures.

"You see," she said to me at Montefiascone, "that it is only by chance or from thoughtlessness that my lover is without money, for he has a big bill of exchange."

"I believe it is forged."

"That is spiteful."

"I judge it from his behavior. Twenty years ago I should have thought it genuine. If his bill of exchange is on Rome, why did he not discount it in Siena, in Florence, in Leghorn?"

"Perhaps he did not have time enough. He was in a hurry to leave. Oh, if only you knew all!"

"I do not want to know anything, my dear Betty, but what you are pleased to tell me; but in the meanwhile I will tell you that all the things I have said to you are

neither suspicions nor conjectures, but truths which follow from all that I have seen.''

"You persist in the idea that he does not love me.''

"He loves you only in a way to deserve your hatred.''

"How can that be?''

"Would you not hate a man who would keep you only
in order to live by your charms?''

"I resent your believing that.''

"I can convince you of it this evening at Viterbo, if
you are willing.''

"I beg you to convince me, but with positive proof. It
will hurt me to the quick, but I shall be obliged to you.''

"And when you are convinced, do you think you will
stop loving him?''

"Certainly, for I fell in love with him only because I
think him honest.''

"You are mistaken. You will still love him when you
have found that he is a scoundrel, for the fellow has
turned your head; he has deprived you of the ability to
reason. But for that, you would see as clearly as I do.''

"What you tell me is more than unlikely, but it may be
true. Show me beyond doubt that he does not love me,
and then it will be for me to convince you that I shall be
able to despise him.''

"You shall see proof this evening; but tell me if you
have known him long.''

"About a month. But we have been together only five
days.''

"And before those five days had you granted him your
favors?''

"Not even a kiss. He spent every night under my
windows, and during the day I never looked out of them
into the street without seeing him pass by. Do you think
it likely that a young man who does that can be only
pretending to love?''

"I admit, my dear Betty, that he loved you, but in the
way I have already told you—to make his fortune at the

cost of your happiness; and perhaps without even being aware of it, for it is possible that the fellow thinks that prostituting yourself would not make you unhappy.''

''How can you assume that a man whom, after all, you do not know, is such a villain?''

''Would to God that I did not know him! I am sure that, unable to enter your house, he persuaded you to run away with him.''

''That is true. He wrote to me, and I will show you his letter. He is to marry me in Rome.''

''And who vouches to you for his constancy?''

''His love.''

''Are you afraid you may be followed?''

''No.''

''Did he take you from a father, a lover, a brother?''

''From a lover, who will not return to Leghorn for a week or ten days, who has gone to London on business, and who left me with a reliable woman who, though she had no authority over me, would never have let me receive visits from a new lover.''

''Now I see and know everything. I am most sorry for you. Tell me if you loved the Englishman who is to return to Leghorn and if he was worthy to possess you.''

''Alas! I loved him alone until the moment when, after he left, I was in Boboli[21] and saw this Frenchman, who, for good or for ill, made me become unfaithful to a man who adored me and who will be in despair when he does not find me.''

''Is he rich?''

''Not very, but he is well enough off; he is a merchant.''

''Is he young?''

''No. He is your age, a kind, honest man who was only waiting for the death of his wife in order to marry me and take me back to London; and his wife, who is consumptive, may be dead now.''

"How sorry I am for him! Have you given him a child?"

"No. But I must say that God had not destined him for me, for Monsieur de l'Étoile has conquered me irresistibly; he has positively taken possession of my will."

"That is what everyone thinks who has been led astray by love."

"Now you know all, and I am not sorry to have hidden nothing from you, for twice yesterday I found that you were truly my friend."

"My dear Betty, you will find me so in the future too, and you will need me very much; and I give you my word of honor that I will not abandon you. I love you, I have told you so, and I repeat it; nevertheless, so long as you love this Frenchman you will not find me asking to be anything to you but a true friend."

"Very well, I accept your assurance and I promise that I will never hide anything from you."

"Tell me why you didn't bring even a little luggage with you."

"I escaped on horseback, but my trunk, filled with dresses and shifts, will be in Rome two or three days after we get there, together with the Count's. I had it taken from my house the day before I left, and the man who received it, and whom I knew, had his instructions directly from him."

"Good-by to your trunk!"

"Oh, my dear friend, you foresee only evils!"

"It will be enough for me, my dear Betty, if my foresight does not have the power to make them arrive. I shall be happy if I am mistaken. But despite your having come as far as Siena on horseback, it seems to me that you should have worn a cloak and have a few things in a night bag."

"All that is in the small trunk, which I will have brought up this evening."

After dining well, we slept until four o'clock, and at seven we arrived at Viterbo, where we found the Count in high spirits, and where I was to convince Betty that he did not love her as she believed he did. To that end, I began to put on a show of being enchanted by Betty, to congratulate myself in exaggerated terms on my good fortune in having met her, and him on his possessing such a treasure, and him again on his heroism, which even rose above any fear that leaving her in the company of another man might lead to her breaking her conjugal vows. The harebrained fellow thereupon began to go even further than I had done in my praise of him; he said that jealousy was so little in his nature that he could not conceive either how a man who truly loved a woman could be jealous of her or how he could love her constantly unless he saw her inspiring desires in all the men who came near her. He began a dissertation on the subject, and I let him talk on as he pleased, never contradicting even one of his statements. Satisfied with what I had thus learned about my man, I saved the second part of my plan for after supper, for that would be the opportunity I must seize to bring it off.

At supper I got him to drink a great deal, I constantly made remarks which would encourage him to declare his libertine principles, always praising the strength of mind it took to trample on all prejudices; and it was at dessert that I returned to the subject of love and of the various perfections it must have in order to make two lovers truly happy. He laid it down that two perfect lovers must above all do everything possible to further each other's wishes.

"Betty, who loves me," he said, "must procure me Fanny's favors if she discovers that I have a liking for her, and I, who love Betty, must procure her the pleasure of sleeping with you if I find that she loves you."

Betty listened to her lover's extravagances in the utmost astonishment, staring at him and never saying a word.

"I admit, my dear Count," I said, "that your principle is sublime and that it appears to be the only one which could establish perfect happiness on earth, but it is chimerical. All the beautiful and lofty things you have said to me are superb in theory, but impossible and ridiculous in practice. I believe you have great courage, but I do not believe you have enough of it to put up calmly with the certainty that another man was enjoying your mistress's charms. I wager twenty-five zecchini—here they are—that you would not let your wife sleep with me."

"Permit me to laugh. I wager fifty that I have the strength of mind to be present at the performance. Meanwhile I accept your wager. Betty, my dear Betty, let us punish this skeptic; be so good as to go to bed with him."

"You are joking."

"No. Please do as I say. I will only love you the more."

"I think you are mad. I will never go to bed with anyone but you."

At that, the Count took her in his arms and, with the fondest caresses and the most sophistical arguments, tried to persuade her to do him the favor, not so much for the twenty-five zecchini as to prove to an Italian, in my person, how far the daring of such a Frenchman as he could go. He talked to her for half an hour, giving her, in my presence, caresses which she modestly repulsed, for she thought them improper; but Betty, still gently refusing his importunities, told him that he had already won the wager (and perhaps she was right); giving him the fondest kisses, she begged him to stop trying to persuade her to do what she would never do, even under the threat of death. The beast suddenly loses patience, pushes her away, begins to rage, calls her a f . . . . . . fool, treats her to the vilest insults for a quarter of an hour, and ends by telling her that her reluctance was mere hypocrisy, for he was sure that during these three days she had already granted me all that a wh . . .[22] of her sort could grant me.

At these words, seeing Betty trembling, I spring for my sword to run it through his body, but the scoundrel makes off into the next room and locks the door. In despair at having been the cause of the pitiful state in which I saw the charming innocent, I go to her to try to soothe her distress. She was shaking all over, her throat was swollen, her chin trembled, but her staring eyes could not shed the tears which would have relieved her heart. Everyone was asleep in the inn, I had water, and I knew nothing else to do but to bathe her temples and say to her all that I thought could possibly comfort her. She looked at me, she answered nothing, now and again she gave a deep sigh, she seemed to need to cry, but she could not. After an hour of this despair, her eyelids closed, and she sank into sleep, refusing to lie down on the bed despite my urging. So I spent two full hours beside her, watching her sleep, hoping that when she woke she would not be forced to remain at the inn either by the fever which might overtake her, or by convulsions, or by any of the natural infirmities which I feared in the state in which I saw her.

At daybreak I heard her tyrant leave, and I was very glad of it. Betty came out of her lethargy when the inn servant knocked at the door to tell us it was time to dress. He thought we had gone to bed. I asked her if she was able to leave, and she replied that she felt well and only begged me to have tea made for her, taking a sufficient quantity of it from an ivory box which she had in her pocket. I left her there in order to go and make the tea myself, but it proved to be a hard nut to crack. Going upstairs again, I found her in the other room, where she had opened the windows to breathe the air while she watched the sun rising above the horizon. I saw that she was calm, and I thought I could hope that I had cured her. She drank three or four cups of tea, which restored to her face the freshness of which the terrible night she had spent had robbed it. Hearing someone in the next room, in which we had supped, she broke her silence to ask me if I had taken my purse, which I had left on the table. I had forgotten it when I had offered to wager the madman twenty-five zecchini. I also found there a paper, which I at once unfolded. I read a bill of exchange for three thousand écus. The impostor had taken it from his pocket to match my stake; I read it through and I find that it was issued in Bordeaux and drawn on a wine merchant in Paris to the order of a name which was also written on the back of the bill to make it over to Count de l'Étoile. It was at sight, and it was dated six months earlier. Nothing could be more irregular. I take it to Betty, who replies that she knows nothing about it, and who begs me in God's name not to mention the man to her again.

"For pity's sake," she said, "take care of an unfortunate girl who until now has known none but honest people."

I again vowed that I would never abandon her, and we left.

Exhausted by her grief, poor Betty fell asleep, and I did the same. We both woke very much surprised when the coachman told us we were at Monterosi.[23] He had driven for six hours, making eighteen miles without our once waking. We were to rest until four o'clock, and we were very glad of it, for we had to decide on a course. I at once inquired if the wretch had passed through, and I was told that he had said he would spend the night at La Storta.[24] He had eaten and he had paid. I told all this to Betty, who was looking well, which filled me with joy.

After dining with a fairly good appetite, it was she who said to me that we must again discuss the wretch who had brought her to the verge of ruin.

"Be a father to me," she said, "and do not advise me

but command me. I will do exactly what you tell me to do. You have guessed a great deal, and perhaps everything, except that I shall continue to love the cutthroat even after discovering his black character. I can assure you that he fills me with horror.''

''Can you count on your first lover's forgiving you?''

''I think so.''

''Then we must go back to Leghorn. Tell me if you think it sound advice, if it pleases you, and if you feel prepared to follow it. I warn you that if you adopt it, it must be put into execution immediately. Young, pretty, and the honest girl I have seen you to be, you must not suppose that I would consider letting you go alone, or in company with people for whom I could not vouch as for myself. No, my poor Betty, I love you dearly, and the proof which I owe you of the love you have inspired in me is to take you to Leghorn myself. If doing that will convince you that I love you, and that I am not unworthy of your esteem, I am happy, and I ask you for nothing more as my reward. I will live with you like a father with his daughter, if you are reluctant to give me tokens of a stronger feeling which does not come from your heart. Be sure of my good faith. It is my duty to teach you that there are men in the world as honest as the young libertine who seduced you is depraved.''

After my short discourse Betty remained for a good quarter of an hour with her elbows on the table and her head resting on her hands, staring at me fixedly without saying a word. She looked neither sad nor surprised; I was very glad to see her waiting to give me her answer until she was ready to give me a final one. Here is what she said to me:

''Do not think, my dear friend, that my silence arises from an irresolution which would make me contemptible to myself; believe me, it does not. I have judgment enough to recognize both the wisdom of your advice and the beauty of its source. I adopt it; and I consider it a

great blessing of Providence that I have had the good fortune to have fallen into the hands of a man of your character, and to have inspired in you a concern for me
which leads you to do everything for me that you could
do to help a dear daughter for whom you felt a father's
affection. So let us go back to Leghorn, and let us leave
at once. What has kept me in doubt, and still does so, is
how I am to go about making sure that Sir B. M.[25] will
forgive me. I am certain that he will forgive me, but the
way to it is difficult; for, though gentle, affectionate, and
in love, being very delicate on the point of honor, he is
apt to yield to the violence which is the first impulse of a
pure soul which finds itself outraged. The thing is to
avoid that fatal moment, for he might kill me and he
would kill himself afterward. You must think it over on
the way, and tell me what you consider the best course. I
should tell you that he is highly intelligent and that he
will not be taken in by any lie. I think he should be informed of the whole story in a letter, without concealing
the slightest detail, for disguising the truth angers him;
and when he thinks it is being concealed from him he becomes furious. If you are thinking of writing him, you
must take care not to tell him that I deserve his forgiveness, for he must be left to decide if I deserve it or not.
He will judge of my repentance by the letter I will write
him in English, in which he will see my soul and my
tears; but he must under no circumstances know where I
shall remain in hiding until he writes me that he has forgiven me; after that there will be nothing to fear from
him. The slave of his word, noble, and honest, he will live
with me another fifty years; but he will never reproach
me for my folly. He is a generous soul. Alas for me! How
can I have failed him as badly as I have done!''

"Be so good as to tell me if you ever failed him
before.''

"Never, my dear friend; but I know his whole history.
His first wife caused him great unhappiness, he fought

Madame Sarah Goudar

Grape Harvest near Sorrento

two duels in the Antilles, where he was serving in the army; then he married again; but weighty reasons made him separate from his wife. I made his acquaintance two years ago at our boarding school, which he visited with Nancy's friend. My father having died then, and his creditors having seized all his possessions, I had to leave the school, since I could not pay what it cost, and Nancy, Sophie, and all the other girls were distressed, for everyone liked me. Sir B. M. undertook to provide for me and settled a small income on me, enough to save me from poverty for the rest of my life. Gratitude made me fall in love with him. It was I who asked him to take me with him when I learned that he had decided to leave England for some time; my request surprised him; like the honest gentleman he is, he told me that he loved me too much to take me with him and expect it of himself that he would treat me as if I were his daughter. He thought it impossible that I loved him as one loves a lover. You see that his declaration, instead of raising difficulties, removed them. I told him that, in whatever way he loved me, I could only be happy, and thereupon he gave me a written undertaking that he would marry me as soon as the laws would allow him to do so. I never failed in my duty to him.''

''Yes, charming Betty, he will forgive you; dry your tears and let us leave. I have friends in Leghorn, and no one can know that I have made your acquaintance. I will put you in safe and honorable hands, where you shall want for nothing, and where I will never go to see you. I promise you that I will not leave Leghorn until I see you restored to the arms of Sir B. M., whom I already love, and, if it turns out that Sir B. M. is inexorable and refuses to forgive you, I promise I will never forsake you and will even take you to England if you command me to do so.''

''How can you abandon your occupations for me in this way?''

"I will not lie to you, my dear Betty, to make it appear that I am more than I am. Nothing summons me to Rome except my wanting to see again the beautiful things that are to be seen there. That is not an occupation; but saving you from ruin is one."

"Then what am I to do for you?"

I called the coachman and told him that I absolutely must go back to Viterbo, where I had left my portfolio on the bed.

"Send a postilion for it."

"I cannot trust one. If he makes off with my portfolio, I am ruined."

"Take post horses, and I will wait here; but you must pay me for the day."

"Here is a zecchino. Order post horses at once; but follow us slowly with your own horses, for we shall leave again early tomorrow morning."

The zecchino instantly persuaded him, the horses were harnessed at once, and at seven o'clock we arrived in Viterbo, where I pretended to be in despair over not finding my portfolio. The maid swore that no one but she had entered the room. I calmly ordered supper, making Betty understand that I must act as I was doing in order to keep the coachman from protesting against taking her back to Siena, since he could consider that she had been put in his charge by her husband. At ten o'clock he arrived with his horses, and he brought up the small trunk as soon as she asked for it. I easily forced open the little padlock which was on the end of a chain, and Betty took out her cloak and a package in which she had four shifts, stockings, handkerchiefs, and nightcaps. The other things belonged to the villain; but I was too curious not to look at his possessions. Perhaps it was all that he owned in the world.

We found old breeches, old stockings, five or six torn shirts, a powder bag in which there were combs and pomade, and eighteen or twenty part-books, all either comedies or comic operas. There was also a packet of letters, which promised to be very interesting, and which Betty said she would read with me. The first notable thing we found was that all the letters were addressed to "Monsieur l'Étoile, Actor," well known in Marseilles, Montpellier, Toulouse, Bayonne, and several other cities in southern France. I pitied Betty. She could not laugh. She saw that she had been duped by a base actor, and her shame over it was bitter. I told her we would read the letters the next day, and she breathed again.

"Be so good," she said, "as to go out until I can get into bed, for at last I can change my shift."

"Whatever you please, my angel, and if you like I will have a bed made in the other room."

"No, my friend, I cannot but love and cherish your company; you have convinced me of your friendship only too well. Without you, what would have become of me?"

I did not come back until she was in bed, and, having gone to her, kissed her, sat down on the bed, and seen that she was not alarmed, I thought she might forgive me if, doing justice to her charms, I tried to satisfy the desires they inspired in me. Either from fear of seeming unjust, or because she felt what she made me feel, Betty showed herself amenable. On discovering this, I asked her if she would make my happiness complete by allowing me to undress.

"Will you still love me afterward?"

A charming answer when it comes from the heart, and whose falsity is apparent when it comes only from the mind. She offered so little resistance to my perfect happiness that she gave me reason to conclude I was making her happy too. Since Doña Ignacia, I had enjoyed only imperfect pleasures, for I had never seen them shared; but Betty gave me a proof of love which left me in no doubt. She sweetly opposed me when she suspected that I wanted to spare her. We had scarcely fallen asleep before the inn servant knocked at our door.

I dressed to talk to the coachman, who thought he was to take us to Rome, whereas we wanted to go back to Siena.

"Listen," I said, "I absolutely must recover my portfolio, and I feel certain that I shall find it at Acquapendente."

"I guessed it, by God! Pay me for the journey as if I had taken you to Rome, and then give me a zecchino a day, and I'll take you to England if you like."

"You have your wits about you, my lad; I will give you six zecchini now, and you shall give me a receipt; and tonight at Acquapendente I will give you another, and I will do the same every evening."

Ink and writing desk were at hand, the thing was done at once. I told him that I wanted to stop in Montefiascone, where I had business; and we arrived there at seven o'clock. The business was the letter I wanted to write to Sir B. M., in which I was to prepare him to forgive Betty by telling him all her unhappy story. Betty sat down to write him in English. I had already decided to lodge her with the Corsican Rivarola,[26] of whose intelligence I had had proof, and who had a beautiful and discreet woman staying in his house. Betty had acquired a look of satisfaction and assurance which delighted me; she told me again and again that she no longer feared anything, and she laughed when she thought of the deceiver who would vainly wait for us in Rome. She hoped that we would meet the carriage which was carrying her big trunk and that we could easily recover it; and when I said that he might pursue us, she maintained that he would not dare, and I agreed with her. In any case, I was prepared to give him a reception which would make him tremble, for there was no question of my doing him the honor to let him draw his sword. I had excellent pistols, ready to give

him the treatment he deserved. Before I began my letter,
Betty repeated her warning to tell him the whole truth.

"Always excepting the reward which you have granted
my fervent friendship."

"Alas! It is the one thing which he must not know."

In less than three hours we had finished writing, and
Betty was very well satisfied with my letter. But Betty's
was a masterpiece; it could not fail. I was thinking of
taking post horses as soon as I got to Siena, in order the
sooner to put her in a safe place before her lover arrived.
The only difficulty was the mad actor's bill of exchange,
which, whether genuine or forged, I must try to find a
way to return to him—but how to go about it? We left
immediately after dinner, despite the heat, and we arrived at Acquapendente just as day was giving place to
a night which we spent in the delights of love, which is
always innocent when it is sincere and disinterested. In
the morning I learned that a coach from Leghorn, bound
for Rome, was about to leave, and Betty guessed that it
was the one on which her trunk and the actor L'Étoile's
must be. She went downstairs with me, and she recognized it at once. She talked to the coachman much better
than I could have done to persuade him to let her have it;
but he was not to be moved, and, since the arguments he
used were excellent, she had to give in. The only thing she
did, with the help of a notary of the city, was to se-
questrate the trunk at the Roman customs office for a
month, which would give her time to prove her right to
prevent its being delivered to anyone who might come to
get it. The notary had the order of sequestration legalized
by the city magistrate, and the driver had to accept it and
give a receipt for it. He also assured us that he had not
received any other trunk from the same sender, which
convinced us that the actor was a beggar whose only
possessions were those we had seen in the small trunk.

After this achievement, Betty became perfectly charming. She saw herself able to make amends for all the

wrongs which her misguided love had made her commit.
I congratulated her on so quickly being cured of a passion
which had completely deprived her of her reason. She
shuddered when she recollected the monster. However,
she told me that she would not have come to her senses
and been convinced that he did not love her, if the wretch
had not finally told her that she was a mere hypocrite and
that he was sure she had granted me everything that such
a wench as she could not have refused me.

"It was then," she said, "that I saw the monster in all
his ugliness, and that I expected to see him fall, run
through by your sword. I would have helped you to
pierce his heart, if that had been necessary. So he did
well to take to his heels. But it's better that it did not
happen, for now we should be in a most grievous quan-
dary. I am sure that the scoundrel won't dare to show his
face again, either to you or to me."

We arrived in Radicofani about ten o'clock, and we
busied ourselves adding to the letters which were to make
Sir B. M. see reason. We were at the same table, Betty on
one side, facing the door, which was shut, and I on the
other side, with my back to the door and so close to it
that anyone who opened it to come in could see me only
by looking around it. Betty was fully dressed and very
modestly; but I, having taken off my coat, was in shirt-
sleeves—the heat was torrid. However, at that season I
could have been as I was in the presence of the most
respectable of women.

I hear heavy steps in the hall, my door is opened, and
the man who comes bursting in, seeing Betty, says:

"*There you are!*"

But I do not give him time to turn and see me. I take
him around the chest, pinning his arms, just at the moment when, seeing me, he would have fired the pistol in
his right hand at me. As I spring on him, the impact
shuts the door, and just as he was shouting to me, "*Let
me go, traitor!*" and struggling to free himself, Betty fell

on her knees before him, saying, *"You are wrong, he is my savior!"*

But Sir B. M., whose fury deprived him of both hearing and reason, kept saying, *"Let me go, traitor!"* and struggling, while, as long as he still held the pistol, I would have died before I would let him go. Trying to escape from my arms by force, he fell, and, naturally, I fell on top of him. Outside there was a noise of people trying to get in, but they could not, for we had fallen in front of the door. Betty bravely snatched the pistol from his hand, whereupon, seeing that his other hand was empty, I let him go, saying, *"You are wrong,"* while Betty kept repeating, *"He is my savior, calm yourself, listen."*

"What do you mean by 'your savior'?"

At that Betty takes the letter which I had in front of me, hands it to him, tells him to read it, and the Englishman, without getting up, begins to read. At that, sure of the outcome, I get up, I open the door, I tell the innkeeper to serve dinner for three and to leave and take his people with him.

CHAPTER IX

Rome. The perfidious actor punished. Lord Baltimore. Naples. Sarah Goudar. Betty's departure. Agata. La Callimena. Medini. Albergoni. Miss Chudleigh, Duchess of Kingston. The Prince of Francavilla. The swimmers.

FALLING DOWN with the Englishman, I had struck my left hand so violently against the leg of the table that I had made a deep cut on the back of it at the joint of my fourth finger. Blood was coming out as if the vein had been opened by a surgeon. Miss Betty helped me to wrap up my hand in a handkerchief and tie it very tightly, while Sir B. M. read my letter with the utmost attention. The girl's confidence that her lover would come back to his senses pleased me greatly. I took my night bag and my coat and went to the next room to change my shirt and get dressed. I was the happiest of men, seeing that the thing had taken a turn which left me with nothing to fear for Betty. I was not at all vexed to find myself at the end of an amour whose sweets I had only begun to taste. My certainty that I had given her back a happiness which she had lost made up to me for all the distress I knew I should suffer from leaving her.

I had already been dressed for half an hour, and I

still heard her talking forcefully to her lover, who answered her at intervals; they were speaking English, and I did not understand what they were saying, but their dialogue was calm. I thought I should not go in. After a long silence, he knocked lightly on my door, he came in, looking sad and mortified, and saying magnanimously that he clearly saw I had saved Betty, and, what was more, had cured her of her aberration.

"I could not guess," he said, "that the man I should find with her would be her savior, nor that the carriage which I saw here, and in which I was told that a young lady and a man had arrived, had come from Rome. If I had been told that, I would not even have come upstairs. I come up, I see Betty, I have no more doubts, you very sensibly catch hold of me, for, if you had delayed even an instant, my seeing you and killing you would have been simultaneous. And now I should be the unhappiest man alive. God be praised that you were not sitting where Betty was. Be my friend, Monsieur, and forgive me for my mistake."

At that I embraced him cordially, assuring him that what he had done was exactly what I should have done myself in his place. We went back to the other room, where Betty was sitting beside the bed in tears. We remained there for more than a quarter of an hour, saying nothing, while Sir B. M. carefully read my long letter over again. Since my hand was still bleeding, I sent for a surgeon, who, to stop the flow of blood, had to put on a compress and a bandage and make a sling from two handkerchiefs. The cut had severed the vein, but there was no danger. Betty continuing to weep, I took the liberty of telling Sir B. M. that she fully deserved his forgiveness.

"What, Monsieur! Do you think I have not forgiven her already? I should be the most savage of men if I did not know that she deserved it. My poor Betty! She saw her error as soon as you convinced her of the truth. I am sure that her tears have their source in nothing but the grief she feels at having had the weakness to commit a crime for which she cannot forgive herself. In three or four days you cannot have learned to know her as I know her.''

At these words she sprang up and, clasping the angelic man to her bosom, gave way so completely to her emotion that I have never seen repentance shed such a flood of tears. Sir B. M. could not hold back his, and at that I gave in and let mine flow, though I could not keep from varying them from time to time with a little laugh when the happy ending to the tragedy rejoiced my soul. Sir B. M. pleased me when, analyzing our situation, he declared that our tears, since they sprang solely from virtue, could not but be closely allied to laughter. He laughed when he saw his coat all stained with blood. It was of pekin,[1] and he at once sent it to be washed. We sat down to the table where, Sir B. M.'s caresses having calmed his mistress, she ate and pleased her lover by drinking all the muscat he pressed on her. As he was no longer in a hurry, he said that we might as well stay in Radicofani until the next day, for, having ridden fifteen stages at a gallop, he was exhausted. He had arrived in Leghorn the day before, and, not finding Betty at his apartment, had immediately learned by whom her trunk had been taken to the ''Maltese Cross'';[2] the same man had told him that it had been sent to Rome and that the officer who had sent it, after addressing it to Roland,[3] innkeeper, on the Piazza di Spagna, Rome, had hired a horse, leaving the man from whom he had hired it a watch as security. He had gone there at once and had recognized Betty's watch. Thus made certain that Betty must be either in the carriage which was carrying the trunk or on horseback with the officer, he had not hesitated a moment before deciding to follow them.

''I was sure,'' he said, ''that I would overtake you on the road. I took only a good pair of pistols; but not with the intention of killing my sweetheart. Yes, my dear Betty; my soul's first impulse was to pity you; the second, which will last until it is satisfied, was to blow out the villain's brains. We will leave tomorrow for Rome."

I was happy to see Betty delighted by the conclusion of her lover's story. The thought of revenge rejoiced her soul.

"We shall find him," she said, "staying at Roland's."

At that Sir B. M. looked at me and smiled, his eyes shining with content, holding Betty in his arms, as if he wanted to force me to admire the greatness of an English soul, whose natural strength far exceeded the weaknesses to which it might occasionally succumb.

"I understand you," I said, "and you shall not carry out your plan without me. Let us embrace, but promise me that you will follow my advice blindly. Otherwise I will start at once, I will arrive in Rome before you, and I will save the villain who tried to ruin Betty. Remember that if you had killed him before he got to Rome, it would have been nothing; but if you think you can safely blow out his brains in Rome now that you have recovered Betty, you are mistaken. You could have reason to repent; you do not know Rome and priestly justice. Come, Sir B. M., give me your hand and your word of honor that you will do nothing without my consent, or I shall leave you here and now."

Sir B. M. was of my height, somewhat thinner, younger than I by four or five years, and of a character with which my reader must already be so well acquainted that I need not describe it. The rather overbearing tone of my harangue must have surprised him, but, instantly recognizing the source of it, he could not refuse to shake hands with me. I immediately knew that he was a brother,[4] and his brow cleared. We embraced cordially.

"Yes, dear heart," he said to Betty, "let us entrust our revenge to the friend whom Heaven has sent us."

"I consent, provided that we remain together and always act in concert."

Thereupon he went off to bed, and I left him with Betty. I went downstairs to pay the coachman for his day and to tell him that we would leave the next morning for Rome.

"For Rome? Then you have found your portfolio? You would have done better not to have come looking for it."

Seeing me with my arm in a sling, the coachman, like everyone else in Radicofani, thought that I had fought a duel.

Sir B. M. having gone to bed, I spent the whole day with Betty, whose sense of her extraordinary good fortune in having been reconciled with him had left her incapable of any but the most exalted sentiments. She told me that we must remember what had happened between us only to remain good friends until death, without the slightest amorous intercourse, and I consented without much urging. As for her desire to be avenged for the insult the actor had put on her, I made her understand that she must persuade her lover to renounce any idea of violence in such a city as Rome, since it might cost him too dear. I promised her that the day after we arrived in Rome I would have him locked up, which I could do easily and, above all, without causing talk, for otherwise her reputation might suffer. After sleeping until seven o'clock, Sir B. M. woke much less angry with Betty's seducer, and adopted my plan, on condition that he should have the pleasure of paying him a visit, for he wanted to know him. After agreeing on this, and eating a good supper, I went to bed in another room, not without regret.

We set out at daybreak the next morning, Betty sitting on Sir B. M.'s lap; but the Englishman could bear the boredom of the slow pace of the carriage only as far as Acquapendente. We agreed that we should do better to travel post to Rome, hiring a carozzino[5] in which there

was room for four, on which I at once had my trunk put.
In this way we covered in twelve hours a distance which
would have cost us three days if we stayed in the same
carriage. We arrived there at daybreak the next morning,
and as soon as we came to the customs office[6] I gave the
chief clerk the notarized document authorizing Betty to
recover her trunk. He told us that, after the necessary
formalities, he would send it to us at whatever inn we
might choose, and it was done the next day. After a polite
search of my trunk by two clerks, the postilion took us to
an inn opposite the Church of San Carlo,[7] where, after
having my trunk taken to a separate room, I begged Sir
B. M. to remain calm, assuring him that I would attend
to the whole matter in the course of the morning and that
we should dine together well satisfied. He replied with a
laugh that he was going to bed.

I went straight to the Bargello's.[8] The Bargello in
Rome is a person who can do a great deal, who takes on
all sorts of business, and who is very expeditious when
he sees clearly and when his clients are not afraid to
spend money. In consequence he is rich, surrounds himself with a certain ceremony, and has immediate access
to the Cardinal Vicar,[9] the Governor of Rome,[10] and even
the Holy Father. Having been granted a private audience
at once, I laid the whole matter before him, not concealing the slightest detail. I ended by telling him that all we
wanted was to have the scoundrel put in prison, and to
be certain that he would leave it only to be banished from
Rome.

"What we demand," I said, "is perfectly just, and
you see that we could obtain it by the ordinary legal procedures; but, being in a hurry, I have come to ask you to
take the whole matter in hand, and, to help you to look
into it speedily, I offer you the fifty scudi which we shall
save in court costs."

He at once asked me for the bill of exchange for three
thousand écus and for the entire contents of the adven-

turer's small trunk, including his letters. I gave him the
bill of exchange, taking a receipt for it; as for the contents of the trunk, I told him to send to our inn for it at
one o'clock. He assured me that it would all be done in
the course of the day, after he had made him admit in
someone's presence the principal facts of which I had
informed him. He already knew that he was staying at
Roland's, and that he had called at the customs office to
get his trunk. He laughed when he saw me astonished
that he knew all this. He said that the thing was grave
enough to send him to Civitavecchia[11] (to the galleys), if
we would give a hundred scudi instead of fifty, and I
replied that it might be possible. He was very glad to
learn that the horse did not belong to him; he told me to
call on him at nine o'clock in the evening, when he would
certainly have news for me. I promised I would do so in
company with the Englishman, which pleased him.

In pursuit of my intentions, I had a great deal to do
in Rome, and above all to see Cardinal de Bernis;[12] but
I put everything off for the sake of the business in hand.
It had become my only concern. So I went back to the
inn, where I found a local valet whom Sir B. M. had
already engaged to serve us and who told me that after
breakfasting he had gone to bed. It was only eight
o'clock. Since we needed a carriage, I thought I should
speak to the innkeeper, and I was not a little surprised
when I saw that he was none other than Roland. I
thought the actor was staying at his inn.

"I thought, my dear Roland, that you still had your
inn on the Piazza di Spagna."

"I gave it to my eldest daughter, whom I married to a
Frenchman who is making a good thing of it; and I took
this palazzo, where I have splendid apartments."

"And are there many foreigners staying at your
daughter's now?"

"There is only a Frenchman, who calls himself Count

de l'Étoile, who is waiting for his luggage, and who has a good horse which I expect to buy."

"I advise you to wait until tomorrow to buy his horse, without telling anyone who gave you the advice."

"Why should I wait?"

"I can tell you no more."

Roland was the father of Teresa, whom I had loved nine years earlier and whom my brother Giovanni married in 1762,[13] a year after I left, as my reader may remember. He told me that my brother was in Rome with Prince Beloselski,[14] the Russian Ambassador at the Court of Dresden.

"I thought my brother could not come to Rome." [15]

"He is here with a safe-conduct which the Dowager Electress of Saxony[16] obtained from the Holy Father through her Ambassador. He wants to have the case which went against him tried over again, and there he is making a mistake, for if he had it tried a hundred times the case would go the same way and he would receive the same sentence. No one sees him, everyone avoids him. Even Mengs refuses to see him."

"Then Mengs[17] is here? I thought he was in Madrid."

"He was granted a year's leave of absence; but his whole family are in Madrid."

"I need a hackney carriage by the day for as long as the foreigners I am with stay here."

"You shall have it."

After hearing all this sufficiently unwelcome news, for I did not want to see either Mengs or my brother, I went to bed to sleep until dinnertime. I was waked for dinner at one o'clock, being told at the same time that someone was waiting to deliver a note to me; it was a servant of the Bargello's, come to take all the actor's belongings. I sent them to him, together with the trunk.

At table I informed Sir B. M. of all that I had done, and he promised to be with me at nine o'clock. We spent

the afternoon driving to see some villas, and, after taking
Betty to the inn, we went to call on the Bargello, who
told us that our man was already locked up and that, if
we wished it, such a bad case could be made for him that
he would certainly be sent to the galleys. Sir B. M. said
that he would first like to speak to him, and the Bargello
told us how to go about seeing him the next day. He said
that he had made no trouble about confessing everything,
laughing all the while and saying that it was a trifle
which could bring him to no harm, for the young lady
had gone with him of her own free will. He had given
him back his bill of exchange, which he had received with
the utmost indifference; he had told him it was true that
his passion was acting, but that he was nevertheless a
man of rank, and, as for the horse, that he was at liberty
to sell it, since the watch he had left as security was
worth more. I had forgotten to tell the Bargello that the
watch belonged to Betty. After paying the worthy representative of Rome's summary justice fifty Roman scudi,
we went to sup with Betty, who had already received her
trunk. She was very glad to learn that the scoundrel was
in prison, but she did not care to pay him a visit. We
went there the next day after dinner. The Bargello had
provided us with an advocate, who at once made out a
document in which he summoned the prisoner to pay the
costs of the journey and of his arrest, and a pecuniary
compensation to the young woman he had deceived, unless he could prove within six weeks, on the testimony of
the French Ambassador,[18] that his title of Count was
genuine; meanwhile he was to remain in prison.

We found him holding the document, which had been
translated into French for him. The first thing he said
when he saw me was that I owed him twenty-five zecchini
on the wager I had lost, for he had let Betty sleep with
me. On my informing the Englishman of this, he said
that it was a lie, but that he knew that she had slept with

him. The actor, hearing his English accent, asked him if he was Betty's lover.

"Yes, and if I had overtaken you on the road I would have killed you, for you deceived her and you are nothing but a beggarly actor."

"I have three thousand écus."

"I will put up six thousand which will be yours if the bill is not forged; but you shall stay in prison until the answer comes; if it is forged, you shall go to the galleys."

"I accept your proposal."

"I will speak to the advocate."

We left him and went to the advocate's, for Sir B. M., sure that the bill was forged, wanted to have the pleasure of seeing Betty's seducer in the galleys; but the thing could not be arranged, for, though the actor was willing to hand over the bill, he insisted on being given a scudo a day for his expenses until the answer came.

Wanting to see Rome, since he was there, Sir B. M. had to have clothes made for him, even down to shirts. Betty had everything she needed. Becoming their inseparable companion, I never left them; I put off embarking on a regular life until after they were gone. There was nothing any more between Betty and me, but I still loved her, and I had taken a liking to Sir B. M., whose intelligence and English uprightness made him a pleasant companion. He was thinking of spending two or three weeks in Rome, and then going back to Leghorn; but, Lord Baltimore[19] having arrived five or six days after we did, and being an old friend of Sir B. M.'s, he persuaded him to go to spend two weeks in Naples. His Lordship, who had a pretty Frenchwoman and two menservants with him, undertook to arrange the little excursion, and insisted upon my being one of the party. My reader may remember that I had known him in London. I seized the opportunity to see Naples and my old acquaintances there again; I left with them, we arrived there in two days, and we went to lodge

at the "Crocelle," [20] at Chiaia. The first thing I learned
was that the Duke of Matalona[21] had died and that the
Duchess his widow had become the Princess of Caramanica. This put an end to my renewing the acquaintances I had made at the Palazzo Matalona;[22] so I thought
of nothing but amusing myself and calling on no one, as
if I had never been in Naples. Lord Baltimore had been
there several times, but his mistress, who had never been
there, wanting to see everything, as did Betty and Sir
B. M., we went everywhere with our traveling companions, dispensing with guides. His Lordship and I were far
better informed than they.

On the day after we arrived I was surprised to see the
too well-known Chevalier Goudar,[23] whom I had known
in London, come to call on Lord Baltimore. The famous
libertine was in Naples, living in style in a house in
Posilipo[24] with his wife, and his wife was the same Irish
Sarah who had been a barmaid in a beer house[25] in London. Since he knew that I knew her, he had to forewarn
me. He invited us all to dine at his house on the next day
but one.

Sarah Goudar was not surprised to see me, for he had
told her to expect me, but it was I who could not get over
my surprise. Seeing her dressed with all the elegance a
French or an Italian woman could have commanded,
carrying herself well, receiving her guests even better,
without constraint but with perfect dignity, speaking
Italian with all the eloquence of a born Neapolitan, ravishingly pretty, and finding myself unable to forget what
she had been when I had last seen her in London, I was
stupefied; she saw it and laughed heartily; she seemed
to me to be disguised as a princess; but she wanted me to
think that it was when I saw her in London that she had
been in disguise. In less than a quarter of an hour we
saw five or six ladies of the highest standing in the town
and at Court arrive at Madame Goudar's house, as well
as ten or a dozen dukes, princes, and marquises, with

foreigners from every country. Before a table was laid for more than thirty, she sat down at the harpsichord and sang an air with the voice of a nightingale and a brilliance which did not surprise the company, for they knew her, but which astonished me and my traveling companions, for her talent was amazing. Goudar had done it all. Such was the education he had given her in six or seven years. Having begun by marrying her in order to have an unquestionable right to her, he had taken her from London to Paris, where he would have given her to Louis XV as his mistress if La du Barry[26] had not found a way to forestall her. He had then taken her to Vienna, to Venice, to Florence, and to Rome, and having nowhere found the fortune for which he hoped, he had gone to settle in Naples, where, to launch the fair Sarah, he had made her abjure the Anglican heresy and turn Catholic under the sponsorship of the Queen.[27] The amusing thing is that Sarah was Irish and a Catholic. The conversion was a trick.

What I found strange, inconsistent, and unworthy was that all the highest nobility of both sexes went to Goudar's house, and that Madame Goudar could go nowhere, for she was invited nowhere. It was Goudar himself who informed me of all this before dinner. He could not wait to tell me that he supported himself by gambling. Faro and biribissi supplied all his income; and it must have been considerable, for everything in his establishment was splendid. Invited to become his partner, I took good care not to refuse, certain that I should share in all the profits which I could bring to the association by pursuing an activity with whose rules and principles I was already well acquainted and to which my discreet behavior would lend the proper tone. My purse was rapidly reaching the point of emptiness, and I very probably had no other way of maintaining my accustomed style of life. Having come to this decision, I declined to return with Betty. Sir B. M. wanted to reimburse me for all that I had spent on her behalf, and I was in no situation to insist on being more generous than he.

Two months after he left, I learned from the Bargello in Rome that L'Étoile, released from prison by the intervention of Cardinal de Bernis, had also left Rome; and the next year I learned at Florence that Sir B. M. was no longer in Leghorn. He had gone to England with his dear Betty, who presumably became his wife on the death of the one he had.

As for the famous Lord Baltimore, the suzerain of Boston,[28] he left a few days after they did, bent once again on making a tour of Italy, where he died three or four years later[29] from exposing himself to the pestilential air of August in the Roman Campagna, which at that season mercilessly kills all travelers who, not fearing it, dare to spend the night and sleep there. It is enough to sleep a single night in Piperno or its vicinity never to wake again.[30] Those who have to pass that way, going from Rome to Naples or from Naples to Rome, either do not stop there or refrain from sleeping if they value their lives. Lord Baltimore paid with his life for his English skepticism.

Continuing to stay at the "Crocelle," where all rich foreigners came to lodge, I easily got to know them all, and I did them the favor of sending them to lose their money at the beautiful Madame Goudar's. I was sorry for it, but such is the nature of things.

Five or six days after Betty left, I happened on the Abate Gama[31] at Chiaia, very much aged, but in good health and as gay as ever. After we entertained each other for half an hour with accounts of our respective adventures, he told me that, all the differences between the Holy See and the Court of Rome having been settled by the courage of Pope Ganganelli,[32] he would return to Rome in a few days, but that before he left he wanted to take me to call on a person whom I should be very glad to see again.

I thought of Donna Leonilda, or her mother Donna Lucrezia;[33] or who else could it be? But what a pleasant surprise when I saw the dancer Agata,[34] with whom I had been in love in Turin after I left La Corticelli to her fate! The Abate had not forewarned her, though he could have done so, for he did not take me to see her until the next day. After all the astonishment on either side which unexpected recognitions always inspire, and all the words which spring from the satisfaction one feels at those sweet moments, we calmed ourselves in order to tell each other of our vicissitudes. Agata's story, which could have been very short, took a long time; mine, which should have been very long, took only a quarter of an hour. Agata had danced in Naples for only a year. An advocate who had fallen in love with her had married her; and she showed me four children, and their father, who arrived at suppertime. She had talked of me to him so often that she had scarcely spoken my name before he fell on my neck. He was quick-witted, like every Neapolitan *paglietta*.[35] He assured me that he was most eager to know me. We went down to the quay to sup by moonlight, and, the Abate Gama having left, I remained alone with Agata and her husband. I left them at midnight, promising that I would go to dine with them the next day.

Though Agata was in the bloom of youth, she did not kindle the least spark of the old fire in me; but such was my nature. In addition I was ten years older. My coldness pleased me. I was very glad to find that I need not fear that the power of love would force me to trouble the peace of so happy a family.

Not being far from Posilipo, where Goudar lived, knowing that there was play there, and having a considerable share in the bank, I go there. It was not an unusual hour. I see the table surrounded by ten or a dozen punters, and I am surprised when I see the banker. It was Count Medini.[36] It had been only three or four days since he had been ejected from the house of the French

Ambassador, Choiseul,[37] because he had been caught
cheating at play. In addition, I had an old grudge against
him. My reader may remember that we had fought a duel,
and that I might not have forgotten our difference. He had
made his way into Goudar's circle. I glance at the bank,
and I see that it is at its last gasp. It ought to contain
six hundred once,[38] and I see scarcely a hundred. I had a
one-third interest in it. I study the face of the punter who
had wreaked this havoc, and I guess everything. It was
the first time the sharper had been seen in Goudar's
house. At the end of the deal Goudar takes me aside and
tells me he is a rich Frenchman whom Medini himself
had brought there, that he was able to lose a great deal,
and that I should not be distressed if chance had made
him lucky the first time, for he would not be so the next.
I reply that it was all a matter of indifference to me, for I
had told him that I would not have a share in the bank
when Medini was dealing; he replied that, telling Medini
so, he had wanted to reduce the bank by a third, but that
he had taken offense and had told him to leave it as it
was, and that if he lost he would repay me the amount of
the loss.

"If he does not repay me tomorrow morning, there will
be trouble; but in any case it is for you to repay me; for
I told you in so many words that I will have no share in
the bank when Medini insists on dealing."

"You can certainly claim your two hundred once from
me, but I hope you will listen to reason, for it would be
very hard on me to have to lose two thirds."

I did not believe a word of all this, for Goudar was
even more of a scoundrel than Medini; and I waited im-
patiently for the end of the game to clear the matter up.
An hour after midnight it was all over; the lucky punter
left, laden with gold, together with the others, and Medini, affecting a most inappropriate cheerfulness, said
that the victory would cost the victor very dear. I at once
asked him if he would pay me two hundred once, for I

was not in the game, as Goudar must have told him; he replied that he admitted he owed them to me, if I was determined to leave the partnership, but that he asked me to tell him for what reason I did not want to have a share in the bank when he dealt.

"Because I have no confidence in your luck."

"You must see that the reason you give me is specious, and that I might put an unpleasant interpretation on your unwillingness."

"I cannot prevent you from misinterpreting, and what I see or do not see is for me to say. I want two hundred once, and I leave you to enjoy all the victories you may win over the gentleman. You have only to arrange matters with Monsieur Goudar, and you, Monsieur Goudar, will return me my two hundred once at noon tomorrow."

"I cannot return them to you until Count Medini gives them to me, for I have no money."

"I am sure that you will have them at noon tomorrow. Good-by."

Not wanting to listen to arguments which could not but be beside the point, I went home, still considering them clearly a pair of cheats and determined to see no more of the gambling den after recovering my money peaceably or by force. At nine o'clock the next morning I receive a note from Medini in which he asks me to come to his lodging to finish our business. I answer that he should settle the matter with Goudar, asking him to excuse me if I could not go to see him. An hour later he enters my room, and he uses all his eloquence to persuade me to accept his note for two hundred once, payable in eight days. I refuse, saying that I would deal with no one but Goudar, from whom I wanted my money at noon, determined to do everything if he did not return it to me, for he had it only on deposit. Medini raises his voice, saying that my refusal insults him; and I take up a pistol, ordering him to leave, which he does, turning pale and not saying a single word in reply.

At noon I go to Goudar's without a sword but with good pistols in my pocket, and there I find Medini, who reproaches me with having tried to murder him in my room. I do not answer him, and, remaining on my guard, I tell Goudar to give me back my two hundred once; Goudar asks Medini for them, and here the quarrel would have broken out, if I had not prevented it by taking to the stairs, threatening Goudar with unrestrained hostilities which would do him the greatest harm. When I was outside the house, I saw the beautiful Sarah at the window, begging me to come up by the back stairs to talk with her privately. I ask her to excuse me, and she says she will come down. She tells me that I am in the right, that her husband is in the wrong, but that I must wait, for he has no money, and she vouches for it that I will have my money in three days. I reply that nothing can pacify me but the money, and that she will not see me in her house again. At that she takes from her finger a ring which I recognized, and which was worth more than twice the amount, and offers it to me as security; I take it, I look at it, and I accept, making her a bow and leaving her there astonished, for she was in a state of undress in which she had probably never suffered a refusal.

Well pleased with my victory, I go to the house of the advocate, Agata's husband, where I was to dine. I tell him the whole story in detail, and at the same time I ask him to find me someone who will give me two hundred once, keeping the ring as security and writing me a note guaranteeing that the bearer can recover the ring on payment of two hundred once. At that he acts in his professional capacity, having me do everything in accordance with the forms of law; he himself gives me the two hundred once, and he sends a note in my name to Monsieur Goudar, in which he names the depositary of the ring, and sets forth the undertaking by which it will be returned upon payment of the same amount.

After dealing with this matter I recover all my good

humor, and I enter Agata's apartment, where I find her with a charming company of men and women and the Abate Gama. Before dinner Agata took me into her dressing room, where, opening a jewel case, she showed me, besides the beautiful girandole earrings, all the other pieces of jewelry I had given her when I was rich and in love with her. She tells me that she is rich, and that, since she owed me all her good fortune, it will make her happy if I will take back everything I had given her; she assures me that what she has proposed had been agreed upon that morning between her and her husband; and, to overcome my scruples, she shows me her diamonds, which had belonged to her husband's first wife; their value was greater than that of mine. Admiring so much generosity and a proposal so delicate and so magnanimous, I reply only by a silence which could not but make her understand the depth of my gratitude and the justice which I did her.

Her husband comes in, Agata shuts the jewel case, and with a pleasant laugh he tells me that I must not scruple to do what Agata had proposed, and, so saying, he embraces me. We go to join the company, which numbered ten or twelve; but the only person I notice among the men is a youth whom at the first glance I see is in love with Agata. He was Don Pasquale Latilla;[39] and he had everything to make him loved and everything to make him happy, for to intelligence he added a sweet and attractive manner. We became well acquainted at table. Among the women I was surprised by a girl of rare beauty. At fourteen years of age, she was already as well formed as if she were eighteen. Agata told me that she was studying music, so that she could earn her living by it on the stage, for she was poor.

"Such a beauty, and poor?"

"Yes, for she does not want to give herself piecemeal, and the man who would want to possess her entirely would have to assume too heavy a burden, for since she has nothing he would have to do everything for her. Men who would bring themselves to do that are very scarce in Naples.''

"It is impossible that she has not a lover, for she is striking.''

"If she has, no one knows of it. You can make her acquaintance and go to see her. In three or four visits you will learn everything.''

"What is her name ?''

"La Callimena ;[40] she lives on the Largo del Castello del'Ovo.[41] The person who is speaking to her now is her aunt, and I am sure they are talking of you.''

We sit down at table, the dinner is of game, fish, and shellfish, all exquisite, with delicious wines, and I saw Agata's heart leap for joy at the thought that Fortune had so favored her that she could prove her happiness to the man but for whom she would never have been happy; old Gama was congratulating himself on having brought me there, Don Pasquale Latilla could not be jealous of the attentions his idol bestowed on me, for he considered them due to me as a foreigner, and Agata's husband showed that he prided himself on having a mind above common prejudices. But amid all the attentions which were showered on me, Callimena, who was across the table from me, caused me distractions for which I could not forgive myself. Dying to find her witty, I often addressed some remark to her, she answered politely, but so briefly that I could not start a subject which would give scope for repartee. The girl's eyes were such a brilliant black that, try as she might, she could neither prevent them from making any man who looked into them fall in love nor keep them from saying more than they said despite herself. For this reason she never let them rest on any man who wanted to awaken their interest.

I asked her if Callimena was her family name or a nickname, and she replied that it was her baptismal name.

"It is a Greek name," I said, "and no doubt you know what it means."

"No."

"It means beauty in a rage, or beautiful moon." [42]

"I am very glad to have learned that I have nothing in common with my name."

"Have you brothers and sisters?"

"I have only a married sister, whom you perhaps know."

"What is her name? Whom did she marry?"

"Her husband is Piedmontese, but she does not live with him."

"Is she Signora Sclopis, who is traveling with Sir Aston?" [43]

"None other."

"Then I will give you news of her which you will not be sorry to hear."

After dinner I asked Agata what entitled the charming girl to come to dine with her.

"My husband was her godfather, and he does something for her. He pays the master who is teaching her to sing."

"What is her age exactly?"

"She is fourteen."

"She is a prodigy. What beauty!"

"But her sister is even more beautiful."

"I know her only by name."

But at this juncture Monsieur Goudar is announced and comes in. He asks the advocate to hear something he has to tell him, and they go into another room. A quarter of an hour later the advocate came back and told me that, having received the two hundred once, he had given him back his ring. So that was the end of the matter, much to my satisfaction. I saw that I had made an eternal enemy, but I did not care. The company sat down to cards, and Agata made me play with Callimena, whose calm put the finishing touch to my enchantment. Her

character was like her beauty, completely without artifice. I told her everything I knew about her sister, and I
promised I would write to Turin to learn where she was
then, and give her the information afterward. I told her
that I loved her, and that if she was willing I would pay
calls on her, and I was very well satisfied with her answer.

The next day I could scarcely wait to go to her house
at breakfast time. I found her at the harpsichord with
her music master; her talent was mediocre, but love
made me find it superlative. After the master left, I was
alone with her. She launched into apologies for her
frowzy dress, her inadequate furniture, her inability to
offer me a dinner. I said that it all conspired to make her
more beautiful in my eyes, and that I deeply regretted I
was not rich enough to make her fortune. When I began
to praise the beauties of her face, she did not resist a
storm of kisses which saluted her eyes, her lips, the roses
of her cheeks; she stopped me when my daring hand tried
to uncover a bosom of which I saw only half, but, even
while resisting, she gave me her lips to assure herself
that I should not hold her resistance against her. I accepted the kiss, and by an effort assumed a calm which I
did not feel.

"Charming Callimena, tell me the truth and earn my
gratitude. Have you a lover?"

"No."

"Have you had one?"

"Never."

"But for a time . . . a passing fancy?"

"Not even that."

"What! Formed as you are, with eyes and a countenance which assure me that your heart is tender, how can
I believe that there is not a man in Naples who has inspired desires in you?"

"Not one, for no man has ever tried to inspire them.
No one on earth has ever made such a declaration to me
as you did a moment ago. That is the simple truth."

"I believe you; and I see that I must hasten to leave Naples, for otherwise I should become the unhappiest of men."

"How so?"

"By loving you with no hope of possessing you."

"Love me, and stay. Why cannot you believe that I will love you? Only restrain your ardor, for you must see that I cannot fall in love with you unless I see that you can control yourself."

"As I am doing now, for example?"

"Yes. Seeing you calm, I think that you are denying yourself in order to please me, and love often follows gratitude."

It was as much as to tell me that she did not yet love me, but that she would come to love me little by little; I saw that to win her heart I must pursue no other course than the one she pointed out to me. I had reached the age when a man begins to have the strength to wait. After kissing her beautiful eyes, and being ready to go, I asked her if she was in need of money; in answer she blushed, and a moment later she told me to go and ask her aunt, who was in the next room.

I go in by myself, and I am amazed to find her with two unassuming Capuchins, who were amusing her with small talk while she sewed; some little distance away three very young girls were also sewing. She starts to rise, I stop her, I ask after her health, I laughingly congratulate her on her company, she laughs too, the Capuchins do not vouchsafe me even a look and remain where they are. I take a chair and sit down facing her.

The aunt might be fifty years old, she was well preserved for her age, she had a frank expression and traces of a beauty which had left her with her youth. I had scarcely looked at her at dinner the day before. Though I am free from prejudices, the presence of the two bearded men, in their monstrous habit, sweating great drops and giving off a more than unpleasant odor, very much annoyed me; I thought their not leaving was an insult to me. I knew that, being men as I was, they must have the same desires as I; but I could not forgive them for the effrontery with which they encroached on my privileges, despite their knowing that I had the right to send them about their business. I saw clearly that my mortifying them would displease the lady, and I felt sure that the two impostors counted on a consideration which I could not fail to show except to my own disadvantage. No one is more adept at such calculations than a priest. After a long acquaintance with the whole of Europe, I can say that I have never seen the regular clergy remaining within the bounds prescribed by their vows, except in France; there I have never found monks at social gatherings; I have never dined in decent houses with priests or bishops brazen enough to eat meat on the days when the Church forbids it to them; I have never seen monks or abbés in public resorts or at theaters except in secular dress. In Italy, on the contrary, in Spain, and in some German cities, priests, monks, and the whole tribe of abbés appear freely in all the places where it would seem that no one should go but those who, having taken no vows, are sure that they will scandalize no one by their presence there.

After being patient for a quarter of an hour, I could not help telling the worthy aunt that I had something to say to her in private; whereupon I thought the stinking monks would leave; but not a bit of it, she herself rose and took me into the next room to hear what I wanted to say to her. On my asking her if she was in need of money she replied that she was only too much in need of twenty ducati del regno[44] to pay the rent of the house. Twenty Neapolitan ducati come to eighty French francs. She was astonished, and full of gratitude, at my unhesitatingly giving her the amount. I went back to the "Crocelle" without giving her time to thank me.

Something which happened to me on the same day is

worthy to be recorded. While I was dining alone in my room, I was told that a Venetian hermit, who said that he knew me, had come to speak to me. I have him shown in, and I see a face which was not unfamiliar but which I could not place. Of my height, but thin, gaunt, showing all of his sixty years, with hunger, poverty, and weariness depicted in his every feature, with a long beard, a bald head, a brownish-gray robe hanging down to his heels and fastened by a rope from which hung a rosary, a dirty handkerchief, a hood falling down on his back, a long cylindrical basket in his left hand, and a staff in his right, he strikes me as being not a servant of God, a penitent sinner, a humble seeker of alms, but a man in despair perhaps come to murder me in my room.

"Who are you? I seem to have seen you before; but I cannot pretend that I remember you."

"I will tell you who I am, and I will surprise you with the story of my misfortunes; but first have food and drink brought for me, for since day before yesterday I have eaten nothing but some thin soup at the hospice."

"Certainly. Go down and let them give you dinner, and come up afterward, for you cannot talk to me while you are eating."

My local valet goes down with him to order him given something to eat, and I order him not to leave me alone with the man, who really terrified me. Sure, however, that I must know him, I could not wait to learn who he was. Three quarters of an hour later he came up again, looking as if his face were on fire with fever. I tell him to sit down and speak freely, for my servant would stay on the balcony, where he could hear nothing of what he should say to me. He began by telling me his name.

"I am Albergoni." [45]

I instantly remember him. He was a Paduan gentleman with whom I had been on terms of close friendship twenty-five years earlier, when, Signor Bragadin having granted me his protection, I had given up earning my

living as a violinist. The Paduan nobleman had only a
very small fortune, but he had intelligence, a strong
character, great knowledge of the world, and a splendid
constitution able to withstand every debauch in the
service of Bacchus and Venus; if his morals were unbridled, so was his tongue, which mocked now the government, now religion; he was brave to the point of temerity,
a gamester who did not confine cheating to the bounds of
prudence, a disciple of the antinaturalism which long
ago brought the fires of Heaven down on the five cities.[46]
In addition, the man whom I had before me and who presented me with the veritable image of ugliness had been
handsome until the age of twenty-five; but that is not
surprising: the way from beauty to ugliness is very
short, much shorter than the way from ugliness to beauty.
In the first change Nature descends, in the second she
rises. It was twenty-five years since I had seen Albergoni,
and fifteen since I had heard any news of him. I saw him
before me dressed as a hideous hermit. Here is what he
told me.

"A club of five or six young men of whom I was one
had a casino on La Giudecca[47] where we spent delightful
hours without harming anyone. Somebody took it into
his head that our gatherings were enlivened by illicit relations forbidden by the law. We were indicted in the
greatest secrecy, the casino was closed, and all the members of it ran away except myself and a certain Branzardi. We were arrested. Two years later Branzardi was
sentenced to be burned after being beheaded, and I was
sentenced to ten years in prison. In the year '65 I was
released, and I went to live in Padua, where I was not left
in peace. I was accused of the same crime, and, thinking
it best not to wait for the bolt to fall, I went to Rome.
Two years later the Council of Ten sentenced me *in absentia* to perpetual banishment. One can bear banishment
patiently if one has an income, and I should have had
enough to live on if my brother-in-law, who had taken

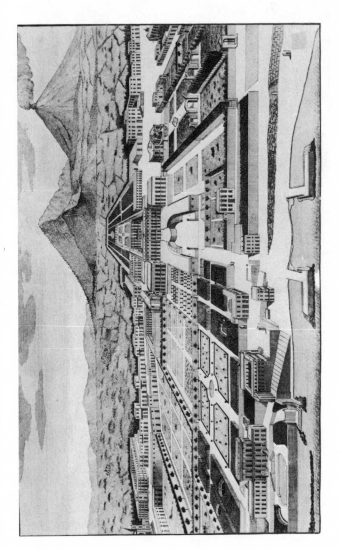

The Palace in Portici at the Foot of Vesuvius

Loving Attendance

over my estate, did not decide to profit by my misfortune
to obtain full possession of it. A lawyer in Rome was
ordered to pay me two paoli a day if I would sign an
undertaking assuring them that I would never make any
further claims. I refused to accept the two paoli on this
unjust condition, and I left Rome to come here to be a
hermit. It is as such that I have lived for two years, and
I am at the end of my tether, for misery kills. Anyone
who defies it can only be some wretch who has never experienced it.''

"Go back to Rome. I think that with two paoli a day
you can manage to live."

"I would rather die than submit to injustice."

I condoled with him, I gave him a zecchino, and I told
him that as long as I remained in Naples he could come to
eat at my inn every day, and I thought I saw him leave
satisfied; but two days later his name was on every
tongue in Naples. My valet told me when he entered my
room in the morning that the hermit to whom I had had
dinner given for two days was lying stark naked at the
door of an inn on the Via Toledo.[48] The innkeeper had
found him dead, hanging in the room in which he had
slept, and, having immediately informed the magistrate,
had been ordered to expose him publicly to find out who
he was. I quickly dress to go and see the spectacle. I see
the wretch who had strangled himself, and who made the
spectators tremble. His face was black and livid, and his
scrotum was so swollen that he appeared to have a very
big hernia. I go to speak with the innkeeper, who tells
me that for two days he had supped very well and drunk
even better, paying him in advance as was the practice in
the case of all mendicants. He took me to the room in
which he had killed himself (he did not know at what
hour), leaving the door unlocked. He had given his basket
and all his rags to the magistrate, and he could not wait
to have them come to fetch his body and bury it in the
carrion pit. On the floor I see a sheet of paper, I pick it

up, and I read my name at the head of eight or ten others, among which was that of Count Medini. After giving us the flattering title of his benefactors, he tells us that, life having become a burden to him, he thought it best to free himself of it and deserve our approbation. In recompense for what we had done for him, he gave us five numbers. I gave the paper to the innkeeper, who received it as if it were a treasure. The death of the wretched madman was very advantageous to the Neapolitan lottery. All the players staked on the five numbers, not one of which came out; but experience has never had power to dispel superstition. Five numbers written down by a man who hanged himself a quarter of an hour later could not but be those which would come out at the first drawing.

I go into a coffeehouse for breakfast, and hear someone discoursing at length on the reason why a man who was determined to commit suicide should choose to hang himself; he claimed that it was a delightful death, and the great proof he alleged was that every hanged man at his last moment had an erection and an ejaculation of sperm. As I left the coffeehouse, I finally seized the hand of a pickpocket just as he was spiriting away my handkerchief. In less than a month I had been robbed of at least twenty handkerchiefs. Any number of rogues live in Naples by nothing else, and their skill is admirable. As soon as the rascal saw that he was caught, he begged me not to raise a row, assuring me that he would give me back all the handkerchiefs he had stolen from me, and he confessed that he had robbed me of seven or eight.

"You have robbed me of twenty, and more."

"Not I, but some of the others. Come with me, and perhaps you'll find them all, and whoever has them will let you have them very cheap."

"Is it far?"

"On the Largo del Castello;[49] but let go of me, for people are looking at us."

The rascal took me to a shabby inn ten paces from

Callimena's house, and a minute later he shows me into a room where a very wide-awake man asks me if it is true that I want to buy secondhand goods. Hearing that I want to buy handkerchiefs, he opens a cupboard which looked like a door and he shows me at least two hundred, among which I found ten or a dozen of mine, which I bought for ten times less than they were worth. In the course of the following days I bought several more, feeling restrained by no scruple despite my being sure that everything I bought was stolen. Two or three days before I left, by which time he had got to know me well and concluded it was not in me to betray him, this honest Neapolitan merchant told me confidentially that if I would invest ten or twelve thousand ducati in his merchandise I would make a profit of thirty thousand by selling it in Rome or elsewhere.

"What sort of merchandise have you?"

"Watches, snuffboxes, and rings which I dare not sell here, for they are all stolen."

"But are you not afraid?"

"I haven't much to fear, but I do not confide in everyone."

I thanked him, but I would not even look at his jewelry; I was too much afraid that I could not resist the temptation to buy for ten what was worth fifty. I should have run the risk of somewhere running into the owner of the thing I bought.

Back at the inn, I found that among the newly arrived foreigners were some people whom I knew. Bertoldi[50] had arrived from Dresden with two young Saxon gentlemen whose tutor he was. The young Saxons were handsome and rich and looked as if they were bent on pleasure. I had known Bertoldi for twenty-five years. He had played the role of Arlecchino in the company of Italian actors[51] in the service of the King of Poland, and after the King's death he had been appointed a Councilor with the duty of superintending the *opera buffa,* which was much to the

taste of the Dowager Electress, who loved music. They
were given rooms near mine, and we were soon very well
acquainted.

The other foreigners, who had arrived at the same time
with a large suite of servants, were Miss Chudleigh,[52]
who had become Duchess of Kingston, with an English
Lord and a Knight whose name I have forgotten. The
lady at once recognized me and did not hesitate a moment
to accept the homage which I proposed to offer her; an
hour later Monsieur Hamilton[53] came to see her, and I
was delighted to make his acquaintance. We all dined
together. Hamilton was a genius; I have been told that
he is now married to a young woman who had the skill
to make him fall in love. This misfortune often overtakes
men who have managed to guard against it all their lives;
age weakens the heart as it does the mind. Marrying is
always a folly, but when a man who is getting old is
guilty of it it is deadly. The woman whom he marries can
offer him only grudging favors, for which he pays with
his life, which he certainly shortens; or if it happens that
she is in love with him, he is in an even worse situation.
He will infallibly die in two or three years. Seven years
ago I came very near to succumbing to this folly in
Vienna,[54] *a qua me servavit Apollo* ("from which Apollo
saved me").[55]

After dinner I presented the two Saxons to the Duchess of Kingston, to whom they gave news of the Dowager
Electress of Saxony, of whom she was very fond. We all
went to the theater. As chance would have it, Madame
Goudar was in the box next to ours; Hamilton entertained the Duchess by telling her the beautiful Irishwoman's story. The Duchess showed no wish to make her
acquaintance.

After supper she got up a game of quinze,[56] with herself, the two Englishmen, and the two Saxons; the stakes
being small, not much was lost, the Saxons won; I decided to play another time. The next day we all went to

dine at the Prince of Francavilla's;[57] he gave us a splendid repast and toward nightfall took us to a small pool which he had by the seashore, where he showed us a wonder. A priest[58] dived into the water stark naked and swam, resting from time to time without sinking. He used no artificial means to keep afloat. We were forced to conclude that it could only be due to his internal organization. After that the Prince gave the Duchess a very agreeable spectacle. He had all his pages swim naked before her; they were charming boys fifteen, sixteen, and seventeen years of age, all of them minions of the amiable Prince, whose nature made him prefer the male to the female sex. The Englishmen asked the Prince if he would give them the same spectacle with girls as the swimmers, and he promised that he would do so the next day at a house he owned near Portici, where he had a pool in the garden.

CHAPTER X

My amour with Callimena. My journey to
Sorrento. Medini. Goudar. Miss Chudleigh.
The Marchese della Pettina. Gaetano. Mrs.
Cornelys's son. Anecdote about Sarah Goudar.
The Florentines blanketed by the King. My
happy journey to Salerno, my return to
Naples, my departure thence, and my arrival
in Rome.

THE PRINCE of Francavilla was a rich, lavish, extremely intelligent Epicurean, whose favorite motto was *Fovet et favet* ("He forwards and fosters").[1] He was in favor in Spain, but the King had thought it best that he should live in Naples, because he foresaw that he might easily have initiated the Prince of Asturias[2] and his brothers into his antinatural practices. At his little palace on the afternoon of the next day he showed us his small lake enlivened by ten or twelve young peasant girls, who swam in our presence until nightfall; Miss Chudleigh and two other ladies found the treat as boring as they had found the one on the day before delightful. The English visitors and the two Saxons did not prevent me from paying two visits a day to my dear Callimena, with whom, the more she kept me languishing, the more I found myself in love. Agata, whom I saw every day, was the confidant of my passion, and would have been glad to find a way to forward my desires; but her dignity did not per-

mit her to act openly; she promised to include her in the
party one day when we were to go to Sorrento, where I
could easily make progress during the night we should
spend in that charming countryside.

But before the party with Agata could be arranged,
Monsieur Hamilton arranged the same excursion with the
Duchess of Kingston, and, since it was to be a picnic, I
paid my respects to her by joining it with the two Saxons
and a charming Abate Giliani,[3] with whom I became better acquainted later in Rome. We left Naples at four
o'clock in the morning in a twelve-oared felucca, and at
nine o'clock we arrived at Sorrento. There were fifteen
of us, all in high spirits, and all enraptured by the pleasures of the place, which we thought truly a terrestrial
paradise. Monsieur Hamilton took us all to a garden
which belonged to the Duke of Serracapriola,[4] who happened to be there with his wife the Duchess, a Piedmontese lady, beautiful as a star, and in love with her
husband.

The Duke had been banished there with her for two
months because he had appeared in public with too fine
a carriage and liveries; the Minister Tanucci[5] had in-
timated to the King that it was necessary to punish a
nobleman who, by breaking the sumptuary laws, had set
a very bad example; and the King, who had not yet
learned to oppose Tanucci's will, had banished the couple
to the most delightful prison in all his kingdom; but for
the most delightful place in the world to become distaste-
ful, one has only to be obliged to live there. The Duke
and his beautiful wife were bored to death. When they
saw Hamilton leading a numerous party, they sighed
with relief and recovered from their gloom. An Abate
Bettoni,[6] whose acquaintance I had made nine years
before at the late Duke of Matalona's, came to call on the
Duke and was delighted to see me. He was a Brescian
gentleman, and he had chosen Sorrento as his permanent
residence. With an income of three thousand scudi, he

lived in luxury, enjoying all the gifts which Bacchus, Ceres, and Venus could bestow on him. Whatever he wanted he could have, and he could want no more than nature offered him at Sorrento; he was content, and he laughed at the philosophers who said that man could not be so, since he enjoyed moderate but sufficient wealth, had no ambition, and was in perfect health. What displeased me was to see him accompanied by Count Medini, who, after the scene which had taken place at Goudar's, could not but be my enemy. We scarcely bowed to each other. At table we were twenty-two or twenty-four, and we enjoyed delicious fare without needing the offices of a cook, whose art consists in nothing but making tasty what would not be so without it. Everything at Sorrento is delicious—greenstuff, all the products of the dairy, red meat, veal, and even the flour, which gives all the pastries a delicate flavor which is found nowhere else. We spent the afternoon strolling about villages whose tree-lined streets were more beautiful than those of all the gardens of Europe and Asia.

At the Abate Bettoni's house we found ices flavored with lemon, with chocolate, with coffee, and pot cheeses than which nothing more delicious could be imagined. Naples excels in these delicacies, and the Abate Bettoni saw to it that his table was well served. He had five or six young peasant girls, all of them pretty, so nicely dressed they looked anything but servants. Their beauty astonished me, and when I asked him privately if it was a seraglio he replied that it might be, but that jealousy had no place in it, as I was free to learn for myself by spending a few days in his house. I looked at the fortunate man, but with a sigh, for he was at least twelve years older than I. His happiness could not last much longer.

Toward nightfall we went back to Serracapriola's, where a supper of ten or twelve different kinds of fish and shellfish had been prepared. The air of Sorrento

never leaves those who live there without an appetite.
After supper the English Duchess wanted to play faro;
the Abate Bettoni, who knew that Medini was a professional gamester, suggested that he be banker; but Medini
declined, saying that he had not money enough. However,
the Duchess had to be satisfied, and I offered myself.
Cards were brought, I emptied my purse on the table; it
contained all I possessed, which did not amount to more
than four hundred once. The whole company took gold
from their pockets and accepted livrets.[7] One of the
Saxons asked for counters, and I begged him to excuse
me from carrying him on his word, whereupon his friend
gave him fifty ducati. Medini asked me if I would let him
take a share in my bank, and I replied that since I did
not want to count my money it was impossible. I dealt
until an hour after midnight, and stopped only because
I had but thirty or forty once left; the two Duchesses and
almost all the other punters were lucky, except a Sir
Rosebery,[8] who, instead of gold, smilingly staked London
bank notes. I put them in my pocket without examining
them, while the whole company thanked me warmly for
the favor I had done them. Medini did not play. In my
room I looked at the English notes, and I found four
hundred and fifty pounds sterling, which came to about
twice what I had lost. I went to bed very well pleased
with my day, determined to tell no one the amount I had
won.

The Duchess of Kingston having said that we should
leave at nine o'clock, Signora Serracapriola invited her
to drink coffee before going on board the felucca. After
the breakfast Bettoni and Medini arrived, and the latter
asked Hamilton if he might intrude so far as to return
to Naples with us; the Englishman replied that his company would be an honor. At two o'clock we arrived at our
inn, where, about to enter my room, I was surprised to
see in the antechamber a young lady, who, coming toward
me with a sad look, asked me if I knew her. She was so

changed that she might well have asked me the question, but I had no difficulty in recognizing her. She was the eldest of the five Hanoverian sisters whom I had loved in London, the one who had run away with the Marchese della Pettina.[9] I imagine that my reader will remember the whole episode. My curiosity is as great as my surprise. She tells me that if I am alone she will be glad to dine with me, and I order for two.

Her story was not long. She had arrived in Naples with the Marchese, whom her mother had refused to see. He had taken lodgings with her at a miserable tavern, where he had sold everything she possessed, and two or three months later he had been sent to prison in the Vicaria[10] for seven or eight different charges of forgery. She had been supporting him in prison for seven years, and, being at the end of her resources, and having learned from the Marchese himself that I was in Naples, she had come to ask me, not to help by giving her money, as the Marchese wished, but to use my influence with the Duchess of Kingston to persuade her to take her back to England with her in her service.

"Are you married to the Marchese?"

"No."

"How have you managed to support him for seven years?"

"I have had lovers. Imagine anything, and it will be true. Can you arrange for me to speak to the Duchess?"

"I will mention you to her, and I warn you that I will tell her nothing but the truth."

"Good. And I will do the same. I know her character."

"Come tomorrow."

About six o'clock I went to ask Hamilton how I could exchange the English notes I had won the evening before, and he did it for me himself at the current rate of exchange. Before supper I spoke to Miss Chudleigh about the Hanoverian, and, remembering the five girls, she said that she must have made her acquaintance, for she had come to her with her sister to ask for her protection. She told me she would speak with her and would make up her mind afterward. So I introduced her the next morning and left her alone with her. The result of the interview was that she engaged her to take the place of a Roman chambermaid, whom she dismissed, and took her to Rome a week later, and that winter left to return to England with her. I never learned what became of her.

But when two or three days after she left Naples Pettina begged me in a very well-written letter to come to see him in prison in the Vicaria, where he was, I could not refuse. I found him with a young man whom, since they looked exactly alike, I at once recognized as his brother; but despite their striking resemblance the elder brother was ugly and the younger handsome. Between beauty and ugliness there is often no more than an almost imperceptible point. The visit, in which curiosity played a greater part than magnanimity, did not amuse me: I had to put up with a very long and very boring account of all his misfortunes and of all the mistakes which had brought him to a prison from which he had no hope of being released until the death of his mother, whom he called his bitterest enemy and who was only fifty years of age. He thought he had a right to reproach me for having arranged the departure from Naples of the woman without whom he would die of starvation, for he had only two carlini[11] a day, which were not enough to satisfy his hunger. His brother had been in prison with him for two years because of his kind heart. He had persuaded him to circulate bank notes which he had forged; they had been recognized, he had been discovered to have been the source of them, and he had been sent to prison; he would have been hanged if their mother had not paid; but it was on their mother's complaint that he was being kept in prison, where, like himself, he had only two carlini a day.

What astonished me at the end of his story was a pro-

posal which he made to me with no idea that it was insulting. He assured me that he could forge the signatures
of the ministers Tanucci and Di Marco,[12] on the strength
of which he tried to persuade me to go to Palermo with
papers which he would give me, stay there for only three
days, and receive a hundred thousand ducati. He would
trust me completely, giving me the papers and the necessary instructions, certain that on my return to Naples I
would give him twenty thousand ducati, with which he
would pay his debts and get out of prison despite his
mother.

It would have been a mistake to take offense at his con-
fiding in me and to pick a quarrel with the poor youth for
insulting me by making me a proposal which he could
make me only if he assumed that I was a thief; for, being
himself a scoundrel and a forger, he was simply treating
me as an equal. Indeed he thought he was honoring me
with a mark of the greatest consideration. So I declined
politely, telling him that, since I had to go to Rome, I
had not time to go to Palermo. He ended by asking me
for money, but I could find no good reason to give him
even a carlino. I left, telling him to change his way of
life or to prepare to die on the gallows. My advice made
him laugh, but his younger brother was impressed by it;
I saw him turn pale and, a moment later, red as fire.

At the foot of the stairs a prison official told me that a
prisoner wanted to speak to me.

"Who is he?"

"He's a relative of yours, his name is Gaetano."

A relative of mine, named Gaetano—I thought it must
be my brother the Abate,[13] whom some strange chance
might have sent to prison in Naples. I go up to the third
floor with the official, and I see eighteen or twenty
wretches sitting on the floor, singing bawdy songs in
chorus. In prisons and the galleys gaiety is the resource
of misery and despair; nature provides this relief by
the instinct which commands it to preserve itself. I see

one of the unfortunates coming toward me; addressing me as "godfather," he makes to embrace me. I fall back at once and I recognize him as the Gaetano who, under my sponsorship twelve years earlier in Paris, had married a pretty girl whom I had later helped to escape from him. I think my reader will remember the incident.[14]

"I am sorry to see you here. How can I be of use to you?"

"By paying me the nearly a hundred écus which you owe me for goods you bought from me on several occasions in Paris."

The thing being completely false, I turn my back on him, saying that prison had apparently driven him mad. I go downstairs and inquire of the jailer, and I learn that he is sentenced to prison for the rest of his life and that he had escaped the gallows only because of a flaw in the criminal proceeding which was to have sent him there. But what surprised me was an advocate who came to me that afternoon to demand a hundred écus which I owed Gaetano, and, to prove that I really did owe them to him, showed me a thick book belonging to his client in which my name appeared under ten or twelve different dates as owing him for such-and-such goods which I had bought from him in Paris and for which I had not paid. I answer the advocate that I owe the scoundrel nothing and that his having written my name in his book was no proof.

"You are mistaken, Signor, it proves a great deal, and the courts in this country are very favorable to poor creditors in prison. I am their advocate, and I warn you that if you do not pay, or do not come to some arrangement today, I will have you summoned to court tomorrow."

I control myself, and I ask him his name, which he writes down; then I tell him to go, assuring him that I will arrange everything in less than twenty-four hours. I at once went to Agata's, and her husband laughed heartily when I told him all that the advocate had said to me. He at once had me sign a power of attorney by virtue of which he became my surety in any proceedings, after which he sent the scoundrelly *paglietta* who had threatened me official notice that he must now deal only with him. This ended the whole affair. The rabble of chicaning lawers in Naples is extremely dangerous, for the tricks by which they evade the law are beyond counting, especially when they have to deal with foreigners.

Sir Rosebery having stayed on in Naples, through him I became acquainted with all the English people who arrived. They all came to stay at the "Crocelle," we often went on excursions with the two Saxons, and I passed the time very pleasantly; nevertheless, I should have left Naples after the Fair[15] if my love for Callimena had not detained me. I saw her every day, I made her presents, but her concessions to my desires were of the slightest. The Fair was about to end, and Agata arranged the excursion to Sorrento which she had promised me, choosing a three-day holiday so that her husband could share in the pleasure without hurt to his business. Agata asked her husband to invite a woman he had loved before he had married her; for his own part, her husband invited Don Pasquale Latilla;[16] and they did me the kindness to invite my dear Callimena. So we were three men with three women whom we loved, and the expense of the excursion was to be divided equally between the three of us; Agata's husband the advocate was to direct everything. But before the day on which we were to start I saw, to my great surprise, Joseph, Mrs. Cornelys's son,[17] appear before me, delighted to have found me in Italy, as he had expected to do.

"What chance," I asked him, "brings you to Naples, and whom are you with?"

"I am here alone. I wanted to see the whole of Italy, and my mother has made it possible. I've seen Turin, Milan, Genoa, Venice, Bologna, Florence, Rome, and now here I am in Naples. When I've seen everything worth seeing here, I'll return to Rome, and from there I'll go to see Loreto, then Parma, Modena, Ferrara, Mantua, Switzerland, Germany, the Netherlands, and Ostend, where I will take ship for home."

"And how long will you have devoted to the journey?"

"Six months."

"You will return to London able to give a full account of all the things worth seeing in your journey through this beautiful part of Europe."

"I hope I shall be able to convince Mama that she won't have thrown away what my journey is costing her."

"How much do you think that will be?"

"The hundred guineas she gave me, and no more."

"What! You will have supported yourself for six months and made this long journey, and you will have spent only a hundred guineas? It passes belief."

"If one will take the trouble to economize, one can spend even less."

"Perhaps. And to whom did you have letters of recommendation in all these countries you now know so well?"

"To no one. I have an English passport, and I let people suppose that I am an Englishman wherever I go."

"Aren't you afraid of bad company?"

"I neither let such people come near me, nor approach them myself. I confide in no one; when I am addressed I answer only in monosyllables, I eat and engage lodgings only after having come to an agreement, and I travel only in public conveyances, where the places are at a fixed tariff."

"Here, in the meanwhile, you will economize, for I will pay all your expenses, and I will give you an excellent guide, for you cannot do without one."

"You will excuse me if I accept nothing. I gave Mama my word of honor that I would accept nothing from anyone."

"You must see that that would not apply to me."

"No exceptions. I have relatives in Venice,[18] whom I saw, and my vow to my mother kept me from accepting a dinner. I have never broken a promise I have given."

I knew that he was a fanatic on the point, and I did not press him further. Joseph was twenty-three years of age, he was very short, very handsome, and he would have been taken for a girl if he had not let his whiskers grow so that they covered his cheeks. Despite all its patent absurdity, there was something about his journey which I could not help admiring. Since I was curious to know what his mother's situation was, and what had become of my daughter, he told me everything he knew straightforwardly. His mother was more in debt than ever, her creditors sent her to prison five or six times a year, she always got out by finding sureties or making new arrangements with her creditors, who had to let her come out so that she could pay them in part by the profits from the balls and assemblies which she gave, and which she could not have given if she had stayed in prison. My daughter, who must have been seventeen years old at the time, was pretty, full of talent, and enjoyed the protection and esteem of all the most highly placed ladies in London. She gave concerts and was still living with her mother, who mortified her every day, and over the merest trifles, which made poor Sophie shed tears. I asked him whom she had been supposed to marry when her mother took her out of the boarding school in which I had put her; and he replied that he had never heard of any marriage.

"Have you any employment?"

"None at all. Every year my mother wants to send me to the Indies in a ship loaded with merchandise belonging to me, by which she supposes I will lay the foundations of a great fortune; but it will never happen, for to get merchandise takes money, and my mother has nothing but debts."

Despite his promise I persuaded him to accept the services of my manservant as his guide. In a week he saw everything, and he insisted on leaving; all that I said to persuade him to stay for a week or ten days more was of no avail. He wrote me from Rome that he had left behind six shirts, which must be in one of the drawers of the chest in his room, and his greatcoat; he asked me to get them and bring them to him in Rome, but he failed to tell me where he was staying. He was a scatterbrain, yet he was confidently traveling through half of Europe, and, with the help of three or four well-tried maxims, he was coming to no harm.

I had an unexpected visit from Goudar, who, knowing that I had made my way into distinguished company, came to ask me to invite him and his wife to dinner with the Saxons and the English people, the diversions I was sharing with whom he knew did not include cards. He said that it was a pity not to introduce gaming among them, for they were born to lose. Being of the same opinion myself, I promised to do him the favor, on the understanding that there should be no play in my apartment, for I did not want to risk any unpleasantness. It was all that he asked of me, being sure that his wife would attract them to his lodgings, where he could play, he said, without fear of ill consequences. I undertook to give the dinner upon my return from Sorrento, for which we were to leave the next day.

The excursion to Sorrento was the last real pleasure I enjoyed in all my life. The advocate took us to a house where we were lodged as comfortably as we could wish. We had four rooms, one of which was occupied by Agata and her husband, another by Callimena and the advocate's former mistress, a very charming woman though no longer young, and the two others by Don Pasquale Latilla and myself. We went to call on the Duke of Serracapriola and the Abate Bettoni, though we declined their invitations to dinner and supper. After supper we went to bed early, and we rose in the morning to go walking, the advocate and his former mistress in one direction, Don Pasquale and Agata in another, while I took Callimena in yet another. At noon each day we were all back at the house for a dinner which was always delicious, and after it, leaving the advocate to take a siesta, Don Pasquale set out with Agata and her husband's former flame, and Callimena accompanied me along shaded walks where the least ray of the by then fiery sun could not penetrate. It was there that Callimena rewarded my passion, after struggling with herself for two days. On the third day, at five o'clock in the morning and in the presence of the rising Apollo, we sat down side by side on the grass and yielded to our desires. Callimena sacrificed herself neither to cupidity nor to gratitude, for I had given her only trifles, but to love, and I could have no doubt of it; she gave herself to me, and she was sorry that she had so long put off making me the gift. Before noon we changed our altar three times, and we spent the whole afternoon going everywhere on foot and stopping as soon as the least spark of passion inspired us with the desire to quench it.

On the fourth day, the wind being too strong, we returned to Naples in three carriages. Callimena persuaded me to confide to her aunt all that had happened between us, which would enable us to have the pleasure of spending some nights together in perfect freedom. Convinced that it would be my best course, and sure that her aunt would raise no objection in view of an arrangement of which I had already thought, I brought her niece back to her and then took her aside.

"Callimena," I said, "whom, as you know, I love dearly, has satisfied all my desires; but I do not feel entirely happy because I am not in a position to make her fortune. However, I can do something for her, under your guidance, by supplying her with such things as she needs and which she seems to be without, and by giving

you enough to pay a master, who will perfect her in the
art which she intends to practice, until she is accomplished enough in it to appear on the stage. So it is for
you, my dear aunt, to tell me if you have any small debts,
which I will pay to put your mind at ease, and what you
will need to equip her with all the linen she needs as well
as dresses to put her on an equal footing with all the
other young ladies in the companies which she fre-
quents.''

The aunt, who was a most worthy woman, was delighted by my frankness, and she told me that she would
give me a written list of all the things Callimena needed
the first time I should call on her; I told her that, having
to go back to Rome in a few days, I would sup with Callimena every evening, and, finding her more than willing
to grant me that favor, I went with her to her niece, who
was delighted to hear of our arrangements. I began that
same day to sup and sleep with her and indeed to win her
heart completely, for I spent at least six hundred Neapolitan ducati to put her beyond want. I thought I had
bought my happiness very cheaply. Agata, to whom I
confided everything, was delighted to have been the agent
of it.

Two or three days later I gave a dinner for the Englishmen, the Saxons, and the Saxons' tutor Bertoldi, with
Madame Goudar, who came with Medini, which very
much displeased me, for after the trick he had played on
me I could not bear him; however, I immediately concealed my feelings, waiting for her husband, with whom
I had it out. We had agreed that his wife should come to
my house with no one but himself. The master scoundrel
beat about the bush and tried to assure me that Medini
had nothing to do with breaking my bank, but he wasted
his eloquence.

Our dinner was choice and gay, and the beautiful Irish
Sarah shone. She was a woman who had everything to
please—youth, beauty, grace, intelligence, high spirits,

talent, and, with all that, an air of distinction. After
dinner the Russian Count Buturlin,[19] a great admirer
of the fair sex, entered the drawing room where we were,
which was next to the apartment in which he was staying.
He came drawn by the sweet voice of the beautiful
Madame Goudar, who was humming a Neapolitan song,
accompanying herself on the guitar. The rich nobleman
fell in love with her that day. It was he who, ten months
after I left, obtained her favors in consideration of five
hundred pounds sterling which Goudar needed to obey
the order he received to leave Naples with his wife within
three days.[20] This thunderbolt was launched by the
Queen, who discovered that the King had had an interview with her in Procida,[21] and that the thing might go
much further. She came upon her royal husband laughing heartily over a note and refusing to show it to her.
The Queen's curiosity made her insist, and, the King
yielding at last, the Queen read:

*"Ti aspetterò domani nel medesimo luogo ed all'ora
stessa con l'impazienza medesima che had una vacca, che
desidera l'avvicinamento del toro"* ("I will expect you
tomorrow at the same place and the same time with all
the impatience of a cow desiring the approach of the
bull").

The Queen pretended to laugh, but on her own authority she signified to the cow's husband that he had only
three days to go to live elsewhere. But for this order,
Count Buturlin would not have been cured so cheaply.

Goudar invited the whole company to sup at his house
in Posilipo the next day, and the supper was magnificent;
but when Count Medini sat down at a large table and
took up the cards to deal at faro before a heap of gold
pieces which might come to five hundred once, no one
chose to sit down to punt. Madame Goudar tried in vain
to distribute livrets; the Englishmen and the Saxons told
her that they would punt if she would hold the bank
herself, or would have me deal for her, for they all feared

Count Medini's too lucky hand. At that, Goudar took it
upon himself to ask me if I would deal, taking a one-
fourth share in the bank, but he found me inflexible. I
told him that I would have dealt on equal shares with
him, and putting up my half of the bank in cash. On
hearing my answer, Goudar spoke to Medini, who, fearing to lose the opportunity of winning a great deal, did
no more than rise and take back his money, leaving
Goudar's on the table. Having only two hundred once in
my purse, I took two hundred more from Goudar, and
I sat down in the place which Medini had vacated. In less
than two hours all my money was gone, and I went
quietly home to console myself in the arms of my dear
Callimena.

Thus left without money, I the next day determined to
lighten the conscience of Agata's husband, who with his
wife continued to urge me to take back the earrings and
all the other pieces of jewelry which I had given her in
Turin and Alessandria.[22] I told Agata that I would never
have consented to such meanness if Fortune had not used
me ill. When she told her husband the news he came out
of his office with open arms to thank me as if I had made
his fortune.

I told him that I would accept the value of the jewelry
in cash, and he undertook to arrange it. The next morning he handed me the equivalent of fifteen thousand
French livres, about fifteen hundred ducati. With this
money I prepared to leave for Rome, intending to spend
eight months there; but before I left, the advocate wanted
to have me to dinner at a charming house he owned in
Portici. What food for thought it gave me when I found
myself in the very house in which, twenty-seven years
earlier, I had made a small fortune by confounding the
honest Greek with my false augmentation of mercury![23]

The King being then at Portici with the whole Court,
we went there, and we witnessed an extraordinary spectacle which, though laughable, did not make us laugh.

The King, who was then only nineteen years of age, was amusing himself and the Queen in a large room by all sorts of pranks. He took it into his head to be blanketed, that is, to be thrown up into the air by means of a blanket held by four strong arms which simultaneously pull it taut. But after having made his courtiers laugh, the King wanted to have his turn at laughing. He began by proposing the same sport to the Queen, who protested only by shrieks of laughter, and the King did not press it upon the ladies who were present—for fear, I believe, that they would accept. The older courtiers, who were afraid, stole away, to my regret, for I should have been delighted to see a number of them flying into the air, among others the Prince of San Nicandro,[24] who had brought him up very badly, that is, too much in the Neapolitan way, giving him his own prejudices. So the King, who wanted more of the sublime sport, was reduced to proposing it to the young noblemen who were present and who perhaps hoped to receive such a proof of their playful monarch's favor. I did not fear I should be accorded the distinction, for I was unknown and not of a rank high enough to deserve it.

So after subjecting three or four young courtiers to a tossing, which they took with various degrees of courage and which set the Queen and all the ladies present laughing, and laughing in the Neapolitan manner, which is not the covert laughter of the Spanish Court, nor even has much in common with that of France and of other Courts, where sneezes are stifled and every gentleman is ruined if he dares let himself be seen yawning, his eyes fell on two young Florentine noblemen, brothers or cousins just arrived in Naples, who were there with their tutor, who had not been able to keep from laughing with his precious charges when they saw His Majesty and his favored victims bounding into the air.

The King very graciously approached the two unfortunate Tuscans, both of them hunchbacks, short of stature and ugly of countenance, who were flabbergasted by his proposal that they undress and display themselves to the entire company. Everyone listened in the deepest silence to the eloquence of the King, who, at the same time that he urged them to undress, gave them to understand that it was very unmannerly of them to refuse, for, he argued, they could not be humiliated by doing what he had himself done first. Their tutor, knowing that the King would be angered by a refusal, told them that they should accept the honor which His Majesty was offering them, whereupon the two little misshapen creatures took off their clothes, the silence ceased, and laughter broke out at the sight of their structure, which, offering the eyes of the spectators nothing but bodies with humps before and humps behind, set on long, thin shanks which made up three fourths of their height, drew uncontrollable laughter from everyone present, including their grave tutor, who was doing his best to encourage them and ashamed to see the elder of his hunchbacks crying. The King, assuring him that he ran no risk, took him by the hand, put him in the middle of the blanket, and, to do him as much honor as possible, himself took one corner of it.

How could anyone help shrieking with laughter at the sight of that misshapen body flying into the air three times to a height of ten or twelve feet? After getting through it, he put on his clothes, and the other hunchback submitted to the same ordeal with somewhat better grace. Their tutor, to whom the King was bent on conferring the same honor, had taken to his heels, at which the monarch laughed heartily.

We enjoyed for nothing a spectacle which was worth gold. Don Pasquale Latilla, whom the King had fortunately not seen, told us at table countless anecdotes of the good King, all of which testified to an excellent character and an irresistible bent for gaiety at the expense of the cumbersome gravity and dignity in which royalty is made to consist. He told us that all who came near him could not but love him, because he preferred the pleasure of being treated as a friend to the feeling of pride with which the human heart may be filled when it sees itself surrounded by faces on which nothing is depicted but respect and fear. He was never so unhappy as when his minister Tanucci forced him to be severe in cases where severity was his duty, and he was never so joyful as when he found himself able to do a favor, so that he could be regarded as the fortunate sovereign whom the poet so well depicts in the distich:

> *Qui piger ad poenas princeps ad praemia velox*
> *Quique dolet quoties cogitur esse ferox*

> ("A prince who is slow to punish, quick to reward, and who grieves each time that he has to be severe").[25]

His education had been such that he had read nothing and learned nothing, he had no interest in any kind of literature, but he had an excellent mind and the highest esteem for men who had gained a distinguished reputation either by their probity or by their knowledge. He revered the minister Di Marco, he had the greatest respect for the memory of Don Lelio Caraffa,[26] of the ducal house of Matalona, and he had provided generously for a young nephew of the scholar Genovesi[27] out of consideration for his illustrious uncle.

Gambling being forbidden, he had one day come upon the officers of his guard playing faro. Terrified at the sight of the King, they tried to hide the cards and the money; but he told them not to let him disturb them, but to be very careful that Tanucci did not learn of their foolhardiness, at the same time assuring them that he would tell him nothing. When he was scarcely forty years of age, the King seized the opportunity to make himself loved and esteemed by all Italy and a good part of Germany, everywhere giving proofs of his good character and his virtues. His father loved him dearly until the time came when good reasons of state obliged him to resist the orders he wanted to give him in accordance with the views of his ministers. Ferdinand knew that, though he was the King of Spain's son, he must none the less be King of the Two Sicilies.[28] He had deferred long enough to Tanucci's authority in the Government. A few months after the suppression of the Jesuits he wrote his father a letter[29] the beginning of which is very amusing.

"Of all the things which I do not understand," he wrote, "four astonish me. The first is that not a soldo was found among the suppressed Jesuits, who were said to be so rich. The second is that all the *scrivani*[30] in my Kingdom are rich, though the law forbids their receiving any pay. The third is that all young wives who have young husbands become pregnant one day or another, and that mine[31] never does; and the fourth is that everyone dies when his time comes except Tanucci, who will live, I believe, until the end of the world." [32]

The King of Spain showed this letter to all his ministers at the Escorial to convince them that his son, the King of Naples, was clever, and he was right. A man who writes like that without instruction is clever.

A day or two later the Cavaliere Morosini, the nineteen-year-old nephew of the Procurator and sole heir of that illustrious House, came to Naples with Count Stratico,[33] his tutor, Professor of Mathematics at the University of Padua, who had given me a letter to his brother the monk, Professor at the University of Pisa. He came to lodge at the "Crocelle," and our pleasure in seeing each other again was mutual. The young Venetian was traveling to complete his education by learning to know Italy; he had spent three years at the Academy[34] in Turin; and he had with him a man with whom he could have become everything he could wish in order one day to be capable of filling the most important posts in his country and distinguishing himself from the common run of those who make up the Venetian nobility, which rules the Republic;

but unfortunately the rich, handsome, and not unintelligent youth had no will to learn. He had an animal love of women, he enjoyed rioting with libertines, and good society made him yawn. Detesting study, he devoted himself entirely to inventing ways to amuse himself and to spend money broadcast, more to avenge himself for the economy his uncle wanted him to practice than from natural generosity. He complained that though he had reached his majority his uncle still tried to keep him under tutelage. He had calculated that he could spend eight hundred zecchini a month, and he thought it very unjust that he was confined to spending only two hundred; in this conviction he tried his best to get into debt, and he sent Count Stratico packing when he mildly reproached him for his extravagance and pointed out that, by practicing economy, he could be lavish when he returned to Venice, where his uncle had arranged an incomparable marriage for him with a very pretty girl who was the heiress to the House of Grimani de'Servi.[35] The only thing about him which did not dismay his tutor was that he could not bear cards, either played socially or for money; for this reason I did not hesitate to introduce him to Madame Goudar as soon as, having learned that I knew her, he asked me to do him the favor.

After my bank had been broken I had been at Goudar's house, but I had always refused to play. Medini had become my mortal enemy; he left when he saw me arrive, but I pretended not to notice it. He was there on the day when I introduced Morosini and his tutor, and, forming designs on him, he at once became very intimate with him; but when he found him firmly resolved not to play, his hatred of me redoubled, for he felt certain that if the young man did not play it could only be because I had warned him. Morosini, enchanted by the charms of the beautiful Madame Goudar, thought of nothing but winning her favors by the force of love. He would have hated her if he could have supposed that the only way to con-

quer her was to offer her money. He told me more than
once that, if he was reduced to paying a woman he loved
to obtain her, he would feel so debased that he would
certainly be cured of the love she had inspired in him;
for he maintained, and he was right, that his virtues as a
man were at least equal to any that La Goudar might
have as a woman. Another of Morosini's quirks was that
he refused to be the dupe of a woman with whom he had
fallen in love and who wanted to receive presents from
him before she had granted him her favors, and La
Goudar's particular game was exactly contrary to any
such principle. She wanted her lover to give her credit.
His tutor Stratico was delighted to see him cultivating
this acquaintance, for the great thing was to occupy the
young man, who otherwise would find no way to amuse
himself except riding horseback, not like a gentleman but
galloping ten or twelve stages a day, foundering horses
for which he paid afterward. His worthy tutor every day
expected to hear that he had had an accident.

It was when I had already resolved to leave that Don
Pasquale Latilla came to see me with the Abbé Galiani,[36]
whom I had known in Paris. My reader may remember
that I had made the acquaintance of his brother in Sant'
Agata, that I had lodged in his house, where I had left
Donna Lucrezia Castelli.[37] I at once told him that I intended to pay him a visit, and I asked him if Donna
Lucrezia was still staying with him. He replied that
Donna Lucrezia was living in Salerno with the Marchesa
della C. . . ,[38] her daughter. But for this visit I could
not have had news of my former mistress except at the
Marchese Galiani's, and I should not have had one of
the greatest pleasures my soul has enjoyed in all my life.
I ask him if he knows the Marchesa della C. . . , and he
replies that he knows only her husband, who is old and
very rich. I ask him no more.

A day or two afterward the Cavaliere Morosini gave a
dinner for Madame Goudar, her husband, two other

young men whom he had met gaming at her house, and
Medini, who still hoped to make the Cavaliere his dupe in
one way or another.

Toward the end of dinner it happened that Medini
differed from me on a certain subject. Since he had
expressed his opinion with considerable acerbity, I put
it to him that a polite man ought to speak in a different
tone; he replied that it might be so, but that he had no
intention of taking lessons in good manners from me. I
restrained myself, but I was tired of putting up with
such shafts from a man who might have reason to hate
me, but who, having been originally in the wrong, ought
to conceal his hatred. I thought that he might attribute
my prudence to fear and, on that supposition, would
become constantly more insolent. I resolved to teach him
better once again. My reader may remember over what
we had fought a duel.[39] He was drinking coffee on the
balcony, enjoying the cool breeze from the sea, when,
with my cup of coffee in my hand, I approached him and,
there being no one within earshot, told him that I was
tired of putting up with his bad temper when chance
brought us together in company. He replied that I would
find him still more cutting if we could be alone together
without witnesses. I replied with a laugh that if we were
alone together, I could easily teach him a lesson. He
riposted by saying that he should like to see how easily,
and that our being alone together could be arranged at
once. I invited him to follow me as soon as he saw me
leave, as if nothing were afoot, and he said that he would
not fail to do so.

At that I left him and returned to the company, and a
quarter of an hour later I left the inn, walking slowly toward Posilipo. I saw him following me at a distance, and
then I had no doubt that we should fight, for he was
brave. We were both wearing our swords. I turned right
at the end of the beach, and when I saw that I was in the
country, where we could even hide our encounter behind

trees, I stopped, and when he came up I thought I might
speak to him, and even that he would not be sorry to have
it out in words; but, doubling his pace, the brute came at
me like a madman, with his sword in his right hand and
his hat in his left. I quickly unsheathed, and, without a
thought of giving ground, I stopped him by lunging just
when, instead of parrying, he lunged too, with the result
that we ran our swords halfway up each other's coat
sleeves. We at once withdrew them, but his only pierced
my sleeve in two places, while mine wounded him in the
forearm and in the flesh above the elbow. When I made
to continue, he fell back, and, having seen that his parry
had no vigor, I said that I would give him quarter if the
wound I had given him prevented him from defending
himself. So saying, and seeing that he did not answer me,
I played with his sword, then, with a smart blow near the
hilt, I knocked it to the ground and at once set my foot on
it. Foaming with rage, he said I had got the better of him
that time, because the slight wound I had given him had
deprived him of the strength to hold his sword, but that
he hoped I would give him his revenge. I promised to do
so at Rome, and, seeing that he was losing much blood,
I put his sword in the sheath myself, and I left, advising
him to go to Goudar's house, which was two hundred
paces away, to have his wound dressed at once.

I returned perfectly calmly to the "Crocelle," as if
nothing had happened. The Cavaliere Morosini was flirt-
ing with the beautiful Sarah, and Goudar was playing
quadrille[40] with Stratico and the two others. An hour
later I left, without having said a word to them about
Medini. I went for the last time to sup and sleep with my
dear Callimena, whom I did not see again until six years
later in Venice, performing brilliantly on the stage of
the Teatro San Benedetto.[41] I went to the "Crocelle" at
daybreak, and at eight o'clock I set out, taking leave of
no one, in a post chaise into which I put all my luggage.
At two o'clock in the afternoon I arrived in Salerno,

where, after putting my trunks in an excellent room, I
wrote a note to Donna Lucrezia Castelli in care of the
Marchesa della C. . . . I asked her if I might pay her a
visit, after which I would leave Salerno. I asked her to
answer me at once, while I was dining.

A half hour later, when I was in the middle of dinner,
I see Donna Lucrezia herself enter my room with her face
the picture of joy and run to my arms, declaring herself
happy to see me once more in her country. The enchanting woman was exactly my age, but she looked at least
ten years younger than I. After telling her that it was
from the Abbé Galiani that I had learned where she was,
I ask her for news of our daughter, and she replies that
she was awaiting me with her husband the Marchese, a
worthy old man who was eager to meet me.

"How does he know that I exist?"

"Leonilda has talked to him about you countless times
in the five years since she became his wife. He even knows
that you gave her five thousand ducati; and you shall sup
with us tonight."

"Let us go there at once, my dear friend, I am dying
to see her again, and the kind husband God has given her.
Has she children?"

"No, and it is unfortunate for her, because all of her
husband's estate will go to his nearest relatives when he
dies; but Leonilda will still be rich, for she will have a
hundred thousand ducati."

"And you have never wanted to marry?"

"Never."

"You are beautiful, as you were twenty-six years ago,
my charming old flame; but for the Abbé Galiani, I
should have left Naples without seeing you."

I quickly pick up my hat, I lock all my belongings into
my room, and I go with her to the house of the Marchese
della C. . . . I find Donna Leonilda at least three inches
taller, and, at the age of twenty-five, become a perfect
beauty. Her husband's presence does not trouble her, she

comes to me with open arms, and she saves me from the embarrassment into which I should have been thrown by a prejudice which would have made it impossible for me to act freely. She was my daughter, and nature, far from preventing me from having all the feelings of a lover toward her, forbade me to have only the inconsequential ones of father. After two fond embraces, which lasted only a moment, she introduces me to her husband, who, suffering from gout, could not stir from the chair to which it condemned him. Seeing him with a smile on his handsome face, his nightcap in his hand, and his arms open, I kissed the worthy man on both cheeks, and I was surprised by a third kiss, which he offers to my lips and which I return with a sign which sufficed to tell us that we were brothers.[42] The Marchese expected it, but I did not. A nobleman seventy years of age who could boast that he had seen the light was a rare phenomenon thirty years ago in the Kingdom of Sicily. I sit down beside him, whereupon, our certainty of our divine alliance being renewed, our embraces begin again, and the two women who were their astonished witnesses cannot understand how the recognition could have come about. Donna Leonilda is delighted to find that her husband had long known me, she tells him so, embracing him, and the worthy old man laughed loud and long. Only Donna Lucrezia suspects the truth; her daughter can make nothing of the scene, and saves her questions for another time.

The Marchese della C. . . was a nobleman who had traveled in every part of Europe, who had lived life to the full, and who did not think of marrying until his father died at the age of ninety. Finding himself provided with an income of thirty thousand ducati, which comes to a hundred and twenty thousand French livres, and hence wealthy in a country where everything is cheap, he thought he could still have children despite his advanced age. He saw Donna Leonilda at the theater in

Naples, and in a few days he signed the contract, granting her a dowry of a hundred thousand ducati. The Duke of Matalona having died, and Donna Lucrezia living with her daughter at the time, she went to live with her in Salerno. Her husband, though he lived sumptuously, could never spend half of his income. All his relatives had lodgings in his immense palace; there were three families of them, each living apart from the others. All these relatives were well off, and they were all waiting for the Marchese to die so that they could share his wealth among them, which distressed him, for he did not like them. He had married only to have an heir, and he no longer hoped for one; but that did not lessen his love for his wife, who made him happy by the charm of her intelligence. Like her, he was a freethinker, but in the greatest secrecy, no one thought freely in Salerno, so he lived with his wife and his mother-in-law like a good Christian, adopting all the prejudices of his fellow countrymen. All this I learned from Donna Leonilda three hours later while walking in his beautiful garden, to which he sent us after talking with me for three hours on all sorts of interesting subjects, which could be of no interest either to his wife or to his mother-in-law, though both of them remained with us, delighted to see the worthy man in ecstasies over having someone to talk with who thought as he did.

About six o'clock he asked Donna Lucrezia to take me to the garden and entertain me there until nightfall, and at the same time he asked his wife to remain with him because he had something to say to her. We were in the middle of August, and the heat was intense; but a gentle breeze tempered it in the apartment on the ground floor in which we were. Since I saw through the open window that the air was perfectly still, for the leaves of the trees were not moving, I could not help telling the Marchese that I was astonished to find perfect spring weather in the room in which we were. He told Donna Lucrezia to

take me to the place which would show me what caused
the coolness we had enjoyed.

Fifty paces from the room in which we were, after
passing through a suite of five or six, we came to a closet
in one corner of which was an opening four feet square.
It was this dark window which gave passage to a very
cool wind, which indeed was much too strong, so that it
would have been unhealthy for anyone who stood at the
window too long. The aperture was at the top of a flight
of more than a hundred stone steps, which led to a grotto
in which there was a perpetual spring of ice-cold water.
Donna Lucrezia told me that I should run a great risk
if I went down to the grotto without first dressing as if
in the dead of winter. I have never been foolhardy enough
to risk that kind of danger. Lord Baltimore would have
made light of it. I told my dear friend that I could well
imagine how the thing could be, and indeed understood
how it must be; so we went to the garden, which was
separated from another larger one used by the three
other families; but in this one there was every delight
for which one could wish—flowers scenting the air, foun-
tains, grottoes decorated with shellwork and furnished
with couches stuffed with down, than which nothing could
be softer. A large round pond, more than ten fathoms[48]
deep, contained fish of twenty different kinds and of
every color, which swam sinuously about and which, being
intended only to please the sight, and so not fearing the
rapacity of the epicures who would have liked to catch
and eat them, came fearlessly sporting even into the
hands held close to the surface of their element. The covered walks of this pretty paradise were overhung with
vines and great bunches of grapes as broad as the leaves
which separated them, and fruit trees to left and right
formed the colonnade which supported them.

I told my dear Lucrezia, who was enjoying my delight,
that I was not surprised that the garden aroused more
pleasing sensations in me than the vineyards of Tivoli

and Frascati, for everything extensive is more apt to dazzle than to charm. In half an hour she informed me of all her daughter's happiness and all the good qualities of the Marchese, who, except for the gout, enjoyed perfect health. His only misfortune, his sorrow which he nevertheless had the strength of mind to hide, was that he had no children; it was a hard trial for his philosophy, for, among ten or twelve nephews, he had not found one who promised to be distinguished either in body or mind.

"They are all ugly," she said, "and all dullards, brought up like peasants by boors and ignorant priests."

"But is our daughter really happy?"

"Very happy, even though she cannot find in the husband she adores the lover whom she needs at her age."

"The Marchese seems to me a man incapable of jealousy."

"He is not jealous, and I am sure that if, among the nobility of this city, she could have found a man capable of pleasing her the Marchese would have made a friend of him and would even not have been sorry to see her become pregnant."

"Is he in a position to be absolutely certain that, if she gives him a child, he cannot be its father?"

"Not entirely certain, for when his health is good he comes to sleep with her, and, according to what my daughter has told me, he could flatter himself that he had really done what he had not done. But there is no longer any likelihood that his ardor will have happy results. My daughter had reason to hope so during the first six months of their marriage, but after that his attacks of gout became so much worse that his nerves were weakened to the point that she herself concluded that the transports of conjugal love might be fatal to him. Hence she is never so distressed as when he wants to sleep with her."

In ecstasies of admiration for the unchanging qualities
of my dear former mistress, I was beginning to tell her
what power her charms still had over my amorous soul,
when the Marchesa appeared in the covered walk down
which we were strolling, followed by a page who held up
the train of her dress and a young lady on her left who
kept half a pace behind her. As she approached I went
through all the motions of showing the most profound
respect, to which she responded by affecting the most refined politeness. She said that she had come to negotiate
a matter of the utmost consequence, for if she failed she
would lose all the confidence her husband had in her.

"Where, beautiful Marchesa, is there a negotiator with
whom you can fear not to succeed?"

"It is yourself."

"If it is I," I replied with a laugh, "your reputation
runs no risk, for I give you carte blanche even before I
know what it is all about. I make only one exception."

"So much the worse, for unfortunately the exception
might be the very thing. Tell me what it is, I beg you,
before I speak."

"I was about to leave for Rome on urgent business,
when the Abbé Galiani told me that Donna Lucrezia is
living with you. I made the necessary arrangements so
that sixty extra miles will not interfere with my business."

"And could a short delay put your life or your honor
in danger? Are you no longer your own master? To whom
are you responsible? This is the ruin of my negotiation."

"Wait, I beg you, and let me see that beautiful countenance serene again. Your orders, and even your wishes,
can never endanger either my life or my honor. Yes, I am
still completely my own master, and I will never cease to
be so except at this moment. I am yours to command."

"Very good. You shall come to spend a few days with
us at an estate which is only an hour and a half from here.

My husband will have himself carried there. You will allow me to send to your inn for all your luggage and have it brought here."

"Here, Signora, is the key to my room. Happy the man to whom you grant the opportunity to obey you!"

At that she gave the key to her page, ordering him to go there himself with some menservants to take everything and see to it that nothing was left behind. The page was a very handsome boy; and her chambermaid, or maid-in-waiting, who was following us, was a charming blonde. I told her so, thinking that she did not understand French; she smiled and told her mistress that I knew her but had forgotten her.

"You saw me and talked with me several times, and even made me angry with you, when I was with the Duchess of Matalona, now Princess of Caramanica."

"It is possible; you must have been very different nine years ago from what you are today. I am sorry, Signorina, that I do not remember having done anything to make you angry."

The Marchesa and her mother laughed heartily at the exchange, and urged her to tell what I had done to make her angry, but she blushed and said no more than that I had played jokes on her. I remembered that I had given her a few kisses, almost by force; but the Marchesa and her mother believed what they pleased. Since I had some knowledge of the human heart, it seemed to me that Signorina Anastasia (such was her name) had quite given herself away by reproaching me, and that if she wanted me she should have said nothing.

"You were," I said to her, "much shorter and very thin."

"I was only twelve years old. You have changed too, for it seems to me your eyes were blacker and your complexion lighter."

"That is to say, less dark. I am old, Signorina."

But full of ardor for both the mother and the daughter,

I turned the conversation to the late Duke, and Anastasia left us. We went and sat down in a grotto, where, as soon as were alone, we surrendered to the pleasure of addressing each other by the fond names of daughter and father, which gave us the right to intimacies which, though imperfect, were sinful nevertheless. The Marchesa thought it her duty to calm my transports by saying that when we had given rein to our senses despite the ties of blood she was her own mistress, whereas now she had a master. Donna Lucrezia, who saw me in ecstasies with her daughter in my arms, and who saw that her daughter was moved too and offered very little resistance to my caresses, warned us to restrain ourselves and take good care not to be led into consummating our mutual crime, and, so saying, she went to another part of the walk. But her words, followed by her departure, had the very opposite effect to the advice she had given us. Determined to consummate the so-called crime, we came so close to it that an almost involuntary movement forced us to consummate it so completely that we could not have done more if we had been acting according to a premeditated plan conceived by the free exercise of reason. We remained motionless, looking at each other without changing our position, both of us serious and silent, lost in reflection, astonished, as we told each other afterward, to feel neither guilty nor tormented by remorse. We arranged our clothing, and my daughter, sitting beside me, called me ''husband'' even as I called her ''wife.'' By sweet kisses we confirmed what we had just done, and even if an angel had come to tell us we had monstrously outraged nature we should have laughed at him. Absorbed as we were in this perfectly decorous tenderness, Donna Lucrezia was edified to find us become so calm.

We did not need to discuss it together to know that we must keep our secret. Donna Lucrezia was intelligent, but everything compelled us not to tell her what it was neither necessary nor advantageous to confide to her. It seemed to us that, by leaving us alone, she had wanted only to be sure that she would not witness what we were going to do. But in fact, as she told us immediately, she believed that we had let ourselves indulge in nothing but inconsequential toying, and she laughed when we could not deny it. We recalled the beautiful night we had all three spent in one bed, and Donna Lucrezia was very well pleased by my candor when I told her that my hand had found her daughter almost exactly as she was when she had slept with us nine years before. We left the walk, and we returned to the palace with Anastasia.

The Marchese received his wife very gaily, congratulating her on the success of her negotiation, and telling me that at his country house I should be lodged better than in the apartment to which my luggage had been taken. He told his mother-in-law that he hoped she would not be sorry to have me in the room next to hers. She replied that our good days were over. I was surprised that, knowing that I had wanted to marry Donna Leonilda, he should think that I was sufficiently cured of my passion to prefer her mother to her. Five places were laid on a large table, and scarcely were we served before I saw an old priest come in and sit down without looking at anyone. Nor did anyone ever speak to him. The same handsome page, as he was called, stood behind the Marchesa, and ten or twelve others busied themselves serving everyone. Having dined on nothing but soup, I ate like an ogre. The Marchese had a French cook, who employed his art to give him excellent fare; so, except for the dish of macaroni, the supper was composed entirely of entrées; the Marchese exclaimed with delight when he saw how I ate; he said it was his great misfortune that both his wife and her mother were not hearty eaters. At dessert, our spirits raised by the excellent wines, the conversation became animated, and, since we were speaking French and the priest did not understand a word of what we were saying, he left, after reciting the *Agimus*.[44] The Marchese told me that he had held the post of confessor in his house for fifteen years, but that no one had ever confessed to him; he warned me against saying anything heretical in the ignoramus's presence, but added that I could say anything I pleased in French. Being in the vein, I kept them amused at table until an hour after midnight. Before we parted he told us that we should leave after dining, and that he would arrive an hour after we did. He assured his wife that he felt well, and that he intended to convince her that I had taken ten years from his age. She then kissed him very fondly, begging him to take care of his health; but it had no effect, he promised her a visit.

I then left with Donna Lucrezia, wishing them a fine boy, to be delivered in nine months.

"Draw up the bill," he said, "and tomorrow morning I will accept it."

"I will do everything in my power," said Donna Leonilda, "to keep you from going bankrupt."

Donna Lucrezia showed me to my room, where, after turning me over to a tall lackey, she wished me good night. After sleeping for eight hours in an excellent bed, I got up and I went to find Donna Lucrezia, who took me to breakfast in the apartment of the Marchesa, who was already dressing. I at once asked her if I could venture to draw my bill at nine months, and she replied that it would very likely be paid.

"Really?"

"Really; and it will be to you that the Marchese will be indebted for the only happiness which he lacks, and for which he longs with all his soul. He told me so himself when he left me an hour ago."

What a disappointment not to be able to give her a hundred kisses! She was as fresh as a rose, but we had to restrain ourselves. She was surrounded by pretty girls, all of them in her service. I flirted with Anastasia, and Leonilda pretended to encourage me. Understanding

what she had in mind, I made a show of passion, and I saw
that I should not be dismissed unheard. But I set myself
certain bounds, so that I should not be taken at my word.

We went to breakfast in the apartment of the Marchese,
who was expecting us and who received me joyfully. The
worthy man's health would have been excellent if the
gout had not deprived him of the use of his legs for walking. He could not even stand up, or bear the slightest
touch on his feet: any contact caused him intolerably
acute pain. After breakfast we heard mass, at which I
saw more than twenty menservants and maids, and after
the mass I kept him company until dinnertime. He was
very grateful to me for preferring his company to that
of his wife and his mother-in-law, with whom he believed
I was still in love.

After dinner we left for his country estate, I in a carriage with the mother and daughter, he in a covered litter
carried on two shafts by two mules, one in front of the
other. In an hour and a half we came to his estate, which
was between Picenza and Battipaglia.[45] His ancestral
castle was large and beautiful and very well situated.
While we waited for the Marchesa's chambermaids to
arrive, she took me to her gardens, where, my love having
revived, she abandoned herself to it once again. We
agreed that I was not to enter her apartment except to
flirt with Anastasia, for we must not give anyone the least
occasion for suspecting our love. Indeed, my flirtation
with Anastasia was to amuse the Marchese, whom she
would not fail to keep informed of it. Donna Lucrezia
approved of our measures, for she did not want the Marchese to think that I had stopped in Salerno on her account. My apartment adjoined hers, but I could not enter
hers except through the room in which Anastasia slept
with another of her chambermaids, who was even prettier.

The Marchese arrived an hour after us, with all the
menservants and with mine, who brought me my luggage.
Carried in a comfortable armchair, he himself took me to

see all the beautiful walks of his gardens, while waiting
for his wife and his mother-in-law to arrange everything
in the castle. After supper, being very tired, he withdrew,
leaving me with the ladies. I escorted the Marchesa to her
room, and when I started to leave she told me that I
could go to my room by way of her maids' room, and she
ordered Anastasia to escort me to it. Politeness demanding that I show myself not insensible to this piece of good
fortune, I told the beauty who was lighting my way that
her mistrusting my proximity to the point of locking
herself in would be a reflection on my character which I
hoped she would spare me. She replied that she felt no
mistrust, but that she would lock her door nevertheless,
for it was her duty, and the more so because the room was
her mistress's anteroom and because the maid who shared
it with her would think the worst of her if she dared to
leave her room unlocked. Admitting that she was right, I
asked her to sit down beside me for a moment and remind
me of what I could have done to anger her nine years
earlier. She replied that she did not want to remember it,
and she asked me to allow her to leave, which I did after
she permitted me a kiss which I made her think I wanted.
After she left, my manservant having come in, I told him
that I did not need his services after supper. He understood what I meant, and on the following nights he did
not come. The next day the Marchesa laughingly repeated
to me the whole of the conversation I had had with Anastasia. She had confided it all to her, withholding not the
slightest detail, and she had praised her for refusing to
leave her door unlocked, but she had told her that she
could offer me all her services in my room. The Marchesa
purposely regaled her husband with the story, and he,
believing that I was in love with Anastasia, twitted me
with it good-humoredly after dinner, and that evening
he had her sup with us, which obliged me to play the part
of respectful suitor to the girl, who was much flattered
by my giving her the preference over her charming mis-

tress and by the latter's kindness in showing no disap-
probation either of my passion or of the concessions by
which she might keep it alive. The Marchese enjoyed the
pretty comedy which the intrigue suggested to his imagination, for by making it possible for me to play it he
considered that he was doing me the honors of his house
and making me want to stay there a few days longer.

Anastasia came with a candle to show me to my room,
where, when she learned that I had no servant, she insisted on dressing my hair for the night; gratified that I
did not venture to go to bed in her presence, she sat with
me for a good half hour, during which, since I was not in
love with her, I had no difficulty in playing the timid
suitor. When she wished me good night she was delighted
that my kisses were less bold than those I had given her
the evening before. The Marchesa said to me the next
morning that, if what Anastasia had told her was true,
she concluded that I must find her a trial, for she was
sure that if I loved her I should not be timid.

"She is no trial at all, for the scene we play is pretty
and amusing; but I am amazed that you think I can love
her, when we agreed that it was to be only a feint to
amuse the Marchese and put the servants' suspicions to
sleep."

"Anastasia believes that you adore her, and I am not
sorry that you are giving her a decided liking for coquetry."

"If in the meantime I can bring her to leave her door
unlocked I could easily go to your room without her having the least suspicion, for when I leave her bed, where I
would have done nothing of consequence, she could never
imagine that instead of going to my room I go to yours."

"Take care how you go about it."

"I will open negotiations this evening."

Both the Marchese and Donna Lucrezia credited me
with behaving as became a man of discretion, but at the
same time they were certain that the girl Anastasia slept

with me every night, which delighted them. Meanwhile I spent all day with the Marchese, who insisted that I made him happy. It cost me nothing, for I liked his principles and his intelligence. During the third supper with Anastasia I showed myself more ardent than usual, and she was astonished when she found me cold in my room; she said that she was glad to see me become calm. I replied that the reason for it was that I imagined she thought she was in danger when she was alone with me.

"Not a bit of it. I believe you have learned wisdom; you are very different in that respect from what you were nine years ago."

"But what extravagances did I commit then?"

"It was not that; you simply failed to consider that I was still a child."

"I gave you a few harmless caresses, for which I am sorry because now they make you think you must be on your guard and keep your door locked."

"It is not because I am mistrustful, but for the reasons I told you, which you acknowledged were sound. I could also say that it is a kind of mistrust which keeps you from going to bed while I am here."

"Good God! You must think me a great fool. I will go to bed at once. But you shall not leave until you have come and kissed me."

"Gladly."

So I got into bed; and Anastasia came and spent half an hour with me, during which I had the greatest difficulty in denying myself everything; but I had to act so, for I was afraid that she would tell it all to the Marchesa. When she left, Anastasia gave me such a sweet embrace that I could no longer control myself. Her own hand, guided by mine, convinced her that I loved her, and she went away—whether edified or annoyed by my restraint I do not know.

Very curious the next morning to hear how she had described the scene to the Marchesa, I was not sorry to learn that she had said nothing of her touching me. This made me certain that she would leave her door unlocked for me, and I promised my dear Leonilda that I would come and spend two hours with her. When Anastasia visited me after supper I challenged her to show as much confidence in me as I had shown in her, and she said that she would willingly do so provided that I would blow out my candle and never once put my hand on her. I promised, and I was certain I would keep my word, for I must not risk cutting a poor figure with my dear Marchesa. I put out my candle as soon as she left, and I saw her undress, kneel down in her shift to say her prayers, then get into bed and blow out the candle.

At that I undressed quickly, went into her room barefoot, and sat down beside her, when she at once took hold of both my hands. I made no effort to free them, which she attributed to my great love and the promise I had made her. The only part of us which allowed itself freedom of action was our lips, which in half an hour gave and received a quantity of kisses, but silently for fear that her roommate would hear them. For the same reason we never said a word to each other. The half hour passed very slowly for me and with a discomfort which it is hard to imagine. I had to believe that Anastasia enjoyed it, for she found that she had the power to make me do whatever she pleased. When I left her I went to my room; but as soon as I thought she was asleep, I crossed hers and entered Leonilda's; she was expecting me, but she did not know that I had come in until she felt me embrace her. After giving her the liveliest tokens of my love, I told her, hiding nothing, all that I had done to persuade Anastasia to leave her door unlocked for me, and all that I had done during the half hour I had been beside her on her bed. After spending two delicious hours with my dear Leonilda, I left her, certain that they would not be the last. I returned to my room without making the slightest noise to betray the secret. I slept until noon. The Mar-

chese and Donna Lucrezia twitted me with it at dinner,
and at supper they twitted Anastasia, who played her
role very well. When we were alone together she told me
that she would no longer lock her door, but that it was
useless and even dangerous for me to come to her in her
room, so it would be better if we talked by candlelight
in mine, but that to assure her that she was not incon-
veniencing me I must go to bed. I had to consent. I hoped
that nothing would happen which could prevent me from
going to spend another two hours with the Marchesa
after Anastasia had spent a constrained hour with me;
but I miscalculated, and it was my own fault.

In bed, with Anastasia in my arms and her lips pressed
to mine, I told her that she did not trust me enough to
undress and get into my bed with me; thus challenged,
she replied by asking me if I would promise to be on my
good behavior. Only a fool would have answered no. I
made up my mind, and, answering yes, I prepared to
make her happy, for the poor, pretty girl had fought
against herself quite long enough the evening before.
She took off her dress, she let her petticoat drop, and she
came to my arms, in a surrender which left her with no
thought of demanding that I keep my promise. Appetite,
says the proverb, grows with eating. Her ardor made me
amorous, she threw off all restraint, she displayed all her
beauties to me, and I did not cease to do her justice until
sleep overcame my senses. She then had to leave me.
When I woke, feeling strangely put out, for what had
happened so unseasonably was bound to interfere with my
visits to the Marchesa, I laughed when I saw that I should
have to tell her everything. I saw that I had become
Anastasia's victim despite myself, for, aside from its
being unforgivable if I had sent her away after half an
hour's amusement, she would have locked her door; and
even if she had not locked it, what would I have done with
Leonilda after Anastasia had exhausted me?

When I told Leonilda the whole story she could not but

laugh, and she saw as well as I did that I could have
nothing more for her. We had to resign ourselves. During
the five or six more days that I stayed on there, I had
Leonilda only two or three more times in an arbor in the
garden and in the greatest haste. I had to receive Anastasia in my bed every night, and to end by her thinking
me a traitor when I raised objections to her offer to come
to Rome with me, where she told me she had a very rich
uncle who would take care of her when I no longer loved
her. She declared that if I loved her I could not refuse
her offer; and she was right, but I did not love her enough
to make her my mistress, when my whole fortune
amounted to only a thousand zecchini.

The evening before I left, the Marchese della C. . .
strangely surprised me by a proposal he made to me in
private. Without any long preamble, the generous man,
after thanking me for having kept him such good company, told me that he had learned from the Duke of
Matalona himself the reason why I had not married his
wife, and that he had always admired me for making her
a present of five thousand ducati when I left Naples,
though I was not rich.

"Those five thousand ducati," he went on, "with five
or six thousand more which she had from the Duke's
generosity, made up her dowry, to which I added a hundred thousand, so that she is sure of a fortune even if I die
without having a child. What I now ask is that you be
kind enough to accept the return of the five thousand
ducati you gave Leonilda; it is she who wants to give you
this token of her affection and esteem; I approved of her
noble generosity, but I did not want her to deprive herself: it is from me that you shall receive them today. She
did not dare to express to you what I have just told you,
because of a delicacy for which you must be grateful to
her. She thought you would be offended by her trying to
discharge her obligation to you by this restitution."

"And she would have been right, I should have refused

to accept the five thousand ducati from her, but I do not refuse them from you, for I consider them only a gift inspired by the noblest of all your virtues. A refusal on my part, my dear Marchese, could spring from nothing but a stupid and most inappropriate pride, for I am not rich. What I wish is that your wife and her mother shall be present when you make me this gift.''

''We will do it after dinner.''

The city of Naples was my Temple of Fortune each of the four times that I stayed there. If I went there now, I should die of starvation. Fortune scorns old age. The last time I went there, she sent me two rich and happy women, who gave me back what I had given them, as if it had been lent. Leonilda and her mother wept for joy when the Marchese handed me the five thousand ducati in bank notes in their presence and at the same time gave another five thousand to Donna Lucrezia by way of rewarding her for having been the person who introduced me to him. He was discreet enough not to reveal the more important reason to her. Donna Lucrezia did not know that the Duke of Matalona had told him that Leonilda was my daughter. Gratitude tempered my high spirits all the rest of the day, and Anastasia spent a rather gloomy night with me. When she reproached me with not loving her, I replied only ambiguously. I left the next morning at eight o'clock, after the most refined sentiments on all our parts found expression only in words which interpreted them most inadequately. I very gladly promised the Marchese that I would write to him from Rome. I arrived at Agata's house in Naples at eleven o'clock, finding her amazed to see me, for she thought I was in Rome. Her husband received me with expressions of the greatest friendship, despite *li flati*[46] from which he was suffering severely that day. I told him that I was determined to leave after dinner, and that I had only come to embrace him and ask him to get me a bill of exchange on Rome against the five thousand Neapolitan ducati which I gave him. He promised me that it would be ready before three o'clock, and Agata, who was delighted, at once sent word to Callimena to come to dine with her.

Very much surprised to see me still in Naples when she thought I had been in Rome for two weeks, the good-hearted girl told me all the details of her amour with the young Cavaliere Morosini, which lasted only ten days; but she had nothing to complain of but his inconstancy. He had left her for a dancing girl. My two weeks' disappearance was the puzzle which enlivened our dinner; I satisfied no one's curiosity. I left them at three o'clock after the fondest embraces, and I traveled all night; I stopped at Monte Cassino,[47] which I had never seen, and I was delighted to have done so, for I found there Prince Xavier of Saxony under the name of Count Lausitz,[48] with Signora Spinucci,[49] a lady of Fermo, whom the Prince had married but whose position he did not make known. He had been there for three days. He had had to wait for the Pope's permission for Signora Spinucci, for by the Rule of St. Benedict women were expressly forbidden to enter the monastery, and, since Signora Spinucci refused to comply, the Prince had to send an express messenger to Signor Bianconi[50] in Rome to obtain permission. After seeing everything worth seeing in Monte Cassino and sleeping there, I left to go on to Rome without stopping, for though it was the middle of September it had not yet rained and the air was still noxious. I went to lodge at the inn on the Piazza di Spagna kept by Roland's daughter, the sister of Teresa, the wife of my brother, who was still in Rome with Prince Beloselski.

VOLUME 11 · NOTES

CHAPTER I

1. *La Pichona:* Maria Teresa Palomino (1728-1795), called La Pichona, Spanish actress (see Vol. 10, Chap. XII, n. 67).
2. *Fandango:* Well-known Spanish dance, which C. had been taught by a Spanish actor (see Vol. 10, Chap. XII).
3. *Pareja:* Spanish, "partner" (feminine). C. had picked up the term when the disguised Duke of Medina Celi had encouraged him to find a partner for the next ball (see Vol. 10, Chap. XII).
4. *Plazuela:* C. writes "la plaquella."
5. *Calle del Desengaño:* This street, in the vicinity of the Puerta del Sol, still exists.
6. *Ramos:* Obviously a fictitious name, for C. first began to write a name beginning with Q, then substituted Ramos.
7. *Doblones:* The doblón was a gold coin minted in Spain until 1772; value 4 pesos.
8. *The Mint:* In the 17th century the Mint (Real Casa de la Moneda) was in the Calle de Segovia; it later occupied a building at the corner of the Paseo de Recoletos and the Calle de Goya.
9. *Medina Celi:* Luis Antonio Fernandez de Córdoba, Duke of Medina Celi (died 1768), Grand Master of the Royal Horse.
10. *Pesos duros:* Spanish silver coin worth 8 reales. Four pesos made 1 doblón.
11. *The Duke . . . had died:* The Duke of Medina Celi died in Jan. 1768.
12. *A son:* Pedro de Alcántara Fernandez de Córdoba, Duke of Medina Celi (died 1790); his son was Luis Maria (died 1806).
13. *An intelligent author:* To what author C. refers remains unascertained.
14. *Thirty hats:* Sombrero ("hat") was the term for the right of certain Spanish Grandees not to uncover in the King's presence.

15. *Marazzani:* Antonio Luigi Marazzani (ca. 1740 - after 1780), priest who became an adventurer, assuming the title of Count. He appeared in Venice ca. 1779 and was banished as the result of information supplied by C. in his role of *confidente* ("informer") to the State Inquisitors.

16. *His Majesty:* Carlos III (1716-1788), King of Spain from 1759 (cf. Vol. 10, Chap. XI, n. 47).

17. *Mercury:* Roman equivalent of the Greek god Hermes, the messenger of the gods, often employed by Jupiter as a procurer.

18. Martial, *Epigrams*, 1, 57, 2.

19. *Zapatero de viejo:* C. writes "*viecco*." The meaning is "cobbler" (in contradistinction to "shoemaker").

20. *Accord the "Don" . . . a hidalgo:* A hidalgo (cf. Vol. 10, Chap. XII, n. 72), as a nobleman of the lower class, had the right to be addressed as Don.

21. *Princess of Asturias:* Asturias is a province in northwestern Spain. The titles Prince and Princess of Asturias were borne by the Heir Apparent and his wife. The reference is to Maria Luisa Teresa (1751-1819), daughter of the Duke of Parma; she was married in 1765 to the son of Carlos III, who became King of Spain in 1788 as Carlos IV.

22. *Ratafia:* A sweet fruit liqueur (cf. Vol. 3, Chap. VIII, n. 21).

23. *Doblón de a ocho:* Spanish gold coin worth 8 escudos. (In Vol. 1, Chap. X, n. 29, "gold scudi" should be corrected to "escudos.")

24. *La Soledad:* There were then two churches in Madrid named Nuestra Señora de la Soledad. C. probably refers to the one which still stands in the Calle de Fuencarral, near the Puerta del Sol.

25. *Charlotte:* Charlotte de Lamotte, of Brussels (died 1767), whose acquaintance C. had made in Spa, where she was the mistress of the adventurer Croce (Crosin) (cf. Vol. 10, Chap. XI).

26. *Obligation . . . Count of Aranda . . . done:* As President of the Council of Castile from 1766, the Count of Aranda had issued new regulations governing theatrical performances and had licensed masked balls.

27. *Los padres de la Compañía:* I.e., the Jesuits, whom Aranda expelled in 1767.

28. *Cloaks . . . sombreros gachos:* Long cloaks (*capas largas*) and slouch hats (*sombreros gachos*) had already been forbidden by Aranda's predecessor Squillace (cf. Vol. 10, Chap. XII, n. 44).

29. *Los Caños del Peral:* Theater in Madrid (cf. Vol. 10, Chap. XII, n. 64).

30. *La Mancha:* Old province of central Spain, south of Madrid, famous for its wines, especially that from Valdepeñas; birthplace of Don Quixote.

31. *Marina:* St. Marina (5th century), whose feast is celebrated on July 17, lived in a Bithynian hermitage in men's clothing, first with her father, then as a hermit. Accused of being the lover of a girl to whom she had given religious counsel and who was found to be pregnant, she was sentenced to death. Only after her death was it discovered that she was a woman.

32. Altered from Erasmus, *Adagia,* Chil. III, Centur. IV, Prov. LXXVII. (C. has quoted it several times before.)

33. *I was five inches taller than she:* As C. states several times (e.g., Vol. 3, Chap. VIII), he was 5 feet 9 inches tall.

34. *Alcalde Messa:* An alcalde (from Arabic *al-qadi*) was a Spanish administrative official with judicial and police powers. Aranda had divided Madrid into 64 districts, each of which elected its alcalde from among its inhabitants. Of an Alcalde Messa nothing is known.

35. *Presidios:* Penitentiaries in which persons convicted of serious crimes and sentenced to hard labor were confined. The 4 principal ones were in North Africa.

36. *He was innocent:* C. here added, then crossed out, two sentences in which he expressed his doubt of his page's innocence.

37. *À la maréchale: Poudre à la maréchale* was highly scented.

38. *The Cavaliere di Casanova:* Text: *"le Chevalier de Casanova."* It follows that C. did not call himself de Seingalt in Spain. As a Knight of the Golden Spur, he had a right to the title Cavaliere.

39. *Buen Retiro:* The palace of Buen Retiro was the residence

of the Spanish Kings from the 17th century until the Palacio
Real was built in 1737. Of the 17th-century building almost
nothing remains, so the name now designates the fine gardens
of the former palace.

40. *Philip V . . . the Queen:* Philip V was King of Spain from
1700 to 1746. His first wife was Maria Louisa of Savoy, after
whose death in 1714 he married Elizabeth Farnese of Parma;
C. refers to the latter.

41. *The Parmesan Ambassador:* Piacenza belonged to the
Duchy of Parma, which, however, had no regular representative in Madrid.

42. *The Venetian Ambassador:* Alvise Sebastiano Mocenigo
(1725-1780), Procurator of San Marco, from 1762 to 1768
Venetian Ambassador in Madrid.

43. *Manuzzi:* Son of Giovanni Battista Manuzzi, who, as a spy
for the Venetian State Inquisition, had contributed to C.'s
being imprisoned under the Leads. C. calls the son a Count.
Nothing is known of him or of his title. See Vol. 4, Chap. X,
and Vol. 10, Chap. XII.

44. *Signora Zorzi . . . Condulmer:* Maria Teresa Zorzi, née
Dolfin, married in 1748 to the Venetian patrician Marcantonio Zorzi; according to C.'s account (Vol. 4, Chap. VIII),
she was courted by the patrician Antonio Condulmer, who
was a State Inquisitor in 1755 and who sent C. to prison
under the Leads.

45. *Roda:* Manuel, Marqués de Roda y Arrieta (ca. 1707 -
after 1776), Minister of Justice from 1765.

46. *His Catholic Majesty:* Title conferred on the Kings of
Spain by Pope Alexander VI in 1497.

47. *Rojas:* C. writes "Royas"; Rojas was so common a name in
Spain at the time that no identification is possible.

48. *I did him a wrong:* C. anticipates events of which he will
give an account in Chap. IV of this volume.

49. *Dandolo:* Marco Dandolo (1704-1779), Venetian patrician,
and C.'s faithful friend.

50. *One of the three Inquisitors:* C. followed this by "who had
me imprisoned under the Leads," then crossed it out. The
reference is to Antonio da Mula (1714 - after 1782), who was
a State Inquisitor in 1755, and whom C. names a few lines
further on.

51. *Zulian:* Girolamo Giuliano, Venetian Zulian (1730-1795), Venetian patrician and diplomat; State Inquisitor in 1774.

52. *Aranjuez:* Then a village some 30 miles south of Madrid on the Tagus, with a famous royal palace, built in the 16th century by Juan de Herrera. King Carlos III regularly spent the months of April and May in Aranjuez.

CHAPTER II

1. *Princess Lubomirska:* According to Chap. I of this volume, C. had come to Madrid with a letter of introduction to the Duke of Losada from Princess Lubomirska, née Czartoryska (cf. Vol. 10, Chap. XI).

2. *Béliardi:* Agostino Bigliardi, of Sinigaglia (1723-1803), Italian abate, entered the French service in 1757, after which he spelled his name Béliardi; the Duke of Choiseul appointed him "general commercial and naval agent" on the staff of the French Ambassador in Madrid, the Marquis d'Ossun, where he remained until his patron Choiseul was disgraced in 1770. (C. writes "Bigliardi.")

3. *Campomanes:* Don Pedro Rodríguez, Count of Campomanes (1723-1803), held several important governmental posts; in 1765 he became Director of the Royal Historical Academy; he wrote numerous works on political and economic subjects.

4. *Olavides:* Pablo Antonio José Olavides, Count of Pilos (1725-1803), of Lima, Peru, Spanish statesman and economist, and until 1775 superintendent of the Swiss and German settlements in the Sierra Morena (cf. note 19 to this chapter); he was tried by the Inquisition in 1776 and exiled to a monastery, but was able to escape to France in 1778 and did not return to Spain until 1797.

5. *Strabismics:* C. writes "strabons," an Italianism, augmentative of *strabo*, "squinter."

6. *Mortmains:* Mortmain is the condition of lands or tenements held inalienably by ecclesiastical or other corporations. Many religious orders were the beneficiaries of such testamentary dispositions.

7. *Sarpi:* Fra Paolo Sarpi, called Paolo Veneto (1552-1623), was an adviser to the Venetian Republic and, as an opponent of Papal absolutism, the author of numerous political trea-

tises, which, after being forgotten, were rediscovered in the latter half of the 18th century and found to bear on problems then current.

8. *Campomanes was imprisoned . . . four years later:* There is no record that Campomanes was ever imprisoned; he retired from political life voluntarily in 1791.

9. *Olavides . . . treated more harshly:* Cf. note 4 to this chapter. His condemnation was principally due to his correspondence with Voltaire and Rousseau, as well as to his possession of erotic pictures and pieces of sculpture.

10. *Appointed Ambassador to France:* Aranda was the Spanish Ambassador in Versailles from 1773 to 1786.

11. *Carlos III . . . died mad:* C. exaggerates. Of a melancholy temperament by nature, the King had lost his wife in 1760 and then, one after the other in rapid succession, his daughter-in-law the Infanta of Portugal, her children, and finally his own son the Infante Don Gabriel. All this naturally had its effect on the King's innate melancholy; but there is no evidence that he died insane.

12. *The excesses committed by the Jesuits:* The allusion is to the attempted assassination of the King of Portugal, which took place in 1758, and to the financial crisis in France brought on by the speculations and bankruptcy of the Superior of the Jesuits in Martinique (cf. Vol. 10, Chap. II).

13. *The Jesuit confessor of Don Fernando VI:* Fernando VI (1713-1759), King of Spain from 1746, had as his confessor the Jesuit Francisco de Rávago (1685-1763).

14. *Ensenada:* Zenón de Somodevilla y Bengoechea, Marqués de la Ensenada (1702-1781), Spanish statesman, holder of numerous high offices from 1737 to 1750, in which year he was disgraced and banished to Granada at the instigation of the King's confessor Rávago; however, he was not removed from his last offices until 1754, when his support of the pro-French faction brought the English diplomat Richard Wall into action against him.

15. *Los Teatinos:* English, Theatines; name of an order of monks founded in Italy in 1524 by St. Cajetan (1480-1547) and Pietro Caraffa, then Archbishop of Chieti (in antiquity Teate, whence "Theatines"), later Pope as Paul IV (1555-

1559). But in Spain in the 17th and 18th centuries the name was applied to the Jesuits. (C. writes *"los Theatinos."*)

16. *Cayetanos:* Alternative Spanish name for the Theatines, from their co-founder St. Cajetan. (C. writes "Gaetanos.")

17. Cf. *pia fraus,* Ovid, *Metamorphoses,* IX, 711.

18. *Was given a new confessor:* Until 1760 his confessor was Fray José Casado, called (from his birthplace) Bolanos; when he resigned because of age and illness, the King himself chose the Franciscan Fray Joaquín Eleta (died 1788) as his confessor.

19. *Las sierras de Morena:* Properly La Sierra Morena, a mountain range in southern Spain, running east and west north of the Guadalquivir. The plan for an intensive settlement of the region had originated in 1749. But it was not until 1766 that a Bavarian officer, Johann Caspar Thürriegel, presented a thorough study of the project, which was approved by the Council of Castile in 1767. The settlers came not only from Switzerland but also from Germany, and some of them were Protestants. After great difficulties at the beginning, the colony flourished.

20. *The Bishop:* Probably the Bishop of Córdoba.

21. *Heimweh:* Homesickness. (C. writes "le Heimvèh.")

22. *What the Greeks called* nostalgia: The word *nostalgia* did not exist in classical Greek; it was coined from Greek roots in the 17th century to represent the German *Heimweh* in medical writings.

23. *Customs . . . in regard to making love:* Allusion to the Swiss *Kiltgang* or Bavarian *Fensterln,* which C. has described in Vol. 6, Chap. V (see also note 11 to that chapter).

24. *The Portuguese lady:* In all probability a reference to Pauline (cf. Vol. 9, Chaps. VIII and IX).

25. *Signora Sabatini:* Wife of the Italian architect Francesco Sabatini (1722-1797), who was summoned to Spain in 1760. (Cf. Vol. 10, Chap. XII.)

26. *Medina Sidonia:* Pedro de Alcántara Pérez de Guzmán el Bueno, Duke of Medina Sidonia (died ca. 1777), from 1765 Master of the Horse to the Prince of Asturias, from 1768 to King Carlos III.

27. *Varnier:* Don Domingo Varnier, valet to King Carlos III; two letters from him to C. are extant.

28. *Amigoni:* Jacopo Amigoni (1675-1752), Italian painter and engraver, summoned to Madrid in 1747.

29. *Hospitality to heretics:* Mengs had turned Catholic in 1749 and as a convert was probably particularly strict in matters of religion.

30. *Long Spanish leagues:* In the 18th century the league represented four different distances in Spain. C. probably refers to the *legua nueva* ("new league") introduced in 1760, the length of which was just over 4 miles.

31. *Al sitio:* "At the country seat"; here specifically Aranjuez, one of the Sitios Reales ("royal country seats") which Carlos III regularly frequented at different seasons. The others were El Pardo (February and March), La Granja (July), the Escorial (October). He spent April at Aranjuez.

32. Ovid, *Tristia*, 5, 6, 13.

33. *The coffeehouse where I was staying:* C. was staying at the Café français on the Calle de la Cruz (cf. Vol. 10, Chap. XII, n. 36).

34. *The Tower of Babylon:* The ziggurat Etemenanki, the remains of which, however, were not brought to light until the archeological excavations at Babylon conducted by Robert Koldewey from 1898 to 1917.

35. *His eldest son:* According to the registries of baptisms of the Roman churches, Mengs had at least 14 children; his eldest son, Domenico Raffaello, born in 1750, died in infancy. Another son, Giovanni Antonio, born in 1754, died ca. 1759-1760. Of his other sons only Alberico (the dates of his birth and death are not recorded) is known to have survived and had children.

36. *Cavaliere:* Mengs, like C., had received the order of the Golden Spur and hence had the title Cavaliere.

37. *Correggio:* Antonio Allegri da Correggio (1494-1534), famous painter of the Italian Renaissance.

38. *Raffaello d'Urbino:* Raffaello Santi (Raphael), of Urbino (1483-1520), famous Italian painter of the Renaissance.

39. *Died before . . . fifty years:* Mengs was 51 years of age when he died.

40. *His biography:* C. doubtless refers to the biography by José Nicolas de Azara, which appeared in *Obras de don Antonio*

Rafael Mengs, primer pintor de Camara del Rey (Madrid, 1780).

41. *Naumachia:* In classical antiquity, orginally a mock naval battle, then an artificial basin, usually surrounded by tiers of seats, especially constructed for the exhibition of such battles. The ruins of a Roman amphitheater are still to be seen in Toledo; they must have been more extensive in the 18th century.

42. *Alcázar:* The Alcázar (from the Arabic *al qaṣr*, "castle") of Toledo was first the residence of the Visigothic rulers of Spain, then of the Moorish, and, from the 11th to the 16th century, of the Kings of Castile.

43. *The cathedral:* The celebrated cathedral of Toledo was built from 1227 to 1493. In C.'s time the Archbishop of Toledo was Don Luis III Fernandez de Córdoba.

44. *Collections:* What collections C. can have seen is not known, for the first natural history collection of which records exist was established by the Cardinal-Archbishop of Toledo after 1772.

45. *Grimaldi:* Don Pablo Jerónimo Grimaldi (1720-1786), of the celebrated Genoese patrician family, early entered the Spanish diplomatic service; from 1763 to 1777 he was Minister of Foreign Affairs, and then Spanish Ambassador in Rome until 1783.

46. *My opera:* Nothing is known of this libretto by C. It was not found among his papers.

47. *Pelliccia:* Clementina Pelliccia, Roman singer; documented as appearing in Spain in 1768 and 1769. Her younger sister was Maria Teresa Pelliccia, who was still singing at the opera in Madrid in 1777.

48. *Marescalchi:* Luigi Marescalchi (born ca. 1740), Bolognese impresario and composer of operas; he opened a music shop in Venice in 1770 and in 1785 moved it to Naples.

49. *The Governor of Valencia:* Until 1766 the Count of Aranda was Governor (Spanish, "capitán general") of Valencia (then, of course, no longer a kingdom but a province).

50. *Arcos:* Antonio Ponce de León y Spínola (1726-1780), Duke of Baños, from 1763 Duke of Arcos and personal friend of Carlos III.

51. *Don Diego Valencia:* Don Diego Valencia was a banker in the city of Valencia.

52. *Who now reigns:* The then Prince of Asturias became King of Spain as Carlos IV in 1788.

53. *Every day . . . go hunting:* It is a fact that Carlos III went hunting every day, except on Good Friday and the major ecclesiastical feast days, often continuing to hunt by torchlight after dark.

54. *His brother:* The Infante Don Luis Antonio Jaime, called Don Luis (1727-1785), Archbishop of Seville and Toledo, was made a Cardinal in 1735; in 1754 he renounced all his ecclesiastical offices and in 1776 married Countess Maria Teresa Vallabriga y Rozas. However, it was not he but his brother the King who delighted in Mengs's paintings of the Virgin and saints.

55. *Carrera de San Gerónimo:* In this street, which still exists between the Prado and the Puerta del Sol, there was in the 18th century a small church adjacent to the Franciscan Monastery of Espíritu Santo; it was demolished in 1823.

56. Paraphrased from Luke 11:27.

57. *Pico:* Alessandro Pico (died 1787), cousin of Francesco Maria Pico, Duke of Mirandola, who, after he was deprived of all his estates in Italy, went to Spain with Alessandro. The latter was the friend and adviser of the Marchese Grimaldi and almoner to King Carlos III.

58. *Barbarigo:* Piero Barbarigo was one of the three Venetian State Inquisitors from 1769 to 1770.

59. *St. Luke . . . as a painter:* According to a legend first documented in the 5th century, St. Luke the Evangelist was also a painter; hence he was considered the patron of painters and of artists in general. Numerous portraits of Christ are attributed to him; among the best known is the one (probably of the 6th century) in the Capella Sancta Sanctorum in the Lateran, Rome; the predominant color in all of them is brown. C. had known from his boyhood the well-known painting of the Madonna Nicopeia, attributed to St. Luke, in San Marco, Venice; this may account for his assertion that St. Luke painted with only three colors.

60. *This altar:* C. writes "cet hôtel," obviously a slip for "cet autel."

61. *Origen:* Origen of Alexandria, Christian theologian and apologist of the 2nd-3rd centuries.

62. Paraphrased from Matthew 19:12.

63. *De Ségur:* Probably a member of the old Poitevin noble family of De Ségur, but he has not been identified.

64. Antique maxim, differently expressed by various authors (e.g., Tibullus, 3, 6, 43-44).

65. *The Grand Inquisitor:* From 1761 to 1775 the Spanish Inquisitor General was Archbishop Don Manuel Quintano y Bonifaz (died 1775).

66. *Squillace:* Leopoldo de Gregorio, Marchese di Squillace (died 1785 in Venice), native of southern Italy; from 1759 Spanish Minister of Finance, from 1763 Minister of War; he was dismissed in 1766, but was made Spanish Ambassador in Venice in 1772. On the occasion of the uprising of 1766 in Madrid (cf. Vol. 10, Chap. XII, n. 25) numerous satires accusing him of being an overly uxorious husband were published.

67. *Madame Adélaïde of France:* Marie Adélaïde (1732-1800), daughter of Louis XV of France, whence her title Madame de France; she died unmarried.

68. *Marriage of conscience:* An Infante of Spain was forbidden to marry a woman of lower rank. In 1776 Carlos III made an exception to the rule in the case of his brother.

69. *Carlos III . . . the Queen of Portugal . . . mad:* It is a fact that Maria I Francisca Isabela of Portugal (1734-1816) became insane after the death of her eldest son and her daughter. On the alleged insanity of Carlos III see note 11 to this chapter.

70. *The King of England was mad:* George III of England (1738-1820), of the House of Hanover, became King in 1760; he began to show signs of insanity in 1789, but the fact was kept secret. He was not declared incurable until 1810; his son George Frederick Augustus assumed the regency, and became King as George IV in 1820.

71. *A Biscayan maidservant:* Maidservants from the northern Spanish province of Vizcaya, on the Bay of Biscay, were still the most numerous and sought after in Madrid in the 19th century; they were reputed to be especially capable and clean.

72. *Calle de Alcalá:* The Calle de Alcalá is still one of the most important streets in Madrid; it runs from the Puerta del Sol to the Prado.

73. *Aranjuez . . . Madrid . . . Fontainebleau . . . Paris:* The distance from Aranjuez to Madrid is about 30 miles, from Fontainebleau to Paris about 34 miles.

74. *Bilbao:* Near the northern coast of Spain in the province of Vizcaya, today an industrial city with a population of some 300,000.

75. *Criadillas:* A kind of roll; also a kind of truffle.

CHAPTER III

1. *He had done:* C. writes "qu'il m'avait" (omitting *fait,* "done").

2. *St. Ignatius of Loyola:* Spanish, Iñigo López de Loyola (1491-1556), of the lesser Basque nobility, first an army officer, then converted to the spiritual life in 1521; he founded the Society of Jesus (the Jesuit order) in Rome and obtained papal recognition of it in 1540. He was and still is especially revered in Spain. He was canonized in 1622.

3. *Peso duro:* see note 10 to Chap. I of this volume.

4. *Buen Suceso:* The church of Nuestra Señora del Buen Suceso is a large parish church in the present Calle de la Princesa, near the Puerta del Sol.

5. *Atocha:* The basilica of Nuestra Señora de Atocha, built as a Dominican church in the 16th century, is in the Calle de Atocha near the present southern railway station (del Mediodia).

6. *Don Jaime:* Jaime is the Spanish form of Giacomo and Jacques.

7. *La Soledad:* See Vol. 10, Chap. XII, n. 70.

8. *Duchess of Villadarias:* Dukes or Duchesses of this name are not documented; probably C. refers to the wife of Juan Bautista, Marqués de Villadarias (died 1773), who was made a Grandee in 1760, or perhaps to the wife of his successor Don Francisco (died 1798).

9. *Duchess of Benavente:* María Josefa Alfonsa Pimentel, Countess (not Duchess) of Benavente; she inherited the es-

tates of the Duke of Béjar in 1777, conducted a celebrated literary salon in Madrid, and was a patroness of poets.

10. *Los Balbazes:* C. is in error. There was and is no public garden, promenade, or street of this name in Madrid.

11. *Homer . . . dispute on the subject:* The dispute on the subject between Jupiter and Juno is not in Homer but in Apollodoros's *Bibliotheca* (III, 67).

12. *Tiresias:* According to legend, the blind prophet Tiresias, when he was a young man, was changed into a woman. While a woman he married, and later was changed back into a man. Jupiter and Juno refer their dispute to him, and he decides it in Jupiter's favor, declaring that the woman receives ten times as much pleasure as the man (Apollodoros, *ibid.*).

13. *This creature the womb:* This entire discussion of the influence of the womb on the feminine psyche seems to echo a controversy which took place in Bologna in 1771-72 and into which C. entered with his *Lana Caprina*. He gives an account of the controversy in Vol. 12, Chap. VI.

14. *Canine hunger:* Old medical term for a morbidly voracious appetite.

15. *St. Theresa:* St. Teresa de Jesús, of Ávila (1515-1582), with the support of Juan de la Cruz, reformed the Carmelites; she is considered one of the great mystics, and her writings are classics of Spanish literature.

16. *St. Agreda:* The nun María Coronel (died 1665), of Agreda, was the author of a mystical work *La mística ciudad de Dios* (1670); she was never canonized. C., much to his annoyance, had been given her book to read when he was imprisoned under the Leads (cf. Vol. 4, Chap. XII).

17. *Messalinas:* Valeria Messalina was the third wife of the Roman Emperor Claudius; notorious for her loose life, she was executed in A.D. 48 for having taken part in a conspiracy against the Emperor.

18. *St. Anthony of Padua:* See Vol. 7, Chap. I, n. 2.

19. *St. Aloysius Gonzaga:* See Vol. 7, Chap. I, n. 1.

20. *St. Ignatius:* See note 2 to this chapter.

21. This concept, which the Scholastic philosophy made common intellectual property, goes back to Aristotle (*Eudemian Ethics*, VII, 2).

22. *Great amphitheater:* The great bull ring was erected in

1749 under King Fernando VI outside the Puerta de Alcalá
and was later enlarged. The present building dates from 1874.
From March or April to Oct. 12 corridas were held there
each year, many of them lasting all day.

23. *Picadero:* Now usually *picador;* the mounted *torero* in a
bullfight.

24. *Prado San Jerónimo:* Now the southern end of the Paseo
del Prado. The magnificent street was first laid out under
King Carlos III and the Count of Aranda; so C. saw it when
it was new.

25. *Lyons embroidery:* Embroidery from Lyons was considered
especially choice in the 18th century.

26. *Of your nobility:* As a hidalgo, Don Diego could not give
his daughter in marriage to anyone but a nobleman.

27. *Whence comes:* "D'où vient" is supplied by the editor in
brackets. If the question mark too is his and not C.'s, the
sentence would mean: "My angel, tell me that I am happy"
(which seems more likely).

CHAPTER IV

1. *The late Cardinal:* Probably Joaquín Portocarrero, Count
of Palma (1681-1760), Spanish Grandee, Cardinal from 1743.
Nothing is known of the adventuress who took the name.

2. *Béliardi:* See note 2 to Chap. II of this volume. He had
known Portocarrero when the Cardinal had been the Spanish Ambassador in Rome.

3. *Fraiture:* The family name Fraiture is documented in Liège;
in 1766 a Wilhelm Maria, Baron van Coudenhove, Seigneur
de Fraiture, is recorded as a Deacon to the Prince-Bishop of
Liège.

4. *The Principality:* The Bishops of Liège were also Princes of
the Holy Roman Empire.

5. *Querini:* Zuan Querini (1733 - after 1771), Venetian patrician, went to Madrid on June 28, 1768, to replace his uncle
Alvise Sebastiano Mocenigo as Venetian Ambassador.

6. *Escorial:* Name of the complex of palace, cathedral, and
monastery of San Lorenzo del Real de la Victoria, built
1563-1584) by Philip II north of Madrid on the slopes of
the Sierra Guadarrama. The immense building measures some

660 by 520 feet. The church is modeled after St. Peter's in Rome; it was the burial place of the Kings of Spain from the time of Charles V.

7. *The two Ambassadors:* Venetian protocol prescribed that the retiring Ambassador should not leave until his successor had been presented at Court. Querini had his first audience with King Carlos III on July 3, 1768.

8. *Found myself guilty:* C. added, then crossed out: "of a real betrayal."

9. *Believe myself capable:* C. added, then crossed out: "which I had never committed, and which I never committed again in all my life."

10. *El Pardo:* A royal palace (not to be confused with Prado) some miles north of Madrid, on the Manzanares, built in 1543. It is now the residence of the Head of State.

11. *Soderini:* Gasparo Soderini, from 1767 Venetian Secretary of Embassy in Madrid, from 1775 employed in the State Secretariat of Venice.

12. *He will leave . . . this week:* Mocenigo left Madrid on July 26, 1768.

13. *Sabatini:* Francesco Sabatini (Sabattino) (1722-1797), Italian architect, summoned to Spain in 1760.

14. *Not having received permission:* It would seem that Mocenigo was already in disfavor with the Venetian authorities; he was imprisoned in the Fortress of Brescia from 1775 to 1780.

15. *Without turning Turk:* Allusion to Count Claude de Bonneval (1675-1747), who left the French service for Constantinople in 1729, became a convert to Islam in 1730, and was appointed Governor of the Turkish provinces of Karamania and Rumelia under the name of Ahmed (cf. Vol. 2, Chap. IV). C. had known Bonneval in Constantinople.

16. *Auditor . . . Nuncio:* The Papal Nuncio in 1768 was Monsignore Cesare Alberico Lucigni, of Milan (born 1730). A councilor to a Papal Nuncio had the title Auditor.

17. *Pinzi:* Giuseppe Antonio Pinzi (1713-1769), Professor of Eloquence in the Seminary at Ravenna, from 1759 Auditor to the Papal Nuncio Lucigni, first in Cologne, then in Madrid.

18. *Dishonesty . . . Genoese:* In the 18th century the Genoese were often reputed to be especially untrustworthy.

19. *Tiepoletto:* Giovanni Battista Tiepolo, called Tiepoletto (1693-1770), famous Venetian painter. His son Domenico (1726 or '27 - 1804) was also a painter. C. to the contrary, Domenico's talent was far from being "of the slightest."

20. *The Aragonese:* The old Kingdom of Aragon, whose capital was Saragossa, had become a part of the Kingdom of Spain in 1479.

21. C. writes *"el"* (the Spanish article) *"spadino"* (the Italian noun). *Spadino* properly means "short sword," which is belied by his description of the weapon. Spanish *espadín* was the term for a short dress sword fashionable in the 18th century.

22. *Nuestra Señora del Pilar:* "Our Lady of the Pillar," miracle-working statue of the Virgin Mary, which stands on a pillar (*pilar*) in a chapel of its own in the cathedral church of Saragossa.

23. *Palafox:* Juan Palafox y Mendoza (1600–1659), appointed Bishop in 1639 and Viceroy of Mexico in 1642, was recalled to Spain and made Bishop of Osma (Spain) in 1653. King Carlos III revered him so greatly that he instituted proceedings for his canonization in 1726; they were finally dismissed by the Curia in 1777.

24. *Pignatelli:* Don Ramón de Pignatelli y Moncayo (1734-1793), uncle of the Marquis of Mora, was a Canon, and, from 1762 to 1784, Rector of the University of Saragossa; he was notorious for his libertinism.

25. *Bawd . . . whore:* C. writes "maq ...." and "p ....." (for *maquerelle* and *putain*).

26. *Two years later:* José Maria Pignatelli, Marquis of Mora, did not die until 1774.

27. Altered from Silius Italicus, *Punica*, I, 271 f. Sagunto was orginally an Iberian settlement on a steep hill near the sea, some 15 miles north of Valencia. As an ally of Rome, it was besieged and taken by Hannibal in 219 B.C. during the Second Punic War. Its inhabitants, to escape falling into the Carthaginian's hands, burned themselves with their houses and all their possessions. The Romans rebuilt it from 214 B.C. as Saguntum (or Saguntos). Extensive ruins of the Roman city, especially of the walls and the amphitheater, still remain.

28. *La Condamine:* Charles Marie de la Condamine (1701-1774), celebrated French mathematician and scholar.

29. *Séguier:* Jean François Séguier (1703-1772), French antiquarian and naturalist and friend of Scipione Francesco, Marchese Maffei (Italian writer; cf. Vol. 3, Chap. VIII, n. 4).

30. *Murviedro:* Saguntum continued to flourish during the Middle Ages but then fell into decay and was called Murviedro. (C. writes "Morvedro.") Since 1877 it has been called Sagunto.

31. After Ausonius, *Epigrams,* 35, where the text, instead of *nominibusque* ("to names"), has *marmoribusque* ("to marbles").

32. *Old Castile . . . New Castile:* There was already a County of Castile in the 8th century. Alfonso VI of Castile and León conquered the greater part of the Kingdom of Toledo from the Moors in 1080, called the territory Castilla la Nueva, and moved his capital from Burgos to Toledo (1085). Not until then was the former county called Castilla la Vieja, to distinguish it from the new province.

33. *Claudius . . . Gallienus:* The Roman Emperors Marcus Aurelius Claudius Augustus (reigned 268-270) and Publius Licinius Egnatius Gallienus (reigned 260-268). What inscription and what statue of Hannibal C. hoped to find is not known.

34. *The amphitheater:* The Roman amphitheater, which had been well preserved until the 18th century, was then used as a quarry to such an extent that the Count of Aranda installed a curator to guard it.

35. *Málaga . . . Alicante:* C.'s geography here is erroneous; Alicante is some 110 miles south, Málaga some 430 miles southwest, of Valencia.

36. *Alexander VI:* Rodrigo de Borja (1431-1503) was a native of Játiva, near Valencia. As Pope Alexander VI (from 1492), he made the name Borgia famous and notorious.

37. *Pétau:* Denys Pétau (1583-1652), French Jesuit, theologian, and chronicler, who Latinized his name as Dionysius Petavius. His best-known works were the *Tabulae chronologicae* (1628) and the *Rationarium temporum* (1633-34) (cf. Vol. 4, Chap. XIV, n. 8).

38. *Guadalaviar:* Valencia is situated only a mile or so from
    the sea; the old town lies south of the River Guadalaviar,
    which is now generally called the Rio Turia. The countryside
    around the city is unusually fertile.

39. *Amenum stagnum:* The reference is to the lake of Albufera,
    south of Valencia, a salt lagoon some 20 miles long and
    abounding in fish.

40. *Its university:* The University of Valencia developed from
    the Estudios Superiores de Gramática y Artes, founded in the
    15th century; the library was not opened until 1785.

41. *Five great bridges:* Except for the Puente Nuevo or Puente
    San José, they all date from the 15th or 16th century. Of 12
    old gates only 2 remain after the destruction of the old city
    walls, the Puerta de Serranos and the Puerta de Cuarte. The
    streets of Valencia were not paved until the middle of the
    19th century.

42. *Tarragona:* C. writes "Tarascone," but must mean the city
    of Tarragona, some 150 miles north of Valencia.

43. *Murcia and Granada:* Neither was still a kingdom in the
    18th century, Murcia having been conquered from the Moors
    in 1265 and Granada in 1492.

44. *The mines of Peru and Potosí . . . prejudices:* C. accepts
    the doctrine that the decay of Spain was chiefly due to the
    immense wealth which flowed into the country from her
    South American possessions. Potosí, then part of the Vice-
    royalty of Peru, now a Department of Bolivia, was famous
    for its silver mines.

45. *La Granja:* Royal palace built ca. 1722 in the style of Ver-
    sailles by Philip V in the Sierra Guadarrama, some 45 miles
    north of Madrid.

46. *An Inquisition in Spain:* The Inquisition was not finally
    abolished in Spain until 1834.

47. *You:* C. writes "ostè" (for Spanish *usted*).

48. *Medina Celi . . . La Pichona:* See Chap. I of this volume.

49. *Pini:* Don Almerico Pini (died after 1788), native of
    Parma, was Ayuda de Cámara (valet) to King Carlos III
    until the latter's death. (C. writes "Alberico.")

50. *La Marcucci:* Geltrude Marcucci, called La Galguilla,
    Italian dancer from Lucca; she appeared in Madrid until
    1772 and then retired to Bologna with her two children by

her lover Don Carlos Gutiérrez de los Rios, Count of Fernan Núñez (1742-1795).

51. *Another . . . Spanish Grandee:* See the preceding note.

52. *The Spirito Santo Bank:* Banca dello Spirito Santo. (Vol. 1, Chap. IX, n. 19, should be corrected accordingly.)

53. *Belloni:* Francesco Belloni, from 1761 director of the banking house of the same name in Rome.

54. *Moñino:* José Moñino (1728-1808), from 1773 Count of Floridablanca, Spanish diplomat, from 1776 Minister of Foreign Affairs.

55. *And who:* Canceled: "was disgraced a month ago and." He fell into disgrace in 1792.

56. *A Chevalier of Alcántara:* The order of Alcántara was founded in 1156 as a military-religious order. From 1542 its members had the right to marry. It was dissolved about the middle of the 19th century.

57. *Nina:* Nina Bergonzi (died ca. 1782), Italian dancer.

58. *Ricla:* Ambrosio Funes de Villalpando, Count of Ricla (died 1780), from 1767 Captain-General of Catalonia, from 1772 Spanish Minister of War.

59. *Pimp . . . whore:* Cf. note 25 to this chapter.

60. *Molinari:* Probably a certain Francesco Molinari, Italian singer, about whom nothing more is known.

61. *The scaffold where he sold his balsam:* In Venice the charlatans sold their wonder-working drugs on the Piazza San Marco. The name of Pelandi's oil has not been explained, nor has he been identified.

62. *Beautiful though she was:* C. added, then canceled, "I should not have wanted her even if she had paid me."

63. *Jackanapes:* C. writes "jocrisse," from the name of a stupid servant in old French farces.

64. *Fuc. . . . :* C. writes "fout. . . ." (for *fouterie,* "fucking").

65. *Dildo:* C. writes "gaudm. . . . ." (for *gaudemiche,* "dildo").

66. *Whore:* Cf. note 25 to this chapter.

67. *Primero:* Old card game of Spanish or Italian origin, in which four cards were dealt to each player, each card having three times its usual value; it was widely popular from the 16th century.

68. *The "Santa Maria":* Probably the Fonda Santa Maria, in

344 History of My Life

the Calle de los Ases, near the Plaza del Palacio, mentioned
in 19th-century guidebooks to Barcelona.

CHAPTER V

1. *Cevaillos:* Miguel de Cevaillos, also Zevaillos, presumably a
relative of Don Pedro Ceballos, who was Governor of Buenos
Aires until 1767 and later a Lieutenant-General and Secretary of State, and of Fray Ceballos (1732-1802), author of
several books on religious subjects, who lived in Seville.

2. *Secada:* A Don Domenico della Secada is documented as a
theater director in Barcelona in 1768.

3. *Peralada:* Fernando de Boxadors y Chaves, Count of Peralada (died 1801), Spanish Grandee.

4. *San Gennaro:* The order of San Gennaro, the highest honor
of the Kingdom of Naples, was founded in 1738 by Don
Carlos on the occasion of his marriage to Maria Amalia Wal-
purgis of Saxony. Don Carlos was King of Naples from 1735
to 1759 and became King of Spain as Carlos III in the latter
year.

5. *Usía:* Spanish courtesy title, used in address; it is the contracted form of Vuestra Señoría ("Your Lordship").

6. *The theater:* The only theater in Barcelona was the Teatro
Principal, also called Teatro de la Santa Cruz, originally built
in 1560 and rebuilt more than once, the last time of stone in
1788; it still exists.

7. *Squizza . . . Schizza:* Giovanni B. Gragioli, called Lo
Sghizza or Schizza, Roman dancer, who is documented as appearing in a number of European cities between 1762 and
1777. His byname is derived from *schiacciato* ("squashed,"
"crushed").

8. *Walloon Guards:* Under King Carlos III the King's Bodyguard consisted of two infantry regiments, one Spanish, the
other made up of foreigners, principally Walloons.

9. *Passano . . . Pogomas:* Giacomo Passano (died ca. 1772),
used the anagrams Ascanio Pogomas and Cosimo Aspagona;
son of a Genoese officer, actor, theater director, poet, and adventurer, with whom C. had had several unpleasant encounters (cf. Vol. 7, Chap. VII, and especially Vol. 9, Chaps.
I-IV).

10. *The Palace:* The Palacio Real in Barcelona, originally built in 1444 as a cloth market, was confiscated for the Crown by King Philip IV in 1652 and made the residence of the Viceroys, later of the Captains-General; the building is on the Plaza del Palacio and is not the same as the Palau, the old royal palace, on the Plaza del Rey, which in the 18th century belonged to the Duke of Alba.

11. *The Tower:* The Torre de San Juan, also called Torre de Santa Clara and Torre de la Ciudadela, was probably a remnant of the old Convent of Santa Clara, which was demolished in 1715 to make room for a citadel, the tower being left standing inside it. It was used as a military prison until the beginning of the 19th century; in 1814 the entire citadel was demolished.

12. *Calabozo:* Spanish for "dungeon" (whence American slang "calaboose").

13. *My . . . confutation:* C.'s *Confutazione della Storia del Governo Veneto d'Amelot de la Houssaie* appeared in three volumes at Lugano in 1769 (though the place of publication is given as Amsterdam). This long work, which treats of many more subjects than its title would indicate, was conceived by C. as a pamphlet during his incarceration in the Torre de San Juan and was not written in its extended form until later (see Chap. VI of this volume). C. hoped that its publication would gain him a pardon from the Venetian State Inquisition (see Chap. VII of this volume).

14. *La Houssaye:* Abraham Nicolas Amelot de la Houssaye (1634-1706), French historian, had published his *Histoire du gouvernement de Venise* in 8 volumes at Paris in 1676. He was Secretary to the French Ambassador in Venice from 1669 to 1671. The Venetian Government authorities were so enraged by the work that they succeeded in having its author imprisoned in the Bastille. However, the book was republished at Lyons in 1768 and aroused so much anti-Venetian sentiment in France that C. was all the more encouraged to hope that his confutation of it would gain him the favor of the State Inquisitors.

15. *Tadini:* Nothing is known of him.

16. Cf. John 5:36.

17. According to the regulations for papal elections promul-

gated by Gregory X (1271-1276), the newly elected Pope was and is invested to the accompaniment of the words, *Investio te Papatu Romano ut praesis urbi et orbi* ("I invest thee with the Roman Papacy that thou mayest preside over the city [of Rome] and the world"). The Pope's first formal benediction is given *urbi et orbi*.

18. *Gutta serena:* Amaurosis, a loss or decay of sight from loss of power in the optic nerve.

19. *Catalan laws:* See Vol. 5, Chap. IV, n. 22.

20. *The Holy Innocents:* The children massacred by Herod's order in his attempt to kill the infant Jesus. Their feast is celebrated on Dec. 28.

21. *I read it:* The text of the Brockhaus-Plon edition has "Je le dis" ("I say it"), which, since it makes no sense and is not annotated, would seem to be yet another typographical error or an editorial misreading for *lis* ("read").

22. *Vuestra Señoría:* "Your Lordship" (C. gallicizes to "Votre Seigneurie"). Cf. note 5 to this chapter.

23. *Badillo:* Perhaps a relative of Don Manuel de Vadillo y Velasco, who had been an official of the Spanish Court from 1716.

24. *Grimaldi della Pietra:* Giovanni Agostino Grimaldi, Marchese della Pietra (1734-1784), Genoese patrician and patron of C. (cf. Vol. 9, Chap. I).

25. *The fourth Genoese:* Who the other three were has not appeared.

26. *A thousand zecchini:* In Vol. 9, Chap. I, C. says that the amount he lost to Grimaldi and for which he gave him drafts on himself was 2,000 zecchini.

27. *A Kingdom, not a Principality:* In the 18th century Barcelona was a County and Catalonia a Principality governed by a Captain-General. However, in the 12th century the Counts of Barcelona had become Kings of Aragon.

28. The line does not occur in the works of Petrarch.

29. *A B:* C. first wrote "Bolognini," then crossed it out and substituted "A B." Countess Teresa Attendolo-Bolognini, née Zuazo y Ovalla Zamora, wife of Count Giuseppe Attendolo-Bolognini, was of Spanish descent. (Cf. Vol. 8, Chaps. VI and VII.)

30. *Marchisio:* Giuseppe Filippo Marchisio, diplomat in the

service of the Duke of Modena; from 1769 to 1771 he was in Madrid, and later in Vienna.

31. *San Ildefonso:* The royal palace of La Granja was in San Ildefonso, south of Segovia.

32. *Olivieri:* Giuseppe Francesco Olivieri, Venetian commoner, Secretary of Embassy in Madrid, later Vice-Chancellor of Venice.

33. *The Marchese Grimaldi:* See note 45 to Chap. II of this volume.

34. *The Venetian Ambassador . . . his uncle the Ambassador:* Querini was the nephew of Alvise Sebastiano Mocenigo, whom he had succeeded as Ambassador (cf. note 5 to the preceding chapter).

35. *Prothonotary:* When C. received the order of the Golden Spur, he was also made Apostolic Prothonotary *extra urbem* (see Vol. 7, Chap. IX, and *ibid.*, n. 44).

36. *Grimaldo de' Grimaldi:* C. writes "de." The reference is to the Marchese Grimaldi.

37. *The three Sitios:* Aranjuez, La Granja, and El Pardo.

38. *Forty short leagues from Barcelona:* The distance by road is some 90 miles.

39. *We do not see:* C. writes "ne voyons pas" (omitting *nous*).

40. *D'Argens:* Jean Baptiste de Boyer, Marquis d'Argens (1704–1771), Chamberlain to Frederick the Great and Director of the Academy of Sciences in Berlin from 1744 to 1769.

41. *The "White Horse":* The "Cheval Blanc" inn was opened in Montpellier in 1435 and survived until 1910.

42. *Professors:* The University of Montpellier, founded in 1289, was one of the most celebrated in Europe, especially for medicine.

43. *Apollo:* Here as god of poetry and leader of the Muses, symbolizing literature in general.

44. *La Castel-Bajac:* See especially Vol. 10, Chap. IX.

45. *The Ambassador:* I.e., the French Ambassador in Vienna, the Marquis de Durfort-Civrac (died 1787). See Vol. 10, Chap. IX, n. 38.

46. *Séguier:* See note 29 to the preceding chapter.

47. *Monuments:* C. doubtless refers to the Roman buildings in Nîmes, especially the arena and the small temple known as the "Maison Carrée."

48. *A Parlement:* Under the Old Régime the Parlements in France were essentially judicial institutions. Besides the one in Paris, there were several provincial Parlements, among them the one in Aix-en-Provence.

49. *The "Three Dolphins":* This inn has not been identified. However, Aix in the 18th century had a Rue des Quatre Dauphins (now Rue du Quatre Septembre), to which the name of the inn may have had some reference.

50. *Spanish Cardinal . . . Rezzonico:* Pope Clement XIII (Carlo Rezzonico) died on Feb. 2, 1769. The two Spanish Cardinals who took part in the conclave were Solis, Archbishop of Seville, and Bonaventura de Córdoba Spínola de la Cerda, Patriarch of the Indies and Cardinal, both of whom traveled to Rome by land, so it was possible that C. met them; they reached Rome about the middle of April 1769. C. makes it clear in the next chapter that he refers to La Cerda.

CHAPTER VI

1. *D'Argens:* See note 40 to the preceding chapter.

2. *D'Éguilles:* Alexandre Jean Baptiste de Boyer, Marquis d'Éguilles, Président au mortier ("Presiding Judge") of the Parlement at Aix (died 1785). His country house, Mon Repos, was in Éguilles, some 5 miles northwest of Aix.

3. *The late Frederick II:* Frederick the Great died in 1786.

4. *His writings:* The literary works of the Marquis d'Argens consist of novels, philosophic, aesthetic, and critical essays, and a number of fictitious memoirs and collections of letters; his collected works were published at Berlin in 1768 in 24 volumes.

5. *The actress Cochois:* Barbe Cochois (before 1722 - after 1771), French dancer; she appeared in Berlin in 1742 and married the Marquis d'Argens in 1749.

6. *Lord Marischal:* George Keith (ca. 1693-1778), from 1712 Earl Marischal of Scotland; exiled as a Jacobite, he spent many years at the Court of Frederick the Great and served as the Prussian Ambassador first to Paris and later to Madrid. (In Vol. 2, pp. 100, 314, Vol. 3, p. 156, Vol. 4, pp. 110, 333, "Marshal" should be corrected to "Marischal.")

7. *Jesuit "of the short robe":* The Jesuit order accepted lay affiliates whose high position could make them useful to it; they were not obliged to wear the dress of the order.

8. *Gotzkowski:* Son of an art dealer and banker in Berlin, Johann Ernst Gotzkowski (1710-1775); his sister was married ca. 1764 to the Comte de Canorgue (died ca. 1767), who was a nephew of the Marquis d'Argens. C. writes, variously, "Schofskouski," "Chouskouski," "Choskoski," "Choskouski," "Chofskouski."

9. *Making a mock of eternal bliss: Béatilles,* which also means "small articles of religion," is derived from *béat* ("blissful").

10. *Ganganelli:* Giovanni Vincenzo Antonio Ganganelli (1705-1774), Franciscan friar under the name of Fra Lorenzo, became a Cardinal in 1759 and Pope, as Clement XIV, in 1769.

11. *Pinzi:* See note 17 to Chap. IV of this volume.

12. *Polyeucte:* Tragedy on a Christian subject by Pierre Corneille, first performed in 1643.

13. *Argenis:* Political allegory in the form of a romance, written in Latin and published at Paris in 1621. Its author was the Scotch Humanist John Barclay (1582-1621).

14. *His adopted daughter:* Born in 1754, at the time of C.'s visit to Aix in 1769 she was called Mina Giraud and was said to be the niece of the Marquise d'Argens, née Cochois. Some months after C. left Aix in December of that year, the Marquis d'Argens recognized her, in the presence of a notary and his whole family, as his legitimate daughter by his wife. After that she was recognized by the family as Barbe d'Argens; in 1774 she married the Solicitor-General of the Aix Parlement, Monsieur de Magallon.

15. *Porphyry:* Greek philosopher and scholar of the 3rd century of our era; among his writings were scholia on the *Iliad* and the *Odyssey*.

16. *Buffoonery:* C. writes "un lazzi." *Lazzi* (which C. makes a singular though it is plural) were stereotyped bits of comic business used by the improvising actors of the *commedia dell'arte.*

17. *Written . . . in their proper places:* The incident at Metz is recounted in Vol. 8, Chap. II. The incident in England does not appear in C.'s memoirs.

18. *Santiago de Compostela:* City in the province of Galicia,

History of My Life

northwestern Spain, and site of the shrine which, according
to tradition, contains the bones of St. James the Greater. It
has been a place of pilgrimage since the early Middle Ages.

19. *Cockle shells:* Symbol of a pilgrim, and especially of one
who had made the pilgrimage to the shrine of St. James.

20. *Balsamo:* Giuseppe Balsamo (1743-1795), Italian adventurer from Ballaro, near Palermo; he assumed the name
Count Alessandro Cagliostro in 1776. He married Lorenza
Feliciani, of Rome, in 1768; when he had changed his name
she had changed hers to Serafina. He gained fame and wealth
by practicing magic and alchemy, but in 1790 was sentenced
to death in Rome as a Freemason, his sentence being com-
muted in 1791 to life imprisonment in the papal fortress of
San Leo (near Rimini). There he died insane in 1795. Neither
he nor his wife was ever in Santiago de Compostela.

21. *Our Lady of the Pillar:* See note 22 to Chap. IV of this
volume.

22. *The Most Holy Sudary:* The handkerchief (literally "sweat
cloth") of the legendary St. Veronica, on which Christ is supposed to have wiped his face, leaving the imprint of it, on his
way to be crucified. Several churches in Europe claim to possess it.

23. *Sweating:* Text, "grondant de sueur" (which, if it is not a
misreading, makes no sense).

24. *Testone:* See Vol. 7, Chap. VIII, n. 15.

25. *Rembrandt:* Rembrandt van Rijn (1606-1669), famous
Dutch painter and etcher. (C. writes "Reimbrand.")

26. *"Saint-Omer" inn:* See Vol. 7, Chap. III, n. 2.

27. *I have heard that he is dead:* Cagliostro died in 1795 in the
fortress of San Leo (cf. note 20 to this chapter). His wife,
who is said also to have gone insane after betraying him to
the Inquisition in 1789, was relegated to the Convent of
Sant'Apollonia in Rome and died there in 1794.

28. *King of Sweden . . . assassinated:* Gustav III (1746-
1792), nephew of Frederick the Great, King of Sweden from
1771, was assassinated on March 29, 1792.

29. *All his works:* See note 4 to this chapter.

30. *Account . . . written in his youth:* He had published his
Mémoires in London as early as 1735.

31. *The scoundrels . . . Waldstein's castle:* The major-domo
Feldkirchner, the courier Wiederholt, and the steward Stelzel
leagued together to make life as unpleasant as possible for C.
in Waldstein's castle, where C. was librarian; they even had
him set upon and cudgeled in the streets of Dux (Dec. 1791).
Waldstein, who was away from Dux most of the year, did not
dismiss the three accomplices until July 1793. C. went to Dux
in 1785 and died there in 1798.

32. *When the time comes:* This shows beyond doubt that C.
intended to carry his memoirs down to the time of his residence at Dux.

33. *Corpus Christi:* In 1769 it fell on May 25.

34. *Saturnalia:* Roman festival in honor of the god Saturn and
in celebration of the mythical Golden Age during his reign. It
was held for a week in December; during it masters and
slaves were considered equal.

35. *Saint-Marc:* Perhaps Louis Sauvage de Saint-Marc, Seigneur des Marches (documented in 1757 and 1789), of a
family ennobled in the 18th century for distinguished judicial
service.

36. *Henriette:* See Vol. 3, Chaps. I–V, and Vol. 9, Chap. IV.

37. *Croix d'Or:* Name of a crossroads south of Aix-en-Provence.

38. *He:* The text has "elle," which is either a slip of C.'s or a
misreading. Laforgue gives "il" ("he").

39. *Molinari:* See Chap. IV of this volume.

40. *Proc . . . . ship:* C. writes "maq . . . . . . ge" (for *ma-
querellage,* from *maquereau,* "pimp").

41. *Twenty-two years:* According to C.'s account he parted
from Henriette in Dec. 1749 or Jan. 1750, which would be at
most 20 years before the time of her letter.

42. *Cesena:* It was at Cesena that C. first met Henriette (see
Vol. 3, Chap. I).

43. *D'Antoine:* See Vol. 3, Chap. IV, n. 17.

44. *Marcolina:* See Vol. 9, Chaps. I–V.

45. *Letters which I shall add:* Henriette's letters to C. have not
been preserved.

46. *Madame Audibert:* She maintained a gaming room in Marseilles (see Vol. 9, Chap. III).

47. *Madame N. N.:* C. had saved her from destitution when she

was abandoned by the adventurer Croce and had taken her
to Marseilles as his niece and married her to a Monsieur N. N.
(see Vol. 9, Chaps. I-II).

48. *Croce . . . Charlotte:* See Vol. 10, Chap. XI.

49. *Rosalie:* See Vol. 7, Chaps. IV and V, and Vol. 9, Chap. I.

50. *Grimaldi . . . not have amused me:* See Chap. V of this
volume.

51. *Villars:* Honoré Armand, Duke of Villars (1702-1770); C.
had met him and his physician Tronchin in Geneva and at
Voltaire's house (see Vol. 6, Chap. X).

52. *D'Aragon:* Assumed name of the Italian adventurer Darra-
gon, whom C. had known in Russia and in Spa (see Vol. 10,
Chaps. V and XI).

53. *Colle di Tenda:* Pass on the road from Nice or Ventimiglia
to Cuneo in Piedmont; with an altitude of some 6,200 feet,
it was one of the highest passes over the Alps (but not the
highest) in the 18th century.

54. *Raiberti:* Carlo Adalberto Flaminio Raiberti-Nizzardi
(1708-1771); he held several important posts in the Piedmontese administration.

55. *La Pérouse:* Count Gian Giacomo Marcello Gamba della
Perosa, called Comte de la Pérouse (1738-1817)

56. *Sir XXX:* The English Envoy Extraordinary in Turin from
1768 to 1779 was Sir William Lynch. Turin was then the capital of the Kingdom of Sardinia.

57. *Campioni:* Giustina Campioni-Bianchi (died after 1781),
Italian dancer from Parma.

58. *Nani:* Giambattista Nani (1616-1678), Venetian patrician
and Procurator; by order of the Venetian Senate he composed the *Storia di Venezia dal 1613 al 1671* ("History of
Venice from 1613 to 1671") (2 vols., Venice, 1676-1679).

59. *Inn . . . Taglioretti:* The Albergo Svizzero, opened ca.
1760 and operated by Pietro and Tommaso Taglioretti.

60. *Agnelli:* Giovan-Battista Agnelli (1706-1788), of Milan,
Abate; in 1746 he was granted permission to establish a press
for the cantons of Zurich and Lucerne. The privilege was
renewed for Lugano in 1765.

61. *Bargello:* Title of the Chief of Police in many Italian cities.

62. *Monsieur de ══ :* Urs Victor Joseph, Baron Roll von Em-
menholtz (1711-1786), Swiss statesman. He was Bailiff of

Lugano from 1768 to 1770. C. had known him and his wife earlier (see Vol. 6, Chaps. IV-VII, where he refers to them as Monsieur and Madame . . .).

CHAPTER VII

1. *Offspring . . . four years:* Léontius Victor Joseph de Roll was born in Soleure on Oct. 14, 1761, hence only a year and a half after C. left there. So at the time of which C. is writing the boy was some 8 years old.
2. *Lebel:* Invented name of the major-domo to the French Ambassador in Soleure; he married C.'s housekeeper and mistress, Madame Dubois (see especially Vol. 6, Chaps. VIII and IX).
3. *Riva:* Francesco Saverio da Riva, Count of Mauensee and abbé (1701-1782), of a Venetian patrician family which had been ennobled in 1698 and had acquired citizenship in Lucerne through the purchase of the estate of Mauensee. He lived in Lugano and was a jurist, philosopher, poet, and a member of the Arcadian Academy.
4. *Querini:* Angelo Querini (1721-1795), Venetian patrician and Senator; friend of Voltaire.
5. *Count Giovanni Battista:* Giovanni Battista da Riva, Count of Mauensee (1687-1772), elder brother of Francesco (see note 3); however, C. may mean Count Carlo da Riva, letters from whom to C. have been preserved and who was a nephew of Francesco's.
6. *Borromeo:* Count Federico Borromeo (1703-1779), son of the Viceroy of Naples (see Vol. 8, Chap. V). He owned the Borromean Islands.
7. *Inspectors . . . the thirteen cantons:* Until 1798 Switzerland had 13 cantons (they now number 25). Since the Canton of Appenzell did not take part in the struggle of the Confederation against the French in Lombardy in 1512, it was not given a share in the administration of the four ultramontane bailiwicks, of one of which Lugano was then the capital. The 12 sovereign cantons each year sent 12 representatives, with the title of Syndikus (also Avoyer or Schultheiss), to examine the financial affairs of the bailiwicks and the conduct of their governors and to render decisions in cases on appeal.

8. *The one from Bern:* His name was Karl Steiger and he was Syndikus for the Canton of Bern in 1769. He had been Muralt-Favre's predecessor as Financial Commissioner in London (1758-1762) (see the following note).

9. *M. F.:* Louis de Muralt-Favre (1716-1789), member of the Bernese Council of Two Hundred. For C.'s earlier relations with him and his family, see Vol. 6, Chap. VIII, and Vol. 9, Chap. XIII.

10. *Sara:* Sara or Marguerite de Muralt-Favre married Frédéric de Vatteville (Wattenwyl) in 1785.

11. *Marazzani:* See Chap. I of this volume, and *ibid.*, n. 15.

12. *Presidio:* See note 35 to Chap. I of this volume.

13. *La Bellucci:* Anna Bellucci, also Belluzzi, called La Bastoncina, Venetian dancer; she appeared in St. Petersburg from 1758 to 1759 and in Venice from 1764 to 1765. Her husband was the ballet master Giuseppe Bellucci. C. has not mentioned either of them before.

14. *Bobbio:* In northern Italy, between Piacenza and Genoa.

15. *Sellentin:* Baron von Sellentin (died after 1797), Prussian officer, whom C. had met in Augsburg in 1767 (cf. Vol. 10, Chap. X).

16. *Brézé:* Giovacchino Argentero, Marchese di Bersezio, called Marquis de Brézé (1727-1796), writer, bibliophile, and member of the Academy of Sciences in Turin.

17. *Fair at Lugano:* The cattle market at Lugano, which had been held in the first half of October from the 16th century, was famous and attracted many Italian buyers.

18. *The English Envoy:* See note 56 to the preceding chapter.

19. *Lubomirski . . . Bielinski:* Count Franciszek Bielinski (1683-1766), Grand Marshal to the Polish Crown from 1742, was succeeded in that office by Prince Stanislaus Lubomirski (1722-1783), whom C. had known in Poland (cf. Vol. 10, Chaps. VII and VIII).

20. *Zulian:* See note 51 to Chap. I of this volume.

21. *Berlendis:* Giovanni Berlendis, Venetian Secretary of Embassy in London from 1762 to 1763, Venetian Resident in Turin from 1768 to 1771. He informed the Venetian State Inquisition of C.'s presence in Turin by a memorandum dated Dec. 30, 1769.

22. *The College:* The Pien Collegio ("Full College"), made up

of the most important officers of the Venetian Government. (For its exact composition, see Vol. 4, Chap. X, n. 4.)

23. *The answer he received:* The original of the answer, signed by the Inquisitors Flaminio Corner, Barbarigo, and Alvise Renier, and which is still extant, is of an entirely different tenor. Perhaps C. refers to a private letter from the Secretary to Berlendis.

24. *Andrais:* Nothing is known of him. (C. later writes "Andreis.")

25. *Di Rubione:* Probably a relative of the diplomat Francesco Antonio Caisotti di Rubione (1700-1774), who was in the service of the King of Sardinia.

26. *Rica:* Since there were two branches of the noble family of Rica, or Richa, Rica (Richa) of Castelvecchio and Rica (Richa) of Olcenengo, and since all four Counts of the family were alive at the time, it is impossible to identify the one whom C. mentions.

27. *Baretti:* Giuseppe Baretti (1719-1789), important Italian writer of the Enlightenment, who lived for many years in London and died there; he was famous especially for his periodical *La Frusta letteraria,* which appeared in Venice from 1763 to 1765, in which he scathingly attacked the contemporary Arcadian school of poetry.

28. Horace, *Epistles,* 2, 2, 60. Bion of Borysthenes (fl. 300 B.C.), philosopher famous for his caustic satire. (The Brockhaus-Plon edition has *Bioncis* and *nigra.*)

29. *This time:* C. first wrote "At the beginning of the month of April 1770," then substituted "During this time."

30. *Orlov:* Count Alexei Orlov was appointed Grand Admiral of the Russian fleet which operated in the Mediterranean during the first Russo-Turkish War (1768-1774). He spent much of his time in Leghorn from 1770 to 1772. C. had known him in Russia (cf. Vol. 10, Chap. VI).

31. *Sir XXX:* C. first wrote "Link," then substituted "XXX." See note 56 to the preceding chapter.

32. *Aston:* Perhaps a member of an English family of this name who were traveling on the Continent in 1764 and whom Boswell met in Holland.

33. *Rivarola:* Probably the Corsican Count Rivarola, whom Boswell met in Leghorn in 1765.

34. *Paoli:* Pasquale Paoli (1725-1807), celebrated Corsican patriot.
35. *Sclopis:* A noble family named Sclopis (also Sclopitz) is documented in Turin from the 17th century.
36. *Camerana:* Giulio Vittorio d'Incisa, Count of Camerana, was the Sardinian Resident in Venice from 1749 to 1774. (C.'s "Turin" would seem to be a slip for "Venise.")
37. *The English Resident:* Sir James Wright was the English Resident in Venice from 1766 to 1774. He left Venice in Aug. 1769 and did not return there until 1771. During his absence the merchant Robert Richie took his place as Chargé d'Affaires; so C. must refer to Richie.
38. Terence, *Adelphi*, Act IV, scene 5, line 9.
39. *The Dardanelles:* Strait between Europe and Asiatic Turkey, the gateway to Constantinople.
40. *The presence of Achilles:* In *Iliad* I, 509-510, Thetis prays to Zeus to make the Trojans victorious as long as her son Achilles absents himself from the war.
41. *Bentivoglio:* He has not been identified.
42. *Colorno:* Spring and summer residence of the Dukes of Parma, some 9 miles north of Parma (cf. Vol. 3, Chap. IV, n. 13).
43. *Dubois-Chatellerault:* Baron Michel Dubois-Chatellerault (1711-1776 or '77), engraver in the service of the Duke of Parma from 1742, Director of the Parmesan Mint from 1766 (cf. especially Vol. 3, Chap. IV). Parma had no mint, so his directorship was merely honorary.
44. *The Infante:* In 1770, Ferdinando, Duke of Parma, son of Duke Filippo, who was also an Infante of Spain.
45. *Order of St. Michael:* The order was founded in 1469 by Louis VI of France, but was little esteemed in the 18th century, membership in it having been too freely conferred. From the time of Louis XIV it was chiefly conferred on scientists, scholars, writers, and artists. It was abolished in 1830.
46. *He had spent a year in Venice . . . mint:* See Vol. 7, Chap. XII.
47. *Nestor's age:* Proverbial for a very great age. Nestor, the chief counselor of the Greeks in the *Iliad*, was said to have lived "three generations of men."
48. *Morosini:* Francesco I Morosini (born 1751), of an old

Venetian patrician family, nephew of the Procurator Francesco II Lorenzo Morosini (1714-1793). He was a Cavaliere of the Order of the Stola d'Oro.

49. *Stratico:* Count Simone Stratico (1730-1824), from 1755 Professor of Medicine at the University of Padua, later Professor of Mathematics and Physics in Venice.

50. *His brother:* Count Giandomenico Stratico (1732-1799), Dominican monk and philologist, Professor in Siena from 1763, Professor at the University of Pisa from 1769.

51. *The baths:* The Bagni di S. Giuliano, about halfway between Pisa and Lucca; they had been celebrated since Roman times and were a fashionable resort in the 18th century.

52. *The "Pretender-in-vain"* . . . *Great Britain:* Charles Edward Stuart (1720-1788), son of the Old Pretender James, who died in 1766.

53. *The English Consul:* Sir John Dyck, also Dick (1720-1804), Baronet from 1768, English Consul in Leghorn from 1754 to 1776.

54. *Dall'Oglio:* Giuseppe B. Dall'Oglio (died between 1791 and 1796), Italian musician from Padua or Venice; with his better-known brother Domenico, he played in the orchestra at the Imperial Court in St. Petersburg from 1735 to 1764. In 1765 he was appointed the Polish diplomatic representative in Venice. C. had met him in Berlin (cf. Vol. 10, Chap. IV).

55. *Marucci:* Probably Lambro Marucci, also Maruzzi (died 1799); there were three brothers (Costantino, Tano, and Lambro) of this name, all three of whom were ennobled by Maria Theresa in 1765. Lambro was first a banker in Corfu, later became a Councilor of State in St. Petersburg, and supplied the means for Alexei Orlov's expedition against the Turks. From 1768 to 1783 he was the Russian Chargé d'Affaires in Venice.

56. *Order of St. Anne:* Russian order established by Duke Karl Friedrich of Schleswig-Holstein in 1735 in honor of the Czarina Anna Ivanovna and of his wife Anna Petrovna; it was abolished in 1917.

57. Horace, *De arte poetica,* 390.

58. *Calchas:* Seer and prophet who accompanied the Greeks to Troy.

59. *Two or three years later:* Giandomenico Stratico was made

Bishop of Cittanuova (Istria) in 1776, hence three years after the death of Pope Clement XIV (Ganganelli), who had dissolved the Jesuit order in 1773. Lorenzo Ricci (see the following note) died in 1775, hence in the pontificate of Pius VI.

60. *Ricci:* Lorenzo Ricci (1703-1775), General of the Jesuit order from 1758, was sentenced to imprisonment in the Castel Sant'Angelo in Rome in 1773.

61. *Corilla:* Maria Maddalena Fernandez, née Morelli (1727–1800), Italian poetess; as a member of the Arcadian Academy she bore the name Corilla Olimpica; her fame in her day rested principally on her improvisations. C. had met her and heard her improvise (see Vol. 7, Chap. VII).

62. *Crowned* Poetessa . . . *on the Capitol:* The custom of crowning poets dated from Greek antiquity. The Roman Emperors continued it; from the time of Domitian the Capitol became the scene of these coronations. They seem to have continued late into Roman times, but fell into desuetude during the Middle Ages; Humanism and the Renaissance revived the custom with the coronation of Petrarch on the Capitol in 1341. During the Renaissance many poets were crowned, not only in Rome, but also in Florence and Naples. Later, the honor was accorded so often that it came to be little esteemed.

From the 16th century few traces remained of the ancient Roman Capitol. Pope Paul III (1534-1549) had it restored and modernized; he rebuilt the façade of the Palazzo Senatorio, built under Boniface IX (1389-1404), and erected the two lateral buildings, the Palazzo dei Conservatori and the Museo Capitolino.

63. *Their names . . . their favors:* A strange statement for a man of C.'s reading, who cannot but have known that—not to mention the Sibyls—the Seven Poetesses of the Greeks were famous for their own works, not for the praise bestowed on them by their lovers.

64. *Gonzaga Solferino:* Luigi Gonzaga, Prince of Castiglione delle Stiviere, Marchese of Medole and Solferino (1745-1819), Venetian patrician and lover of Corilla Olimpica; he later married Elisabetta Rangoni

65. *The temple:* Poets were usually crowned in the great hall of the Palazzo Senatorio. The Pope had granted the sponsors of Corilla's coronation the use only of a small room. He had

also specified that the ceremony should be performed at night and as simply as possible. Three days later he ordered Corilla and the Prince to leave Rome. C., of course, uses "temple" ironically.

66. *She-wolf:* Allusion to the she-wolf who nursed Romulus and Remus. There is a play on the two meanings of *lupa:* "she-wolf" and "prostitute."

67. *That Pope:* Count Giovanni Angelo Braschi (1717-1799) became Pope as Pius VI in 1775.

68. *Apollo . . . Priapus:* Apollo, the god of poetry; Priapus, a fertility god of the Romans, usually represented with an enormous phallus.

69. *Pizzi:* Gioacchino Pizzi (1716-1790), Abate and man of letters, from 1771 Procustodian of the Arcadian Academy, later Custodian-General. As a member of the Academy he bore the pastoral name Nivildo Amarinzio. On Jan. 4, 1787, he received Goethe into the Academy under the name of Megalio Melpomenio.

70. *Forests of the Arcadians:* The Accademia degli Arcadi was founded in 1690 by the poet and critic Crescimbeni (1663-1728). Each of its members took a fanciful name intended to suggest that of an Arcadian shepherd or shepherdess. Its purpose was to foster the study of poetry. C. became a member of it in 1771, under the name of Eupolemo Pantaxeno.

71. *The Marchesa Chigi:* Violante Teresa, Marchesa Chigi Zondadari (1723-1792), née Gori Pannilini.

72. *Ciaccheri:* Giuseppe Ciaccheri (ca. 1723–1804), Abate and librarian of the University of Siena.

73. Horace, *Odes,* 1, 11, 8. C. often quotes it.

74. *Vico:* The Marchesa's country house was called Vico Bello and had been built by the architect Baldassare Peruzzi (1481-1536) on a hill near Siena.

75. *Pistoi:* The Abate Candidus Pistoi was Professor of Mathematics at the University of Siena and wrote a treatise on mechanics (1775).

76. *Bouts-rimés:* Literary game, in which the contestants are furnished with rhymed endings to which they must make verses in the order given.

77. *Maria Fortuna:* C. to the contrary, this was only her family name; her name as a member of the Arcadian Academy was

Isidea Egirea. She was born ca. 1742, and was a well-known poetess.

78. See note 32 to Chap. I of this volume.

79. *Its Academy:* The Florentine Accademia della Crusca. See Vol. 7, Chap. VII, n. 17.

80. *Palladio:* Like the Marchesa Chigi's country house (see note 74 to this chapter), her town house was built by Baldassare Peruzzi, not by the celebrated Andrea Palladio (1508-1580).

81. *The Bargello:* See note 61 to the preceding chapter.

82. *Coltellini:* Marco Coltellini (1719-1777), Italian poet; he lived in Leghorn, Vienna, Berlin, and, from ca. 1773, in St. Petersburg. C. had probably met him in Vienna in 1763.

83. *Tabarrani:* Pietro Tabarrani (1702-1780), Professor of Anatomy at the University of Siena from 1759; his principal work, the *Observationes anatomicae,* was published at Lucca in 1753.

84. *Piccolomini:* Name of an old Sienese noble family; but to which Count Piccolomini C. refers has not been ascertained.

85. *Chevalier of St. Stephen:* There were two orders of St. Stephen: the Italian Ordine di Santo Stefano di Toscana, founded by Cosimo I de' Medici in the 16th century, which survived until 1859, and a Hungarian one, founded by Maria Theresa in 1764 (abolished in 1919).

86. *Bianconi:* Giovanni Lodovico Bianconi (1717-1781), Bolognese physician and philosopher; he was a member of the Berlin Academy of Sciences from 1749, and for many years physician-in-ordinary to the Hereditary Prince of Saxony and from 1764 Saxon Chargé d'Affaires in Rome. He spent much of his time in Siena.

CHAPTER VIII

1. *Soufflet:* C. has earlier called it a calèche; both were light carriages with seats for two and a folding hood.

2. *Buonconvento:* Post station on the road from Florence to Rome, some 17 miles south of Siena.

3. *Three miles an hour:* The Italian mile was about 1.16 English miles.

4. *San Quirico:* San Quirico d'Orcia, small town on an important crossroads some 10 miles southeast of Buonconvento.

5. *Count de l'Étoile:* Probably the stage name of a French actor, of whom nothing is known except what C. relates.

6. *Pudding:* C. writes "blancputing," possibly for "plum pudding."

7. *Montepulciano:* Wine from the hill town of the same name, considered the best in Tuscany.

8. *Montefiascone:* Muscat wine from the town of the same name (see note 19 to this chapter).

9. *Sophie . . . seventeen years old:* C. first wrote "nineteen," then crossed it out and substituted "seventeen." Sophie Pompeati, C.'s illegitimate daughter by Teresa Imer Pompeati, who lived in London under the name of Mrs. Cornelys, was born between Dec. 1753 and March 1, 1754.

10. *Paoli:* The paolo was a coin which chiefly circulated in the Papal States and in Tuscany; it was worth one-third of a testone, a silver coin minted in Rome.

11. *Nancy Stein . . . given my daughter a ring:* See Vol. 10, Chap. I.

12. *Pi. .:* C. writes "maq. . . . . ." (for *maquereau,* "pimp").

13. *Radicofani:* Town (altitude ca. 2,600 feet) on the road to Rome, some 18 miles south of San Quirico d'Orcia.

14. *B. . . . . .:* C. writes "b. . . . ." (for *bougre,* "bugger").

15. *La Scala:* Post station some 7 miles southeast of San Quirico d'Orcia.

16. *A third horse:* The steepness of the road to Radicofani (cf. note 13 to this chapter) made it necessary to use three horses to drive up it.

17. *Centino:* Ponte Centino, village and post station some 8 miles south of Radicofani.

18. *Acquapendente:* Hill town and post station north of the Lago di Bolsena, some 6 miles southeast of Ponte Centino.

19. *Montefiascone:* Town on the Lago di Bolsena. The distance from Acquapendente to Montefiascone is some 21 miles.

20. *Viterbo:* Town between Lakes Bolsena and Vico, with mineral springs nearby used since the time of the Etruscans.

21. *Boboli:* Village near Leghorn.

22. *F. . . . . ., wh. . . .:* C. writes "f. . . . ." and "p. . . . ." (for *foutue* and *putain*).

23. *Monterosi:* Village and post station at an important cross-roads some 25 miles south of Viterbo.

24. *La Storta:* Last post station on the road from Siena to Rome, some 11 miles north of the ancient Etruscan city of Veii.

25. *Sir B. M.:* Possibly a Sir B. Miller, whose name appears in the list of subscribers to C.'s translation of the *Iliad*.

26. *Rivarola:* See Chap. VII of this volume.

CHAPTER IX

1. *Pekin:* A silk fabric, usually flowered, originally from China.

2. *The "Maltese Cross":* La Croce di Malta was located on the Via Fernanda (now Via Grande) in Leghorn until the middle of the 19th century.

3. *Roland:* Charles (Carlo) Roland (died 1785), of Avignon, owned the "Ville de Londres" inn on the Piazza di Spagna, Rome (cf. Vol. 7, Chap. VIII). His daughter Anne Marie Roland (1744-1779) married François Lafont, of Carcassonne, in 1766, in which year Roland ceded the inn to his son-in-law. Also called "Albergo Inglese" and "Hôtel Lafont," it remained one of the most expensive and well-patronized inns in Rome until well into the 19th century. In 1770 Roland opened another inn, the "Ville de Paris," on the Piazzetta Caetani, near the Corso.

4. *A brother:* Freemasons recognized, and still recognize, one another by a particular grip when shaking hands.

5. *Carozzino:* A light carriage, usually with seats for only two passengers.

6. *The customs office:* The Roman customs office, the Dogana di Terra, was on the Piazza di Pietra in the building now occupied by the Exchange; its façade contains 11 columns from the temple of Marcus Aurelius.

7. *San Carlo:* That is, the Church of San Carlo al Corso, adjacent to the mausoleum of the Emperor Augustus.

8. *The Bargello:* See note 61 to Chap. VI of this volume.

9. *Cardinal Vicar:* The official temporal representative of the Pope in the Bishopric of Rome, which comprised the whole city and a considerable territory outside it.

10. *Governor of Rome:* He was chief judge of the criminal court

(Congregazione criminale) of the city, and in charge of the
police of the ecclesiastical domain. In 1770 the post was held
by Cardinal Antonio Casali.

11. *Civitavecchia:* The port at which the Papal fleet was
stationed. The parenthetical gloss is C.'s.

12. *Bernis:* François Joachim Pierre de Bernis (1715-1794),
abbé, writer, and diplomat; French Ambassador in Venice
from 1752 to 1755, then in Madrid and Vienna; from 1757
Secretary of Foreign Affairs in Paris, from 1769 to 1791
French Chargé d'Affaires at the Roman Curia. He was made
a Cardinal in 1758. C. had known him in Venice (cf. Vol. 4)
and in Paris (cf. Vol. 5).

13. *Teresa . . . whom my brother Giovanni married in 1762:*
Teresa Roland (1744-1779) was married to Giovanni Ca-
sanova in 1764, not in 1762 (cf. Vol. 7, Chap. VIII). It was
C.'s brother Francesco who married in 1762.

14. *Beloselski:* Prince Andrei Mikhailovich Beloselski-Belozer-
ski (died 1779), was Russian Ambassador at the Court of
Saxony from 1766 until the year of his death. C. had known
his younger brother Prince Aleksandr in Dresden (cf. Vol. 10,
Chap. VI).

15. *Could not come to Rome:* Giovanni Casanova was sentenced to prison *in absentia* at Rome in 1767 in connection
with a forged bill of exchange. He was then in Dresden, where
he held the post of Director of the Academy of Fine Arts.

16. The *Dowager Electress of Saxony:* Maria Antonia Walpur-
gis (1724-1780), daughter of the Emperor Charles VII, from
1763 widow of the Elector Friedrich Christian of Saxony. Her
Ambassador at the Holy See was then Lodovico Bianconi. The
reigning Pope was Clement XIV.

17. *Mengs:* The celebrated painter Anton Raphael Mengs
(1728-1779) did not return to Rome from Madrid until Feb.
1771 and remained there until 1774. C. cannot have seen him
until after his visit to Naples. For C.'s earlier relations with
him, see Vol. 7 and Chaps. I and II of this volume.

18. *The French Ambassador:* De Bernis (cf. note 12 to this
chapter).

19. *Baltimore:* Frederick Calvert, 7th Earl Baltimore (1731–
1771) ; C. had known him in London (cf. Vol. 10, Chap. I).

20. *The "Crocelle":* This inn, which was still considered one of

the best in Naples in the 19th century, belonged to the monks of the order of the Holy Cross (Padri Crociferi, whence "Crocelle"). The Riviera di Chiaia, with a striking view of the Bay of Naples, had become a fashionable suburb in the 18th century.

21. *Matalona:* Carlo Caraffa, Duke of Matalona (Maddaloni), died in 1765 (cf. especially Vol. 7, Chap. X). His widow married Francesco Palena d'Aquino, Prince of Caramanica (1736-1795), after 1765.

22. *Palazzo Matalona:* See Vol. 7, Chap. X, n. 6.

23. *Goudar:* Ange Goudar (1720 - ca. 1791), of Montpellier, adventurer and journalist, married the Irishwoman Sarah in 1764 (cf. especially Vol. 9, Chap. XI).

24. *Posilipo:* Name of a range of hills, now part of Naples.

25. *Sarah . . . beer house:* See the reference in note 23 to this chapter.

26. *Du Barry:* Née Marie Jeanne Bécu (1743-1793), the celebrated mistress of Louis XV, who married her to Count Guillaume Du Barry in 1768. C. writes "la Bari."

27. *The Queen:* Maria Carolina Luisa (1752-1814), daughter of the Empress Maria Theresa; she was married to King Ferdinand IV of Naples in 1768.

28. *Suzerain of Boston:* So C. ("seigneur de Boston"), no doubt from a confused recollection of the American connections of the Baltimores, the first Baron Baltimore (George Calvert, ca. 1580-1632) having been granted what is now the state of Maryland by Charles I.

29. *Three or four years later:* The 7th Baron Baltimore died at Naples in Sept. 1771.

30. *Piperno . . . never to wake again:* Piperno was a post station in the Pontine Marshes, on the road from Naples to Rome. However, C. had not hesitated to spend part of a night there in 1761, and the Signora Diana whom he had left to sleep out the night there reappeared in Rome in perfect health a few days later (cf. Vol. 7, Chap. XI).

31. *Gama:* Giovanni Patrizio da Gama de Silveira (1704 or '05 - ca. 1774), of Lisbon; abbé and diplomat (cf. especially Vol. 7, Chap. VIII).

32. *Differences . . . Ganganelli:* The expulsion of the Jesuits

from Portugal in 1759 had created tension between the Holy See and the King of Portugal (for which C.'s "Rome" is obviously a slip). The difference was resolved by the suppression of the Jesuit order by Pope Clement XIV (Giovanni Ganganelli) in 1773.

33. *Leonilda . . . Lucrezia:* For C.'s amour with Donna Lucrezia Castelli, see Vol. 1, Chaps. IX and X, and Vol. 7, Chap. X. Donna Leonilda was C.'s daughter by Donna Lucrezia.

34. *Agata:* C.'s invented name for an Italian dancer from Lucca (cf. Vol. 8, Chaps. V and VI), who married the advocate Aniello Orcivolo, of Naples.

35. *Paglietta:* Neapolitan term for a chicaning lawyer.

36. *Medini:* Count Tommaso Medini (1725 - ca. 1788), writer and adventurer. C. had fought a duel with him in Padua in 1746 (cf. Vol. 2, Chap. VIII).

37. *Choiseul:* Viscount Louis César Renaud de Choiseul (1735-1791), from 1785 Duke of Praslin; from 1766 to 1771 French Envoy Extraordinary in Naples.

38. *Once:* The oncia (plural, once) was originally a silver coin of the Kingdom of Naples (= 30 carlini). From 1749 a gold oncia, having twice that value, was also minted.

39. *Latilla:* Perhaps a relative of Archbishop Benedetto Latilla, Confessor to King Ferdinand IV of Naples.

40. *La Callimena:* Agata Carrara, called "La Callimena," who is known to have sung in Venice and Turin in 1776; she later became the mistress of the Venetian patrician Zuan Carlo Grimani.

41. *Castello dell'Ovo:* Fortress on an egg-shaped island off the Santa Lucia quarter of Naples, with which it was connected by a bridge. *Largo* is the Neapolitan term for *piazza* ("square").

42. *It means . . . moon:* The first etymology (from Greek *kalon*, "beautiful," and *menos*, "madness") is far-fetched; the second is incomprehensible.

43. *Sclopis . . . Aston:* See notes 32 and 35 to Chap. VII of this volume.

44. *Ducati del regno:* Singular, ducato: gold coin of the Kingdom of Naples (= 10 carlini).

45. *Albergoni:* Lodovico Albergoni (ca. 1724-1768), of Padua; he was tried by the Venetian State Inquisitors in 1741 and again in 1750. C. has not mentioned him before.

46. *The five cities:* Of the five cities of the plain, Sodom, Gomorrah, Admah, Zeboiim, and Zoar, only Zoar escaped destruction (see Genesis, Chaps. XIV and XVIII).

47. *La Giudecca:* Venetian, Zuecca; island south of central Venice, a favorite place of resort.

48. *Via Toledo:* Built in the 16th century by the Viceroy Don Pedro de Toledo, it is still one of the principal streets of Naples. Its official name is now Via Roma, but it is still popularly known as the Via Toledo.

49. *Largo dell'Castello:* See note 41 to this chapter.

50. *Bertoldi:* Antonio Bertoldi (died 1787), Italian actor, long a member of the Italian troupe at the Court of Saxony and from 1762 directly in the service of the Elector of Saxony, Friedrich August II (died 1763), who was also King of Poland as Augustus III. C. has not mentioned Bertoldi earlier, but his mother Zanetta was also a member of the troupe.

51. *Company of Italian actors:* See the preceding note.

52. *Miss Chudleigh:* Elizabeth Chudleigh (ca. 1720-1788); she married Augustus John Hervey, 3rd Earl of Bristol, secretly in 1744, but separated from him and in 1769 married Evelyn Pierrepont, Duke of Kingston-upon-Hull; in 1776 she was found guilty of bigamy and fled from England.

53. *Hamilton:* Sir William Hamilton (1730-1803), English diplomat, antiquarian, and art collector; in 1764 Envoy Extraordinary and from 1767 to 1800 English Ambassador in Naples. His second marriage, in 1791, was to Emma Lyon Hart (ca. 1765-1815), the celebrated Lady Hamilton.

54. *Came very near . . . in Vienna:* C. probably refers to an episode with an actress, Caton M., whom he wanted to marry in Vienna in 1785. Cf. Vol. 1, p. 76, of the present translation. There is a reference to the episode in Lorenzo da Ponte's *Memoirs*.

55. Altered from Horace, *Satires*, 1, 9, 78.

56. *Quinze:* A card game in which the player who ends with 15 points or the closest approximation to it is the winner.

57. *Francavilla:* Michele Imperiali, Prince of Montena and

Francavilla (before 1736-1782), Spanish Grandee and Major-domo to the King of Naples.
58. *A priest:* Don Paolo Moccia, whose extraordinary natural buoyancy was the subject of scientific studies at the time.

CHAPTER X

1. A favorite motto of C.'s too (cf. Vol. 5, Chap. IX).
2. *Prince of Asturias:* Title of the eldest son of the King of Spain; but in this instance, the eldest son having been declared insane, it devolved upon Carlos III's second son, the later Carlos IV. His brothers were Don Fernando (born 1751, King of Naples from 1759), Don Gabriel (born 1752), Don Antonio (born 1755), and Don Francisco (born 1757).
3. *Giliani:* Saverio Giliani, two letters from whom were found among C.'s papers.
4. *Serracapriola:* Antonino Maresca, Duke of Serracapriola (1750-1822); Neapolitan Ambassador in St. Petersburg 1782. He was married to Maria Adelaide del Carretto (died before 1788).
5. *Tanucci:* The Marchese Bernardo Tanucci (1698-1783), Professor of Law at the University of Pisa, from 1735 Minister, from 1767 Prime Minister of the Kingdom of Naples.
6. *Bettoni:* Count Giuseppe Bettoni (1722 - after 1777), Somaschian priest in Rome and Auditor of the papal court of the Rota.
7. *Livrets:* In basset and faro, a *livret* is the 13 cards given to each punter.
8. *Rosebery:* Perhaps Neil Primrose, Earl Rosebery; since C. writes only "un chr. [for 'chevalier'] Rosburi," the identification is not certain.
9. *Hanoverian sisters . . . Marchese della Pettina:* See Vol. 10, Chaps. I and II.
10. *The Vicaria:* The fortress of Castel Capuano, built in the 13th century in the northeastern quarter of Naples, was also known as La Vicaria from its having at one time been the viceregal residence. From the 15th century it served as the seat of the supreme court and as a prison.
11. *Carlini:* The carlino was a Neapolitan coin worth 1/10th of a ducato del regno.

12. *Di Marco:* Carlo, Marchese di Marco (died after 1799), of Brindisi; Neapolitan Minister of Justice from 1759 and favorite of Tanucci.

13. *My brother the Abate:* Gaetano Alvisio or Luigi Casanova (1734-1783), subdeacon from 1755, from 1767 to 1769 imprisoned in Venice by order of the Council of Ten, from 1771 preacher in Rome (cf. especially Vol. 9, Chaps. II and III).

14. *The incident:* See Vol. 5, Chap. VI.

15. *The Fair:* Probably the Festa di Santa Maria di Piedigrotta, celebrated at Posilipo in September with parades, music, fireworks, and so on.

16. *Latilla:* See note 39 to the preceding chapter.

17. *Mrs. Cornelys's son:* Giuseppe (Joseph) Pompeati (1746-ca. 1797), son of Angelo Pompeati and his wife Teresa, née Imer, who later lived in London under the name of Mrs. Cornelys. (See especially Vol. 9, Chaps. VII and VIII.)

18. *Relatives in Venice:* His uncle Giacomo Zuan Battista Pompeati, merchant, and the latter's son Giovanni.

19. *Buturlin:* Count Pyotr Aleksandrovich Buturlin (1734-1787), Russian diplomat; Envoy Extraordinary in Vienna, Stockholm, and Madrid.

20. *Leave . . . within three days:* The Goudars were expelled from Naples on a date before Sept. 17, 1774. C. has confused this with their earlier departure from Naples in 1770; they left a few months after he did, to travel with Sarah's lover Count Buturlin.

21. *Procida:* Island in the Bay of Naples with an old castle.

22. *I had given her in Turin and Alessandria:* See Vol. 8, Chaps. V and VI, where, however, C. says nothing of making her presents in Alessandria, a town in northern Italy.

23. *Made a small fortune . . . mercury:* See Vol. 1, Chap. VIII.

24. *San Nicandro:* Domenico Cattaneo, Prince of San Nicandro, Duke of Termoli and Count of Aversa, appointed Grand Master of Crown Prince Fernando's household in 1755 and President of the Council of Regency in 1759.

25. Altered from Ovid, *Ex Ponto,* 1, 2, 121f (where the text has *sed piger* and *quotiens*).

26. *Caraffa:* Don Lelio Caraffa, who had befriended C. during

the latter's first visit to Naples (cf. Vol. 1, Chap. IX), had
died in 1761.

27. *Genovesi:* Antonio Genovesi (1712-1769), celebrated philosopher and economist at the University of Naples and, from
1754, at the University of Milan.

28. *The Two Sicilies:* Alternative name for the Kingdom of
Naples, which included Sicily. When the Saracens conquered
almost all of Sicily in the 9th century its Byzantine rulers
called their territory on the Italian mainland "Sicily beyond
the Straits."

29. *A letter:* Fernando, born in 1751, was only 17 years old
when he wrote his royal father this letter; the expulsion of
the Jesuits from the Kingdom of Naples took place in 1767,
Fernando was married in 1768.

30. *Scrivani:* Court clerks.

31. *Mine:* Maria Carolina, daughter of Maria Theresa; she
later bore him 17 children, of whom one was born dead and 9
died in infancy.

32. *Tanucci . . . live . . . until the end of the world:* Tanucci
died in 1783 at the age of 85.

33. *Morosini . . . Stratico:* See notes 48 and 49 to Chap. VII
of this volume.

34. *The Academy:* No doubt the Real Accademia Militare,
founded in Turin in 1669.

35. *Marriage . . . de'Servi:* Francesco Morosini's marriage to
Loredana Grimani de'Servi took place in 1772.

36. *Galiani:* Fernando Galiani (1728-1787), of Naples, known
as the Abbé Galiani, served as his country's Secretary of
Embassy in Paris from 1759 to 1769; writer and political
economist, he was a leading figure of the Enlightenment. C.
had known him in Paris (cf. Vol. 5, Chap. IV).

37. *His brother . . . left Donna Lucrezia Castelli:* See Vol. 7,
Chap. X.

38. *Marchesa della C. . . .:* Leonilda, natural daughter of C.
and Donna Lucrezia, must have married the Marchese della
C. . . after 1760.

39. *Over what we had fought a duel:* The duel took place in
Padua in 1746 or 1747 (cf. Vol. 2, Chap. VIII).

40. *Quadrille:* Old card game played with two packs of cards
from which the 8's, 9's, and 10's have been removed.

41. *Teatro San Benedetto:* Built by the patrician family of Grimani de San Luca and opened in 1756, it soon became the chief theater in Venice; from this position it was displaced after 1792 by the new Teatro La Fenice. It is now the Cinema Rossini in San Luca.

42. *We were brothers:* A particular kind of kiss was a sign of recognition among Freemasons.

43. *Ten fathoms:* C. writes "toises" ("fathoms"), perhaps in error, since 60 feet would be an unusual depth for a pond in a garden.

44. *The Agimus:* I.e., grace (from *Gratias tibi agimus, o Domine . . .*).

45. *Picenza . . . Battipaglia:* Picenza is a village some 7 miles southeast of Salerno on the hills above the Plain of Paestum; Battipaglia, now an important railway junction some 13 miles from Salerno, is on the Plain. C., however, writes "Vicence," so the identification is not certain.

46. *Li flati:* The vapors (cf. Vol. 1, Chap. IX, n. 2).

47. *Monte Cassino:* The celebrated Benedictine monastery, on a steep hill above the place of the same name, founded in the 6th century, was destroyed during the Second World War but has since been rebuilt.

48. *Lausitz:* Prince Franz Xaver of Saxony and Count von der Lausitz (1730-1806) was the second son of Augustus III, Elector of Saxony and King of Poland.

49. *Signora Spinucci:* Countess Chiara Rosa Maria Spinucci (1741-1792), Lady-in-Waiting at the Court of the Elector of Saxony; she married Prince Franz Xaver in 1765. The marriage was not recognized by the Courts of Europe until 1777.

50. *Bianconi:* Giovanni Lodovico Bianconi (1717-1781), Bolognese physician, scholar, and diplomat; from 1764 he represented the Elector of Saxony as Resident in Rome.

HISTORY OF MY LIFE

Volume 12

CONTENTS

Volume 12

LIST OF PLATES

Volume 12

Between pages 236–237

VOLUME 12

CHAPTER I

1770. Margherita. La Buonaccorsi. The Duchess of Fiano. Cardinal de Bernis. The Princess of Santa Croce. Marcuccio[1] and his sister. The excommunication attached to the visiting room is abolished.

HAVING ALREADY made up my mind to spend a quiet six months in Rome, confining my activities to learning to know the city and making such acquaintances as doing that should bring me, on the day after I arrived I took a pleasant apartment opposite the palace of the Spanish Ambassador, who was then Monsignor Azpuru;[2] the apartment was the one which had been occupied twenty-seven years earlier by the teacher of languages to whom I had gone for lessons when I was in the service of Cardinal Acquaviva.[3] The landlady of the apartment was the wife of a cook,[4] who came to spend the night with her only once a week. She had a daughter sixteen or seventeen years of age, who, despite her rather too dark complexion, would have been very pretty if smallpox had not deprived her of one eye. She wore a false eye, which, being of a different color from the other and also larger, made her face repulsive. The girl, whose name was Margherita, made no impression on me; even so, I

could not refrain from giving her a present, than which
none other could have gratified her more. An English
oculist who was known as the Chevalier Taylor[5] being in
Rome, and lodging on the same square, I took Margherita
and her mother to him and, for six zecchini, had her
fitted with a porcelain eye which matched the other and
could not have looked better. My generosity made Margherita think that, overwhelmed by her beauty in twenty-
four hours, I had already fallen in love with her; her
mother, being a devout woman, feared to burden her conscience by judging my motive too unfavorably. I was not
long in learning all this from Margherita herself, when
we reached the point of an intimate acquaintance. I came
to terms for dinner and supper without any luxury. Rich
in the possession of three thousand zecchini, I determined to pursue a course of conduct which would assure
me that I could live in Rome not only without needing
anyone but even cutting a respectable figure.

The following morning I found letters at almost all the
post offices,[6] and found, too, that the head of the Banca
Belloni,[7] who had long known me, had already received
notice of the bill of exchange of which I was the bearer.
Signor Dandolo,[8] always my faithful friend, sent me two
letters of recommendation written by the same Venetian
nobleman, Signor Zulian,[9] who had recommended me to
the Venetian Ambassador in Madrid, Signor Mocenigo,
with the consent of the State Inquisitors. One of his letters was addressed to Signor Erizzo,[10] the Venetian Ambassador, which greatly pleased me. He was the brother
of the Erizzo who had been Ambassador in Paris. The
other was addressed to his sister, the Duchess of Fiano.[11]
I saw that I should soon make my way into all the great
houses in Rome; I was delighted at the thought of presenting myself to Cardinal de Bernis after I had become
well known in the city. I engaged neither a carriage nor
a servant; it is not necessary in Rome, where both can be
procured at a moment's notice when they are needed.

The first person to whom I presented my letter was the Duchess of Fiano, who, having heard from her brother that I would call on her, received me most graciously. She was an extremely ugly woman, not at all rich, but with an excellent heart; having very little wit, she had taken the course of being amusingly malicious to prove that she had a great deal of it. Her husband the Duke, who used the name of Ottoboni, to which he had a right, and who had married her to obtain an heir, was impotent, which, in the language of Rome, is *babilano;*[12] this was her first confidence to me, vouchsafed the third time I saw her; but she did not say it in a way to make me conclude that she did not love him or that she wanted to present herself as a woman to be pitied, for it appeared that she said it only to make fun of a confessor she had who had threatened to refuse her absolution if she continued to do everything she could to make him potent. She gave a supper every evening to her circle of intimates, composed of some seven or eight people, to which I was not admitted until a week or ten days later, when, all of them having met me, they seemed to value my company. Her husband, who did not like society, supped alone in his room. The cavalier who danced attendance on the Duchess was the Prince of Santa Croce,[13] whose wife's cavalier was Cardinal de Bernis. The Princess, daughter of the Marchese Falconieri,[14] was very young, pretty, extremely animated, and a woman to please all who came near her; however, proud of possessing the Cardinal, she let no one hope for the honor of taking his place. Her husband the Prince was a handsome man, elegant in his manners and with a sufficiency of intelligence; but he used it only in commercial speculations; he believed, and rightly, that a nobleman does not derogate from his birth by availing himself of all the advantages to which it entitles him. Not liking to spend, he attended the Duchess of Fiano because he spent nothing, and he felt that he was in no danger of falling in love with her.

Though not bigoted, he was a fanatical Jesuit, and indeed
a Jesuit of the short robe,[15] like Président d'Éguilles,[16]
brother of the Marquis d'Argens, whom I had known in
Aix. As soon as, two or three weeks after I arrived, he
heard me complain of the difficulties a man of letters encountered when he went to work in the Roman libraries,[17]
the Minerva, for example, or still more the Vatican, he
offered to introduce me to the Superior of the professed
house at Il Gesù and at Sant'Ignazio.[18] One of the librar-
ians presented me once and for all to all the assistants,
and from then on I found I could not only go to the
library on any day and at any hour but could also take
home whatever books I needed, only writing the title of
the book on a sheet of paper which I left on the table at
which I was writing. I was brought candles when it appeared that I did not have light enough, and the courtesy
I was shown even extended to my being given the key to
a small door by which I could enter the library at all
hours, very often without being seen. The Jesuits were
always the most courteous of all the regular ecclesiastics
of our religion, and even, if I may say so, the only courteous ones; but during the crisis in which they were then
involved they carried their courtesy so far that they impressed me as servile. The King of Spain[19] wanted the
order suppressed, and they knew that the Pope had promised [20] him that he would do it; but, sure that the final
blow would never fall, they were unafraid. They could
never persuade themselves that the Pope could have a
courage which, according to them, surpassed the moral
strength of mankind. They even managed to have him
indirectly warned that he did not have the necessary
authority to suppress their order without convoking a
Council; but all was in vain. The Pope found it difficult
to make up his mind because he knew that decreeing the
suppression of the Company would be decreeing his own
death. He did not bring himself to it until he saw that his
honor was seriously endangered. The King of Spain, who

was the stubbornest of all sovereigns, wrote him in his
own hand that, if he did not suppress the order, he would
print and publish in every language of Europe the letters
he had written him when he was a Cardinal and on the
strength of which he had had him created Supreme
Pontiff of the Christian religion. A man of a different
stamp from Ganganelli could have answered the King
that the Pope was not obliged to do what he had promised as a Cardinal, and the Jesuits would have supported
the doctrine, which is not the most specious of all those
put forward by the adherents of probabilism;[21] however,
in his heart Ganganelli had no love for the Jesuits, he
was a Franciscan, he was not born a gentleman, his manners were rustic, and he was not strong-minded enough
to defy the shame he would have felt at finding himself
exposed as a man of ambition and capable of breaking the
promise he had made to a great monarch in order to become the occupant of the Chair of St. Peter.

I laugh at those who say that the Pope poisoned himself by taking counterpoisons. It is true that, always
afraid that he would be poisoned, he took antidotes and
preservative drugs. Being wholly ignorant of pharmacy,
he was gullible in that respect; but I am in a position to
say that it is morally certain (if there is such a thing as
moral certainty) that Pope Ganganelli died from being
given poison[22] and not from his alexipharmics.[23] The
grounds for my certainty are as follows:

At the time when I was in Rome, which was the third
year of Ganganelli's pontificate, a woman from Viterbo,[24]
who made enigmatic predictions with surprising particulars, was sent to prison. In obscure terms she predicted the destruction of the Company of Jesus without
naming the time at which it was to occur; but what she
said perfectly clearly was this: *"The Company of Jesus
will be destroyed only by a Pope who will reign five
years, three months, and three days, exactly as long as
Sixtus V,[25] not a day more, not a day less."* Most of those

who read this prophecy made light of it, and nothing
more was said of the Sibyl, who was nevertheless imprisoned. I ask my reader to tell me if a man of judgment, if
a man who can think, can doubt that the Pope was poisoned when, at his death, the prophecy was found to have
been fulfilled. In such a case moral certainty becomes the
same as material certainty; the mind which made the
woman from Viterbo its mouthpiece was clever enough to
inform the world that, if the Jesuits were suppressed,
they would not fail to avenge themselves. The very powerful man who poisoned the Pope could certainly have poisoned him before he suppressed the order; but we must
believe that he never thought he would be capable of it. It
is obvious that, if he had not suppressed the order, he
would not have poisoned him, and so the prophecy would
not have been false. Let us note that Ganganelli was a
monk of the Order of St. Francis, like Sixtus V, and that
the one was no more of noble birth than the other. The
strange thing is that after the Pope's death the Sibyl was
declared insane and released from prison and nothing
more was heard of her, and that, despite the fact that the
prophecy I have mentioned was widely known, men of
learning and noblemen alike all insisted on saying that
it was true that the Pope had been poisoned, but that it
was by his alexipharmics, which he constantly took and
even without his faithful friend Bontempi[26] being present. I ask any thinking man what inducement the Pope,
unless he was insane, could have to fulfill the woman of
Viterbo's prophecy to the letter. Those who will tell me
that the whole thing could have been the result of pure
chance will strike me dumb, for it is a possibility which I
cannot deny, but I shall continue to argue as I have
always argued. The poisoning of Pope Ganganelli was the
last example of their power to which the Jesuits, even
after their extinction, treated the world. The unpardon-
able mistake they made was not to have killed him before

that, for true policy consists only in foresight and precaution, and the worst of all politicians is he who does
not know that there is nothing on earth which, in case of
doubt, precaution must not sacrifice to foresight.

The second time that the Prince of Santa Croce saw
me at the Duchess of Fiano's he asked me *ex abrupto*
("without preamble") why I did not go to see Cardinal
de Bernis; I replied that I intended to go there the next
day.

"Go, for I have never heard His Eminence speak of
anyone with as much regard as he does of you."

"He put me under an infinite obligation to him eighteen years ago;[27] and I would gladly risk my life to convince His Eminence that I have not forgotten what I owe
him."

"Then go to see him, and we shall all be delighted."

The Cardinal received me the next day with every sign
of the unfeigned pleasure it gave him to see me again.[28]
He praised me for my reticence in speaking of him to the
Prince of Santa Croce at the Duchess's, being sure that I
would say nothing about the circumstances of our friendship in Venice. I told him that, except for having grown
stouter, I found him as handsome and fresh-looking as
when he had left Paris twelve years earlier, but he
replied that he felt different in every way.

"I am fifty-five years old," he said, "and I am reduced
to a vegetable diet."

"Is it in order to keep down the inclination of the
flesh for the work of love?"

"I wish people believed it; but I do not think it
deceives anyone."

He was delighted when he learned that I had a letter
to the Venetian Ambassador, which I had not yet delivered. He promised me that he would approach him in a
way which would assure me of a good reception from
him.

"Meanwhile," he said, "I will begin breaking the ice tomorrow. You shall dine with me, and he shall learn of it."

I told him I had plenty of money, and I saw that he was delighted to know it, and even more pleased when I told him I was all alone and determined to be on my good behavior and to live without ostentation. He said that he would write M. M.[29] of my presence in Rome and my resolve. I amused him very much by telling him the story of my adventure with the nun in Chambéry.[30] He said that I should not hesitate to ask the Prince of Santa Croce to introduce me to the Princess, with whom we could spend pleasant hours, but not of the sort we used to spend in Venice, for she had no resemblance to M. M.

"Yet she provides Your Eminence with your only agreeable occupation."

"Yes, for want of anything better. You will see."

The next day as we rose from table the Cardinal told me that Signor Zulian had mentioned me to the Ambassador, Erizzo, who had shown the greatest desire to make my acquaintance; and I was very well satisfied with the reception he gave me. The Cavaliere, brother of the Procurator Erizzo, who is still alive, was a man of great intelligence, a good citizen, very eloquent, and a consummate politician. He congratulated me on being on my travels, and on being protected by the State Inquisitors instead of persecuted by them, for Signor Zulian had recommended me to him with their consent. He kept me for dinner, and he told me to come there whenever I had nothing better to do.

It was at the Duchess's on that same evening that I asked the Prince of Santa Croce to introduce me to the Princess; he replied that she wished it, the Cardinal having talked of me for an hour on the previous evening. He said that I could go there every day, either at eleven o'clock in the morning or at two in the afternoon. I went there the next day at two o'clock; she was in bed, where

she took a siesta every day, and, since I had the privilege of being a person of no importance, she had me
shown in at once. In a quarter of an hour I saw everything that she was: young, pretty, gay, animated, curious, merry, always talking, asking questions, and never
having the patience to hear out the answers. I saw that
the young woman was a perfect plaything to amuse the
mind and the heart of a voluptuous and discreet man
who was burdened with important affairs and needed
distraction. The Cardinal saw her only on the three
regular visits he paid her every day: when she rose in
the morning and he went to see if she had slept well;
every afternoon, when he went to drink coffee with her
in her apartment; and every evening at the assembly in
her palace. He played a game of two-handed piquet with
her, at which he saw to it that he lost six Roman zecchini[31] every day, neither more nor less. This made the
Princess the richest young woman in Rome. Her husband,
though so lacking in magnanimity as to be jealous, had
practical intelligence enough not to object to his wife's
enjoying an income of eighteen hundred francs a month
without doing anything which could lead either her to
reproach herself or others to speak ill of her, for the
thing was done in public and the money was honestly won
at a game success in which could be attributed only to
luck.

So the Prince of Santa Croce could not but cultivate
and set the highest value on the Cardinal's friendship for
his charming Princess, who, being extremely fecund,
gave him a child not only every year but sometimes every
nine months, despite the fact that the physician Salicetti[32] had assured her that proper care for her health
demanded that she should not become pregnant again
until after the six weeks of discharge after her lying-in
had elapsed.

In addition the Prince enjoyed the advantage of being
able to receive all the fabrics he wanted from Lyons,

without giving any occasion for objections on the part of the Grand Treasurer,[33] who was then Monsignor Braschi[34] (now the Pope), since they were addressed to the Cardinal-Ambassador of France. Add, too, that the Cardinal's friendship for his house protected him against all those who would have annoyed him by courting his wife. The man who was in love with her at that time was the Constable Colonna,[35] whom he had taken by surprise in a room in his palace conversing with her during one of those quarters of an hour when she was morally certain that the ring at the door did not announce the arrival of the incumbent Eminence. No sooner had the Prince-Constable left than the offended husband told the Princess to be ready to leave for the country with him the next day. The Princess protested that such an unexpected, unwonted, and unprepared departure was only a whim to which her honor did not permit her to yield; but his mind was made up, and she would have had to obey if the Cardinal himself, having arrived and heard the whole story from the ingenuous and innocent beauty, had not proved to the husband that he could, and under the circumstances must, go to the country alone, leaving his Princess in Rome, where she would take greater care in future to avoid encounters which were always troublesome and of a nature to give rise to unfortunate misunderstandings likely to destroy the peace of the family.

In less than a month I became the person whose presence discommoded none of the three chief actors in the play. Taking no part in the dispute while it raged, listening, approving everything, and, when it was over, always declaring that the victor was in the right, I became almost as necessary to them as the marker is to the billiard player. I occupied the dreary time which follows such quarrels with stories or amusing comments; everyone felt better, everyone attributed it to me that the thing had been patched up so quickly, and I was rewarded by never being unwelcome at any time and in any situation.

In the Princess, the Prince, and the Cardinal, I saw three nobly innocent and inoffensive souls going their[36] way without harming anyone or doing anything to subvert the peace and the just laws of society in general.

The Duchess of Fiano, conceiving that her possessing the husband of her whose possession he allowed the Cardinal to enjoy showed that her own merits were of the highest, and not a little vain of what she thought Rome must be saying in consequence, whereas in fact no one was taken in, was angry with me for being stupid enough to see everything through rose-colored glasses. She would never have supposed me so lacking in intelligence, she was amazed that I did not see that only an unconquerable jealousy kept the Princess of Santa Croce from ever calling on her; she spoke to me one day so hotly to convince me that such was the case that I saw that if I did not admit it I should lose her good graces. As for the Princess's charms, I had had to grant her from the beginning that it was incomprehensible how they had succeeded in dazzling the Cardinal, for she was the thinnest creature alive and none of her sex in Rome had a mind that was giddier or more incapable of reasoning. What was, however, the incontrovertible truth was that the Princess of Santa Croce was a jewel perfectly adapted to make a voluptuous and philosophical lover like the Cardinal happy. At certain moments I was more inclined to wonder at his good luck in possessing such a treasure than at the eminent dignity to which Fortune and his innate qualities had raised him. I loved the Princess, but, never allowing myself to hope, I remained within the bounds which assured me that I should forever keep the place which I then held. Trying to attain something more, I should have risked losing everything, for I should have offended the lady's pride and shocked the delicacy of her lover, whom age and the sacred purple had, despite his philosophy, made a different man from what he had been when we had shared possession of M. M.[37] It must be

added that the Cardinal had always told me that he
felt for her only the fondness of a father; it was enough
to show me that he would have taken offense at my at-
tempting to be, or to become, anything more than the
favorite among all her most humble servants. I had to be
satisfied and consider myself very fortunate that she
feared me no more than she did her chambermaid. Indeed, to be as agreeable to her as I could, I pretended not
to be looking at her when she knew that I saw her. The
course one must pursue to gain the good graces of a
woman who pampers herself is not easy to find, especially
if she has a king or a cardinal dancing attendance on her.

The life I had been leading during the month I had
been in Rome was everything I could want in the way of
tranquillity. At my lodging Margherita had found the
way to capture my interest by her attentions. Since I had
no servant, she was in my room morning and evening; I
looked at her, very well pleased with the present of the
false eye I had made her, which looked natural and real
to all who had not known her as one-eyed. The girl was
extremely intelligent, though completely uneducated,
and enormously vain in the matter of dress. With no particular intention, I played up to her by holding long,
amusing conversations with her morning and night and
making her little presents; and, by giving her money, I
catered to her love of finery which made her looked at
in the Church of the Holy Apostles[38] every feast day and
Sunday when she went to mass. In a few days I became
aware of two things: first, that she was astonished that,
loving her, I never came to a declaration in words or in
acts; second, that, if I loved her, I could conquer her
without much difficulty. The latter I could not but divine
when, urged to tell me the story of all the little adventures she must have had from the age of eleven to her
then age of seventeen or eighteen, she told me anecdotes
which I greatly enjoyed and which she could not have
told me without trampling on every feeling of modesty. I

had reached this point with her by giving her three or
four paoli every time I thought she had been frank; I told
her so; and I gave her nothing when I felt sure that she
concealed the most interesting circumstances of the intrigue. By this course I forced her to confess to me that
she no longer had her maidenhead, that a charming girl
whose name was Buonaccorsi and who came to see her
every Sunday and feast day no longer had hers either,
and what man it was who had conquered them both. She
assured me that she did not make love with the Abate
Ceruti,[39] whose room was next to mine and to whom she
had to go whenever her mother did not have time enough.
This Piedmontese Abate was handsome, learned, and in
general a man of prepossessing qualities, but he was poor,
burdened with debts, and in very ill repute in Rome because of an ugly story which everyone had heard and
of which he was the unfortunate hero. It was said that
he had confided to an Englishman who was in love with
Princess Lanti[40] that she was in need of two hundred
zecchini, and that the Englishman had given them to him
to give to her, but that the Abate had kept them for himself. This black fraud had been revealed in the course of a
conversation between the lady and the Englishman, who,
after telling her that he was ready to do anything for her,
had assured her that he considered the two hundred
zecchini he had sent her nothing. The lady, very much
surprised, having denied all knowledge of it, the Englishman had prudently not insisted; but the Abate had been
suddenly banished from the Lanti palace and the magnanimous Englishman had done no more than refuse to
see him again.

The Abate, who was one of the people Bianconi
employed to write the *Roman Ephemerides*[41] which came
out every week, had become my friend as soon as I came
to stay in Margherita's house. I had noticed that he was
in love with her, and it was a matter of indifference to me,
for I did not love her, but I should not have believed that

Margherita treated him unkindly. The girl assured me that she could not bear him and that she was very much displeased whenever she had to enter his room. The Abate was already under obligations to me. He had borrowed some twenty scudi from me, promising that he would return them three or four days later, and three weeks had passed without his giving them back; but I did not ask him for them, and I would even have lent him another twenty without his asking me for them, but for what happened next.

When I supped at the Duchess of Fiano's I came home late, and Margherita would be waiting for me. Her mother would be asleep, and, wanting to be diverted, I would keep her with me for an hour or two, regardless of the fact that our amusements made noise enough to disturb the Abate Ceruti, who, separated from the room in which we were entertaining ourselves only by a board partition, could not but hear even what we said and painfully resent our gay conversations when Margherita did nothing to quench the fire with which he burned for her.

Coming home one evening toward midnight, I was very much surprised to find, instead of Margherita, her mother.

"Where is your daughter?"

"My daughter is asleep. It goes against my conscience to let her stay in your room all night."

"She stays only until, being ready to go to bed, I tell her to leave, and this change offends me, for it shows me only too clearly your unjustified suspicions. What can Margherita have said to you? If she has complained, she lied, and I will leave your house tomorrow."

"You would be wrong. Margherita has said nothing to me, on the contrary she maintains that you only joke with her."

"Exactly so. Do you see any harm in joking?"

"No, but you might do something else."

"And on that assumption, meanwhile, you base an unworthy suspicion which should burden your conscience, if you are a good Christian."

"God keep me from suspecting my neighbor, but I was informed that your laughter and joking are carried to such extremes that there can be no doubt that your meetings are immoral."

"So it was my neighbor the Abate who was indiscreet enough to set you worrying."

"I cannot tell you from whom I know it, but I know it."

"So much the better for you. I shall remove to other lodgings tomorrow, and thus put your conscience at rest."

"But cannot I render you the services my daughter does?"

"Certainly not. Your daughter amuses me, and I need it. You are not a woman to amuse me. I leave tomorrow, I tell you. You have insulted me, and it must not happen again."

"I should be sorry to have you leave, because of my husband, who would ask me the reason, and I should not know what to tell him."

"What your husband may say about it is nothing to me. I shall leave tomorrow. Be so good as to go, for it is time I went to bed."

"Permit me to serve you, to take off your shoes."

"Neither that nor anything else. If you want me to be served, send Margherita."

"She is asleep."

"Wake her."

At that she left, and three minutes later in comes Margherita, with nothing much on but her shift and without her false eye, which she had not had time to put in, at which I burst out laughing.

"I was asleep, and my mother told me to come and

persuade you not to leave our house, for my father would think the worst of it.''

''I will stay, but you shall continue to come to my room alone.''

''Gladly, but we must not laugh any more, for the Abate complained of it.''

''So it was the Abate who told your mother?''

''Can you have any doubt of it? Our joy made him bitter. Our gaiety offended his passion.''

''He is a wretch who needs to be punished. If we laughed day before yesterday, we will laugh even more tonight.''

She agreed; whereupon we played every imaginable trick, accompanied by constant laughter, which must have driven the talebearer to despair. At the height of our romp, which must have gone on for an hour, the door opens; it was Margherita's mother who entered, expecting to catch us in the act. She sees me with Margherita's cap on my head, and Margherita with a pair of mustaches which I had painted with ink. She could not help laughing too.

''Well,'' I said, ''do you think us great criminals?''

''No, and I see that you are right; but consider that your innocent orgies keep your neighbor from sleeping.''

''Let him go and sleep somewhere else. I shall do as I please. I will even tell you that you have only to choose between him and me. I will stay in your house only on condition that you turn him out, and I will take his room for myself.''

''I cannot turn him out until the end of the month; but I foresee that he will say things to my husband which will make trouble in our household.''

''He will say nothing to your husband, of that I am sure. Let me take care of it. I will speak to the Abate myself tomorrow morning, and he will leave your house of his own free will without your having to say anything to him. And that, my good woman, will save you from even greater worries. In future, fear for your daughter when you know that she is alone in a room with a man and they are not talking and not laughing. Then you can be sure that they are doing something serious.''

After this little sermon she left well satisfied and went off to bed. Margherita, congratulating me in advance on the brilliant move that I had promised to make the next day, became so gay that I could not keep from doing her the justice she deserved; she spent an hour in my bed without laughing, then left, proud of her victory.

The next morning early I entered the Abate's room, where, after reproaching him for his talebearing, which he could not deny, I told him in so many words that he must find other lodgings at once or take the consequences of my declaring myself his enemy, beginning by implacably demanding the twenty scudi he owed me, undeterred by the fact that he could not pay them. After beating about the bush for some time, he told me that he could not leave without paying what he owed the innkeeper and without having money to pay a month in advance on another room which he would at once go to look for; and to get rid of all these difficulties I gave him another twenty scudi. So the whole affair ended well;[42] I found myself better lodged, in full possession of Margherita, who soon put me in that of the charming Buonaccorsi, whose attractions were much greater than hers.

The two girls introduced me to the young hero who had had the art to seduce them both. He was a tailor's apprentice fifteen years of age, handsome, short, but so generously endowed by nature that I had to say they were right when I saw the object the sight of which had deprived them of the power to resist. The youth was very well-mannered; I found in him a refinement which declared him to be above his station. He loved neither Margherita nor La Buonaccorsi. Seeing them together,

and hence without constraint, he had thought they were
curious about what they did not see, and he had satisfied
their curiosity. But the satisfaction of their sight was
followed by desires for something more tangible; the
youth became aware of it, and, being polite and magnanimous, he took the first step by offering them everything in his power. Thereupon the two girls consulted
together, and, pretending only to humor him, obtained
the enjoyment of the splendid object.

Loving them both, and feeling the greatest friendship
for the youth, I often arranged to have the pleasure
of watching him performing amorous exploits, very glad
to see that, instead of being jealous of his enjoyment and
his abilities, I felt their beneficent influence to the point
of sharing in the festivities with an increase in enjoyment
which the sight of the youth, handsomer than Antinoüs,[43]
procured me. I outfitted him with linen and some fine
coats, and before long he trusted me completely, confid-
ing to me all that filled his heart, in love with a girl on
whom his entire happiness depended and whose love
made him miserable, because she was cloistered; and,
since he could obtain her only by marrying her, he was in
despair, for, earning only a paolo a day, he had not
enough even to live on alone. Constantly telling me of the
rare beauty of the girl he adored, he made me want to
see her, and I saw her; but before telling my reader how
it came about I must give him an account of my situation
in Rome at the time when I made this acquaintance.

Having gone to the Capitol on the day on which prizes
were to be conferred on young students of painting and
drawing,[44] I saw the painter Mengs, who, with Pompeo
Battoni[45] and two or three others, was to decide which
students deserved the preference. Not having forgotten
how Mengs had treated me in Spain,[46] I was going to
pretend I did not see him, when, greatly to my surprise,
he came up to me.

"Despite what happened between us in Madrid," he

said, "we can forget it all in Rome and speak without tainting our honor."

"Why not?" I replied, "provided we do not raise the subject of our quarrel, for I, at least, could not discuss it coolly."

"If you had known Madrid as I do, and the necessity I was under to give no opening to evil tongues, you would not have forced me to do what I did. Learn that I was believed to be a Protestant, and that to add color to the suspicion I had only to show myself unconcerned by your behavior. Come to dine with me tomorrow, and we will make peace under the auspices of Bacchus. It will be a family dinner; I have heard that you do not see your brother, and I can assure you that you will not find him in my house,[47] for if I received him all the decent people who frequent it would forsake it."

I did not fail to go there. My brother left Rome some time later, still in company with Prince Beloselski, the Russian Envoy to Dresden, with whom he had gone there, and still without having obtained what he demanded to clear his honor. Senator Rezzonico[48] was inexorable. We saw each other only three or four times.

Five or six days before he left, I was surprised to see my brother the Abate[49] appear before me, dirty, in rags, and unbashedly demanding that I help him.

"Where have you come from?"

"From Venice, where I could no longer make a living."

"And how do you expect to make a living in Rome?"

"By saying mass and teaching French."

"You, teach French? You don't even know your own language."

"I know it, and I know French, and I already have two pupils."

"Who are they?"

"The son and daughter of the proprietor of the inn where I am staying; but you must help me at first."

"I will not give you a soldo; leave my presence."

I paid no attention to his protests, I finished dressing, and I left, telling Margherita to lock my apartment. The wretch went to the Duchess of Fiano's and sent in his name; she received him to find out what it was about. He implored her to take pity on him and persuade me to help him, and she dismissed him, promising that she would speak to me. I felt ashamed and annoyed when she mentioned it to me that evening. I begged her not to speak of it again, and even not to receive him again. I gave her a brief account of all the base acts to which he had descended and told her what I had to fear from him, and she refused to listen to him after that. He went about reviling me to all my friends, even the Abate Gama,[50] who had rented the fourth floor of a house opposite the Church of Trinità dei Monti; everyone told me I ought to help him or make him leave Rome, and it annoyed me. It was the Abate Ceruti who, ten or twelve days after going to lodge elsewhere, came to tell me that if I did not want to see my brother begging in the streets I must do something for him; he said that I could make provision for him outside of Rome, and that he was willing to go there if I would give him three paoli a day. I consented; but the Abate Ceruti arranged the thing in a way which greatly pleased me. He spoke to a parish priest who was then in Rome and who served a church belonging to a Franciscan nunnery. The priest took my brother with him and promised him a testone[51] a day to say a mass in his church every day, in payment for which he would receive the testone, and other worthwhile perquisites if he was a success at preaching, of which the nuns in his convent were passionately fond. So my brother left, and I did not care if he knew that his three paoli a day came from me. I gave the Abate Ceruti all my old shirts to give to him and an old black coat, and I refused to see him. The place to which he went was

Palestrina,[52] the ancient Praeneste, which was the site of the famous Temple of Fortune. As long as I remained in Rome he never failed to receive the nine scudi a month; but after I left he went back to Rome, then left it for another convent, where he died suddenly, thirteen or fourteen years ago.[53] He may have poisoned himself.

Medini[54] had been in Rome ever since I arrived there, but we never saw each other. He lodged on the Strada delle Orseline[55] in the house of one of the Pope's light-cavalrymen, where, living on gaming, he tried to cheat all the foreigners who arrived. Having accumulated some money, he had sent to Mantua for his mistress and her mother and another daughter she had, twelve or thirteen years of age. Thinking that he could do much better in furnished lodgings, he had taken a fine apartment on the Piazza di Spagna, five or six houses away from the one in which I was staying. I knew nothing of all this.

One Sunday when I had gone to dine at the Venetian Ambassador's, His Excellency told me that I should be dining with Count Manuzzi,[56] who had just arrived from Paris and had been delighted to learn that I was in Rome.

"I imagine you know all about him; be so good as to tell me who the Count is, for I am to present him to the Holy Father day after tomorrow."

"I met him in Madrid with Ambassador Mocenigo; he makes a good impression, he is modest, handsome, polite —that is all I know."

"When he was in Madrid was he presented at Court?"

"I believe so."

"I think not. You are not telling me all you know— but it doesn't matter. I risk nothing by presenting him to the Pope. He says he is descended from the famous thirteenth-century traveler Manuzzi[57] and from the famous printers[58] of the same name who did so much honor to literature. He showed me the anchor[59] in his coat of arms, which has sixteen quarterings."

Greatly astonished that a man who had carried vengeance to the point of trying to have me assassinated
should speak of me as of an intimate friend, I determined
to conceal my feelings and wait to see what turn the thing
would take. So I saw him appear without showing any
sign of my justified resentment, and when, after paying
the Ambassador the usual compliments, he came to me
ready to embrace me I received him with open arms and
asked him for news of the Ambassador.[60] He talked a
great deal at table, telling any number of lies, all of them
to my honor, about everything I had done in Madrid,
flattering himself (I conclude) that by lying he obliged
me to lie and thus inviting me to do as much for him. In
no position to do anything else, I swallowed all these
bitter pills, but I was determined to have it out with him
the next day at the latest.

The person who interested me, and who had come to
dine at the Ambassador's with Manuzzi, was a Frenchman who went by the name of the Chevalier de Neuville.[61] He had come to Rome to obtain the annulment of
the marriage of a lady who was in a convent in Mantua;
he had a special recommendation to Cardinal Galli.[62]
Telling us a quantity of amusing stories, he diverted the
entire company; and when we left the Ambassador's
house I did not refuse to get into his carriage with Manuzzi to take a drive until evening. Toward dusk he told
us that he would take us to the house of a pretty woman
where we would sup and where there was a bank at faro.
The carriage stops at a house on the Piazza di Spagna,
not very far from mine, we go up to the third floor, and
I find myself face to face with Count Medini and his mistress, whom the French Chevalier had praised and whom
I think of little account. Medini gives me a friendly greeting and thanks the Frenchman for having persuaded me
to forget the past and come to his house. The Frenchman
says that he knows nothing about it, but I change the sub-

ject and begin observing the company, which was gradually assembling.

When Medini thought there were punters enough he
sat down at a big table, put five or six hundred scudi in
gold and notes in front of him, and began dealing.
Manuzzi lost all the money he had, Neuville won half the
amount in the bank, and I did not play. After supper,
Medini having asked the Frenchman for his revenge,
Manuzzi asked me for a hundred zecchini, or for what I
had if I did not have that much. I gave him a hundred
zecchini, which he lost in less than an hour, and Neuville
came within twenty or thirty zecchini of breaking the
bank. We all went home. Manuzzi was lodging at my
sister-in-law's,[63] Roland's daughter. I saw him in my
room the next morning just as I was dressing to pay him
a visit with an intention which would have put us both
in danger. After returning my hundred zecchini, he embraced me, and, showing me a letter of credit for a large
sum on Belloni, he offered me all the money I might need
and, not giving me a chance to say anything, he argued to
me that we should forget everything and be good friends
for the rest of our lives. My heart betrayed my mind, as
has happened to me on many other occasions, and I
agreed to the peace which he offered me and asked of me.
On the next day but one I went to dine with him alone.
The French Chevalier arrived at the end of our dinner,
and after him the unlucky Medini, who persuaded the
three of us to play, each dealing in turn. We played until
nightfall, and the winner was Manuzzi. He won twice
what he had lost the evening before; my losses were in-
considerable. Neuville, however, lost four hundred zecchini, and Medini, who had lost only fifty, wanted to
jump out the window.

A few days later Manuzzi left for Naples, after giving
two hundred zecchini to Medini's mistress, who had gone
to sup with him alone; but the two hundred zecchini did

not keep Medini from being arrested for debts amounting
to more than a thousand scudi. He wrote me some very
urgent letters from prison, trying to persuade me to help
him; but the only effect they had on me was to induce
me to look after what he called his family, in return for
the favors granted me by his mistress's young sister. At
this time the Emperor arrived in Rome with his brother
the Grand Duke of Tuscany;[64] and, some gentleman in
the suite of one or the other of the two princes having
made the girl's acquaintance, Medini was released from
prison and left Rome a few days later. We shall return to
him in five or six months.

I continued the same course of life; in the evening at
the Duchess of Fiano's, every afternoon at the Princess
of Santa Croce's, and at my inn, where I had Margherita,
La Buonaccorsi, and the young tailor, whose name was
Marcuccio[65] and who talked to me so much about his
heart's desire that I became curious to know the object
of his passion.

The girl he loved was in a sort of convent, which she
had charitably been allowed to enter at the age of ten
years and which she could not leave except to marry with
the permission of the Cardinal who superintended the
economy and directed the policy of the pious foundation.
When the girls who were kept there left the establishment
they were given two hundred Roman scudi, which they
brought as their dowry to the men they married. Marcuccio also had his sister in the convent and sometimes
went to see her. She came to the grating with the governess who was in charge of her and who saw to her education; even though Marcuccio was her brother, the regulations of the convent did not allow her to go to the grating
alone. One day five or six months earlier his sister had
come to the grating with a schoolmate, a young girl whom
Marcuccio had never seen. It was on that day that he fell
in love with her. Having to stay in his shop at work on
working days, he went to see his sister every holiday, but

she came to the grating with the object of his devotion
only when chance decreed it. In five or six months he had
had the good fortune to see her no more than eight or
ten times. His sister knew that he adored her, and she
was more than willing to do anything she could for him;
but she had no authority to bring her down to the grating, and she did not dare ask her governess, who could
do her the favor, to grant it, for if she had had any suspicion that love entered in she would no longer have allowed her to go down even by chance. So I decided to
pay Marcuccio's sister a visit with him.

On the way he told me that the establishment was very
poor; that the women who directed it could not properly
be called nuns, for they had taken no vows and they did
not even wear a regular habit; nevertheless, they were
not tempted to leave their prison, for poverty would
reduce them to begging for their bread or trying to find
positions as servants in some house or other. The girls
who had reached the age of puberty would run away if
they could; but the house was so well guarded that it was
impossible to escape from it.

We arrived at a vast, ill-built house standing near one
of the gates of Rome[66] in a square which, because it led
nowhere and so had to be sought out purposely, was solitary and deserted. On entering the visiting room, I was
surprised to see the structure of the cruel gratings. The
square apertures were so small that one could not put
one's hand in except at the risk of scraping the skin from
the back of it from wrist to knuckles; nor was that
enough: the barbaric, tyrannous, and scandalous grating
had another of exactly the same construction a foot behind it; but it was not easy to see it, for, though the visiting room was light enough for us who had come to call
on the poor recluses, the inner part of it, where they received their callers, was nearly dark. The sight made me
shudder.

"Where and how," I asked Marcuccio, "did you see

the mistress of your heart, whereas I see nothing inside there but darkness?''

''By means of a candle, which the nun is not allowed to light on pain of excommunication except to receive relatives.''

''So she will come with a candle this time?''

''I doubt it, for the portress must have announced that I have someone with me.''

''But how did you have the privilege of seeing your mistress, to whom you are not related?''

''The first time she came down she had slipped away, and my sister's governess, who is goodhearted, said nothing; and the other times she came because my sister begged her governess to let her.''

What happened was that they came down without a light and that there were three of them. I could never persuade the governess to go for a candle, not so much for fear of excommunication as for fear of being betrayed by a spy and punished by the Superioress. I saw that it was on my account that poor Marcuccio could not see his idol. I offered to leave, but he would not let me. I spent an infuriating hour, but one not without interest. The voice of my young friend's sister went to my soul; I concluded that it must be by the voice that the blind fall in love, and that their love would become as strong as that which had its origin in sight. The governess in charge of Marcuccio's sister was a young woman still under thirty years of age. She told me that when the girls reached the age of twenty-five they were made governesses of the younger girls, and that at the age of thirty-five they could leave their prison not to return; but that those who took that course were very few, for they feared destitution.

''Then you have many old women?''

''There are a hundred of us, and the number never decreases, for at every death a new recruit is brought in.''

Dell' Iliade d'Omero
Ridotta in Veneziano
Canto quarto
Divin Consiglio - Patti rotti - Guerra.
Il castigo di Dio ...
Argomento

Per opra di Giunon Donna, a tributo
Nega il Troian, nè ... si ...
Il Re di Sparta dalla strale ...
Di Pandaro è ferito. ...
...
...
...
Strage s'accresce ... Marte.

1 - ... Dei nel gran palazzo incomparabile
De Giove era redutti in concistoro.
El nettare ghe dava Hebe adorabile;
Tutti bevean allegri in coppa d'oro
Con tanto bon umor, che ...
Che la andava ... el divin coro
... d'una volta. Tutti i Dei pensava
A Troia che ...

Casanova's Translation of the Iliad

Anton Raphael Mengs

"And the girls who leave to marry—how have they managed to fall in love with their husbands?"

"In all the twenty years I have been here, I have seen only four girls leave to marry, and they did not meet their husbands until after they left. Any man who asks our protector the Cardinal for one of us is a desperate fool who needs a hundred zecchini; but the Cardinal will not grant him the favor he asks unless he is sure that he practices a trade which will enable him to live well with his wife."

"And what choice is he given?"

"He states the age the girl must be, and the abilities he expects her to have, and the Cardinal leaves it to the Superioress."

"I suppose you are well fed and comfortably lodged?"

"Neither. Three thousand scudi a year cannot feed a hundred people and supply their clothing and all their needs. The ones who earn by the work of their hands are the most fortunate."

"And who are those who ask permission to put a poor girl in this prison?"

"A poor relative, a devout mother or father, who fears that the girl will succumb to sin. For this reason girls are not accepted here unless they are already very pretty."

"Who pronounces on their prettiness?"

"Relatives, some ecclesiastic, a monk, the priest of the girl's parish, and in the last instance the Cardinal, who, if he does not think the child pretty, sends her away, for an ugly girl is believed to run no risk by remaining in the world. So you can be sure that, unhappy as we are here, we curse all those who declared us pretty."

"I am sorry for you. I am amazed that a man cannot obtain permission to see you openly so as to have a reason for asking for one of you in marriage."

"The Cardinal says that even he cannot give such a permission, since breaking the conditions of the foundation entails excommunication."

"Whoever established this house must be in hell."

"We all think so; and Our Lord the Pope ought to take the thing in hand."

I gave the girl ten scudi, saying that, since it was impossible to see her, I could not promise to come again, and I left with Marcuccio, who was all apologies for having made me waste my time.

"My dear friend," I said, "I foresee that I shall never see either your young mistress or your sister, whose voice greatly interested me."

"I cannot believe that your ten scudi will not work wonders."

"I cannot believe that there is not another visiting room."

"There is; but anyone who is not a priest and dares to enter it is excommunicated, unless he has permission from the Most Holy Father."

I could not understand how the house could be tolerated, for I saw how hard it must be for the recluses to find husbands, and I thought it impossible that it would be allowed to exist once it was known that the regulations of the establishment seemed made on purpose to prevent their marrying. I saw that since each of the recluses was assigned a dowry of two hundred scudi, the founder of the house must have counted on at least two marriages a year, and hence that someone must be stealing all that was saved by the girls not marrying. I communicated my thoughts to Cardinal de Bernis in the presence of the Princess, who, very much concerned for the unfortunate girls, said that the Pope must be presented with a petition signed by them all in which they would ask His Holiness for permission to receive callers in the visiting room under the same honorable and decent conditions which were in force in all the establishments in which women were cloistered. The Cardinal told me to write the petition, get it signed, and bring it to the Princess; in the meanwhile, he said, he would find an opportunity to mention the matter to His Holiness and would think of someone to present the petition to him officially.

Not doubting that most of the recluses would sign, I composed the petition and, the second time I went to the grating with my friend, I left it with the girl, his sister's governess, with whom I had talked on the previous occasion. She assured me that I should have it back, signed by all the recluses, the first time I came to see her. The petition asked His Holiness only to abolish the excommunication affecting the visiting room where it was light enough to see; but I also briefly recounted the whole history of the house.

When the Princess of Santa Croce received the petition she went directly to the Protector, Cardinal Orsini,[67] who had to promise her that he would speak to the Pope, who, informed beforehand by Cardinal de Bernis, at once issued a papal brief abolishing the excommunication. The convent was first informed of it when someone was sent to remove the notice announcing it from the visiting-room door. The chaplain was instructed to inform the Superioress that in future she must permit all the girls who were asked for to receive callers in the light visiting room, though they must always be accompanied by their governesses. It was Marcuccio who brought me the news, which the Princess herself had not heard, and she was delighted to learn it from me. But Pope Ganganelli did not stop there. He ordered that the administration be put on trial at once and forced to account for all the money it had saved in the century and more which had elapsed since the house was founded. He reduced the number of recluses from one hundred to fifty, he set the dowry at four hundred scudi, and he ordered that every girl who had reached the age of twenty-five without having found a husband should be dismissed with the four hundred scudi which would have been given her if she had married, and that twelve mature women of good repute should be engaged at a salary as governesses of the girls in the house, each having four of them, and that twelve other serving women should be paid to do the housework.

CHAPTER II

Supper at an inn with Armellina and Emilia.

INTRODUCING ALL the innovations I have just explained took six months; what was done at once was to abolish the prohibition against entering the visiting room and even the convent itself, which, since the inmates were not cloistered, the Superioress was free to direct as she saw fit. Marcuccio had received the news in a note his sister had written him; he brought it to me joyously, begging me to go with him, as his sister requested, to please her governess. She told him also to ask at the grating for her young friend, who would come down either alone with her or with her own governess; it was I who was to ask for her. Delighted to fall in with this arrangement, I had Marcuccio leave his shop and take me to the convent, which was not far from San Paolo.[1] We asked for the two girls in the light visiting room, which we had no sooner entered than we saw the gratings occupied, one by the Abate Guasco,[2] whom I had known in Paris at Giulietta's[3] in 1751, the other by a Russian nobleman, Count Ivan Ivanovich Shuvalov,[4] and by Father Jacquier,[5] a Minimite friar of the Church of Trinità dei Monti, a famous astronomer. Inside I saw some very pretty girls.

All four of ours having come to the same grating, we began a most interesting conversation, but in whispers, because we could be overheard. We did not feel at our ease until the other visitors left. The object of my young friend's love was very pretty, but his sister was surprising. Fifteen or sixteen years of age, with a figure already voluptuously well developed, she cast a spell on me. I thought I had never seen a whiter complexion or such black eyes and eyebrows and hair; what gave her charms an irresistible power was the sweetness of her look and the ingenuous simplicity of her remarks. Her governess, who was ten or twelve years older than she, was also very likable, and very interesting by reason of a sadness which seemed to be the effect of a quantity of desires which she had to suppress. She amused me greatly by telling me all the particulars of the confusion which the abolition of the excommunication had brought about in the establishment. The Superioress was as pleased with it as the girls were; but the old bigots were scandalized. She told us that the Superioress had already ordered windows made to give light in the dark visiting rooms, even though the bigots insisted that she had no right to go beyond the permission the Father-Director had given her. The Superioress argued, and rightly, that as soon as everyone was allowed to enter the light visiting room the dark ones became ridiculous. She had also decided to have the double grating removed, since there was only a single one in the light visiting room. The Superioress's intelligence made me want to make her acquaintance, and Emilia arranged for me to have that pleasure the next day. Such was the name of Marcuccio's sister Armellina's sad friend. This first visit lasted two hours, which I found passing very quickly while Marcuccio availed himself of the opportunity to go and talk with his beloved at another grating, though she was still accompanied by her governess.

I left, after giving them ten Roman scudi, as I had done at my first visit, and kissing Armellina's hands, at which, though she made no attempt to deny them to me, she blushed scarlet. No man had ever touched her hands, and she was amazed when she saw the sensuous delight with which I covered them with kisses.

I went home in love with Armellina, surrendering to my budding passion, and not at all disheartened by the difficulties I foresaw I should encounter in obtaining her. But Marcuccio, more in love than ever, was in an ecstasy of bliss. He had made his declaration to his beloved, and she had replied that she asked nothing better than to become his wife as soon as he could obtain permission from the Cardinal-Protector. He was sure to obtain it if he could set up shop as a master tailor; he had finished his apprenticeship; he needed only a sum of money to furnish a small house, and the assurance of a sufficient number of customers. I promised him a hundred scudi as soon as he required them, and I congratulated him on his certainty of becoming happy, whereas I, in love with his sister and unable to marry her, was in despair.

"Then you are married?"

"Alas, yes! But you must say nothing, for I mean to go to see her every day, and if it were known that I am married my visits would become suspect."

It was not true, but it was what I had to say.

I was obliged to tell this lie, both to assure myself that I would never commit the folly of marrying and to keep Armellina from flattering herself that I was seeing her with no other intention. I found the Superioress polished, frank, reasonable, and not at all prejudiced. After the first time that she came down to the grating to please me, she sometimes came without being summoned; she knew that I was the prime mover in the happy reformation of the establishment, both the economy and the good order of which were under her direction, and she expressed all her obligation to me, which increased by leaps and bounds every day. In less than six weeks three of her girls had left, all to make good marriages, and she had been allowed an additional fifty scudi a month for the expenses of the house. She confided to me that she was not satisfied with the Dominican confessor, who, unlike the three others, made his penitents go to communion every Sunday and feast day, kept them in the confessional for hours, and condemned them to austerities and abstinences which made them ill and hence lose the time they needed to do their work. Having undertaken to see that her complaint was placed in the Cardinal's hands, I wrote it out for her, and she had the satisfaction of seeing no more of the Dominican and of distributing his penitents among the three other confessors, who were reasonable priests who did not dampen their devotion.

Marcuccio went alone on every feast day to see his fiancée. I went at nine o'clock almost every morning to see his sister with Emilia; I breakfasted with them, and I stayed with them until eleven o'clock in a visiting room in which there was only one grating, so that when I was there I fastened the door; however, it had another door giving access to the interior of the convent. Instead of a window being made, that door had been left open, admitting light enough; this was a great annoyance to me, for I constantly saw some of the recluses, both young and old, passing by the door, and, though they did not stop, they always glanced at the grating, which prevented Armellina from surrendering her hand to my amorous lips.

It was toward the end of December that, the weather having turned very chilly, I asked the Superioress to let me send her a screen, which alone could keep me from catching the cold which the draft from the door was sure to give me. The Superioress saw that, since she could not allow the door to be shut, she could not deny me the protection of the screen; so we were more at our ease, but within such narrow limits so far as the desires Armellina aroused in me were concerned that I could bear it no longer. For New Year's 1771 I gave each of the two girls a fine winter coat, and coffee and sugar to the Superioress, who was infinitely obliged to me. Emilia having often come to the grating half an hour before Armellina, who was not yet ready, so that I should not have to wait alone, Armellina too began often coming alone, waiting for Emilia, who, busy with something else, had not been able to come down with her. It was in the quarter hours of my being alone with her that Armellina's sweetness made me hopelessly in love with her.

Emilia was as fond of Armellina as Armellina was of her; but modesty in respect to everything to do with sensual pleasure was so strong in them that I had not yet succeeded in getting them to consent to listen to licentious talk or to pardon the freedoms which I wanted them to grant to my hands, and theirs too, to say nothing of letting my avid eyes look at what their education had taught them they must hide not only from the sight of all men but from themselves. They were astonished when I once asked them if, to exchange tokens of true friendship, they sometimes went to bed together. They blushed, and Emilia asked me what I could suppose friendship had in common with the discomfort of being two together in a very narrow bed. I took good care not to explain the reason for my question, for I saw that they were both frightened by the thought which must have led me to ask it; they were both made of flesh and blood, but I was convinced that they were sincere; they had never confided their secret mysteries to each other, and they had perhaps not even talked of them to their confessor, whether because of an unconquerable sense of shame or because it never occurred to them that they had sinned in what they might have let their hands do. I brought them white silk stockings lined with plush for winter, which they accepted with signs of the liveliest gratitude; but it was in vain that I asked them to put them on in my presence. It was no use my telling them that there was no essential difference between a girl's legs and a man's, that it could not even be a venial sin, that their confessor would consider them fools if they confessed it to him as a crime; they replied, always blushing and in concert, that it could not be permissible for girls, who, unlike men, had been given skirts for no other reason than to teach them that they must never raise them above the ground. I could have replied that skirts were made for nothing but to be turned up. The embarrassment with which Emilia advanced these arguments, which Armellina seconded, proved to me that it was neither artifice nor coquetry which made her speak as she did, but education and a sense of decency. I thought she believed that if she had done otherwise she would have lowered herself in my judgment and that I would have conceived a very unfavorable opinion of her. Yet she was twenty-seven or twenty-eight years of age, and she was not prejudiced by any excessive devotion. As for Armellina, I saw that she felt ashamed to adhere to her duty less strictly than her friend; it seemed to me that she loved me and that, unlike what I had experienced with several other girls, I should find it easier to bring her to abandon some of her moral strictness in Emilia's absence than in her presence.

I made the experiment one morning when she appeared at the grating, telling me that Emilia would come down soon. I told her that, adoring her, I was the unhappiest of men, for, being married, I could not hope to marry her and thus gain the right to hold her in my arms and cover her all over with my kisses.

"Is it possible," I asked, "that I can live, with no other relief than kissing your beautiful hands?"

At these words, uttered with all the fire of passion, she looked at me steadily with her beautiful eyes and, after thinking for a moment, she began kissing my hand with

the same eagerness which I showed when I kissed hers. I
begged her to put her mouth to the grating; she blushed,
she looked down, and she would not. I complained bitterly, but in vain. Armellina was deaf and dumb until
the arrival of Emilia, who at once asked us why we were
not gay as usual.

During these days, which were the first of the year
1771, I saw in my room Mariuccia, whom I had married
ten years earlier to the worthy youth who had opened
a wigmaker's shop. My reader may remember how I had
made her acquaintance at the Abate Momolo's, *scopatore*[6] to Pope Rezzonico. All the inquiries I had made to
learn something about Mariuccia during the three months
I had been in Rome had been fruitless; I saw her before
me with the greatest pleasure, the more so because I
thought she had scarcely changed. She told me that she
had seen me at St. Peter's at mass on Christmas Eve, and
that, since she had not dared to approach me because of
the company I was with, someone who was with her had
undertaken to follow me and to send her word where I
lived, and that, he having fulfilled his promise, she had
come to see me. She told me that she had been in Frascati[7]
for eight years, having a shop and living there very happily with her husband and her children, of which she had
four, the eldest being a girl nine years of age. After asking Margherita to keep her company and making sure
that she would dine with me, I went, as I did every day,
to breakfast with Armellina, then I returned to Mariuccia, with whom I dined, and I spent the whole day de-
lightfully without ever feeling tempted to renew the consequences of our old fondness with her. Our adventures
were the subject of our talk, and the interesting news that
my valet Costa had returned to Rome three years later
with all the trappings of prosperity and had married
Momolo's daughter, with whom he had fallen in love
when he was in my service.

She said she had guessed that he had robbed me,[8] that

he had left his wife two years after he married her, that no one knew where he was, and that she was in Rome in poverty, her father having died. I did not see fit to go to see her, for I could have done nothing but grieve her by telling her that I would have her husband hanged where-ever I found him. This remained my intention until the year 1785, when I found him in Vienna, valet to Count Hardegg.[9] When we come to it fourteen years hence, my reader will learn what I did. I promised Mariuccia that I would pay her a visit in Lent and bring presents to her children, especially her eldest daughter, who, according to Mariuccia, would interest me more than the others.

In love with Armellina, and unhappy, I inspired pity in the Princess of Santa Croce and Cardinal de Bernis, whom I often amused with a detailed account of all my sufferings. The Cardinal told the Princess that she could easily do me the favor of obtaining permission from Cardinal Orsini to take Armellina to the opera or the play and that, being of the party, I could make her less severe by my attentions. He said that she need have no doubt of the Cardinal's consent, since Armellina was neither a nun nor bound by any kind of vow, and that, since she must make her acquaintance before making her the offer, it could quickly be arranged.

"You have only to tell the Cardinal that you are curious to see the inside of the house."

"Will he give me permission?"

"Immediately, for they are cloistered only by the rules of the house. We will go with you."

"You will come too? A charming party!"

"Ask the Cardinal for permission, and we will set the hour afterward."

I thought I was dreaming when I heard this fine plan; I saw that the gallant Cardinal was curious to see the beautiful Armellina, and his curiosity did not alarm me, for I knew that he was not fickle. In addition, if Armellina pleased him, I was sure that both he and the Princess

would use their influence to get her a suitable husband
by procuring her a charitable stipend, of which there are
many to be had in Rome.

Three or four days later the Princess summoned me to
her box in the Teatro Aliberti,[10] and she showed me the
Cardinal's written permission to visit the house with
what company she chose to bring. She said that we would
decide the day and hour after dinner the next day. The
next morning the Superioress came to the grating to tell
me that the Cardinal-Protector had sent her word that
the Princess of Santa Croce would come to visit the house
with a party, which gave her great pleasure. I told her
that I knew it and that she would see me with the Princess. She wanted to know when, but I had no idea; I
promised to inform her as soon as I knew. She said playfully that the news had set the whole house topsy-turvy,
and turned the heads of all the prudes, for, except for
some priests, the doctor, and the surgeon, no one since
the house was founded had entered it simply to see it. I
told her that there was no longer any question of excommunication, so she must put the idea of reclusion out of
her mind, from which it followed that she could receive
personal visitors herself without permission from the
Cardinal. She replied with a smile that she would not
dare.

After dinner we agreed on the hour for the next day,
and I informed the Superioress in the morning. The
Duchess of Fiano was one of the party, and we drove to
the house, arriving there at three o'clock. The Cardinal
wore nothing to show his exalted rank. He at once recognized Armellina from the description I had given him of
her, and he talked to her of her charms and congratulated
her on having made my acquaintance. Poor Armellina
blushed again and again, and I thought she would faint
when the Princess, after telling her that no one in the
house was as pretty as she, gave her fond kisses. Poor
Armellina was completely abashed, both because of the

Princess's praise, which all the other girls heard, and because of her kisses, which were forbidden by the regulations anywhere in the house. After caressing the girl,
the beautiful Princess began making herself agreeable to
the Superioress; she said I had told her she was intelligent, and that she saw it in the order which she maintained throughout the big house; she promised to speak
of her to the Cardinal, doing her all the justice she deserved. After seeing all the rooms and the refectories,
she complimented Emilia, whom I presented to her. She
told her that she knew she was sad, and that she would
do her best to find her a husband who would know how to
make her gay. The Superioress seconded the compliment
with an approving smile; but I saw ten or twelve old
bigots who raised their eyes to heaven. Emilia, however,
at once kissed her hand, as if to beg her to keep her promise.

What filled me with satisfaction was that none of the
inmates could bear away the prize from Armellina; not
even my young friend Marcuccio's mistress could cast
doubt on her superiority, for she was not tall. When we
went down to the visiting room the Princess told Armellina that she would ask the Cardinal's permission to take
her with her to three or four of the theaters in Rome during the Carnival, and at that I saw the whole community
horror-stricken, except the Superioress, who said that His
Eminence was free to end all severities in a house in which
the girls were kept only in order to make good marriages.
Armellina, blushing with shame and joy, was completely
at a loss. She did not know where to find words to thank
her. Just as we left, the Princess commended Armellina
and Emilia to the Superioress's good graces, and gave
her a note of hand so that she could make the two girls
presents of what little things they most needed. The
Duchess of Fiano told her that she would entrust me with
a small present which she, too, wanted to give the two
girls.

My reader can imagine all that I said to the Princess as soon as we were in the carriage to show her my feelings. Gratitude almost made me eat her up. Neither she nor the Cardinal had a moment's doubt of Armellina's intelligence, despite the fact that she had been too much taken aback to shine. She could be only what her education had made her. The Princess was impatient to see her at the theater with her, and at supper at an inn, as is the custom in Rome. She at once wrote the two girls' names on her tablets,[11] wanting to obtain all the charitable stipends possible for them. I thought of my poor Marcuccio's mistress, but it was not the moment to recommend her; it was to Cardinal de Bernis that I the next day confided my great interest in the young man, and, after seeing him, he took up his cause to such purpose that before the end of the Carnival he got him married to his fiancée with a dowry of five hundred scudi, which, with the hundred I let him have, gave him enough to furnish a house and set up shop.

But my moment of triumph came the next day after the visit to the grating, when the Superioress came down at once to thank me. The note of hand had been for fifty Roman scudi, with which she was going to provide both Armellina and Emilia with an ample supply of linen. They were astonished when I told them that the fat Abate was the Cardinal de Bernis, for they did not know that a Cardinal was ever permitted to doff the purple. The Duchess of Fiano had sent them a cask of wine; so much bounty led them to hope for more, and, since they considered me the sole cause of their good fortune, I thought I could aspire to everything.

Three or four days later the Princess thanked Cardinal Orsini, and, having told him that she was interested in arranging marriages for some of his girls and wanted first to give them a little knowledge of the world, she asked his permission to take them to the theater with her sometimes, promising to see that they should always return to their house properly accompanied. The Cardinal had replied that the Superioress would receive whatever instructions she might wish in the matter. I told the Princess that I should be able to tell her what orders the Superioress received.

The Superioress herself told me the next day that the Cardinal's auditor had come to tell her that His Eminence left the care of the girls in her house entirely to her discretion and to order her to show the Princess of Santa Croce every consideration, letting her take them out, either coming for them herself or sending trustworthy people whom she knew. She had also been ordered to send him the names of those who, having passed the age of thirty, wanted to leave the place, receiving two hundred scudi. She had not yet made this last order public, but she was certain that she would get rid of at least twenty in this way.

As soon as I informed the Princess of what the Superioress had been ordered to do, she declared that the Cardinal could not have acted more generously. Cardinal de Bernis told her that the first time she wanted to take the girls to a play or the opera she should go to fetch them in person and tell the Superioress that she would never send for them except by sending one of her own carriages with her livery. She acted accordingly, and a few days later she went by herself for Armellina and Emilia and took them to her palace[12] on the Campo di Fiore, where I was waiting for her with the Cardinal, her husband the Prince, and the Duchess of Fiano.

They were made much of, questioned kindly, encouraged to answer, to laugh, to express themselves freely; but it was no use; finding themselves for the first time in a splendid room, and in such company, they did not have the strength to speak, they were overwhelmed with shame and with fear of saying something stupid. Emilia did not dare to answer without rising, and Armellina shone only by her beauty; urged by the Princess to return her

kisses of the sort she was giving her, she could never
bring herself to do it. Armellina smilingly excused herself, kissed her hand ecstatically, and, when the Princess
pressed her lips to hers, Armellina seemed to have no
idea of how to give a kiss. The Cardinal and the Prince
laughed, the Duchess of Fiano said that so much reserve
was unnatural, and I suffered the torments of the
damned, for such awkwardness seemed to me to verge on
stupidity, for Armellina had only to kiss the Princess's
lips as she was kissing her hands. She thought that to kiss
her so would be to fail in respect to her, and that she had
no right to take such a liberty despite the Princess's permission.

The Cardinal said to me privately that he thought it
impossible that in the course of two months I had not
initiated the girl; but he had to believe it and recognize
the power of education. For this first time the Princess
wanted to take them to the comedy at the Tor di nona,[13]
where they were sure to laugh, and that made us hope.
After the play we went to sup at an inn, and at table,
whether because they were hungry or because of my
remonstrances, they unbent a little. They let themselves
be persuaded to drink wine, and that gave them courage.
Emilia shook off her sadness, and Armellina at last gave
the beautiful Princess some proper kisses and, when she
rose from the table, scores of them, and the acclamations
of the company convinced her that she had done nothing
wrong.

It was to me that the Princess entrusted the delightful
task of escorting them back to the convent. The moment
had come for me to take the first step toward the goal
which every lover sets himself. The carriage was of the
kind which has a seat for two and a folding seat; but
scarcely had it set off before I saw that one must never
reckon without one's host. When I tried to bestow kisses
a head was turned away, when I tried to extend my hands
a dress was drawn tight, when I tried to use force I was

repulsed, when I complained I was even told that I was in the wrong, when I grew angry I received no reply, and when I threatened never to show my face again I was not believed.

As soon as we arrived at the convent, a maid opened the small door, and, seeing that she did not shut it after the girls had gone in, I went in too, and, seeing that I was not stopped, I went up to the fourth floor with them to the Superioress's room, finding her in bed but apparently not surprised to see me. I told her that I considered it my duty to deliver her young charges to her in person; she thanked me; she asked them if they had had an amusing evening and a good supper, after which she asked me to make as little noise as I could going down the stairs. So I wished them a good night's sleep, and I left, giving the maid a zecchino, and the coachman another when I got out at my inn. I found Margherita asleep in an armchair; she woke and began calling me names, but she changed her tone when my fond caresses gave her reason to conclude that I had not been guilty of any infidelity. I sent her away two hours later after thoroughly convincing her that I loved her alone. I slept until noon and, after dining with her, at three o'clock I went to the Princess's, where I found the Cardinal. They were expecting me to narrate a triumph, and they were surprised to hear the opposite, and especially to find me unperturbed.

I may have appeared to be so, but I was far from being so in reality. It was simply that, having outgrown childishness, I gave a comic turn to my bad luck, ending by saying that, since I had no love for Pamelas,[14] I had decided to abandon the enterprise. The Cardinal said that he would congratulate me on it in three days.

Not seeing me that day, Armellina thought that I had slept late; but when she did not see me on the day after that she sent to her brother to ask if I was ill, for I had never gone two days without seeing her. So Marcuccio, come to tell me that his sister was anxious, was of course delighted that he could go back to tell her that I was in good health.

"Yes, my dear friend, go and tell her that I will continue to ask the Princess's good graces for her, but that she will see no more of me."

"But why?"

"Because I mean to try to get over my unhappy passion. Your sister does not love me, I am only too sure of it. I am no longer young, and I do not feel inclined to become a martyr to virtue. However virtuous a girl may be, love does not permit her to carry virtue so far. She has never granted me even the trifling favor of a kiss."

"I'd never have believed it."

"Believe it. I must end the thing. Your sister is too young, and she does not know what risks she runs by acting as she does toward a man in love at my age. Tell her all that, and refrain from giving her any advice."

"You cannot imagine how this grieves me. Perhaps Emilia's presence embarrasses her."

"No, for I have often urged her when we were alone. In short, I must get over it; if she does not love me, I will not have her yield either to seduction or to gratitude. The practice of virtue costs no effort at all to a girl who is not in love; she may feel that she is ungrateful, but she takes pleasure in sacrificing gratitude to prejudice. How does your fiancée treat you?"

"Very well, ever since she has been sure that I will marry her."

Hearing this, I was sorry that I had begun by saying that I was married, for, in the state to which I had been brought, I would have given her a promise of marriage, without any intention of deceiving her. Marcuccio went away troubled, and I went to the meeting of the Arcadians[15] at the Capitol, where the Marquise d'Aout[16] was to recite her diploma poem upon becoming a member. She was a young Frenchwoman who had been in Rome for six months with a husband as pleasant and likable

as herself but very much below her in intelligence. The
Marquise even possessed genius; on that day I began an
intimate friendship with her, but with no thought of
love; I left the coast clear for a French Abbé who was
madly in love with her and who gave up his fortune for
her.

The Princess of Santa Croce told me every day that
she would give me the key to her box whenever I wanted
to take the two girls to the opera, even without her; but
when she saw that a week had passed without my returning there she began to believe that I had broken off completely. The Cardinal thought I was still in love, and he
praised my behavior; he predicted that the Superioress
would write to me, and he guessed rightly. At the end
of a week she wrote me a short, polite note in which she
asked me to come to the visiting room and send for her.
I thought I could not avoid going.

Since I asked for her alone, she came down alone at
ten o'clock in the morning. She began by asking me why
I had so suddenly stopped my visits.

"Because I love Armellina."

"That was the reason which led you to honor her with
a visit every day; it is hard to understand how one and
the same reason can have an entirely opposite consequence."

"It cannot but have it, Signora; for when one is in
love one desires, and when one desires vainly one suffers,
and constant suffering makes men unhappy; so you see
that I must do everything in my power to cease to be so."

"I am sorry for you, and I see that you are acting
wisely; but if matters are as I think them to be, permit
me to tell you that you must esteem Armellina and so
you must not, by abandoning her, lead all the girls in this
house to conclude what is not the truth."

"And what can they conclude?"

"That your feeling was only a whim, and that you left
her as soon as you had satisfied it."

"That would be the height of malice; but I do not know what to do about it, for I have no other way to cure myself of my folly. Do you know any other? Be so good as to tell me it."

"I do not know very much about that disease; but it seems to me that little by little love becomes friendship, and then one is at peace."

"That is true; but to become friendship love must not be handled roughly. If the loved object does not treat it tenderly, it becomes contempt or indifference. I do not want either to become desperate myself or to condemn Armellina, who is an angel of beauty and virtue. I want to continue to be useful to her, and not to see her, and I am sure that cannot be displeasing to her, for she must have been aware of my anger. It must not happen again."

"To tell you the truth, I am completely in the dark. They have always assured me that they did not fail in their duty toward you and that they cannot possibly divine the reason which may have induced you to stop coming to see them."

"Whether from shyness, or prudence, or fear of wronging me, they have lied to you; but you deserve to know all. My honor itself demands that I inform you."

"Please do so, and you can be sure of my discretion."

I then told her the whole story in detail, and I saw that she was greatly moved. She said that her principle was never to think evil unless the likelihood of it was very strong, but that, knowing human weakness, she would never have believed that we would have kept ourselves under such severe restraint for almost three months during which we saw each other every day.

"I think," she said, "that there is less harm in a kiss than in the scandal your abandoning her is causing."

"But I am sure that Armellina does not care at all."

"She cries every morning."

"Her tears may spring from vanity, or perhaps from the reason which people give for my inconstancy."

"No, for I have had everyone in the house told that you are ill."

"And what does Emilia say?"

"She does not cry, but she is very sad, and I think that by constantly saying that if you do not come any more it is not her fault she means that it is Armellina's. Do me the favor to come tomorrow; they are dying to go at least once to the opera at the Aliberti and to the *opera buffa* at the Capranica." [17]

"Very well, Signora, I will come to breakfast tomorrow, and tomorrow evening they shall see the opera."

"I am delighted and I thank you. May I tell them the news?"

"I even beg you, Signora, to tell Armellina that I have decided to come to see her again only because what you have said has persuaded me."

How glad the Princess was when I told her the news that afternoon! The Cardinal knew that the thing was bound to turn out as it was doing. She at once gave me the ticket for her box for the next day, and ordered her stableman to put her carriage and liveried servants at my disposition.

The next day when I sent for Armellina Emilia came down first in order to have time to reproach me for my behavior; she said that a man could not act as I had done if he was really in love, and that I had done wrong to tell the Superioress everything.

"I should have told her nothing if I had had anything of consequence to tell her."

"Armellina has become unhappy since she has known you."

"Why, may I ask?"

"Because she does not want to fail in her duty, and she sees that you love her only to turn her from it."

"But her unhappiness will end as soon as I cease to urge her."

"And at the same time cease to see her."

"Exactly. Do you think it does not cost me pain? But my peace of mind demands the effort."

"Then she will be convinced that you did not love her."

"She may think as she pleases. Meanwhile, what I know is that, if she loved me as I love her, we should be of one mind."

"We have duties which you men consider that you do not have."

"Then be faithful to your pretended duties, and do not blame a man of honor for respecting them by avoiding your company."

Armellina appeared, and I found her changed.

"You do not look yourself, you are pale and downcast. Why?"

"Because you have hurt me."

"Then calm yourself, be cheerful again, and let me try to cure myself of a passion which by its very nature tries to turn you from your duty. I will be your friend despite everything, and I will come to see you once a week as long as I remain in Rome."

"Once a week! You shouldn't have begun by coming every day."

"That is true. Your face deceived me into thinking what is not so; but I hope that, at least from gratitude, you will permit me to become reasonable again. To help the remedy to take effect, I must see you as seldom as possible. Consider it a little, and you will conclude that the course on which I have embarked is wise, virtuous, and worthy of your esteem."

"It is a pity that you cannot love me as I love you."

"That is to say calmly. Without desiring anything."

"I don't say that—but practicing the art of checking desires which are contrary to our duty."

"That is an art which at my age I should not want to learn. Will you be so good as to tell me if you suffer very much from suppressing the desires which your love for me arouses in you?''

''I should be very sorry to suppress my desires every time I think of you. On the contrary, I cultivate them, I foster them. I wish you would be made Pope, I sometimes wish you were my father so that I could give you countless caresses in perfect freedom, in my dreams I wish you could become a girl as I am, so that I could live with you every hour of the day.''

At that I could not keep from laughing.[18] After telling them that I would come to take them to the Teatro Aliberti, I left them with the joy which a man in love must feel when he is certain that he will succeed, even though with great difficulty, for in all that Armellina had just said to me I found not the least trace of artifice or coquetry. She loved me and she persisted in not admitting it to herself, and consequently she was reluctant to grant me pleasures in which her nature would have forced her to share, whereupon she would have become convinced that she loved me. She reasoned thus unconsciously. Experience had not taught her that she must either flee me or prepare to fall a victim to love.

At the hour for the opera I went to fetch them in the same carriage and with the same footman. When the portress saw the Santa Croce livery, she had them come down, and they found me sitting on the folding seat. They were not surprised to find me alone. Emilia brought me compliments from the Superioress, who asked me to come to speak with her the next day. I took them to the opera, where I never interrupted the attention they should give to a spectacle they were seeing for the first time. Neither gay nor sad, I undertook nothing except to answer all their questions. As Romans, they must have been more or less acquainted with the physical characteristics of castrati; nevertheless, Armellina insisted that the one who was singing the second role was a woman: his bosom proved it to her. I asked her if she would dare to go to bed with him, and she answered that she would not, because a decent girl must always be in bed alone.

So strictly had the girls in the house been brought up. This silence and mystery about everything which could stimulate the pleasure of love could only have led them to attach the greatest importance to everything concerning the senses of sight and touch; that was why Armellina would only surrender her hands to me after defending them for a long time, and would never let me see if the stockings I had given her were a good fit. The prohibition against sleeping with another girl must have made her consider that letting herself be seen naked was a dreadful sin, and if it was a sin with a girl like herself, what could she not but think if it were ever a case of her being with a man? The mere idea must make her shudder. Every time that, seeing them at the grating, I had allowed myself a certain freedom in referring to the pleasures of love, I had found them deaf and dumb. I was furious. I felt no wish to lighten Emilia's gloom, though she was fresh and rather pretty; but I was in despair when I saw Armellina's face lose all its cheerfulness when I asked her if she knew in what the difference between a girl and a man consisted.

After the opera Armellina told me she had a good appetite after a week during which she had eaten next to nothing because of her grief at seeing no more of me. I replied that if I had known it I would have ordered a good supper, whereas we should eat only what the innkeeper had to give us.

"How many shall we be?"

"Just the three of us."

"So much the better. We shall be more at liberty."

"Then you don't like the Princess?"

"I like her, but she wants me to give her kisses which amaze me."

"But you gave her some, and very loving ones."

"I was afraid that if I didn't she would think me a fool."

"Will you be so good as to tell me if you think you sinned by giving her those kisses?"

"Certainly not, for I took no pleasure in them."

"Then why haven't you made the same effort for me?"

She did not answer, and we arrived at the inn, where I had a good fire made and ordered a good supper. The waiter asked me if I wanted oysters and, seeing that the girls were curious to find out what they were, I asked him the price of them. He said that they came from the Arsenal [19] at Venice, and that he could not sell them for less than fifty paoli a hundred, and I assented. I insisted on their being opened in my presence.

Armellina, astonished that her whim was going to cost me five Roman scudi, asked me to countermand the order; but she said no more when I told her that nothing seemed expensive to me when I saw that it enabled me to give her a pleasure. At my reply she took my hand, which I angrily withdrew when she raised it to her lips; but, having done it a little too roughly, I saw that Armellina was hurt. I was seated in front of the fire between her and Emilia; her dismay pained me; I begged her pardon, saying that my hand was not worthy of her kisses; but despite my excuse Armellina could not prevent two small tears from welling from her beautiful eyes. It made me very sad. Armellina was too much the dove to be treated harshly. I could renounce her love, but, if I was not to make her either fear me or hate me, which I did not want, I must either stop seeing her at all or completely change my approach. Made certain by the two tears that I must have wounded her delicacy to the utmost, I rose and went downstairs to order champagne.

Coming up again five or six minutes later, I saw that she had really cried and that she would come to supper in no frame of mind to enjoy it, and it distressed me. I had no time to lose. I repeated my excuses, and I begged her to resume her smiling countenance unless she wanted to mortify me extremely. Emilia backed me up, I took her hand, I kissed it tenderly, and she cheered up. The hundred oysters were brought and opened, filling four large dishes. The poor girls' astonishment would greatly have amused me if I had had reason to be happy; but I was desperate with love. I pined, and Armellina begged me to be as I had been when I first knew her—as if one's state of mind depended on one's will.

We sat down at table, where I taught the two girls to eat oysters by setting them the example. They were swimming in their liquid. Armellina, after swallowing five or six of them, said to Emilia that anything so delicious must be a sin; Emilia replied that it would not be a sin because the taste was exquisite but because with each oyster we swallowed we swallowed half a paoli.

"Half a paoli?" said Armellina. "And Our Lord the Pope does not forbid it? If it isn't a sin of gluttony, I'd like to know what gluttony means. I eat these oysters with pleasure; but I assure you that I will accuse myself of it in confession to see what my confessor will say."

This simplicity rejoiced my soul; but it was in my body that I needed to rejoice. My love which was dying of starvation envied the luck of my mouth. In the course of eating fifty oysters we emptied two bottles of sparkling champagne, which aroused laughter in the two girls who had to commit the indecency of belching. How I regretted that I could not laugh my fill, and devour Armellina with kisses instead of only with my eyes! I told the waiter to serve the supper, keeping the rest of the oysters for dessert. They were surprised to find their appetites keener after eating sixteen such excellent tidbits. Armellina seemed to me to have become amorous; I needed to believe it and to hope. Counting somewhat on Bacchus, I forbade water. We had a supper of the first quality for an inn. My poor heroines let themselves go. Even Emilia was on fire. I ordered up lemons, a bottle of rum, sugar, a big bowl, and hot water, and, after having the other fifty oysters put on the table, I dismissed the waiter. I made a large quantity of punch, which I enlivened by pouring a bottle of champagne into it. After we each swallowed five or six oysters and drank some punch, at which the two girls exclaimed, for they were carried away by so charming a beverage, I took it into my head to ask Emilia to put an oyster into my mouth with her own lips.

"You are too intelligent," I said, "to suppose that there is any harm in it."

Astonished at my proposal, Emilia sank into thought. Armellina watched her attentively, curious to hear what answer she would give me.

"Why," she asked, "don't you propose it to your Armellina?"

"Give him one first," Armellina said to her, "and if you have the courage I will have it too."

"What courage does it take? It's a child's game, there's no harm in it."

After receiving this propitious answer, I thought I could count on victory. I put the shell to her mouth, I told her to suck in the liquid and keep the oyster between her lips. She performed the feat to the letter after laughing heartily, and I took the oyster by pressing my lips to hers with the greatest decency. Armellina applauded her, saying that she had not thought she had it in her to do it, and she imitated her to perfection. She was delighted by the delicacy with which I took the oyster from her lips. She astonished me by saying that it was my turn to pay them back for their gifts, and God knows how much I enjoyed fulfilling the duty.

Playing this pretty game, we ate all the oysters, meanwhile emptying glass after glass of punch. We were sitting in a row with our backs to the fire, I in the middle, our heads were whirling, never was intoxication either gayer or more justified or more complete. But the punch was not finished. We felt the heat. Unable to bear it any longer, I took off my coat, and they had to unlace their dresses, which were lined in front with fur. I told them that there was a water closet near the door of our room to which they could go, and they quickly rose and took hands, delighted that I had guessed their need, which they dared not impart to me. They came back bursting with laughter, for they could not stand straight. I left them for a moment for the same reason, but a little less drunk than they. They were sitting by the fire, doing nothing but laugh at the condition they were in. I served as their fire screen, telling them nothing of the pleasure I took in seeing them in a state of disorder, which, allowing me to gaze at the beauty of their bosoms, enchanted my soul. I thanked them both for the pleasure they gave me by their charming company. I told them we must not leave the inn until we had drunk all the punch. They replied, with shrieks of laughter, that it would be a shame to leave it, and we drank. I made bold to tell them that their legs were so pretty that I could not say which pair deserved the preference, and at that their laughter redoubled, because they had not noticed that their open skirts and short petticoats let me see half of their legs.

After finishing the punch we stayed for another half an hour, talking aimlessly, while I silently congratulated myself on having the firmness not to undertake anything. Just as we left I asked them if they had any cause to complain of me, and Armellina was the first to say that if I wanted her as my soul's daughter she was ready to follow me everywhere.

"Then you no longer fear that I will urge you to fail in your duty?"

"No, I believe I am safe with you."

"And you?" I asked Emilia.

"As for me, I will love you when you do for me what the Superioress will tell you tomorrow."

"I will do everything, but I shall not go to see her until toward evening, for it is now three o'clock."

It was then that they laughed. "What will our mother say, what will our mother say?" I quickly paid for everything on the reckoning, rewarding the waiter generously, and I took them back to their convent, where the portress was very well pleased with the new order of the establishment when she received two zecchini. It being far too late to go upstairs, I at once went home, whence I sent back the Princess's carriage, to the great satisfaction of the coachman and the footman. But the one who was satisfied was Margherita, who would have scratched my eyes out if I had not repeatedly convinced her of my perfect fidelity. I told her, and she had to believe me, that I had been detained playing cards until that hour.

The next day I amused the Princess and the Cardinal with a detailed account of all that I had done. The Princess said that I had missed the moment, but the Cardinal declared that I had laid the foundation for a complete victory another day.

I went to the convent to learn what the Superioress wanted and what I could do for Emilia. The kindly Superioress received me by congratulating me on my having been able to amuse myself in the company of her two charges until three o'clock in the morning without having done anything with them which was not perfectly decent. They had told her how we had eaten fifty oysters, and she declared it a most innocent game. After this preamble, she told me that I could make Emilia happy by persuading the Princess to procure her a dispensation from publishing the banns of her marriage to a merchant who lived in Civitavecchia, and who would long since have married her but for the need to publish the banns, for there was a woman who claimed that he was under an obligation to marry her, though she had no legitimate reason for it. Her opposition would give rise to a suit which would never end.

"Emilia," she said, "would be made happy, and she would owe it entirely to you."

I took the man's name, I promised her I would use my best eloquence on the Princess. She asked me if I was still firm in my resolve to try to cure myself of my love for Armellina, and I said that I was, but that I would not begin to stop seeing her until Lent. She congratulated me on the Carnival being a very long one that year.

The next day I spoke to the Princess about the dispensation from publishing the banns, which of course was not to be asked for without a certificate from the Bishop of Civitavecchia[20] that the man was free. The Cardinal told me to have the man come to Rome, and he would see to the matter, provided he could have two reputable witnesses testify that he was not married. The Superioress wrote to him accordingly, and a few days later I saw the man in another visiting room at a grating with the Superioress and Emilia. Earnestly begging for my good offices, he said that before he could marry he must be sure of having six hundred scudi. He needed to obtain a charitable stipend of two hundred scudi, for the convent gave him four hundred; and I succeeded; but before that I arranged to have a very different supper with Armellina, who every morning at her grating asked me when I would take her to the *opera buffa* which was being given at the Teatro Capranica. I replied that I feared my love would force me to infringe on duties which she cherished more than she did *opera buffa*. They said that experience had taught them they need not fear me. Armellina said with a smile that her confessor had laughed at her when she had told him that she had eaten oysters by taking them from a man's lips with hers. He had told her that it was no more than a piece of nastiness.

CHAPTER III

The Florentine. Emilia married. Scholastica.
Armellina at the ball.

IF BEFORE supping with Armellina I was in love
with her to the point of being forced not to see her again
if she was not to drive me mad, after the supper I found
myself absolutely obliged to obtain her if I was not to die.
Having seen that she had consented to the small liberties
to which I had urged her only by taking them as inconsequential trifling, I decided to pursue my object as far as
possible by the same means. I began playing the role of
indifference to the best of my ability; I went there only
every other day, I did not give her amorous looks, I pretended to forget to kiss her hand, I did the same with
Emilia, I talked to her of her engagement, and I told her
that if I were sure of obtaining some favor from her I
would go to stay in Civitavecchia for a few days after her
marriage was celebrated. I made believe I did not notice
that this talk hurt Armellina, who could not bear my
showing a desire for her friend. Emilia answered me that,
once she was married, she would feel less strictly bound

Lover Calling on His Lady

Young Schoolgirl

by her duties, and Armellina, annoyed that she made bold to let me hope for some favors in her presence, told her that a married woman's duties were more binding than those of a spinster. I reproved her by alleging a false doctrine. I said that a wife's great duty was only not to risk making her husband's progeny illegitimate, that anything else was a trifle, and that I would never demand anything of Emilia but trifles to amuse hands and eyes. I even told Emilia that if I was to act to good purpose in obtaining charitable stipends for her she must not only make me hope that she would be kind when I was in Civitavecchia but must give me some pledge of her future kindness before she was married. On one such occasion she answered that she would give me no pledges except those which Armellina would give me, and that I should think of getting her married too. Despite the troubled state into which this conversation put her, Armellina told me that I was the only man she could say she had seen since the day she was born, and that, not hoping to be married, she would never give me any pledge, though she could not imagine what such a pledge could be. I had the strength to go, leaving her troubled. It was killing me to have to play this role toward an angel whom I adored; but I knew no surer way of overcoming her prejudices.

I engaged a box at the Capranica when I saw some magnificent oysters which were delivered to the Venetian Ambassador's major-domo, who let me have a hundred of them for what they had cost him. Taking them to the inn at which I had supped the first time, I asked the waiter for a room in which there was a bed; but he replied that it was not permitted in Rome; he said that on the fourth floor I could have two rooms in which there were long sofas, which I was free to consider beds, and, finding that it was so, I engaged them. I told him to light fires in both rooms and to serve me with the most delicate fare in Rome.

Entering the third-tier box I had taken with the two

girls, in the box next to mine I saw the Marquise d'Aout, and I did not have time to escape her. She at once greeted me, congratulating herself on being my neighbor. She was with her French Abbé, her husband, and a young man as handsome as he was well-mannered, whom I had never seen at her house. She at once asked me who the two girls she saw with me were, and I said that they belonged to the household of the Venetian Ambassador. She praised their beauty, without making any invidious distinction between them; but she began talking a great deal to Armellina, who was on her side and who replied very prettily to all the remarks she addressed to her until the performance began. The young man also began speaking to her, and, after asking my permission, he gave her a large paper of sweetmeats, asking her to share it with her neighbor. Having learned from his accent that he was a Florentine, I asked him if the sweets were from his country, and he replied that they were from Naples, whence he had arrived three days earlier.

After the first act I was surprised to hear him tell me that he had a letter which the Marchesa della C. . .[1] had charged him to deliver to me.

"I have just learned your name," he said, "and I shall have the honor to bring it to you tomorrow, if you will be so good as to tell me where you are staying."

After the usual exchange of politenesses, I feel obliged to tell him. I ask him for news of the Marchese, of his mother-in-law, of Anastasia, saying that I am delighted to receive letters from the Marchesa, from whom I had been awaiting an answer for six months.

"It is precisely the answer to your letter with which that charming lady has charged me."

"I cannot wait to read it."

"I can give it to you now, without prejudice to the pleasure I shall have in seeing you at your lodging tomorrow. I will bring it to you in your box, if I may."

"Pray do so."

He could have handed it to me directly from where he sat, but what of that?

He comes in, I yield him my place next to Armellina, he takes a portfolio from his pocket and gives me the letter. I open it, I see that it is four pages long, I tell him I will read it at home because the box is dark, and I put it in my pocket. He tells me that he intends to stay in Rome until after Easter, since he wants to see everything, though he could not hope to see anything more beautiful than what was before his eyes.

Armellina, who was looking at him very attentively, blushes and turns away her head; as for me, I am annoyed and feel in a manner insulted by his compliment, which was polite, but as insolent as it was unexpected. I make no reply, and I decide that the handsome young man must be a fool and a fop of the first water. Seeing that we have fallen silent, he realizes that he has offended me; and after some disconnected remarks he leaves.

I at once congratulate Armellina on the fine conquest she has made in half an hour, and I ask her what she thinks of the man she has so thoroughly enchanted.

"He seems to me very handsome, but I thought the compliment he paid me showed deplorably bad taste.[2] Please tell me if it is the fashion to make a girl one sees for the first time blush like that."

"No, my dear Armellina, it is neither the fashion nor polite nor behavior permissible to anyone who wants to frequent good society and who has had any experience of the world."

Sunk in silence, I appeared to be doing nothing but listen to the beautiful music, but the truth was that the worm of base jealousy was gnawing at my heart. I examined the feeling of resentment which was upsetting me, and I exerted my mind to find it well founded, for it seemed to me that the Florentine must have supposed me to be in love with Armellina and should not have begun by making the most well-turned of declarations of love to

her in my presence without fear of displeasing me, unless
he took me for a man who would be in the company of
such a pretty girl only as her lap dog. At the end of half
an hour of this silence, the ingenuous and sincere Armellina put me in an even worse state by saying with a fond
look that I ought to calm myself and be sure that the
young man had not given her the slightest pleasure by
his flattery. She did not understand that it was to tell me
exactly the opposite. I replied that, on the contrary, I
wished that he had pleased her. The dear child continued
to torment me by saying that he had probably thought I
was her father.

What reply could I make to an argument as cruel as it
was plausible? None. I could only fume, remain silent,
and finally, unable to bear more, ask Armellina and
Emilia to leave with me. It was at the end of the second
act, and certainly if I had had my wits about me I should
never have made the sweet girls a proposal all the tyranny
and injustice of which I did not see until the next day.
Nevertheless, they looked at each other for a moment,
then they were ready. I told them by way of excuse that
I had to make sure that the Santa Croce carriage was not
recognized, as it would be if we left the theater with the
crowd, and that we would go there again on the next day
but one. I prevented Armellina from leaning out of the
box to greet the Marquise d'Aout. At the door I found
the lackey who was serving me talking with one of his
fellows, which led me to conclude that the Princess was
at the opera. We got out at the inn. I whispered to the
lackey to return to the palace and to come back at three
o'clock in the morning. The weather was cold, so I had to
consider the horses.

We at once sat down in front of the fire, where for half
an hour I gave no thought to anything but the excellent
oysters, which a deft scullion opened in our presence,
taking great care not to lose a single drop of the savory
liquid in which they were swimming. We ate them as

they were opened, and the laughter of the girls, who were
thinking of the game of exchanging them, began to dissipate my ill-humor. In Armellina's sweet gentleness, I
thought I saw the innocence of her beautiful soul, and I
was angry with myself because, envious of the justice a
man more fit to please her than I had done to her charms,
I had permitted a hateful feeling to trouble my peace of
mind. Armellina, drinking champagne as I had taught
her to do, looked at me as if she were begging me to add
my gaiety to hers. Emilia talked to me about her future
marriage; and, without saying again that I would go to
Civitavecchia, I promised her that her fiancé would have
the dispensations in a few days, at the same time kissing
Armellina's beautiful hands again and again, while she
seemed grateful to me for being loving once more.

Put in high spirits by the oysters and the champagne,
we supped deliciously. We had sturgeon and exquisite
truffles, whose delicacy I savored more by enjoying the
voluptuous appetite with which the girls were eating
them than by eating myself. A natural and well-founded
feeling informs the thinking man that a sure way to make
a woman love him is to procure her some new pleasure.
When Armellina saw me filled with joy and once again
ardent, she could not but recognize her handiwork and
delight in the power she had over me. She gave me her
hand of her own free will. She kept me from turning my
head to the left to look at Emilia, constantly keeping her
eyes on mine. Emilia ate and did not care. It seemed to
me impossible that Armellina could refuse herself to my
love after supper, when we came to the orgy of oysters
and punch.

After serving the dessert, the remaining fifty oysters,
and bringing me everything I needed to make punch, the
waiter left, saying that the water was on the fire in the
other room, where there was everything necessary for the
young ladies to retire. The room being small, we were too
hot; I urged them to go into the other room and get rid

of their fur-lined dresses, and come back to eat oysters
in perfect freedom. Their dresses were fitted to their
figures with whalebone stays, they returned in white
corsets and short dimity petticoats which came only halfway down their calves. They returned with their arms
around each other, laughing over their state of undress.
I had the strength to conceal all the emotion which this
enchanting costume aroused in me, and even to refrain
from fixing my eyes on their bosoms while they were complaining that they had neither fichus around their necks
nor jabots at the top of their shifts. I said nonchalantly
that I would not look at them, for the sight of a bosom
left me perfectly indifferent. Knowing nature, I had to
lie. I was sure that they could no longer set much value
on what I valued so little.[3] The two girls, who knew that
they had very beautiful bosoms, were astonished by my
disdain; they had to suppose that I had never seen
beautiful bosoms; and the truth is that in Rome beautiful
breasts are scarcer than pretty faces. Despite their good
morals, Armellina and Emilia could not but undertake
to convince me that I was wrong; it was my part to put
them at their ease and in a frame of mind to feel ashamed
of nothing. I delighted them by saying that I wanted to
see them make the punch themselves. The lemon juice
had already been squeezed into a big goblet. They were
charmed when I told them that I found the punch better
than the one I had made the first time they drank it.

At the game of passing oysters from mouth to mouth
I chided Armellina for swallowing the liquid before I
took the oyster. I admitted that it was difficult to do
otherwise, but I undertook to show them how to go about
keeping both the oyster and the liquid in their mouths
by raising a rampart behind it with the tongue to stop it
from entering the throat. Having to set them the example,
I taught each of them to insert the oyster and the liquid
into the other's mouth as I did by simultaneously inserting the full length of the tongue. I did not object when

they took no offense at my extending mine, nor did
Armellina object when I lingered over sucking hers,
which she gave me most generously, laughing heartily
afterward at the pleasure afforded by the game, than
which they agreed with me nothing could be more innocent.

It was by chance that a fine oyster which I gave Emilia,
putting the shell to her lips, dropped into her bosom; she
made to recover it; but I claimed that it was mine by
right, and she had to yield, let me unlace her, and gather
it with my lips from the depth to which it had dropped.
In the course of this she had to bear with my uncovering
her bosom completely; but I retrieved the oyster in such
a way that there was no sign of my having felt any
pleasure except that of having recovered, chewed, and
swallowed it. Armellina watched the whole procedure
without smiling, surprised that I appeared to show no
interest in what I must have seen. Four or five oysters
later I gave one to Armellina, who was sitting on my lap,
and I cleverly dropped it into her bosom, which brought
a laugh from Emilia, who at bottom was annoyed that
Armellina had escaped a test of an intrepidity such as
she had shown me. But I saw that Armellina was delighted by the mishap, though she refused to give any
sign of it.

"I want my oyster," I said.

"Take it."

I unlace her whole bodice, and, the oyster having
dropped as far down as possible, I complain that I shall
have to bring it up with my hand. Good God! What torment for a man in love to have to hide the excess of his
delight at such a moment! Armellina had not the slightest pretext to accuse me of anything, for I did not touch
her beautiful breasts, hard as marble, except in searching
for the oyster. After retrieving and swallowing it, I took
hold of one of her breasts, demanding the liquid from the
oyster which had spilled on it; I seized the rosebud with

my avid lips, surrendering to all the voluptuous feelings inspired in me by the imaginary milk which I sucked for a good two or three minutes. I saw that she was surprised and moved; but when I let her go, it was only to recover my soul, which my great pleasure had made to exhale where I did not know if she could suspect it. But when she saw me fix my eyes on hers as if in a stupor, she asked me if I had very much enjoyed imitating the babe at the breast.

"Yes, for it is an innocent game."

"I do not believe so, and I hope you will say nothing about it to our Superioress; what you did is not innocent for me, and we must retrieve no more oysters."

Emilia said that such little weaknesses were wiped out with holy water.

"We can swear," she added, "that we have not given one another a single kiss."

They went into the next room for a moment, and, after I went there myself, we moved the table away and sat down by the fire on a sofa which we pulled up to it, with a stand on which were the bowl of punch and glasses beside us. We had no more oysters.

Sitting between them, I spoke of our legs, which were exactly alike yet which women insisted on concealing under their skirts, and, so saying, I touched their legs, adding that it was just as if I were touching my own, and seeing that they had not opposed my examining them up to the knee, I told Emilia that I wanted no reward from her but her permission to judge the thickness of her thighs in comparison with Armellina's.

"Hers," said Armellina, "must be thicker than mine, though I am the taller."

"There's no harm in letting me see."

"I think there is."

"Then I will just measure them with my hands."

"No, for you would look, too."

"No, on my word of honor."

"Let us blindfold you."

"Gladly. But you must let me blindfold you as well."

"Very good. We'll play blindman's-buff."

After drinking, we all three blindfolded one another, and then the great game began and, standing in front of me, they let me measure them several times, falling on me and laughing each time I measured too far up. Having taken off my handkerchief, I saw everything, but they had to pretend they had no idea of it. They must have cheated me in the same way too, to see what it was that they felt between their thighs when they laughed so hard that they fell on me. The charming game did not end until nature, overcome with pleasure, deprived me of the strength to go on. I then restored myself to a state of decency before they took off their blindfolds, which they did when they heard my decision.

"Emilia," I said to Armellina, "has her thighs, her hips, and everything more developed than yours, but you have still to grow."

Speechless and laughing, they sat down beside me again, thinking, I know not how, that they could disavow all they had let me do. It seemed to me, though I said nothing, that Emilia had had a lover, but Armellina was untouched in every way. She seemed more humiliated than Emilia, and there was a look of far greater gentleness in her big black eyes. I wanted to take a kiss from her beautiful lips, and I found it very strange that she turned away her head, though at the same time holding my hands with all her strength.

We had spoken of the ball. They were very curious about it; it had become rather the madness than the passion of all the girls in Rome after Pope Rezzonico had kept them starved for that pleasure during all the ten years of his reign. Though he had permitted the Romans every kind of gambling game, he had forbidden them to dance; his successor Ganganelli, having different views, had forbidden gaming and given unrestricted permission for dancing. He saw no reason to prevent his subjects from hopping about. So I promised I would take them to the ball, after finding one in a quarter as far as possible from the most frequented part of Rome, where they would run no risk of being recognized. I took them back to the convent at three o'clock in the morning, well enough satisfied with all that I had done to calm my desires, though I had thereby increased my passion; I felt more convinced than ever that Armellina was a girl to be adored by any man over whom beauty had the right to exercise absolute dominion. I was one of beauty's subjects, and, to my sorrow, I am so still, destitute, even in my state, for the exhaustion of the incense had made the censer pitiable.

I reflected on the sort of enchantment which forced me again and again to fall in love with an object which, seeming to be new, inspired me with the same desires that had been inspired in me by the last object I had loved, and which I had not ceased to love until it had ceased to inspire them in me. But the object which seemed to be new—was it really so in essence? Not at all—for it was always the same play, with nothing new but its title. But when I succeeded in possessing it, did I know that it was the same object which I had enjoyed so many times before? Did I complain? Did I feel that I had been tricked? Not at all. The reason is that, enjoying the play, I kept my eyes on the playbill, on the charming title given it by the enchanting face with which I had fallen in love. But if the entire illusion comes from the title of the play, would it not be better to go to see it without having read the playbill? Of what consequence is it to know the title of a book one wants to read, the name of a dish one wants to eat, of a city whose beauties one wants to visit?

All this is literally true in the case of a city, a dish, a play; the name means nothing. But every comparison is a sophism. Man, in distinction from all the other animals, cannot fall in love with a woman except through the

medium of one of his senses, all of which, except the sense
of touch, have their seat in the head. For this reason, if
he has eyes, it is the face which casts the all-powerful
spell of love on him. The most beautiful of female bodies,
offered to his eyes stark naked, but with the head covered,
might excite him to lust, but never to what is called love,
for if, just as he was surrendering to instinct, the woman
uncovered her head, the crown of that beautiful body,
and it proved to have one of those really ugly faces
which inspire disgust, repugnance to the pleasure of love,
and often hatred, he would flee, with a sort of horror for
the animality to which he was surrendering. It is the
exact opposite which occurs when a face which he finds
beautiful has made a man fall in love. If he succeeds in
enjoying the possessor of it, no deformity or ugliness in
her body repels him; he even manages to find beauty in
what, if he examines it, is ugly; but he does not care.

The empire of the face, then, being thus established in
the nature of the animal man, the human race, being in
intuitive possession of moral calculation in respect to all
that it needs, has in every civilized country decided that
the whole body must be concealed by clothing except the
face, and not only the bodies of women but those of men
too, who, however, in the course of the centuries, have in
several provinces of Europe adopted the habit of dressing
in a manner which makes it very easy for women to imagine them as they must be when they are naked. The advantage accrued to women by the establishment of this
rule is incontestable, despite the fact that beautiful faces
are scarcer than beautiful bodies, for art can easily give
charms to a face which has none, whereas there is no cos-
metic to correct the ugliness of a bosom, a belly, and all
the other parts of the human body. However, I admit
that the Spartan phainomerides[4] were right, like all
women whose faces are repulsive though they have very
beautiful bodies, for, though the play is beautiful, because of the playbill they find themselves without an

audience; but it does not matter, man needs to love, and in order to fall in love he must have a title which arouses his curiosity. Woman bears it on the surface of her face. Fortunate and thrice fortunate the Armellinas, whose play is so beautiful that it surpasses expectation!

Very well satisfied with my conquest and with my certainty that I should achieve perfect happiness, I entered my room, where I found Margherita sound asleep on the sofa. I quickly undressed, and, making no noise, put out the candle, got into bed, and at once surrendered to sleep, of which I was in the greatest need. When I woke at noon Margherita told me that a very handsome gentleman had come to see me about ten o'clock and that, not having dared to wake me, she had entertained him until eleven.

"I made him coffee," she said, "which he found very good; he said he would come back tomorrow, and he would not tell me his name. He is one of the pleasantest men I have ever met. He made me a present of this coin, which I don't recognize; I hope you won't be angry."

It was the Florentine; he had given her a two-once piece.[5] It made me laugh, and, not being in the least jealous of Margherita, I told her that she had done well to entertain him and still better to accept the coin, which was worth forty-eight paoli. She kissed me fondly, and, thanks to the incident, spared me the reproaches with which she would otherwise have assailed me for coming home so late. Curious to know who this Tuscan paragon of generosity was, I read Donna Leonilda's[6] letter. He was Signor XXX,[7] a merchant established in London, who had been recommended to her husband by a Knight of Malta who was in Marseilles, from which he had arrived by sea; he was rich and his own master, amiable, well educated, and generous; she assured me that I should like him. After giving me all the news of her husband, her mother, and the whole family, she ended her letter by saying that she was happy to be six months with child, and that she would be even happier if God (for God does all things) would grant her the boon of bearing a boy. She asked me to congratulate the Marchese on it.

Whether it was due to nature or to education, the news made me shudder. I answered her a few days later, sending my letter unsealed and enclosed in a letter of congratulation which I wrote to her husband, saying that God's bounties never arrive too late and that no news had ever concerned me more. In May Leonilda gave birth to a son, whom I saw in Prague at Prince Rosenberg's[8] when I was there for the coronation of the Emperor Leopold.[9] He is called the Marchese della C. . . , like his father, who lived to the age of eighty years. Though he did not know my name, I arranged to be introduced to him, and I enjoyed his conversation on another occasion at the theater. He was with a very learned Abate who was called his tutor; but he did not need one, for at the age of twenty he had a wisdom which few men possess at sixty. What pleased me most particularly was the youth's resemblance to the late Marchese, his mother's husband. It was this thought which drew tears from me when I reflected on the satisfaction which the resemblance must have caused both that excellent man and the youth's mother. I wrote to her, and I entrusted her son with the letter. She did not receive it until he returned to Naples during the Carnival of the year 1792, and I at once received an answer in which she invited me to come to her son's wedding and to spend the rest of my days in her house. Perhaps I shall go there.

At three o'clock I found the Princess of Santa Croce in bed, with the Cardinal keeping her company. The first thing she asked me was what had made me leave the opera at the end of the second act. I replied that I should have to tell her a story six hours long, the circumstances of which were most interesting, but which I could not tell without being granted *carte blanche* in advance, for there were details which I should have to describe too much after nature. The Cardinal asked me if it was something in the nature of the evenings with M. M.,[10] and, having heard that it was of just that nature, he asked the Princess if she would turn a deaf ear. She replied that I could count on it, and I told them the whole story, more or less in the terms in which I have written it. The recovered oysters and the blindman's-buff made her laugh despite her deafness. At the end she agreed with the Cardinal that I had gone about it the right way, and she was sure that I would crown my labors at the first opportunity. The Cardinal told me that in two or three days I should have a dispensation from the banns for Emilia's fiancé, with which he could marry her wherever he pleased.

The next morning at nine o'clock Signor XXX came to see me, and I found him such as the Marchesa had described him to me; but I had a grudge against him because of the compliment he had paid Armellina, and it grew stronger when he asked me if the young lady who was with me was married or engaged and if she had parents or other relatives who could dispose of her. I asked him with a rather sour smile to excuse me from giving him any information about the young lady, since she had been masked at the theater. He blushed and begged my pardon. Thanking him for the honor he had done Margherita by accepting a cup of coffee from her, I asked him to do me the same favor, assuring him that I would go to breakfast with him the next day. He was staying at Roland's,[11] opposite San Carlo, another of whose guests was the famous singer Gabrielli,[12] known as La Cochetta, who was being assiduously courted by Don Giovanni Battista Borghese.[13]

As soon as the young Florentine left, I flew to San Paolo, where I could not wait to see what reception my vestals, whom I had so well initiated, would accord me. They appeared before me with their faces wearing precisely the opposite expressions to those they had worn during the preceding days. Emilia had become gay, and Armellina sad. I at once told Emilia that in three days I would bring her a full dispensation from publishing the banns, and that in a week at the most the Superioress would have a note from Cardinal Orsini to pay her four hundred scudi and dismiss her, and that on the same day I would bring her an order for a stipend of two hundred scudi, which I would collect as soon as I had her marriage certificate. Beside herself with joy over the news, she left the grating to run and tell it to the Superioress.

I thereupon took my poor Armellina's hands, and, covering them with kisses which came from my soul, I implored her to stop looking sad.

"What shall I do here," she said, "without Emilia? What shall I do here when you have gone? I am wretched. I detest myself."

I thought I should die of grief when I saw her weep after saying those few words. I could not contain myself. I promised her on my honor that I would not leave Rome before I had seen her married and procured her a dowry of a thousand scudi.

"I don't care about the thousand scudi; your promise that you will not leave Rome before you have seen me married brings me back to life, and I ask nothing more; but if you fail me it will kill me. Be sure of that."

"I give you my word, and I will die rather than fail you. Forgive the love, my dear Armellina, which perhaps led me too far astray yesterday."

"Be my faithful friend, and I forgive you everything."

"Let me for the first time kiss your beautiful lips."

After the kiss, which promised me all that I could desire, she dried her tears, and Emilia appeared with the Superioress, who spoke to me in the most flattering way possible. She said that I must prepare to take an interest in another girl whom she intended to give Armellina as a companion as soon as Emilia left. I promised her I would do whatever she bade me, and at the same time I asked her to let them go with me that evening to the play at the Tor di nona.[14]

As soon as they were alone I asked them to forgive me if I had made plans for them without their consent. Emilia replied that they would be absolute monsters if they could refuse me anything after all I had done for them.

"And you, my beautiful Armellina, will you refuse yourself to my love?"

"No, my friend, but within the limits which morality prescribes. No blindman's-buff, for example."

"Oh God, it's such a charming game! You distress me."

"Think of another," said Emilia.

Emilia had become ardent, and I did not like it, for I feared that it would make Armellina jealous. Knowing the human heart, I could entertain that fear without being conceited.

On leaving them, I went to engage a box at the Tor di nona, then to the inn to order supper in the same rooms, not forgetting the oysters, even though I was sure I should not need them again. After that I went to find a fiddler to get me three tickets for a ball where I could hope that no one would recognize me. I told him that I should be alone with two young ladies who would not dance.

Back at my lodging, and intending to dine alone, a note from the Marquise d'Aout, reproaching me for never coming to dine with her, changed my mind; I went, and I found the Florentine there. It was during the dinner that I came to know a good part of his worth; I found him such as Donna Leonilda had described him to me. Toward the end of dinner the Marquise asked me why I had not stayed until the end of the opera.

"Because the young ladies were bored."

"They do not belong to the Venetian Ambassador's household, as you told me they did; I am sure of that."

"You are right, Madame; excuse my little lie."

"It was a subterfuge to avoid telling me who they are; but it is known."

"So much the better for those who are curious."

"The one who talked to me deserves to arouse anyone's curiosity; but in your place I would have her put a little powder on her hair."

"I have no such authority, but God preserve me from imposing my will on her."

The Florentine pleased me by saying nothing. I made him talk at length about England and his business there. He told me that he was on his way to Florence to take possession of his inheritance and at the same time to look for a wife, so that he could return to London married. When I left, I told him that I should not have the honor of calling on him until the next morning but one, because of urgent business which had arisen for me. At that he had sense enough to ask me not to come until noon, so that he could have the pleasure of dining with me.

Full of my happiness, I went to fetch my girls, who enjoyed the whole comedy as I did, without the slightest interruption. On arriving at the inn, I ordered the carriage to come back at two o'clock, and we repaired to the fire, where the scullion worked away at opening oysters, which no longer interested us as they had done the first two times. The girls had each adopted the attitude toward me which was appropriate to the actual state of her affairs. Emilia had the manner of someone who, having sold excellent merchandise on credit, maintains an air of superiority because of the good bargain she has given the buyer. Armellina, tender, smiling, and a little humbled, spoke to me with her eyes and reminded me of the promise I had given her. I replied only with passionate kisses which reassured her but which at the same time made her foresee that I should want greatly to increase my obligation to her. I thought she seemed resigned; and, profoundly content, I sat down at table, confining all my attentions to her. Emilia, on the eve of marriage, had no difficulty in believing that I neglected her only because of a feeling of respect I considered due to the sacrament by which she was to bind herself.

After supper, which was as gay and voluptuous as always, I sat down on the wide sofa with Armellina, where I spent three hours which I could have made delicious if I had not insisted on obtaining the final favor. The girl would never consent to it. Yet neither my caresses nor my words nor my occasional rages could ever perturb her unvarying sweetness. Tender in my arms, now laughing, now amorously sad in the most eloquent silence, she never granted me what I persisted in demanding, yet she never appeared to refuse it to me. This may seem an enigma, but it is not one. Her failure to consent was not a refusal on her part; it was one only in respect to its result. She left my arms a virgin, perhaps sorry not to have had the courage to fail in her duty. Driven by Nature to make an end, still amorous, and little satisfied, asking her to forgive me was my only resource. It was the only way, so Nature told me, to make sure of her consent on another occasion.

We dressed, half sad, half gay, we woke Emilia, who was sleeping as if she were in her own bed; and, after taking them home, I went to recover my strength in mine, laughing at all the reproaches with which Margherita assailed me.

The Florentine gave me a little dinner for two, at which the choice and delicate fare took the smallest part of my attention. What impressed me was his protestations of friendship, his obliging expressions, his generous offers of money if I were in need of it. There must be a reason for all this, and I could not discover it. He had seen Armellina, she had pleased him, I had been short with him once when he had mentioned her to me, he had not mentioned her again, and at the dinner her name never came up. I found myself reduced to believing in sympathy; I even thought I ought to be grateful to him for it, and to do as much for him. I returned his dinner at my lodging, and I included Margherita, with whom, since I was no longer jealous of her, I wished that he might fall in love. He would not have found her making difficulties, for he pleased her, and they would both have found me willing; but nothing of the sort happened. She had praised a small ring which he wore on his watch chain, and he asked me to allow him to make her a present of it; I consented; and that was to give him a free hand; but it went no farther.

In a week everything was arranged for Emilia's marriage. I discounted her stipend, so that I could give her the money in advance, and on the same day that she left the convent she was married and went to Civitavecchia with her husband. Three days later Marcuccio married his mistress, and the next day Armellina came to the grating with the Superioress and a new girl, perhaps three or four years older than she, who was very pretty; but she interested me only a little; still in love with Armellina, and hoping to conquer her completely, I could only be indifferent to any other object. The Superioress told me that the girl, whose name was Scholastica,[15] would thenceforth be Armellina's inseparable companion, and that she was sure she would win my esteem, for she was as good as Emilia; but that in return I must do what I could to forward her in her inclination for a young man who had lucrative employment and who would be ready to marry her if he had the three hundred scudi he needed in order to do so. He was the son of a third cousin of Scholastica's; she called him her nephew, though he was older than she; the stipend could easily be bought; but to obtain it for nothing I should have to find someone who would ask the Holy Father for it. I promised her I would speak on his behalf.

The Carnival was nearing its end, and Scholastica had never seen either an opera or a play. Armellina wanted to see a ball, and I had finally found one at which I thought I could be certain that no one would recognize us; but since being recognized could have consequences, it was necessary to take precautions; I asked them if they were willing to dress as men, which I would arrange for them, and they eagerly consented. I had a box at the Teatro Aliberti for the day after the ball, so I told them to ask the Superioress for permission, and to expect me toward dusk, when I would come to fetch them as usual in one of the Santa Croces' carriages. Though disheartened by Armellina's resistance and by the presence of her new companion, who I thought was neither a girl to be hurried into anything nor one to be left to stare at the wall, I nevertheless had everything we needed to dress the two girls as men taken to the inn to which we always went.

Getting into the carriage, Armellina told me the bad news that Scholastica knew nothing about our relation and that we must not permit ourselves the slightest liberty in her presence. I did not have time to answer her. The other girl got in, and we went to the inn, where we had no sooner entered the room in which there was a good fire than I said in a tone which betrayed ill-humor that if they insisted upon being perfectly free I would go into the other room, though it was cold there. So saying, I showed them the men's clothing. Armellina replied that it would be enough if I would turn my back, adding:

"Isn't that so, Scholastica?"

"I'll do as you do; but I'm very sorry, for I'm sure I'm in your way. You love each other, and it's perfectly clear: I prevent you from giving each other tokens of it. I am not a child. I am your friend, but you do not treat me like a friend."

At this discourse, which proceeded from common

sense, but which required a good deal of intelligence to be so well expressed, I breathed again.

"You are right, beautiful Scholastica," I said, "I love Armellina and she is looking for an excuse not to give me tokens of it, for she does not love me."

So saying, I left the room and shut the door. I fell to making a fire. A quarter of an hour later Armellina knocked and asked me to open the door. She was wearing breeches. She said that they absolutely needed me because, the shoes being too small, they could not get them on. I sulked, so she threw herself on my neck, and she had no difficulty in soothing me; I was justifying myself to her, at the same time covering everything I could see with kisses, when Scholastica broke in on us, giving a great laugh.

"I was sure," she said, "that I was in your way; but if you do not trust me completely I warn you that I shall not have the pleasure of going to the opera with you tomorrow."

"Very well," said Armellina, "embrace my friend too."

"Here I am."

I was displeased by such generosity on Armellina's part; but that did not keep me from giving Scholastica the kisses which she deserved, and which I would have given her even if she had been ugly, for so much such kind consideration was not to be scorned. I even gave her amorous kisses, intending to punish Armellina; but I was deceived. I saw that she was delighted, she kissed her friend fondly, as if to thank her for her readiness to help, and at that I went to the other room with them to see what was the matter. I made them sit down, and I saw there was nothing for it but to send out for shoes for them; I sent the waiter on the errand, with orders to come back with a shoemaker who would bring all the shoes he had in his shop. While we waited for the shoe-

maker, love imperiously commanded me not to confine
myself to kisses with Armellina. She did not dare to refuse either me or herself; but as if in exculpation, she
insisted that I give Scholastica the same caresses I had
given her, and Scholastica, to make her easy, eagerly
accepted anything I could have demanded of her if I had
been in love with her. The girl was charming, she fell
short of Armellina only in sweetness and a delicacy of
features which was Armellina's alone. The toying, all in
all, was not displeasing to me, but my reflections filled me
with bitterness. What I saw made me certain that Armellina did not love me, and that if Scholastica made me no
resistance it was only to put her friend at ease and to
convince her that she could trust her completely. I saw
that, before the shoemaker arrived, I must by hook or
crook make myself desire Scholastica. I at once became
curious to see if Armellina would not change her attitude
when I showed that I was really in love with her friend,
and if the latter would continue to grant me what could
not but seem to her too much, for until then my hands
had never gone beyond the boundaries which the belt of
her breeches opposed to their reach.

The shoemaker arrived, and in a few minutes they had
shoes which fitted them perfectly. After that I helped
them on with their coats, and I saw two very pretty
girls dressed as elegant young men and such as to make
anyone who saw them with me envy my good fortune.
After I ordered that supper should be ready at midnight,
we went downstairs and on to the house which was to be
the scene of the ball and where it was a safe bet that I
would not be recognized, for the fiddler whom I had paid
for the three tickets had assured me that the company
consisted entirely of shopkeepers.

I enter the ballroom with my two metamorphosed
beauties, and the first person who strikes me is the
Marquise d'Aout with her husband and the Abbé. The
usual exchange of compliments follows, and the expected

persiflage on the subject of my two companions, who, having no acquaintance with society, stood there as if stricken dumb; but what annoyed me to death was a tall young lady who, finishing a minuet, came and bowed to Armellina to invite her to dance with her. The young lady was the Florentine, who had taken it into his head to dress as a girl. He made a perfect beauty. Armellina, thinking that she should not let herself be taken for a dupe, said that she recognized him, and he replied with no little quickness that she was no doubt mistaken for he had a brother who looked just like him, just as she must have a sister with the same face as hers to whom his brother had spoken in a box at the Teatro Capranica. This well-sustained riposte by the Florentine set the Marquise laughing, and, though reluctantly, I laughed too. Armellina having declined the honor of dancing with him, the Marquise made her sit down between herself and the Florentine, and the Marquis made off with Scholastica; politeness demanded that I devote all my attention to the Marquise and not even look at Armellina, to whom the Florentine was talking in a way which occupied her completely. Jealous as a tiger, and having to dissimulate, my reader can imagine how much I suffered and how greatly I repented of having come to the ball. But the cruelty of my situation increased when, a quarter of an hour later, I saw Scholastica leave the Marquis d'Aout and stand talking in a corner to a respectable-looking man of indeterminate age who seemed to be treating her to a most interesting discourse.

The minuets over for the time being, lines are formed for a contradance, and I am surprised to see Armellina beside the Florentine, she as a man, he as a girl. I approach them to compliment them, and in the sweetest of tones I ask Armellina if she is sure she knows how to dance a contradance.

"The Signore told me," she replied, "that I cannot go wrong if I will just do whatever he does."

I am left without an answer. I go toward Scholastica,
very curious about the man who was speaking to her. She
timidly introduces him to me, saying that he is her
nephew, the man who wanted to make her happy by
obtaining permission to marry her. My surprise was
great, but I conceal it perfectly; I say all the polite and
encouraging things I can to him, telling him that the
Superioress had informed me and that I had already
thought of such a way to obtain it from the Holy Father's
bounty that permission for them to marry would cost
neither him nor her a soldo. He commends himself to my
good offices, saying that he is not rich, and I am comforted to see that he feels not even a twinge of jealousy.

I leave Scholastica with him, and I look in amazement
at Armellina, who is dancing very well and never at a
loss in a figure. The Florentine, who was a master, guided
her superbly; they had all the air of a happy couple;
I fumed inwardly; but I did not let it keep me from
congratulating Armellina after the contradance and
praising the Florentine, who played the lady to perfection; he was so skillfully dressed that one would have
said he had a bosom. It was Madame d'Aout who had
tricked him out so well. Since I could not bring myself
not to observe everything that Armellina did, I declined
to dance, but managing always to show not a trace of
ill-humor. Scholastica, still with her fiancé and occupied
in talk of great interest to them both, gave me no uneasiness. She conversed with him for three hours, until
the time when I went to ask her if she was willing that
we should leave. It was getting on toward midnight,
an hour which I could not wait to see arrive, for the
anguish I had endured had made me heap a thousand
curses on the ball and my kindness in taking the girls
to it.

But I was no little embarrassed at half past eleven
o'clock. It was a Saturday, and the whole company was
waiting for midnight to go to eat meat, either at an inn

or wherever each of them had decided to go. The Marquise d'Aout, enchanted by Armellina's ingenuous talk, told me pleasantly, and at the same time commandingly, to come to supper at her house with my two companions.

"Madame, I cannot have that honor, and my two companions know the reason for it."

"This one" (Armellina) "has just told me that it is entirely for you to say."

"It is a subterfuge, believe me."

I turn to Armellina, and I say with a smile and all the sweetness I was able to counterfeit, that she well knew she had to be at home at the latest by half an hour after midnight; and she replies with unfeigned sweetness that it is true, but that nevertheless it is for me to decide. I reply a little sadly that it is not for me to decide to break my word, but that she has the power to decide me to do it. At that the Marquise, and the Marquis, seconded by the Florentine, urge Armellina to use her power and oblige me to break the promise I claimed to have made, and Armellina ventures to urge me accordingly. I was furious, but resolved to do anything rather than give her the slightest reason to think me jealous. I say to Armellina in the most natural manner that I am willing if her friend will consent; and, with a satisfaction which rends my soul, she replies by sending me off to ask her for the favor.

Sure that I am safe, I go to the other end of the room, and, in her fiancé's presence, I tell Scholastica the whole story, at the same time asking her not to consent but without involving me. Her relative praises my prudence; but Scholastica does not need me to ask her to play the role, she tells me clearly that she would never consent to go to sup with anyone. She then comes with me, and, on the way, I tell her that she must speak to Armellina privately. So I take her to the Marquise, complaining that I have not succeeded. Scholastica asks to be excused and tells Armellina to come and hear what she has to say to her. They talked together for some time, then they came back downcast, and Armellina said she was sorry, but it was absolutely impossible. At that the Marquise stopped insisting, and about midnight we left. I urged silence on Scholastica's lover, asking him to come to dine with me on the second day in Lent. He was a man forty years of age, modest, pleasing, who greatly interested me in his favor.

The night being very dark, as it was bound to be at the end of the Carnival, I left the house with the two girls, sure that I should not be followed and going to find the carriage where I knew it would be. Escaping from a hell in which I had suffered like one of the damned for four hours, I arrived at the inn without saying a word to either girl, and not answering the reasonable questions which the too natural Armellina put to me. Scholastica avenged me by reproaching her for having obliged me to appear either rude or jealous or ready to break my word.

When we were in our room Armellina all at once changed my jealous rage to pity; I saw her beautiful eyes showing unmistakable signs of the tears which the truths Scholastica had told her had made her shed in the carriage. Supper being already served, they had time only to take off their shoes. I was sad, and I had reason to be so, but Armellina's sadness distressed me; it was a barrier; I had to dissipate it, though the source of it could not but drive me to despair, for I could find it nowhere but in the liking she had taken to the Florentine. Our supper was exquisite, Scholastica did it justice, but for once Armellina ate scarcely anything. Scholastica gave rein to a natural gaiety, she kissed her friend, she begged her to share in her happiness, for, her lover having become my friend, she was sure that I would use my influence for him and for her, just as I had done for Emilia. She blessed the ball and the chance which had brought him there. She proved to Armellina that she had no reason to be sad, since she was sure that I loved her alone.

But Scholastica was mistaken; and Armellina did not dare to enlighten her friend by telling her the real cause of her sadness. On my side, self-esteem prevented me from telling her, for I knew that I was in the wrong. Armellina was thinking of marriage, I was not the sort of man for her, and the handsome Florentine was. Our supper ended without Armellina's having been able to recover her good humor. She drank only one glass of punch, and, since she had eaten very little, I did not urge her to drink more, for fear it would make her ill. Scholastica, on the contrary, who was tasting the delicious beverage for the first time, helped herself to it freely and thought it amusing that instead of going into her stomach it had risen to her head. In this state of gaiety she thought it was her duty to make perfect peace between us and to assure us that she would be no hindrance even if she were present at all the proofs of love which we could give each other.

She rose from the table and, controlling her legs with difficulty, she carried her friend to the sofa, pressing her to her bosom and giving her countless kisses, which made Armellina laugh despite her sadness. She called me, she made me sit down beside her, and put her into my arms. I gave her amorous caresses, which Armellina did not refuse but to which she did not accord the return which Scholastica hoped to see and for which I did not hope, for she would never have granted me in Scholastica's presence what she had not granted me during the three hours I had had her in my arms while Emilia was sound asleep. Scholastica, who did not want to fail in her mediation, put the blame on me: she reproached me with a coldness which I was far from feeling. I told them to take off their disguises and put their dresses on again. So saying, I helped Scholastica to take off her coat and her vest, whereupon Armellina did the same. I offered them their shifts, and at that Armellina told me to go and stand by the fire; but two minutes later the sound of kisses made me curious. Scholastica, more than gay from the punch, was covering Armellina's bosom with kisses, while Armellina, at last become cheerful, did as much to her ardent friend in my presence. The sight so worked upon Scholastica that she did not object to my doing justice to the beauty of her bosom and becoming a babe at the breast. At that Armellina felt ashamed to be less generous to me than her friend, and Scholastica triumphed when she saw for the first time the use to which I put Armellina's hands, whereupon, fearing for her good repute, Armellina demanded that Scholastica serve me in the same way. She did everything, and her astonishment, for though the girl was twenty years of age she knew nothing about such matters, delighted me.

After the explosion I put on their shifts and with the utmost decency took off their breeches. They went to the water closet with their arms around each other, and when they came back they sat on my lap. Scholastica, far from being annoyed at the preference I at once showed for the secret beauties of Armellina, seemed to be fascinated; she watched my maneuvers, and the way in which Armellina lent herself to my undertaking, with the greatest attention, hoping to see the thing which I should have been very glad to show her, but which Armellina would not grant me. Unable to conclude where I wanted to, I called a halt, remembering that I had duties to Scholastica, whose beauties, which were hidden under a long shift, I also wanted to bare for my eyes. Armellina's obliging friend offered me no resistance. She was too sure that she would leave the question unanswered. It was too hard to decide which of the two was the more beautiful; but Armellina had the advantage of being loved, Scholastica's advantage was the beauty of her face. My hand felt that she was as untouched as Armellina, and from the way in which she held herself I clearly saw that she left me the lord of everything; but I hesitated to take advantage of the moment. It was too fine a triumph to owe it to intoxication. However, I ended by doing everything which a skilled practitioner can do to give all the pleasure possible to the charming object whom he deprives of the final pleasure. Scholastica succumbed, voluptuously overcome, and convinced that I had only failed to fulfill her desires from respect and delicacy.

Armellina, all smiles, ingenuously congratulated us both. I felt ashamed. Scholastica begged her pardon. I took them back to their convent, assuring them that I would call for them the next day to take them to the opera, and I went home to bed, unable to decide whether I had won or lost in the game I had played. It was not until I woke the next morning that I was able to decide the question.

AFTER THE opera on *Shrove Sunday Armellina,
urged on by Scholastica's example, yields to my love; and
I enjoy their company again for the last time on the last
day of the Carnival, after appearing on horseback on the
Corso[2] dressed as Pierrot, thinking that no one recognized me. But this is what happened to me. I stop beside
a triumphal car, and I am surprised to see a masker disguised as a warrior in the costume of the ancient Romans
put his left hand on my horse's reins and with his right
hand give a pen and paper to a woman masker dressed as
a queen who sat beside him. The queen writes, hands the
paper to the warrior, who hands it to me and at the same
time lets go of my horse's reins. At the same moment a
musical prelude strikes up and all the maskers in the car
throw handfuls of sweetmeats at me. After that they fall
in with the procession. I read the note, expecting only an
ordinary pasquinade, but I am surprised to read the following:*

Pierrot audacieux, tremble: voici ton sort,
Je t'ai sauvé du Muran à Venise,
Mais cette nuit, je te condamne à mort,
Tu rendras l'âme en changeant de chemise.

("Audacious Pierrot, tremble: this is your
fate. I saved you from Murano, Venice, but
tonight I sentence you to death. You shall
give up your soul when you change your
shirt.")

I instantly guessed that the warrior could be only Car-
dinal de Bernis and the Queen only his beautiful Prin-
cess. There was no one but he who could remind me of
what had happened to me seventeen years before.³ Only
he could be the author of the impromptu. I leave the
Corso, I go to the door of a coffeehouse, and I write the
following four lines; then I return to the Corso and hand
them to the queen.

Je signe à ta sentence, adorable déesse;
Mais de ma mort laisse-moi donc le choix.
Mon crime, en bon chrétien, au guerrier je confesse.
J'expierai content, mais sur la sainte croix.

("I accept your sentence, adorable goddess; but
leave me the choice of my death. As a good Christian, I confess my crime to the warrior. I will gladly
expiate it, but on the holy cross." ⁴)

On the second day in Lent I received from the Su-
perioress all the papers I needed for Scholastica's mar-
riage, and the Princess and the Cardinal exerted them-
.selves to such purpose that she left the convent after
Easter and was married.

On the first Sunday in Lent the Marquise d'Aout had
me to dinner with the Florentine XXX, who, informing
me of his honorable intentions in regard to Armellina,
had no difficulty in persuading me to play the leading
role in the matter by taking the place of her father. I
arranged the whole thing in one week. He provided her

with a dowry of ten thousand scudi, which he deposited
in the Spirito Santo Bank,[5] and after Easter he married
her, then he took her with him to Florence and from there
to England, where she now lives happily.

It was on this occasion that I presented myself to Cardinal Orsini, who, being Prince of the Accademia degli
Infecondi,[6] arranged for me to receive the honor of becoming a member of it. He stipulated that I should recite
an ode in honor of the Passion of Our Lord Jesus Christ
at the next meeting, which was to be held on Good Friday.
To compose the ode, I decided to spend a few days in the
country, and I chose Frascati, where I thought I could
live a solitary life. I had promised Mariuccia that I
would visit her. She had assured me that I would enjoy
making the acquaintance of her family, and I was curious
to do so. I left three weeks before Easter; I arrived in
Frascati toward nightfall, and the next day, having sent
for a wigmaker, I saw before me Mariuccia's husband,
who at once recognized me.

After telling me that he dealt in grain, that he was
prospering in his business, and that he practiced the
trade of wigmaker only because he enjoyed it, he offered
me a room and very modestly invited me to dinner. I was
extremely surprised when he told me that he would introduce me to my daughter, to whom he had given the name
Giacomina at her baptism. I thought I ought not to admit
it, I laughed, I told him the thing was impossible, and
he calmly told me that I would admit it when I saw her.
This makes me extremely curious; here is yet another
intrigue which may have consequences; but in any case
the girl can be only a child nine or ten years old, and my
being her father must be extremely doubtful, for the wigmaker had married Mariuccia only four weeks after my
first amorous interview with her.

But at noon her face struck me. She had my features
beautified; and she was much more beautiful than Sophie,

Confessor and Penitents

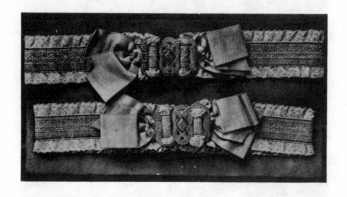

Garters

whom I had had by Teresa Pompeati[7] whom I had left in London.

Giacomina was very tall for her age and very well built. I looked at her very little; but I saw that she was examining me attentively, in the silence of concentration. I seized the first opportunity to ask Mariuccia on what grounds her husband could have told me that Giacomina was my daughter, and she replied, as if it were nothing at all, that he was as sure of it as she was, and that it did not prevent him from loving her more than all his other children.

"But the child does not know she is not your husband's daughter."

"Of course not. One does not confide such secrets to children."

I found Mariuccia's house very clean, and the room which her husband, Clemente, offered me having pleased me, I let him have my portmanteau brought there from the inn.

Mariuccia informed me privately that I would dine with an unmarried woman called Signora Veronica,[8] who kept a drawing school, at which Giacomina was studying and making astonishing progress.

"The woman," she told me, "will come with her supposed niece, a pretty, very clever girl and a great friend of Giacomina's. She is thirteen years of age. Her aunt knows you; but she knew your brother Zanetto[9] much better. We have talked about you a great deal, and she will be very pleasantly surprised when she sees you."

And so she was when she saw me; but not more than I when I saw her niece, who resembled my brother in the most telltale way imaginable. I guessed all. Signora Veronica, seated beside me at the table, after telling me that the girl was the daughter of a sister of hers who was dead, said to me at dessert that I would be her brother-in-law if my brother had been a man of honor. She could

*not say more to lead me to suppose that her pretended
niece was her daughter and that I was her uncle. At this
news, I made up my mind to love the niece; and what I
found amusing and extraordinary was that I found that
what had decided me to pursue this passing amour was a
kind of vengeance. I leave it to physicians who are more
learned than I to interpret phenomena of this kind. My
pretty niece was named Guglielmina, and throughout the
dinner I constantly found her charming. Giacomina said
very little, but she seemed to me to be thinking a great
deal. After dinner I took a solitary walk at the Villa
Ludovisi.*

*How many were my reflections when I found myself
in the place where precisely twenty-seven years earlier I
had been with Donna Lucrezia!* [10] *I saw the place, and
found it more beautiful, whereas I found myself not only
not the same but diminished in all my faculties, except
experience, which I abused and which made up to me
for nothing except when it gave me a better right to
reason. Wretched gain! Reasoning led me to melancholy,
the pitiless mother of the horrible idea of death, which I
had not the strength to face like a Stoic. Strength beyond my strength, which I was never able to acquire, and
which I shall never acquire! This weakness has never
made me a coward, but, even though abhorring its cause,
I have never been able to understand how a thinking man
can be indifferent to it.*

*As always, I put aside these somber ideas, reflecting
that, except for La Corticelli, I had bestowed happiness
on every girl I had loved. Lucia from Pasiano had ended
in ignominy only because, obeying my finer feelings, I
had respected her. She had become the victim of a base
courier who could lead her nowhere but to ruin.*

*Toward dusk I went home, and I remained in my room
until suppertime. I spent four hours vainly trying to
begin the ode on the Redemption which I had promised
Cardinal Orsini. The ode is a kind of composition which*

*does not depend on the poet's will. It can come neither
from his brain nor from his pen, unless Apollo sends
it to him. This time, Apollo scorned me, for, as I invoked
him, I was thinking of Guglielmina, for whom the god
cared nothing. I supped with Clemente and his wife, who
was with child; he hoped for a boy. I could not but wish
him that satisfaction.*

*He left me alone with his wife, which was most con-
siderate; but at that moment I thought her too much the
bourgeoise. I spent a very pleasant hour, but only in conversation. Mariuccia was full of her happiness, and, believing that she owed it to me, she could forbid herself to
love the bestower of it, but not to adore him. These are
natural feelings, which cost nothing; but the greater
includes the lesser. I saw Mariuccia at my disposal, but
I wanted only Guglielmina. She told me that her aunt
had left her with Giacomina.*

*"They are upstairs," she said, "together in the same
bed. I am sure they're sound asleep; would you like us
to go up and see them?"*

"Let us go, but we must not wake them."

*We go up on tiptoe. I see two beds; her two younger
daughters were asleep in one of them; in the other I see
Guglielmina and my daughter, both asleep on their
backs, both pretty and both with the heightened color of
those roses which blush on the cheeks of young girls and
boys only when they are asleep. The coverlet allowed a
view of the two little maids' bosoms. My daughter's was
ungarnished; but the other resembled the swellings one
sees on the head of a calf which is about to grow its horns.
Neither their hands nor their forearms were exposed.
What a vision! What enchantment! Mariuccia laughs at
my admiration, but she wants to increase it. She takes it
upon herself to raise the coverlet slowly and display to
my covetous soul two charming images which, to make a
perfectly new picture, needed only that I could not expect it. I see the two innocents, each with an arm reaching*

*down her belly and a hand just curved over the tokens of
her puberty, which were beginning to show. The middle
finger, still more curved, was held motionless on the little
piece of almost imperceptibly rounded flesh. It was the
only moment in my life when I knew for a certainty the
true temper of my soul, and I was satisfied with it. I felt
a delicious horror. This new feeling forced me to cover
the two nudities myself; my hands shook. What a betrayal! It was of a kind as new as it was cruel. Mariuccia
did not have a mind able to comprehend the greatness of
it. She had in all good faith betrayed the greatest secret
of two innocent souls at the moment of their greatest confidence. They might well have died of grief if they had
waked when I was contemplating their beautiful posture.
Only the most invincible ignorance of one thing could
have saved them from death, and I could not suppose they
were ignorant of it.*

*I at once left the room, and Mariuccia followed to
show me to mine, where what happened would certainly
not have happened save for the picture by which I had
just been overwhelmed; but Mariuccia, instead of taking
it as a punishment, chose to consider it a recompense for
the pleasure she thought she had procured me. I let her
believe whatever she pleased, and she went off to bed
with her husband. Alas! The thing had not been premeditated. If she had not calmed me, I could not have gone to
sleep.*

*I woke at daybreak, and I laughed as I thought of my
ode. I found myself Guglielmina's slave. I could have
composed no verses except for her. With his arrows Cupid
defied a gloomy Apollo who could only have unstrung his
bow with the lugubrious subject of the death of the Creator. Just as Clemente was dressing my hair, the two
charming friends entered. Giacomina brought me my
chocolate on a tray, the other was carrying a roll of paper.
It contained drawings. In both their faces was depicted a
gaiety which sprang from innocence, candor, and confi-*

dence. *If they had known what had happened to them during the night, they would not have dared to appear before me. Guglielmina would have been inconsolable if she had been told that what I had seen had made me fall in love with her.*

The earliest sentiment of a girl who has the true seed of intelligence is coquetry; it is the only sentiment she values, for it is the only one which assures her that she can make a lover constant. Guglielmina at her age would have hated me if she had known that, so far as my eyes were concerned, I had already become her lord and master despite her. As for my daughter, at nine years of age she could not have such mature ideas. I asked them to let me see the products of their pencils.

After showing some little reluctance, they handed me the notebook. Nearly all the figures were naked—men, women, statues, groups of children—all were pretty and all copied after excellent studies from the nude. The Apollo Belvedere, Antinoüs, Hercules, and that reclining Venus of Titian's who holds her hand just where I had seen those of the dear girls. The psychological phenomenon which I observed at that moment, and which gave me the greatest pleasure, was a dispute between Guglielmina and my daughter.

My daughter did not want me to linger over the Venus, and Guglielmina laughed at her. She claimed that I should not linger over the Antinoüs or the Apollo, for, being a man, I could find nothing new in the drawings of them; then too, they ought not to let me know that they had ventured to draw them. The pleasure I took in their dispute filled my soul; but I was at a loss when they chose me to decide between their opinions.

"I do not know," I said at last, "which of you is right; but if I consider the pleasure your drawings give me I will say that the Venus interests me more than Antinoüs."

The amusing thing is that each of them thought she

was the victor, and Guglielmina refused to hear any further explanation. I have all my life attributed the greatest importance to these trifles, which served to show me the course I must follow to enter the hearts of those whom I sought to conquer.

They went off to school, and when I was dressed I went to call on Signora Veronica. There I saw seven or eight girls, all very young. None of them could take my mind from Guglielmina. To have a reason for going to the school often, I asked the mistress of it to paint my portrait in miniature; as she was not rich, she could not but be delighted to earn six zecchini; and the next day I promised Guglielmina six zecchini too to make a crayon portrait of me in my dressing gown and nightcap. To do so, she had to come to my room very early. But when, the next day, she kept me waiting, Giacomina told her she ought to stay and sleep with her, her mother Mariuccia agreed, and her aunt willingly consented. At that I hoped for everything. On the fourth day of my stay in Frascati, Guglielmina came alone to sup with us, and, to banish any notion of jealousy from my dear Giacomina's mind, I bought a gold watch with a clasp from her father and made her a present of it after supper. The child was mad with joy; on the pretext of gratitude, she began giving me countless caresses, which I had some difficulty in receiving as became a father. The whole little town was whispering that I was certainly her father, and Mariuccia and her husband were not sorry to have it believed. Giacomina suspected it; but she did not know what direction to give to the ideas which were floating in her young mind. Boldly accepting my challenge, she began coming into my bed after I had lain down in it, and making fun of the clear-sighted Guglielmina, who was afraid to do likewise. I did no more than give my daughter fond kisses on her beautiful lips and on her eyes in Guglielmina's presence, while Guglielmina laughed at our trifling. I said to her carelessly that four years' difference in age

*meant nothing, and that I would treat her as a child too
if she were in Giacomina's place. This slighting attitude
finally had the effect it was meant to have after three or
four days. I gave her six zecchini for her drawing, which
her aunt retouched, and that evening she got into bed
with me, where my daughter, on my other side, was delighted when she saw that I treated her in the same way
—plenty of kisses, but nothing more. When they were
tired they went off to their room and to bed; but I was
sure that Guglielmina knew from the kisses I gave her
that, though I restrained myself, I had expectations of
more solid fare. The next morning before leaving for
school they told Mariuccia in my presence how they drove
me frantic in my bed before they went off to theirs. The
worthy woman laughed, knowing already how the thing
would end.*

*Three or four days later Giacomina fell asleep, or pre-
tended to, and a few minutes afterward Guglielmina did
the same and let me do whatever I pleased up to a certain
point, at which she thought it best to wake. She saw me
looking so content that she thought she would gain most
by making no complaint. She wanted to let me believe
that, having been asleep, she had not been aware of anything at all; she woke Giacomina and they left together;
but the next morning I made her a present of a pretty
ring which was worth at least fifty scudi, and which
earned me the thanks of her aunt the same evening at
supper. The crayon being finished, she proposed to take
the girl home with her, and I was in terror. My daughter
protested to the point of tears, and Signora Veronica
smilingly yielded. She said to me that I had good reason
to love her niece, the same reason, she went on, which
Giacomina had for loving her. She thought she had pro-
pounded an insoluble enigma.*

*After she had gone, the two girls, left alone with me,
let themselves be persuaded to do the honors to another
bowl of punch and, after seeing me in bed, came to drive*

*me frantic, as they put it; but as soon as my daughter
really went to sleep, I did not sink to letting my dear
Guglielmina employ the same stratagem a second time.
I clearly saw that I could count on her affection, and I
was not mistaken. I spoke the language of love to her,
using its most eloquent terms without waiting for her
answers and not coming to the crowning act until I heard
her moaning. She gave herself to me heedless of the fact
that Giacomina had sat up and was watching our performance with equal attention and astonishment. When
the sweet combat ended, Giacomina became the object of
all our caresses, and we had no difficulty in assuring ourselves of her silence; but she wanted to be instructed in
everything and to see at close range just how the thing
was done. During the following days we had to satisfy
her curiosity in every respect. I vainly tried to convince
her that, because of her age, I could not possibly treat
her in the same way; she summoned me to the lists, and
she roused me to pity. Guglielmina finally felt obliged to
tell her that she was very probably my daughter, and
that I must not take the risk of committing a dreadful
crime which would make us both unhappy for the rest of
our lives. She was horrified at the thought, and so became
reasonable, stifling her passion as well as she could. What
Nature excited her to do could only increase my voluptuous enjoyment, and Guglielmina could not take exception
to a toying of which she became the chief beneficiary.
But now for a very fortunate event, not unlike a number
of others which have made me superstitious.*

*The next day at table Mariuccia reminded me that she
had had the good fortune in Rome to give me a number
on which I had staked and which, having been drawn,
had made the whole company win.[11] Giacomina said that
she had a number she was sure of, and, without waiting
to be asked what number it was, she named twenty-seven.
Mariuccia cried out, remembering, as I did, that the num-*

ber that she had given me ten years earlier was twenty-seven.

No more was needed; I said that I would stake on it then and there; Clemente said that it was too late to stake in Frascati, and that I must send the number to be staked on in Rome. The drawing for the lottery was to take place on the next day but one. I declare that a trustworthy man must be sent to Rome at once, and Clemente says that he will go himself. I encourage him, and he at once goes to order a horse and to put on riding clothes.

I at once write down the number twenty-seven, on which twenty-five Roman scudi are to be staked uncondi-tionally for the benefit of five partners. The partners were Mariuccia, Clemente, Giacomina, Guglielmina, and Signora Veronica. I then add twenty-five scudi for my-self, ordering that it be staked on the twenty-seven at the second drawing. I give the fifty scudi to Clemente, who sets off at once, promising that he will be back by supper-time.

Mariuccia said she was sure she would win, but my daughter looked sad.

"We shall win," she said to me, "and you will not. Why do you insist that the number will be drawn second rather than first, third, fourth, or fifth?"

"Because it pleases me to trust Fortune without reser-vations. Because this is the second time I have been given the twenty-seven. And because I want to win five times as much as the rest of you."

"But it is five times as difficult. It seems to me that your reasoning is faulty."

"If the twenty-seven comes out at the second drawing, I will take you all to Rome and keep you there through all of Holy Week."

"God grant that it comes out!"

Clemente was back at eleven o'clock and gave me my receipt, keeping the other himself. After supper Mariuc-

cia whispered to me that she had not failed to change my sheets. I thanked her, embracing her fondly and assuring her that we should go to Rome.

Guglielmina had become my angel. On this second night I found her so amorous that I forgave my brother for all follies. I hoped I should find him still in Rome, so that I could express my gratitude to him and thank him for having created such a jewel for my soul's consolation. Guglielmina sighed in my arms, thinking of the cruel day when I should leave her. I thought I could venture to promise that I would marry her, provided that her aunt would consent. She replied that she was sure her aunt would consent; but I was sure of the contrary. The poor child did not know that she was my brother's daughter.

But what joy the next day when the five numbers drawn in the Roman lottery were posted! The second number drawn was twenty-seven. Giacomina fell on my neck, and then all the household. Signora Veronica came and struggled to express her gratitude. She saw that, through me, she had come into possession of a hundred and fifty Roman scudi, as Clemente had of two hundred and twenty-five. I had won eight hundred and seventy-five, a sum of money to which I could not be indifferent, for after the expenses of the Carnival my exchequer was reaching its end.

The Roman scudo is worth half a zecchino. My daughter made the whole company laugh by asking me why I had not staked on twenty-seven at the second drawing for everyone. Clemente came and embraced me and admitted that he had staked on the twenty-seven too—ten scudi that it would be drawn second. He won seven hundred and fifty scudi; I congratulated him most sincerely. I then repeated my promise that I would keep them in Rome for the whole of Holy Week at my expense. Signora Veronica excused herself because of her school, and Clemente because of his shop. The party consisted of Ma-

*riuccia, with Giacomina and Guglielmina, and me; and
we left at daybreak on Sunday.*

*What pleasure to find myself adored by three such
creatures! These good moments in my life were the ones
which made me a hundred times happier than the bad
ones made me unhappy. I took them to my lodging, regardless of Margherita, who pouted when I ordered her
mother to put two beds for me in the room next to mine,
in which Ceruti had lodged. After ordering Margherita's
mother to prepare dinner and supper for five until the
day after Easter, I took them to St. Peter's in one of
Roland's carriages, and everywhere during the course of
the week. What calmed Margherita was my granting her
the favor of dining with us; and she could not object
when I told her I could not let her enter my room after
supper during all of that week. I left her to suppose that
it would be Signora Mariuccia who would come to sleep
with me. Seeing Giacomina, she did not find it hard to
guess that she was my daughter and that I must have
loved her mother ten years before. I let her suppose what
she pleased about Guglielmina. After supper Mariuccia
went to bed, and the two girls came to my room as they
had done in Frascati. I spent a very happy week, though
at great cost, for I spent more than four hundred zecchini
for fabrics, linen, and all sorts of jewelry, not forgetting
Signora Veronica, to whom Guglielmina took all the
presents I bought expressly for her.*

*It was on the night of Holy Thursday that I composed
the ode which I recited the next day at the meeting of the
Infecondi, where I saw Cardinal de Bernis and Cardinal
Giambattista Rezzonico,[12] who asked me to give him a
copy of my ode, which I recited by heart, shedding a
torrent of tears. All the Academicians wept. The only
way to draw tears is to shed them oneself; but one must
have grief depicted on a face which is able to arouse
emotion without making grimaces; I had such a face,*

*and the poetry gave me (as poetry still gives me today)
the essential nature of the subject treated. Cardinal de
Bernis, who knew my cast of mind, told me four days
later that he had never believed that I was so great an
actor. I swore to him that, at the moment, I had felt that
I was sincere, and, after thinking about it for a little, he
admitted that it was possible.*

*On the day after Easter I went back to Frascati with
Mariuccia and her daughter and Guglielmina, whose
despair rent my soul.*

*I dined, supped, and slept there for the last time, and
Signora Veronica showed a lively sense of my generosity
when Guglielmina gave her all the presents I had chosen
for her; but she greatly distressed me the next day when
I went to take leave of her an hour before my departure.
She took me aside to tell me that, seeing Guglielmina's
tears, she could not help concluding that I had made her
fall in love with me, and, after presenting a number of
very sad considerations for my reflection, she demanded
that I tell her on my word of honor if anything too serious had taken place between her and me. I assured her on
my word of honor that her tears could derive only from
a love born of gratitude, and she seemed to be satisfied.*

*Can one put a gentleman on his honor to reveal a secret
which honor itself forbids him to reveal? God knows what
I suffered at that cruel parting. All partings are heart-
breaking, and the last one always seems worse than
all those which have gone before; I should have died a
hundred times if God had not given me a well-tempered
soul, which easily comes to terms with the inevitable and
in a few days is calm. They who call this forgetting are
wrong. Forgetting comes from weakness; to calm oneself
by adopting another course comes from a strength which
may be reckoned among the virtues. As for Guglielmina,
she was fortunate. Four years later she became the wife
of a painter who is still distinguished today. It was
Clemente who gave me news of her whenever I grew*

curious enough to write to him. He became rich and seven or eight years later returned to Rome, where he entered into partnership with a grain merchant who married Giacomina; but the marriage was not happy. She was widowed at the age of twenty years, and she left Rome with a Count from Palermo who married her after the death of his wife.

When I left Venice in the year 1783 God ought to have sent me to Rome or Naples or Sicily or Parma, and in all likelihood my old age would have been happy. My Genius, which is always right, took me to Paris to save my brother Francesco, whom I found sunk in debt and on the verge of going to the Temple.[13] That he owes me his restoration is of no moment to me, but I congratulate myself on having accomplished it. If he were grateful to me, I should consider myself repaid; I prefer that he should bear the burden of his debt, which must weigh heavily on him from time to time. He deserves no greater punishment. Today, in the seventy-third year of my life,[14] I need only to live in peace and far from anyone who can suppose that he has rights over my moral freedom, for that supposition cannot but be accompanied by a kind of tyranny.

After my too lively stay in Frascati I spent six weeks in Rome enjoying the society of the Palazzo Santa Croce, frequenting my Academy, and without any new love affair. Margherita, who always made me laugh, was enough for me.

During this time Father Stratico, who is today Bishop of Lesina and who had introduced me to the beautiful Marchesa Chigi in Siena,[15] came to Rome to pass the examination for Maestro. This is the Doctor's degree of the Dominican monks. I had the pleasure of being present at the examination he had to take to be accepted as a theologian-at-large. The four examining theologians and the General of the Order[16] were present. The four monks, who are very strict, give the candidate the thorniest ques-

*tions in all theology; they think that they cannot appear
very learned in their General's eyes unless they embarrass the candidate, who, if he happens to be more learned
than they, must take great care to conceal the fact, for
they refuse him, and their decision is without appeal; and
my reader knows, I believe, what the science of theology
is. Being very curious about this ludicrous doctorate, at
which Stratico himself laughed in secret, I called on him
in the morning, expecting to find him with St. Thomas
in hand, conferring with a pack of friars;[17] but instead I
find him with a hand of cards, absorbed in a game of
piquet against another monk who was cursing Fortune.*

*"I thought," I say, "that I should find you deep in
study."*

He replies:

"Oportet studuisse ['One has to have studied']."

*I left him, assuring him that I should soon be present
at his trial, where I was looking forward to hearing the
famous Mamachi[18] argue. Oh, how I suffered! The candidate was not on an ordinay stool, but on a stool-of-peni-
tence like a condemned criminal. He had to sum up the
arguments in forma ("formal arguments") of his four
torturers, whose amusement it was to give their syllo-
gisms endless majors. I saw that they were all in the
wrong, for they were all absurd; but I congratulated
them on my not being allowed to speak. Without being a
theologian, I flattered myself that I should have annihi-
lated all of them with common sense; but I was mistaken:
common sense has no part at all in theology, and especially in speculative theology; and Stratico proved it to
me theologically the same day in a house to which he took
me to sup with him.*

*His brother, Professor of Mathematics at the Uni-
versity of Padua, arrived in Rome at this time, coming
from Naples with the young Cavaliere Morosini,[19] whose
tutor he was. He had broken a leg on one of the rides his
wild pupil made him take; he had come to Rome to finish*

curing it. The company of these two brothers, the Counts Stratico, both men of honor, learned, and without prejudices, was my delight until, upon their departure, I too left Rome, where I had greatly enjoyed myself but had spent too much. I went to Florence after taking leave of all my acquaintances and especially of the Cardinal, who still hoped that Louis XV would recall him to Versailles.[20]

Such is the fate of all men, who, after having been Ministers at a great Court, find themselves in disfavor and compelled to live elsewhere, whether with no official position or with some commission which puts them in dependence upon the Ministers who have succeeded them. There is no wealth, no sort of philosophy, no image of peace, of tranquillity, or of any other happiness which can console them; they languish, they sigh, and they live only to hope that they will still be recalled. Indeed, by comparison we find in history that monarchs who have abdicated the throne are more numerous than Ministers who have voluntarily renounced their ministry. This observation has more often made me wish to be a minister than to be a king; one must believe that being a minister has inconceivable charms; and I am curious about them, for I cannot clearly picture what they may be.

I left Rome at the beginning of June 1771,[21] *all alone in my carriage, with four post horses, well outfitted, in good health, and fully resolved to adopt a manner of life entirely different from the one I had so far pursued. Tired of the pleasures I had enjoyed for thirty years, yet glad that I had had them, I thought not of renouncing them altogether but of confining myself in future to entering into them lightly, forbidding myself any serious entanglements. In pursuit of this plan I was going to Florence without a single letter, determined to see no one and to devote myself entirely to study. Homer's* Iliad, *which since I had left London had delighted me for an hour or two each day in the original language, had made* me want to translate it into Italian stanzas;[22] it seemed to me that its Italian translators had falsified it, except for Salvini,[23] who was so dry that no one could read him. I had scholiasts, I knew the merits of Pope;[24] but I felt that in his notes he could have said much more. Florence was the city in which I intended to occupy myself with this, living there in retirement from the world.

Other circumstances urged me to decide on this course.

I thought I had grown old. Forty-six years seemed to me a great age. There were times when I found the pleasures of love less intense, less seductive than I had imagined them before the act, and for eight years already my potency had been diminishing little by little. I found that a long bout was not followed by the soundest of sleep, and that my appetite at table, which before then love had sharpened, became less when I was in love, just as it did when I had enjoyed. In addition, I found that I no longer interested the fair sex at first sight, I had to talk, rivals were preferred to me, I was made to feel that it was already a favor if I was secretly allowed to share with another man; but I could no longer expect that sacrifices would be made for me. Finally, it angered me when I saw some young blockhead take no offense at the eagerness I showed for the object of his love, and when the object herself, to do me a favor, tried to make it appear that I was of no account. When I heard someone say of me, "He's a man getting on in years," I admitted it, but it was a truth which annoyed me. All this, at the times when, being alone, I reflected seriously on myself, convinced me that I must think of a dignified retirement. I even felt that I was forced into it, for I saw that I was on the verge of having nothing left to live on after my exchequer was exhausted. All my friends whose purses were open to me were dead. Signor Barbaro, who had died that year of consumption, had been able to leave me in his will no more than six wretched zecchini a month for life; and Signor Dandolo,[25] my only remaining

*friend, could give me only six more, and he was twenty
years older than I. When I left Rome I had seven or eight
hundred Roman scudi and my jewelry in the way of
watches, snuffboxes, pretty rings of little value which did
me more harm than good, for they made people think me
rich, and ambition drove me to spend in a manner which
proved that they were not wrong. My knowledge of this
truth determined me to take the wise course of always
appearing in Florence simply dressed and with no show
of luxury. If I do that, I said to myself, when lack of
money forces me to sell my possessions no one will be the
wiser.*

*With this plan I got to Florence in less than two days,
stopping nowhere and going to lodge at an inn of no
reputation and sending my carriage to the post house,
since the innkeeper, whose name was Gian Battista Allegranti, had no place to put it. It was on the next day
that I went to have it put in a coach house.*

*Well enough lodged in a small room, finding the inn-
keeper modest and reasonable, and seeing only old and
ugly women, I thought I could live there very peacefully
and without any risk of making seductive acquaintances.
The next morning I dressed in black,[26] and, wearing my
sword, went to the Pitti Palace[27] to present myself to the
Archduke–Grand Duke. He was Leopold,[28] who died the
Emperor seven years ago. He gave audience to all who
presented themselves, I thought I should go to him directly without troubling to go to Count Rosenberg's[29]
first. Wanting to be left in peace in Tuscany, I thought
that to guard myself against the misfortunes which result
from the activities of spies and the natural suspicious-
ness of the police, I should present myself directly to
their master. So I went to the anteroom and I wrote
down my name after those of the others who were there
waiting to be granted an audience. A Marchese Pazzi[30]
who was one of them, and who had made my acquaintance in Rome at the house of a Marchesa[31]—I forget*

whether she was born a Frescobaldi of Florence or was
the widow of a Marchese of that name—approached me
with polite expressions of the pleasure it gave him to see
me again in his country. He told me that he had traveled
as far as Bologna with Signor XXX, who was returning
to England with a young Roman wife who would eclipse
all the beauties in London. He said that he mentioned
him because, during the time he spent in Florence, he
had talked about me a great deal, hoping to find me on
his return to Rome. I thanked him for giving me this
good news, since I was very much interested in the hand-
some couple's happiness.

I should have been sorry to find Armellina still in Flor-
ence, for, still loving her, I could not have seen her again
possessed by another except in the greatest bitterness of
soul.

My reader must have noticed that in the passage where
I mentioned her marriage to the generous and charming
Signor XXX, I did not dwell upon any of the circum-
stances which accompanied it. The reason is that I have
never had the strength to write well about something the
memory of which is painful to me. The intrigues of the
Marquise d'Aout, the tears of Armellina, who was in love
with the Florentine, and my word of honor which I had
given her to make her his wife when I demanded her final
favors on that humiliating condition both for her and
for me, were the powerful motives which forced me to
act against the interests of my heart. Repenting of my
promise, I found myself reduced to offering Armellina
my hand in the Superioress's presence, after I had made
her perfectly certain that I was not married. Armellina
refused my offer not in words but by tears; and one
sentence from the Marquise d'Aout crowned my abase-
ment. She asked me if I was in a position to give the ex-
cellent girl ten thousand Roman scudi.

This haughty question brought me back to reason, but
with the utmost grief in my soul. I then wrote to the

*Superioress and to Armellina herself that I recognized
how unjust I had been and I hoped that she would forgive me and lay my errors of judgment to the passion
which filled my mind, wishing her all possible happiness
with Signor XXX, who I admitted was a far better
match for her and far worthier of her than I. The only
favor I asked of her was to excuse me from being present
at her wedding, and she granted me the favor, despite
the insistence of the Marquise d'Aout, who, declaring all
amorous feelings to be trifles, claimed that men of intelligence should shake off their influence. The Princess of
Santa Croce was of the same opinion, but Cardinal de
Bernis took my part, for he was more the philosopher
than the Frenchman. The wedding was celebrated at the
Marquise's, and Marcuccio was present at it with his
wife, for Armellina had no other relatives in Rome.*

*It was with this grief that I went to Frascati, thinking
that it would increase my enthusiasm for my ode on the
Man-God; but my guardian Genius had prepared an entirely different kind of consolation for me.*

*Vice is not synonymous with crime, for one can be
vicious without being a criminal. Such I was all my life
long, and I even venture to say that I was often virtuous
in the act of vice; for it is true that every vice cannot
but be opposed to virtue, but it does not infringe on the
universal harmony. My vices have never burdened anyone but myself, except the cases in which I have seduced;
but seduction was never characteristic of me, for I have
never seduced except unconsciously, being seduced myself.*

*The professional seducer, who deliberately sets out to
accomplish it, is an abominable creature, inevitably the
enemy of the object on which he has designs. He is a true
criminal who, if he has the necessary qualities to seduce,
renders himself unworthy of them by abusing them to
make a woman wretched.*

CHAPTER VI

*La Denis. Medini. Zanovich. Zen. My enforced
departure and my arrival in Bologna. General
Albergati.*

IN A few words I asked the young Grand Duke[1] for
safe asylum so long as I should remain in his domains,
and, anticipating the questions which I foresaw, I told
him for what reason I could not return to Venice. I told
him that for the necessaries of life I needed no one, and
that I intended to spend my time in study. He replied
that, if my conduct was good, the laws of his country
were enough to assure me that I should enjoy all the
peace I needed, but that he was glad that I had presented
myself to him. He asked me what acquaintances I had in
Florence, and I replied that I had frequented several
distinguished houses ten years earlier, but that, wanting
to live in strict retirement, I was not thinking of renewing my acquaintance with anyone.

This was the entire conversation I had with the sovereign. It was all that I thought I need do to guard me from
any misfortunes. What had happened to me ten years before must have been forgotten, or else have no bearing,

for the old government[2] had nothing in common with the new. I went to a bookseller's shop, where I bought the books I needed, and where a man with the air of good breeding, seeing that I was concerned with Greek literature, addressed me and interested me. I told him that I was working on a translation of the *Iliad,* and, confidence breeding confidence, he told me that he was compiling an anthology of Greek epigrams,[3] which he wanted to publish translated into Latin and Italian verse. When I expressed my interest in it, he asked me where I was lodging, and I gave him my address and my name, then asked him for his, intending to make the first call. Having gone to see him the next day, I had the honor of a visit from him on the day after that; we showed each other our work, and, exchanging our views, we became friends, and we remained so until my departure from Florence, without ever having to eat or drink together or even to go walking in each other's company. An intimacy between two men who love letters often excludes all the pleasures which they can enjoy only by stealing the time for them from literature. This worthy Florentine gentleman was named (or is named if he is still alive) Averado de' Medici.[4]

At the end of the month I resolved to leave Gian Battista Allegranti's. I was comfortable there, I enjoyed all the solitude and all the quiet I needed to study Homer, but I could bear it no longer. His niece Maddalena,[5] who, though very young, was well developed, pretty, and cleverness itself, drove me to distraction when I saw her, when she wished me good morning, when she sometimes came into my room to ask me if I needed anything. Her presence, her graceful ways seduced me. It was my fear of her seduction which saved her from mine. A few years later the girl became a celebrated musician.

So I left her uncle's inn, taking two rooms in the house of a townsman who had an ugly wife and no nieces. Maddalena Allegranti became the leading actress

of all Europe and has always lived virtuously. She and
her husband are now in the service of the Elector of
Saxony.

In my new lodging I lived very peacefully for only
three weeks. Count Stratico arrived in Florence with the
Cavaliere Morosini,[6] his pupil, then eighteen years of
age. I could not but go to see him. The leg he had broken
had not yet regained its strength, he could not go out
with his pupil, who, having all the vices of youth, kept
him in continual fear of mishaps. He asked me to try to
gain his good will and even, if necessary, to become his
companion in his pleasures, so that he should not be left
to go alone where he might encounter evil and dangerous
company.

This interrupted my studies and played havoc with my
determination to live quietly; goodheartedness forced me
to take part in the young man's debauches. He was a
frenzied libertine who cared nothing for learning, good
society, or sensible people; riding until he galloped his
horse to death without any fear of dying himself, drinking all kinds of wines, never satisfied until he had drunk
away his reason, obtaining a brutish pleasure from loose
women, whom he often beat, were his only passions. He
had a local valet who was obliged by contract to supply
him every day with some girl or woman who was not
known as a public prostitute in the city of Florence.
During the two months he spent in Tuscany I saved his
life twenty times; I suffered under it, but my sense of
decency forced me not to abandon him; as for the expense, I had to pretend to look the other way, for he
always wanted to pay for everything, which often gave
rise to violent quarrels between us, for, since he was paying, he insisted that I must drink as much as he did and
keep up with him in the work of the flesh, either with the
same girl or with another; but in these two respects I
only half satisfied him. Even this did not happen until
we began going to see the opera in Lucca,[7] where he often

had two dancers go out with us, one of whom was of a caliber to please the most refined taste. The Cavaliere, who, as usual, had drunk too much, could do her only small justice; but I avenged her, and since she thought I was the sleeping young man's father, she told me that I ought to bring him up better.

After his departure, which took place when his tutor was entirely cured, I returned to my studies, but going every evening to sup at the dancer La Denis's,[8] who, after leaving the King of Prussia's service, and even the stage, had retired to Florence, where she is perhaps still living. She was about my age, but despite it she still inspired love. She did not look more than thirty, she had a childish charm which became her, the manners of good society, a gentle disposition, and she dressed very well. In addition she had a most comfortable apartment on the Piazza, above the best-known coffeehouse[9] in Florence, with a balcony where on hot nights one enjoyed a coolness which went to the soul. My reader may remember how I had become her lover in Berlin in 1764.[10] Now, meeting again in Florence, our old fires were rekindled.

The leaseholder of the house in which she lived was the Signora Bregonzi[11] whom I had met in Memel that same year, when I was on my way to Petersburg. La Bregonzi, who claimed that I had loved her twenty-five years before, often came up to see her tenant with the Marchese Capponi,[12] her former lover, a most agreeable and well-read man. Seeing that he enjoyed talking with me, I took the first step toward our becoming better acquainted by paying him a visit, which he returned, leaving a note because he had not found me at home. He introduced me to his family, he invited me to dinner, and it was the first day on which I dressed elegantly and appeared with my jewelry. At his house I made the acquaintance of Corilla's[13] famous lover, the Marchese Ginori,[14] who took me to a house in Florence where I could not escape my destiny. I fell in love with Signora XX,[15] a widow, still young, well read, rather well off, and acquainted with the manners of nations from having traveled and spent six months in Paris. This unhappy love made the last three months I spent in Florence a burden to me.

At this same time Count Medini arrived; it was the beginning of October, and, the Count having no money to pay his coachman, the latter had had him arrested. He had gone to lodge at an Irishman's who was poor though he had been a rogue all his life, and Medini wrote me begging me to come at once and deliver him from the constables who surrounded him in his own room and who wanted to take him to prison. He said that I did not need to pay, but only to stand surety for him, assuring me that I ran no risk, since he was certain that he would himself be able to pay what he owed in a few days.

The reader may remember the reasons I had for disliking the man, nevertheless I did not have the strength of mind not to go to his rescue, even resolved to stand surety for him as soon as he showed me that he would be able to pay within a few days. In any case, the amount, I thought, could not be large. I did not understand why the innkeeper himself did not do him the favor. But I saw and understood everything as soon as I entered his apartment.

He received me by running to me with open arms, begging me to forget all and help him out of his scrape. I saw three trunks, empty because all the clothes they contained were scattered about the room, his mistress, whom I knew and who had reasons not to like me, his sister, who was eleven or twelve years old, and his mother, who was cursing and swearing, calling Medini a scoundrel, and saying that she would go to the magistrate to protest, for it was not right that her dresses and her daughter's should be taken from her because of the debt he had incurred to his coachman. I at once asked the innkeeper why he did not stand surety when, having the persons and all their possessions in his house, he ran no risk. The

innkeeper replied that everything I saw there was not
enough to pay the coachman, and that he would no longer
keep the new arrivals in his house. Surprised that all I
saw there was not enough to cover the debt, I ask what it
came to, and I see an exorbitant sum signed by Medini
himself, who said nothing, leaving me to find out whatever I could. The amount came to two hundred and forty
Roman scudi; but it no longer surprised me when he told
me that the coachman had been in his employ for six
weeks, having taken him from Rome to Leghorn, then to
Pisa, then through the whole of Tuscany, paying his expenses everywhere. I told Medini that the coachman
could not accept me as surety for such a large sum, but
that even if he were fool enough to do so, I would never
consent to act in that capacity. Medini then told me to go
into another room with him, assuring me that he would
persuade me. Two constables wanted to go in too, giving
me as their reason that the debtor might escape by way
of the windows; after I assured them that I would not let
him leave they let us go in alone, and just then the coachman arrived and, coming to kiss my hand, said that if I
would stand surety for the Count he would release him
and would give me three months to pay. The coachman
was the same one who had driven me from Siena with the
English girl whom the French actor had seduced.[16]

Medini, a great talker, bold as brass, a liar, fertile in
schemes, and never despairing of anything, thought he
could persuade me by showing me a number of unsealed
letters which introduced him in high-flown terms to the
leading noble houses of Florence; I read them, but in
none of them did I find an order to give him money; he
told me that there was play in all these houses, and that,
if he dealt, he was sure to win immense sums.

Another resource which he showed me, and which he
kept in a large portfolio, was a quantity of notebooks in
which he had three quarters of Voltaire's *Henriade*,[17]
very well translated into Italian stanzas.[18] His stanzas

and his lines were equal to Tasso's. He expected to finish his fine poem in Florence and to present it to the Grand Duke; he was sure he would not only receive a munificent present but would become his favorite. I laughed to myself, for I knew that the Grand Duke only pretended to love literature. An Abate Fontana,[19] a man of some talent, amused him with natural history; for the rest, the sovereign never read anything and preferred bad prose to the most beautiful poetry. What he loved was women and money.

After spending two very wearisome hours with this unfortunate exemplar of great intelligence but poor judgment, and having thoroughly regretted that I had gone to see him, I told him in the fewest possible words that I could not stand surety for him, and I was making for the door, when he had the audacity to take me by the collar.

Despair reduces men to such extremes. Medini, in a blind fury, took me by the collar without having a pistol in his hand, without remembering that I was probably a better man than he, that I had drawn blood from him for the second time in Naples, and that the constables, the innkeeper, and the servants were in the next room; but I was not so cowardly as to call out, I put my two hands around his neck to strangle him, being six inches taller than he, which meant that since I was holding him away he could not do the same to me. He let go of me at once, whereupon I took him by the collar, asking him if he had gone mad; I opened the door, and the constables, of whom there were four, came in. I told the coachman that I would stand surety for nothing, and, just as I was making to leave for good and all, Medini sprang to the door, saying that I must not abandon him. Since I persisted in forcing my way out, the constables tried to lay hands on him; the ensuing struggle held my attention. Medini, unarmed and in a dressing gown, began bestowing buffets, blows, and kicks on the four cowards, though each of

them had a sword. This time it was I who, standing at the
door, prevented the Irishman from leaving to summon
help. The bloodstained Medini, for his nose was bleeding,
with his shirt and his dressing gown torn, did not stop
fighting the four henchmen until they let him alone. At
that moment I inwardly pitied the poor wretch, and I
esteemed him. In the silence which fell I asked the two
servants in livery who were there why they had not lifted
a finger to defend their master. One of them replied that
he owed them six months' wages, and the other was base
enough to say that he wanted to put him in prison on his
own account. The scene touched me. Medini was trying to
stanch his bleeding with cold water.

The coachman said quietly that if I did not vouch for
the Count he would consider it a warning from me to
have him put in prison.

"Give him two weeks' respite," I said, "and I will
undertake in writing that if he absconds during that time
I will pay you the entire amount."

After thinking for a moment the coachman said that
he was satisfied, but that he would not pay a copper of
the legal costs; after learning what the costs were, I
decided to pay them, laughing at the constables who demanded damages for the beating he had given them. His
servants then said that if I would not give them the same
guarantee they would have their master arrested, and
Medini told me to let them do as they pleased. After I
wrote everything necessary to satisfy the coachman and
paid the constables four or five scudi to leave, Medini said
that he had something more to say to me, but without
even answering I turned my back on him and went to dinner. Two hours later one of his two servants came to my
lodging to tell me that if I would promise him six zecchini he would come to warn me as soon as he saw signs
that his master intended to escape. I told him curtly that
I had no need of his services, for I was sure that the
Count would pay all his debts before the time ran out.

The next morning I informed the Count of the proposal
his lackey had made to me. He replied in a long letter
full of gratitude, appealing to my friendship to enable
him to honor his obligations; but I did not answer him.
His guardian angel sent someone to Florence to get him
out of his difficulty. He was Premislas Zanovich,[20] who
later became as famous as his brother,[21] who, after swin-
dling the merchants of Amsterdam, took the title of Prince
Scanderbeg. I will speak of him in the proper place. Both
of these great swindlers came to bad ends.

Premislas Zanovich was then at the flourishing age of
twenty-five years, the son of a gentleman who was a native
of Budua,[22] the last city in the former Venetian Dal-
matia on the border of Albania, now under the rule of
the Turks; it is the ancient Epirus.[23] A young man of
brilliant intelligence, after being brought up in Venice,
completing his studies there, frequenting the best society,
and acquiring a taste for the pleasures which one enjoys
in that beautiful capital, he could not make up his mind
to return to Budua with his father when the supreme
guardians of law and order saw fit to order him to return
to his native city, there peacefully to enjoy the great fortune he had made at cards in the capital, where he had
spent fifteen years. Premislas could not conceive of himself as a citizen of Budua. He would not have known what
to do there. He would have found nothing there but its
coarse Slavonic inhabitants—dull or ferocious, having no
more than the rudiments of reason, neither happy nor
unhappy, as insusceptible to pain as to pleasure, with
no knowledge of the arts or of letters, and indifferent to
all the events which interest Europe and of which they
hear only when some ship arrives from the east or the
west with news. So Premislas, and his even more talented
brother Stepan,[24] made up their minds to become adventurers, in perfect accord and always maintaining a
correspondence, one of them going to the north, the other
to the south of Europe, which they had determined to lay

under contribution by their cleverness, making dupes
wherever they could find victims ready to fall into the
snares they would spread for them.

Premislas, whom I knew only from having seen him
when he was a boy, and who even then had made himself
a reputation from having duped the Cavaliere Morosini
in Naples by persuading him to put up a surety of six
thousand ducati for him, arrived in Florence in a fine
carriage, with his mistress, two tall lackeys, and a valet
who served as his courier. He took splendid lodgings, he
engaged a fine coach, he took a box at the opera, he hired
a cook, he gave his beautiful mistress a lady-in-waiting,
and he went to the casino of the nobility, all alone, mag-
nificently dressed and bejeweled. Everyone knew that he
was Count Premislas Zanovich. The Florentines have
what they call a casino of the nobility; any foreigner is
free to go there without being introduced by anyone, but
so much the worse for him if he does not have at least the
outward appearance of belonging there, for the Florentines to the manner born leave him as solitary as if he
were not there; he does not dare to come back a second
time. The newspapers are there to be read, all kinds of
games of chance are played, one can indulge in gallantry
if one wishes to, and breakfasts and light refreshments
are to be had if one pays for them. The Florentine ladies
go there too.

Zanovich, all affability, did not wait to be spoken to
before speaking, he bowed to everyone in turn, congratulating himself on having come to see them, talked of
Naples, from which he had arrived, made comparisons
flattering to those present, cleverly gave the conversation
such a turn as to bring out his name, played for high
stakes, lost good-humoredly, paid after pretending that
it had slipped his mind, and pleased everyone. I learned
all this the next morning at La Denis's from the intelligent Marchese Capponi. He told me that he had been
asked if he knew me, and he had replied that when I left

Venice he was in school, but that he had often heard his
father speak of me with great esteem; the Cavaliere
Morosini was his intimate friend, and Count Medini, who
had been in Florence for a week and who was mentioned
to him, was also an acquaintance of his, and he spoke
well of him. Asked by the Marchese if I knew him, I replied in the affirmative, not considering myself obliged to
tell what I knew which could be harmful to him. La Denis
having expressed a wish to make his acquaintance, the
Cavaliere Puzzi[25] promised to present him to her.

This was done three or four days later. I saw a young
man whose command of the situation made him certain
to succeed in his undertakings. Though not handsome,
and arresting attention neither by his face nor his figure,
he had polished and easy manners, a talent for conversation, the ability to amuse, a gaiety which was infectious,
he never talked about himself, and, asked about his native
country, he gave a comic account of it, describing his
estate, half of which was within Turkish territory, as a
place which would make anyone who tried to live there
die of melancholy. As soon as he learned who I was he
complimented me in the highest terms, but without ever
lapsing into flattery. In short, I saw in the young man a
budding adventurer who, with discipline, could hope to
achieve greatness; but I thought his luxury would prevent him from practicing it. I thought I saw in him my
own portrait when I was fifteen years younger, and I
pitied him, for I doubted if he had my resources.

Zanovich came to see me. He told me offhandedly that
he had felt sorry for Medini and had paid all his debts. I
praised him for doing so, and I thanked him. This piece
of generosity led me to suppose that the two adventurers
had laid some plots together. I congratulated them, but
did not want to have any part in it. The next day I returned his call. I found him at table with his mistress,
whom I had known in Naples, and whom I should have
pretended not to know if she had not been the first to call

me Don Giacomo, saying that she was delighted to see me
again. I called her Donna Ippolita rather uncertainly,
and she replied that I was not mistaken and that, though
she had grown three inches taller, it was she. I had
supped with her at the Crocelle[26] with Lord Baltimore.
She was extremely pretty. Zanovich invited me to dinner
on the next day but one, and I declined; but Donna Ippolita persuaded me to accept, saying that I should find
company and that his cook had undertaken to do himself
honor.

Somewhat curious to see who would make up the company at this dinner, and wanting to show Zanovich that I
was not in a situation to become a drain on his purse, I
dressed in my best for the second time in Florence. I
found Medini with his mistress, two foreign ladies with
their gentlemen, and a very well-dressed and rather
handsome Venetian about thirty-five or forty years of
age, whom I should never have recognized if Zanovich
had not named him to me as Alvise Zen.[27] Since Zen was a
patrician family, I thought it my duty to ask him by
what titles I should address him, and he replied by those
which one gives to an old friend, though I could not remember him for he was then only ten years of age. He
said that he was the son of the Captain Zen whom I had
known when I was imprisoned in the Fortress of Sant'
Andrea.[28]

"That was twenty-eight years ago," I replied, "and I
recognize you, Signore, even though you had not had the
smallpox then."

I saw that he was annoyed to have to admit it, but it
was entirely his own fault, for he had not needed to tell
me that he had known me there and that the Adjutant
was his father. He was the son of the natural son of a
Venetian nobleman. As a boy he had been the greatest
scamp in the Fortress, a rascal of the first water. He had
just come from Madrid, where he had won a great deal of
money, keeping the bank at faro in the house of the Vene-

tian Ambassador, Marco Zen.[29] I was delighted to make
his acquaintance. During dinner I perceived that he had
neither culture nor the slightest education, he had neither
the manners nor the speech of a gentleman, but he would
not have given his talent for correcting the vagaries of
fortune in exchange for all that. Medini and Zanovich
were an entirely different sort. The two foreigners were
the victims on whom they had designs; but I was not
curious about the performance. When I saw the table
made ready for play, and a pile of gold which Zanovich
poured from a large purse, I took my leave.

This was the manner of my life during all of the seven
months I stayed in Florence. After that dinner, I did not
see Zanovich or Medini or Zen again, except by chance
in public places. But here is what happened to me about
the middle of December.

Lord Lincoln,[30] at the flourishing age of eighteen years,
fell in love with a Venetian dancer named La Lamberti.[31]
She was the daughter of the innkeeper in the Via del
Carro[32] and admired by everyone. At the opera the young
Englishman was seen to visit her every day in her dressing room, and all the connoisseurs observed with surprise
that he did not go to her lodging, where he was sure to
be well received not only as an Englishman but because
of his youth and his wealth, for he was, I believe, the
only son of the Duke of Newcastle.[33] The observation was
not lost on Zanovich. Within a few days he became an intimate friend of La Lamberti's, then he struck up an
acquaintance with Lord Lincoln, and took him to call on
the beauty as a man of the world takes his friend to see
his mistress.

In collusion with the rogue, La Lamberti was not chary
of her favors to the young Englishman. She had him to
supper every day with Zanovich and Zen, whom Zanovich
had brought to her, apparently needing him either to
make the bank at faro in visible gold, or to cheat, perhaps
not being skillful enough to do it himself. In the begin-

Carnival Ball in a Private House

The Sleeper

ning they let the young lord win a few hundred zecchini after supper, at which he got drunk, to wake the next morning in ecstasies to find himself as much in favor with Fortune as with Love and with the pleasant gentlemen who were his opponents at La Lamberti's, where he got drunk and nevertheless always won. But he stopped being in ecstasies when they finally cleaned him out. Zen won twelve thousand pounds sterling from him, and it was Zanovich who lent them to the young lord three or four hundred at a time, because he had promised his tutor that he would not play on his word. Zanovich, in luck, won from Zen all that His Lordship lost, and so it went on until they had done their worst to the Englishman and Zanovich reckoned up the amount that he had lent him. The Englishman arranged matters then and there. He promised to pay him three thousand guineas the next day, and he signed three bills of exchange for three thousand each, payable at intervals of two months and drawn on a banker in London. I learned the whole story of the transaction from His Lordship himself three months later in Bologna.

But at Florence his loss became the talk of the town the next day. The banker Sasso Sassi had paid Zanovich six thousand zecchini by His Lordship's order. Medini came to see me, furious that Zanovich had not cut him in, whereas I was congratulating myself on having had no part in the thing. But I was not a little surprised when three days later I saw in my room a man who, after asking my name and having heard me speak it, ordered me on behalf of the Grand Duke to leave Florence within three days and Tuscany within a week. I at once sent for the innkeeper to be a witness to the unjust order I was given.

It was December 28th; on exactly the same day three years before I had been ordered to leave Barcelona[34] within three days. I dress quickly and, since it was raining in torrents, I send for a carriage. I go to see the

Auditor,[35] to obtain some light on my banishment, which
seemed to me incomprehensible. The Auditor, being the
Chief of Police, must know everything. I go there, I find
the same man who had banished me from Florence eleven
years before because of the Russian Ivanov's forged bill
of exchange.[36] I ask him for what reason he had sent me
an order to leave, and he replies coldly that such is the
will of His Royal Highness.

"But," I replied, "His Royal Highness cannot so will
without a reason, and I think I have a right to ask what
it is."

"Then go and ask him, for I do not know it. The sovereign left yesterday for Pisa, and he will remain there
three days; you are free to go there."

"And if I go, will he pay for my journey?"

"That I do not know, but you will see if he seems inclined to do you the favor."

"I will not go to Pisa, I will simply write to him, if
you will promise to send my letter on to him."

"I will send it to him at once, for that is my duty."

"That is enough, you shall have it before noon, and
before daybreak tomorrow I will be in the Pope's dominions."

"There is no need for you to make such haste."

"There is the greatest need, for I could not sleep in a
country of despotism and violence where the law of nations is disregarded and where the sovereign breaks his
word to me. I shall write him all this."

I leave, and at the foot of the stairs I come upon Medini, who tells me that he is going to ask the Auditor why
he had sent him an order to leave. I reply with a laugh
that I have just asked him the same question, and that he
had told me to ask the reason of the Grand Duke, who
was in Pisa.

"Then you have been ordered to leave too? What have
you done?"

"Nothing."

"No more have I. We must go to Pisa."

"You may go there if it amuses you. For my part, I shall leave before nightfall."

I go home, and I at once send the innkeeper to the post house to inspect my carriage with a cartwright and to order four post horses to be ready for me at nightfall. After giving a few other little orders, I amused myself writing the Grand Duke this little letter, which I now translate word for word.

"Jupiter, Monseigneur, did not entrust you with the thunderbolt except on condition that you hurl it only at the guilty, and you are disobeying him by hurling it at my head. Seven months ago you promised me that I should enjoy perfect peace in your domains, provided that I did nothing to disturb the social order and would obey the laws; I have scrupulously kept that just condition; and consequently Your Royal Higness has broken your promise to me. I write to you, Monseigneur, only to let you know that I forgive you. In consequence of that forgiveness, I will complain to no one and will not accuse you of injustice either in writing or by word of mouth in any house in Bologna, where I shall be day after tomorrow. Indeed I should wish that I could forget a stain on my honor which is visited on me by your arbitrary will, were it not that I must remember it in order never again in my life to set foot on the soil of which God has made you the master. The Auditor has told me that I could go to speak to Your Royal Highness in Pisa; but I feared that my doing so would seem a piece of temerity to a prince who, according to common justice, must talk to men not after he condemns them but before. I am, etc. . . ."

After sealing my letter, I sent it to the Auditor, then I began packing.

Just as I was about to sit down at table, in comes Medini to inveigh against Zanovich and Zen. He complains that, whereas the misfortune which had befallen him was

entirely because of the twelve thousand guineas they had
won from the Englishman, they now refused him the mere
hundred zecchini without which he could not leave. He
told me that they had also received orders to leave, and
that they were all going to Pisa, and he said he was surprised that I was not going there too. Laughing at his surprise, I asked him to leave, since I had to pack. As I
expected, he thereupon asked me to lend him money; but
I refused him so curtly that he left without pressing the
matter.

After dinner I went to return some pieces from his
anthology to Signor de' Medici and to embrace La Denis,
who already knew everything and who could not conceive how the Grand Duke could confuse the innocent
with the guilty as he was doing. She told me that La
Lamberti the dancer had also been ordered to leave, together with a little hunchbacked Venetian Abate who
knew La Lamberti but who had never gone to supper
there. In short, the Grand Duke had made a clean sweep
of all the Venetians who were then in Florence.

On my way home I met Lord Lincoln's tutor, whom I
had known in Lausanne eleven years earlier.[37] I disdain-
fully told him what had happened to me because of his
pupil's having let himself be cleaned out. The worthy
Englishman told me that the Grand Duke had told the
young Lord not to pay the amount he had lost, and that
he had sent the Grand Duke word that not to pay would
be dishonorable, and the more so since the money he owed
was borrowed money, for he had never played on his
word. It was true. It was also true that the lender and
the gamester were in collusion, but His Lordship could
not be sure of that.

My leaving Florence cured me of a very unhappy love
which would have had disastrous consequences if I had
stayed there longer. I have spared my reader the sad
story of it, because it makes me sad every time I recall it.
The widow whom I loved, and to whom I had been weak

enough to declare myself, kept me tied to her triumphal chariot only to seize every opportunity to humiliate me; she despised me, and she wanted to convince me of it. I had persisted in continuing to see her, always thinking that I should succeed; but I saw, when forgetfulness had cured me, that I should have been wasting my time.

I left Florence poorer by about a hundred zecchini; I had run into no expense there, in short I had lived there like a wise man. I stopped at the first post house[38] in the Pope's dominions, and on the next to the last day of the year I arrived in Bologna, going to lodge at the "San Marco" inn.[39] I at once went to call on Count Marulli,[40] who was the Florentine Chargé d'Affaires, to beg him to write His Royal Highness that wherever I might be during the rest of my life I would praise his virtues.

He supposed I was not speaking as I thought, for he had received a letter informing him of the whole matter, but I told him that if he knew everything he would see that my obligations to His Royal Highness were vital. He assured me that he would write the Prince how I spoke of him.

On the first day of the year 1772 I went to present myself to Cardinal Branciforte;[41] he was the Legate. I had known him in Paris twenty years earlier when he was sent by Benedict XIV to convey the consecrated swaddling clothes to the newly born Duke of Burgundy. We had been together at Masonic lodges, and had enjoyed choice suppers with Don Francesco Sersale[42] and Count Ranucci[43] in company with pretty girls. The Cardinal was a wit and what is called a *bon vivant*.

"Oh, here you are!" he exclaimed as soon as he saw me; "I was expecting you."

"How could you have been expecting me, Monsignore, when nothing obliged me to choose Bologna in preference to some other city?"

"Bologna is better than any of them, and then too I was sure that you would think of me; but there is no need to tell people here the life we led when we were young. Count Marulli told me last evening that you pronounced the most flowery eulogy on the Grand Duke, and you are very right to do so. But speak to me in confidence, for nothing will go beyond this room. How many of you shared in the twelve thousand guineas?"

I thereupon told him the whole true story, ending by showing him the copy of the letter I had written the Grand Duke. He replied with a laugh that he was sorry I was innocent. When he learned that I was thinking of staying in Bologna for some months, he said that I could be sure of enjoying the greatest freedom there, and that as soon as the first gossip had died down he would give me proofs of his friendship.

After taking this precaution, I prepared to lead the same kind of life in Bologna as I had led in Florence. There is not a city in Italy in which one can live with greater freedom than in Bologna, where living is not expensive and where one can procure all the pleasures of life at little cost. In addition, the city is beautiful, and nearly all the streets are lined with arcades.[44] As for society, I did not trouble myself about it. I knew the Bolognese: the men of the nobility, ill-natured, proud, and violent; the rabble, the *birichini*[45] as they are called, even worse than the Neapolitan *lazzaroni;*[46] but the citizenry in general are decent people. All that, however, was of no concern to me. My plan was to devote myself to study, and to spend my time with few men of letters, whose acquaintance it is nowhere difficult to make. In Florence people are generally ignorant even of the Italian language, which is spoken well, but to be ignorant of its principles is as much as not to know it at all; and in Bologna everyone has some appreciation of letters. It is a university[47] at which there are three times as many professors as in all the others; but all with very small salaries; some have only fifty scudi a year; but they have many pupils and they live well. Printing is cheap there

should avoid England, for he could be sure that if he
went there he would die in prison. If he went there to
prove the prophet false, he did ill, for the alternative was
the cruel one of proving the prophecy true. He was a man
who had birth, education, and intelligence, but who,
being poor and loving luxury, could maintain himself
only by gaming, correcting the vagaries of Fortune or
incurring debts which, since he could not pay them,
always obliged him to decamp. Yet he lived in this fashion for seventy years, and he might still be alive if he
had heeded my advice. Eight years ago Count Tosio[52]
told me that Medini, in prison in London, said to him
that he would never have gone to England if I had not
made him that cruel prophecy. That may be so; however,
I shall never abstain from giving good advice to any poor
wretch whom I see on the verge of ruin. On the same
principle I told Cagliostro, twenty years ago in Venice,
when the ignorant scoundrel was calling himself Count
Pellegrini, that he should beware of setting foot in Rome.
If he had believed me he would not have died in the
Fortress of San Leo. The same sort of thing happened to
me thirty years ago, when a wise man told me to beware
of Spain; I went there nevertheless. And I came very
near to perishing there.

A week or so after I arrived in Bologna I was in the
shop of the bookseller Taruffi,[53] where I made the
acquaintance of a young Abate with a squint whom in a
quarter of an hour I found to be possessed of intelligence,
learning, and taste. He made me a present of two
pamphlets, the recent fruit of the genius of two young
professors at the University. He said that reading them
would make me laugh, and he was right. One of the pamphlets, which had been published the previous November,
undertook to prove that women must be forgiven all the
wrongs they did because they were the work of the womb,
which made them act despite themselves. The second
pamphlet was a critique of the first. The author claimed

that the uterus was indeed an animal, but that it had
no power over woman's reason, since anatomy had never
found the slightest channel of communication between
that organ, the matrix of the fetus, and the brain. I took
it into my head to print a diatribe against the two pamphlets. I wrote it in three days; I sent it to Signor
Dandolo in Venice to have five hundred copies of it
printed for me immediately, which I received in Bologna
and which I at once gave to a bookseller to sell on my account. The whole thing was done in two weeks; and at the
expense of the two witty young doctors I made some
thirty zecchini. The first of the two pamphlets was called
L'Utero pensante[54] ("The Thinking Uterus"); the
second, which criticized it, was in French and its title
was *La Force vitale*[55] ("The Vital Force)." Mine was
called *Lana Caprina*[56] ("Goat's Wool"). I made fun of
the authors of the dissertations, and I treated the subject
lightly, but by no means superficially. I had given it a
preface in French, but using only idioms of the Parisian
rabble, which made me unintelligible. The joke gained me
many close acquaintances among the young men of the
city. The squinting Abate, whose name was Zacchiroli,[57]
introduced me to his friend the Abate Severini,[58] who
in ten or twelve days became my friend too. He got me
out of the inn, making me rent two fine rooms in the
apartment of a retired *virtuosa* who was the widow of
the tenor Carlani,[59] and had me make an arrangement
at so much a month with a pastry cook for dinner and
supper, which he sent me at my lodging. For lodging,
food, and a servant I had to take, I did not spend as much
as ten zecchini a month. The Abate Severini was the cause
—and the very agreeable one—of my losing all interest in
study and leaving the *Iliad,* to return to it when the
fancy took me again.

The first thing he did was to introduce me to his
family, and in a few days I became the most intimate of
the friends of his household and the favorite of his sister,

who, aged thirty years and rather ugly, but intelligent enough, declared herself proud of her spinsterhood and railed at marriage. During Lent the Abate introduced me to the cream of the singers and dancers in Bologna, which is the nursery of the breed, and all these heroines of the stage are very amenable and to be had very cheaply when they are in their native city. Severini introduced me to a new one every week; and, like a true friend, he kept watch over my finances. Being very poor, he never spent anything for the parties which he arranged for me and at which he was always present; but without him everything would have cost me twice as much.

A Bolognese nobleman, the Marchese Albergati Capacelli[60] by name, was getting himself talked about at the time; he had opened his theater to the public, and himself displayed great talent as an actor; he had made himself famous by obtaining the annulment of his marriage to a very noble lady whom he could not bear, in order to marry a dancer by whom he already had two sons. Despite that, he had had his marriage to his first wife annulled on the ground of impotence, and he had brazenly proved it by means of the tribunal whose use is still the barbarous and absurd custom in the greater part of Italy. Four expert, equitable, and uncorrupted judges subjected the naked Marchese to every experiment calculated to show if he was capable of erection, and the worthy Marchese, resisting their utmost diligence, remained perfectly flaccid. The marriage was pronounced null and void on the ground of "conditional" impotence, for he had had bastards.

But why the tribunal if his potency or impotence was to be pronounced "conditional"? He had only to swear that he could not be a man with the Marchesa, and the Marchesa had only to confirm it, and the tribunal would have been seen to be supererogatory, for, even if the stimuli had had power to resuscitate the Marchese, he

could have said that he defied the Marchesa to apply
them to him and obtain the same result.

So, the thing having made me curious to know the
eccentric Marchese, I wrote Signor Dandolo to get me a
letter to present to him as soon as I learned that he was
back in Bologna, for at the time he was in Venice. A week
or ten days later Signor Dandolo sends me a letter addressed to the Bolognese Marchese and written by a
Venetian nobleman named Zaguri,[61] and he assures me
that this patrician Zaguri was his intimate friend. Reading the letter, which was closed but not sealed, I am
enchanted by its style; it was impossible to recommend
a person unknown to the recommender more courteously
or more ingeniously. I could not help writing Signor
Zaguri a letter of thanks in which I told him that from
that day I began to hope to be pardoned and to return to
Venice for no other reason than to make the acquaintance
of the noble patrician who had written such a fine letter
in my honor. Signor Zaguri wrote me in reply that he
considered my wish so flattering that he would at once
set about procuring my return to Venice. After two and
a half years of effort, and the help of others, he succeeded; but I shall speak of it when I come to that time.

Signor Albergati arrives in Bologna with his wife and
his children; Severini informs me of it, the next day I
go to his palace to send my letter in to him, and the porter tells me that His Excellency (for in Bologna they all
assume the "Excellency") had gone to his country
house,[62] where he would spend the whole of the spring.
Two or three days later I have post horses harnessed to
my carriage and I go to the gentleman's country house.
It was a charming building on a hill. Finding no one at
the door, I go upstairs and I enter a drawing room in
which I see a gentleman and a pretty lady, about to sit
down to dinner at a table to which the dishes had already
been brought and which was laid for only two. After

politely asking the gentleman if he was the person to whom the letter I had in my hand was addressed, and having heard him reply that he was, I give it to him. He reads the address, then he puts the letter in his pocket, saying that he will read it and thanking me for having taken the trouble to bring it to him. I instantly reply that it had been no trouble at all, but an honor, and that I begged him to do me that of reading the letter with which Signor Zaguri had honored me and for which I had asked because I wished to make myself known to him. At that the Marchese, with an air of smiling affability, told me that he never read letters when he was about to sit down at table, that he would read it after dinner, and that he would obey the orders which his friend Zaguri gave him.

This whole brief exchange having taken place standing, and everything having been said, I turn without bowing to him, I leave the room, I go downstairs, and I arrive still in time to keep the postilion from finishing unharnessing the horses. Promising him a double *mancia* ("tip"), I gaily tell him to take me to some village where, while waiting for his horses to eat their oats, I could eat something too. So saying, I get into my carriage, which was a very pretty and comfortable coupé. Just as the postilion was about to mount, a valet appears at the door and tells me that His Excellency asks me to come up. Silently pronouncing the stupid Marchese a very poor actor, I reach into my pocket, and I give him a card on which was my name and the place where I was lodging. I hand it to the valet, saying that it was what his master wanted. The valet goes upstairs with my card, and I tell the postilion to whip up.

In half an hour we stopped at a place where we refreshed ourselves, and then we went on to Bologna. The same day I informed Signor Zaguri of the incident, giving him all the details in a running narrative, and sending my letter to Signor Dandolo unsealed to convey to him. I ended my letter by asking the Venetian nobleman to write the Bolognese that, considering myself insulted, he must prepare to undergo all that my resentment would prompt me to do in accordance with the laws of honor.

I laughed a little the next day when, on my returning to my lodging to dine, my landlady handed me a card on which I read: "General the Marchese Albergati." She said that he had left it in person after learning that I was not at home.

I was very far from being satisfied; it was nothing but bravado. I awaited the result of the letter I had written Signor Zaguri in order to decide what sort of satisfaction I could demand. Just as I was studying the card which the ill-bred man had left for me, unable to conceive for what reason he assumed the title of General, in comes Severini, who tells me that three years earlier the King of Poland had accorded the Marchese the ribbon of the Order of St. Stanislas and the title of his Chamberlain;[63] Severini could not tell me if he was also a General in that monarch's service, but I instantly understood everything. According to the custom of the Polish Court, a Chamberlain had the title of Adjutant-General. So the Marchese called himself General. He was right, he was so, but General what? The adjective without the noun was used only to deceive readers, for the adjective by itself must seem the noun to all who did not know better. Delighted that I could avenge myself on my man by exposing his absurdity, I wrote a comic dialogue[64] and had it printed the next day. I made a present of it to the bookseller, and in three or four days he sold all the copies of it at a baiocco[65] apiece.

CHAPTER VII

The Dowager Electress of Saxony and Fari-
nelli. La Sclopitz. Nina. The midwife. La
Soavi. The Abate Bollini. La Viscioletta. The
seamstress. Sad pleasure of a revenge. Severini
goes to Naples. My departure. The Marchese
Mosca at Pesaro.

ANY WRITER who attacks a proud man by comico-
satirical compositions is almost sure to triumph, for the
laughers are at once on his side. In my dialogue I asked
if a Field Marshal could call himself simply a Marshal,
and a Lieutenant-Colonel a Colonel. I asked if a man who
preferred to the titles of nobility which birth confers
titles of honor bought for cash could be considered wise.
The Marchese thought it best to ignore my dialogue, and
the thing was over; but from then on the whole city never
called him anything but the General. I saw over the door
of his palace the arms of the Republic of Poland,[1] which
greatly amused Count Mischinski,[2] Ambassador from the
King of Poland to the Court of Berlin, who arrived in
Bologna at this time, coming from the baths at Pisa. I
persuaded him to leave a visiting card showing his title
at his door, and Albergati returned the courtesy, but for
once I saw no title of General on his card.

The Dowager Electress of Saxony[3] came to Bologna

soon afterward, and I paid my court to her. She had
come only to see the famous castrato Farinelli,[4] who,
after leaving the Court of Madrid a rich man, was living
quietly in that city. He gave her a magnificent collation,
and an air of his composition which he sang to his own
accompaniment on the harpsichord. The princess, who
was an enthusiastic musician, embraced Farinelli and
told him that now at last she could die content. Farinelli,
who was known as the Cavaliere Don Carlo Broschi, had
so to speak reigned in Spain. The Parmesan Queen,[5] the
wife of Philip V, had fomented intrigues which forced
Broschi to leave the Court after the disgrace of the Marquis of La Ensenada.[6] The Electress, looking at the
standing portrait of the Queen painted by Amigoni,[7]
praised her and spoke to the castrato about something
which must have taken place during the reign of Ferdinand VI.[8] In answer the musical hero, shedding tears
which he quickly wiped away, said that Queen Barbara[9]
was as good as Elizabeth of Parma was bad. When I saw
him in Bologna, Broschi might have been seventy years
of age. He was extremely rich, and in very good health;
despite that, he was unhappy because, having nothing to
do, he was bored, and he wept every time he remembered
Spain. Ambition is far more powerful than avarice. In
addition Farinelli was unhappy for another reason,
which was, I have been told, the cause of his death. He
had a nephew[10] who was to inherit all his wealth. He had
him marry a young lady of a noble Tuscan family,[11]
thinking thus to attain the happiness of seeing himself
the head of a family which, because of its wealth, would
easily be ennobled by the second generation at the latest,
and it might well have happened; but this was precisely
the cause of his unhappiness. Poor old Farinelli fell in
love with his nephew's wife, and, what is worse, became
jealous, and, what is still worse, hateful to his niece, who
could not imagine how an old animal of his species could
flatter himself that she would prefer him to her husband,

too, and though the Inquisition[48] exists, it is easy to deceive it.

On the fourth and fifth days of the year all the exiles from Florence arrived. La Lamberti stayed only one day and went on to Venice. Zanovich and Zen stayed five or six days, but apart, because they had quarreled over the division of the stolen money. Zanovich refused to make one of His Lordship's bills payable to Zen because he did not want to run the risk of becoming liable himself if the Englishman did not pay; he wanted to go to England, and he told Zen that he was free to go there too. They left for Milan without having made up their quarrel, the Milanese Government ordered them to leave, and I have never learned how they settled the matter between them; but I did learn that His Lordship's bills were punctually paid.

Medini had come to lodge at the inn in which I was staying, with his mistress, his little sister, his mother, and a servant, but still without money. He told me that the Grand Duke would give no one a hearing, that he had received another order to leave, so he had returned to Florence, where he had had to sell everything. He implored me to help him, but in vain. I never saw the man except in desperate straits for money, yet for all that never bringing himself to spend in moderation, and getting out of his scrapes *per fas et nefas* ("by fair means or foul"). The luck he had in Bologna was to find a Slavonian Franciscan friar named De Dominis[49] who was on his way to Rome to obtain a brief of laicization from the Pope. The friar fell in love with Medini's mistress, who made him pay very dearly, as was only right, for her favors. At the end of three weeks Medini left and went to Germany, where he printed his *Henriade*,[50] having found a good Maecenas in the Elector Palatine.[51] After that he wandered all over Europe for a dozen years, until at last he went to die in the prisons of London in the year 1788. I had always told him that he

who was a man like other men and to whom she owed her
affection by all human and divine laws. Farinelli, angry
with the young woman, who refused him concessions
which, after all, amounted to nothing, for they could not
have any serious consequences, had sent his nephew
traveling, and he kept his niece in his house as if in
prison, having taken away the diamonds he had given
her, and never going out so that he should never lose
sight of her. A eunuch in love with a woman who detests
him becomes a tiger.

Lord Lincoln[12] having come to Bologna with a letter
of recommendation to the Cardinal-Legate, he gave a
dinner for him and invited me to it. He had the pleasure
of convincing himself that I had never been with his
Lordship, and hence that the Grand Duke had committed
a crying injustice in banishing me. It was on that day
that I learned from his own lips how the snare had been
set for him, but he never told me that he had been
cheated. He assured me that it was he himself who had
wanted to stop playing. It is easy to cheat an Englishman; but it is very difficult to make him admit that he
has been cheated. The young Lord died of debauchery in
London three or four years later. At this same time I also
saw in Bologna the Englishman Aston, with the beautiful
Sclopis, sister of the charming Callimena.[13] La Sclopis
was by far the more beautiful. She had two small children with her, fathered by Aston and pretty as angels.
Charmed by all that I said to her about her sister, she
understood that I had loved her, and she told me she was
sure she would go to sing in Florence during the Carnival
of the year 1773. I found her in Venice in 1776, and I will
speak of her when I come to that time.[14]

La Nina, the fatal Nina Bergonzi,[15] who had made
Count Ricla lose his reason and who had been the cause
of all the misfortunes which had befallen me in Barcelona, had been in Bologna since the beginning of Lent.
She had rented a house, she had an open letter for a

banker who was ordered to supply her with all the money
for which she should ask; she had carriages, horses, and
many servants; and, having declared that she was with
child by the Captain-General of the Kingdom of Barcelona, she demanded that the good Bolognese pay her
the honors due to a queen who, for her convenience, had
come to be brought to bed in their city. She had a particular recommendation to the Cardinal-Legate, who
often went in the greatest incognito to visit her, and the
time of her lying-in drawing near, a confidential secretary of Count Ricla named Don Martino[16] had arrived
from Barcelona with a power of attorney from the Spanish madman who was the vixen's dupe authorizing him
to have the infant baptized and recognized as a natural
child of the Count's. Nina made a spectacle of her pregnancy. She showed herself at the theater and in the
public promenades with an enormously big belly, insisting on being supported on either side by the intrepid
Bolognese noblemen who paid her court and to whom
she often said that she would always receive them but
that they must be on their guard, for she did not answer
for the tolerance of her lover, who might have them
murdered; and she shamelessly told them what had happened to me in Barcelona, not knowing that I was in
Bologna. She expressed great surprise when Count Zini,[17]
who knew me, told her that I was there, and it was Count
Zini who, having found me at the evening promenade on
La Montagnola,[18] saw fit to approach me and learn from
my own lips the whole of the unhapppy story.

In my turn I saw fit to tell him that it was a fairy tale,
which Nina, whom I did not know, had invented for him,
wanting to see if he had the courage to expose his life
to a great risk in order to give her a great proof of his
love. I did not deny the fact to the Cardinal-Legate when
he told me the same story; I astonished him when I recounted all of the shameless vixen's extravagances to
him, and when I told him that she was her sister's

daughter; but I could not keep him from laughing when I told him that I did not believe she was with child.

"What possible reason," he said, "can you have for not believing she is with child? Nothing could be easier or more natural. She may not be with child by the Count, but she is with child, and even on the verge of being brought to bed. It cannot be untrue, for if she is with child she needs must lie in. Besides, I do not see what reason she can have had to pretend she is with child."

"Your Eminence does not know the woman's infamous character; she wants to make herself famous by dishonoring Count Ricla, who was a paragon of virtue until he met the monster."

Eight hours later, an hour after midnight, I hear a great noise in the street, I look out of my window, and I see a woman, naked to the waist, mounted astride an ass, followed by the executioner, who was whipping her, surrounded by constables, and followed by all the *birichini* of Bologna, who were enjoying the show and hooting incessantly. Just then Severini comes upstairs and tells me that the woman who was being treated in this fashion is the most celebrated midwife in Bologna, that her punishment was by order of the Cardinal-Archbishop,[19] that the reason for it was not yet known, but that it would be known very soon. It could only be for some great crime. He said that she was the midwife who two days earlier had delivered La Nina, who had given birth to a fine dead boy. Here is the story, exactly as it was known to the whole city the next day.

A poor woman went to complain to the Archbishop that the midwife Teresa, known as Teresaccia, had four or five days earlier led her astray by promising her twenty zecchini. She had persuaded her to sell her a fine boy whom she had borne two weeks earlier. The woman, who had not received the twenty zecchini, and who was in despair over having caused the death of her baby, demanded justice from the Archbishop, undertaking to prove that her son was the dead child whom Nina was said to have borne. The Archbishop ordered his chancellor to proceed at once and in the greatest secrecy to make all the investigations necessary to substantiate the allegation, and as soon as he was sure of the scandalous crime he had the midwife summarily sentenced and punished, in accordance with the Valerian law,[20] *Punire et deinde scribere* ("First punish, then write"). A week later Don Martino left for Barcelona, but the shameless Nina stuck to her guns, even ordering her servants' red cockades[21] made twice as big, and having the gall to tell those who called on her that Spain would avenge her for the calumny by which the Cardinal-Archbishop had dishonored her; and, to play her bad role well, she remained in Bologna for six weeks after her pretended lying-in; but the Cardinal-Legate, who felt ashamed to have protected her, secretly took every step to force her to leave. However, Count Ricla settled a considerable annual income on her, on condition that she never again dare appear in his presence in Barcelona. Some months later he was summoned to the Court, to assume the post of Minister of War, and a year later he died.[22] Nina died two years after him, in poverty and of the pox. Her sister herself told me in Venice the whole wretched story of her last two years, which would sadden my reader and which I spare him.

The infamous midwife did not lack protectors. A pamphlet came out, printed no one knew where, in which the unknown author proved that the Cardinal-Archbishop should be disciplined for having sentenced a citizen to the most harrowing of punishments, in contravention of all established legal procedures. His conclusion was that the midwife was unjustly punished even though she was guilty, and so in her turn she could appeal to Rome, demanding the fullest compensation from the Archbishop.

The Archbishop circulated a reply through Bologna, in which he said that the midwife, whom he had punished only by whipping, would have paid the extreme penalty three times if the honor of three illustrious Bolognese families had not prevented him from publishing her crimes, all attested by official documents preserved in his chancellery. They concerned forced abortions, from which the guilty mothers had died, living children substituted for infants stillborn, and a boy substituted for a girl, the said boy being now unjustly in possession of the family's entire estate. This reply silenced all the infamous creature's protectors, for several young noblemen whose mothers had been attended in childbed by the guilty midwife feared the disclosure of secrets which would have proved them bastards.

During this time I saw the dancer La Marcucci,[23] who had been banished from Spain a little time before I left for the same reason which had brought about the banishment of La Pelliccia.[24] The latter had gone to settle in Rome, La Marcucci went to live in opulence in her native Lucca.

The Bolognese dancer Soavi,[25] whom I had known in Parma when I was living there happily with Henriette, then in Paris, where she was dancing at the Opéra and being kept by a Russian nobleman, then in Venice as the mistress Signor Marcello,[26] came to settle in Bologna at this time with her eleven-year-old daughter, a love-child, whom she had had by Monsieur de Marigni,[27] Musketeer. The girl, whom she had named Adelaide,[28] was a perfect beauty, and to beauty she added all the graces, the sweetness, and the talents which the choicest education can confer. La Soavi came to Bologna, where, finding her husband [29] whom she had not seen for fifteen years, she introduced this perfect treasure to him.

"She is your daughter," she said.

"She is pretty, my dear wife, but she cannot be mine."

"She is yours, you silly, as soon as I give her to you. Let me tell you that she has an income of two thousand scudi, and that I shall be her only cashier until the time comes when I marry her to a dancer, for I want her to learn the whole art of the dance and to shine on the stage. On holidays you shall take her to the promenade.''

''And if I am asked who she is?''

''You will say she is your daughter, and that you are sure of it because the person who gave her to you is your own wife.''

''I don't understand that.''

''Because, my dear friend, having never traveled, you know nothing.''

Having been present at this dialogue, which made me laugh heartily, I now amuse myself by writing it. Enchanted to see so rare a jewel, I at once offered my services to increase her talents; but her mother replied that she was afraid I would give her too many. Adelaide had become the wonder of Bologna. A year after my departure Count Du Barry,[30] brother-in-law of the famous Madame Du Barry, the last mistress of the last King of France,[31] now become infamous, passing through Bologna fell so in love with Adelaide that her mother, fearing that he would carry her off, sent her into hiding. Du Barry wanted to give her a hundred thousand écus for her. The mother refused them. Five years later I saw her dance in Venice. When I went to congratulate her, the charming Adelaide found an opportunity to tell me that her mother, who had brought her into the world, also wanted to send her out of it, for she felt that the profession of a dancer was killing her. And in fact she lasted only six or seven years more. All her money coming from an annuity, her mother was left in poverty; she would have lost nothing if she had invested her capital in an annuity with a reversion to her survivor on her death.

At this time I saw in Bologna the famous Afflisio,[32] who, having been dismissed from the Imperial service, had turned opera impresario. Going steadily from bad to worse, five or six years later he was guilty of forgeries for which he was sentenced to the galleys, where he died six or seven years ago.

In Bologna I was struck by seeing another man descended from a great family and born to be rich. He was Count Filomarino.[33] I found him destitute and crippled in every limb by venereal disease. I often went to see him, both to leave him a few paoli for food and to study the human heart in the remarks he made to me with his malevolent tongue, the only one of his members of which the pestilential disease had left him the use. I always found him the same scoundrel and slanderer, and angry to have been reduced to a state which prevented him from going to Naples to massacre his relatives, all decent people, but according to him the basest of mortals.

The dancer Sabbatini,[34] having returned to Bologna rich enough to rest on her laurels, gave all her money to the Professor of Anatomy and became his wife. I found her with her sister, who had no talent and was not rich, but who had prepossessing ways. I noticed an Abate whose modesty seemed to me more unusual than his pretty face, who attracted the sister's entire attention; he seemed to respond to it only from gratitude. When I addressed him on I forget what subject, he replied very sensibly, but with the tone of uncertainty which always pleases. Having taken leave of the company at the same time, we walked away together at random, and, merely from politeness, we told each other where we were from and what small concerns we had in Bologna. We parted, promising to call on each other.

Between twenty-four and twenty-six years of age, he had nothing of the Abate except the dress. He was the only son of a noble family of Novara,[35] who were not rich. With his small income, he lived in Bologna more comfortably than in Novara, where living was dearer, and where everything was a burden to him; his parents interfered with him, friendships had no substance, and ignorance was general. He could not bear being there, he seemed not to be free, though, having no decided inclinations, he made almost no use of what a man of strong passions calls freedom. The Abate Bollini (such was his name) was a man of peaceable disposition who loved nothing but quiet; other things he enjoyed, but they were not of great moment to him. He liked men of letters better than letters; he was satisfied not to be thought stupid, not to be set down as ignorant by the learned men he sometimes frequented because he did nothing but listen to them. He was sober by nature, a good Christian by education, not at all a freethinker, for he never reasoned about religion; nothing shocked him; rather kindly than inclined to criticism, which is almost always malevolent, he seldom praised, but he never blamed. To womankind he was almost indifferent. He avoided ugly women and those who tried to dazzle by their wit; those who fell in love with him and made advances, he did not leave to languish; as soon as he found some merit in them he acceded to their wishes from gratitude, never from love, having, in any case, so little temperament that he thought women apt rather to diminish the happiness of life than to increase it.

This last aspect of his character was the one which interested me, and so much so that, after we had been acquainted for two or three weeks, I made bold to ask him how he could reconcile it with his obvious attachment to Signorina Brigitta Sabbatini. He went to sup with her every day, for she did not lodge with her sister, and she came to breakfast with him every morning. I kept seeing her there, for she would arrive while I was there myself. She always looked content, and her behavior was unexceptionable, but I saw love in her eyes and in her every movement. In the Abate I found only the extreme complaisance which is never without a certain constraint, which, for all the Abate's politeness, did not escape me. She was at least ten years older than he, and she treated me in the most obliging manner possible. She did not

want to make me fall in love with her, but to convince
me that the Abate was happy in the possession of her
heart and that she well deserved the most perfect return.

So when, in the state of sincerity which a bottle of good
wine after dinner inspires between two friends, I questioned the Abate Bollini about the nature and the quality
of his connection with Brigitta, he smiled, he sighed, he
blushed, he looked down, and he told me that the connection was the misfortune of his life.

"The misfortune of your life? Does she make you sigh
in vain? You must recover your happiness by leaving
her."

"I cannot sigh in vain, for I am not in love with her.
On the contrary, it is she who, declaring that she is in
love with me, and constantly giving me the most convincing proofs of it, is threatening my freedom. She
wants me to marry her, I promised her I would from a
feeling of pity, and she is in a hurry; she torments me
every evening, she urges me, she cries, she demands that
I keep a promise which I made her only to calm her despair, and she rends my soul every day by saying that I
am deceiving her. You cannot but see all the misery of
my situation."

"Have you contracted obligations to her?"

"None at all. She is poor, she has only thirty baiocchi
a day, which her sister allows her and which she will no
longer allow her after she marries."

"Perhaps you have given her a child."

"I have been very careful not to. She loathes my precautions. She claims they are clear proofs that I am not
thinking of marrying her, and at that, not knowing what
to say, I say nothing or beat around the bush."

"But you mean to marry her one day or another."

"I feel, my dear friend, that I shall never in my life
bring myself to it. The marriage would make me at least
four times poorer, and I should make a laughingstock of
myself in Novara if I married her and brought her there,

for, though she is respectable, not ugly, and has a sufficiently good manner, she is not a woman to be my wife,
for she has neither wealth nor birth, and in Novara at
least the first is demanded.''

''As a man of honor even more than as a man of good
sense, you must break it off, you must leave her today
rather than tomorrow.''

''I see that, and since I can only do it by moral force,
I tell you I have not enough of that to do it. If I did not
go to sup with her this evening she would instantly come
to my lodging to find out what has happened to me. You
can understand that I can neither have her turned away
from my door nor send her away myself.''

''That I see, but you must see too that you cannot live
in this state of turmoil. You must come to a decision, you
must cut this knot with Alexander's sword.[36] You must
say nothing to her, and go to live in some other city,
where she will not be fool enough, I imagine, to go looking for you.''

''That would be the best solution, but running away
is very difficult.''

''Difficult? You are laughing at me. Do as I tell you,
and I will arrange for you to go as easily as you please.
She will not know you are gone until, not seeing you at
supper, she will hurry to your lodging and not find you.''

''I will do whatever you tell me, and you will be ren-
dering me a service which I will never forget. Her grief
will drive her mad.''

''Come now! I begin by forbidding you to think of her
grief. That is all you need to do; leave everything else to
me. Do you want to go tomorrow? Have you debts? Do
you need money?''

''I have enough money, and I have no debts; but the
thought of leaving tomorrow makes me laugh. I need at
least three days. I have to get my letters from the post
tomorrow, and I have to write home to say where I will
be.''

"I will see to getting your letters from the post, and to sending them to you where I send you, which you will know when you are setting off. Trust in me. I will send you where you will be very comfortable. The only preparation you have to make is to leave your trunk with your landlord, ordering him to deliver it to no one but me."

"I will see to that. So you want me to leave without my trunk, and you won't tell me today where I shall be going. It's odd. But I'll do it."

"Don't fail to come to dine with me on all these three days, and above all tell no one that you are leaving."

He had become radiant. I embraced him, thanking him for having confided in me; I thought he had become a different man on the instant.

Congratulating myself on having done this work of charity, and laughing at the fury which poor Brigitta would vent on me after her lover's flight, I wrote Signor Dandolo[37] that in five or six days he would see a Novarese Abate who would give him a letter from me; I asked him to find him a decent room, with board, but at the lowest price possible, for, though a nobleman and well mannered, he was not rich. I wrote the other letter which the Abate would deliver to him personally. The next day the Abate told me that Brigitta was very far from guessing his intention, for she had found him most amorous. She had all of his linen, but he hoped to get the greater part of it back on some pretext.

On the day set for his departure he came to my lodging at the hour I had appointed the previous day, bringing in a night bag whatever he might need during the four days he would be without his trunk. I took him to Modena by post, and, after we had dined, I gave him my letter addressed to Signor Dandolo, to whom I promised him I would send his trunk the next day. He was most agreeably surprised when he learned that he was to stay in Venice, which he very much wanted to see, and when I assured him that the gentleman to whom I was sending him would arrange for him to live as he had been living in Bologna. After seeing him leave for Finale,[38] I returned to Bologna, where I at once obtained the Abate's trunk from his landlord, having it taken to the post addressed to Signor Dandolo in Venice.

The next day, as I expected, I saw before me the poor abandoned Brigitta dissolved in tears. It was the moment to treat her with pity. I should have been cruel if I had pretended not to know the cause of her despair. I preached her a very long sermon intended to persuade her that, so far as she was concerned, I could not but feel sorry for her, but that I could not abandon my friend, who was on the verge of ruining himself by marrying her. She fell on her knees before me at the end of my discourse, begging me to make him come back, promising that she would say no more to him of marriage, and to calm her I said that I would try to persuade him to do so. I told her that he had gone to live in Venice, and, as was to be expected, she did not believe me. There are occasions when a man who is sure he will not be believed should tell the truth. It is a kind of lie which cannot but be approved by the strictest moralists. Twenty-seven months later I saw my dear Abate Bollini in my native city. I shall speak of him when I come to that time.

After my friend's departure I made the acquaintance of the beautiful Viscioletta,[39] and I fell so much in love with her that, not wanting to take the long way round, I had to resolve to buy the enjoyment of her. Try as I would, women no longer fell in love with me; I had to make up my mind to renounce love, or to submit to paying for it, and nature forced me to accept the latter course, which love of life finally makes me reject today. The sad victory I have won obliges me, at the end of my career, to forgive all my successors and to laugh at all those who ask me for advice, for I see beforehand that most of them have no intention of following it. This foresight results in my giving it to them with more pleasure than I should feel if I were sure they would follow it, for man is an animal who can only be taught by cruel experience. Because of this law, humanity will always exist in disorder and ignorance, for wise men make up at most a hundredth part of it.

La Viscioletta, whom I went to see every day, and to whom I had been introduced by the Quaranta Davia,[40] who was reputed to be a little mad, treated me as the Florentine widow had done; but the widow demanded a respect which I did not think I owed to La Viscioletta, who was a professional courtesan under the guise of a *virtuosa*. In three weeks I had obtained nothing, and I was laughingly repulsed when I tried to steal anything more. Her secret lover was Monsignor Buoncompagni,[41] the Vice-Legate. The whole city knew it, despite which he visited her in secret, for his position did not allow him to court her publicly. La Viscioletta herself made no mystery of it.

At this same time I put up my coupé for sale. I needed money, and I preferred selling my carriage to selling some other possession which I liked better. I set the price of it at three hundred and fifty Roman scudi. The proprietor of the stable where it was came to tell me that the Vice-Legate offered me three hundred scudi for it; I took real pleasure in thwarting the wish of a prelate who possessed the object of my vain desires. I replied that I did not care to haggle and that I had already announced the price.

Having gone to the stable at noon to make certain that my carriage was in good condition, I found there the Vice-Legate, who knew me from having seen me at the Cardinal's and who must have known very well that I called on his beauty. He said to me in an insolent tone that my carriage was not worth more than three hundred scudi, that he knew more about it than I did, and that I ought to seize the opportunity to get rid of it, because it was too fine for me.

The originality of these expressions made it necessary for me to be silent, for I feared that too acid a reply might anger him. I left him there, saying that I would not lower the price by a copper.

The next day La Viscioletta wrote me that my giving my carriage to the Vice-Legate at the price he had offered would be doing her a great favor, for she was sure he would make her a present of it. I replied that I would go to speak with her that afternoon, and that it would depend on her to persuade me to do whatever she wanted. I went there, and after a short but forceful conversation, she surrendered to me. I wrote her a note in which I sold her my carriage for the sum of three hundred Roman scudi. She had the carriage the next day, and I the money and the pleasure of having given the prelate good reason to guess that I had found a way to avenge myself for his stupid pride.

About this time Severini, who was unemployed, managed to secure a place as tutor to a young nobleman of an illustrious Neapolitan family, and he left Bologna as soon as he received money for the journey.

After my friend left, I began to think of leaving that beautiful city too. Signor Zaguri, who had maintained an interesting correspondence with me from the time of the affair of the Marchese Albergati, thought of obtaining permission for me to return to my native country by joining with Signor Dandolo, who asked nothing better. He told me that to obtain a pardon I should go to live as near as I could to the Venetian State, to make it easy for the Tribunal of the State Inquisitors to observe my good behavior. Signor Zulian,[42] brother of the Duchess of Fiano,[43] who also wanted to see me back in Venice, was of the same opinion and promised to use all his influence in favor of the plan.

So, determined to change my place of refuge, and having to choose one near the borders of the Republic, I did not care for either Mantua or Ferrara. I decided on

Trieste, where Signor Zaguri told me he had an intimate friend to whom he would recommend me. But since I could not go to Trieste by land without passing through the State of Venice, I thought of going there by sea. I chose Ancona, from which ships left for Trieste every day. Having to pass through Pesaro, I asked for a letter to someone who could introduce me to the Marchese Mosca,[44] a man of letters whose acquaintance I wanted to make, and Signor Zaguri procured one for me himself. The Marchese had just got himself much talked about because of a treatise on almsgiving which he had published and which the Roman Curia had caused to be put on the Index. Both devout and learned, he was imbued with the doctrine of St. Augustine, which, carried to the extreme, is that of the so-called Jansenists.[45]

I left Bologna with regret, for I had spent eight delicious months there. On the next day but one I arrived in Pesaro alone, in perfect health, and reasonably well provided for.

Having sent my letter in to the Marchese, I saw him at my lodging the same day, delighted with the letter I had brought him. He said that his house would always be open to me, and that he would leave me in his wife the Marchesa's hands to be introduced to all the nobility of the city and shown everything worth seeing there. He ended his short visit by inviting me to dine at his house the next day with his whole family, where I should, he said, find myself the only stranger; but that did not prevent him from inviting me to spend the morning in his library, where we would drink a cup of chocolate together. I went there, and I had the pleasure of seeing an immense collection of scholiasts on all the known Latin poets from even before Ennius[46] down to the twelfth century. He had had all their productions carefully and accurately printed, in his house and at his expense, in four large folio volumes; but the edition was not beautiful, and I ventured to tell him so. He admitted it. This want of beauty, which had saved him twenty thousand scudi, had prevented him from gaining fifty thousand. He presented me with a copy of it, which he sent to my inn together with a large folio the title of which was *Marmora Pisaurentia*,[47] and which I did not have time to examine. I should have learned everything about the town of Pesaro.

The great pleasure I had was at table, where I sat next to his wife, in whom I discovered a great deal of merit, and opposite to his five children, three girls and two boys, all pretty and well brought up. They interested me infinitely, yet I can give my readers no account of them. I never inquired what became of them.

The Marchesa Mosca was the perfect pattern of a woman of the world, and her husband cared for nothing but literature; hence they were not in agreement, and the harmony of the household suffered; but a stranger was not aware of it. If I had not been told as much, I should not have known it. "All families," a wise man said to me fifty years ago, "are privately at odds over some comedy which mars the peace of the household. It is the part of the head of the family, in his prudence, to see that the comedy does not become public, for one must not give occasion for laughter and for the malicious comments and catcalls of the public, which is always spiteful and ignorant." Signora Mosca-Barzi devoted her entire attention to me during all the five days I spent in Pesaro. She took me in her carriage to see all the country estates, and in the evening she presented me at all the entertainments of the nobility.

The Marchese Mosca might then have been fifty years of age. Cold by nature, his only passion was study and his morals were pure. He had founded an academy, of which he had reserved the presidency to himself. His device was a fly, in allusion to his family name of *Mosca,* with the two words *deme ce* ("take away c"). Removing the letter *c, Musca* became *Musa*.[48] The worthy noble-

man's one fault was what the monks considered his finest
quality. He was too much a Christian. This "too much"
of religion could not but make him go beyond the bounds
where *nequit consistere rectum* ("what is fitting cannot
exist").[49] But is there less harm in going beyond than in
falling short? That is a question on which I will never
pronounce. Horace said: *Nulla est mihi religio* ("I have
no religion"),[50] and he began an ode in which he condemns the philosophy which keeps him from worshiping
the gods.[51] Every "too much" is bad.

I left Pesaro enchanted by the fine company I had seen
there, and sorry not to have met the Marchese's brother,[52]
whom everyone praised to me.

CHAPTER VIII

I take a traveling companion in the person of a Jew from Ancona named Mordecai, who persuades me to lodge in his house. I fall in love with his daughter Leah. After a stay of six weeks, I go to Trieste.

I DID not examine the Marchese Mosca-Barzi's collection of all the Latin poets until I was at leisure in Ancona. I found neither the *Priapeia*[1] nor the *Fescennina*[2] nor several other fragments of the ancient poets which exist in manuscript in several libraries. It was a work which showed that the man who had produced it loved literature but not that he was learned in it, for all that he had done himself was to arrange the authors' works in chronological order. I should have liked to find it supplied with notes and often with glosses. In addition, as a product of the printing press it was undistinguished, the type was ugly, the margins scant, the paper poor, and there were too many typographical errors, a fault which is rightly held to be unforgivable. So the work had little success; and, the Marchese not being rich, it was one of the reasons for the couple's lack of harmony.

What showed me the quality of the Marchese's learning, intelligence, and judgment was reading his treatise

on almsgiving and, even more, his apology.[3] I saw that all
that he had said must have given offense in Rome, and
that with his exquisite judgment he should have foreseen
it. The Marchese Mosca was right, but in Rome only those
are right whom Rome declares to be so, and she does that
only of those whose opinions are not at variance with
the abuses which she has made customary practice. The
Marchese's treatise was full of erudition, and still more
so his apology, which must have done him more harm
than the treatise. He was a rigorist, and though he leaned
toward Jansenism, he often refuted St. Augustine. He
absolutely denied that the fixed penalty for sins could be
made good by almsgiving; and he accepted as alone meri-
torious the alms given in accordance with the letter of the
Gospel precept: "Let not thy left hand know what thy
right hand doeth."[4] In sum, he laid it down that giving
alms was a sin unless it was done in the greatest secrecy,
for otherwise vanity was bound to enter in.

Wanting to go to Trieste, I ought to have seized the
opportunity to cross the Gulf[5] by taking ship at Pesaro
on a tartan[6] which was leaving that very day and which,
with the wind blowing as it was, would have landed me
there in twelve hours. I ought to have gone there, for,
aside from my having nothing to do in Ancona, I was
making the journey a hundred miles longer; but I had
said that I would go to Ancona, and for that reason alone
I thought I ought to go there; a strong tincture of superstition was always characteristic of me, and it is clear to
me today that it had an influence on all the strange vicissitudes of my life.

Perfectly understanding what it was that Socrates
called his "Demon,"[7] which seldom prompted him to
take some decisive action and very often prevented him
from making up his mind to it, I easily thought I had
the same Genius, he having chosen to call his Genius his
"Demon." Sure that this Genius could only be good and
bent on my best welfare, I turned to him every time I

was in doubt how to choose because I had no compelling reason. I did what he wanted, without asking him the reason for it, when a secret voice told me to abstain from an act toward which I felt inclined. The secret voice could only be the action of my demon. I have paid him this tribute countless times in my life, and I often inwardly complained of him because he very seldom prompted me to do something which, having consulted my reason, I was determined not to do. Following this course, I have more often had cause to congratulate myself on having laughed at my reason than on having obeyed it. But that has neither humiliated me nor kept me from always and everywhere reasoning to the best of my ability.

At Sinigaglia, three posts before Ancona, just as I was about to go to bed, my coachman comes to ask me if I will let him take a Jew in the carriage who also wanted to go to Ancona. I coldly reply that I want no one, least of all a Jew. The coachman leaves, and I instantly feel that I ought to take the Jew with me, despite the reasonable repugnance which had made me say I did not want him. So I call the coachman back, and I say that I am willing. He then tells me that I must prepare to leave earlier than usual, for, it being Friday, the Jew could travel only until sunset. I reply that I have no intention of putting myself out, and that it is for him to make his horses go faster.

The next morning in the carriage the Jew, who looked not unprepossessing, asked me why I did not like Jews.

"Because," I said, "your religion makes it your duty to be our enemies. You think it your duty to cheat us. You do not consider us your brothers. You set no limit to your usury when, needing money, we borrow it from you. In short, you hate us."

"Signore," he replied, "you are mistaken. Come to our assembly with me this evening, and you will hear us

praying together for all Christians, beginning with our
master the Pope.''

At that I could not but burst out laughing, for it was
true; however, I told him that what prayed must be the
heart, not the mouth, and I threatened to throw him out
of the carriage if he would not admit that the Jews would
certainly not pray for Christians if they were the rulers
of the countries in which they lived, and he was surprised
to hear me quote to him in Hebrew passages from the Old
Testament in which they were commanded to seize every
opportunity to do all the harm they could to all non-Jews,
whom they constantly cursed in their prayers. The poor
man did not open his mouth again. At dinnertime I invited him to dine with me, and he replied that his religion forbade it, for which reason he would eat only eggs,
fruit, and goose sausage, which he had in his pocket. His
superstition made him drink only water because, he said,
he was not certain the wine was pure. That afternoon in
the carriage he told me that if I would like to lodge in
his house, and would be content to eat only food that
God has not forbidden, he would feed me more delicately,
more substantially, and more cheaply than at an inn, all
by myself in a fine room facing the sea.

''So you lodge Christians?'' I asked him.

''Never, but I will make an exception this time to enlighten you. You shall give me only six paoli a day, and
I will have dinner and supper served you, but without
wine.''

''But you will have your cook prepare all the kinds of
fish I like and want to eat, which of course I will buy
on my own account.''

''Certainly. I have a Christian maid-of-all-work, and
my wife always oversees the cooking.''

''You will give me goose liver every day, but on condition that you will eat it with me in my presence.''

''I know what you are thinking. But you shall have
your wish.''

So I put up at the Jew's, thinking it very strange. Not being comfortable there, I should have left the next day. His wife and children were eagerly awaiting him, to celebrate the Sabbath. On that day consecrated to the Lord, all servile labor being forbidden, I see with pleasure the holiday look in their faces, their attire, and the cleanliness of the whole house. I am greeted like a brother, and I respond as well as I can; but a single word spoken by the master (whom I shall call Mordecai)[8] instantly changes the whole nature of their politeness; at first it was genuine, what followed was only policy based on interest. Mordecai shows me two rooms to choose between, and, one being next to the other, I take them both, saying at once that I will pay him an extra paolo. The mistress of the house orders a Christian maid to do everything necessary for me, and to make me supper. In an instant Mordecai has told her everything. While waiting for the maid to arrange all the things the coachman had brought in, I am pleased to go to the synagogue with Mordecai, who, having become my landlord, seemed to me another man, and the more so because I had seen his family and his house, where I had found everything very clean.

After attending the short ceremony, at which the Israelites paid not the least attention either to me or to some other Christians, both men and women, who were present, I went alone to stroll by the Exchange,[9] giving way to gloomy reflections, as they cannot but be when they recall a past time of happiness which one cannot hope will return. It was in this city that I had begun to enjoy life to the full, and I was astounded that it was almost thirty years earlier,[10] an immense length of time, and that I nevertheless felt more young than old. But what a contrast when I took the measure of my moral and physical existence in those days of my youth, and compared them with the present! I found myself a wholly different person, and the more I saw that I was perfectly happy then, the more I had to admit that I had become

unhappy, for the whole beautiful prospect of a happier
future no longer stretched before my eyes. Despite myself, I knew, and I was forced to admit, that I had wasted
all my time, which meant that I had wasted my life; the
twenty years I had still before me, and on which I
thought I could count, seemed to me gloomy. Being forty-
seven, I knew that I was at the age which Fortune scorns,
and this in itself was all that I needed to sadden me, for
without the Blind Goddess's favor no one on earth can
be happy. Working as I was to be able to return to my
country a free man, I thought I was limiting my desires
to obtaining the favor of retracing my steps, of undoing
what I had done for good or for ill. I understood that it
was only a matter of making less unpleasant a descent
the final term of which was death. It is on his descent
that a man who has spent his life in pleasures makes
these somber reflections, for which there is no place in
his flourishing youth, when he needs to foresee nothing,
when the present occupies him completely, and when an
ever unchanging and rose-colored horizon makes his life
happy, and keeps his mind so happily illuded that he
laughs at the philosopher who dares to tell him that, behind the charming horizon, there is old age, wretchedness,
repentance, which always comes too late, and death. If
such were my reflections twenty-six years ago,[11] my
reader can imagine what those must be which today obsess
me when I am alone. They would kill me if I did not find
ways to kill the cruel time which brings them to birth in
my soul, which, fortunately or unfortunately, is still
young. I write in order not to be bored; and I am delighted, I congratulate myself, that I enjoy doing it; if
I write nonsense, I do not care, it is enough for me to
know that I am being amused:

> *Malo scriptor delirus inersque videri*
> *Dum mea delectent mala me vel denique fallant,*
> *Quam sapere et ringi*

("I would rather appear to be a scatterbrained
and unskillful writer, so long as my faults please
me or escape me, than be wise and chafe").[12]

Back at the house, I found Mordecai at table with his
family, consisting of eleven or twelve persons, one of
them his mother, who was ninety years old and in good
health. Another Jew, a middle-aged man, was the husband of his elder daughter, who struck me as not pretty;
but I found much to admire in his younger daughter,
whom he was going to marry to a Jew from Pesaro,
whom she had not yet seen.

"If you haven't seen him," I said to her, "you can't
be in love with him."

She replied in a serious tone that being in love was not
a necessary condition for marriage. The grandmother
praised her answer, and my landlady said that she had
not fallen in love with her husband until after she had
borne her first child. I will call the pretty Jewess Leah,[13]
having reasons for concealing her name; I said things to
her to make her laugh; but she did not even look at me.

I found a supper without meat, but exquisite, and with
everything perfectly Christian, and I retired to an excellent bed. The next morning Mordecai came and told me
that I could give my linen to the maid to wash, and that
Leah would see to making it ready for me. I thanked him
for the shellfish, and I told him I had a dispensation
which permitted me to eat both meat and fish every day,
and above all not to forget the goose liver. He said that I
should have it the next day, but that no one in his family
ate it except Leah.

"Then Leah," I said, "shall eat it with me, and I will
give her the purest wine from the Kingdom of Cyprus[14]
to drink."

I asked the Venetian Consul[15] for some that same
morning, going to his residence to take him a letter from
Signor Dandolo. The Consul was a Venetian of the old

school. He had heard of me, and he seemed very glad to make my acquaintance. He was a real Pantalone[16] without a mask, lively, full of experience, and an epicure. He took my money and gave me some genuine Scopolo wine[17] and some very old muscat from Cyprus; but he protested loudly when I told him I was lodging at Mordecai's, and what chance had taken me there. He said that he was rich but that, being a great usurer, he would treat me badly if I needed money. After telling him that I did not want to leave until the end of the month, and on a good ship, I went back to my room, where I found myself very comfortable. The next morning I wrote down all the linen and silk stockings which I gave to the maid, as Mordecai had told me to do; but a moment later he came with Leah, for she wanted to know how I wanted her to wash the laces which were attached to my shirts, then he left her with me. Between eighteen and twenty years of age, and appearing before me in perfect candor in a bodice which could not better reveal a firm bosom as white as alabaster, the girl troubled me, and she would have seen it if, having any suspicion of it, she had looked at me. Mastering myself, I told her to take care of my linen as diligently as possible, for I was not a man to pinch pennies. She said that she would attend to it all herself, if I was not in a hurry. I replied that it was in her power to keep me in her house as long as she pleased, to which declaration she paid not the slightest attention. I told her I was satisfied with everything, except the chocolate, which I liked whipped and foamy, and she answered that she would prepare it herself.

"In that case," I said, "I will give you twice the quantity, and we will drink it together."

She said she did not like it.

"But you like goose liver?"

"Very much, and today I am to eat it with you, my father tells me. Am I to take it you are afraid you'll be poisoned?"

"Certainly not. On the contrary, I wish we could die together."

Leah pretended not to understand me, and left me full of desires and resolved to lose no time. I must either make sure of her that same day, or tell her father not to send her to my room any more. The Jewess in Turin[18] had taught me what to think of Jewesses in the matter of love. As I saw it, Leah must prove to be both more beautiful and less difficult, for gallantry in Ancona must be entirely different from gallantry in Turin. Such is the reasoning of a libertine, and he is often wrong.

I was given a meat dinner prepared entirely in the Jewish fashion, and Leah herself came in with the liver and sat down opposite me without any ado, but wearing a fichu over her beautiful bosom. The liver was exquisite, and since it was not large we ate it all, washing it down with Scopolo wine, which Leah declared was even better than the liver; then she got up to leave; but I objected: dinner was only half over. Leah said she would stay, but that her father would not like it. I told the maid to ask him to come up, for I had something to say to him. I told Mordecai that his daughter's appetite doubled mine, and that he would be doing me a favor if he allowed her to eat with me whenever we had goose liver. He replied that her doubling my appetite was precisely what he did not want, for he would lose money on boarding me, but that she should stay if I would pay him double, that is, a testone more. No logic could have pleased me better. I told him that I accepted his condition, and I presented him with a bottle of Scopolo, which Leah assured him was of the purest. So we dined together, and seeing her enlivened by the good wine, which, having diuretic properties because of its taste of tar, perfectly produces the effect which love seeks, I told her that her eyes set me on fire and that she must let me kiss them. She replied that her duty forbade her to permit it.

"No kissing, and no touching," she said; "let us eat

and drink together, and I shall enjoy it as much as you do. But that must be all. I am entirely dependent on my father, and can have no will of my own."

"Must I ask your father to allow you to be kind?"

"I don't think that would be proper, and my father might well take it as an insult and not let me come to your room again."

"And if he told you that you need not be scrupulous about such trifles?"

"I should despise him, and I should continue to do my duty."

So clear a declaration showed me that she would not be easy, and that, if I persisted, I might find myself committed, fail, repent, and lose sight of my chief business, which obliged me to make no more than a very short stay in Ancona. So I did not answer her, and, finding the Jewish pastries and compotes excellent at dessert, we drank some Cyprus muscat, which Leah declared superior to all the liqueurs on earth.

Seeing her so carried away by drink, I thought it impossible that Venus should not have as much power over her as Bacchus; but her head was strong; the wine did not go to it; her blood was fired, but her reason remained unaffected. I encouraged her high spirits, and after coffee I took her hand to kiss it, and she resisted; but her refusal was of a kind at which I could not take umbrage. She told me wittily that it was too much for honor and too little for love. I at once felt certain that she was no novice. I put off my design until the next day, and I informed her that I should sup with the Venetian Consul. He had told me that he never dined, but that he would always be very glad to have me come to supper.

I came home at midnight; everyone was asleep, except for the maid, who was waiting for me and whom I tipped well. I got her to talk about Leah, but she told me nothing to the purpose. Leah was a good girl, always working, the whole family loved her, and she had never listened to a suitor. It was just the sort of thing she would have said if Leah had paid her.

But Leah came in the morning to bring me my chocolate, and sat down on my bed, saying that we had an excellent liver and that, since she had not supped, she would dine with a very good appetite. She said that what had kept her from supping was the excellent Cyprus muscat, about which her father had been very curious. I said that we would give him some. Leah was there, as she had been on the evening before. Her breasts drove me to despair, and I thought it impossible that she should not be aware of their power. I asked her if she knew that her bosom was very beautiful. She replied that all girls' bosoms were like hers.

"Do you know," I asked, "that the sight of it gives me extreme pleasure?"

"If that is true, I am very glad of it, for it is a pleasure I can give you without having any reason to reproach myself. In any case a girl does not hide her bosom any more than she does her face, except when she is on parade in company."

As she said this, the minx looked at a small gold heart pierced by an arrow and covered with little diamonds which I used to fasten my jabot.

"Do you think my little heart is pretty?" I asked her.

"Charming. Is it pure gold?"

"Yes. And that is what gives me the courage to present it to you."

With that, I unfasten it to give it to her, but she says, thanking me sweetly, that a girl who intends to give nothing must accept nothing. I beg her to accept it, and I give her my word of honor that I will never ask her for the slightest favor; she replies that, even so, she would consider herself in my debt, and that she would never accept anything.

After this declaration I saw that there was nothing to be done, or too much to do, and that in either case I must come to a decision. I scornfully rejected the idea of employing a violence which might have made her laugh at me or anger her; in the first case it would both have degraded me and made me more in love to no purpose, and in the second case, since the right would be on her side, I should have given her the right to take steps which would have humiliated and offended me. She would have stopped coming to bring me chocolate, and I could not have complained of it. I decided to keep my eyes in check, and not to speak another amorous word to her. We dined in very high spirits. I was served shellfish which her religion forbade her, I urged her to eat some, and I horrified her, but when the maid was gone she ate some with surprising relish, assuring me that it was the first time in her life that she had enjoyed the pleasure.

"This girl," I said to myself, "who breaks the law of her religion so easily, who is passionately fond of pleasure, who does not hide the relish with which she enjoys it, tries to make me think that she is insensible to the pleasure of love, or that she can conquer it by treating it as a trifle. It is impossible. She does not love me, or she loves me only to amuse herself by keeping me in love with her; and to satisfy the needs of her temperament, she apparently has other resources."

I thought of having her to supper, counting on the strength of the Scopolo wine, and she excused herself, assuring me that if she ate in the evening she could not sleep.

She came to bring me chocolate, and the first thing that strikes me is that her too beautiful bosom is covered by a white kerchief. She sat down beside me on the bed, and I reject the stale idea of pretending not to notice it. I say in a melancholy voice that she had come with her bosom covered only because I had told her it gave me pleasure to see it. She replies carelessly that she had not thought about it and had only knotted a kerchief over it because she hadn't had time to put on her bodice. I say with a laugh that she had done well, for it might be that, seeing her whole bosom, I should not think it so beautiful after all. She makes no answer, and I finish my chocolate. I think of the miniatures and engravings of lascivious nudes which I had in my jewel case, and I ask Leah to give it to me, saying that I want to show her pictures of the most beautiful bosoms in the universe. She says they would not interest her; but after bringing me my case she stays where she is.

I take the picture of a woman lying on her back stark naked and masturbating, but I cover it up to the navel with a handkerchief, and I show it to her, holding it in my hand. She says that it is a bosom like any other, and that I can uncover the rest. I hand her the miniature, saying that it disgusts me. Leah laughs, and she says it is well painted, but that it is nothing new to her, for it was all that girls did, though secretly, before they married.

"Then you do it too?"

"Every time I feel like it. Then I go to sleep."

"My dear Leah, your sincerity drives me to distraction, and you are too intelligent not to know it. So either be kind and obliging, or stop coming to see me."

"You must be very weak. So in future we will see each other only at dinner. But show me another miniature."

"I have some engravings which you won't like."

"Let me see."

At that I give her the collection of illustrations for Aretino,[19] and I admire the calm though very attentive way in which she looks at them, going from one to another, and returning to the one she has already examined.

"Do you find it interesting?" I asked her.

"Very much so, and it's only natural; but a decent girl mustn't look long at these things, for you can imagine that they arouse a strong emotion."

"I believe it, my dear Leah, and I feel it as you do. Look."

At that she smiled, and she quickly got up and went to

look at the book by the window, turning her back to me and leaving me to call to her as much as I pleased. After calming myself like a schoolboy, I dressed, and, the hairdresser arriving, Leah left, saying that she would return my book to me at dinner.

I then believed I should have her on the next day at the latest. My libertine approach had not offended her, the first step was taken. We dined well, we drank still better, and at dessert Leah drew the collection from her pocket, and she inflamed me by asking for commentaries but at the same time preventing me, on threat of leaving, from proceeding to the demonstration which would have given life to the explanation, which was only for the eyes, and which I perhaps needed more than she did. Out of patience, I took the book away from her, and I went for a walk, counting on the hour when she would bring me my chocolate.

Leah told me that she needed to ask me for explanations, but that if I wanted to please her I must give them to her only in words and with the engraving in my hand. She would not look at any living demonstrations. I said that she must likewise answer all the questions I might ask her in regard to her sex, and she promised she would do so; but on the same condition that our observations should concern only what we saw in the pictures.

Our lesson lasted two hours, during which I cursed Aretino countless times, for the pitiless Leah threatened to leave each time I tried to put one of her arms under my coverlet. But the things she said to me concerning her sex, and which I could pretend not to know, drove me to distraction. She told me the most voluptuous truths, and she put such sincerity and animation into explaining the internal and external movements which must take place during the cohabitations we had before our eyes that it seemed to me impossible that theory alone could lead her to reason so correctly. What seduced me completely was the fact that no shame obscured the clarity of her sublime teaching. She philosophized on the subject far more learnedly than the Genevan Hedwig.[20] Her intellect was in such perfect accord with the rest of her being that it seemed to be detached from it. I would have given her all that I possessed to reward her prodigious talent with the great exploit. She swore to me that she knew nothing from experience, and I thought I must believe her when she confided to me that she could not wait to be married in order to learn all. She grew sad, or she pretended it, when I took it into my head to tell her that the husband her father Mordecai had chosen for her might be a man poorly equipped by Nature, or one of those ill-constituted cacochymics[21] who do their conjugal duty only once a week.

"What!" she answered in alarm. "Then are not all men alike, as we are? Are they not all able to be amorous every day, as they must eat and drink and sleep every day?"

"On the contrary, my dear Leah, men who are amorous every day are very scarce."

So cruelly exasperated every morning, I was furious that there was no decent place in Ancona where a gentleman could have his pleasure by paying for it. I trembled to realize that I was falling in love with Leah; I told the Consul every day that I was in no hurry to leave. I indulged in all the paralogisms[22] of a true lover; I thought Leah was the most virtuous of all girls; she became my model of virtue; it was upon her that I built my definition of it. She was all true, unstained by hypocrisy as by imposture; unable to escape her nature, she satisfied her desires only by herself, and she forbade herself all that was forbidden her by the law to which she was determined to remain obedient despite the fire which burned her from morning to night and from night to morning. It was in her power to make herself happy, and she resisted for two long hours in my company, adding fuel to the fire which devoured her, and being strong enough to refuse ever to do anything to extinguish it. Ah, the virtuous Leah! Every day she risked defeat, and every day she gained the victory, assuring herself of it by the one sovereign remedy of never yielding to the first step. No looking and no touching.

After nine or ten days I began to be violent with the girl, not in action but by the force of eloquence. She was abashed, she admitted that I was right and that she did not know how to answer me, and she ended by saying that it would be a wise resolve on my part to forbid her to enter my room in the morning. At dinner, she insisted, we ran no risk. I decided to ask her to continue to come to my room, but always with her bosom covered and never again talking of the illustrations for Aretino or of anything to do with love. She replied with a laugh that she would not be the first to break those conditions. I did not break them either, but three days later, tired of suffering, I told the Consul that I would leave at the first opportunity. Under our new compact, Leah's gaiety was making me lose my appetite. But this is what happened.

Two hours after midnight I woke, feeling a need to go to the water closet. It was on the ground floor and Mordecai always saw that it was kept very clean. I go downstairs barefoot and in the dark, and, after doing my business, I go back to the stairway to return to my apartment. At the top of the first flight of stairs I see light through a crack in the door of a room which I knew should be unoccupied. I go there to see who could be in the room at such an hour with a light. My curiosity was not inspired by any idea of seeing Leah, for I knew that she slept on the other side of the house; but to my great surprise I see Leah lying stark naked on a bed, practicing postures with a young man in the same state. They were no more than two paces from the door, I saw everything perfectly. They were talking in whispers, and every four or five minutes they presented me with a new tableau. This change of posture showed me Leah's beauties from every angle. The pleasure somewhat soothed my fury, which however was not little when what I saw left me in no doubt that Leah was only imitating the illustrations for Aretino, which she had learned by heart. When they came to the essential act they set themselves limits and, working with their hands, procured the ecstasies of love, which, imperfect though they were, nevertheless tried me cruelly. When the young man assumed the straight tree[23] position, Leah unashamedly played the Lesbian, and he devoured her jewel, and, not seeing her spit at the end of the act, I was sure that she had imbibed the nectar of my fortunate rival. Her lover then laughingly showed her his flaccid instrument, whose death Leah appeared to mourn. She was about to restore it to life; but the base fellow looked at his watch, paid no attention to her protests, and put on his shirt. She did not do likewise until after she had spoken to him in a way from which I guessed that she was reproaching him. When I saw that they were nearly dressed, I went to my room and stationed myself at a window which overlooked the door of the house. Four or five minutes later I saw the fortunate lover come out and leave. I went back to bed, not delighted to have been disabused, but indignant and feeling debased. Since I no longer saw Leah as virtuous, she seemed to me nothing but a wanton who hated me. I went to sleep intending to drive her from my room after reproaching her with all that I had seen.

But when she appeared with my chocolate I suddenly changed my mind. Seeing her gay, I forced my features to assume a corresponding expression, and, after drinking my chocolate, I told her without the slightest show of anger the story of all her exploits which I had been able to see during the last hour of her orgy, dwelling on the straight tree and on the excellent food which, like a true Lesbian, she had taken into her stomach. I ended by saying that I hoped she would give me the next night, not only to satisfy my love but also to oblige me to keep her secret safe.

She replied unabashedly that I could not expect the least favor from her, for she did not love me, and, as for keeping her secret, she defied me to reveal it out of revenge.

"I am sure," she said, "that you are not capable of so base an act."

Having said which, she turned her back on me and left.

And in fact what she had said was the truth. I should have been guilty of a very base act, and I was far from resolved to commit it; I was not even thinking of it. She had made me see reason by a great truth, which, hard as it was to swallow, demanded respect: she did not love me; there was no answer to that, she owed me nothing, I could demand nothing. It was she, on the contrary, who could demand satisfaction from me, for I had no right to spy on her or to insult her by telling her what I should never have known except from an indiscreet and indefensible curiosity. I could only complain of her because she had deceived me. So what could I do?

I did what I ought to do. I dressed hastily, I went to the Exchange, where I found that a peota[24] was leaving that day for Fiume. Fiume is on the other side of the Gulf, opposite Ancona. From Fiume to Trieste is only forty miles by land; I decided to go to Fiume, I go to the port, I see the peota, I speak to the captain, who tells me that the wind is astern, and that he is sure that the next morning we shall be at least in the Canal.[25] I engage the best place, I have a folding seat put in it, then I go to take leave of the Consul, who wishes me a good journey. From there I return to the house, where I pay Mordecai all that I owed him, and I go to my room to pack my trunks. I have plenty of time.

Leah comes to tell me that she cannot possibly give me

my linen and my stockings that day, but that she could give me everything the next. I reply calmly and quietly that her father need only take whatever belonged to me to the Venetian Consul, who will send it on to me in Trieste. She makes no answer.

A moment before I sat down at table the captain of the peota[26] himself came with a sailor to take my belongings, I give him the trunk I had packed, and I tell him that the rest will go on board with me when he is ready to leave. He says that he will leave an hour before nightfall, and I reply that he will find me ready.

When Mordecai learned that I was going to Fiume, he asked me to take charge of a small box which he wanted conveyed to a friend of his, together with a letter which he would write him; I replied that I should be glad to oblige him.

Leah sat down to dinner with me as if nothing had happened. She spoke to me in her usual way, she asked me if I was satisfied with what I was eating, and my short answers no more put her out of countenance than my determined attempt never to let her look me in the eye. She must have believed that I took her attitude for strength of mind, firmness, noble confidence, whereas it seemed to me nothing short of exaggerated effrontery. I hated her because she had deceived me and had then dared to tell me that she did not love me, and I despised her because she believed I ought to esteem her because she did not blush. She may also have believed that I ought to esteem her because she had avowed that I was incapable of telling her father what I had seen. She could not understand that I owed her nothing for her confidence.

As she drank Scopolo, she said that I still had two flagons of it and two bottles of muscat. I answered that I left them to her as excellent means of increasing her fire during her nocturnal debauches. She replied with a smile that I had enjoyed for nothing a spectacle which she was sure I would have paid gold to see, and that she was so glad of it that she would arrange for me to enjoy it again if I were not going to leave.

This reply made me want to hit her in the face with the bottle which stood before me. I picked it up in a way to show her what just anger was about to make me do, and I should have committed the shameful crime if I had not seen on her face the unmistakable expression of a defiant assurance. I poured wine into my glass, very awkwardly, as if I had picked up the bottle only for that purpose; but when one is going to pour wine one simply picks up the bottle, one does not seize it in one's inverted fist. Leah noticed it.

I rose and went into my bedroom, unable to bear more; but a quarter of an hour later she came to drink coffee with me. This most insulting persistence seemed to me monstrous. I calmed myself a little when I reflected that such a proceeding on her part must spring from a spirit of revenge; but she had avenged herself enough by telling me that she did not love me and proving it to me. She said that she wanted to help me pack, and at that I asked her to leave me alone, taking her by the arm, leading her to the door, and locking it after her.

We were both in the right. Leah had deceived, humiliated, and scorned me. I had every right to loathe her. I had discovered that she was supremely hypocritical, deceitful, and shameless. She had every right to loathe my existence, and she would have wished that I would practice some crime on her which would make me repent of having discovered her secret. I have never been in a state more violent.

Toward evening two sailors came for my belongings, I thanked my landlady, and I calmly told Leah to wrap my linen in waxed cloth and deliver it all to her father, who had already gone ahead to put his box in the peota. He gave me the letter, I embraced him and thanked him, and we sailed at once with a fresh breeze, which dropped two hours later. We had gone twenty miles. After a quarter of an hour of calm, the wind began blowing from the west, and then the little ship, which was almost empty, began pitching and tossing so cruelly that my stomach was upset and I began to vomit. At midnight, the wind having become completely contrary, the captain told me that the best thing for him to do was to go back to Ancona. With a head wind it was impossible to go to Fiume or to any port in Istria. So in less than three hours we were back in Ancona, where the officer on guard, having recognized us as the same persons who had left about nightfall, was kind enough to let me go ashore.[27]

While I was talking to the officer, thanking him for allowing me to go and sleep in a good bed, the sailors picked up my luggage and, instead of waiting for me to tell them where they should take it, the captain told me they had gone with it to the same place from which they had fetched it. I wanted to go to the nearest inn, it made me furious that I must see Leah again, but the thing was done. Mordecai got out of bed and congratulated himself on seeing me again. It was three hours after midnight. I went to bed, exhausted and badly in need of rest. I told him that I was very ill, and that I would dine alone in my bed when I called him. A light dinner, and no liver. I slept for ten unbroken hours, with my whole body aching but feeling that I had an excellent appetite. I rang, and it was the maid who came to tell me that Leah was in bed with a severe headache; I thanked Providence for saving me from the pain of seeing the brazen creature again.

I had found my dinner very scanty, I told the maid to make me a good supper. The weather was dreadful. The Venetian Consul came to spend two hours with me, assuring me that the weather would remain bad for at least a week—a warning which distressed me both because of Leah whom I could not possibly see again, and because I had no more money; but I had articles of value. Not having seen Leah at suppertime, I thought she would not come again; but my hope was vain. She came the next morning and asked me for chocolate so that she could prepare it for me; but the look she wore was neither cheerful nor calm. I told her that I would drink coffee, that I wanted no more goose liver, and so I should eat alone, and to tell her father that in consequence I would pay him only seven paoli a day; and that in future I would drink only Orvieto wine.

"You still have four bottles."

"No, I haven't, for I gave them to you; I beg you to leave and to enter this room as seldom as possible, for your sentiments and the style you are pleased to use to express them are such as to make the most philosophical of men lose all moderation. Add that your presence disgusts me. Your exterior no longer has any power to blind me to the fact that it contains the soul of a monster. You may be sure, too, that the sailors brought my luggage here while I was talking to the officer on guard, otherwise I should not have come here; I should have gone to an inn, where I should not have feared being poisoned."

Leah left without answering me, and I felt certain that I had seen the last of her. Experience had taught me that girls of Leah's sort were not uncommon; I had known her like in Spa, in Geneva, in London, and even in Venice, but this Jewess was the worst of them all. It was a Saturday; on his return from the synagogue Mordecai came to ask me smilingly why I had mortified his daughter, who swore to him that she had not given me the slightest reason to complain of her.

"I had no intention of mortifying her, my dear Mordecai; but, needing to diet, I told her that I wanted no more goose livers; from which it follows that I can eat alone, and so save three paoli."

"Leah is prepared to pay them to me, and she wants to dine with you to rid you of any fear of being poisoned. She told me that you feared it."

"Your daughter, my friend, is fooled by her own cleverness. I have no need either for her to pay you three paoli, or not to spend them myself, and to convince you of it I will pay you six, but on condition that you will eat with me too. Her offering to pay the three paoli is an impertinence of a piece with her character. In short: either I will eat alone and pay you seven paoli a day, or I will pay you thirteen and eat with both father and daughter. That is my final word."

He left, saying that he had not the heart to let me eat alone. I got up for dinner; I talked only to Mordecai, never once looking at Leah or laughing at the witty things she said from time to time. I would drink only Orvieto wine. At dessert Leah filled my glass with Scopolo, saying that if I persisted in not drinking it she would not drink it either. I replied that if she knew what was good for her she ought never to drink anything but water, and that I would accept nothing from her. Mordecai, who was fond of wine, laughed heartily, and saying that I was right, drank for the three of us.

The weather being bad, I spent the day writing, and, after being served supper by the maid, I went to bed and at once fell asleep. A little later a slight noise wakes me, I say "Who's there?" and I hear Leah answering in a whisper that she has not come to trouble me but to justify herself in half an hour and then let me sleep. So saying, she lies down beside me, but on top of the coverlet.

This visit, which I did not expect, since I thought it was not in accord with the girl's character, pleases me, for, having no feeling in respect to her but a desire to be revenged, I was sure that I should not succumb to anything she might do to gain the victory. So, far from being curt with her, I tell her mildly that I consider her justified, and I beg her to leave, since I needed to sleep. She replies that she will not let me sleep until I have heard her out.

She followed this by a harangue which I never once interrupted and which went on for a good hour. Whether trumped up, or proceeding from genuine feeling, it was calculated to persuade me, for, after admitting that she had done very wrong, she maintained that at my age and with my experience I ought to forgive everything in a girl of eighteen, weak because of the irresistible dominion over her of a temperament [28] whose instinct for love deprived her of the use of her reason. According to her, I ought to forgive so fatal a weakness for everything, even for crimes, for, if she went so far as to commit them, it would only be because she had no power over herself. She swore to me that she loved me, and that she would have given me the most telling proofs of it if she had not had the misfortune to be in love with the Christian I had seen with her, who was a beggar and a libertine who did not love her and whom she paid. She assured me that, despite her temperament, she had never let him cull her flower. She swore that it had been six months since she had seen him, and that it was I who was the cause of her having summoned him that night, for I had set her soul on fire with my engravings and my wines. The conclusion of her long apology was that I must restore peace to her soul by forgetting everything and granting her my sincere friendship during the few remaining days I should spend in her house.

When she stopped talking I chose not to refute any of the points in her harangue by the slightest objection. I pretended to be convinced that I had wronged her by showing her too lascivious pictures, I condoled with her on her misfortune in having fallen in love with a beggar, and on the irresistible force with which Nature had endowed her senses, which left her with no power over herself, and I ended by assuring her that she would see no more signs of even the slightest resentment in my behavior.

But since this declaration did not end in what the minx

wanted, she went on talking to me about the weakness of
the senses, the strength of self-esteem, which often bound
fond love in fetters and led a heart to act against its dear-
est wishes, for she wanted to persuade me that she loved
me and that she had only confined me to trifles to make
my love stronger by conquering my esteem. It was her
nature which had driven her to act so, and it was not her
fault if she had been unable to act otherwise.

How many answers I could have given her! I could
have answered that it was precisely because of her loath-
some and accursed nature that I ought to hate her and
that I hated her; but I did not want to discourage her
completely, for I wanted to see her advance to the as-
sault, so that I could overwhelm her with humiliation;
but the minx never went so far. She never held out her
arms, she never put her face close to mine. But after the
contest, and as soon as she was gone, I was very glad
that she had never really engaged me, for she would have
been the victor, even though we were without a light.
Segnius irritant animos demissa per aures ("The mind
is less strongly affected by what enters through the
ears").[29] When she talked to me about the prodigious
power which Venus had over her, I remembered what I
had seen her do in the straight tree position, and if Leah
had attacked me then I should have found it difficult to
resist. She left after two hours defeated, but with every
appearance of being content. I thought I had to promise
her that she could make my chocolate. She came very
early for a stick of it, in the most lascivious undress,
walking on tiptoe for fear of waking me, whereas if she
had ever once looked at my bed she would have seen that I
was not asleep. Finding her as false and artful as ever, I
congratulated myself on being equal to all her wiles.

She came with my chocolate, and, seeing two cups, I
said that it must not be true that she did not like it. She
replied that she thought it her duty to relieve me of my
fear of being poisoned. What I also thought worth re-

marking on was that she had come to bring my chocolate
with her bosom well covered and wearing a dress, whereas
half an hour earlier she had come in only a shift and
petticoat. The more I saw that she was bent on catching
me by the bait of her attractions, the more I felt resolved
to humiliate her by indifference. I considered that the
only alternative to my victory was my dishonor and my
shame; so I felt ready to meet every contingency.

Nevertheless, my palate began to get the better of me
at dinner. Against my orders, Leah had me served a goose
liver, saying that it was for her and that, since it was
poisoned, she would die alone; Mordecai said that he
would die too, and he ate some of it; at that I laughed
and ate some, and Leah said that my resolves were not
strong enough to stand up in the presence of the enemy.
This judgment annoyed me. I said to her that she had
given herself away, which showed a lack of intelligence,
and that I was strong enough to defy temptation.

"Try," I said, "to get me to drink Scopolo or muscat.
Yet I should have drunk some now if you had not reproached me with the weakness of my resolves. I will
convince you that they are invincible."

"The agreeable man," she replied, "is the one who
often lets himself be conquered."

"But the agreeable girl is the one who does not reproach him with his weaknesses."

I sent to the Consul's for Scopolo and muscat, and
Leah, who could not contain herself, annoyed me again
by saying with a knowing smile that I was the most
agreeable of men.

After dinner I left the house despite the bad weather,
and I walked to the coffeehouse. Feeling sure that Leah
would come that night to attack me again, I went there
to see if I could find someone who could take me somewhere to buy amorous pleasures. A Greek who a week
before had taken me to a house which I had found dis-

gusting took me to another where a countrywoman of his, covered with rouge, displeased me even more. I went home, where, after supping alone as usual, I decided that my only course was to bolt my door, which I had done only twice before. But it made no difference. A minute later Leah knocks and calls to me that I have forgotten to give her chocolate. I open the door, and, taking a stick of chocolate, she begs me to leave my door unbolted, for she needed urgently to talk to me and it would be for the last time.

"Tell me now what you want."

"No. It's rather long, I can't come until everyone in the house is asleep. In any case you have nothing to fear, even if you go to bed, for you are your own master, and for you I am no longer a danger."

"Certainly not. You will find the door unbolted."

Still resolved to resist all her artifices, I thought it best not to blow out my candles, for, since I was sure she would come, my putting them out would show her that I was afraid. The light would make my triumph the greater, and allow me to enjoy her humiliation and shame all the more. So I got into bed.

Leah arrives at eleven o'clock in shift and petticoat, she bolts the door, and when I ask her, "Well, what have you to say to me?" she comes to my bedside, she lets her petticoat drop, then her shift, and lies down close to me, throwing the covers aside. Sure of her triumph, she does not hesitate, she says nothing, she clasps me to her bosom, she bestrides me, she deluges me with kisses, and in short in a single instant she deprives me of all my faculties except the one I do not want to have for her. I use my only remaining moment of reflection to tell myself I am a fool, that Leah was nothing if not intelligent and that she knew human nature far better than I did. In no time my caresses become as ardent as hers, she lets me devour her breasts, and she brings me to the point of death on the surface of the tomb, in which to my astonishment she convinces me that she could not bury me except by unlocking it.

"My dear Leah," I said to her after a short silence, "I adore you, how can I have hated you, how can you have wanted me to hate you? Is it possible that you came here into my arms only to humiliate me, to win a vain victory? If that is your idea, I forgive you; but you are wrong, for my enjoyment is far more delicious, believe me, than any pleasure you can feel from your revenge."

"No, my dear friend. I am here neither to triumph, nor to avenge myself, nor to win a shameful victory; I am here to give you the greatest proof of my love, and to make you my true conqueror. Make me happy in an instant: break this barrier which I have preserved unbroken until now despite its weakness and despite Nature; and if the sacrifice I make you allows you still to doubt the sincerity of my affection, it will be you who will become the most wicked, the most unworthy of men."

At that, without losing any more time than was demanded by a small arrangement dear even to an impatient love, I gathered a fruit the greatest novelty of which was its sweetness. On Leah's beautiful face I saw the extraordinary symptom of a delicious pain, and in her first ecstasy I felt her whole person trembling with the excess of pleasure which flooded it. The pleasure I felt seemed to me entirely new; determined not to let it reach its climax until I could not possibly prevent it, I kept Leah inseparable from me until three hours after midnight, and I aroused all her gratitude by making her receive my melting soul in the palm of her beautiful hand. Seeing me dead a moment later, she said that it was only justice, and we parted content, in love, and sure of each other. I slept until noon, and, when I saw her reappear, the thought of my leaving made me sad. I told her so, and she begged me to put it off as long as I possibly could. I told her that we would settle it that night. I got up, and

meanwhile she carried away the sheet on which the maid
would have seen the signs of our criminal connection. We
dined most voluptuously. Mordecai, having become my
table companion, prided himself on showing me that he
was not miserly. I spent the afternoon at the Consul's,
with whom I arranged to leave on a Neapolitan warship
which was in quarantine and which, after being released,
was to go to Trieste; so I was to spend another month
in Ancona, and I adored Providence. I gave the Consul
the gold box which I had had from the Elector of Cologne,
removing his portrait from it. Three or four days later
he gave me forty zecchini for it; it was all I needed. My
stay in Ancona cost me a great deal; but when I told
Mordecai that I should spend another month in his house
he peremptorily declared that he would have no more of
my feeding him at my table; so Leah was left to dine with
me alone. I have always believed that the Jew knew that
his daughter did not refuse me her favors. Jews are not
difficult in this respect, for, knowing that a son which
one of us might give to one of their women would be a
Jew, they think that letting us do so is getting the better
of us. But I spared my dear Leah.

What tokens of gratitude and increased affection when
I told her that I should stay in her house another month!
What blessings on the storm which had kept me from
going to Fiume! We went to bed together every night,
even on those on which the Jewish law[30] excommunicates
the woman who indulges in love. I left Leah the little
heart, which might have been worth ten zecchini; but she
would accept nothing for having taken care of my linen
for six weeks. In addition, she gave me six fine Indian
handkerchiefs; I met her again in Pesaro six years later.
I will speak of her then. I left Ancona on November 14th,
and I arrived at Trieste on the 15th, going to lodge at the
Locanda Grande.[31]

CHAPTER IX

*Pittoni. Zaguri. The Procurator Morosini. The
Venetian Consul. Görz. The French Consul.
Signora Leo. My devotion to the Tribunal of
the State Inquisitors. Strasoldo. The Carniolan girl. General Burghausen.*

THE INNKEEPER comes to ask my name, I strike
my bargain with him, I find I am very well lodged on the
third floor, and my bed is good. The next day I go to the
post office for my letters, which had been awaiting me
for a month. In one from Signor Dandolo I find another,
unsealed, from the patrician Marco Donà[1] to Baron Pittoni,[2] the Chief of Police, recommending me in strong
terms. I take a conveyance to his house, I present the
letter to him, naming myself, and, without reading it, he
tells me that Signor Donà had written him about me, and
that he would show me every consideration at every opportunity. I then take a letter from Mordecai to the Jew
Moses Levi,[3] in which I did not know that he had mentioned me; so I leave it at his office in his house. The Jew
Levi, who proved to be sensible, amiable, and very well
off, came to my apartment the next morning to offer me
his services in every respect. He gave me the letter to
read; I was the only subject of it; he told him that if I

happened to need a hundred zecchini he would vouch for me, and that any favors he would do me he would consider done to himself.

I felt it incumbent on me to write Mordecai a most cordial letter of thanks and to offer him all my credit in Venice if he needed it. What a difference between Baron Pittoni's cold reception[4] and the Jew Levi's! Baron Pittoni, who was ten or twelve years younger than I, was amiable, amusing, well versed in literature, and without prejudices. At odds with all economy, he disapproved of the law of mine and thine, he left the conduct of his small house to his valet, who robbed him; but he did not protest, for he knew it. He was a bachelor on principle, a great panegyrist of celibacy, gallant with the fair sex, and the friend and protector of all libertines. Lazy and indolent, he was prone to an unforgivable absent-mindedness, which subjected him to the misfortune of often forgetting very important business of the greatest consequence to his official functions. He was said to be given to lying, but it was not true; he did not tell the truth because, having forgotten it, he could not tell it. I have portrayed his character as I learned to know it a month after making his acquaintance. We were good friends, and we are still good friends.

After announcing my arrival in Trieste to my friends in Venice, I spent a week or ten days in my room putting together the notes I had collected in Warsaw on everything that had happened in Poland after the death of Elizabeth Petrovna. I embarked on a history of the troubles[5] down to the partition which was being made at the time I was writing. This event, of which I had published a prediction[6] when, on the election of King Poniatowski, the Polish Diet recognized the Czarina who has just died as Empress of All the Russias, and the Elector of Brandenburg as King of Prussia, inspired me to write the whole history down to the partition; but I published only the first three volumes of it because of the dishonesty

of the printer,[7] who did not fulfill the conditions on which
we had agreed. The other four volumes will be found in
manuscript after my death,[8] and whoever comes into possession of my papers may publish them if he pleases. It
has become a matter of indifference to me, like so many
other things since my time has shown me stupidity en-
throned in absolute supremacy.

Poland, which no longer exists today, would still exist
as it was at the death of Augustus III, Elector of Saxony,
but for the ambition of the Czartoryski family, which
Count Brühl, the King's Prime Minister, humiliated. To
avenge himself, Augustus Czartoryski, Palatine of Russia, ruined his native country. Passion so blinded his profound intelligence that he forgot that the power of axi-
oms, and especially in politics, is invincible. Having made
up his mind not only to deny the House of Saxony any
possibility of succeeding to the throne of Poland but also
to dethrone the reigning monarch, and needing the
friendship of the Czarina and the Elector of Brandenburg[9] to accomplish his design, he made the Diet recognize them, the former as Empress of All the Russias and
the latter as King of Prussia. Failing that, the two sovereigns, who were perfectly in agreement, would not
treat with the Republic. The Republic was right in not
wanting to give them those titles, for it was the Republic
which possessed the principal Russias, and the Republic
which was King of Prussia, since the Elector of Brandenburg possessed only the Duchy of Prussia.[10] The Palatine
of Russia, Czartoryski, blinded by his desire for revenge,
proved to the Diet that the recognition meant nothing if
the sovereigns wanted only the honor of the titles and
undertook never to exercise their prerogatives. The sovereigns declared that they demanded only the titles; and
the Republic acceded and granted them, and the Palatine
of Russia had the pleasure of seeing Stanislaus Poniatowski, the son of his sister Constance, on the throne. I
told the Palatine at the time that the titles granted gave

Summer Amusements on the Piazza Navona, Rome

blici ſuffragj il nobile Sig. Lapo Niccolini, paſſato all'altra vita il giorno antecedente in età di anni 60. in circa.

Nello ſcorſo venerdì 13. corrente condu cendoſi per Arno da un navicellaio molte perſone di qui partite per trovarſi alla teſta della Beata Giovanna nella Pieve di S. Giovan Batiſta, fu da eſſo inveſtita col na vicello una delle baſi degli archi del Pon te a Signa; per lo che ſi aperſe il legno, e ſarebbero periti tutti quegli che vi erano ſopra, ſe non foſſe ſtato preſtato loro un pronto ſoccorſo di chi ſi trovò preſente al caſo. Nel ſuſſeguente lunedì eſſendo ſalito un contadino ſopra uno dei pilaſtri del can cello oppoſto alla porta principale della Pieve ſuddetta, per vedere il gioco della gioſtra ſolito farſi ſu quella piazza, ne ca gionò la rovina, per la quale reſtarono fe rite diverſe perſone, e tre morirono im mediatamente.

Avendo predicato nella ſcorſa Quareſi ma nell'Inſigne Real Baſilica di S. Lorenzo il Molto R. P. Maeſtro Lorenzo Fuſconi, gli è ſtato meritamente ſtampato, e diſpenſato al Pubblico il ſeguente Elogio:

LAVRENTIO · FVSCONIO

Domo · Ravenna

In · Sacra · Minorum · D · Francisci

Qvos · Conventuales · Vocant · Familia

Divinae · Facultatis · Magistro

Principvm · Postarvm · Svi · Temporis

Nelli, Secundo

Apvd · Regiam · Lavrentianam · Basilicam

An. A · Chr. N. MDCCLXX

Esorialibvs · Feriis

Coelestia · Aperienti · Mysteria

Loculentissimis · Orationibvs

Delectv · Rervm · Dicendi · Copia

Stylo · Ad · Etrosci · Sermonis · Elegantiam

Svadendi · Qve · Facilitatem · Accommodato

Miro · Jvdicio · Refersis

Viro · Pietate · In · Deum · Svavitate · Morvm

Avctoritate · Ervditione

Scripsi · Qve · Cedro · Vere · Linendis

Praestantissimo, Digno · Propter · Ea

Qvi · Famige ·ath · Ramanae · Artealvm

Qviritum · Qvae

Patriae · Insvper · Ac · Florentinae

Academiis · Fverit · Adscriptvs

Animarvm · Proctvm · Religionis · Incrementvm

Itervm · Gratvlata · Florentia

Martedì 24. ſi venderanno per via dell' Incanto de' Pupilli alcuni mobili, d'atte nenza del fù Signor Dottor Conte Felici, eſiſtenti nella di lui caſa di Via Larga, per intereſſe de' ſuoi figli.

Nel dì 16. giunſe da Vienna un carriaggio con diverſe robe deſtinate per queſta Real Corte.

Caterina Moglie di Gaſpero Lori abitante in Borgo Ogniſſanti fù ſorpreſa dalle doglie del Parto nel ſettimo meſe della ſua gravi danza, le quali la tennero per tre giorni in gran travaglio, nè potè ſgravarſi, ſe non coll'aiuto del Chirurgo la ſtra de' 4. del cor rente Aprile. Il Profeſſore trovò che il Fe to eraſi alquanto ritirato e raggruppito ver ſo la parte deſtra a motivo della corrugazione dell'utero procedura dall'eſſere il me deſimo teſtato privo delle ſue acque fino dal giorno innanzi. Ambe le mani della picciola creatura erano quelle, che ſi pre ſentavano nel farſi dal Cerulico le debite eſplorazioni; ed appariva all'eſterno una porzione del funicolo umbelicale. Queſta poſitura e circoſtanza rendeva il caſo pur troppo ſcabroſo, e di pericolo pel feto; il quale per altro fu eſtratto vivo, e ricevu te fortunatamente le acque batteſimali mo rì tre ore dopo. Seguitando poi un' indebi ta emoragia e altri ſintomi pericoloſi, nè vedendoſi le naturali conſeguenze del par te, convenne paſſare anche all'eſtrazione della Placenta. E tutto queſto fu una delle ſolite operazioni celeri, e felici del Sig. Giuſeppe Galletti aiuto del Sig. Domenico Maſotti nella Real Corte. La Donna ſi è già riſtabilita in perfetta ſanità, ed è ritor nata alle ſue domeſtiche faccende.

Si trattiene tuttora in Firenze quel Sig. che nella paſſata Gazzetta fu detto eſſere il Sig. Giacomo Caſanova di S. Gallo nobile Vene ziano. Siamo in dovere di riſarire che il men tovato ſoggetto è venuto a dirci in perſo na chiamarſi egli Giacomo Caſanova di Seingalt, ed eſſere Veneziano, e non già Nobile nè eſſerſi mai attribuita queſta qua lità eccedente di molto la ſua condizione, i di cui limiti ſon quelli di eſſer un buon Suddito di quella Nazione, e non già un Nobile di quel Dominio.

Dai torchi della Stamperia del Giglio è uſcita la riſtampa dell' = Opere ſpirituali dell'

Casanova's Denial of His Having Claimed to Be of Noble Birth them a real right, and that the promise never to make use of them would be meaningless or illusory, and that they would not have demanded them if they had not understood their importance. Though laughingly, for I could not discuss it except in a jesting tone, I told him again and again that, in consequence of the recognition, the whole of Europe must thenceforth regard Poland as no more than the depositary of White, Red, and Black Russia and of the Kingdom of Prussia, and that sooner or later the successors of the recognized sovereigns would relieve the depositary Republic of the burden of the deposit. It was not their successors but the sovereigns themselves who dismembered the Republic, but not on the strength of their titles. Policy, which always maintains a decent exterior, made it unnecessary for them to use them. The same sovereigns who then dismembered it finally divided it between them last year. The second extraordinary blunder which Poland, of which Czartoryski was then the soul, committed was not remembering the fable of the man and the horse[11] and applying it to protection. The Roman Republic became mistress of the entire then known world only by first becoming the protector of the countries which she appropriated. For this reason alone every sovereign asked for protection does not hesitate for an instant before granting it; it is the first step toward becoming the guardian, and from guardian the father, and then the master of his dear ward, if only to look after the latter's inheritance. It was thus that my mistress the Republic of Venice became mistress of the Kingdom of Cyprus, which the Grand Turk later took away from her in order to dispose of the good wine which is made there, despite the fact that the Koran ought to make him hate it.[12] Venice today exists only to her eternal shame.[13]

In short, ambition, revenge, and stupidity were the ruin of Poland, but most of all stupidity. The same stupidity, often the child of kindliness and indolence, began to ruin France on the accession of the too unfortunate Louis XVI.[14] Every king who has been dethroned must have been stupid, for no nation on earth has a king except by force. For this reason a stupid king must have an intelligent prime minister and make him very powerful. The King of France perished because of his stupidity, and France will perish because of the stupidity of that ferocious, mad, ignorant nation, blinded by its very intelligence and always fanatical. The disease which now reigns in France would be curable in any other country, but France it will lead to the tomb, and I have not intelligence enough to guess what she will become. The French *émigrés* may inspire pity in some, but not in me, for I hold that, if they had remained steadfastly in the kingdom, they could have opposed force to force and have spent their money having the firebrands killed without giving them time to kill the nation. History shows us no example of an assembly of imbecile peasants who, blinded by their position, imagine that that is possible which forty centuries prove to be impossible.[15] A headless body can endure only for a time, for reason lies in the brain, whose seat is the head.

On the first day of December Baron Pittoni sent me his valet to ask me to go to his house, where there was someone who had come from Venice expressly to see me. Extremely curious, I hastily dress, and the Baron introduces to me a prepossessing man thirty-five or forty years of age, elegantly clad, with a handsome, smiling face, who looks at me with what appears to be the greatest interest.

"My heart tells me," I said to him, "that Your Excellency is Signor Zaguri, for I see the style of your letters in your handsome countenance."

"Exactly so, my dear Casanova; as soon as my friend Dandolo told me, three days ago, that you are here, I decided to come and embrace you and congratulate you on your return to your country, which will certainly be an accomplished fact if not this year then next year at the latest, when I hope to see installed as State Inquisitors two men whom I have sometimes found not to be deaf and even to speak out. What must give you no slight proof of my friendship is that I have come to see you despite the fact that, being now an Avogador,[16] the law does not allow me to leave the capital. We shall spend all of today and tomorrow together.''

After replying appropriately, making a particular point of the great honor his visit did me, I hear Baron Pittoni asking me to excuse him for not having gone to call on me, assuring me that it had slipped his mind, and a handsome old man asking His Excellency to persuade me to come to dinner at his house with him, though he had not the honor of knowing me.

''What!'' Signor Zaguri said to him, ''Casanova has been in this small city for ten days, and the Venetian Consul does not know him?''

''It is my fault,'' I said very quickly. ''I thought I should insult him by going to make my bow to him, since the Consul might consider me contraband merchandise.''

He replied wittily that from then on he would consider me merchandise which was in Trieste only under quarantine before returning to its country, and that his house would always be open to me, as the Venetian Consul's had been in Ancona.

By this answer the Consul intended to inform me that he knew all about me. His name was Marco Monti.[17] He was a man full of intelligence and experience, very amiable in company, making very amusing remarks, very eloquent, graceful in narrative, and always giving his stories a turn which made his listeners laugh, and at the same time having the gift of not laughing himself at what he was narrating and deliberately making ridiculous. Since I had something of the same gift myself, we were instantly on good terms, becoming rivals in the art of anecdote. Though he had the advantage of me by thirty years, I was a not unworthy match for him, and when we were together at gatherings there was no need for play to pass the time. This worthy man's friendship, which I was able to win, was extremely useful to me during the two years I spent there,[18] and I have always believed that he contributed greatly to my obtaining a pardon, the one object of my wishes at that time, for I was attacked by the malady which the Germans call *Heimweh*, "return." The Greeks called it nostalgia.[19] Its power is so great that the Swiss and the Slavonians die of it in a very short time. I might not have died of it if I had treated it with scorn, and I should not have gone to waste nine years in the ungrateful bosom of my stepmother.[20]

So I dined with Signor Zaguri at the Consul's with a numerous company, and the next day at the Governor's, who was a Count Auersperg.[21] This visit from a Venetian Avogador made me a personage entitled to the greatest consideration. I could no longer be regarded as an exile. I was treated as a man whom the Venetian Government itself could not demand, for, having left my country only to escape from an illegal imprisonment, the Government, none of whose laws I had broken, could not consider me guilty.

On the next morning but one I accompanied Signor Zaguri to Görz, where he stayed for three days, since he could not refuse the honors which the very distinguished nobility of that city wanted to accord him. I was included in all their invitations to him, and I saw that a foreigner in Görz could live there in great freedom and enjoy all the pleasures of society. There I made the acquaintance of a Count Cobenzl,[22] who may still be alive, wise, generous, and a man of wide reading without the least pretension; he gave a formal dinner for Signor Zaguri, and it was there that I was introduced to four ladies in every respect worthy of all homage. I made the acquaintance of Count Torres,[23] whose father, a Lieutenant-General in the Imperial service, was Spanish. He had taken a wife at the age of sixty, and, having married a woman as prolific as she was intelligent, he had five children all as ugly as himself. His daughter, who had been very well brought up, was very attractive despite her ugliness, for in intelligence and character she resembled her mother. The eldest son, who squinted, was so intelligent that it made him a fool. A libertine, a swaggerer, an inveterate liar, never mincing his words, malicious, a gossip, his company was sought because he told stories well, he said witty things, and he made people laugh. If he had studied he would have been a great scholar, for his memory was prodigious. It was he who vainly guaranteed the contract[24] I made with the printer Valerio de' Valeri to publish my *History of the Troubles in Poland*. During those two days I also made the acquaintance of a Count Coronini,[25] who had made a name for himself in the *Journal des Savants*[26] by publishing essays on diplomacy which he wrote in Latin. No one read them; people preferred according him the name of scholar for nothing to taking the trouble to read them.

I made the acquaintance of a young gentleman, Morelli,[27] who had written a history of Görz and who was then about to publish the first volume of it. He gave me the manuscript, asking me to read it at my leisure in Trieste and to correct what needed correcting, and I did it for him. I returned it to him after finding nothing to criticize in it, and thus I gained his friendship. He would have liked me less if I had taken the trouble to write critical remarks on it separately. I became a great friend of Count Karl Coronini,[28] who had every talent. He was an only son. Having married in the Netherlands a woman with whom he could not live, he had retired to his estate, where he amused himself pursuing little love affairs, hunting, and reading the political and literary news of the day. He laughed at those who said that there was not a happy man on earth, whereas he was happy and he was sure that he was so because he felt it. He was right; but he died of an apostem[29] of the head at the age of

thirty-five years. The pains which killed him will have
taught him better. Besides, it is not true either that there
is a man in the world who feels happy at every hour, or
that there is one who always feels unhappy. Whether
happiness or unhappiness is more or less cannot be
judged, for each is relative and depends upon character,
temperament, and circumstances. Nor is it true that virtue makes a man happy, for there are virtues the practice
of which brings suffering, and all suffering excludes happiness.

I accompanied the charming Zaguri as far as the
border, together with Baron Pittoni, and I returned to
Trieste with him. The Abate Pini,[30] an ecclesiastical advocate well versed in the dissolution of marriages, was
with the amiable Venetian whose coming set the tone for
all the courtesies which the society of Trieste showed me
until I left. In three or four days Pittoni introduced me
at every house, and at the Casino, to which no one could
go except the select of the city. The Casino was in the
inn at which I was staying. The woman who struck me
was a Lutheran Venetian, the daughter of a German
banker and the wife of David Büchelin,[31] a Swabian man
of business established in Trieste. Pittoni was in love with
her, and remained so until her death. Like Petrarch his
Laura, he loved her for twelve years, always sighing,
always hoping, and never obtaining anything. This rare
woman, whose baptismal name was Zanetta, and whose
husband was not jealous, was pretty, sang very well, accompanying herself on the harpsichord, and did the
honors of her house to perfection; but the sweetness of
her character and the evenness of her temper distinguished her even more than all the other gifts which
Nature and education had bestowed on her. I needed no
more than three days to discover that the woman was
unconquerable, and, though vainly, I gave due warning
of it to poor Baron Pittoni, whom she always distinguished above all her other suitors, though never stray-

ing from the conjugal fidelity which she had promised
to her husband and, far more inviolably, to herself. She
did not enjoy good health, but one would have found
it hard to believe it of her if everyone in the city had not
known it. She died young, very peacefully.

A few days after Signor Zaguri left, I received a note
from the Consul telling me that His Excellency the Procurator Morosini[32] had arrived in Trieste during the
night and was lodging at my inn. He was informing me
of this, he said, because, if I knew him, I should seize the
opportunity to pay my court to him. I was greatly
obliged to my dear Consul for giving me this advice, for
Signor Morosini was very much of a bigwig, both because
of his eminent station as Procurator of San Marco and
because it had become his turn to be a Savio Grande.[33]
He had known me from my boyhood, and my reader may
remember that in the year 1750 he had presented me to
the Maréchal de Richelieu at Fontainebleau[34] when the
self-styled Signora Querini was there to make a conquest
of Louis XV.

So I quickly dressed as if I were to appear before a
monarch, and I went to his anteroom to have myself announced, telling him who I was in a note. He came out
of his room to receive me, and he expressed his pleasure
in seeing me in the most gracious terms. When he learned
for what reason I was staying in Trieste, and my desire
to return to my country after so many vicissitudes, he
assured me that he would do everything in his power to
obtain me that favor from the redoubtable Tribunal,
from which he thought that a subject like myself could
ask it after seventeen years. He thanked me for looking
after his nephew in Florence,[35] and he kept me with him
all that day, which I spent giving him a detailed account
of the principal adventures which had befallen me in my
lifetime. Delighted to learn that Signor Zaguri was prepared to do everything for me, he told me to write to
him that they should lay plans together, and he most

cordially recommended me to the Consul, who, constantly
writing to the Secretary of the Tribunal of the State
Inquisitors, was delighted to be able to inform him of the
marks of esteem which the Procurator had bestowed on
me, at the same time letting him know that he himself
was under an obligation to treat me with the greatest
consideration.

After Signor Morosini left, I began to enjoy life in
Trieste as I needed to if I was to stay there for any considerable length of time and in accordance with the economy which I must practice, for my only certain income
was fifteen zecchini a month. So I never played cards,
and at dinnertime I went every day to take pot luck at
the houses of those who had invited me once and for all
and who I was sure would enjoy my company. They were
the Venetian Consul, the French Consul,[36] who was eccentric but a man of honor and who had a good cook,
Pittoni, and a number of others; as for the pleasure of
love, I sought out young girls of no consequence, thus
spending very little and running no risk to my health.

It was toward the end of the Carnival that, at a ball
given in the theater after the play, a masker dressed as
Harlequin introduced me to his Harlequiness. They
played pranks on me, and, the Harlequiness having interested me, I wanted very much to make her acquaintance. After a great many fruitless inquiries, Monsieur
de Saint-Sauveur, the French Consul, told me that the
Harlequin was a young lady of rank, and the Harlequiness a handsome youth, and that if I wished he would
introduce me to the family of the Harlequin, who, dressed
in girl's clothes, would interest me much more than her
young male companion. In the course of the pranks they
played on me until the end of the ball, I politely and
decently convinced myself that the Consul had not
deceived me in regard to the false Harlequin, and, curious to see her face, I demanded that he keep his promise on the second day of Lent. Thus it was that I made the

acquaintance of Signora Leo,[37] a clever woman who had led a fast life but who was still attractive. She had a husband, an only son, and six daughters, all rather pretty; but the one who particularly pleased me was the Harlequin.[38] I fell in love with her, but, being thirty years older than she, and having begun by showing her only a fatherly fondness, a sense of shame which was something entirely new in my character prevented me from doing anything to convince her that my affection was that of a lover, so I never asked anything of her which went beyond the limits which may be considered the boundary line between the two feelings.

After Easter of the year 1773 the Governor of Trieste, Count Auersperg, was summoned to Vienna, and Count Wagensperg[39] came to take his place. His eldest daughter, Countess Lantieri,[40] who was as beautiful as a star, kindled a fire in my soul which would have made me unhappy if I had not had the strength to hide it under the veil of a great respect. I celebrated the new Governor's arrival in some verses which I published,[41] and, enumerating the virtues of the father, I praised the daughter's rare qualities. My homage pleased them, I began paying assiduous court to them, the Count-Governor took a liking to me, and proved it by confidences which he intended I should use to forward my own affairs. He did not tell me so, but it was easy to guess what he had in mind.

The Consul told me that he had been vainly trying for years to persuade the Government of Trieste to allow the diligence which made the journey between Mestre and that city once a week to lengthen it only one stage[42] by passing through Udine, the capital of Venetian Friuli. Its going through Udine, he said,[43] would be of great advantage to the commerce of the two States,[44] and the Council of Trieste would not agree to it for a reason as specious as it was irrelevant. The members of the Commercial Council of Trieste, all of them profound political

schemers, said that if the Republic of Venice was so much
in favor of the thing it was the clearest proof that it
would be of advantage to it, and that, if that were so, it
could not but be disadvantageous to the people of Trieste.
The Consul assured me that if I could get the thing done I
should so ingratiate myself with the Inquisitors that, if it
did not obtain me a pardon, I should at least have earned
their consideration, and that I should trust to his friendship for guidance in the matter as well as for his report-
ing my efforts in terms which would give me all the credit
I should deserve from them. I replied that I would think
it over.

I let no grass grow under my feet before I broached
the matter to the Count-Governor, who, being acquainted
with it, assured me that he considered the stubbornness
of the Commercial Council scandalous; but he added
that there seemed to be nothing he could do about it, for
the decision did not lie with him. He told me that Councilor Rizzi[45] was the most pig-headed of them, and indeed
was the one whose sophisms led all the others to think as
he did. He advised me to submit a memorandum to him,
in which, treating the subject from every point of view,
I should prove that by going through Udine the diligence
would be of much greater advantage to Trieste, which
was a free port,[46] than to Udine,[47] whose commerce was
very small. He said that he would send my memorandum
to the Council without saying who had submitted it to
him, and that, asserting that he was convinced himself, he
would lay it on the dissenting Councilors to refute my
arguments by convincing reasons, and he assured me that
he would say in full Council that, if the thing was not
done, he would send the memorandum to Vienna with
his recommendation.

Seeing that I was on sure ground, I wrote a memorandum to which no one could reply except by tergiversat-
ing. The Council decreed that in future the diligence
should pass through Udine both going and returning,

and it was to me that Count Wagensperg gave the copy of their decree. I at once took it to the Consul, and, following his advice, I wrote the Secretary of the Tribunal that I considered myself fortunate to have succeeded in giving the Tribunal a proof of my eagerness to be useful to my country and worthy to be granted the favor of being allowed to return to it when Their Excellencies should decide that I had finally deserved it.

The Governor did not publish the new decree concerning the diligence until a week later, so the Government of Udine learned from the Tribunal that the thing was done before the city of Trieste was informed of it. It was thought that the Tribunal, which does everything secretly, had accomplished it by dint of money. The Secretary did not answer me, but he wrote the Consul a letter, which he showed me, in which he ordered him to give me an honorarium of a hundred silver ducati, which is equal to four hundred francs in French currency. He told him that it was to encourage me, and that I could hope for everything from the clemency of the Tribunal if I could resolve the great problem of the Armenians,[48] of which the Consul could give me the details.

He set it forth to me in a quarter of an hour, and I at first thought I could not resolve it; but I was not ready to despair; nothing, I told myself, is beyond hope.

Four Armenian monks had deserted [49] from the Monastery of San Lazzaro in Venice, tired of suffering under the tyranny of their Abbot. They had very rich relatives in Constantinople, and, making light of the excommunication which their Abbot had fulminated against them, calling them apostates, they had gone to Vienna to ask for asylum and protection, promising to be useful to the State by setting up a press which would supply books in Armenian to all the monasteries of Armenians established in the vast domains of the Turkish Empire. They undertook to expend the sum of a million florins in whatever place Their Imperial and Royal Majesties of Austria

would permit them to settle both to establish their press
on a large scale and to buy or build a house in which they
proposed to live in community, though they were without
a head. The Austrian Government not only acceded to
their request at once but also granted them privileges. It
was a matter of ousting Venice from her place in this
branch of commerce and giving it to Austria. The Cabinet in Vienna hit upon the idea of sending them to Trieste
with a strong recommendation to the Governor, and they
had been there for six months. The State Inquisitors
justifiably wanted to make them return to Venice, and,
having failed to accomplish it by direct means, that is,
through the action of their Abbot, who had offered them
great compensations, they were using all secret means to
raise obstacles to them in Trieste which would discourage
them from remaining there. The Consul told me sincerely
that he had declined to undertake the business because he
had thought it impossible, and he predicted that if I
undertook it I should waste my time.

It was certain that in a matter of this nature I could
not count on the Governor's friendship, and that I must
not even mention it to him or give him any reason to
suspect that I would try to make the monks abandon their
project, for, aside from his duty, his particularly zealous
interest in forwarding the commerce of Trieste impelled
him to do all that he could to make the monks succeed in
their project. Despite all this, I began by striking up an
acquaintance with them on the pretext of going to see
their Armenian types,[50] which they had already had
cast, and a stock of precious stones and minerals which
had come to them from Constantinople. In a week or ten
days I became intimate with them. One day I said to
them that, if only to free themselves from their excommunication, their honor demanded that they return to
the obedience they had vowed to their Abbot. The most
obstinate of them replied that he was sure that their
Patriarch,[51] absolving them from their excommunication,

would give them a head, and that a number of monks
would come from the Levant to found a new monastery
in Trieste. Another day I asked them what conditions
they would impose on their former Abbot as the price of
returning to Venice; and the most reasonable of them
replied that their first condition would be that the Abbot
should recover the four hundred thousand ducati which
he had entrusted to the Marchese Serpos[52] at four per
cent interest.

The four hundred thousand ducati constituted the
capital of the Monastery of San Lazzaro, where the
Armenian Basilians had been established for three centuries.[53] It was the nation which had raised the capital;
the Abbot could not dispose of it even with the consent of
the majority of his monks. If the Marchese Serpos went
bankrupt, the monastery would be left destitute. Yet it
was true that the Abbot had transferred the amount to
him on his own authority.

The Marchese Serpos was an Armenian merchant,
established in Venice, who dealt entirely in precious
stones; he was an intimate friend of the Abbot.

I then asked the monks what their other conditions
would be, and they replied that they concerned only
discipline and would give rise to no difficulties which
could not be settled; but they said that they would put
them all in writing when I could assure them that the
Marchese Serpos was no longer in possession of their
capital.

So began my negotiations; I wrote everything down, I
gave the Consul my memorandum, which he sent to the
Tribunal, and six weeks later I received the answer that
the Abbot would find means to deposit the amount in
question in a bank, but that he wanted first to know exactly what the matters of discipline were.

When I read this counterproposal, which was in direct
contradiction to what I had written, for the parties were
completely at odds, I determined to abandon the business.

But what impelled me to get rid of it very quickly was a
few words which Count Wagensperg said to me.[54] He
gave me to understand that he knew I was trying to
reconcile the monks with their Abbot, and that he regretted it, for I could not succeed except by harming
the country in which I was living and which I should
treat as a friend, for it treated me as such. At that I
immediately told him in all sincerity just where the matter stood, assuring him that I should never have entered
into negotiating it if I had not been inwardly certain
that I should never succeed, for I had learned directly
from Venice that there was absolutely no doubt that the
Marchese Serpos could not return the four hundred
thousand ducati to the Abbot. He understood my position. The Armenians bought Councilor Rizzi's house for
thirty thousand florins and went to live in it; I went to
see them from time to time, but never again spoke to
them about returning to Venice. But now for the last
proof of his friendship which Count Wagensperg gave
me, for he died that autumn at the age of fifty years.

One morning he stopped after reading a long memorandum which he had just received from Vienna, and
he said he was sorry I did not understand German, for
he would give it to me to read.

"Here is the substance of it," he said, "and a way to
make you honored in your country at no risk of displeasing those whose official position obliges them to secure
every possible advantage to our commerce. I am going
to confide something to you which you must never say
you learned from me, but which can be of great profit
to you whether you succeed or fail in your efforts, for
your patriotism will be appreciated, the diligence with
which you communicate the matter will earn you thanks,
and your cleverness in discovering the thing will be set
to your credit. At the same time, there will be no need for
you to say how you discovered it. Say no more than that

you would not communicate it if you were not certain of
it.

"All merchandise," he went on, "which is sent from
our country to Lombardy goes through the Venetian
State, and through Venice itself, where, after having
passed through the customs, it is placed in warehouses
as merchandise in transit. This has always been the case,
it is so now, and it can be so in the future if the Venetian
Government will make up its mind to diminish by at
least one half what it makes us pay for storing our goods.
The four per cent it makes us pay is too much. A project
has been presented to the Court, which has immediately
approved it, and here is the order I have received to execute it without even notifying the Venetian Government
beforehand, for the operation is not such that we consider
it our duty, as a friendly Power, to communicate it before putting it into execution. In the matter of shipment,
every State is free; if it ships through, it pays; if it does
not ship through, the place it avoids can neither demand
anything of it nor complain if it ships through some other
place. Such is the present case. In future whatever we
send to Lombardy will no longer pass through the Venetian State. Everything will be put on board here, and will
be taken to La Messola[55] to be unloaded. That port, which
belongs to the Duke of Modena, is opposite to us. The
Gulf is crossed in a night, and our merchandise will be
stored there in warehouses which we shall build at once.
You see that we shorten the voyage by more than half,
and that the State of Modena will demand only the usual
small toll, which does not come to a quarter of what we
pay the Venetians. Add to that the smaller costs for
cartage, and also the time we save. I am certain that if
the Republic will inform the Minister of Finance or the
Council of Commerce in Vienna that she is ready to
diminish the amount she demands by a half, the offer will
be eagerly accepted, for new things are always attended

by difficulties, demand extraordinary expenditures, and are subject to irregularities due to events which are not foreseen. I will not present this matter to the Council for three or four days yet, for there is no hurry; but it is you who should hurry, for as soon as I make the thing public the Venetian Government will immediately be informed of it by your Consul, and the whole corporation of merchants by their correspondents. I should like to have you be the cause of my receiving an order from Vienna to suspend the operation just when I am about to put it into effect.''

I at once saw how greatly it would conduce to my credit if I should be the first to convey this news to the State Inquisitors. Their foible is to astonish by knowing everything before anyone else by means which can never be guessed. After returning His Excellency all the thanks I owed him, I told him I would go to write a report on the matter, which I would send to the State Inquisitors by express messenger after giving it to him to read. He said he would be very glad to read it, which greatly pleased me.

I did not dine that day. In five or six hours I got through everything—draft, copy, and second copy— and I took it all to the Governor, who was delighted by my promptness. He declared it excellent. It was then that I took my report to the Consul. Looking at me in astonishment, he asked me if I was sure it was not all a myth, for he thought it impossible that such a piece of news could have escaped his knowledge and that of all Trieste. I thereupon assured him, as I had written at the end of my report, that I staked my life on the truth of it, at the same time asking him not to insist on my telling him how I had come to know of it. After thinking it over carefully, he said that my report, if it was to be sent by him, would have to go to the Magistracy of the five Savi alla Mercanzia,[56] since, as Consul, he was its agent, and that in consequence he could send it to the State Inquisitors only if I expressly demanded that he do so. So he told me to deliver it to him sealed, and to write him a polite note in which I requested him to send my packet to the Tribunal, asking him to excuse me for not sending it to him unsealed.

"Why," I asked him, "do you want me to show this lack of confidence in your good faith?"

"Because otherwise I should have to vouch for the truth of the thing, and, then too, if I were aware that it was true, the five Savi alla Mercanzia would have reason to blame me, for I am here to serve them, rather than Their Excellencies the State Inquisitors, to whom I owe nothing. So permit me to insist on remaining ignorant of the matter until it comes to my ears as public knowledge. It seems to me that, if it is true, His Excellency the President[57] must know of it, and that before the week is out it will no longer be a secret. Thereupon I will make my report to the five Savi alla Mercanzia, and my duty will be done."

"Then I could send my memorandum directly to your Magistracy, without sending it through you?"

"No. For in the first place you would not be believed. In the second place it would injure me, for, when I transmitted the news, I should be accused of negligence. In the third place my dear master the Magistracy would not give you a copper, and perhaps would not even thank you. If you are certain of this strange novelty, you will play a master stroke by sending it to the Tribunal, and you are sure not only to gain great credit but a fresh reward in money, which should assure you of your credit. If the thing is true I congratulate you with all my heart, but if it is an invention you are ruined, for you lead the redoubtable and infallible Tribunal to make a strange blunder, you can be sure that an hour after the Tribunal is informed of the thing the Magistracy of the five Savi alla Mercanzia will have a copy of it."

"Why a copy?"

"Because you name yourself; and no one is allowed to know the names of Their Excellencies' *confidenti*." [58]

I did everything that my wise friend advised me to do, and I instantly wrote him the note for which he had asked, I sealed my report in a cover, addressing it to Signor Marcantonio Businello,[59] Secretary to the Tribunal, who was the brother of the one under whose reign I had escaped from the Leads, seventeen years earlier.

The President was pleased the next morning when I told him that I had done everything before midnight. He assured me again that the Venetian Consul should know nothing about the matter until Saturday. But my dear Consul's uneasiness during the five days which passed before the thing became known distressed me: his delicacy kept him from saying anything to me, and on my side I was sorry that I could not reassure his noble soul.

On Saturday when the session of the Council ended, it was Councilor Rizzi who told me the news at the Casino, announcing it as most disadvantageous to Venice, which delighted him, for he claimed that the port of Trieste would very soon reduce the port of Venice to nothing.[60] The Consul arrived while we were still discussing the news; he said that the loss to Venice was only a small matter, but that at the first shipwreck in crossing the Gulf all that the tax for storage cost in ten years would be lost. He said further that the German shippers would lose all that the cartage would cost them for goods which would have to travel back again from La Messola to Venetian Lombardy, and to all our fairs. In short the Consul simply made light of it. His office demanded that he do so. In all small commercial cities like Trieste trifles are magnified out of all proportion.

I went to dine with the Consul, who, when he was at last alone with me, unburdened his soul and confessed all his doubts and fears. On my asking him what he thought the Venetians would do to turn away the blow, he said that they would hold great discussions, after which they would decide on nothing, leaving the Austrian Government to send its merchandise by whatever route it pleased.

And in fact the Consul's prediction was verified. He wrote the news to his Magistracy the same day, and the following week he was told in reply that Their Excellencies had learned of the thing some days earlier through private channels, and that he was to continue to inform the Magistracy of the consequences. It was not until three weeks later that he received a letter from the Secretary of the Tribunal in which he ordered him to give me an honorarium of a hundred silver ducati and to allow me ten zecchini a month to encourage me to deserve well of the Tribunal. It was then that I had no more doubt that I should be granted a pardon before the end of the year; but I was mistaken. I did not receive it until the year following, and I shall speak of it when that time comes. My circumstances were now easy. What I had of my own was not enough to live on, for certain pleasures of which I could not deprive myself cost me a great deal. I was not displeased to find myself in the pay of the same Tribunal which had deprived me of my freedom and whose power I had defied; on the contrary, I felt that I was the victor, and my honor demanded that I make myself useful to it in anything which did not infringe the Law of Nature and the Law of Nations.

A little incident which made the city of Trieste laugh will not fail to amuse my readers. It was at the beginning of the summer; I had just eaten some sardines at the seaside, and I returned to my lodging two hours before midnight. I was about to go to bed, when I see a girl enter my room whom I at once recognize as the maidservant of young Count Strasoldo.[61]

The young Count was handsome, poor, like almost all the Strasoldos, fond of expensive pleasures, and hence in debt; his post brought him only six hundred florins a year, and he spent four times as much. He was polite and generous, and I had several times supped at his house with Pittoni. He had in his service a Carniolan[62] girl of the greatest beauty, whom his friends saw but whom none of them dared to approach, for they knew that he was in love with her and jealous. Bowing to the circumstances, I had seen her, admired her, and praised her in her master's presence, congratulating him on possessing such a treasure; but I had never said so much as a word to her.

Count Strasoldo had been summoned to Vienna by Count Auersperg, who was fond of him and who when he left had promised to keep him in mind. He was to be employed in Poland as Captain of a District;[63] he had taken leave of everyone, he had sold his furniture at auction, and he was on the verge of leaving. Everyone in Trieste knew that he was taking his Carniolan beauty with him; that very morning I had gone to wish him a good journey. So the reader can imagine how surprised I must have been to see his maidservant, who had scarcely even looked at me, in my room at such an hour. I ask her what she wants, and she tells me in a few words that, not wanting to leave with Strasoldo, and not knowing where she could go to hide, she had thought that she could nowhere be as safe as in my room. No one, she said, could guess that she was there, and Strasoldo would set off alone. After he was gone she would at once leave Trieste and go home; she hoped that I would not be cruel enough to send her away; she assured me she would leave the next morning, for Strasoldo was to set off at daybreak, as I should be able to see from my window.

"Charming Lenzica" (such was her name), "you are not a girl to be sent away by anyone, least of all by me, who have always thought you adorable. You are safe here, and I give you my word that no one shall enter this room as long as you are in it. I thank my good fortune which made you think of me; but if it is true that, as everyone says, the Count is in love with you, you'll see that he will not leave. He will stay here at least all of tomorrow looking for you.''

''He will look for me everywhere except here. Will you promise me that you will not make me leave this room even if the devil tells him I am here?''

''I give you my word of honor for it a hundred times over. You understand, I hope, that you cannot avoid sharing my bed?''

''Alas! If I shall not be a burden to you, I consent to it.''

''Be a burden to me, you say? You shall see. So, my charming Lenzica, go and undress. Where are all your belongings?''

''Everything I have is in a small trunk which has already been tied to the carriage, but I don't care about that.''

''He must be in a fury at this moment.''

''He will not come back until midnight. He is supping with Signora Bissolotti,[64] who is in love with him.''

So saying, she got into bed, and, after eight months of abstinence, I spent a delicious night. After Leah I had had only casual pleasures which lasted but a quarter of an hour and on which I did not congratulate myself afterward. Lenzica was so perfect a beauty that, if I had been rich, I would have set myself up in a house in order to keep her in my service. We did not wake until seven o'clock, when she got up and, seeing the carriage at Strasoldo's door, she said to me sadly that I had guessed right. I comforted her, assuring her again that she was free to stay with me as long as she pleased. I was sorry not to have a closet, for I could not hide her from the waiter who would have brought us coffee. We had to go without breakfast. I needed to think of some way to bring her food, but I had plenty of time. But there was a surprise in store for me. At ten o'clock I saw Strasoldo enter the inn with his intimate friend Pittoni. I go out into the hall, and I see them both talking to my landlord.

Then I see them go into the Casino and afterward enter and leave a number of apartments on every floor; I see what must be afoot, and I laughingly tell Lenzica that they are looking for her and that they will certainly come to pay us a visit; she urges me to keep my promise, and I reassure her. I understand very well that I cannot keep them from entering my room without giving them reason to guess the truth.

I hear them coming, and at that I go out and close my door, asking them to excuse me if I could not let them enter, for I had a piece of contraband.

"Only tell me," said Strasoldo in a pitiable voice, "that you haven't got my Carniolan in your room. We are certain that she entered the inn at ten o'clock last night; the guard at the door saw her."

"Very well. She is in my room, and I have given her my word that no one shall use violence on her. And you can be sure that I will keep it."

"I don't want violence used on her either; but I am sure that she will come with me of her own free will if I can talk with her."

"I will see if she is willing. Wait outside here."

She had heard everything. She told me that I could bring them in. She was the first to speak, proudly asking Strasoldo if she had contracted any obligation to him, if he could accuse her of having robbed him, in short if she was not free to leave him. He gently replied that, on the contrary, it was he who owed her a year's wages, and that he had her trunk with her belongings, but that she was wrong to leave him for no reason as she was doing.

"The reason," she replied, "is my will. I do not want to go to Vienna. I have been telling you so for a week. If you are a man of honor you will leave me my trunk, and, as for my wages, if you have no money now you can send them to me at Laibach[65] in care of my aunt."

Strasoldo then put an end to my pitying him, for after descending to the most groveling entreaties, he burst into tears. It disgusted me. But I was very near to losing patience when Pittoni told me I ought to turn the hussy out of my room. I said to him firmly that it was not for him to teach me my duty, and that I did not agree that the girl was a hussy. Changing his tone, he began to laugh and asked me if I could possibly have fallen in love with her in the short space of a night. Strasoldo interrupted him to say he was sure she had not slept with me, and she told him he was mistaken, for there was only one bed.

Toward noon they left, and poor Lenzica could not find words enough to thank me. The need for secrecy being thus ended, I had dinner for two sent up, and, the carriage still being there, I promised that I would stay with her and never go out so long as Strasoldo remained in Trieste.

At three o'clock the Venetian Consul came to tell me that Strasoldo had come to him and implored his good offices to persuade me to give him back Lenzica. I told him that it was to her that he should address himself, and, when he had heard the whole story, he left, saying that we were both in the right. Toward nightfall a porter brought the girl's trunk to my room; at which I saw that she was touched but still firm in her resolve. She supped and slept with me for a second night, and Strasoldo left at daybreak. I then hired a carriage and I escorted my dear Lenzica two stages on the road to Laibach, where, after eating a good dinner with her, I left her in the house of a woman whom she knew. Everyone in Trieste declared that I had acted well, and even Pittoni said that in my place he would have done no differently. But poor Strasoldo came to a bad end. He had a post in Leopol, he got into debt there, and he was sentenced for misappropriation of funds. To save his head he escaped to Turkish territory, where he took the turban.

The Venetian Proveditor General of Palmanova,[66] who was a patrician of the Rota family, came to Trieste at this time to pay a visit to the President-Governor Count

Wagensperg; the Procurator Erizzo[67] was with him. In
the afternoon the Governor presented me to Their Excellencies from Venice, who seemed surprised to see me in
Trieste. The Procurator asked me if I was managing to
enjoy myself as much as I had done in Paris sixteen years
earlier;[68] I replied that sixteen years more and a hundred
thousand francs less had perforce made me a different
man. The Consul came in to tell them that the felucca was
ready, and Signora Lantieri, seconded by her father the
Count, said that I could be of the party; the three noble
Venetians who were there, the third of whom I did not
know, said together that I must be of it. After making a
bow which meant neither yes nor no, I ask the Consul
what this party on a felucca might be. He replied that
we were going on board a Venetian warship which was
at anchor in the mouth of the harbor, and of which His
Excellency, whom I saw there, was the commander. I then
told the charming Countess, with a modest smile, that an
earlier engagement prevented me from paying my court
to her on this pleasant occasion.

"I am forbidden, Signora, to set foot on Venetian territory."

There was a chorus of oh's and ah's.

*"You have nothing to fear. You are with us. We are
men of honor. Indeed, your suspicion is a trifle insulting."*

"That is all to the good," I said to them,[69] "and I will
comply, provided that one of Your Excellencies will
assure me that the State Inquisitors will not know, and
perhaps no later than tomorrow, that I had the boldness
to make one of this delightful party, which of course is
the greatest honor to me."

At that I saw them all dumb, looking at one another,
and no one insisted any longer. The noble commander of
the ship, who did not know me, then approached, and
they spent five or six minutes talking together in low
voices.

The next day the Consul told me that the commander of the ship had thought it extremely prudent on my part to refuse to join the party, for if he had chanced to be told my name and my complaints while I was on board his ship he would not have let me leave. When I repeated what the Consul had told me to the Governor of Trieste he gravely replied that he would not have allowed the vessel to leave. The Procurator Erizzo told me that evening that I had done very well, and that he would see that the Tribunal was informed of it.

During those days in Trieste I saw one of the most beautiful of the Venetian women who were then much talked about. She had come there with a party of her admirers, on pleasure bound. She was by birth a Venetian lady of the Bon family, and she was the wife of Count Romili,[70] of Bergamo, who allowed her complete freedom, at the same time being her intimate friend. She was dragging behind her chariot an old gout-ridden General, Count Burghausen,[71] a famous libertine and spendthrift, who had forsaken Mars ten years earlier in order more freely to devote the remainder of his life to Venus. Very gay and full of experience, he remained in Trieste after the rest of the party had gone; he insisted on making my acquaintance, and ten years later he did me a service, as my reader will see in the next volume, which will perhaps be the last.

CHAPTER X

*Adventures in Trieste. I do the Tribunal of
the Venetian State Inquisitors good service.
My journey to Görz and my return to Trieste.
I renew my acquaintance with Irene, become
an actress and a skilled gamester.*

ABOUT THAT time the ladies of Trieste wanted to
see how well they could do in the way of acting French
comedy, and they put me in charge of everything, leaving
it to me not only to choose both the plays and the actors
and actresses but also to distribute the parts. It was a
task which cost me a great deal of effort and did not yield
me the pleasures for which I had hoped. They were all
novices in the art of the theater, I had to train them, go
to see them all every day to rehearse them in their parts,
which they were to learn by heart; but since they were
never able to fix them in their memories properly I had
to resign myself to serving them as prompter. I very soon
learned all the woes by which that occupation is beset.
The prompter is in the most ungrateful of positions, the
actors never admit their obligations to him and, when
they stumble, always blame him for it. A physician in
Spain is treated no better; if his patient gets well it is by
the protection of some saint, if he dies it is the physician's

remedies which killed him. A Negress who was in the service of the prettiest of my actresses, to whom I showed great attentions, made one of those observations which it is not easy to forget.

"I don't understand," she said to me one day, "how you can be so much in love with my mistress when she is as white as the devil."

I asked her if she had never loved a white man, and she replied that she had, but it was because she had never encountered a Negro, whom she would certainly have preferred. A few months later the African maidservant, yielding to my urging, granted me her favors; on that occasion I learned the falsity of the maxim which says that *sublata lucerna nullum discrimen inter feminas* ("when the lamp is taken away, all women are alike").[1] Even with the lamp taken away, one cannot but know whether a woman is black or white. Negroes are of a different species, there is no doubt of it; they have the peculiarity that their women, if they have been taught, are able not to conceive, or even to conceive males or females as they choose. If my reader does not believe this he is in the right, for in creatures of our nature the thing is incredible, but he would be convinced of it, as I am, if I instructed him in the theory of it.[2]

Count Rosenberg,[3] Grand Chamberlain to the Emperor and later created a Prince, who died last year, came to Trieste at that time on pleasure bent, accompanied by the Abate Casti,[4] whose acquaintance I wanted to make because of two or three little poems, of unexampled impiety, which he had composed. I found him an ignoramus, brazen and shameless, whose only talent was a knack for versification. Count Rosenberg always took him with him because he needed him. He made him laugh, and he procured girls for him. In those days the pox had not yet eaten away his uvula. I have been told that he has now been made poet to the Emperor;[5] his succession to the post dishonors the memory of the great Metastasio, who

had no vices and all the virtues; Casti has not one virtue
and all the vices. As for his poetical ability, he possesses
neither nobility of language nor any knowledge of the
theater. Two or three comic operas[6] which he has produced prove it; they contain nothing but buffooneries
badly strung together; and one of them is conspicuous
only for its calumnies against both King Theodore[7] and
the Republic of Venice, which he attempts to ridicule by
lies. In another, called *The Grotto of Trophonius*,[8]
he made himself the laughingstock of all men of letters,
parading a far-fetched erudition which contributes nothing to the humor of his plot.

Among the people of rank who came from Görz to see
the French plays, which were given in the house of Baron
Königsbrunn,[9] whose charming wife, née Countess Attems, played the leading parts, I made the acquaintance
of a Count Luigi Torriano,[10] who was able to persuade
me to go to spend the autumn with him in a country house
which he had six miles from Görz. If I had heeded my
Genius, I would not have gone there. The Count was not
yet thirty, and was unmarried. He was not handsome, but
he could not be called ugly, despite his having the countenance of a gallows bird. In it one read cruelty, treachery, pride, and brutal sensuality. I also saw hate and jealousy in it. This dreadful mixture made me believe that I
was mistaken. A gracious invitation seemed to me incom-
patible with the horrible characteristics which his face set
before my eyes. Making inquiries about him before promising to go there, I heard nothing but good. I was told
that he loved the fair sex, and that he became ferocious
when he had to avenge himself on someone who had insulted him; but, considering these two qualities not unworthy of a gentleman, I promised him I would go there.
He told me he would expect me in Görz on September 1st,
and that we would leave the next day for Spessa, which
was the name of his estate. So I took leave of everyone
for a couple of months, and of Count Wagensperg, who

was seriously ill with the disease which is easily cured by mercury when the physician knows how to administer it, but which becomes mortal when the patient falls into incompetent hands. The poor Count suffered that misfortune. He died a month after my departure.

I leave Trieste in the morning, I dine at Prosecco,[11] and I arrive at Count Luigi Torriano's house in Görz in good time; he was not there; but I am allowed to unload my few belongings when I say that the Count had invited me. I go out, I go to call on Count Torres,[12] I stay there until suppertime, then I return to the house of my new host. I am told that he had gone to the country and that he would be back the next day. I am told that my trunk has been taken to the post house inn,[13] where supper and a room had been ordered for me. This surprises me; but I go there, I find myself poorly lodged and poorly fed; but what of that? I conclude that he could not lodge me in his house, and, that being the case, he could not do otherwise. I blame him only for not having told me so. Could I suppose that a nobleman who has a house hasn't a room in it for a friend?

The next morning Count Luigi Torriano comes to see me, thanks me for my promptness, congratulates himself on the pleasure he will take in having me with him at Spessa, and tells me that he is only sorry that we cannot leave until the next day but one, because he is on the eve of the decision which was to be handed down in a suit he had against a rascally old farmer who had served him and who, being in his debt, not only refused to pay him but made claims himself. The case was to be argued the next day in the court of last appeal, which would render justice where it was due. I told the Count that I would go to hear the advocates, which would be an amusement for me. He left, not only without asking me where I should dine but without offering me the least excuse for having been unable to lodge me in his house. I think that perhaps according to his way of thinking I had been wrong simply to appear and expect to be lodged in his house. He had invited me to the country. I decide to overlook it all. It may have been from tact that he had said nothing to me about it, for if I had been in the wrong it would have been my part to ask him to excuse me.

I dine alone. I spend the afternoon making visits, I sup with Count Torres, I speak of the pleasure it will give me to hear the eloquence of the advocates of Görz the next day; and Torres tells me that he will be at the session too, for he is curious to see how Torriano will take it if the peasant wins.

"I am acquainted with the case," he went on, "and everyone knows that Torriano cannot lose unless the account book he has put in evidence, and according to which the peasant appears to be in debt to him, is forged. The peasant, on his side, cannot lose unless the Count's receipts are for the most part forged. The peasant has already lost in the two lower courts; but he has continued to appeal, paying the costs, and note that he is poor. If he loses tomorrow he is not only ruined but risks being sent to the galleys; but if he wins it will be a sad day for Torriano, for then it would be he who would deserve to go to the galleys, together with his advocate, who has already deserved it several times."

Since I knew that Emanuel Torres was a scandal-monger, his discourse had little weight with me, but my curiosity increased. So the next day I went to the court-room, where I saw the judges, the opposing litigants, and their two advocates. The peasant's was old and looked honest. My host's looked like a bold-faced scoundrel. His client the Count was beside him, and had the scornful look and the sneer of the proud man who is willing for once so far to lower himself as to consolidate his victory over an upstart whom he had already twice defeated. The peasant was there with his wife, a son, and two daughters born to win every suit on earth. I was astonished that such a family could have lost twice. There they were, all four of them, shabbily dressed, keeping their eyes cast down, showing every sign of being the victims of oppression. Each advocate was allowed to speak for two hours.

The appealing advocate spoke on behalf of his peasant for only half an hour. He used it to lay before the judges the book of receipts authenticated by the Count's signatures down to the day when he had dismissed him because he would not let his daughters go to his house; and, continuing to speak with the utmost coolness, he showed the judges the book which the Count had put in evidence and according to which the peasant was in debt to him, and he proved that all the peasant's receipts had been declared forged by experts under oath. In addition he proved that there were anachronisms and parachronisms everywhere, and he ended by saying that his client was in a position, by proceeding in criminal court, to reveal the two forgers whom the Count had paid and who were the authors of the shamelessly fraudulent papers (*scartafacci*) which the opposing advocate had dared to present to the magistrate to deceive his good faith and ruin an honest family, whose only fault was poverty. He ended by demanding reimbursement of all the costs paid and to be paid, and compensation for loss of time and reputation.

The harangue by my dear Count's advocate would have lasted more than two hours if he had not been made to cut it short. There are no insults which he did not spew out against the other advocate, the experts, and the poor peasant, whom he more than once addressed directly, saying that he would go to look at him in the galleys, where no one would pity him. During these exchanges I should have been bored to death if I had been blind, for my only pleasure lay in watching the faces of the litigants and the audience. My dear host's face was always smiling and unafraid.

We all withdrew to an adjoining room to await the verdict. The peasant was in a corner with his family,

shunned, distressed, with not a soul to speak a word to
him, either in friendship or as a covert enemy. Count
Torriano was surrounded by a dozen or more personages
of distinction, all telling him that he could not lose; but
that if anything so unlikely should happen he would have
to pay, but at the same time making the peasant prove the
alleged crime of forgery. I listened but said nothing.
Torres, who was the sworn enemy of prudence, asked me
what I thought. I replied that my dear Count ought to
lose even if he were in the right, because of his advocate's
shameless harangue.

An hour later the magistrate's clerk came in with two
papers, one of which he gave to the peasant's advocate
and the other to Count Torriano, who, after reading it,
burst out laughing. He read it aloud. The court sentenced
him to recognize the peasant as his creditor, to pay all
the costs, and to give him a year's wages, all without
prejudice to the peasant's right to appeal *ad minimum*
on account of any other complaints he could bring before
the court. The advocate appeared, looking gloomy, but
Torriano consoled him by giving him six zecchini. Everyone left. I remained with him to ask him if he would appeal to Vienna, and he replied that his appeal would be
of a different sort. I did not want to know more. We left
Görz the next morning. When the innkeeper presented
my account he said that Count Torriano had ordered him
not to insist if I should decline to pay, for in that case
he would pay for me himself. The revelation made me
laugh. These three or four samples convinced me that I
was going to spend six weeks with a dangerous eccentric.

We arrived at Spessa in less than two hours. It was a
large house on a little hill, with nothing about its archi-
tecture to distinguish it. We went upstairs to his apartment, which was furnished neither well nor ill, and, after
showing me all the others, he escorted me to mine, which
was a room on the ground floor, badly furnished, poorly
ventilated, and not very light. He told me that it had

Carriage-building

*Illustrations from Forbidden Literature
of the 18th Century*

been the favorite room of his father,[14] who, like me, was fond of study, and that I could be sure that I should enjoy perfect quiet there, for I should never see anyone. We dined very late, so on that day there was no supper. I found the food and the wine tolerable, as was the company of a priest who served as the Count's steward and part of whose duty it was to eat with him when he was at Spessa. A thing which offended me was that, eating very fast, he made bold to tell me, though with a smile, that I ate too slowly. After dinner he said that he had a great deal to do, and that we should see each other the next day.

So I go to my room to put my papers in order. I was working on the second volume of my *Troubles in Poland.* Toward dusk I go out to ask for a light, and a manservant brings me a tallow candle. I think it disgraceful, for I was entitled to wax candles or an oil lamp, but I am discreet enough to say nothing. I only ask the servant if one of them had been ordered to wait on me; he replies that the Count had said nothing to them, but that of course they would be at my orders whenever I summoned them. It would have been a troublesome task, for to find them I should have had to leave the house and go around it by way either of the street or of the courtyard. I ask him who will take care of my room, and he says it will be the duty of the maidservant.

"Then she has another key?"

"There is no key; but to lock yourself in at night you have the bolt."

At that I wanted to laugh, for it was really intolerable; but I have the firmness to say nothing; the manservant leaves, I bolt my door, and I set to work; but after half an hour I have the bad luck to put out my candle in snuffing it; I laugh and curse, and I see that I am reduced to going to bed in the dark. The bed was good; which, as I did not expect it, soothes me a little, and I sleep perfectly well. In the morning I see no one. I dress,

I lock up my papers, and, in nightcap and dressing gown, I go to wish my host good morning. I find him having his hair dressed by his second lackey, who served as his valet. After saying that I had slept well, I tell him I have come to breakfast with him. He replies politely enough that he never breakfasts, and not to trouble myself to call on him in the morning, for he was always busy with his peasants, who were all thieves.

"For your breakfast," he said, "since you take breakfast, I will send word to my cook to make coffee for you when you wish it."

"You will also be so good as to order your servant to dress my hair after he has attended to you."

"I am surprised that you have not a manservant of your own."

"If I could have foreseen that my small need of a servant who can dress hair in a village where there is no hairdresser, and in your house, could be an inconvenience to you, I should have procured one."

"It will not inconvenience me; but you may often lose patience waiting for him."

"I will gladly wait. A thing that I must have is a key to the door of my room, for I have papers for which I am responsible, and which I cannot lock up in my trunk every time I need to go out."

"Everything is safe in my house."

"So I suppose, but you must understand that it would be absurd in me to claim that you were responsible for a letter which I might find missing; it could be a great misfortune for me, and I certainly should not tell you about it."

He makes no answer, and after thinking for five or six minutes he tells his hairdresser-lackey to tell the priest to put a lock on the door of my room and give me the key to it. While he was thinking I notice on his night table a wax candle with a snuffer on it, and a book. I go to the table, asking him, of course, if I might see what reading

beguiled him to sleep; he replies politely, but asking me
not to touch the book. I promptly draw back, and I say
with a laugh that I am sure it is a prayer book; but I
swear I will tell no one of my suspicion. He replies, laughing too, that I had guessed rightly. I leave, asking him to
send me his lackey when he has finished with him, and a
cup of coffee or chocolate or broth.

Nettled by behavior such as I had never before experienced, and especially by the tallow candle while he used
a wax one, I return to my wretched room, and I fall into
serious reflections. My first impulse urged me to leave at
once. Though I commanded only forty or fifty zecchini, I
had as much courage as when I was rich. But I rejected
that expedient, since I thought I could not execute it
except by affronting him most signally. The one crying
wrong being the tallow candle, I decided to ask the lackey
if he had not been ordered to bring me wax ones; I had
to do this, for the thing might be nothing but an oversight
on the Friulian lackey's part. It was he who an hour later
brought me a cup of coffee, poured out into the cup and
sugared according to his taste. I burst out laughing, for
I had either to laugh or to throw it in his face, I tell him
that is not the way to serve coffee, and I leave it untouched, taking off my nightcap so that he could dress
my hair. At the end of my patience, I ask him why he had
brought me tallow and not wax. He modestly replies that
the person who had charge of the wax candles was the
priest, and that he had given him only one for his master.
I make no answer. I think that the wretched priest may
have thought it a sin against economy to give me wax, or
had supposed that it would make no difference to me. I
decide to question the priest that day.

As soon as I was dressed I go out for a stroll, and I
come upon the priest with a locksmith. He tells me that,
having no lock ready, he will put a padlock on my door
and give me the key to it. I reply that it makes no difference, provided that I can lock my door, and I abandon

my stroll and go back with him to watch the work. While the locksmith hammered away, I ask the priest why he had sent me a tallow candle and not one or two of wax. He replies that he would never have dared to do that without an express order from the Count.

"Doesn't that," I asked him, "go without saying?"

"Nothing goes without saying here. It is I who buy the wax candles, and he pays me for them with no fear of being cheated, for the candle is entered in the account each time he needs another one."

"Then you can let me have a pound of wax candles if I pay you what they cost you?"

"That's the least favor I can do you, but I warn you that I cannot avoid telling the Count about it, for you understand——"

"Yes, I understand perfectly, but I do not care."

I paid him for a pound of them; and I went for a walk, after learning from him that dinner was at one o'clock. But I was very much surprised when, returning at half past twelve, I was told that the Count had been at table since noon. Not knowing what could account for this accumulation of impertinences, I control myself again, and I go in, saying that the Abate had told me dinner was at one o'clock; he replies that so it is usually, but that, wanting to pay calls on his neighbors and present me to them, he had decided to dine at twelve; but that I should have time to dine nevertheless, and he orders the dishes which had been taken away brought back to the table. I make no reply, and I eat from what dishes were on the table, affecting good humor and refusing the soup, the boiled beef, and the ragouts which had been brought back. He urges me to help myself to them, he says he will wait; but in vain. I calmly reply that I always punished myself in this way when I committed the fault of arriving late at a nobleman's dinner.

However, concealing all my ill-humor, I get into his

carriage with him to accompany him on the calls he wanted to make. He took me to the house of a neighbor who lived only half an hour away. He was Baron del Mestre,[15] who stayed there all year, who kept up a good establishment and had a numerous family, all high-spirited and likable. The Count spent the whole day there, putting off the other visits he meant to make until another day, and we returned to Spessa, where the priest, a half hour later, gave me back the money I had paid him for the pound of wax candles. He said that the Count had forgotten to tell him that I was to be served like himself. For better or worse, the slight was patched up; and I pretended to take his reparation at face value. When supper was served it proved to be as bountiful as if we had not dined, and, eating enough for four while the Count ate almost nothing, I congratulated him on his perspicacity.

The lackey who showed me to my room having asked me at what hour I wanted breakfast, I told him, and he observed it punctually. The coffee was in a coffeepot, and the sugar separate. The other lackey came to dress my hair, the maid came to tidy up my room, everything was changed. I thought I had taught him manners, and that I should have no more unpleasantness; but I was mistaken. Three or four days later the priest came to ask me at what hour I wanted to dine alone in my room.

"Why alone in my room?"

"Because the Count left for Görz yesterday after supper, saying that he did not know when he would return. He ordered me to have dinner served you in your room."

"I will dine at one o'clock."

Freedom is everyone's right, but I thought he ought to have told me that he was going to Görz. He remained there a week. Boredom would have driven me to despair if I had not gone on foot every day to spend two hours with Baron del Mestre. I was without company; the

priest was an ignorant rustic; not even a pretty peasant
girl; I thought I could not possibly have the stamina to
spend four more weeks there.

When he came back I talked to him without mincing
my words. I told him that I had gone to Spessa with him
to keep him company and that, seeing that he had no
need of it, I asked him to take me back to Görz the first
time he went there, and to leave me there, for I was as
fond of company as he was. He assured me that it would
not happen again, and he told me he had gone there because he was in love with an actress in the *opera buffa*
named Costa.[16] She had left Trieste expressly to see him,
and good manners as well as his feelings had obliged him
to spend the whole week she was in Görz with her. In
addition he had signed a marriage contract with a young
lady,[17] the daughter of a castellan of Venetian Friuli,
whom he would marry during the coming Carnival. All
these reasons persuaded me to stay on with the eccentric
Count.

His entire estate consisted in vineyards of white
grapes; the wine he made was excellent; it brought him
an income of about a thousand zecchini and, bent on
spending two thousand, he was ruining himself. Convinced that all the peasants robbed him, he prowled about
everywhere, he entered their cottages, and wherever he
found a few bunches of grapes he caned all those who,
unable to deny that they had taken them from his vineyards, fell on their knees begging for pardon. After being
present several times at these cruel scenes, it fell to my lot
one day to witness the blows which two peasants rained
on him with broomsticks; he saw fit to withdraw after
receiving a sound thrashing. He chided me bitterly for
having remained only a spectator of the affray. I proved
to him by irrefutable arguments that I had no occasion
to interfere in it, first because it was he who, as the ag-
gressor, was in the wrong, and in the second place because
I did not know how to fight with sticks, especially against

peasants who, better skilled than I in that kind of duel, could have let me have one on the head which would have felled me like an ox. In his fury over a bruise on his face, he told me that I was a great coward and a booby who did not know the law that a man must defend his friend or die with him. To this dictum I replied only by a look whose meaning he must have understood.

The whole village heard of the affray; the peasants who had beaten him abandoned the estate; as soon as it became known that in future he would visit their cabins with pistols in his pockets the community assembled and sent him two speakers who told him that all the peasants would abandon the estate that week if he would not promise not to visit their cabins either alone or in company. In the eloquence of these proud boors I admired a philosophical argument which I thought sublime and which the Count thought ridiculous. They told him that the peasants had a right to eat a bunch of grapes from the vine which would have produced none if they had not cultivated it, just as his cook had the right to taste the stew which he had made in his kitchen for his master before he sent it to his table.

The threat of abandoning the estate, just at the time of harvest, terrified the brutal Count. They left, proud to have made him listen to reason.

One Sunday we went to the chapel to hear mass, and we found the priest at the altar, his *Credo* already said. I saw the Count's eyes flashing with anger. After the mass he went into the sacristy and gave the poor priest, who was still in his surplice, three or four blows with his cane; the priest spat in his face, and four or five people came running at his cries. We left. I told him that the priest would go to Udine[18] at once and would get him into very serious trouble; I soon persuaded him to prevent him from going there, even if he had to use force.

He called his servants, and he ordered them to bring the priest to his room, willingly or by force. The priest,

foaming with rage and calling him a contumacious ex-
communicate, told him the most cutting truths; he ended
by saying that neither he nor any other priest would
celebrate mass in his chapel again, and that the Archbishop would avenge the crime he had committed. The
Count let him talk on, and, preventing him from leaving
the room, made him sit down at table, where he was weak
enough not only to eat but to let himself get drunk.
This disgusting behavior brought peace. The priest forgot everything.

A few days later two Capuchins came to call on him
at noon. Seeing that they were not leaving, and not wanting to tell them to go, he had dinner served without ordering two more places set. The bolder of the two, when he
saw that there was no intention of giving them food, said
that they had not dined. At that the Count sent him a
plate of rice; the Capuchin refused it, saying that he was
worthy to dine not only with him but with a monarch.
The Count, who could hardly keep from laughing, told
him that their quidditative[19] epithet being "unworthy,"
they were worthy of nothing, and that furthermore the
humility which they professed forbade them any pretensions. The Capuchin defending himself badly, and the
Count being right, I thought I should support him. I
told the Capuchin that he ought to be ashamed of breaking the rule of his Order by committing the sin of pride.
He replied by insults, and the Count thereupon called for
scissors to be brought, so that he could cut off the beards
of the two impostors. At this dreadful threat they took to
their heels, and we laughed heartily.

It was a joke, and I could easily have forgiven the
Count if his vagaries had all been of this sort; but far
from it. His intestines produced a chyle which infuriated
him, and during the hours of digestion the fury which
overcame him made him ferocious, cruel, unjust, blood-
thirsty. His appetites became rages, he ate, and because
it was from anger, it seemed an act of hatred when he de-

voured a succulent woodcock, of which I was voluptuously praising the exquisite delicacy. He one day gravely told me in so many words to eat and hold my tongue, for the praise I bestowed on the dishes which were served irritated him. I stopped praising for, after all, I had to submit to his decrees or else leave.

La Costa, with whom he had been in love, told me three months later in Trieste that she had not believed a man of such a character could exist before she knew Torriano. She told me that in amorous intercourse, though he was full of vigor, he was always angry because he could not achieve the pleasure which leads to the crisis which marks its end, and that he threatened to strangle her if she could not keep herself from showing physical signs of the voluptuousness which flooded her soul during the act. She pitied the lot of the woman who was destined to be his wife. But now for what finally exhausted my patience and forced me to part company with the poisonous creature.

In the boredom and idleness of Spessa, where I had not a single pleasure, I found myself attracted by a poor and very young widow, I gave her money, some tokens of the tender feelings she inspired in me, and, after obtaining her consent to minor pleasures, I persuaded her to grant me the principal ones in my room. She came at midnight, unseen by anyone, and she left at daybreak by a small door which opened onto the street. It was my only relief; she was in love, and amenable as a lamb, a very rare thing among the peasant women of Friuli, and I had had her seven or eight times. We were both perfectly unapprehensive in regard to our relationship, for we supposed that it must be unknown to everyone; we had no fear of masters or of jealousy or envy; but we were mistaken.

One fine morning Sgualda (such was her name) left my arms, and, after getting dressed, woke me as usual to go to lock the door by which she went out to return home.

I go; she leaves; but no sooner have I closed the door
than I hear her screaming. I open the door, and I see
the atrocious Count Torriano holding her by the dress
with his left hand and caning her with his right. To see
it and to spring on him was the work of an instant. We
both fall, he underneath, I on top of him, and Sgualda
runs off. In my nightshirt as I was, with one hand I was
holding his arm with the stick, while I tried to strangle
him with the other. For his part, he held me by the hair
with his free hand and struggled to free himself. He did
not let go until he felt that I was strangling him, and,
instantly seizing his cane and rising, I rained blows at
his head which he was lucky to ward off with his hands,
taking to his heels and snatching up stones, which I did
not wait to have strike me. I go back into the house and
I lock myself in my room, not knowing whether we had
been seen or not, and I throw myself on the bed out of
breath and sorry that my hand had not been strong
enough to strangle the barbarian who I thought was
determined to murder me.

I take my pistols and I load them on the table, after
refilling the pans; then I dress, and after shutting everything up in my trunk I put my pistols in my pocket and
I go out, intending to find some peasant with a carriage to
take me back to Görz. Without knowing it, I take a road
which leads me past poor Sgualda's house; I enter, and
I see her sad but calm; she comforted me by saying that
she had been hit only on the shoulders by blows which had
not hurt her very much; but she said that the thing
would become public knowledge, for two peasants had
seen the Count beating her, and had seen me, as she herself had seen me from a distance, struggling with him. I
gave her two zecchini, I asked her to come to see me in
Görz, where I intended to stay for two or three weeks,
and to tell me where I could find a peasant who had a
carriage, for I wanted to leave immediately. Her sister
offered to take me to a farm where I would find a car-

riage and horses, and on the way she told me that Count
Torriano had a grudge against Sgualda because as long
ago as when her husband was alive she would never have
anything to do with him.

At the farm I found what I wanted. The carriage was a
good cart, and the peasant promised to have me in Görz
by dinnertime. I gave him half a scudo on account, and
I left, saying that I would wait for him. I go to the
Count's house, I enter my room, and I put everything
which I had left out in a portmanteau. The cart arrives.

One of the Count's servants comes to tell me that he
requested me to go up to his room, where he wanted to
talk with me. I instantly write him in clear French that
after what had taken place between us I could not speak
to him again except outside his house. A minute later he
comes in, saying that if I would not speak with him in his
room he has come to speak with me in mine, and he shuts
the door.

He begins by telling me that my leaving his house in
such a way would dishonor him, and that he would not let
me go.

"I am curious to see how you will set about stopping
me, for you will never persuade me to remain here of my
own free will."

"I will prevent you from leaving alone, for honor demands that we leave together."

"I understand you. So go for your sword, or a pair of
pistols, and we will leave at once, armed alike. In my carriage there is room for two."

"It is you who must leave in mine with me, after we
have dined together."

"You are very much mistaken. Everyone would think
me a fool to dine with you now, when our ugly meeting is
known to the whole village and will be the talk of all Görz
tomorrow."

"Then I will dine alone with you here, and people may
say what they please. We will leave after dinner. Dismiss

your carriage, and so prevent a scandal, for, I tell you
again, you shall not leave."

I had to yield. I dismissed the carriage, and the
wretched Count remained with me, beating about the
bush until noon, trying to convince me that the wrong
was all on my side, for I had no right to stop him from
beating a peasant woman in the street to whom, after all,
I had no possible title. I asked him, laughing at the sav-
agery of his argument, what right he thought he had to
beat a free woman in the street, and how he could suppose that the free woman would not find a defender in
some man whose heart she had engaged, as had been the
case, and how he could have imagined that I would stand
patiently by while he killed a girl who had just left my
arms, and for that reason alone. I asked him if I should
not have been a vile coward, or a monster like himself,
if I had remained indifferent to the scene. I ended by
asking him if in my place he would not have done as I
did without stopping to consult reason, even if he had
had to deal with a great prince.

A little before we sat down at table he said that a duel
over the matter would do no honor to the one of us who
killed the other, for he was determined not to fight except
to the death. I replied with a laugh that, so far as I was
concerned, I did not agree, and if he thought that the
matter stood so on his side he was perfectly free not to
engage in the duel, for I considered myself satisfied already. As for fighting to the death, I said that I hoped
to leave him among the living despite his rage, driving
him to the wall, and that on his side he might do as he
saw fit. He said that we would go to a wood, and that he
would order his coachman to take me wherever I pleased
if I came back to the carriage alone, and that he would
bring no servant with him. After praising his noble attitude, I asked him if he wanted to fight with swords or
pistols, and he said that swords would suffice. I then

promised him that I would get rid of the pistols I had in my pocket when we were ready to leave.

It seemed to me impossible to see this savage creature become polite and reasonable, when the idea of an imminent duel ought to have troubled him to the soul, for I was certain that a man of his character could not be brave. Finding myself perfectly cool, I felt sure that I would lay him low instantly by my infallible right lunge, and then cripple him by pinking him in the knee if he wanted to go on. I thought I could take refuge in the Venetian State, from which, not being known, I could easily make my escape; but I thought I foresaw that nothing would come of it, and that the duel would dissolve into thin air like so many others when one of the heroes is a coward. I set the Count down as such.

After dining well, we left. He without anything, and I with all my small stock of possessions securely tied to the back of the carriage. In his presence I had emptied my pistols, and he had shown me that he had none. I had heard him order his coachman to take the road to Görz; but I kept expecting an order to turn left or right, for we were to fight in a wood. On the way I was careful not to ask him the slightest question. I understood what was afoot when I saw Görz, and I laughed heartily when we arrived there. The Count ordered the coachman to drive to the post house inn, and as soon as we got there he told me that I had been right, that we must remain good friends, and that we must promise each other not to mention the matter to anyone, only to laugh at those who should mention it to us, and not to take the trouble of relating it correctly to those who, when they told the story, changed its details. I gave him my promise, we embraced, and his carriage went to fetch him after the innkeeper Bailon[20] had had my luggage taken down from it.

The next day I went to lodge in a very quiet street to finish the second volume of my *Troubles in Poland,* but the time I spent on it did not prevent me from enjoying life until the time when I resolved to return to Trieste and there await the pardon of the new State Inquisitors. Remaining in Görz, I could give them no proof of my zeal, and it was my duty to pursue their interests, for they paid me for nothing else. I stayed in Görz until the end of the year 1773. During the six weeks I spent there I enjoyed all the comforts and pleasures I could wish for.

My adventure at Spessa being known to the whole town, everyone talked to me about it during the first days; but seeing that I only laughed at it as a thing of no consequence finally put an end to the questioning, and Luigi Torriano made much of his friendship for me wherever we met. However, I politely declined each time he invited me to dinner; he was a dangerous man, to be avoided at all costs. During the Carnival he married the young lady[21] I mentioned above; he made her unhappy for thirteen or fourteen years, until he died insane[22] and in poverty. What delighted me during those six weeks was Count Franz Karl Coronini,[23] of whom I believe I have spoken. He died three or four years later of an abscess in the head. A month before he died he sent me his will in Italian verses of eight syllables, which I still preserve as a specimen of his philosophical mind and the gaiety of his soul. Everything in it is comic and enlivened by the most subtle wit. If he had known that he was to die four weeks later he could not have written it, for the thought of death can inspire gaiety only in a madman.

A Monsieur Richard,[24] of Lorraine, came to settle in Görz at that time. He was a bachelor forty years of age who, after serving the Court of Vienna well in financial matters, had received permission to retire with a very good pension. He was handsome, he had the manner of the best society, some literary accomplishment, though without the least pretension, and he was received and made much of in all the houses in Görz. I met him in the house of Count Torres, which he frequented more than any of the others because of the intelligence of the young Countess, whom he married some time afterward.

At the beginning of October, as was customary, the new Council of Ten[25] had assumed its functions in my illustrious country; hence the new State Inquisitors had replaced the three who had reigned during the preceding twelve months. My protectors—that is, the Procurator Morosini, Senator Zaguri, and my loving friend Dandolo —wrote me that if they did not succeed in obtaining my pardon during the twelve months during which they were to sit they must give up hope of ever attaining it in their lives, for, aside from the virtues of the new Inquisitors, as chance would have it they honored them with their esteem and friendship. The State Inquisitor Sagredo[26] was a friend of the Procurator Morosini, the second Inquisitor, Grimani,[27] loved my faithful friend Dandolo, and Signor Zaguri assured me that he would personally persuade the third,[28] who by law had to be one of the six Councilors who are members of the Council of Ten. Though called "of Ten," that powerful Council was made up of seventeen personages, for the Doge was at liberty to sit with it whenever he pleased. So I went back to Trieste, thoroughly resolved to make every effort to serve the Tribunal well and thus deserve to obtain from its justice the pardon for which I longed after nineteen years which I had spent traveling all over Europe. At the age of forty-nine years which I had then reached, it seemed to me that I had nothing more to hope from Fortune, who loves only youth and is the declared enemy of ripe years. It seemed to me that in Venice I could not but live happily, without needing the blind Goddess's favors. I counted on being self-sufficient, profiting by my talents, feeling sure that I should succumb to no more misfortunes, armed as I was with immense experience, and cured, furthermore, of all the vanities which had led me to the verge of ruin. I thought I could be certain too that the State Inquisitors would find me some post in

Venice itself, the emoluments from which would amply
suffice for me to live in perfect comfort, being alone, with
no family, and prepared to content myself with having
what I decently needed, gladly resigning all superfluity.
I was writing my *History of the Troubles in Poland*; the
first volume was already printed; I was at work on the
second, and I had enough material to present the whole
history to the public divided into seven volumes.[29] After
finishing this task I was thinking of publishing a translation of Homer's *Iliad* [30] in rhymed stanzas, and I had no
doubt that after finishing these I should not find it difficult to produce other works. In short I did not fear that
I could risk starving to death in a city where a hundred
resources kept alive people who could live nowhere else
except by begging. So I left Görz on the last day of the
year 1773, and I put up at the principal inn on the
Piazza in Trieste on the first day of 1774.

I could not have hoped to be better received. Baron
Pittoni, the Venetian Consul, all the Councilors, the men
of business, the ladies, and all the members of the Casino
of the city saw me again with the greatest show of their
pleasure in seeing me again. I spent the Carnival there
in the utmost gaiety, enjoying perfect health, without
interrupting my *History of the Troubles in Poland*, the
second volume of which I published at the beginning of
the Carnival.

The first thing which interested me in Trieste was the
second actress of the troupe of comedians which was
playing there.[31] I was surprised to see in her the Irene,
daughter of the self-styled Count Rinaldi,[32] whom my
reader doubtless remembers. I had loved her in Milan, I
had neglected her in Genoa on account of her father, and
I had been of use to her in Avignon, where I had come to
her rescue with Marcolina's approval.[33] Eleven years had
gone by during which I had never learned what had become of her. I was surprised to see her, and at the same
time sorry, for, seeing her still pretty, I saw that she

Satirical Representation of the Partition of Poland

The Doge's Palace, Venice

The Author at about Forty-nine Years of Age

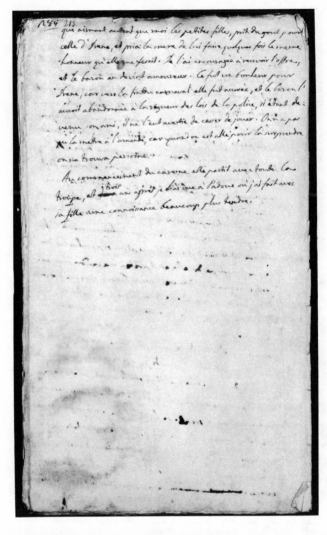

234 218

qui aimant autant que moi les petites filles, prit du goût pour
celle d'Irene, et pria la mere de lui faire quelques fois le meme
honneur qu'elle me faisoit. Je l'ai encouragée à recevoir l'offre,
et le baron en devint amoureux. Ce fut un bonheur pour
Irene, car vers la fin du carnaval elle fut accusée, et le baron l'
auroit abandonnée à la rigueur des lois de la police, si étant de-
venu son ami, il ne l'eut avertie de cesser de jouer. On n'a pas
pu la mettre à l'amande, car quand on est allé pour la reprendre
on ne trouva personne.

Au commencement du careme elle partit avec toute la
troupe, et j'irai avec j'irai même à Padoue où j'ai fait avec
sa fille une connoissance beaucoup plus tendre.

The Last Manuscript Page of Casanova's Memoirs

might please me again, whereas, not being in a position
to be of use to her, I ought to be on my guard. Thinking
that I could not avoid paying her a visit, and in any case
very curious to learn her story, I appeared before her the
the next day an hour before noon.

She received me with a cry, saying that she had seen
me in the parterre and that she was sure I would come to
see her. She at once introduced her husband, who always
played the role of Scapino,[34] and her daughter, who was
nine years of age and showed talent for dancing. Her
story was not long. The same year that I had seen her in
Avignon she had gone to Turin with her father and, having fallen in love with the man she had introduced to me,
she had left her parents to become his wife, and she had
turned actress to join him on the stage. She knew that her
father was dead, and she did not know what had become
of her mother. She told me that she remained faithful to
her duty as a wife, but without being so absurdly strict
as to let her coldness discourage a man who declared that
he loved her and who was worth listening to. At Trieste,
however, she assured me that she had no one, and that
her only pleasure was to give a little supper for some
friends, which was not a drain on her resources, for she
made more than enough by holding a small bank at faro.
It was she who dealt, and she asked me to join in the
game from time to time. On leaving, I assured her that
she would see me that same day after the play and that,
since the bank was small, gaming being forbidden in
Trieste,[35] I would play like the others, for small stakes.

I went there, I supped with a company of coxcombs,
young merchants, all in love with her. After supper she
made a small bank, and we all began punting. But my
surprise was not small when I saw, beyond the possibility
of doubt, that she was cheating very skillfully, and always at just the right juncture. I felt like laughing when
I saw her exercising her talent against me. It was a trifle,
but I did not want Irene to suppose me a dupe. I saw

her the next day at a rehearsal at the theater, and I congratulated her on her skill; at first she pretended not to
understand me, and when I told her what I meant she
had the impudence to say that I was mistaken; but when,
turning my back on her, I said that she would repent of
not having admitted it, she laughed and said it was true
and that if I would tell her how much I had lost she was
ready to give me back my money and even to let me have
a share in her bank without anyone's knowing it except
her husband. I said that I wanted neither, and even that
I would no longer make one at her game, but to be very
careful not to clean out any of her friends, for it would
become known, and then she would be fined, for gaming
was strictly forbidden. She said that she knew it, that she
never carried anyone on his word, and that all the young
men had promised her they would keep the secret. I told
her that I would no longer go to sup with her, but that I
should be pleased if she would come to breakfast with me
when she had time. She came a few days later, with her
daughter, who pleased me and who did not refuse me
some caresses. One fine morning she made the acquaintance of Baron Pittoni, who, being as fond of young girls
as I was, took a liking to Irene's daughter and asked her
mother to do him the same honor sometimes that she
granted me. I encouraged her to accept his offer, and the
Baron fell in love with her. It was fortunate for Irene,
because toward the end of the Carnival she was accused,
and the Baron would have abandoned her to the rigor of
the law and the police if, having become her friend, he
had not warned her to stop gaming. She could not be
fined, for when the police went to surprise her no one was
to be found there.

At the beginning of Lent she left with the whole
troupe, and three years later I saw her in Padua, where
I resumed my acquaintance with her daughter on far
more tender terms.[36]

VOLUME 12 · NOTES

CHAPTER I

1. *Marcuccio:* Though C. writes "Marcuccio" in the chapter heading, when the personage figures in the text he usually writes "Menicuccio," probably to conceal the identity of his sister. (In the translation the form "Marcuccio" has been used throughout.)

2. *Azpuru:* Tomás Azpuru y Jiménez (1712-1772), Auditor of the Papal Rota, from 1769 Archbishop of Valencia; from 1765 to 1772 he was the Spanish Chargé d'Affaires in Rome.

3. *The teacher of languages . . . Cardinal Acquaviva:* C. refers to the episode of Barbara Dalacqua and her father (see Vol. 1, Chaps. IX and X).

4. *Landlady . . . a cook:* Probably Francesco Poletti and his wife Maria Angela, née Abbondi; the couple, who lived at No. 32, Piazza di Spagna, had two sons and a daughter Margherita, who in 1771 was about 16 years old.

5. *Taylor:* John Taylor (1708 - ca. 1776), English oculist from Norwich; physician in ordinary to the Grand Duke of Tuscany from 1769, author of several works on diseases of the eye.

6. *All the post offices:* In the 18th century at least each of the more important countries had its own postal system, with offices in the larger cities of Europe. The Roman Curia also had its own post.

7. *Banca Belloni:* In 1761 the Marchese Francesco Belloni succeeded his father Girolamo as director of the bank of that name.

8. *Dandolo:* See Vol. 11, Chap. I, n. 49.

9. *Zulian:* See Vol. 11, Chap. I, n. 51. He was a brother of the Duchess of Fiano.

10. *Erizzo:* Niccolò Marcantonio Erizzo (1723-1787), Procurator of San Marco and a Cavaliere of the Stola d'Oro, was the Venetian Ambassador in Rome from 1766 to 1771. His brother Niccolò Erizzo (1722-1806) held the corresponding post in

Paris from 1754 to 1760. The residence of the Venetian Ambassadors in Rome was the Palazzo Venezia.

11. *The Duchess of Fiano:* Lucrezia Ottoboni-Buoncompagni-Ludovisi, née Zulian (died 1782), married to the Duke of Fiano in 1758.

12. *Babilano:* Slang for "impotent"; from the Genoese Marchese Babilano Pallavicini, whose marriage was annulled by reason of his impotence about the middle of the 17th century.

13. *Santa Croce:* Antonio Publicola, Prince of Santa Croce (1736 - after 1800).

14. *Princess . . . Falconieri:* Giuliana, Princess of Santa Croce ca. 1750 - after 1802), was the daughter of the Marchese Orazio di Falconieri.

15. *Jesuit of the short robe:* The Jesuit order accepted lay affiliates whose high position could make them useful to it; they were not obliged to wear the dress of the order.

16. *D'Éguilles:* See Vol. 11, Chap. VI, n. 2.

17. *The Roman libraries:* In addition to the famous Vatican Library (cf. Vol. 7, Chap. IX, n. 16), there were several large libraries in Rome, of which C. mentions only two: the Biblioteca Casanatense, or Biblioteca alla Minerva (because connected with the Church of Santa Maria sopra Minerva), and the Library of the Collegio Romano, which belonged to the Jesuits and was connected with the churches of Il Gesù and Sant'Ignazio.

18. *Il Gesù . . . Sant'Ignazio:* The former, completed in 1575, became the model for all the Jesuit churches in the Baroque style; the latter was not dedicated until 1626.

19. *The King of Spain:* Carlos III.

20. *The Pope had promised:* Pope Clement XIV (Giovanni Vincenzo Antonio Ganganelli) suppressed the Jesuit order in 1773.

21. *Probabilism:* The doctrine, upheld by the Jesuits, that culpability does not attach to an action based upon judgment of its probable moral lawfulness where certainty does not exist.

22. *Died . . . poison:* C. accepts the view, widely held in his time but not proven, that the Pope was poisoned.

23. *Alexipharmics:* Counterpoisons.

24. *A woman from Viterbo:* Bernardina Bensi (or Rensi or

Baruzzi), from the village of Valentano, near Viterbo, known as the Prophetess (or Pythoness) of Valentano. She was said to have had several interviews with Ricci, the last General of the Jesuits.

25. *Exactly as long as Sixtus V:* Pope Sixtus V was elected on Apr. 24, 1585, and died on Aug. 27, 1590; Clement XIV was Pope from May 19, 1769, to Sept. 9, 1774. Hence the prophecy was inaccurate.

26. *Bontempi:* Innocenzo Bontempi, also Buontempi, Franciscan friar, friend and confidential secretary to Pope Clement XIV; he died in poverty after 1775.

27. *Eighteen years ago:* C. wrote "seventeen," then substituted "eighteen." He first met De Bernis in Paris in 1752 and entered into closer relations with him in Venice during the winter of 1753-54. (Cf. Vol. 4, Chaps. I-X.) The probable date of C.'s arrival in Rome is May 1770.

28. *See me again:* C. had not seen De Bernis since he had left Paris in 1759.

29. *M. M.:* C. wrote "to the nun at the Angels," then substituted "M. M." The first version shows that M. M. was a nun in the Convent of Santa Maria degli Angeli in Murano.

30. *The nun in Chambéry:* See Vol. 6, Chap. XI, and Vol. 7, Chap. I.

31. *Roman zecchini:* The Roman zecchino was a gold coin worth 2 scudi.

32. *Salicetti:* Natale Salicetti (1714-1789), born in Corsica; physician and Professor at the University of Rome.

33. *The Grand Treasurer:* The Tesoriere Generale della Camera Apostolica had charge of the finances of the Roman Curia; infractions of the laws relating to finance and commerce, especially usury, were also under his jurisdiction.

34. *Braschi:* Giovanni Angelo, Count Braschi, was Tesoriere Generale from 1766 to 1773. He became Pope, as Pius VI, in 1775.

35. *Colonna:* Lorenzo Colonna, Prince and Duke of Pagliano and Castiglione (1723-1779), hereditary Grand Constable of the Kingdom of Naples.

36. *Their:* C. writes "son" (a slip for "leur").

37. *Shared possession of M. M.:* See Vol. 4, Chaps. VII and VIII.

38. *Church of the Holy Apostles:* The Basilica dei Santi Apostoli, on the square of the same name, goes back to the 6th century; it was restored several times, and at the beginning of the 18th century was almost completely rebuilt by Francesco Fontana. It was given a neo-classic façade in the 19th century.

39. *Ceruti:* Giacinto Ceruti (or Cerutti), Piedmontese Abate and journalist (ca. 1734 - ca. 1791). His better-known brother, Giuseppe Antonio Gioacchino Ceruti (1738-1792), collaborated with Mirabeau.

40. *Princess Lanti:* Princess Lanti della Rovere; either the Prince's first wife, Maria Virginia Emilia, née Altieri (born 1704), or his second wife, Faustina, Duchess of Capranica (died after 1807).

41. *The Roman Ephemerides:* The *Effemeridi letterarie* appeared from 1772 to 1795, with Bianconi as director and Ceruti as editor.

42. *Ended well:* According to the parish registers, Ceruti did leave the inn in 1771, but he seems to have returned to it in 1774, after Margherita married an Englishman named Goodman.

43. *Antinoüs:* A beautiful Greek youth, from Claudiopolis in Bithynia, favorite of the Emperor Hadrian; he was drowned in the Nile in A.D. 130.

44. *Prizes . . . students of painting and drawing:* Prizes were awarded to students at the Accademia di San Lucca every three years from 1715; Mengs was its director.

45. *Battoni:* Pompeo Girolamo Batoni (Battoni) (1708-1787), Italian painter, friend of Winckelmann.

46. *How Mengs had treated me in Spain:* See Vol. 11, Chap. II.

47. *Your brother . . . in my house:* In 1761 Giovanni Casanova had offered Winckelmann two of his own paintings as works of antiquity which he had found near Rome, and Winckelmann was taken in. He bought the paintings and described them in his *History of Painting in Antiquity* (1764). After discovering the fraud, Winckelmann tried to revenge himself by suing Giovanni for issuing a forged bill of exchange. He was condemned *in absentia* in 1766. However, he retained his position of Director of the Academy of Fine Arts in Dresden, where he was never prosecuted, and was

able to visit Rome in 1771 without being molested, perhaps because Winckelmann's accusation seems not to have been strictly in accordance with the facts. Apparently C. started to give an account of the affair, then thought better of it, for after Mengs's reported speech there follows a long canceled passage beginning with "Such was the situation of my brother."

48. *Rezzonico:* Abbondio Faustino Rezzonico (1742-1810), Venetian patrician, Procurator of San Marco, and from 1765 Roman Senator.

49. *My brother the Abate:* See Vol. 11, Chap. X, n. 13.

50. *Gama:* See Vol. 11, Chap. IX, n. 31.

51. *Testone:* The Roman testone was worth 3 paoli (the amount which C. had promised the priest that he would allow the Abate).

52. *Palestrina:* Some 25 miles east of Rome; it was already a flourishing town in the 8th century B.C., when it was called Praeneste. It was famous for the Temple of Fortuna Primigenia, the ruins of which are still to be seen.

53. *Thirteen or fourteen years ago:* C.'s brother the Abate died in January 1783.

54. *Medini:* See Vol. 11, Chap. IX, n. 36.

55. *Strada delle Orseline:* The earlier Strada Vittoria received this name toward the end of the 17th century, when Princess Camilla Orsini Borghese founded an Ursuline convent there; it adjoins the Corso.

56. *Count Manuzzi:* See Vol. 11, Chaps. I and IV.

57. *The . . . traveler Manuzzi:* Nothing is known of a 13th-century traveler of this name; C. may refer to a Niccolò Manuzzi (1638 or '39 - ca. 1710), who led an adventurous life in India as confidential agent of Pitt and as physician to the Great Mogul; however, the history of the Great Mogul's domains which he wrote (*Storia del Mogor*) was not published until early in the 20th century.

58. *The famous printers:* Aldo Manuzio (latinized Aldus Manutius; 1449-1515), his son Paolo (1512-1574), and his nephew Aldo the Younger (1547-1597). Aldo established his press in Venice in 1498; the beauty and accuracy of its editions soon made it famous throughout Europe.

59. *The anchor:* The device of the Aldine press, adopted in 1499, was the anchor and dolphin.

60. *The Ambassador:* That is, Alvise Sebastiano Mocenigo, Venetian Ambassador in Madrid during C.'s stay there and Manuzzi's patron.

61. *Neuville:* Nothing more is known of him.

62. *Galli:* C. is in error. Antonio Andrea Galli (born 1697), Cardinal from 1753 and friend of Popes Benedict XIV and Clement XIII, had died in 1767 and so was no longer living at the time of which C. is writing.

63. *At my sister-in-law's:* That is, at the Hôtel Lafont (or Albergo di Londra), the proprietor of which was François Lafont, husband of the sister of Teresa Roland, whom C.'s brother Giovanni had married in 1764.

64. *The Emperor arrived . . . with . . . the Grand Duke of Tuscany:* C. is again in error. The Emperor Joseph II was in Rome in 1769 and 1775; however, his brother Leopold, Grand Duke of Tuscany, was in Rome in 1770.

65. *Marcuccio:* C. here, for example, failed to change the name to Menicuccio (see note 1 to this chapter).

66. *Near one of the gates of Rome:* At the beginning of Chapter II, C. says that the house was near the Basilica of San Paolo fuori le mura. So the gate must be the Porta San Paolo (or Porta Ostiense). The establishment was probably the Istituto di Santa Caterina de' Funari, where girls were taught various manual trades.

67. *Orsini:* Domenico Amadeo Orsini (1719-1789), of the ducal house of Gravina. After the death of his wife (1742) he took orders and was made a Cardinal in 1743.

CHAPTER II

1. *San Paolo:* The celebrated Basilica of San Paolo fuori le mura is a little more than a mile south of the Porta San Paolo on the road to Ostia, and so outside of the Aurelian wall (hence its name). It was built at the beginning of the 4th century by Constantine the Great, as the largest church in Christendom, over the grave of the Apostle Paul and in the course of the centuries became one of the most splendid of churches. A great part of it was destroyed by fire in 1823;

it was rebuilt as nearly as possible in accordance with the original plan.

2. *Guasco:* Ottaviano Guasco, Count of Clavières (1712-1780), native of Piedmont and a Canon of the Cathedral of Tours.

3. *Giulietta:* Giulia Ursula Preato, known as Giulietta and La Cavamacchie (1724 - ca. 1790), singer and courtesan; in 1752 she was married to Francesco Antonio Uccelli (born 1728). See especially Vol. 3, Chap. IX.

4. *Shuvalov:* Count Ivan Ivanovich Shuvalov (1727-1797), favorite of the Czarina Elisabeth and Chief Chamberlain at her Court; he founded the University of Moscow in 1756 and the Academy of Fine Arts in that city in 1758. (In Vol. 10, Chap. VI, n. 55, "Catherine the Great" should be corrected to "the Czarina Elisabeth.")

5. *Jacquier:* François Jacquier (1711-1788), French Franciscan friar. He was well known in his day as a mathematician and astronomer. In Rome he was on terms of friendship with Cardinal de Bernis.

6. *Mariuccia . . . wigmaker's shop . . . scopatore:* See Vol. 7, Chap. IX.

7. *Frascati:* Some 12 miles southeast of Rome, in the Alban Hills.

8. *Costa had returned to Rome . . . robbed me:* See Vol. 7, Chap. IX.

9. *Hardegg:* Johann Joseph Franz de Paula, Count Hardegg (born 1741), was High Steward and Cupbearer of Austria.

10. *Aliberti:* The Teatro Aliberti, built in 1718 near the Piazza di Spagna, was one of the largest theaters in Rome during the 18th century; it was demolished in the 19th century.

11. *Tablets:* See Vol. 3, Chap. XI, n. 14.

12. *Her palace:* The Palazzo dei Santa Croce was near the Campo di Fiore, the flower market in the heart of medieval Rome.

13. *Tor di nona:* This theater occupied the site of an old prison of the same name on the left bank of the Tiber opposite the Castel Sant'Angelo. First built in 1660 by Jacques d'Alibert, it was rebuilt in 1733 and 1798 and finally demolished in 1866. It belonged for a time to the Santa Croce family, who sold it in 1820.

14. *Pamelas:* Pamela is the name of the heroine of Richardson's

novel *Pamela* (published 1740); C. uses it generically for a
girl of the most rigid virtue.

15. *The Arcadians:* See Vol. 11, Chap. VII, n. 70.

16. *Marquise d'Aout:* Wife of the Marquis Anseaume d'Aout
(also Aoust), poetess and member of the Arcadian Academy.

17. *The Capranica:* A small theater, opened in 1678 by the
Marchese Pompeo Capranica in his palace near the Church
of Santa Maria in Aquiro, next to the Pantheon. Performances of *opera buffa* were given there from 1745 to the middle
of the 19th century. It is no longer used.

18. *Keep from laughing:* Crossed out: "I thought Armellina
adorable precisely because she did not love me; but the certainty spurred me on."

19. *Oysters . . . from the Arsenal:* See Vol. 8, Chap. X, n. 12.

20. *Bishop of Civitavecchia:* Cardinal Federigo Marcello Lante
della Rovere (1695-1773) was Bishop of Porto and Civitavecchia from 1763 until his death; friend of Cardinal de Bernis.

CHAPTER III

1. *The Marchesa della C. . . :* See Vol. 11, Chap. X.

2. *Showed . . . bad taste:* Canceled: "showed that he is stupid."

3. *Valued so little:* Canceled: "Woman is avaricious only of
some real beauty, of the effect of which when it is stolen she
is sure."

4. *Phainomerides:* Plural of Greek *phainomeris*, "a woman who
shows her hips." The Greek poet Ibykos (6th century B.C.) so
designated the women of Sparta, whose dresses were open at
the sides.

5. *Two-once piece:* The once, originally a measure of weight,
became the name of a coin in various countries. The reference
here is probably to the Neapolitan gold once.

6. *Donna Leonilda:* See note 1 to this chapter.

7. *Signor XXX:* He has not been identified.

8. *Rosenberg:* Franz Xaver Wolf, Count Orsini-Rosenberg
(1723-1796), Prince from 1790; from 1756 to 1765 Imperial
Ambassador in Madrid, from 1766 Major-domo to the Grand
Duke of Tuscany.

9. *Coronation of the Emperor Leopold:* Leopold II (1747-

1792), who was Grand Duke of Tuscany from 1765, was crowned Emperor in Prague on Sept. 6, 1791. C. first wrote "last year," then crossed it out. This shows that he originally wrote the passage in 1792 and later revised it.

10. *M. M.:* See note 37 to Chap. I of this volume. C. here first wrote "Maria Mathilde," then substituted "M. M."

11. *At Roland's:* At the "Ville de Londres," opposite the Church of San Carlo (cf. Vol. 11, Chap. IX, n. 3).

12. *Gabrielli:* Caterina Gabrielli (1730-1796), celebrated Italian singer, who appeared all over Europe; her sobriquet, "La Cochetta," derived from the fact that her father was a cook.

13. *Borghese:* Prince Giovanni Battista Francesco Borghese (born 1733).

14. *Tor di nona:* See note 13 to Chap. II of this volume.

15. *Scholastica:* Nothing is known of her except what C. relates. The name may well be fictitious.

CHAPTERS IV AND V

1. As stated in the Introduction (Vol. 1, p. 19), these two chapters are missing from the original manuscript. C.'s "Extrait du chapitre [sic] quatre et cinq," found at Dux in 1884 and not published until 1906, takes the place of the missing chapters in the Brockhaus-Plon edition. There, and in the present translation, it is printed in italics to distinguish it from the manuscript. In the manuscript, Chapter III ends on page 92, Chapter VI begins on page 149. The "Extrait" is contained in a notebook, written on twenty-two pages numbered 102–118 and 143–148. It would seem that C. intended either to omit Chapters IV and V entirely or to rewrite them later.

2. *On horseback on the Corso:* The reference is to the Trottata, a feature of the Carnival in all the larger Italian cities from the 17th century and on into the 20th. All the participants were masked, and carriages were usually elaborately decorated. In Rome it took place on the Corso.

3. *What had happened . . . seventeen years before:* The reference is to C.'s relationship with M. M. in Murano (see Vol. 4, Chap. VI). The same events are alluded to in the verses which follow.

4. *Holy Cross:* Punning allusion to the Princess of Santa Croce.
5. *Bank:* See Vol. 11, Chap. IV, n. 52.
6. *Accademia degli Infecondi:* The "Academy of the Sterile" was founded in Rome in the latter part of the 16th century by Father Domenico Spiretti, with purely religious ends. In 1650 it was transformed into a literary academy with a formal constitution. In the 18th century it had a renaissance; it met irregularly in the Palazzo Lancellotti near the Castel Sant'Angelo.
7. *Sophie . . . Pompeati:* See Vol. 11, Chap. VIII, n. 9.
8. *Signora Veronica:* Perhaps a Veronica Rossi, in whose father's house C.'s brother Giovanni (see the following note) and Mengs went to live in 1752; perhaps a Veronica Ruffini, in a house with whom Giovanni was living in 1757. Since C. speaks of a "niece" 13 years old, the second is the more likely candidate.
9. *Zanetto:* Venetian diminutive of Giovanni; here in reference to C.'s brother Giovanni Battista (1730-1795), a celebrated painter in his day.
10. *Villa Ludovisi . . . Lucrezia:* See Vol. 1, Chap. IX.
11. *Give me a number . . . the whole company win:* See Vol. 7, Chap. IX.
12. *Rezzonico:* Giambattista Rezzonico (1740-1783), Venetian patrician and nephew of Pope Clement XIII, Cardinal from 1770.
13. *The Temple:* Originally the headquarters of the Knights Templar in Paris, and occupying more or less the site of the present Square du Temple (3rd Arrondissement), by the 18th century it had become a sanctuary for insolvent debtors, who could not be arrested in its precincts.
14. *The seventy-third year of my life:* It follows that C. wrote this passage in the year before he died.
15. *Stratico . . . the Marchesa Chigi in Siena:* See Vol. 11, Chap. VII.
16. *The General of the Order:* In 1770-1771 the Magister Generalis of the Dominican Order was Juan Tomás de Boxadors (1703 - ca. 1780), made a Cardinal in 1775.
17. *A pack of friars:* C. writes "des padrasses," after Italian *papasso,* a disrespectful augmentative.

18. *Mamachi:* Tommaso Maria Mamachi (1713-1792), Dominican and Secretary to the Congregation of the Index.

19. *Morosini:* See Vol. 11, Chap. VII, n. 48.

20. *Would recall him to Versailles:* Cardinal Pierre de Bernis (1715-1794) had fallen into Louis XV's disfavor in 1758 and in 1769 been sent to Rome as Chargé d'Affaires. He was never recalled.

21. *The beginning of June 1771:* C. is in error, for his extant correspondence shows that he cannot have left Rome before the middle of July 1771.

22. *Translate it . . . Italian stanzas:* Count Giandomenico Stratico had given C. the translation by Giovanni Dal Turco which had just been published. This would seem to have increased C.'s eagerness to publish his own translation. The first three volumes of the contemplated four appeared in Venice from 1775 to 1778 (19 books out of 24) after C.'s return to his native country. (In Vol. 10, Chap. III, n. 33, "from 1755 to 1788" should be corrected to "from 1775 to 1778.") The fact that the complete translation by Cristoforo Ridolfi was published, in a much handsomer edition, at Venice the year after C.'s first volume appeared may have influenced him to abandon the publication before it was completed. By "Italian stanzas" C. means *ottava rima.*

23. *Salvini:* The translation by the Greek scholar Antonio Maria Salvini (1653-1729) had been published in 1723.

24. *Pope:* Pope's English translation of the *Iliad* had been published in 6 volumes at London from 1715 to 1718.

25. *Barbaro . . . Dandolo:* Marco Dandolo (1704-1779) was the only surviving member of the triumvirate of Venetian patricians who had been C.'s faithful friends and patrons from 1746. The two others, Marco Barbaro and Matteo Giovanni Bragadin, had died in 1771 and 1767 respectively.

26. *I dressed in black:* In the 18th century wearing black—except as a sign of mourning—indicated that one was not rich and did not want to mingle in society.

27. *Pitti Palace:* The building of the immense Palazzo Pitti, with some 900 rooms, was begun by Brunelleschi in 1440. It is located south of the Arno and today houses, among other things, a celebrated art gallery. Until 1859 it was the residence of the Grand Dukes of Tuscany.

28. *Leopold:* Grand Duke Leopold resided in the Palazzo Pitti from 1765 to 1790; he then became Emperor as Leopold II. He died in 1792, so C.'s "seven years ago" is an error (C. died in 1798).

29. *Rosenberg:* See note 8 to Chap. III of this volume.

30. *Pazzi:* C. writes both "Pazzi" and "Puzzi." The reference may be to the Marchese Gian Cosimo Pazzi (1706-1773), or to his son Francesco (died 1821), or to a Marchese Domenico Pucci.

31. *A Marchesa:* Marchesa Maria Anna Vitelli (1702-1776), née Frescobaldi, married to Niccolò Vitelli, Marchese di Bucina, in 1720. After her husband's death she moved to Rome in 1747 and received artists and writers in her house.

CHAPTER VI

1. *The Young Grand Duke:* Leopold, Grand Duke of Tuscany from 1765, had been born in 1747, and so was 24 years old at the time of which C. was writing.

2. *The old government:* Tuscany had been under Hapsburg dominion from 1737 and was first ruled by Governors. From 1757 to 1766 the office was held by the Marchese Antonio Ottone Botta-Adorno (cf. Vol. 7, Chap. VIII). In 1765 Tuscany became the "Secundogenitur" (right of the younger son) of the House of Hapsburg, and Leopold, son of the Empress Maria Theresa, became Grand Duke.

3. *An anthology of Greek epigrams:* Its title was *Epigrammi greci scelti tradotti in versi latini e toscani* (Leghorn, 1772).

4. *Averardo de' Medici:* Died 1808, descended from the famous Florentine family, writer of prose and poetry.

5. *Maddalena:* Maddalena Allegranti (ca. 1750 - after 1799), Italian singer; her career began in Venice in 1770. She married an Irish officer in the English service, probably when she was in Ireland in 1781.

6. *Morosini:* Cf. especially Vol. 11, Chap. X.

7. *The opera in Lucca:* There were several theaters in Lucca at the time.

8. *La Denis:* Giovanna Denis, née Corrini (ca. 1728 - after 1797), Italian dancer, known as La Pantaloncina, married to the French ballet master Jean Baptiste Denis. C. had known

her when she first appeared in Venice at the age of 8 (cf. Vol. 10, Chap. IV).

9. *The best-known coffeehouse:* The most frequented coffeehouses in Florence at the time were on the Piazza del Granduca (now Piazza della Signoria) and the Piazza del Duomo. To which coffeehouse C. refers has not been determined.

10. *Her lover . . . in 1764:* See Vol. 10, Chap. IV.

11. *Bregonzi:* Caterina Bregonzi, or Brigonzi, Venetian singer, appeared in St. Petersburg ca. 1750 (cf. Vol. 10, Chap. IV).

12. *Capponi:* Either the Marchese Alessandro Maria Capponi (1720-1788) or Gino Pasquale Capponi (1716-1781), both of whom were Chamberlains to the Emperor Francis I; the first was a member of the Accademia della Crusca, the second Major-General of the troops of the Grand Duke of Tuscany.

13. *Corilla:* See Vol. 11, Chap. VII, n. 61.

14. *Ginori:* The Marchese Lorenzo Ginori (1734-1791).

15. *Signora XX:* In his correspondence with Cäcilie von Roggendorf in 1797 C. gives some details of this "unhappy love," but does not mention the lady's name.

16. *The English girl . . . seduced:* See Vol. 11, Chap. VIII.

17. *Henriade:* Voltaire's epic poem *La Henriade,* in ten cantos, celebrates the life and accomplishments of Henri IV of France, who, by issuing the Edict of Nantes in 1698, became the champion of religious tolerance.

18. *Translated into Italian stanzas:* Medini's translation, *L'Enriade del Signor di Voltaire tradotta in ottava rima . . . dal Conte Tommaso Medini,* was published at Munich in 1774.

19. *Fontana:* Felice Fontana (1730-1805), Italian physician and naturalist, Professor of Philosophy at the University of Pisa and later director of a museum in Florence, was ennobled by the Emperor Joseph II and finally appointed Court Physician to Grand Duke Leopold of Tuscany, later the Emperor Leopold II.

20. *Zanovich:* Premislas Zanovich (ca. 1751 - ca. 1774), Dalmatian adventurer.

21. *His brother:* Stepan Zanovich (ca. 1750-1786), brother of Premislas and also an adventurer, who took the name of Prince Scanderbeg. Scanderbeg (from "Iskander" and "beg"

with the meaning "lord") lived from 1404 to 1466 and was the national hero of the Albanians because of his courageous resistance to the Turks. It was not Stepan but his brother Premislas who, in the role of a rich Dalmatian merchant named Nicola Peovich, cheated two merchants of Amsterdam out of large sums of money.

22. *Budua:* Now Budva on the Adriatic coast south of the Gulf of Cattaro (Kotor) and just north of the present boundary between Albania and Yugoslavia.

23. *Epirus:* Classic Greek province south of the present Albania.

24. *Stepan:* See note 21 to this chapter.

25. *Puzzi:* C. writes both Puzzi and Pazzi. The reference may be to (1) the Marchese Gian Cosimo Pazzi (1706-1773), or, more probably, (2) his son Francesco (died 1821), who was made a Knight of the Order of St. Stephen in 1776 and was Chamberlain to the Grand Duke of Tuscany, or (3) a Marchese Domenico Pucci, who is often mentioned in letters of the period.

26. *The Crocelle:* See Vol. 11, Chap. IX, n. 20.

27. *Alvise Zen:* Descended from a well-known patrician family of Venice, he is several times mentioned as guilty of bad conduct in the registers of the Venetian State Inquisition. His father Francesco was Adjutant of the Fortress of Sant' Andrea.

28. *Captain Zen . . . imprisoned . . . Sant'Andrea:* See Vol. 1, Chap. VII.

29. *Marco Zen:* Venetian patrician (1723 - after 1785), was Venetian Ambassador in Madrid from 1771 to 1775 and Podestà of Treviso from 1781 to 1783.

30. *Lincoln:* Henry Pelham Clinton (1752-1778), Earl Lincoln.

31. *La Lamberti:* Marianna Lamberti (died after 1777), Italian dancer, appeared in Venice from 1764, later in other cities, and in Florence in 1771.

32. *Via del Carro:* The street no longer exists.

33. *Newcastle:* Henry Fiennes Clinton (1720-1794), 2nd Duke of Newcastle-under-Lyne from 1768, father of the Earl Lincoln identified in note 30.

34. *Same day . . . ordered to leave Barcelona:* See Vol. 11, Chap. V.

35. *Auditor:* Auditore fiscale was the title of the official in charge of the entire police of the Grand Duchy of Tuscany; from 1760 the office was held by Count Roberto Pandolfini.

36. *The same man . . . forged bill of exchange:* See Vol. 7, Chap. VIII.

37. *Tutor . . . eleven years earlier:* C. does not mention this tutor in his account of his stay in Lausanne in Vol. 6, Chap. IX.

38. *The first post house:* Probably Loiano, some 22 miles south of Bologna on the road to Florence.

39. *"San Marco" inn:* It was also the post station and survived into the 19th century. In C.'s day it was considered very bad.

40. *Marulli:* A Count Marulli, from 1767 Florentine Ambassador in Rome, was in 1772 Chargé d'Affaires in Bologna. Though Bologna then belonged to the Papal States, it had certain privileges, especially of a diplomatic nature. It was represented in Rome by a Chargé d'Affaires, and several powers had diplomatic representatives in Bologna.

41. *Branciforte:* Antonio Branciforte Colonna, Prince of Scordia (1711-1786), was Cardinal-Legate in Bologna from 1770 to 1777. C. has said nothing of having known him in Paris earlier.

42. *Sersale:* Francesco, Count of Sersale (ca. 1716-1772), of Naples; well-known gamester of the period, lived in Paris from ca. 1751 to 1760. C. here mentions him for the first time.

43. *Ranucci:* Girolamo Ranucci (also Ranuzzi), Count of Porretta (born ca. 1724), was descended from an old Bolognese family. C. has not mentioned him before.

44. *Arcades:* These arcades are still an attractive feature of many streets in the inner city of Bologna.

45. *Birichini:* Properly, the name given to organized bands of ruffians among the populace of Bologna. Each band was drawn from a particular neighborhood and had a captain. The *birichini* were noted for their violence; but protection from them could be bought from their leaders.

46. *Lazzaroni:* The *lazzaroni,* or *lazzari,* were the common people of Naples.

47. *Bologna . . . university:* The University of Bologna, founded in 1119, is one of the oldest in Europe. Its culture was communicated in some measure to the whole city, which

Goldoni called "Mother of the Sciences" and "the Athens of Italy."

48. *The Inquisition:* The Inquisition was still especially redoubtable in the Papal States (cf. Vol. 2, Chap. XI, n. 21).

49. *De Dominis:* Giuseppe de Dominis (died after 1776), monk in the Bolognese monastery de' Zoccolanti (1772); subscriber to the second volume of C.'s *Iliad*.

50. *His* Henriade: See note 17 to this chapter.

51. *The Elector Palatine:* Karl Theodor von Wittelsbach (1724-1799), from 1742 Elector of the Palatinate, from 1777 Elector of Bavaria.

52. *Tosio:* There is a Casa Tosio in Venice, but nothing is known of the family or its representatives.

53. *Taruffi:* Jacopo Taruffi (died after 1780), Bolognese bookseller and poet.

54. *L'Utero pensante:* Its proper title was *Di geniali della dialettica delle donne ridotta al suo vero principio* (Bologna, 1771); its author was Pietro Zecchini, Professor of Philosophy and Medicine at the University of Bologna from 1770.

55. *La Force vitale:* Its proper title was *Lettres de Madame Cunégonde écrites de Bologne à Madame Pacquette à Florence à l'occasion d'un livre qui a pour titre Di Geniali . . .* (Bologna, 1771); its author was Germano Azzoguidi, also a Professor at the University of Bologna. C. obviously passes over the proper titles of both pamphlets in favor of titles of his own invention which briefly indicate their contents.

56. *Lana Caprina:* Full title: *Lana Caprina. Epistola di un Licantropo indiritta a S. A. la Signora Principessa J. L. n. P. C. Ultima Edizione. In nessun luogo. L'Anno 1 000 7 000 702* (Venice, 1772). "Lana Caprina" is from Horace, *Epistles*, 1, 18, 15: *Alter rixatur de lana saepe caprina* ("Another often wrangles over goat's wool").

57. *Zacchiroli:* The Abate Zacchiroli (1750-1826) was a writer and member of the Arcadian Academy under the name of Euripilo Naricio.

58. *Severini:* Giuseppe Severini (died after 1777), lived in Rome in 1775, then in Naples, but returned to Bologna in 1777.

59. *Carlani:* Carlo Carlani, Italian singer, appeared in Venice, Naples, and Vienna. Born in 1738, he is said to have lived

until after 1780, so that the "widow" with whom C. went to stay must rather have been his wife. Carlani was an intimate friend of the celebrated castrato Farinelli.

60. *Albergati Capacelli:* The Marchese Francesco Albergati Capacelli (1728-1804); C. seems to have forgotten that he spoke slightingly of him in one of his conversations with Voltaire (cf. Vol. 6, Chap. X). Albergati's marriage to Teresa Orsi was annulled by Pope Benedict XIV in 1751. He did not marry Caterina Boccabadati until 1772.

61. *Zaguri:* Pietro I Antonio Zaguri (1733-1806), Venetian patrician and Senator; he was a patron of Lorenzo da Ponte, who was his secretary for a time. Most of Zaguri's letters to C. from 1772 to 1798 are extant.

62. *His country house:* Albergati owned three villas: La Vigna, close to Bologna; Zola Predosa, halfway between Bologna and Bassano; and another in Medicina.

63. *Chamberlain:* Albergati was appointed Chambellan (Chamberlain) to the King of Poland in 1767; and in 1768 Adjutant de camp (Field Adjutant) with the title Aide de camp général au service de S. M. le Roi de Pologne (General Aide-de-camp in the service of His Majesty the King of Poland), with permission to wear the uniform but without obligation to serve the King in war. He did not receive the Cross of St. Stanislas until Dec. 17, 1772.

64. *A comic dialogue:* This dialogue has survived neither in manuscript nor in print.

65. *Baiocco:* Copper coin minted in the Papal States (cf. Vol. 1, Chap. VIII, n. 29).

CHAPTER VII

1. *The Republic of Poland:* Such was the official designation of Poland from the time when the Kingdom of Poland was united with the Grand Duchy of Lithuania and the first elective King was proclaimed in 1573.

2. *Mischinski:* C. is in error. From 1771 to 1774 the official Polish Envoy Extraordinary in Paris was Franciszek Kwilecki. Mischinski (so C. writes—perhaps for Miasczynski) may have been an official of the embassy.

3. *The Dowager Electress of Saxony:* See Vol. 11, Chap. IX, n. 16.

4. *Farinelli:* Carlo Broschi, called Il Farinello or Farinelli (1705-1782), Italian singer and member of the lesser Neapolitan nobility; as a castrato he won great acclaim, especially in Spain, where from 1737 he was a familiar of the royal household under Philip V and Isabela and Fernando VI but was exiled from Spain by Carlos III in 1759.

5. *The Parmesan Queen:* Elisabetta, Princess Farnese (1692-1766), became in 1714 the second wife of Philip V of Spain and thus Queen of Spain under the name Isabela.

6. *Ensenada:* See Vol. 11, Chap. II, n. 14.

7. *Amigoni:* See Vol. 11, Chap. II, n. 28.

8. *Ferdinand VI:* Fernando VI (1713-1759), King of Spain from 1746.

9. *Queen Barbara:* Maria Barbara, Princess of Portugal (1711–1758), married in 1729 to Fernando, Prince of Asturias, who became King of Spain as Fernando VI in 1746. During their reign Farinelli had a position of extraordinary influence at Court, which, however, he did not abuse.

10. *A nephew:* Matteo Pisani, son of Farinelli's sister Dorotea; in 1768 he married Anna Gatteschi, of the higher Bolognese nobility.

11. *A noble Tuscan family:* C. is in error. Her family was Bolognese (cf. the preceding note).

12. *Lincoln:* See the preceding chapter, *passim* and n. 30.

13. *Callimena:* See Vol. 11, Chap. IX, n. 40.

14. *When I come to that time:* Another of the many indications that C. intended to continue his memoirs beyond 1774.

15. *Nina Bergonzi:* See Vol. 11, Chap. IV, n. 57, and *ibid.* Chap. V, *passim.*

16. *Martino:* He has not been identified.

17. *Zini:* He has not been identified.

18. *La Montagnola:* A small hill, the public promenade of Bologna, very fashionable in the 18th century.

19. *The Cardinal-Archbishop:* Vincenzo Malvezzi (1715-1775), Cardinal from 1753, Archbishop of Bologna from 1754.

20. *The Valerian law:* The so-called Valerian laws were collections of laws promulgated by several Roman consuls named Valerius between the 6th and 1st centuries B.C.

21. *Red cockades:* Red was the national color of Spain and of the Kingdom of the Two Sicilies.
22. *A year later he died:* Ambrosio Funes de Villalpando, Count of Ricla, was Captain-General of Catalonia from 1767; he was appointed Spanish Minister of War in 1772; but he did not die until 1780.
23. *La Marcucci:* See Vol. 11, Chap. IV, n. 50.
24. *La Pelliccia:* See Vol. 11, Chaps. II and IV.
25. *La Soavi:* Geltruda Soavi, Italian dancer, appeared in Venice, Vienna, and Paris from 1750. C. has not mentioned her before.
26. *Marcello:* The Marcelli di San Polo were a Venetian patrician family. The reference here is perhaps to Piero Marcello (1719-1790), who in 1755 was sentenced to five years' imprisonment under the Leads for dissolute living.
27. *Marigni:* Nothing is known of him. In the 18th century the title Musketeer was reserved for young noblemen serving in the royal forces.
28. *Adelaide:* Adelaide Soavi (died ca. 1784), appeared as a dancer in Venice from 1781.
29. *Her husband:* His name is not known.
30. *Count Du Barry:* Jean Baptiste Du Barry (1723-1794), brother-in-law of Countess Jeanne Du Barry, née Bécu, the celebrated mistress of Louis XV, who married her to Count Guillaume Du Barry in 1768.
31. *Last King of France:* Louis XV was succeeded by his grandson, who reigned as Louis XVI from 1774 to 1791 and was the last King of France in C.'s lifetime. C. seems to have considered Louis XVI unworthy of the title of King; for his admiration for Louis XV, see Vol. 3, Chap. IX.
32. *Afflisio:* Giuseppe Afflisio, also Affligio, who also used the names Don Bepe il Cadetto and Don Giuseppe Marcati (died 1787), Italian adventurer, professional gambler, theater director, and officer in the Austrian army (cf. especially Vol. 3, Chap. XII).
33. *Filomarino:* He has not been identified.
34. *Sabbatini:* Anna Sabbatini, also Sabatini, Bolognese dancer, appeared from 1748 in Milan, Venice, and Naples, and from 1771 in Lisbon. C. calls her sister Brigitta; but the only sister she is known to have had was named Dorotea. C. has not

previously mentioned a Professor of Anatomy in connection
with her.

35. *Only son . . . Novara:* The Abate Carlo Bollini, of Novara, of whom nothing more is known. Novara is some 30
miles west of Milan.

36. *Knot . . . Alexander's sword:* Reference to the Gordian
knot (cf. Vol. 9, Chap. I, n. 16).

37. *Dandolo:* See Vol. 11, Chap. I, n. 49.

38. *Finale:* Finale Emilia, formerly Finale di Modena, station
on the post road from Modena to Ferrara.

39. *Viscioletta:* Margherita Giacinta Irene Gibetti, called La
Viscioletta (1744 - after 1782), Neapolitan singer and courtesan.

40. *The Quaranta Davia:* Quaranta was the name of the Bolognese Senate (cf. Vol. 6, Chap. X, n. 53) and also the title of
its individual members. The reference is either to the Marchese Giuseppe Davia or to Giacomo Davia, both of whom
were members of the Bolognese Senate at the time.

41. *Buoncompagni:* Ignazio Lodovico, Prince Buoncompagni-
Ludovisi (1743-1790), Vice-Legate in Bologna from 1769,
made a Cardinal in 1775.

42. *Zulian:* See Vol. 11, Chap. I, n. 51.

43. *The Duchess of Fiano:* See note 11 to Chap. I of this
volume.

44. *Mosca:* The Marchese Carlo Mosca-Barzi (1718-1790),
owner of a printing press in Pesaro and author of several
theological works. C. refers to his treatise on almsgiving,
*Lettera scritta ad un suo amico di Rovereto in proposito della
limosina* (Rovereto, 1765), which was put on the Index in
March 1766. He was married to Countess Francesca della
Branca Barzi.

45. *Jansenists:* See Vol. 9, Chap. I, n. 25.

46. *Ennius:* Quintus Ennius (239-169 B.C.), considered the first
Roman poet of importance.

47. *Marmora Pisaurentia:* C. refers to *Marmora Pisaurentia
notis illustrata* (Pesaro, 1737), by Annibale degli Abati Olivieri Giordani, a work on the history of Pesaro (Latin,
Pisaurum).

48. *Musa:* Latin *musca* ("fly") yields Italian *mosca*. Deleting

the letter *c* from *musca* gives *musa* ("the Muse"), an allusion
to the Marchese's interest in literature.

49. Horace, *Satires*, 1, 1, 106f: *fines / quos ultra citraque
    nequit consistere rectum* ("the bounds beyond which and
    short of which the fitting cannot exist").

50. Horace, *Satires*, 1, 9, 70. Properly, "I have no scruples";
    but C. takes *religio* to mean "religion."

51. Horace, *Odes*, 1, 34.

52. *The Marchese's brother:* Francesco Mosca, made a Knight
    of Malta in 1738; he inherited the estate of Cardinal Agape-
    tus Mosca.

CHAPTER VIII

1. *Priapeia:* Priapus was a Greek fertility god, also worshiped
   in Rome, whose representations were characterized by an
   enormous phallus. A collection of some 80 Latin poems, late
   literary imitations of inscriptions on his statues, many of
   them obscene, has been preserved under the title *Priapeia.*

2. *Fescennina:* The *Carmina Fescennina*, named from Fescen-
   nium in southern Etruria, were originally an exchange of
   rustic jibes in verse on the occasion of the festivals of Ceres
   and Bacchus. Some time before the Christian era they became a literary genre, sung at weddings.

3. *Apology:* To what apologetic work of Mosca's C. refers is
   not certainly known; perhaps to the essay in epistolary form,
   La matematica fatta guide per credere ("Mathematics made
   a guide to faith") (Rome, 1772).

4. Matthew, 6:3.

5. *The Gulf:* The northern part of the Adriatic was called the
   Gulf of Venice into the 19th century.

6. *Tartan:* A small vessel used in the Mediterranean and
   carrying a mast with a lateen sail and two jibs.

7. *What . . . Socrates called his "Demon":* C. had been introduced to this concept in his youth by Senator Malipiero and
   often refers to it. Cf. Vol. 1, Chap. VI, and *ibid.*, note 8.

8. *Mordecai:* Fictitious name (C. writes "Mardoqué").

9. *The Exchange:* The Loggia dei Mercanti in Ancona, built in
   1459 and still standing.

10. *Almost thirty years earlier:* C. first stayed in Ancona in the autumn of 1743, and then again in the spring of 1744. The year of which he is writing is 1772.

11. *Twenty-six years ago:* It follows that C. wrote this passage in 1798, the year of his death.

12. Horace, *Epistles,* 2, 2, 126–128.

13. *Leah:* C. writes "Lia." It had already served him as the name of the Jewess in Vol. 7, Chap. XII.

14. *Wine from . . . Cyprus:* Wine from Cyprus was considered among the best in the 18th century and fetched very high prices. The island of Cyprus was a kingdom from 1192 to 1489, when the Venetian Cattarina Cornaro, after the death of her husband the King and their son, gave it to the Republic of Venice. It was conquered by the Turks in 1571.

15. *The Venetian Consul:* Giorgio M. Bandiera, properly Venetian Chargé d'Affaires in Ancona. He immediately informed the Council of Ten of C.'s arrival in Ancona by a letter dated Oct. 12, 1772.

16. *Pantalone:* One of the stock characters of the *commedia dell'arte,* an elderly Venetian merchant.

17. *Scopolo wine:* A well-known wine from the island of Skópelos in the Aegean (now Greek, then under Turkish rule).

18. *The Jewess in Turin:* See Vol. 7, Chap. XII.

19. *The collection . . . Aretino:* A collection of engravings illustrating postures for sexual intercourse. Cf. Vol. 4, Chap. IV, n. 22, and Vol. 8, Chap. IV, n. 43.

20. *Philosophized . . . the Genevan Hedwig:* See Vol. 8, Chap. IV.

21. *Cacochymics:* Persons suffering from a vitiated state of the body fluids, especially the blood.

22. *Paralogisms:* Pseudo-syllogisms, in which the conclusion does not follow from the premises.

23. *The straight tree:* See Vol. 4, Chap. IV, n. 22 (where "thirty-two" should be corrected to "thirty-five").

24. *Peota:* A kind of covered gondola (cf. Vol. 1, Chap. VII, n. 28).

25. *The Canal:* The Canale del Carnaro (Quarnero, Quarnaro, or Guarnero), corresponding to the southern part of the present Carnaro.

26. *The captain of the peota:* The text has "poste," which is

either a slip of C.'s or more probably an editor's misreading or a typographical error for *péote*.

27. *Let me go ashore:* An arriving passenger should properly have been put in quarantine.

28. *Over her of a temperament:* C. writes "sur un tempérament" (omitting "elle").

29. Horace, *De arte poetica,* 180.

30. *The Jewish law:* Intercourse during the menstrual period was forbidden; cf. Leviticus, Chap. 15.

31. *The Locanda Grande:* This inn, on the Piazza Grande in Trieste, had been built by the municipality and was let to an innkeeper approved by the magistrates. It provided good food and lodging at unusually low rates.

CHAPTER IX

1. *Donà:* Marco Donà delle Torreselle (1709 - after 1774), Venetian patrician.

2. *Pittoni:* In 1772 Pietro Antonio Pittoni (1730-1807) held the post of Executive Commissary and Assessor of Police; he was not made Chief of Police of Trieste until 1777. He was a member of the Arcadian Academy.

3. *Levi:* Moses Levi (1721-1805), Jewish merchant in Trieste.

4. *Cold reception:* Extant letters show that C. and Pittoni later became good friends.

5. *A history of the troubles:* C.'s *Istoria delle turbolenze della Polonia dalla morte di Elisabetta Petrovna fino alla pace fra la Russia e la Porta Ottomano in cui si trovano tutti gli avvenimenti cagioni della rivoluzione di quel regno* ("History of the Troubles in Poland from the death of Elisabeth Petrovna to the peace between Russia and the Ottoman Porte, in which are recounted all the events which caused the revolution in that kingdom") was published at Görz (Gorizia) in 3 volumes, 1774-1775.

6. *Published a prediction:* Nothing is known of this publication, nor is there any trace of it among C.'s surviving papers. He refers to the partition of 1772.

7. *The printer:* He was Valerio de' Valeri, of Cividale, who established a press in Görz in 1773 and from 1774 also printed the *Gazzetta Goriziana.*

History of My Life

8. *The other four . . . after my death:* These mss. were not found among C.'s papers at Dux.

9. *The Elector of Brandenburg:* I.e., Frederick the Great. Frederick III, Elector from 1688, had adopted the style "King of Prussia" and was crowned at Königsberg in 1701. Frederick the Great called himself "King of Prussia."

10. *The Duchy of Prussia:* East Prussia, which was made a Duchy in the 16th century under King Sigismund I of Poland.

11. *Fable of the man and the horse:* Reference to the Aesopian fable of a young man who mounted a wild horse which ran away with him.

12. *Wine . . . Koran . . . hate it:* The Koran forbids the drinking of any alcoholic beverage.

13. *Venice . . . eternal shame:* This sentence is added between the lines in C.'s ms.; hence he revised this chapter after the final dissolution of the Venetian Republic by the Treaty of Milan (May 10, 1797), by which the Great Council renounced all rights and surrendered Venice to the French troops.

14. *Louis XVI:* Louis XVI, King of France from 1774, was executed in 1793.

15. *Assembly . . . impossible:* C. here inveighs against the French National Assembly.

16. *Avogador:* The Senate of the Venetian Republic regularly appointed three magistrates to serve for 16 months with the title of Avogador del Comun; they exercised supreme judicial authority. Zaguri was made one of the three Avogadori in 1772.

17. *Monti:* Marco de'Monti (died 1782), Venetian Consul in Trieste from 1763.

18. *The two years I spent there:* C. spent not quite two years in Trieste. He arrived there Nov. 15, 1772, was pardoned by the Venetian State Inquisitors on Sept. 3, 1774, and left Trieste for Venice on Sept. 10, 1774.

19. *Heimweh . . . nostalgia:* See Vol. 11, Chap. II, nn. 21 and 22.

20. *Ungrateful . . . stepmother:* C. fell into disgrace with the State Inquisitors again in 1782 by publishing a pamphlet

criticizing the Venetian Patriciate, *Nè amori nè donne, ovvero la stalla ripulita* ("Neither Loves nor Ladies, or the Stable Cleaned"), which appeared in Aug. 1782. On Jan. 13, 1783, C. left Venice never to return, except for a brief stay on his way through the city in June of the same year.

21. *Auersperg:* Count Heinrich Auersperg, Lord of (Herr auf) Schönberg and Saisenburg (1721-1793), had been President of the Intendancy of Trieste from 1764. The title of Governor was not created until 1776.

22. *Cobenzl:* Count Guido Cobenzl, Baron of Prosegg, Luegg, Mossa, and Leitenburg (1716-1797), was a member of the Arcadian Academy under the pastoral name of Eurimante Epidaurico and founded a branch of the Academy in Görz.

23. *Torres:* Count Emanuel Anton Torres (1743-1789), member of the Government Chancellery of Görz and from 1772 its Director. His father, Count Emanuel Torres (ca. 1686-1775), was a Field Marshal in the Austrian service.

24. *Contract:* The contract between C. and the printer Valerio de' Valeri (see note 7 to this chapter) was signed on Sept. 3, 1773.

25. *Coronini:* Rudolf Coronini-Cronberg, Baron of Prebacina and Gradiscuta (1731-1791), author of historical works.

26. *Journal des Savants:* The oldest French, and indeed European, literary and scientific periodical; it was founded in 1665, principally to publish articles and reviews by members of the various French royal academies.

27. *Morelli:* Karl Morelli von Schönfeld (1730-1792), Austrian government official and historian. The first two parts of his history of Görz, *Del saggio storico della Contea di Gorizia dall'anno 1500*, were published in Görz in 1772.

28. *Karl Coronini:* Franz Karl, Reichsgraf Coronini-Cronberg (1736-1775), Austrian Chamberlain and army officer.

29. *Apostem:* External tumor with suppuration. C.'s father had died of the same disease (cf. Vol. 1, Chap. I).

30. *Pini:* The Abate Giovanni Domenico Pini (died after 1796); he corresponded with C. in 1772.

31. *Büchelin:* David Büchelin, of Kempten, merchant (1727-1789), was married to Johanna Rosina, née Pfauz (ca. 1750-1787), of Augsburg (C. writes "Piquelin").

32. *Morosini:* Francesco Lorenzo Morosini (1714-1793), Venetian patrician and diplomat, Procurator of San Marco from 1755.

33. *Savio Grande:* The 6 Savi Grandi, with certain other Savi, made up the Venetian Pien Collegio; their powers could be likened to those of ministers.

34. *Presented me . . . at Fontainebleau:* See Vol. 3, Chap. IX.

35. *His nephew in Florence:* See Chap. VI of this volume.

36. *The French Consul:* André Grasset de Saint-Sauveur (died 1810) was French Consul General in Trieste from 1772 to 1781.

37. *Signora Leo:* Antonio Saverio di Leo (died 1776), patrician of Trieste, married Maddalena, née de' Costanzi, in 1744.

38. *The Harlequin:* Probably Elena, daughter of Antonio Saverio di Leo (see the preceding note).

39. *Wagensperg:* Count Adolf von Wagensperg, Baron of Sauegg and Rabenstein (1724-1773). He did not have the title Governor (cf. note 21 to this chapter). He was married in 1747 to Maria Luise, née Countess von Saurau.

40. *Countess Lantieri:* Countess Luise (Aloisia) Lantieri, née von Wagensperg (ca. 1748 - after 1823), married to Count Federico Lantieri-Puriatico in 1764.

41. *Verses . . . I published: Applausi poetici dovuti dalla felice, inclita ed ossequiosa città di Trieste al merito sovra grande dell'Ill.mo Signor Conte Adolfo di Wagensperg.* C. rewrote it in 1787 as a panegyric on the Archbishop of Prague.

42. *One stage:* A stage was reckoned to be a journey of about two hours. However, Udine is more than 18 miles north of the direct road between Trieste and Venice.

43. *He said:* C. writes "me dit" (omitting "il").

44. *The two States:* Austria and the Venetian Republic.

45. *Rizzi:* Pasquale Rizzi, also Ricco (1721-1791), Baron from 1766; patrician and magistrate of Trieste.

46. *Free port:* Trieste was declared a free port in 1719 by the Emperor Charles VI.

47. *Than to Udine:* Udine was then a possession of the Venetian Republic.

48. *The . . . problem of the Armenians:* The Armenian (or Gregorian) Church has been a separate entity from the 6th century. Some Popes succeeded in obtaining the allegiance of

certain groups in the Armenian Church (the so-called "united Armenians"). Among these was the Congregation of the Mekhitarists, so named after their founder Petro Mekhitar (1676-1749), who devoted themselves to preserving and commenting on the theological literature of Armenia. The Congregation was confirmed by Pope Clement XI in 1712 and adopted the Benedictine Rule. In 1702 the Mekhitarists emigrated to Morea (Greece), which was then under Venetian rule, but the subsequent arrival of the Turks forced them to leave and take refuge on the island of San Lazzaro, near Venice, where they founded a monastery in 1717.

49. *Four Armenian monks . . . deserted:* As the result of a dispute in the monastery, which had become very rich by gifts, a group of dissident monks left it and settled first in Trieste and, in 1810, in Vienna, where they elected an Abbot of their own. Their Abbot at San Lazzaro, Melkonian, would seem to have had all the defects which C. attributes to him. Since the work of printing done by the Armenian monks was of great financial importance to Venice, the Republic did everything in its power, though vainly, to bring the dissidents back to San Lazzaro.

50. *Their Armenian types:* Armenian is an Indo-European language with an alphabet that was established in the 5th century A.D.

51. *Their Patriarch:* Properly the Patriarch of Venice, under whose ecclesiastical jurisdiction the Mekhitarist monastery was; but the monk may have been thinking of the head of the Armenian Church, who resided in the monastery of Echmiadzin, near Vagarshapat (Armenian S.S.R.).

52. *Serpos:* The Marchese Giovanni Serpos (died after 1799), Roman nobleman and banker for the Kingdom of Spain in Venice; he was married to a sister of Abbot Melkonian of San Lazzaro.

53. *Basilians . . . three centuries:* C. is doubly in error. The Monastery of San Lazzaro was not founded until 1717, and the Mekhitarists followed the Benedictine Rule, not that of St. Basil (330-379).

54. *A few words which Count Wagensperg said to me:* C. did not become active in the matter of the Armenian monks until Jan. 1774, but Count Wagensperg died in Nov. 1773.

55. *La Messola:* On the Po di Goro, some 40 miles from Ferrara.

56. *Savi alla Mercanzia:* They were members, with other Savi, of the Pien Collegio (see note 33 to this chapter); their domain was commerce.

57. *President:* That is, Count Wagensperg, to whom C. has before referred as Governor but whose proper title was President of the Intendancy of Trieste (cf. notes 21 and 39 to this chapter).

58. *Confidenti:* The Venetian State Inquisitors had their principal source of information in the *confidenti* ("secret agents") whom they employed. C. himself became one of their *confidenti* when he returned to Venice.

59. *Businello:* Marcantonio Businello, also Busenello, was Secretary of the Council of Ten from 1761. The brother of his to whom C. refers was named Pietro and held the same office in 1755.

60. *Reduce . . . to nothing:* Venice finally lost its primacy as a mercantile port to Trieste in the 19th century.

61. *Strasoldo:* Rudolf, Count Strasoldo (died after 1789), assistant magistrate in Trieste from 1772, Kreishauptmann (see note 63) of Galicia in 1774, was sentenced to death for misappropriation of funds in 1782 but managed to escape. Nothing is known of his conversion to Islam.

62. *Carniolan:* Carniola (chief town Ljubljana, formerly Laibach) now belongs to Yugoslavia.

63. *Captain of a District:* As an Austrian province, Galicia was administratively a "Government" ruled by a Governor and divided into "Districts" (Kreise), each under a Kreishauptmann ("District Captain").

64. *Signora Bissolotti:* Perhaps the wife of Captain Paolo Bissolotti (1727-1779), a nobleman of Trieste.

65. *Laibach:* C. writes "Laubach." (See note 62 to this chapter.)

66. *Palmanova:* Palmanova was a fortress in Venetian Friuli, near Udine. The Provveditore generale of the fortress at the time was Francesco Rota (1724 - after 1772).

67. *Erizzo:* See note 10 to Chap. I of this volume.

68. *In Paris sixteen years earlier:* C. had first met Erizzo dur-

ing the latter's term as Venetian Ambassador in Paris (1754-1760). See especially Vol. 5, Chaps. I and II.

69. *I said to them:* C. writes "leur dise" (a slip for "leur dis-je").

70. *The wife of Count Romili:* Countess Lucia Romili, née Bon, Venetian patrician, notorious for her love affairs.

71. *Burghausen:* Otto Ludwig Heinrich, Count Burghausen (1711-1795), had the rank of Lieutenant-Field Marshal in the Austrian army from 1757.

CHAPTER X

1. Altered from Erasmus, *Adagia*, III; C. has quoted it several times before.

2. *The theory of it:* To what theory C. refers is not known.

3. *Rosenberg:* See note 8 to Chap. III of this volume. Rosenberg was Major-domo to the Grand Duke of Tuscany from 1766 to 1772, and after that became Grand Chamberlain to the Emperor Joseph II in Vienna.

4. *Casti:* Giambattista Casti (1724-1803), Italian Abate and poet; he was Professor of Eloquence in the Seminary at Montefiascone until 1764, after which he lived in Vienna. He was a member of the Arcadian Academy under the name Niceste Abidendo.

5. *Poet to the Emperor:* Casti was appointed to the position of court poet in Vienna in 1790; but the title was no longer conferred after the death of Metastasio (1782).

6. *Comic operas:* C. refers to *Il Re Teodoro in Venezia*, with music by Paisiello, first performed in 1784, and to *La Grotta di Trofonio*, music by Salieri, first performed in Vienna in 1785 (the same text was also set by Paisiello in the same year).

7. *King Theodore:* Theodor Stephan, Baron von Neuhoff, who was proclaimed King of Corsica in 1736 (cf. Vol. 9, Chap. VIII, n. 19).

8. *The Grotto of Trophonius:* The Grotto of Zeus Trophonios, near Lebadeia (now Levadia) in Boeotia, contained one of the most celebrated oracles of Greek Antiquity.

9. *Königsbrunn:* Franz Xaver, Count von Königsbrunn (ca.

1730-1794), Chief of Police of Trieste and at the same time theater director from 1769, had married Countess Ernestine Attems (1753-1830) in that year. (C. writes "Kinigsprun.")

10. *Torriano:* Count Luigi Torriano di Valsassina (1741-1794).

11. *Prosecco:* Some 5 miles northwest of Trieste, on the road to Görz.

12. *Torres:* See note 23 to the preceding chapter.

13. *The post house inn:* The Locanda alla Posta was a well-known hostelry in Görz in the 18th century; the Emperor Joseph II stayed there in 1784.

14. *His father:* Antonio, Count Torriano di Valsassina (ca. 1688-1769).

15. *Del Mestre:* Claudio del Mestre, Baron von Schönberg (died ca. 1794), married to Antonia, née Baroness Gaudens; he lived in Cormons, south of Spessa, which is some 4 miles south of Cividale del Friuli.

16. *Costa:* Anna Costa, later Germoglio, Italian actress in comic operas; she appeared in Trieste in 1774, in Venice in 1775, in Vienna in 1781.

17. *A young lady:* Isabella, née Countess of Brazza and Cergneù.

18. *Udine:* After the dissolution of the Patriarchate of Aquileia in 1751 the Pope established two new archbishoprics, one with its seat in Udine for the Venetian territory, the other in Görz for the Austrian. Spessa is some 10 miles east of Udine, and, according to C., was under the jurisdiction of the Archbishop of Udine.

19. *Quidditative:* "Quiddity," a term originating in Scholastic philosophy, means "the essence of a thing." The allusion is to the name of the Order, Ordo Fratrorum Minorum Capucinorum, where *minor* means "lesser," hence "unworthy."

20. *Bailon:* Antonio Bailon was the proprietor of the Locanda alla Posta in Görz.

21. *The young lady:* See note 17 to this chapter.

22. *He died insane:* Count Luigi Torriano died in Görz in 1794, but he had been declared insane and placed under guardianship in 1786.

23. *Coronini:* See note 28 to Chap. IX of this volume.

24. *Richard:* Joseph Richard (1710-1807), born in Lorraine, entered the Austrian civil service and was made a Baron in

1779. He married Countess Josefa Torres in 1776 or 1779. He was already 60 years of age when C. first met him in Görz.

25. *The new Council of Ten:* The Council of Ten consisted of 10 elected Senators, but the Doge and his 6 Councilors joined them. Two of the State Inquisitors had to be Senators and the third a member of the Council. The retiring State Inquisitors were Flaminio Corner, Piero Barbarigo, and Alvise Renier.

26. *Sagredo:* Francesco Sagredo (1705 - after 1782), Venetian patrician.

27. *Grimani:* Francesco Grimani (died after 1774), Venetian patrician and Senator.

28. *The third:* He was Girolamo Zulian. See Vol. 11, Chap. I, n. 51.

29. *Seven volumes:* C. published three volumes of this work in Görz in 1774-1775; however, the first volume was in two parts, as was the first part of the second volume.

30. *A translation of Homer's Iliad:* See especially note 22 to Chaps. IV–V of this volume.

31. *The troupe of comedians . . . playing there:* Probably the company directed by Onofrio (called Odoardo) Paganini, of which Irene's husband was a member. It played in Trieste during June and July 1774, in a repertory consisting principally of *commedie dell'arte.*

32. *Rinaldi:* Adventurer and professional gambler, who assumed the title of Count; C. has mentioned him several times, especially in Vol. 8, Chap. VII. His daughter Irene (died after 1790) is known to have appeared in Padua in 1779 and in Vienna in 1790, using the name Balzali, which she probably did not assume until after her marriage.

33. *Her rescue . . . Marcolina's approval:* See Vol. 9, Chap. IV.

34. *Scapino:* One of the stock characters of the *commedia dell' arte,* a sly valet.

35. *Gaming . . . forbidden in Trieste:* Gambling was strictly forbidden in Austria and its possessions from 1753.

36. Here Giacomo Casanova's *History of My Life* abruptly ends.

REVISIONS

VOLUME 1

Page 10, lines 15, 16, 19: *for* Angiolini *read* Angioloni; see Vol. 10, p. 370, n. 5

Page 47, line 35: *for* the physician *read* the physician Zambelli

Page 51, line 20: *for* Moncenigo *read* Mocenigo

Page 334, note 4: *after* wife *read* (from 1738) of Carlo IV Borbone, King of Naples (as Carlos III, King of Spain, from 1759).

Page 345, note 19: *for* Banco di Santo Spirito *read* Banca dello Spirito Santo

Page 349, note 29: *for* scudi *read* escudos

VOLUME 2

Page 34, line 23: *for* to do here in *read* to do in

Page 100, line 22 and *passim*: *for* Marshal *read* Marischal

Page 233, line 23: *for* Moscynski *read* Moczynski

Page 310, note 7: *for* (1688-1788) *read* (1688-1758)

Page 311, note 23 *should read*: *Dolfin*: Giovanni (Zuan) Antonio Dolfin (1710-1753), called Bucintoro, Venetian patrician and high official of the Republic, Governor of Zante from 1744. He married Donata, née Salamon, and was the father of Caterina Dolfin-Tron (cf. n. 25 to this chapter).

Page 312, note 6 *last sentence should read*: Here the reference is to Daniele IV Andrea Dolfin, called Andrea (1688 - ca. 1767), who held the office from August 1744 to autumn 1746.

Page 313, note 14: *for* n. 21 *read* n. 25

Page 314, note 42 *should read*: *Andrea*: Daniele IV Andrea Dolfin (cf. n. 6 to this chapter)

Page 319, note 7 *should read*: *Infante the Duke of Parma*: Ferdinand Maria Filippo Luigi Borbone (1751-1802), Duke of Parma from 1765; it was not he, however, who was an Infante of Spain, but his father, Duke Philip I

(1720-1765). Guastalla had belonged to the Duchy of
Parma since 1748.

Page 325, note 4: *for* murdered his *read* murdered by his

Page 326, note 12: *for* χφῶν *read* χθῶν

VOLUME 3

Page 17, line 11: *for* posthouse inn *read* Albergo della Posta

Page 62, lines 14, 17: *for* professor *read* violoncellist

Page 144, lines 14-15: *for* Sarrazin, his wife Grandval *read*
Sarrazin, Grandval, his wife

Page 148, line 21: *for* we *read* me

Page 290, line 29: *for* Parma *read* Padua

Page 304, note 12: *for* Manzonni *read* Manzoni

Page 310, note 19 *should read:* The father of Louis de Saussure
was Georges de Saussure, Baron de Bavois et Bercher
(1704 - ca. 1752), Commander of the Swiss Regiment of
the Duke of Modena; he was demoted in 1748 for serious
derelictions.

Page 320, note 19: *for* 1743 *read* 1752

Page 323, note 74: *for* from 1729; Marie *read* from 1729;
François Charles Racot (de) Grandval (1710-1784), from
1729; his wife, Marie

Page 324, note 5 *should read:* Honoré III Camille Léonor
Grimaldi-Goyon de Matignon (1720-1795), from 1751
Duke of Valentinois, Reigning Prince of Monaco (1731-
1793).

Page 324, note 6 *should read:* Jacques François Léonor Grimaldi-Goyon, Count of Matignon and Thorigny, Duke of
Estouteville and (from 1715) of Valentinois (1689-1751).
In 1715 he married Louise Hippolyte Grimaldi (1697-
1731), daughter of Antonio I Grimaldi (1661-1731), the
last Duke of Monaco from the house of Grimaldi. At the
marriage her father bestowed on his son-in-law the Duchy
of Valentinois and the right to add the name of Grimaldi
to his own of Goyon.

Page 325, note 8 *should read:* Cathérine Charlotte Thérèse,
Duchess of Ruffec, née de Gramont (1707-1755), mother-
in-law of the Prince's brother, Charles Maurice Grimaldi-
Goyon de Matignon (1727-1790), Chevalier of Monaco,

Count of Valentinois, who married her daughter Marie Christine Chrétienne in 1749. C.'s "woman of sixty" exaggerates her age by almost twenty years.

Note 20 *should read:* Maria Caterina (Marie Cathérine), Marchesa di Brignole-Sale (1739-1813), married Honoré III, Reigning Prince of Monaco, in 1757. The marriage was annulled in 1770.

Page 327, note 37: *for* Jacobin *read* Jacobite

Page 331, note 7: *for* Born 1725 *read* First name unknown; lived from 1735 to 1802;

Note 8: *for* du Ronderay *read* Duronceray

Page 334, note 15 *should read:* Marie Christine Chrétienne de Rouvroi de Saint-Simon de Ruffec (1728-1774), married Charles Maurice Grimaldi-Goyon de Matignon (1727-1790), Count of Valentinois, Chevalier of Monaco, in 1749.

Page 338, note 11: *for* 1866 *read* 1806

Page 344, note 7 *should read: XXX:* Recent research has led to the supposition that the convent was that of Santa Maria degli Angeli in Murano.

Page 345, note 15, and page 346, note 17: *for* Padua *read* Vicenza

VOLUME 4

Page 326, note 18 *should read: Convent of the XXX:* Presumably the convent of Santa Maria degli Angeli, on the island of Murano.

Page 327, note 1: *for* Countess Coronini-Cronberg *read* née Countess Salburg

Page 331, note 7: *for* (1579-1639) *read* (Jean de Meurs, the Younger, 1613-1654)

Page 332, note 22: *for* thirty-two *read* thirty-five

Page 335, note 8: *for* "*Mersius*" *read* "*Meursius*"

Page 336, note 12: *for* (ca. 1714-1755) *read* (ca. 1714-1775)

Page 350, note 19: *for* Giovanni and *read* Giovanni Boldrin and

VOLUME 5

Page 110, line 19: *for* "*patina*" *read* "*platina*"

Page 235, line 13, and page 309, note 45: *for* Lieutenant *read* Magistrate

Pages 253-4, *passim: for* earrings *read* buckles (see Vol. 9, p. 404, n. 40)

Page 265, line 15, and page 313, note 47: *for* Moerdick *read* Moerdijk

Page 269, note 2: *for* 1756 *read* 1755

Page 277, note 46: *for* Filingieri *read* Filingeri

Page 294, note 52: *for* in 1745 *read* before 1744

Note 58: *for* Frederike *read* Friederike

Page 304, note 19 *should read:* Anton Gabriel Herrenschwandt (died 1785), of Swiss descent. He succeeded his brother Johann Friedrich (cf. Vol. 6, p. 301, n. 29, below) as physician to the Swiss Guards Regiment in Paris, and as physician in ordinary to the Duke of Orléans and to King Stanislaus II Poniatowski.

VOLUME 6

Page 119, line 23: *for* friend of mine. *read* friend of mine.[30] Line 25: *for* brother.[30] *read* brother.

Page 158, line 34, and page 305, n. 5, *for* Smerdis *read* Smerdies

Page 245, line 2: *for* cursed *read* crushed

Page 253, lines 9-10, and page 320, note 4: *for* lisbonini *read* lisbonines (Portuguese, lisbonina; another designation for the dobra, the Portuguese gold coins minted from 1722 and worth 4 escudos or 4000 reis)

Page 291, note 2: *for* Comics *read* Conics

Page 293, note 26: *for* (1745-1777) *read* (1727-1777), Elector from 1745.

Page 301, note 29 *should read:* Johann Friedrich von Herrenschwandt (1715-1798), physician to the Swiss Guards Regiment and to the Duke of Orléans in Paris, 1750-1755; physician in ordinary to King Stanislaus II Poniatowski, 1764-1773; medical Consultant to the City of Bern, 1779-1784. He invented the *Herrenschwandtsches Pulver* which he apparently prescribed for C.'s baths.

Page 301, note 30 *should read: Friend of mine:* Anton Gabriel Herrenschwandt (cf. Vol. 5, p. 304, n. 19, above).

Page 304, note 15: *for* Barton *read* Barbon

Note 18: *for* Agnèse Thérèse, née Mazzade *read* Agnès Thérèse, née Mazade

Page 307, note 29 *should read: Bavois:* Louis de Saussure,

Baron de Bavois (1729-1772), C.'s friend (cf. Vol. 3, Chaps. V and VI), had become lieutenant-colonel in the Bala (Palla, cf. Vol. 2, Chap. III, n. 20) regiment in Venice in 1752. His uncle and aunt were David de Saussure, Baron de Bercher et Bavois (1700-1767), a commander of the Militia in Bern, and his wife, first name unknown, née Mannlich de Bettens.

Page 308, note 37 *should read: Herrenschwandt:* See above, Vol. 6, p. 301, n. 29; he lived in the château of Greng, near Murten.

Page 310, note 21 *should read: Bercher . . . Bavois.* See above, Vol. 6, p. 307, n. 29.

VOLUME 7

Page 46, line 5: *for* Breyden *read* Treyden

Page 126, line 22: *for* with Marchese *read* with the Marchese

Page 141, line 21: *for* Derici *read* Lerici

Page 194, line 11, and page 324, note 28: *for* Smerdias *read* Smerdies

Page 304, note 34, *second sentence should read:* By his wife Benigna Gottliebe von Trotha, known as von Treyden, he had two sons, Peter (1724-1800), who received the Duchy in 1769 upon his father's resignation, and Karl Ernst (1728-1801), the Prince Charles of Vol. 10, Chaps. V-X.

Page 304, note 2: *for* Lim as *read* Limas

Page 306, note 24: *for* "*Where*" *read* "*Whore*"

Page 314, note 22, lines 5 and 6 *should read:* present chapter he gives her son the surname Lanti and her husband's name as Palesi; it is not until

Page 322, note 12: *for* Mariuccia's family name; Righetti's daughter Tecla *read* his daughter Tecla's family name, who Tecla read Tecla (C.'s Mariuccia)

Page 326, note 9: *for* Marzo *read* Marzio

Page 328, note 31: *for* (1710 - before 1766) *read* (1734-1780)

Page 329, notes 5 and 6: *for* Ferdinando *read* Fernando

Page 332, note 42: *for* Clement IV *read* Clement XIV

Page 336, note 4: *for* Charles Emmanuel III *read* Carlo Emmanuele I

Note 5: *for* Emanuele *read* Emmanuele

Page 337, note 7: *for* d'Aglie *read* d'Aglié

VOLUME 8

Page 58, line 14: *for* Lescaris *read* Lascaris
Page 232, line 4, and page 234, line 10: *for* Teresa *read* Theresa
Page 288, note 41 *should read: The physician Herrenschwandt:*
     See above, Vol. 5, p. 304, n. 19, and Vol. 6, p. 301, n. 29
Page 292, note 81: *for* Trautsmannsdorf *read* Trautmannsdorf
Page 293, note 16: *for* Ingnaz *read* Ignaz
Page 303, note 27: *for* Zamorra *read* Zamora

VOLUME 9

Page 25, line 2: *for* Bressa *read* Brescia
Page 36, line 18: *for* Coralline *read* Corallina
Page 70, line 18, and page 375, note 49: *for* Teresa *read* Theresa
Page 100, line 21: *for* providing *read* proving
Page 197, line 11, and *passim: for* Malignan *read* Malingan
Page 370, note 18 *should read: Prince of Monaco:* Honoré III
     Camille Léonor Grimaldi-Goyon de Matignon (1720-1795),
     Duke of Valentinois from 1751, Reigning Prince of Monaco
     (1731-1793).
     Note 20 *should read: Duchess of Ruffec:* Cathérine Char-
     lotte Thérèse, Duchess of Ruffec, née de Gramont (1707-
     1755), mother-in-law of Charles Maurice Grimaldi-Goyon
     de Matignon (1727-1790), Count of Valentinois, Chevalier
     of Monaco (cf. Vol. 3, Chap. IX).
     Note 22: *for* The Prince of Monaco *read* Honoré III (1720-
     1795), Reigning Prince of Monaco
Page 393, note 92: *for* Zulestein *read* Zuylestein
Page 399, note 26: *for* sont *read* sort
Page 406, note 28: *for* Earl Bristol *read* Earl of Bristol
     Note 30: *for* Fernando IV *read* Ferdinand IV

VOLUME 10

Page 23, line 4: *for* Lavallette *read* Lavalette
Page 25, line 25: *for* longed *read* longer
Page 35, lines 7 and 20: *for* Theresa *read* Thérèse
Page 179, line 24: *for* 1776 *read* 1766
Page 316, line 17: *for* Frederick I *read* Frederick II

Page 325, note 7: *for* Chamberlain *read* August Wilhelm
Page 326, note 18: *for* Mansell *read* Maunsell
Page 330, note 35: *for* "*Teresa*" *read* "*Thérèse.*" (She was, however, not the niece of Tiretta's mistress, La Lambertini, but of the stout woman, Madame XXX.
Page 331, note 49: *for* Jacobin *read* Jacobite
Page 333, note 8: *for* 1791 *read* 1781
Page 334, note 33: *for* 1788 *read* 1778
Page 335, note 44: *for* Offray *read* Offroy
Page 337, note 1: *for* George *read* James Francis Edward
Page 340, note 33: *for* Oliviera *read* Olivieri
Page 346, note 31: *for* *Czernichev read Chernichev*
Page 348, note 59: *for* Giosetta *read* Gioseffa
Page 349, note 70: *for first two lines read:* Elisabeth Karlovna Sievers (born after 1745), daughter of Karl Sievers (1710 or '16 - 1774 or '75), a; *add, before last sentence:* From her first marriage to Jacob Efimovich Sievers (1731-1808) she had three daughters.
Page 354, note 48: *for* Biliotis *read* Bilioti
Page 355, note 55: *for* Catherine the Great *read* the Czarina Elisabeth
Page 361, note 53: *for* Michal Fryderyk *read* Fryderyk Michal
  Note 57: *for* Konstanzia *read* Konstancja
Page 370, note 75: *for* Calvalcabo *read* Cavalcabo
Page 382, note 65: *for* zum Putz *read* zum Pütz
Page 385, note 47: *for* 1735 *read* 1734
  Note 53 *should read:* *Brumoy:* Armand Louis Joseph Pâris de Montmartel, Marquis de Brumoy (1748-1781), son of Jean Pâris de Montmartel (cf. Vol. 5, Chap. VII, n. 19)
Page 386, note 2: *for first two lines read:* Étienne François Choiseul, Count of Stainville, Duke of Choiseul-Stainville-Amboise (1719-1785), had returned to
  Note 9: *for* (1775) *read* (1785)
Page 391, note 63: *for* Giacoma Annetta *read* Giacoma Antonia

INDEX
OF PERSONS AND PLACES

INDEX
OF PERSONS AND PLACES

The Index excludes fictional characters. In rare cases an un-known first name is indicated by the letter N. Saints appear under their proper names rather than under Saint, San, etc. Authors quoted by C. but not named in the text are indexed by reference to the notes where they are identified. All geographical features are indexed, but not individual buildings, streets, etc.

Hedwig ("the beautiful theologian"; probably Anne
Marie May, born in 1731,
later by marriage Madame
von Wattenwyl) **6,** 220–
222, 312 n. 44; **8,** 83, 85–
92, 96–116, 299 ns. 18, 26;
9, 362, 400 n. 35, 414 n.
37; **12,** 171

Hedwig's cousin, *see* Helena

Hedwig's uncle (the pastor)
6, 219–222; **8,** 83, 85–87,
90–93, 97, 101, 103, 105–
107, 109–110, 113–114

Heinitz, Friedrich Anton von
10, 222(?), 372 n. 23

Heinrich IV, *see* Henry IV

Helena (Agnes; cousin of
Hedwig) **8,** 84–86, 88–93,
96–102, 107–116, 299 ns. 19,
21

Helena's mother **8,** 89, 92–93,
96–97, 101–102, 105, 107–
108, 113–115

Helvétius, Anne Cathérine,
née Ligneville-d'Autricourt
(1719–1800) **5,** 264, 312 n.
43

Helvétius, Claude Adrien
(1715–1771) **3,** 321 n. 45;
5, 264–265, 307 n. 26, 312
n. 43

Henau, Baron (self-styled) **9,**
363, 414 n. 42; **10,** 27–29,
31–32, 93

Henau's mistress **9,** 363; **10,**
27–31

Hennin-Liétard, Gabrielle de,

Princess of Chimay, née de
Beauveau **5,** 186, 302 n. 63

Hennin-Liétard, Philippe Gabriel Maurice de (born
1736), **7,** 245(?), 331 n. 31

Hennin-Liétard, Thomas Alexandre Marc de, Prince of
Chimay **5,** 302 n. 63; **7,**
331 n. 31

Henri IV, King of France **1,**
42, 325 n. 15; **2,** 315 n. 61;
3, 131, 320 n. 26

Henriette (probably Jeanne
Marie d'Albert de Saint-
Hippolyte [1718–1795],
who used name of Anne
d'Arci) **3,** 13, 15–23, 25–
36, 38–40, 42–47, 49–79, 82,
93, 104, 112, 305 n. 2, 310
n. 7; **4,** 50; **6,** 220; **7,** 333
n. 52; **9,** 68, 79–87, 248,
376 n. 7, 401 ns. 46–47;
11, 171–173, 182–183, 200;
12, 144

Henriette's father, *see* Albert
de Saint-Hippolyte, Michel
d'

Henriette's father-in-law, *see*
Boyer de Fonscolombe,
Honoré

Henriette's husband, *see*
Boyer de Fonscolombe, Jean
Baptiste Laurent

Henriette's mother, *see* Albert
de Saint-Hippolyte, Jeanne
Marie d', née de Margalet

Henriette (1727–1752), Madame de France **3,** 158, 327
n. 44; **6,** 214

92–93, 95–96, 98–101, 103–
104

Mariuccia's father **7**, 200, 248,
250, 253

Mariuccia's father-in-law **7**,
249–250

Mariuccia's mother **7**, 191,
198, 200–201, 203, 205, 242–
243, 253

Mariuccia's husband, *see* Clemente

Marivaux, Pierre Carlet de
Chamblain de (1688–1763)
3, 125, 319 ns. 10–11

Mark, Evangelist, St. **2**, 186,
267, 325 n. 1; **4**, 64, 151,
154, 245, 247, 276–277, 289–
290, 301, 347 n. 37; **10**, 148,
201, 358 n. 18

Maroli (Major in Corfu) **2**,
66, 104, 107, 111, 132

Marolles, Antoine Alexandre
(died 1751 or '52) **3**, 230,
339 n. 38

Maron (Maroni), Anton (Antonio) (1733–1808) **7**, 192,
323 n. 22

Mars **2**, 46, 269, 289; **5**, 222;
9, 61, 372 n. 11; **10**, 252,
379 n. 34; **12**, 213

Marseilles **3**, 204; **5**, 110; **6**,
221, 247; **7**, 50, 63, 75, 78,
82, 88, 91, 97, 108–109, 112,
285, 298; **8**, 66, 116, 184,
225–226, 273, 275, 278, 280;
9, 4, 9, 13, 21, 27–28, 33,
43–45, 50–51, 53, 56–57, 60–
61, 69–74, 101, 139, 141;
10, 271, 299; **11**, 107, 162,

170, 173, 183–184, 205, 247;
12, 72

Marsigli, Sebastiano (died
1783), advocate (= XXX)
3, 342 n. 21; **4**, 184, 340 n.
2; **5**, 21

Marta, *see* Savorgnan, Marta

Martelli, Pier Giacomo (Jacopo) (1665–1727) **3**, 123,
319 n. 6; **4**, 141, 337 n. 23;
6, 242–243, 318 ns. 71–73

Martial, Marcus Valerius **1**,
42, 323 n. 9, 325 n. 8, 340
n. 6, 348 n. 13; **3**, 26, 306
n. 7; **7**, 312 n. 7; **11**, 326 n.
18

Martin III, Pope **1**, 41, 325
n. 3

Martin V, Pope **1**, 325 n. 3

Martin, Pierre Henri (banker)
6, 211, 311 n. 27; **8**, 121,
142, 302 n. 11

Martin, Madame **6**, 211, 311
n. 27; **8**, 121, 302 n. 11

Martin (Englishman in Aix-
la-Chapelle) **8**, 64

Martinelli, Vincenzo (1702–
1785) **9**, 164–167, 181–182,
186, 191, 199, 210, 244, 251–
254, 262, 339, 386 ns. 16–
17, 387 ns. 19–20, 23–24,
401 ns. 3, 6

Martinengo da Barco, Paolo
Emilio, Count of (1704–
after 1795) **4**, 250, 253, 348
n. 43

Martino, Don **12**, 141, 143,
256 n. 16

Martorano (Calabria) **1**, 157,